JOURNAL FOR THE STUDY OF THE OLD TESTAMENT
SUPPLEMENT SERIES

49

Editors
David J A Clines
Philip R Davies

JSOT Press
Sheffield

Theophoric Personal Names in Ancient Hebrew

A Comparative Study

Jeaneane D. Fowler

Journal for the Study of the Old Testament
Supplement Series 49

To Merv

Published by JSOT Press
JSOT Press is an imprint of
Sheffield Academic Press Ltd
The University of Sheffield
343 Fulwood Road
Sheffield S10 3BP
England

Typeset by Sheffield Academic Press
and
printed in Great Britain
by Billing & Sons Ltd
Worcester

British Library Cataloguing in Publication Data

Fowler, Jeaneane D.
Theophoric personal names in ancient Hebrew : a comparative study.— (JSOT supplement series, ISSN 0309-0787; 49).
1. Names, Personal—Jewish 2. Names in the Bible
I. Title
929.4′4′0321 CS3010

ISBN 1-85075-038-6
ISBN 1-85075-039-4 Pbk

CONTENTS

ACKNOWLEDGMENTS

I should like to express my deep gratitude to all those who have made this work possible. I am indebted to Dr J.G. Harris, formerly of Gwent College of Higher Education, who kindled in me a love for Old Testament study. It would be impossible for me to express the debt I owe to Alan Millard of the University of Liverpool, under whose guidance the doctoral dissertation upon which this work is based was undertaken. No student could wish for a more erudite scholar or a kinder and more considerate man for a tutor. This work owes so much to his sound academic advice and everything to the confidence he created in a student filled with self-doubt: any mistakes which remain in the work are entirely my own.

I wish to thank also the publishers and editorial staff for their skilful and careful production of such a difficult text.

On a personal level I am indebted to my parents and my husband for their constant support, but particularly to my husband, Merv, for his tireless help in the proof reading of the work and for his patience throughout the decade of study which this work encompasses. It is to him that I dedicate this work, with love and gratitude.

ABBREVIATIONS

1. *Bibliographical*

AHw	W. von Soden (ed.), *Akkadisches Handwörterbuch*, Unter Benutzung des lexikalischen Nachlasses von Bruno Meissner (1868–1947), Wiesbaden: O. Harrassowitz, 3 vols. (1965, 1972, 1981).
AI	Y. Aharoni, *Arad Inscriptions*, Judean Desert Studies. The Insitute of Archaeology, The Hebrew University of Jerusalem: Israel Exploration Society (1981).
ANET	J.B. Pritchard (ed.), *Ancient Near Eastern Texts Relating to the Old Testament*, 3rd edn with Supplement, Princeton (1969).
APN	K.L. Tallqvist, *Assyrian Personal Names*, Hildesheim: G. Olms (1966). First published 1914.
APNM	H.B. Huffmon, *Amorite Personal Names in the Mari Texts. A Structural and Lexical Study*, Baltimore: Johns Hopkins (1965).
Barr *Cp. Ph.*	J. Barr, *Comparative Philology and the Text of the Old Testament*, Oxford (1968).
BASOR	*Bulletin of the American Schools of Oriental Research*.
BDB	F. Brown, S.R. Driver, C.A. Briggs, *A Hebrew and English Lexicon of the Old Testament*, 1972 edn, Oxford: Clarendon Press (1974).
BEUP	*The Babylonian Expedition of the University of Pennsylvania, Series A: Cuneiform Texts*, Philadelphia (1983–).
BL	P. Bordreuil, A. Lemaire, 'Nouveaux Sceaux Hébreux, Araméens et Ammonites', *Semitica* 26 (1976), 45-63.
BL *JA*	P. Bordreuil, A. Lemaire, 'Deux Nouveaux Sceaux Nord-Ouest Sémitiques', *Journal Asiatique* (1977), 18-19.
BO	*Bibliotheca Orientalis*, Leiden: Nederlands Instituut voor het Nabije Oosten.
CAD	I.J. Gelb, B. Landsberger *et al.*, *The Assyrian Dictionary of the Oriental Institute of the University of Chicago* (1956-).
CBQ	*The Catholic Biblical Quarterly*.
Coogan	M.D. Coogan, *West Semitic Personal Names in the Murašû Documents*, Harvard Semitic Monographs No. 7, F.M. Cross, Jr (ed.), Missoula, Montana: Scholars Press (1976).

Cowley	A. Cowley, *Aramaic Papyri of the Fifth Century B.C.*, Oxford (1923).
CSL	M.H. Goshen-Gottsein (ed.), *Comparative Semitic Linguistics*, Jerusalem (1974).
Dir	D. Diringer, *Le Iscrizioni Antico-Ebraiche Palestinesi*, Firenze, Felice le Monnier (1934).
Driver	G.R. Driver, *Aramaic Documents of the Fifth Century BC*, Oxford: Clarendon Press (1957), revised edn (1965).
EAEHL	M. Avi-Yonah, E. Stern (eds.), *Encyclopedia of Archaeological Excavations in the Holy Land*, 4 vols. London: OUP (1975–1978).
EI	*Eretz-Israel*, Israel Exploration Society, Jerusalem.
Eph	M. Lidzbarski, *Ephemeris für semitische Epigraphik* II, Giessen (1903–1907).
Geh	H.S. Gehman (ed.), *The New Westminster Dictionary of the Bible*, Philadelphia: Westminster (1970).
Gelb Lingua	I.J. Gelb, 'La lingua degli Amoriti', *Atti della Accademia Nazionale dei Lincei*, Rendiconti della classe de scienze morali, storiche e filologiche, Serie 8, XIII (1958), 143-64.
Gibson	J.C.L. Gibson, *Canaanite Myths and Legends*, 2nd edn, Edinburgh: T. & T. Clark (1978).
GKC	*Gesenius' Hebrew Grammar*, 2nd English edn (1910), trans. A.E. Cowley, Oxford: OUP (1976).
Gray	G.B. Gray, *Studies in Hebrew Proper Names*, London: A. & C. Black (1896).
Grelot	P. Grelot, *Documents Araméens d'Égypte*, Paris: Les Éditions du Cerf (1972).
Herr	L.G. Herr, *The Scripts of Ancient Northwest Semitic Seals*, Harvard Semitic Monograph Series No. 18, F.M. Cross, Jr (ed.), Missoula, Montana: Scholars Press (1978).
HTR	*Harvard Theological Review*.
IEJ	*Israel Exploration Journal*.
IH	A. Lemaire, *Inscriptions Hébraïques. I Les Ostraca*, Paris: Les Éditions du Cerf (1977).
IPN	M. Noth, *Die israelitischen Personennamen im Rahmen der gemeinsemitischen Namengebung*, Hildesheim: G. Olms (1966), reprint of Stuttgart (1928) edn.
IR	*Inscriptions Reveal: Documents from the time of the Bible, the Mishna and the Talmud*. Revised 2nd edn, Winter (1973). Cat. No. 100.

JAOS	*Journal of the American Oriental Society.*
JBL	*Journal of Biblical Literature.*
JNES	*Journal of Near Eastern Studies.*
JSS	*Journal of Semitic Studies.*
KAI	H. Donner, W. Röllig, *Kanaanäische und Aramäische Inschriften*, II & III, Wiesbaden: Otto Harrasowitz (1964).
KB	L. Koehler, W. Baumgartner, *Hebräisches und Aramäisches Lexikon zum Alten Testament*, 3rd edn (2 vols.), Leiden: Brill (1967, 1974).
KB (1953)	L. Koehler, W. Baumgartner, *Lexicon in Veteris Testamenti Libros*, Leiden: Brill (1953).
Krael	E.G. Kraeling, *The Brooklyn Museum Papyri*, New Haven: Yale (1953).
Lipiński	E. Lipiński, *Studies in Aramaic Inscriptions and Onomastics I*, Leuven: Leuven U.P. (1975).
M	S. Moscati, *L'epigrafia Ebraica Antica 1935–1950*, Rome: PIB (1951).
MEU	H.W. Fowler, *Modern English Usage*, 2nd edn, revised by Sir Ernest Gowers, Oxford (1968).
NBD	J.D. Douglas (ed.), *The New Bible Dictionary*, London: The Inter-Varsity Fellowship (1962).
NEATC	J.A. Sanders (ed.), *Near Eastern Archaeology in the Twentieth Century*, New York: Doubleday (1970).
OA	*Orientis Antiqui Collectio.*
OED	*The Concise Oxford Dictionary*, 5th edn (1964), Oxford (1970).
OL	*Orientalische Literaturzeitung.*
OMA	C. Saporetti, *Onomastica Medio-assira*, I & II, Rome: PIB (1970).
PEFQS	*Palestine Exploration Fund Quarterly Statement.*
PEQ	*Palestine Exploration Quarterly.*
PNCP	A.T. Clay, *Personal Names from Cuneiform Inscriptions of the Cassite Period*, New Haven (1912).
PNPPI	F.L. Benz, *Personal Names in the Phoenician and Punic Inscriptions*, Studia Pohl Dissertationes Scientificae de Rebus Orientis Antiqui, VIII, Rome (1972).
PS	I.N. Vinnikov, *Palestinskii Svornik*, 3 (1958), 171-216, 4 (1959), 196-240, 7 (1962), 192-237, 9 (1962), 140-58, 11 (1963), 189-232, 13 (1965), 217-62.

PTU	F. Gröndahl, *Die Personennamen der Texte aus Ugarit*, Studia Pohl Dissertationes Scientificae de Rebus Orientis Antiqui, I, Rome (1967).
RB	*Revue Biblique*.
RHR	*Revue de l'Histoire des Religions*.
Roberts	J.J.M. Roberts, *The Earliest Semitic Pantheon*, Baltimore: Johns Hopkins (1972)
RSO	*Revista Degli Studi Orientali*.
SSI	J.C.L. Gibson, *Textbook of Syrian Semitic Inscriptions, I Hebrew and Moabite*, Oxford: Clarendon (1971).
SSI II	*idem*, *Textbook of Syrian Semitic Inscriptions II Aramaic*, Oxford: Clarendon (1975).
SSI III	*idem*, *Textbook of Syrian Semitic Inscriptions III Phoenician*, Oxford: Clarendon (1982).
Stamm	J.J. Stamm, *Die Akkadische Namengebung*, Darmstadt (1968). First published 1939.
Stark	J.K. Stark, *Personal Names in Palmyrene Inscriptions*, Oxford (1971).
Torcz	H. Torczyner, *et al*., *Lachish I: The Lachish Letters*, Oxford: OUP (1938).
UT Glossary	C.H. Gordon, *Ugaritic Textbook Glossary*, Rome: PIB (1965).
V	Seals 1–252: F. Vattioni, 'I sigilli ebraici', *Biblica*, 50 (1969), 357-88. Seals 253–441: *idem*., 'Sigilli Ebraici III', *Annali dell' Istituto Universitario Orientale di Napoli 38 NS 28* (1978), 227-54.
V. Aug	*idem*, 'I sigilli, le monete e gli avori aramaico', *Augustinianum* 11 (1971), 47-87, 173-190.
VH	Th. C. Vriezen, J.H. Hospers (eds), *Textus Minores XVII Palestine Inscriptions*, Leiden: Brill (1951).
WO	*Die Welt des Orients*.
WZKM	*Wiener Zeitschrift für die Kunde des Morgenlandes*.
ZA	*Zeitschrift für Assyriologie*.
ZAW	*Zeitschrift fur die alttestamentliche Wissenschaft*.
ZDMG	*Zeitschrift der deutschen morgenländischen Gesellschaft*.
ZDPV	*Zeitschrift des deutschen Palästina-Vereins*.

2. *General*

A	Arad
abb.	abbreviation
acc.	accusative

Akk.	Akkadian
Ammon.	Ammonite
Amor.	Amorite
approx.	approximately
Arab.	Arabic
Aram.	Aramaic
Ass.	Assyrian
B	Beer-sheba
Bab.	Babylonian
BH	biblical Hebrew
coll.	collective
constr.	construct
cun.	cuneiform
Df(f)	difficult form(s)
DN	divine name
E	Elephantine
EB	extra-biblical
Eg.	Egyptian
f.	feminine
gen.	genitive
Gib.	Gibeon
Gk.	Greek
Heb.	Hebrew
Hurr.	Hurrian
ideog.	ideogram
imf.	imperfective(s)
imv.	imperative(s)
inscr.	inscription(s)
KM	Khirbet El Meshash
L	Lachish
lw	loan word
m.	masculine
MH	Meṣad Hashavyahu
MA	Middle Assyrian
M. Bab.	Middle Babylonian
Moab.	Moabite
Mur.	Wadi Murabaat
n.	noun; note
NA	New Assyrian
NH	New Hebrew
N/L Bab.	New/Late Babylonian
n. f.	feminine noun
n. m.	masculine noun
no.	number

n. pr. div.	divine proper name
OA	Old Assyrian
O. Akk.	Old Akkadian
O. Bab.	Old Babylonian
Palm.	Palmyrene
part.	participle
pass.	passive
perf.	perfective
pers.	person
Pers.	Persian
pron.	pronoun
Q	Tell Qasile
Q.	Qal
R	Ramat-Rahel
sf(f).	short form(s)
sing.	singular
SO	Samarian ostraca
SS	Samarian ostraca 1931-1935
Syr.	Syriac
Ug.	Ugaritic
vent.	ventive
Y	Yahweh
Yavn	Yavneh-Yam

Hebrew transliteration

See T.O. Lambdin, *Introduction to Biblical Hebrew*, London: DLT (1973), pp. XXII, XXIII, XXV.

'ālep	*'*
bêt	*b*
gîmel	*g*
dālet	*d*
hē	*h*
wāw	*w*
zayin	*z*
ḥēt	*ḥ*
ṭēt	*ṭ*
yōd	*y*
kap	*k*
lāmed	*l*
mēm	*m*
nûn	*n*
sāmek	*s*

'ayin	*'*
pēh	*p*
ṣādēh	*ṣ*
qōp	*q*
rēš	*r*
śîn	*ś*
šîn	*š*
tāw	*t*

Vowels

		with *yōd*	with *wāw*
pataḥ	*a*	*ay*	*aw*
qāmeṣ	*ā/o*	*â/āy*	
hîreq	*i*	*î*	*iw*
ṣērê	*ē*	*ê*	
s^e^gōl	*e*		
ḥōlem	*ō*		*ô*
qibbûṣ	*u*		*û*
š^e^wā	*e*		
ḥāṭep pataḥ	*ă*		
ḥāṭep s^e^gōl	*ĕ*		
ḥāṭep qāmeṣ	*ŏ*		

Chapter 1

INTRODUCTION

To the ancient Semitic mind, the name borne by an individual was more than a mere means of identification since each name revealed some aspect concerning the nature of the person who bore that name. Frequently, Semitic names incorporated the name of the deity, so illustrating the beliefs which the name-bearer or name-giver held concerning his god. It is with these theophoric names that this study is concerned.

A study of Hebrew theophoric names has both a theological and technical value. Each name which is compounded with a divine element reveals some aspect of the divine character, or some relationship between that divine character and the originator of the name. It is therefore to be hoped that a study of all theophoric names will construct a detailed picture of what the Hebrew man conceived his God to be. At the same time, however, the grammatical study of such names will, in some ways, enrich the present knowledge of the structure of the Hebrew language.

The principle studies of Hebrew are those by G.B. Gray, *Studies in Hebrew Proper Names*, London: A. & C. Black (1896), and M. Noth, *Die israelitischen Personennamen in Rahmen der gemeinsemitischen Namengebung*, Hildesheim: Georg Olms (1928). However, the early date of both these works has resulted in an omission of the large number of subsequently discovered extra-biblical names, particularly in the case of the earlier work of Gray. It is felt, too, that the German work of Noth is far too restrictive in its treatment of theophoric names. Noth divided Hebrew theophoric names into four groups, *Bekenntnisnamen, Vertrauensnamen, Danknamen*, and *Wunschnamen*, although many of the names are capable of interpretations which would widen such categories considerably. For example, the placing by Noth of all theophoric names with imperfective elements in the category of 'wish names' (May God . . .), denies the Hebrew verb one of its basic functions in which it is used to express habitual or customary action (cf. T.O. Lambdin, *Introduction to Biblical Hebrew*, London: DLT [1973], 91). This has confined the names to the context of birth events and limited the acts and characteristics of the deity to the past and future, without allowing a timeless quality and permanence to the divine personality. It is to be hoped that the names will be seen in the wider context of being applicable to the nature of the Hebrew deity.

This study has set out to examine Hebrew personal names with a view to determining what concepts of God are revealed within those names and to what extent such concepts may be distinct from those displayed in other ancient Semitic onomastica. All the personal names contained in the Old Testament have been collected and from these have been selected those names which contain a theophoric element. Excluded are names of foreigners, although foreign names, when borne by Hebrew persons, are included, since such names throw some light upon the question of the degree of syncretism in Israelite religion and also portray some aspect of divine character. Possible abbreviated names have also been collected from the Old Testament with a view to determining whether in fact they can be accepted as abbreviated forms of theophoric compound names, or whether the evidence for such abbreviations is unsubstantiated.

Extra-biblical names have been gathered from a variety of sources. F. Vattioni[1] has provided the majority of names on seals (i.e. seals, seal impressions and seal stamps), while inscriptional names from Lachish, Tell Arad, Samaria etc., have been gathered from a variety of sources, which are indicated in the text. From all these extra-biblical names, theophoric names have again been extracted, as well as possible abbreviated forms.

Initially, any onomasticon should be studied from within rather than from a comparative point of view. This factor is expressed clearly by M.H. Silverman, 'Such comparative studies, in our opinion, ought to be undertaken only after the situation in the group of personal names has become clear. Even though the contrary belief is often held, we think that such wider studies are meaningless unless the onomasticon is known and comprehended by itself.'[2] Part of the purpose of this work is to examine Hebrew names in isolation from other languages, before discovering what light the latter throw upon certain aspects of the Hebrew onomasticon.

It would also seem to be important from the outset, to examine Hebrew theophoric names without any presuppositions. Nowhere is this more apparent than in the case of biblical names, and many will consider, as Gray (*op. cit.*) did, that it is necessary to examine these names from the point of view of source analysis. However, this is to say that at the outset one must begin with a set of presuppositions which cannot fail to affect considerably any conclusions reached. While it is not possible to ignore totally the question of source analysis, this question should not be allowed to interfere with the argumentation in such a way that conclusions reached can only be reliable as long as the premise of the existence of docmentary sources is tenable. Rather, it is hoped that conclusions will be obtained which hold true irrespective of this problem. Thus, in the main, we should allow the material to speak for itself.

This study of Hebrew theophoric names falls into two divisions, the first of which is an analysis of ancient Hebrew names, while the second part is a comparison between those names and the theophoric names of other Semitic onomastica. The research for these comparative sections has been greatly facilitated by other studies in onomastics, in the fields of Ugaritic, Phoenician, Amorite, Aramaic, Old Akkadian, Akkadian and Palmyrene.

Since the main purpose of this work is to discover what concepts of the deity are revealed in Hebrew personal names, and to find out to what extent Hebrew ideas concerning the deity are distinct from those of other Semitic religions, the purpose is a theological one. It is for this reason that technicalities of comparative Semitic linguistics have largely been avoided.

Notes to Chapter 1

1. 'I sigilli ebraici', *Biblica* 50 (1969), 357-88; 'I sigilli ebraici II', *Augustinianum*, 11 (1971), 447-54; 'Sigilli ebraici III', *Annali dell' Istituto Orientali di Napoli*, 38 NS 28 (1978), 227-54.

2. *Jewish Personal Names in the Elephantine Documents: a study in onomastic development*, Ph.D. Dissertation Brandeis University (1967), University Microfilms, p. 2.

Chapter 2

ANALYSIS OF HEBREW PERSONAL NAMES

2.1 *The Problem of Source Material*

As soon as one is involved with a discussion concerning the dissemination throughout the Old Testament of the various theophoric elements which occur in the Hebrew onomasticon, the problems of dating and source analysis of the Old Testament literature become evident. However, it is obvious that to confine Hebrew theophoric names within the limits of such theories, places upon them, from the start, a set of presuppositions which would influence considerably any following conclusions. Nevertheless, it is felt that certain parts of the Old Testament material need careful examination in order to establish whether or not the spread of names throughout the Old Testament is affected by problematic dating of source material. In fact, the only real difficulty is presented by the work of the Chronicler.

Names included in 1 and 2 Chronicles were discussed by G.B. Gray in his work *Studies in Hebrew Proper Names* (1886). The wide acceptance of Gray's theory that names in 1 and 2 Chronicles lack, in the main, any authenticity has made it exigent in the present study to point out some serious anomalies in the foundations upon which Gray built his evidence. Since it is felt that this question is of considerable importance, the evidence is given in some detail, in order to clarify the incongruities of his argument.

Gray based his argument upon the numbers concerned in the following tables (*ibid.* 159, 160):

TABLE 1

THE NUMBER OF NAMES FIRST REFERRED BY APPROXIMATELY CONTEMPORARY LITERATURE[1] TO

	A	B		Totals	Names in *'l*
Period I	(1-)5	1	=	6(at most)	15
Period II	4	6	=	10	11
Period III to cent. 8	8	18	=	26	6
Period III from cent. 7	4	27	=	31	9
Period IV	1	42	=	43	18
TOTALS	22	94	=	116	59

TABLE 2

THE NUMBER OF NAMES FIRST REFERRED BY ANY OT WRITER[2] TO

	A	B		Totals	Names in *'l*
Period I 1(P)+(2-)	6	14	=	21	44
Period II	11	42	=	53	34
Period III to cent. 8	4	13	=	17	9
Period III from cent. 7	4	17	=	21	7
Period IV	1	29	=	30	7
TOTALS	27	115	=	142	101

Table 1, Gray explained, includes all names in the Old Testament literature compounded with *yh* with the exception of those names found only in Chronicles and only one or two other exceptions (see Gray, 159 n. 2). Table 2, he observed, includes *all yh* compounds i.e. the whole of the Old Testament literature *and* Chronicles.

Table 1 shows a gradual development of A compounds (*yh* prefixed) and B compounds (*yh* suffixed) through the various periods of Israelite history, Period I being pre-Davidic, Period II Davidic, Period III the time of the later kings down to the 8th century BC and, secondly, from the 7th. century BC, and Period IV the post-Exilic period. Table 2, involving the addition of those names found only in Chronicles, upsets this pattern of gradual development considerably, and in Chapter III of his work Gray used this contrast to indicate a lack of authenticity in the names of Chronicles.

However, a careful examination of the two tables shows that as a basis for such a conclusion, they are hopelessly at variance. Indeed, the statistics indicated by these tables are more of an embarrassment to Gray's mathematics than to the Chronicler's lack of authentic nomenclature! To begin with, Table 1, *excluding* the names in Chronicles, has 116 as the total number of *yh* compounds. (The total indicates *name-types*, not numbers of persons bearing name-types. The following numbers are also concerned with name-types unless indicated.) Table 2, *including* names occurring only in Chronicles, has a total of 142. This indicates, by subtracting the former total from the latter, *26 yh compounds which occur only in Chronicles*. If Table 1 lists the *yh* compounds cited by contemporary Old Testament literature but excludes such names in Chronicles for each period, then we should expect the totals for each period in Table 2, in which the Chronicler's names are included, *to be at least equal to, and sometimes more than*, the totals for each period in Table 1. However, let us examine each period, bearing in mind that we have an extra 26 names to account for in Table 2.

Table 1 shows that in Period I, 6 *yh* compounds are attested. Table 2, including the evidence of Chronicles, has a total of 21. This indicates that 15 of the Chronicler's names are assigned to Period I. Table 1 shows that in Period II, 10 *yh* compounds are attested. Table 2, including the evidence of the Chronicler, indicates 53! This would suggest that 43 of the Chronicler's names were assigned to Period II. This is preposterous, since the total number of *yh* compounds occurring solely in Chronicles is only 26.

Table I indicates that in Period III down to the 8th century, 26 *yh* compounds have been attested. Table 2, with the addition of the Chronicler's names, has a total of 17! We should expect at least the 26 from the evidence of the rest of the Old Testament literature.

Table I indicates that in Period III from the 7th century BC, 31 *yh* compounds are attested in Old Testament literature. Table 2, with the addition of any names from Chronicles, has a total of only 21! Again we have the impossible situation whereby fewer names occur in Table 2 than in Table 1. We should expect at least the same 31 compounds of Table 1 to be included in the total for this period in Table 2.

Again, Table 1 indicates a total of 43 *yh* compounds attested by contemporary Old Testament literature for Period IV, and Table 2 a total of 30! We should expect at least the same 43 names, even if none of the Chronicler's names was to be assigned to this period.

It is to be hoped that these discrepancies are clear, for they are of considerable import. Gray was particularly concerned with the names in Periods I and II, the pre-Davidic and Davidic eras, for he was anxious to show that in writing of such times the Chronicler used the personal names of his own time (Gray, 170 suggested about 300 BC) and superimposed these on the earlier period. As has been shown, however, Gray's statistics for this period are entirely erroneous. It is impossible to add 58 names from Chronicles to the 16 attested in other Old Testament literature for the pre-Davidic and Davidic periods, when the Chronicler only records 26 *yh* compounds in all! Moreover it remains unclear why the totals in Table 1 should not have been carried over to Table 2 if, as Gray stated, 'the difference of the two tables practically consists simply in this—that in the first the evidence of Chronicles is disregarded, in the second it is admitted' (p. 159). Thus, in no way should the totals in Table 2 be *less* than those in Table 1.

Gray's second set of tabular evidence, Table 3 and Table 4 (p. 162) displays equally erroneous mathematics. Table 3 contains the number of persons who bear names compounded with *yh* mentioned in approximately contemporary writings, while Table 4 contains the number of persons mentioned only in Chronicles. The totals Gray gives for *yh* compounds are worth repeating here to make the point clear.

TABLE 3

HEBREW PERSONS BEARING A *YH* NAME, AND MENTIONED IN APPROXIMATELY CONTEMPORARY LITERATURE NUMBER IN

	A	B		Totals	Persons bearing a name in *'l*
Period I	1-5	1	=	6	16
Period II	10	7	=	17	18
Period III to cent. 8	19	31	=	50	7
Period III from cent. 7	8	65	=	73	12
Period IV	27	169	=	196	50
TOTALS	69	273	=	342	103

TABLE 4

HEBREW PERSONS BEARING A *YH* NAME AND MENTIONED *ONLY* IN CHRONICLES NUMBER IN

	A	B		Totals	Persons bearing a name in *'l*
Period I	2	13	=	15	3
Period II	19	67	=	86	59
Period III to cent. 8	12	43	=	55	22
Period III from cent. 7	4	11	=	15	4
Period IV	27	170	=	197	50
TOTALS	64	304	=	368	138

It will be seen to begin with that all persons in the Old Testament bearing *yh* compound names number 710 according to Gray (by the addition of the 342 names referred to in approximately contemporary literature and the 368 names referred to only by the Chronicler). This total, however, exceeds the *actual* number of *yh* compounds borne by individuals (a total of 638) by 72. Gray's mistake lies in Table 4, Period IV, where he has indicated a total of 197 individuals to whom the Chronicler alone assigns a *yh* compound name. Yet in fact, very few post-Exilic names are found in the books of Chronicles (only 37 persons in all), for this is a period with which the Chronicler is not predominantly concerned. It would seem that for some unknown reason, Gray has repeated the statistics for Table 3, Period IV. The numbers for the two periods in the two tables are, indeed, practically identical as Gray has them.

Similarly, Gray's statistics showing the use of the theophoric element *'l* (pp. 167-68) indicate far more *'l* compounds from the post-Exilic period (Period IV) mentioned only by the Chronicler, than can possibly be the case. Compare:

TABLE 3

HEBREW PERSONS (OR TRIBES) BEARING A NAME COMPOUNDED WITH *'L* AND MENTIONED IN APPROXIMATELY CONTEMPORARY LITERATURE NUMBER IN

	A	B		Totals
Period I	8	8	=	16
Period II	13	5	=	18

Period III to cent. 8	4	3	=	7
Period III from cent. 7	5	7	=	12
Period IV	22	28	=	50
TOTALS	52	51	=	103

TABLE 4

HEBREW PERSONS (OR TRIBES) BEARING A NAME COMPOUNDED WITH *'L* AND MENTIONED *ONLY* IN CHRONICLES NUMBER IN

	A	B		Totals
Period I	2	1	=	3
Period II	19	40	=	59
Period III to cent. 8	6	16	=	22
Period III from cent. 7	0	4	=	4
Period IV	22	28	=	50
TOTALS	49	89	=	138

Few names of the post-Exilic period are recorded in the books of Chronicles (only 37, see Appendix Table 4:1) and certainly fewer *'l* compounds than for the same period in other Old Testament literature (only about 5, *ibid.*). Yet Gray assigned identical totals for Period IV to both Tables 3 and 4.

The same discrepancies that were evident in the statistics concerning *yh* compound name-types are evident also in those concerning *'l* compounds in the tables included by Gray on pages 166-67 of his work. These are:

TABLE 1

THE NUMBER OF (PERSONAL OR TRIBAL) NAMES FIRST REFERRED BY APPROXIMATELY CONTEMPORARY LITERATURE TO

	A	B		Totals
Period I	7	8	=	15
Period II	7	4	=	11
Period III to cent. 8	4	2	=	6
Period III from cent. 7	2	7	=	9
Period IV	1	17	=	18
TOTALS	21	38	=	59

TABLE 2

THE NUMBER OF NAMES FIRST REFERRED BY ANY OT WRITER TO

	A	B		Totals
Period I	11	33	=	44(in P-A 4, B 25)
Period II	14	20	=	34
Period III to cent. 8	6	3	=	9
Period III from cent. 7	2	5	=	7
Period IV	0	7	=	7
TOTALS	33	68	=	101

Between Table 1, showing the number of names first referred to by approximately contemporary literature (i.e. excluding the names found only in Chronicles and those mentioned only by the Priestly source P) and Table 2, which supposedly includes the evidence of Chronicles and the Priestly source, there is no agreement. Table 1 has a total of 59 names, Table 2 a total of 101, the difference 42, being the number of *'l* compounds mentioned only in Chronicles and P.

Table 1 indicates that in Period I, 15 *'l* compounds have been attested. Table 2, with the addition of names found only in Chronicles and P, has a total of 44 such compounds, accounting for 29 of the extra names in Chronicles and P. For Period II, Table 1 has a total of 11 names and Table 2 a total of 34 names, accounting for 23 extra names in Chronicles and P. At this point, the addition of these extra names from Period I and Period II in Table 2, amounting to 52, has already exceeded the 42 extra names to be found in Chronicles and the Priestly source. For Period III up to the 8th century BC, Table 1 has a total of 6 attested *'l* compounds, and Table 2 for the same period shows a total of 9 such names with the addition of names in Chronicles and P, accounting for an extra 3 names. For Period III from the 7th century BC on, Table 1 has a total of 9 compounds with *'l*, while Table 2, *with the addition of names found only in Chronicles and P*, has a total of 7, which is *less* than the total in Table 1! This shows an inexplicable loss of 2 names. Similarly, Table 1 Period IV shows a total of 18 names, while for the same period in Table 2 a total of 7 names is given, although Table 2 is concerned with *the addition* of names from Chronicles and P.

According to Gray, the final totals of Tables 1 and 2 show that names attested only in Chronicles and P total 42, yet we find a total difference of 55 names attested only by Chronicles and P in the actual figures for each period in Table 2. At the same time, there is an inexplicable *loss* in the totals of Table 1 Period III (from the 7th century BC on) and Period IV, when these totals are carried over to Table 2, where the names recorded only by the Chronicler and the Priestly source are supposedly added.

It is unfortunate that much of Gray's argumentation was based upon such erroneous statistical analyses, the incongruity of which has meant that much of this argumentation is nullified. This can be seen, for example, in the conclusion Gray reached on page 171, where he attempted to show that the proportion of *yh* compound names which the Chronicler refers to the pre-Davidic and Davidic periods is far in excess of the proportions attested for the same periods by the rest of the Old Testament literature. However, if of the 143 *yh* names 27 are mentioned *only* in Chronicles, then these latter names amount to under a fifth of the total number. Now Gray claimed that of the remaining 116, less than one seventh belong to the Davidic and pre-Davidic periods. Yet with the addition of the names occurring only in Chronicles (i.e. one fifth), he arrived at the conclusion that the proportion of *yh* names in these periods is more than one half! Even were we to assign *every one* of the 27 compounds in Chronicles to the Davidic or pre-Davidic periods we could arrive only at a fraction of just over one third when they are added to their complement in other Old Testament literature. Other similar discrepancies are frequently evident (cf. p. 173 concerning the proportions of names found in the pre-Davidic and Davidic periods, p. 174 concerning prefixed and suffixed *yh* compounds, and the proportions of forms on p. 176 etc.) and are a direct result of Gray's inaccuracies in the above eight tables. The incorrect statistical analysis of occurrences of the theophoric element *'l*, moreover, militates rather drastically against Gray's argument that names from the Priestly documents are not authentic reflections of nomenclature of the periods in which they occur.

Another serious flaw in Gray's work concerns his drawing of conclusions from statistics concerning only one name-type, as opposed to statistics involving the names of individuals. This methodology has led to erroneous conclusions, particularly in his analyses of prefixed and suffixed theophoric elements. For example, Gray used statistics concerning *name-types* (Table 1 p. 159) to conclude that names prefixed with *yh* became extinct in the post-

Exilic period (p. 175). He seems to have ignored the statistics of names of individuals, where he totals 27 persons in the post-Exilic period bearing a name prefixed with *yh* (Table 3, p. 162) a total which is the equivalent of the number of persons bearing such names in the whole of the period of the divided Monarchy (Period III in Gray's Table 3, p. 162). It is precisely these *individuals* whose names indicate the relative use or non-use of any theophoric element: one name-type alone can reveal very little.

In summary, Gray's argument that the names in Chronicles reflect those of the post-Exilic period remains unconvincing. Although a separate analysis of those names found only in Chronicles, undertaken by the present writer, has revealed discrepancies in the correlation between these names and those referred to by other Old Testament literature, this lack of correlation, although problematic, is not explained by Gray's conclusions. Indeed, there seems to be no reason why, in the absence of evidence to the contrary, the names referred to by the Chronicler should not, on the whole, be accepted at their face value, or at least treated separately without a preconceived opinion of where such names belong.

2.2 *Theophoric Elements*

Hebrew theophoric compounds usually consist of a divine name which is prefixed or suffixed to a non-theophoric predicate. For the majority of names, as will be illustrated below, abbreviated forms of the divine name *yhwh* and, to a somewhat lesser extent, *'l* occur as the theophoric name-element. Other theophoric elements, synonymous with forms of *yhwh* and *'l*, are also attested. These are *'b* '(divine) Father', *'ḥ* '(divine) Brother' and *'m* '(divine) Kinsman' which provide alternative names for the God of Israel. The Old Testament also indicates the use of the divine name *šdy* (Num. 24.4, 16; Ps. 68.15 etc.) which is found as a theophoric element in names like *šᵉdê'ûr* 'Shadday is a flame or light'.

However, there are also instances in which a divine appellation is used as a theophoric element instead of the divine name. The title *'dn* is used in names such as *'ădōnîrām* 'The Lord is exalted', and is frequently attested elsewhere in the Old Testament as a title for Yahweh (Josh. 3.11, 13; Ps. 97.5 etc.). In the same way, the appellation *mlk* 'King' is also found, particularly in the Psalms (Pss. 5.3; 10.16; 29.10; 44.5; 48.3 etc.). Some names also contain this title *mlk* as a substitute for the more usual divine names Yahweh and El, for example *nᵉtan-melek* 'The King has given'. The biblical text also attests the use of *ṣûr* 'Rock' as a divine appellation (e.g. Deut. 32.4, 18) which is found in biblical names like *pᵉdāhṣûr* 'The Rock (i.e. El/Y) has ransomed'. In some cases it is also probable that the element *b'l* 'Lord' is used as a divine designation for Yahweh, certainly in the name *ba'alyāh* 'Y is Lord' and probably also in a number of other cases (see the discussion on the element *b'l* below).

Such divine names and appellations are often combined together, as in *'ădōnîyāhû* 'Y is Lord', *malkîyāhû* 'Y is King', *'ăḥîmelek* 'The (divine) Brother is King', *'ammî'ēl* 'The (divine) Kinsman is El' etc. It is probable that in names of this type, *both* elements should be retained as divine elements, so that a translation of *'ădōnîyāhû* for example, is preferably 'Y is Lord' rather than 'Y is a lord'. (Cf. Phoen. 'DNB'L [*PNPPI*, 289] 'Baal is Lord' [not 'Baal is a lord'].) Similarly, *'ĕlî'āb* would mean 'El is (divine) Father' rather than the more temporal sense of 'El is (a, or like a) father'.

In any assessment of the theophoric elements in Hebrew proper names, it is important to recognize how these are spread throughout the Old Testament. Before studying this aspect, however, it must be emphasized that such a distribution of theophoric elements involves not just each type of name, for example *y(ᵉh)ônātān*, *y(ᵉh)ôyādā'*, *y(ᵉh)ôzābād* etc. but *the number of persons bearing each name*, for example *y(ᵉh)ônātān* borne by 17 persons, *y(ᵉh)ôyādā'* borne by 4 persons, *y(ᵉh)ôzābād* borne by 13 persons. If cases of the use of the prefix *y(ᵉh)ô* in the exemplified names above are enumerated, we should find not 3, but 34 examples of the prefix *y(ᵉh)ô* with the elements *ntn*, *yd'*, and *zbd*. Similarly, with all theophoric names, failure to take into account each individual and to enumerate only types of names, results in a total disregard of as many as three-quarters of the individuals in the Old Testament who bore a theophoric compound name! Failure to incorporate all such names in any assessment of the use of the theophoric element, particularly when assigning these names to a specific period, can only result in a nonsensical view of the spread and use of the divine compound in the Hebrew onomasticon. While this may seem obvious, it was clearly not contained in the statistical findings put forward by Gray (*op. cit.*, pp. 159 and 160 etc.) or by Noth (*IPN*, *passim*). Indeed, Gray cited the total number of compounds with *yhwh* as 157 (p. 158) whereas the number of individuals bearing names compounded with forms of *yhwh* is more than four times that number.

With these clarifications in mind we must turn to examine the spread of the theophoric elements in personal names, by determining their popularity in the various stages of Israelite development as portrayed by the Old Testament. For this purpose, the Old Testament has been divided into four periods, the pre-monarchical period, the period of the united Monarchy, the period of the divided Monarchy and the Exilic and post-Exilic period.

As noted above in Section 1, the books of 1 and 2 Chronicles present no small difficulty in the present assessment of the use of the theophoric elements. For this reason the spread of theophoric elements with regard to the four previously mentioned periods will be examined in two ways. First, we shall study them in the contexts in which they have been transmitted, that is, including the evidence of Chronicles. Secondly, we shall exclude names of individuals which occur only in Chronicles, unless the occurrence of the latter does not affect the trends shown by the names in general. Only concerning 1 Chr. 23–27 does there seem to be some agreement that these chapters belong to a later period of history than their Davidic context suggests. Nevertheless, rather than assign these chapters to either the Davidic or post-Exilic period, names occurring here will be treated separately, so that they can be assessed with both periods when necessary. Where the addition of these names to either the Davidic or post-Exilic period is sufficient to suggest alternative conclusions, this will also be noted.

The majority of biblical names with which this study is concerned, occur in the post-Exilic period and are contained in the books of Ezra and Nehemiah. Such an extensive listing of names at this time would seem quite natural after the return of the exiles to Jerusalem in view of the formation of the new community. The next largest group of names is extracted from the period of the divided Monarchy followed by a considerable number from the the pre-Monarchical period. Finally, the period of the united Monarchy provides the smallest number of names.[3] When names found only in Chronicles are excluded from each period, this general spread of names is exactly the same. It should be noted here, that is is not possible, in the main, to compare those names found only in Chronicles vis-à-vis those names found in the rest of the Old Testament. This is because the Chronicler assigns, in all, only 37 names to the Exilic and post-Exilic period while the rest of the Old Testament totals 330 for this time.[4] The Chronicler's names, then, will always be at variance with those of the rest of the Old Testament for the Exilic and post-Exilic period.

Only with this background in mind is it possible to assess the relative spread and use of the various theophoric elements: where types of theophoric compounds, for example with *'l* prefixed or *yh* suffixed, do not reflect this general spread of theophoric compound names, then such types are markworthy. However, where such types do conform to the general spread of all names throughout the Old Testament, it is important to note that meaningful conclusions cannot be drawn. The fact that names suffixed with forms of *yhwh*, for example, are more frequent in the Exilic and post-Exilic period may seem in itself an important fact, but such 'importance' is seen in its correct perspective when it is remembered that more names are attested in the post-Exilic period than in any other and we should therefore *expect* more names suffixed with *yhwh* to be attested for this time. The general spread of *all* names, therefore, must continually be borne in mind in order to avoid misleading conclusions. Similarly, we should not expect an agreement as far as mere numbers are concerned between biblical and extra-biblical Hebrew names. Extra-biblical names, which are mainly datable to the period of the divided Monarchy, are more than twice as many as those attested by the Old Testament for the same period. This needs to be borne in mind when the two sets of evidence, biblical and archaeological, are compared.

YHWH as a theophoric element in compound names
(cf. Appendix, Tables, 4.1, 4.3, 4.4, 4.15 and 4.16)

The commonest biblical and extra-biblical theophoric element is *yhwh*, which occurs in various abbreviated forms. Its biblical use, with or without *yhwh* compounds found only in Chronicles, corresponds in distribution to the way in which theophoric compounds in general are spread throughout the Old Testament, as outlined above, with the exception that it was less popular in the early pre-Monarchical period than in the period of the united Monarchy. This is indeed significant, for the pre-Monarchical period is the only time in which another theophoric element, *'l*, was more widely used than forms of *yhwh*. Otherwise, generally speaking, names compounded with *yhwh* in the Old Testament occur more than twice as frequently as theophoric compounds affixed with *'l* (639 *yhwh*, 318 *'l*).

It is in the pre-Monarchical period that compound names with forms of *yhwh* recorded by the Chronicler differ very markedly from the same compounds attested by the rest of the Old Testament for this period. In fact, of the 62 individuals bearing a name compounded with *yhwh* in the pre-Monarchical period, 58 of these are mentioned only by the Chronicler. The main formal characteristic of these 58 names, that of the Qal perfective in the suffixed position, led Gray (*op. cit.*, 176-78) to conclude that they bore the stamp of the post-Exilic period, for in this period the largest number of Qal perfectives is found. However, here we see the importance of relating such statistics to the general spread of names: because most of the names in the Old Testament are attested for the Exilic and post-Exilic period the fact that more Qal perfectives occur in compound names from this time is exactly what one would expect. In fact, compound names composed of the Qal perfective amount to about half of all the names *in each period* except the pre-Monarchical era. Thus one could justifiably claim that the 58 names in Chronicles show characteristics of names not only in the Exilic and post-Exilic period, but also of the period of the united Monarchy as well as the period of the divided Monarchy.

Nevertheless, the reason for the discrepancy between the Chronicler's names and those of the rest of the Old Testament for the pre-Monarchical period is still unclear. To accept the Chronicler's names for the early period as authentic is to admit a large number of names compounded with forms of *yhwh* in the period prior to the revelation of that name at Sinai (Exod. 3.13ff.). Although the rest of the Old Testament is comparatively, though not entirely, silent in attesting such compounds before the events at Sinai, it does attest a large number of abbreviated names for the pre-Monarchical period,[5] some of which, if they are abbreviations of theophoric compounds, as is very probable, may show signs of having originally borne a Yahwistic element.[6] At this point, however, it would be advantageous to consider the problem through a closer examination of the relationship between names attested by the Chronicler and those of the rest of the Old Testament with regard to other periods and other theophoric elements.

Suffixed occurrences of YHWH

Instances of names suffixed with forms of *yhwh* represent by far the most popular type of theophoric compound name, both biblically and extra-biblically. The spread of such names throughout the Old Testament corresponds to the general spread of all names,[7] but as noted above concerning *yhwh* compounds, we find that of the 46 names suffixed with forms of *yhwh* occurring in the pre-Monarchical period, as many as 45 are mentioned only by the Chronicler, so that without these names there would be fewer occurrences suffixed with *yhwh* in the pre-Monarchical period than in the period of the united Monarchy.

The suffixed abbreviations of the divine name *yhwh* occur in biblical names in two forms *yāhû* and *yāh*, and in several cases (44) both *yāhû* and *yāh* terminate, interchangeably, the names of the same individuals. Biblical names containing the suffixes *yāhû* or *yāh* show a marked preference for the latter (340 *yāh* as opposed to 123 *yāhû*) and the use of the suffix *yāh* conforms, in the main, to the general spread of all names, although only the Chronicler assigns names with this suffix to the pre-Monarchical period. Without the Chronicler's evidence, names suffixed with *yāh* are more frequent in the period of the united Monarchy than in pre-Monarchical times.

The alternative suffix *yāhû* is met less frequently than *yāh* but seems, nevertheless, to have been just as popular at the time of the divided Monarchy, when it was mostly used (see below, Appendix Table 4.4) and thus it does not conform to the general spread of all names. Neither does the inclusion or exclusion of the Chronicler's evidence affect this conclusion, so that it is possible to state with certainty the popularity of the suffix *yāhû* during this time. Excluding the evidence of the Chronicler only two names suffixed with this form are cited by the rest of the Old Testament before the division of the Kingdom, while for this period the Chronicler records 15 persons with names suffixed with *yāhû*. However, the evidence of the Old Testament excluding Chronicles, for the period of the united Monarchy shows that the popularity of names suffixed with both *yāh* and *yāhû* referring to the same individual, is second only to that of the time of the divided Monarchy, and thus shows that instances of the suffix *yāhû* were certainly in existence before the division of the Kingdom.

The use of both forms *yāhû* and *yāh* as suffixed elements referring to the same individual does not conform to the general spread of all names and so may be regarded as a special characteristic of the time of the divided Monarchy, and to a somewhat lesser extent of the time of the united Monarchy, irrespective of the evidence of the Chronicler.

In extra-biblical names, suffixed forms of the divine name *yhwh*, which considerably outnumber prefixed forms[8] occur as *yhw*, *yh* and *yw*. Unlike biblical compounds of the same type, the most popular suffix is *yhw* which occurs widely on both seals and inscriptions. This may well be due to the fact that the majority of extra-biblical seals and inscriptions are datable to the period of the divided Monarchy, a period in which biblical names themselves reveal a popularity for the suffix *yāhû*. The suffix *yw* occurs on a number of seals and a few inscriptions, but it is used exclusively as a suffix on the Samarian ostraca.

Amongst those biblical names suffixed with forms of the divine name *yhwh*, the Qal perfective is the most prevalent form and conforms in proportion to all names as far as its spread throughout the Old Testament is concerned.[9] Again, however, it is only the Chronicler who assigns Qal perfective forms suffixed with *yhwh* to the pre-Monarchical period. Other forms conform in the main to the general spread of all names and reveal nothing markworthy. Extra-biblical names suffixed with forms of *yhwh* show the same preference for the Qal perfective.

Prefixed occurrences of YHWH

In the case of biblical compound names prefixed with forms of *yhwh*, which are far fewer than their suffixed counterparts (132 prefixed, 507 suffixed), we find a dissimilarity with the usual spread of names. Instead of the largest number of such names being found in the period of the Exile and post-Exile, we find names prefixed with *yhwh* occurring more frequently in the period of the divided Monarchy, while fewer names of this type are attested for the Exilic and post-Exilic period. Neither do the earlier periods coincide with the general spread of names, for more forms prefixed with *yhwh* occur in the period of the united Monarchy than in the pre-Monarchical period.[10] However, once the evidence of Chronicles is excluded, the names conform in dissemination according to the spread of all names except that, as is usually found when the Chronicler's names are excluded from the pre-Monarchical period, compounds with *yhwh* at this time were far fewer than in the period of the united Monarchy.

The prefixing of names with *y*^{e}*hô* and *yô* does not appear to have been indiscriminate. Prefixed occurrences of *y*^{e}*hô* occur mainly in the time of the divided Monarchy and to a somewhat lesser extent in the period of the united Monarchy, thus not conforming to the usual distribution of names. Moreover, the evidence for the use of *y^ehô* in these times is not affected by the exclusion of the evidence of Chronicles and so may be regarded as a certain feature of the prefix.

The most popular prefixed form of the divine name *yhwh* is *yô*. Names prefixed with this form are, as expected in view of the general distribution of all names, most popular in the Exilic and post-Exilic period. However, they do not conform to the usual pattern in that they are fairly frequent in the period of the united Monarchy, occur to a somewhat lesser extent in pre-Monarchical times, and are least frequently attested for the period of the divided Monarchy. Excluding those names found only in Chronicles, however, names prefixed with *yô* correspond to the general distribution of all names, except that they are commoner in the time of the united Monarchy, than in pre-Monarchical times. As was found with suffixed cases of *yhwh*, interchangeability of the prefixes *yô* and *y^ehô* when referring to one individual, seems to have had considerable popularity in the period of the divided Monarchy, a factor which is not affected by the inclusion or exclusion of the Chronicler's evidence and which is not characteristic of the general spread of all names.

It would seem that the divine element *y(h)w* in the initial position could be abbreviated further to *yē*, a practice indicated by a few cases in the Exilic and post-Exilic period and by only slightly fewer in the time of the divided Monarchy. Only the Chronicler assigns such forms to the earlier periods (*yēhû'*, 1 Chr. 2.38 and 12.3).

Extra-biblical occurrences show the same preference for names suffixed, as opposed to prefixed, with *yhwh* (a ratio of more than 8:1) and amongst the latter, the prefix *yhw* is shown to be more prevalent than any other prefix. This supports the biblical evidence for the popularity of this prefix in the period of the divided Monarchy, since the extra-biblical material is, in the main, similarly dated. Prefixed instances of *yw* are not as frequent as *yhw* (see Appendix, Table 4.16). Also evident is the possibility of a prefix *yō* which in biblical names is found only in *yōrām* (1 Chr. 26.25).

Like suffixed forms, biblical names prefixed with forms of the divine name *yhwh* show, in general, a preference for the use of the Qal perfective (54 instances), a factor which is not influenced in any way by the Chronicler's evidence. Although the Qal perfective is the predominant form used with names prefixed with *yhwh*, nominal forms account for a much higher percentage of this type of compound than was the case with those suffixed with *yhwh*, and predominate over the use of the Qal perfective in the pre-Monarchical period (14 cases of nominal forms compared with 7 verbal Qal perfectives). Again, the Chronicler's evidence does not affect these characteristics whether it is included or excluded. The same applies to the use of the stative aspect of the Qal perfective which was used in a far greater percentage of names prefixed with forms of *yhwh* than in names suffixed with such forms (20% of prefixed forms compared with 7.5% of suffixed forms).

In extra-biblical names prefixed with forms of the divine name *yhwh* we find a slight preference for nominal forms, followed by the use of the Qal perfective. The use of the stative Qal perfective is also more prominent in names prefixed with forms of *yhwh* than those suffixed with *yhwh* (see Appendix, Table 4.15).

In summary, certain characteristics of the use of forms of the divine name *yhwh* in names become clear irrespective of problems of dating or authenticity:

1. Forms of *yhwh* were the most popular in theophoric compound names and suffixed forms of *yhwh* were more frequent than prefixed forms both biblically and extra-biblically.
2. In the pre-Monarchical period compounds with *'l* were more frequent than compounds with *yhwh* but in every other period compounds with *yhwh* predominate.
3. Biblical names suffixed with forms of *yhwh* occur with a terminating *yāh* more frequently than a terminating *yāhû*. The contrary is true for extra-biblical names, which portray features of names in the divided Monarchy.
4. The suffix *yāhû* was a characteristic of the divided Monarchy and of extra-biblical names.
5. The use of both forms *yāhû* and *yāh* as suffixed elements and of *y*^{e}*hô* and *yô* as prefixed elements, referring to the same individual is a special characteristic of the time of the divided Monarchy.
6. The suffix *yw* is only attested in extra-biblical names and is used exclusively on the Samarian ostraca. Prefixed occurrences of *yhwh* in extra-biblical names on Samarian ostraca also show exclusive use of *yw*.

7. Prefixed occurrences of *yᵉhô* occur mainly in the time of the divided Monarchy and to a somewhat lesser extent in the period of the united Monarchy.
8. The Qal perfective is the commonest form with prefixed and suffixed forms of *yhwh* in biblical names. In extra-biblical names suffixed with *yhwh*, the Qal perfective is the most frequently attested form, whereas extra-biblical names prefixed with *yhwh* show a preference for nominal forms. Although nominal forms are more noticeably characteristic of biblical compounds prefixed with forms of *yhwh* they are rarely sufficient to outnumber instances of the Qal perfective. Only in the pre-Monarchical period with names prefixed with *yhwh* are nominal forms slightly predominant over Qal perfectives.
9. The use of the stative Qal perfective is a feature of biblical and extra-biblical names prefixed with forms of *yhwh*.

The theophoric element 'L
(cf. Appendix, Tables 4.1, 4.5 and 4.15)
In comparison with names compounded with *yhwh*, biblical names compounded with *'l* occur about half as frequently, and extra-biblically occur only in the ratio of nearly 1:5 with *yhwh* compounds. *'l* names reveal a marked difference between their distribution throughout the Old Testament and the spread of all names in general. This is because names compounded with *'l* are more frequently found in the pre-Monarchical period than in any other. The Exilic and post-Exilic period contains the second largest number of such names[11] followed by the period of the united Monarchy. The least number of *'l* names is attested for the time of the divided Monarchy. Statistical comparisons between those names recorded only by the Chronicler and those in the rest of the Old Testament are never really possible because the Chronicler assigns very few names to the Exilic and post-Exilic period—the main source of names external to the books of Chronicles. However, excluding the Exilic and post-Exilic period, the rest of the Old Testament without the evidence of Chronicles still reflects the prevalent use of *'l* as a theophoric element in the early, pre-Monarchical period.

Since the pattern of names compounded with *'l* differs completely from the usual spread of names, it is necessary to assess in what ratios *'l* names were used in each period in relation to other theophoric elements. This is important since mere numbers alone for each period will not relfect a true image: the fact that more names as a whole are attested in the Exilic and post-Exilic period, minimizes the extent to which *'l* names are attested in other periods. The presence of 72 *'l* compound names in the Exilic and post-Exilic period, for example, is greater than the 62 attested for the united Monarchy. The 72 later names, however, are 72 out of 367 attested for that period, while the 62 attested for the united Monarchy are 62 out of only 199 names in all for that time. This factor has a considerable affect on the conclusions reached. The ratios of compound names in *'l* to other theophoric compounds are as follows:

	'l		Others
pre-Monarchical period	1	:	2
united Monarchy	1	:	3
divided Monarchy	1	:	5½
Exilic & post-Exilic	1	:	5

What these ratios show is a decline in the use of *'l* as a theophoric element in compound names until the divided Monarchy but then, a slight increase in the Exilic and post Exilic period. When names found only in Chronicles are excluded, however, the picture is quite different:

	'l		Others
pre-Monarchical period	1	:	1¾
united Monarchy	1	:	4
divided Monarchy	1	:	11
Exilic & post-Exilic	(1	:	5)

This shows a far more pronounced decline in the use of the element *'l* in names up to the divided Monarchy followed by a seemingly considerable revival of such names in the Exilic and post-Exilic period. But it must be remembered that since the Chronicler assigns so few names to the Exilic and post-Exilic period, the ratio for this period when the Chronicler's names are excluded is not a true indication in comparison with the other periods. However, the most outstanding difference between the two sets of ratios is that shown for the divided Monarchy, a period in which, when all names are included, 46 *'l* compounds are attested out of which as many as 34 (74%) are mentioned by the Chronicler alone.

With names compounded with *yhwh* the most prevalent form used was found to be the Qal perfective. Compound names with *'l*, however, are found in general to be predominantly nominal (88 instances) and only secondarily Qal perfective (76 instances). However, if names occurring only in Chronicles are excluded, the converse is found to be the case (38 nominal forms and 41 instances of the Qal perfective). When names attested only in Chronicles are retained, biblical names compounded with *'l* indicate a preference for nominal forms until the time of the divided Monarchy. At this time Qal perfective forms become slightly more frequent and this frequency is retained and increased in the Exilic and post-Exilic periods. This preference for the use of the Qal perfective in the later periods is, nevertheless, not sufficient to alter the fact that nominal forms are the main general characteristic of compounds with *'l*. Construct forms are seen to be almost as prevalent as Qal perfective forms in the pre-Monarchical period, the exclusion of the Chronicler's evidence making no difference to this fact. Extra-biblical compound names with *'l* reveal a preference for the Qal perfective as opposed to nominal forms in a ratio of 2:1, but these, of course, appertain to a more specific period of time. Interestingly, this ratio does not coincide with that of the close ratio between Qal perfective and nominal forms of biblical names for the period of the divided Monarchy, with or without the evidence of the Chronicler.

Suffixed occurrences of 'L

In the pre-Monarchical period, which contains more *'l* compound names than any other period, more names suffixed with *'l* also occur than at any other time. The Exilic and post-Exilic period contains the next highest number of such names followed by the period of the divided Monarchy. The least number of compound names suffixed with *'l* is attested for the united Monarchy.[12] Again, however, ratios are important because of the affect of the high percentage of names attested for the post-Exilic time. The approximate ratio of names suffixed wih *'l* in relation to all other theophoric compounds is as follows:

	'l		Others
pre-Monarchical	1	:	3
united Monarchy	1	:	7[13]
divided Monarchy	1	:	8
Exilic & post-Exilic	1	:	7½[14]

This indicates that suffixed occurrences of *'l* reflect a decrease in popularity until the divided Monarchy followed by a slight increase in use in Exilic/post-Exilic times. Excluding those names found only in Chronicles produces different results:

	'l		Others
pre-Monarchical	1	:	2½
united Monarchy	1	:	17
divided Monarchy	1	:	27
Exilic & post-Exilic	(1	:	7¼)

Once again, the last ratio cannot be taken into consideration because the Chronicler assigns so few names to the Exilic/post-Exilic period. Nevertheless this table shows an even greater decline in the use of the suffixed element *'l* for the other periods, mainly because it excludes the high percentage (81%) of compounds suffixed with *'l* which the Chronicler alone assigns to the period of the divided Monarchy.

Biblical names suffixed with *'l* in general, show a preference for nominal forms (45), followed closely by construct forms (41) and then by the Qal imperfective (33) and the Qal perfective (30). Excluding the names found only in Chronicles, however, there appears to be a considerable preference for construct forms (22) and, to a much lesser extent, Qal perfective (15) and nominal forms (15). The use of the Qal imperfective (9) is not a pronounced feature of this type of name when names found only in Chronicles are excluded.

In the pre-Monarchical period, names suffixed with *'l* occur predominantly in the construct form and in the Exilic and post-Exilic period in the Qal perfective. These two facts remain true irrespective of the Chronicler's evidence. In the other two periods there is not such a correlation between the Chronicler's evidence and the rest of the Old Testament. For the period of the united Monarchy the evidence of the whole of the Old Testament including Chronicles attests a preference for nominal forms while, with the exclusion of those names found only in Chronicles, both nominal (2) and construct forms (2) are seen to be equally prevalent, although few in number. For the period of the divided Monarchy the whole of the Old Testament, including Chronicles, attests the prevalent use of the Qal imperfective for names suffixed with *'l*. When the Chronicler's names are excluded, however, very few names suffixed with *'l* are attested for this period and we find no more than one Qal imperfective form, one construct, one Piel imperfective and one prepositional form. Indeed, of the 31 names suffixed with *'l* attested for the divided Monarchy, as many as 26 are recorded only by the Chronicler.

Although suffixed cases of *'l* in general are more frequently attested than prefixed occurrences (208 suffixed and 110 prefixed), in the period of the united Monarchy the latter outnumber the former considerably (34 prefixed and 28 suffixed). This is even more pronounced when names occurring only in Chronicles are excluded (18 prefixed and 6 suffixed instances). In all other periods suffixed cases of *'l* are in the majority. The exclusion of names found only in Chronicles for the period of the divided Monarchy, however, alters the balance in favour of a marginal predominance of prefixed forms (7) over suffixed forms (5). Relevant here, is the extra-biblical material which shows a distinct preference for prefixed forms (see below, Appendix, Table 4.15). In these extra-biblical names, forms suffixed with *'l* reveal a preference for the Qal imperfective.

Prefixed occurrences of 'L

Biblical names prefixed with *'l* amount to just under one third of all *'l* compounds. Although they occur less frequently than names suffixed with *'l*, in the period of the united Monarchy, as noted above, they considerably outnumber names suffixed with *'l*. It is, in fact, in the period of the united Monarchy that more names prefixed with *'l* (34) occur than at any other time, which is to say that such names do not conform in frequency to the normal spread of names throughout the Old Testament. The pre-Monarchical period provides the next highest number of names prefixed with *'l* (29) followed by the post-Exilic period (24),[15] the lowest number of such names being attested for the time of the divided Monarchy (15). The ratios of names prefixed with *'l* to all theophoric compound names for each period is as follows:

	'l		Others
pre-Monarchical	1	:	8
united Monarchy	1	:	6[16]
divided Monarchy	1	:	17
Exilic and post-Exilic	1	:	15

These ratios reveal that the prefixing of the theophoric element *'l* in names shows a rise in popularity from the pre-Monarchical time to the united Monarchy in which they were most popular, followed by a sharp decline in use and then a slight revival in Exilic and post-Exilic times. When the Chronicler's names are excluded these trends are barely affected:

	'l		Others
pre-Monarchical	1	:	7
united Monarchy	1	:	6
divided Monarchy	1	:	19
Exilic and post-Exilic	(1	:	14½)

The relative paucity of names prefixed with *'l* in the time of the divided Monarchy, to which the Chronicler alone assigns 8 and the rest of the Old Testament 7, is not reflected in the extra-biblical material. This material shows a ratio of names prefixed with *'l* to all other theophoric compounds as approximately 1.10, whereas the biblical ratio of such names to all others in the time of the divided Monarchy is 1.17. Names prefixed with *'l* occurring on seals and inscriptions, which mainly date to the time of the divided Monarchy show, in fact, a marked preference for prefixed as opposed to suffixed *'l* in compound names of this type (see below, Appendix, Table 4.15). Even when those names found only in Chronicles are excluded from the biblical total of names prefixed with *'l* in this period, we find only the slightest preference for such prefixes (7 prefixed and 5 suffixed).

Biblical names prefixed with *'l* occur most frequently in the Qal perfective (46) followed by nominal forms (43) and, worthy of mention, some Hiphil imperfectives (10). The evidence of Chronicles makes no difference to this order. In the early pre-Monarchical period, names prefixed with *'l* are found mainly in the Qal perfective (16) followed by the use of nominal forms (12). In the period of the united Monarchy, these characteristics are reversed, for nominal forms are preferred to Qal perfectives, (16 nominal 11 Qal perfective). The Exilic and post-Exilic names with this prefix are equally divided in form between Qal perfectives (8) and nominal forms (8), followed by a few names in the Hiphil imperfective (6).

Extra-biblical names prefixed with *'l* show a marked preference for the Qal perfective. Nearly half of the names have this form and only approximately 1 in 4 is a nominal form.

Characteristics of names compounded with *'l* which obtain regardless of the evidence of those names occurring only in Chronicles, may be summarized as follows:

1. Names compounded with *'l* are far less frequent than those compounded with forms of *yhwh*.
2. *'l* was more popular as a theophoric element in names occurring in the pre-Monarchical period than any other theophoric element, including forms of *yhwh*.
3. Like *'l* compounds in general, names suffixed with *'l* occur more frequently in the pre-Monarchical time than at any other. Names prefixed with *'l*, however, occur more frequently in the period of the united Monarchy.
4. In the time of the divided Monarchy and the exilic/post-Exilic period, Qal perfective forms occur as the most prevalent form with *'l* compound names.
5. In the pre-Monarchical period names suffixed with *'l* occur predominantly in the construct form and in the Exilic and post-Exilic period in the Qal perfective.
6. Names prefixed with *'l* rise in popularity from pre-Monarchical times to the time of the united Monarchy when they were most frequently in use and then sharply decline by the period of the divided Monarchy. A slight revival of these names occurs in the Exilic and post-Exilic times.
7. Names prefixed with *'l* occur predominantly in the Qal perfective.
8. Nominal forms are a characteristic of names prefixed with *'l* in the time of the united Monarchy.
9. Extra-biblical names prefixed with *'l* show a preference for the Qal perfective.
10. In extra-biblical names, prefixed occurrences of *'l* are in excess of suffixed occurrences.

The theophoric element 'B
(cf. Tables 4.1, 4.6 and 4.17 of the Appendix)

In a number of Hebrew names the divine element *'b*, meaning 'Father' (cf. BDB, 3) is used instead of the more usual *yhwh* or *'l*, to refer to the God of Israel.

Only 1 in 20 of the theophoric names in the Old Testament is compounded with the theophoric element *'b*. Such compounds occur quite contrary to the normal distribution of names for they are found predominantly in the pre-Monarchical period and secondarily in the time of the united Monarchy, although the ratios of names in *'b* to all theophoric compounds in each of these periods is 1:9 for both. Only 6 such names are attested for the divided Monarchy and only 3 for the Exilic and post-Exilic period. If those names found only in Chronicles are excluded, more compound names with *'b* occur in the time of the united Monarchy than the pre-Monarchical period but otherwise the pattern is the same. Thus, with or without the Chronicler's evidence, it is possible to conclude that names compounded with *'b* were characteristic of the period before the divided Monarchy and were fairly rare after that time (1 in 44 during the divided Monarchy and 1 in 122 in the Exilic and post-Exilic period).

Extra-biblical occurrences of the element are not infrequent; nevertheless, it is often difficult to determine whether such occurrences are, in reality, Hebrew names. The possibility of a non-Hebrew origin, therefore, needs to be borne in mind when these extra-biblical names compounded with *'b* are discussed.

Names compounded with *'b*, both biblically and extra-biblically, show a preference for the use of nominal forms, which is also a factor unaffected by the Chronicler's evidence. From the biblical evidence, *'b* appears to be used more frequently than any other theophoric element apart from forms of *yhwh* and *'l*. However, extra-biblical names may illustrate the popularity of *'ḥ* rather than *'b* (see Appendix, Table 4.17).

Suffixed occurrences of 'B

Both biblical and extra-biblical names suffixed with *'b* are far fewer in number than their prefixed counterparts, a fact not affected by the Chronicler's evidence as far as biblical names are concerned. Names suffixed with *'b* occur less frequently in the pre-Monarchical period (1 in 48) than in the period of the united Monarchy (1 in 39). Here, also, the Chronicler's evidence makes no difference to this conclusion. Only one name suffixed with *'b* is attested elsewhere and this is found in the Exilic and post-Exilic time. This paucity of suffixed *'b* in compound names is also reflected in extra-biblical material.

Like *'b* compounds in general, a preference for nominal forms (10) is evident in biblical names but the exclusion of those names found only in Chronicles (4) reveals a preference for verbal forms in the stative Qal perfective (7). Extra-biblical names suffixed with *'b* retain the preference for nominal forms.

Prefixed occurrences of 'B

Names prefixed with *'b* are far more numerous, both biblically and extra-biblically, than those suffixed with *'b*. Biblical names with this prefix, including names found only in Chronicles, occur predominantly in both the pre-Monarchical time and the period of the united Monarchy or, if the Chronicler's evidence is excluded, slightly more frequently in the time of the united Monarchy. The ratio of such names to all theophoric compounds for these periods is important, for fewer names are attested for the united Monarchy than the pre-Monarchical period. Including the Chronicler's evidence, approximately 1 in 12 names is prefixed with *'b* both in the pre-Monarchical time and in the time of the united Monarchy while, excluding those names found only in Chronicles, 1 in 9 names is prefixed with *'b* in the pre-Monarchical time, and 1 in 6 in the period of the united Monarchy.

Again, nominal forms are more frequent amongst names prefixed with *'b* both biblically and extra-biblically.

In summary, the following conclusions may be drawn concerning the use of *'b* as a theophoric element in Hebrew names:

1. Biblical names compounded with *'b* were mainly current up to the division of the Kingdom. From this time on they were relatively infrequent and rarely found after the Exile.
2. Names compounded with *'b*, both biblically and extra-biblically, are mainly found in nominal form.
3. In both biblical and extra-biblical occurrences, names prefixed with *'b* outnumber those suffixed with *'b*, the latter being rare.
4. Names suffixed with *'b* were less popular in the pre-Monarchical period than in the time of the united Monarchy.

The theophoric element 'Ḥ

(cf. Appendix, Tables 4.1, 4.7 and 4.17)

Old Testament names compounded with *'ḥ*, 'Brother', occur mostly in the time of the united Monarchy (1 in 11). They are less frequent in pre-Monarchical times (1 in 14), while a small number is attested for the time of the divided Monarchy (6), and only 2 for the Exilic and post-Exilic period. Thus the spread of these names throughout the Old Testament does not conform to the general spread of all names. These facts remain valid irrespective of the Chronicler's evidence. Clearly, then, names with this element are fairly early and occur with any frequency only before the division of the Kingdom, after which time they are not widely attested and are very rare by the post-Exilic period.

The most prevalent form used with both prefixed and suffixed names compounded with *'ḥ* was the nominal form which was characteristic of biblical and extra-biblical names of this type. Those names found in Chronicles reflect the same pattern.

Suffixed occurrences of 'Ḥ

Suffixed occurrences of *'ḥ* are far fewer than prefixed occurrences in biblical names (7 suffixed compared with 36 prefixed) and are non-existent in extra-biblical names. Indeed, in biblical names the suffix *'ḥ* is so rare that it is not really possible to draw any conclusions as to the spread of the element. 2 such names are attested for the pre-Monarchical period, both being mentioned only by the Chronicler, who is also the only source for the name suffixed with *'ḥ* recorded for the time of the united Monarchy. 1 such name occurs only in 1 Chr. 23–27 and 3 names suffixed with *'ḥ* are attested for the period of the divided Monarchy, 2 of which are found only in Chronicles. No names suffixed with *'ḥ* are attested for the Exilic or post-Exilic period. Of the names suffixed with *'ḥ* nominal forms are the most frequent.

Prefixed occurrences of 'Ḥ

Prefixed occurrences of *'ḥ* are found most frequently in the period of the united Monarchy (1 in 12) followed by the pre-Monarchical period (1 in 16), a fact which is unaffected by the exclusion of those names found only in Chronicles. Outside these periods, prefixed occurrences of *'ḥ* in names are quite rare, only 2 being attested for the time of the divided Monarchy and 2 for the Exilic and post-Exilic period, 1 of the latter being attested only by the Chronicler. Approximately 1 in 25 of the biblical Hebrew names is prefixed with *'ḥ*.

With regard to the use of *'ḥ* as a theophoric element in Hebrew names, it may be concluded:

1. *'ḥ* was used in names mainly before the divided Monarchy, and was particularly prevalent in the time of the united Monarchy. After the division of the Kingdom it was no longer prevalent and very rare during and after the Exile.

2. Both biblical and extra-biblical compound names with *'ḥ* were mainly nominal in form.
3. Suffixed occurrences of *'ḥ* are very few in biblical names (7) and entirely absent in extra-biblical Hebrew names.

The theophoric element 'M
(cf. Appendix, Tables 4.1, 4.8 and 4.17)
Hebrew names compounded with the element *'m*, meaning 'Kinsman' or 'Paternal Uncle' (cf. BDB, 769) occur less frequently than compounds with *'b* and *'ḥ*. Biblical names compounded with *'m* amount to about 25 in all. They occur mainly in the time of the united Monarchy (1 in 22) and in the pre-Monarchical period (1 in 24). 3 are recorded by the Chronicler in 1 Chr. 23–27, while 2 are attested for the time of the divided Monarchy and 2 for the Exilic/post-Exilic period, one of the latter being attested only by the Chronicler. Like *'b* and *'ḥ*, then, the use of the theophoric element *'m* in biblical names is an early phenomenon, a fact which the Chronicler's evidence does not affect. Only 6 names compounded with *'m* occur extra-biblically; in 4 the element is suffixed and in 2, prefixed.

In biblical names compounded with *'m*, the form of the non-theophoric element is predominantly nominal (12 instances), while a secondary feature of these names is the use of the stative Qal perfective (5 instances). These characteristics are not affected by the Chronicler's evidence. Of the extra-biblical names compounded with *'m*, 3 are nominal, 1 is a Qal perfective, 2 stative Qal imperfective and 1 a Hiphil perfective.

Suffixed occurrences of 'M
In biblical names, *'m* occurs as a suffixed element less frequently than as a prefixed element (10 suffixed as opposed to 16 prefixed instances). However, suffixed cases of *'m* are more frequently attested for the time of the united Monarchy than for any other period. During this period such suffixed occurrences slightly outnumber prefixed occurrences (5 suffixed, 4 prefixed), factors which are unaffected by those names found only in Chronicles. Elsewhere, cases of names suffixed with *'m* are sporadic, 2 in the pre-Monarchical period (1 of which is attested only by the Chronicler), 1 in 1 Chr. 23–27, and 2 in the period of the divided Monarchy. Like all compounds with *'m*, suffixed occurrences are found mainly with a

non-theophoric element which is nominal in form. The use of the stative Qal perfective is not a feature of names suffixed with *'m*.

Prefixed occurrences of 'M

Names prefixed with *'m* (15) are more numerous than those suffixed with *'m* (10), and occur more frequently in the pre-Monarchical period than at any other time, a factor not influenced by those names occurring only in Chronicles. Outside the pre-Monarchical period, in which 8 names prefixed with *'m* are attested (1 of which is mentioned only by the Chronicler), 3 are attested for the time of the united Monarchy (2 of which occur only in Chronicles), 2 occur in 1 Chr. 23–27, and 2 are attested for the Exilic and post-Exilic period (1 of which is mentioned only in Chronicles).

Formally, nominal forms (9) are prevalent among these prefixed occurrences, and the use of the stative Qal perfective (5) is noteworthy. Extra-biblical occurrences of *'m* in the initial position amount only to 2, one prefixed to a non-theophoric element in the nominal form, and one to a verbal Qal perfective.

Concerning the use of *'m* as a theophoric element, one may conclude with certainty that:

1. *'m* was used as a theophoric element mainly in the time of the united Monarchy and secondarily in the pre-Monarchical period.
2. Compound names affixed with *'m* were usually nominal in form, while names prefixed with *'m* also show some notable cases of the use of the stative Qal perfective.
3. Biblical names prefixed with *'m* were more frequent than those suffixed with *'m* (BH = 16 prefixed, 10 suffixed, but EB = 2 prefixed, 5 suffixed).
4. Names suffixed with *'m* were a feature of the united Monarchy, when they outnumbered prefixed cases (5 suffixed, 3 prefixed).
5. Names prefixed with *'m* were found more frequently in pre-Monarchical times.

The theophoric elements *'b*, *'ḥ* and *'m*, therefore, have been shown to be an early phenomenon in the Hebrew nomenclature. Unlike names compounded with *'l* and forms of *yhwh*, these theophoric elements were mainly in currency during the period before the division of the Kingdom. At other times their use is infrequent and sporadic. Also, in contrast to names compounded with *'l* and *yhwh* which occur predominantly in the suffixed position, *'b*, *'ḥ* and *'m* in compound names are more frequently prefixed. This latter phenomenon is particularly contrasted with compound names with *'l* in the pre-Monarchical period when names prefixed with *'l* are greatly outnumbered by their suffixed counterparts. Against this pattern, the popularity of prefixing *'b*, *'ḥ* and *'m* in the pre-Monarchical period stands in sharp contrast. All three elements *'b*, *'ḥ* and *'m* are mainly affixed to non-theophoric elements which are nominal in form.

The theophoric element and divine appellation MLK
(cf. Appendix, Tables 4.1, 4.11 and 4.19)
The Hebrew element *mlk* in personal names usually has the meaning 'King' (cf. BDB, 572f.). Names with this same element and meaning are also found in Phoenician (*PNPPI*, 344), in which 'Milk' is also a theophoric element and possibly a separate deity (*ibid.*, 344-45). The element is also met in Ugaritic *PTU*, 158) where it is also the name of a god, and in Palmyrene (Stark, 95). In Akkadian and Amorite the term *mlk* takes on the meaning 'counsellor' and is also itself a divine name in both these onomastica (cf. *APNM*, 230-31).

In the Hebrew onomasticon, only 32 names are found with the divine appellation *mlk*. The spread of these occurrences conforms to the general distribution of all names in that most of them (10) occur in the Exilic and post-Exilic period. For the other periods, however, we find 5 in the time of the united Monarchy (one of which is attested only by the Chronicler) and 4 in the pre-Monarchical time (one of which occurs only in Chronicles). 2 such names are attested for the time of the divided Monarchy and 1 name is found in 1 Chr. 23–27. Prefixed cases of *mlk* (14), are far more frequent than suffixed cases (8) and, indeed, suffixed cases are questionably theophoric. Nearly all occurrences of the element are with nominal predicates. Only in the period of the united Monarchy are suffixed forms (4) more frequent than prefixed forms (1), while in the pre-Monarchical time the 4 names attested are divided equally between prefixed and suffixed occurrences.

Some of those names compounded with *mlk* have been thought by some scholars to contain the divine name Melek, though in most cases entirely without substantiation. It is for this reason that the names need some discussion, which can at least show the tenuous nature of such a supposition. Biblical names including this element are:

mallûk The name is very likely a short form (sf.). Lidzbarski (*Eph*, 21) suggested a sf. of *malkîyāh* although there is certainly no evidence that the second element would be a form of *yhwh*. Geh (583) also considers the name to be an abbreviation of a theophoric name containing Melek the divine King. Parallel forms in Heb. e.g. *zakkûr* 'He (the deity) has remembered' (see below § 2.10), *yaddû*^{a}*'* and *'aqqûb* (*ibid.*) do not necessarily help to establish the meaning of *mallûk* since they are dubious short forms in themselves, and especially since such parallel forms are non-theophoric as opposed to divine appellations. However, there is certainly no evidence to claim that a foreign deity is implied in the name. The same may be said of the name:

m^{e}*lûkî* Cf. Geh, 606, KB, 556, *IPN*, 249.

Some names indicate more certainly the use of *mlk* as a divine appellation meaning 'King'. These are:

malkî'ēl 'El is King', cf. KB, 561, Geh, 582 etc.

malkîyāh(*û*) 'Y is King', cf. Geh, 582. The name also occurs on seals (V, 176, 326, 406; Herr, 131 no. 113), and inscr. (*AI*, 24, 14; 39.2; 40.3).

'ĕlîmelek 'El is King', cf. BDB, 45, Geh, 262, and inscr. Hazor B 2 cf. *SSI*, 18.19.

In some names the element *mlk* is used instead of the theophoric element, with a non-theophoric element as predicate, as in:

malkîšû^{a}*'* 'The King (i.e. Y/God) is help or salvation', cf. Geh, 582, KB, 561.

malkîrām 'The King (i.e. Y/God) is exalted', cf. BDB, 575, Geh, 582, KB, 561, *IPN*, 145.

In two names *mlk* is suffixed to the early theophoric elements *'b* and *'ḥ* in the names:

ăbîmelek 'The (divine) Father is King', cf. Geh, 6, KB, 5, *IPN*, 141.

'ăḥîmelek 'The (divine) Brother is King', cf. Geh, 24, *IPN*, 141.

For both these names BDB, 4, 27, consider the interpretation to be 'Brother/Father of Melek'. This, however, seems unlikely: both names are borne by 6 individuals all of whom are found to have lived before the division of the Kingdom when compound names with *'b* and *'ḥ* were more frequently found. When these theophoric elements *'b* and *'ḥ* occurred, moreover, they did so far more frequently in the initial position. Indeed, in the second position they virtually occur only when preceded by another theophoric element e.g. *'ĕlî'āb*, *yô'āb*, *yô'āḥ* (exceptions are only *'āhŏlî'āb* and *kil'āb*—if a compound with *'b*) when they are forced into a predicative position. Since prefixed theophoric elements are a feature of the earlier period and suffixed theophoric elements of the later periods, it seems reasonable to assume that in the names *'ăbîmelek* and *'ăḥîmelek*, which are attested biblically only for the early period, the theophoric element is in its expected initial position and *mlk*, in the suffixed position, is a predicate. In addition *'ḥ*, as well as *'b* and *'m*, never occur in construct with a following theophoric element anywhere in the Hebrew onomasticon. This makes the genitive interpretation by BDB even more uncertain. The name *'ḥmlk* seems to have been popular extra-biblically since it occurs frequently on seals (*V*, 139, 154, 292, 324, 358, 424; Herr, 90 no. 17; P. Bordreuil and A. Lemaire, *Sem* 29 [1979], 73 no. 3) and on inscriptions (SO 29, 2 cf. *SSI*, 9, 12 = SO 22,2-3 = 23,2 = 24,1 = 25,2 = 26,1(?) = 27,2 = 28,2 cf. *IH*, 292; SO 48,2 cf. *IH*, 292; *AI*, 72,2).

n^etan-melek This name is more difficult. It is attested for the period of the divided Monarchy during which time, compounds with *mlk* were extremely rare (only one other, *malkîyāhû*, is attested). The form of the name with the Qal perfective predicate prefixed to the second element *mlk* conforms to the abundant examples of predicate-subject names of this pattern, e.g. *n^etanyāh(û)*, *n^etan'ēl*, *'ăḥazyāh(û)*, *'ămaṣyāhû* etc. (with the exception of the use of *maqqēp*). Most accept the second element as representing the god Melek, cf. Geh, 653, KB (1953), 644. It is also possible, however, that the translation 'King' may still be tenable and an interpretation 'The King has given', is not out of the question. In this case, the element *mlk* would be a divine title for Yahweh.

Extra-biblical names compounded with *mlk* which are not attested in biblical Hebrew amount to only two. These are:

yhwmlk (Seal V, 162). 'Y is King'.

gdmlk (Seal V, 64). This feminine name can be variously interpreted. The element *gad* in Hebrew means 'fortune', 'good fortune' (BDB, 151), but it can also refer to the Aram. and Phoen. god of fortune (*ibid.*). As names compounded with *mlk* in the second position usually contain a divine element in the initial position, an interpretation 'Gad is (divine) King', is possibly preferable, although a meaning 'The King is fortune' is not to be entirely excluded. In the latter case *mlk* would be a divine title for Yahweh.

In conclusion it is maintained that compounds with *mlk* contain very little evidence to suggest that the element was used in all but a few names as anything other than a divine appellation for the Hebrew deity.

The theophoric appellation 'DN
(cf. Appendix, Tables 4.1, 4.9 and 4.18)
The element *'dwn* 'Lord', appears only rarely in biblical Hebrew names. In the time of the united Monarchy two individuals have names prefixed with *'dn* and in the time of the divided Monarchy we find one individual with this element prefixed and one with it suffixed, both of whom are referred to only by the Chronicler. Two individuals bearing names prefixed with *'dn* are also attested for the Exilic and post-Exilic period. The element in names is thus rarely attested.

In the biblical names there seems no reason to doubt that the element is a divine appellation for Yahweh, as in the name:

'ădōnîyāhû 'Y is Lord', cf. Geh, 17, or '(My) Lord is Y', cf. BDB, 11, KB, 16.

In other names, the element *'dn* stands as the divine epithet with a suffixed non-theophoric element:

'ădōnîqām 'The Lord has risen', cf. BDB, 12, Geh, 17, KB, 16.

'ădōnîrām 'The Lord is exalted', BDB, 12, Geh, 17, KB, 16, *IPN*, 117, 145.

Unusual is the name:

ṭôb 'ădônîyāh This name, which would mean 'Good is (my) Lord Y', cf. BDB, 375, Geh, 954, occurs in 2 Chr. 17.8 where, since the text produces the difficult *wa'ădōnîyāhû w^{e}ṭôbîyāhû w^{e}ṭôb 'ădônîyāh*, the name may not be authentic.

The name *'dnyh* also occurs extra-biblically on a seal (V, 75) and perhaps in the abbreviated form *'dny* (V, 96). The name *'dnyw* occurs on an inscription (SO 42,3 cf. *IH*, 48). Also attested is the name:

'dn'm (Inscr. SO 8,2; 9,2; 10,2-3; 11,2? 19,4). 'The Lord is (divine) Kinsman or Uncle' seems to be the best interpretation of this name. However, W. Kornfeld (*WZKM* 71 [1979], 41) suggests as an alternative, 'Herr ist Huld'.

The theophoric appellations ṢWR and ŠDY
(cf. Appendix, Tables 4.1, 4.12, 4.13 and 4.19)

For the early pre-Monarchical period 5 names are attested compounded with the element *ṣwr* meaning 'Rock' (cf. BDB, 849) and 3 names compounded with the element *šdy* which is usually translated 'Almighty' (*ibid.*, 994). In one name, the two elements *ṣwr* and *šdy* are combined.

Biblical names in which these elements are found probably all refer to the Israelite God and in some cases occur with other divine names as:

ṣûrîēl 'El is a Rock', cf. Geh, 1027 or '(My) Rock is El', cf. BDB, 849, *IPN*, 140. The term 'rock' is probably used in the sense of 'support' or 'strength'.

ṣûrîšadday 'My Rock is Shadday', cf. BDB, 849 or, better, 'Shadday (the Almighty) is a Rock', cf. Geh, 1027.

'ĕlîṣûr BDB, 45 translate 'Rock is God' in spite of the same translation for *ṣûrî'ēl*. (On the position of subject and predicate in these nominal sentence names, see below, p. 171 n. 18.) More probably, the translation should be 'El is a Rock', cf. Geh, 264.

'ammîšaddāy 'My Kinsman is Shadday', cf. BDB, 770. Geh, 37 prefers 'An uncle or Kinsman is the Almighty'.

Both elements *ṣwr* and *šdy* appear independently as theophoric elements in the names:

p^edāhṣûr 'The Rock (i.e. God/Y) has ransomed', cf. BDB, 804, Geh, 724.

š^edê'ûr 'Shadday is flame or light', cf. BDB, 994, Geh, 862.

These occurrences of the elements *ṣwr* and *šdy* are all attested only for the pre-Monarchical period. Only *'lyṣwr* (inscr. B 2 1 cf. *IH*, 273) and possibly *'ḥṣr* (seal, N. Avigad, *BASOR* 189 [1968], 44-47) occur extra-biblically. In semantic content *ṣwr* and *šdy* are akin to the more anthropomorphic nature of the elements *'b*, *'ḥ* and *'m* previously discussed.

The theophoric appellation B'L
(cf. Appendix, Tables 4.1, 4.10 and 4.18)
In the Old Testament, the element *b'l* is used in its nominal form to mean 'owner', 'lord', or 'husband', apart from being used as the divine proper name of the god of the Canaanites and Philistines etc. (cf. BDB, 127). In Akkadian personal names, the comparable element

has the meaning 'lord' or 'master' and is found in such names as *Adad-bēl* (*APN*, 7) and *Bēl-ibaši-dūri* (*ibid*., 7; see also Stamm, 330-31 and references). In the Phoenician nomenclature the element is abundantly attested (*PNPPI*, 289-90) as also in Ugaritic (*PTU*, 115-17). The element is also found in Amorite names, particularly feminine names (*APNM*, 174) but only rarely in Palmyrene (Stark, 78). It is also attested in early Semitic names like, *'Ay(y)a-bēli* etc. (Roberts, 19) and in the Murašû documents (Coogan, 48-49, 69).

At various times throughout the Old Testament, the Israelites have been accused of worshipping Baal or baalim instead of the Israelite God Yahweh (e.g. Judg. 2.11; 2.13; 3.7 etc.; 1 Sam. 12.10; 1 Kgs 16.31; 2 Kgs 10.18ff.; Jer. 9.14; Hos. 11.2 etc.). This is perhaps the reason why many scholars are so ready to seize upon any name in the Old Testament compounded with *bʿl* as evidence of widespread syncretism within Israelite religion (cf. H. Ringgren, *Israelite Religion*, trans. D. Green, SPCK [1966], 44; B.W. Anderson, *The Living World of the Old Testament*, 2nd edn, Longmans [1968], 106; *IPN*, 121 *et al.*). The question of the extent of such syncretism is one which is beyond the scope of the present study, but what is certainly within its scope is the important consideration as to whether Hebrew names compounded with *bʿl* can, in fact, be used as evidence of syncretistic ideas within Israelite religious thought and practice.

To begin with, even when names in which the element *bʿl* is very obscure are included, one could only find a maximum of 9 names compounded with *bʿl* referring to 15 individuals in the whole of the Old Testament, and 15 persons bearing such Hebrew names occurring extra-biblically. These must all be examined in order to establish the validity of such names as evidence for religious syncretism in Israelite religion. The biblical names prefixed with *bʿl* are

baʿalyāh The meaning of this name, referred to only in 1 Chr. 14.7 is undoubtedly 'Y is Lord', cf. BDB, 128, KB, 139, Geh, 97, *IPN*, 121, 141. The use of the element *bʿl* with the divine name *yhwh* shows that at least for some names, *bʿl* is used to mean 'lord' and is an appellation for the Hebrew deity.

b^{e}*ʿelyādāʿ* Most accept a meaning 'Baal knows', cf. BDB, 128, Geh, 98, KB, 139, *IPN*, 121. The name is given to a son of David (1 Chr. 14.7) and is attested only by the Chronicler. An alternative meaning 'The Lord (i.e. Y) knows' is also possible.

The four remaining names in which *b'l* is allegedly prefixed are very problematic as far as form is concerned although *ba'ănā'*, *ba'ănāh*, *ba'ărā'* and *ba'šā'* are, formally, practically identical. The presence of the final *'ālep/hē* is reminiscent of a number of abbreviated forms, cf. *'uzzā'/'uzzāh*, *'uzzîyā'*, *'b'*, *'ḥ' yišmā'*, etc., but, more specifically, *šim'ā'/šim'āh* and *šebnā'/šebnāh* etc. (see below § 2.10). These abbreviated forms indicate the possibility that the terminating *'/h* is an abbreviation of a divine element. More positively, *mîkā'/mîkāh* have been shown to be abbreviations of *mîkāyāh(û)* (*ibid.*). It would seem reasonable to assume that *ba'ănā'*, *ba'ănāh*, *ba'ărā'* and *ba'šā'* are also shortened forms and that the final *'ālep* is perhaps representative of a theophoric element placing the first element in a predicative position. The presence of the roots *b'n*, *b'r* and *b'š* would simplify the problem immediately, but such roots either do not exist, as is the case with *b'n* and *b'š*, or present semantic difficulties when used in reference to the deity, as is the case with *b'r* 'to burn, consume', cf. BDB, 128. The variety of suggestions put forward for the meaning of these names will further reveal their uncertainty.

ba'ănā' BDB, 128 suggest *ben 'ānāh* 'Son of distress'; likewise, Moscati (M, 45) finds the element *bn* 'son' in the first part. Geh, 84 suggests the possibility of a derivation from *b'l*, while Noth (*IPN*, 119) also saw the name as containing this same element *b'l* though the meaning remained unclear. W.F. Albright (cited in *BASOR*, 143, 5) found in the second part of the name the element *an ant* (Anath), while Lidzbarski (*Eph*, 7) considered the name to be a pet name from *b'lntn* (unattested in Heb.).

ba'ănāh The same suggestions which were offered for the name *ba'ănā'* have also been offered for *ba'ănāh*, with the exception that for this name, Geh, 84 considers 'Baal has answered' to be the probable meaning.

ba'ărā' f. Again, Geh, 85 considers the name probably to be derived from Baal, as also KB, 140. W.F. Albright (*JBL* 63 [1944], 232) considered the form to be a caritative from *ba'alrām* (not attested in Heb. names), while Lidzbarski (*Eph* 7) suggested a shortened form of *b'lrgm* (also not attested in Heb. names). The name also appears as an inscr. (SO 43,2 = 45,2 = 46,2-3 = 47,1 cf. *IH*, 292). Diringer (Dir, 44 no. 19) considered the inscriptional name to be derived from the root *b'r* meaning perhaps 'to shepherd' with an abbreviated divine element of Y or *b'l*. Following Noth (*IPN*, 40), Lemaire considers the name to be a double abbreviated form with a terminating *a* and the original name to have been *Ba'alram* (*IH*, 50).

ba'šā Geh, 85 suggests a contraction of *Baal-shemesh* ('The sun is Baal or Lord'). KB, 140 suggest a sf. of *b'l* +× (*šāma'* or others), or the element *bn* +

'šh. Lidzbarski (*Eph*, 7) considered the name to be a sf. of *b'lšm'* which is also not to be found elsewhere in the Hebrew onomasticon.

Of these four names, a conclusive assertion that they contain the element *b'l* is by no means possible, so that of the 9 biblical and one extra-biblical individuals who were given these names, not one could be accused with any degree of certainty of being a worshipper of Baal.

Thus, of the 6 names in which *b'l* is possibly prefixed, and which account for 11 individuals in the Old Testament, only *one* can be said with any assurance to contain the element *b'l* as a divine proper name, that is, the name *b^e'elyādā'* which is the name of only one individual, a son of David. Yet even for this name, a translation 'The Lord (i.e. Y) knows' is by no means impossible.

Names in which the element *b'l* is suffixed are much smaller in number than names prefixed with *b'l*. There are, in fact, only 3 such names, referring to 3 individuals in the Old Testament. These names are:

'ešbā'al The name is usually taken to mean *'îš ba'al* 'Man of Baal', cf. BDB, 36, Geh, 277, KB, 89, *IPN*, 121. The name may also mean, however, 'Man of the Lord', where 'lord' is used, as in *ba'alyāh* as a divine appellation for *yhwh*. N. Avigad (*IEJ* 14 [1964], 274-76) notes that *yēš* ' there is' in BH appears in the form *'iš* in two passages (2 Sam. 14.19; Mic. 6.10) 'which is apparently a survival of an early spelling related to UG. *'it*, meaning "there is"' (p. 275). Avigad therefore emends Heb. *'ešb'l* to *'išb'l* which he equates with Phoen. *yšb'l* meaning 'Baal exists'. He further equates *'šb'l* with *'šyhw* (see below, § 2.4) and *yiššîyāhû* which he emends to *yēšyāhû*. Against Avigad's argument it should be noted that the vocalization of *'šb'l* is distinctly *ĕš-* not *iš-*, and the corresponding name for the same individual, *'yšbšt*, is even more clearly *'îš* (to which may be added the name *'îšay* [1 Chr. 2.13] in which Avigad also finds *'š* 'exists'). Moreover, to include the name *yiššîyāhû* as an equivalent is to ignore, totally, the dagheshed *šîn* suggesting the root *nšh* 'to forget' (see below, § 2.4).

Many scholars (e.g. Ringgren *op. cit.*, 44; Anderson *op. cit.*, 106 *et al.*) suggest that at some stage the element *b'l* must have been considered degrading in the name *'ešbā'al* (as well as in the two names which follow, *y^erubba'al* and *m^erîb ba'al*) perhaps because of its pagan associations, for the name was changed to *'îs-bōšet* 'Man of shame' (2 Sam. 2.8, 10, 12, 15; 3.8, 14, 15; 4.5, 8, 8, 12). However, an interesting suggestion has been put forward by Matitiahu Tsevat, 'Ishbosheth and Congeners', *HUCA* 46 (1975), 71-78, who does much to expose the 'textbook case of a hypothesis turned fact' (p. 73) concerning the *bōset* substitution. Tsevat notes that *bāštu* features widely in

Akk. names (cf. *CAD*, B 143) in which it has the meaning 'dignity, pride, vigour' or even 'guardian angel, patron saint', and may also characterize or personify a deity (p. 76). However, he further notes that *bōšet* in Heb. names may not have the same meaning as *bāštu*: 'For the explanation of the Hebrew names, one should start from the basic meaning of Akk. *bāštu* 'dignity, pride, vigor' and take *bošet* as a divine feature-turned-epithet of approximately the same meaning which holds the position of a DN as do *'zr* 'Help' in *'zryqm* and *ṣwr* 'Rock' in *pdhṣwr*' (p. 77).[17] Tsevat prefers to treat these names simply as alternatives for one individual, a feature not uncommon amongst Old Testament personalities (p. 85). We should note, also, the presence of the element *bšt* in the Phoen. name YŠBŠT which is unexplained by Benz (*PNPPI*, 293). Indeed, that this practice of changing the element from *b'l* to *bšt* is no proof that the original meaning of the element in names was offensive, is seen in the following name:

y^erubba'al This name was also changed to *y^erubbešet* in 2 Sam. 11.21. But what is important about it, is the situation in which it was given, and the reason for it. In the context of Judges 6.25-32, we find Gideon having *destroyed* the altar of Baal:

> 'Then the men of the town said to Joash, "Bring out your son, that he may die, for he has pulled down the altar of Baal and cut down the Asherah beside it". But Joash said to all who were arrayed against him, "will you contend for Baal? Or will you defend his cause? Whoever contends for him shall be put to death by morning. If he is a god, let him contend for himself, because his altar has been pulled down." Therefore on that day he was called Jerubbaal, that is to say, "Let Baal contend against him", because he pulled down his altar.'
>
> Judg. 6.30-32

What is of significance here, is that the renaming of Gideon as Jerubbaal is given place in the text, not because Gideon was an advocate of Baal, but because he had torn down the altar of the pagan god and opposed him. In this case, although the name is compounded with *b'l* it cannot be used to suggest that such personal names prove religious syncretism in Israel, and it certainly cannot be used to claim that there was little distinction between Yahweh and Baal in Israelite worship at this time, as Helmer Ringgren has suggested: 'During the period of the Judges proper names formed with the element 'Baal' occur even in families that were apparently strict Yahwists. This fact indicates that Yahweh and Baal were not always sharply distinguished in this period. Gideon, for example, is also called Jerubbaal, i.e. Baal contends . . .' (*op. cit.*, 44). Yet it is precisely because Gideon makes a distinction between Yahweh and Baal that he is given the new name.

Tsevat (*op. cit.*, 82) notes that *y^erubbešet* is also damaging to the hypothesis of a scribal *b'l—bšt* change, since the Masoretes did not vocalize the second element to indicate *bōšet* as in the other names, and an expected *y^e^rubbōšet* does not appear. A root *ryb* 'to strive, contend' for this name has been questioned by Geh, 463, and by *IPN*, 206 who prefer an imf. of the root *rbb* with the Aram. and Arab meaning 'to be great'. The meaning of this name would then be 'Let Baal show himself great'. Geh, 463 also suggests the possibility of an interpretation 'Let Baal give increase'. Tsevat also suggests the root *rbb* but with the meaning 'to hurt, shoot'. This meaning is only rarely attested in BH (cf. BDB, 914) and Tsevat does not clarify the reasons for such a choice. The root *ryb* presents difficulties in that an imf. from this root is not found in the same form as the first element of the name.

m^e^rîb ba'al BDB, 937 suggest, questioningly, 'Baal is (our, my, his) advocate' as the meaning of this name, while Gray, 201 considered the original form to have been *mryb'l*, the name given to the same person in 1 Chr. 9.40, and suggested a meaning 'Hero of Baal'. Geh, 610 translates the name to mean 'Baal (i.e. the lord) contends' from the root *ryb*, while *IPN*, 143 indicates that the first element may contain the Aram. *mr* meaning 'lord'. Tsevat (*op. cit.*, 81) seems to put forward the best suggestion of an original *m^e^rîb ba'al* 'since clusters of identical letters at mutual boundaries of two words are more or less frequently simplified as a matter of scribal rule or accepted habit and not necessarily as a result of scribal error'. He considers the initial element to be a Hiphil of the root *ryb*. The name appears as *m^e^pîbōšet* in 2 Sam. 4.4, 9.6 etc. and *m^e^pibōšet* in 2 Sam. 16.5. Tsevat further notes that in the case of *mryb'l—mpybšt*, it is not only the supposedly offensive *b'l* which is different, but also the inoffensive *mry-* becomes *mpy-* which further supports the doubtful nature of the postulated *b'l—bšt* change (*ibid.*). The name was given to a son of Jonathan and to no other individual in the Old Testament, although the name *m^e^pibōšet* is given to a son of Saul and Rispah, according to 2 Sam. 21.8.

These three names account for all occurrences of the element *b'l* in the second position in Hebrew names in the Old Testament. Of the three, *y^e^rubba'al* was a name given to Gideon as the result of an action *against* Baal and so cannot be used in any argumentation that names compounded with *b'l* prove that syncretism existed widely in Israelite religion. Of all the Old Testament names compounded, or seemingly compounded, with this element, only 3, at most, could therefore be used to support the evidence for syncretism, *b^e^'elyādā'*, *'ešbā'al* and *m^e^rîb ba'al*. *B^e^'elyādā'* was a son of David, *'ešbā'al* a son of Saul, and *m^e^rîb ba'al* a son of Jonathan. If the element *b'l* is accepted as referring to the Canaanite god Baal in these three names (and this is not entirely certain) then the evidence for syncretism in

Israelite religion, as far as biblical names are concerned, is confined to a very limited sphere. Certainly, therefore, personal names cannot be used to demonstrate syncretistic ideas in Israelite religion on a large scale and one would doubt the validity of basing any conclusion upon the names of three individuals.

Yet, as noted above, the Old Testament certainly endorses the fact that the Israelites worshipped baalim, but personal names do not show such worship to have been widespread, for biblical names attest such worship, if at all, only for the families of Saul and David. However, we should turn now to extra-biblical names compounded with the element *b'l*, to discover what light these can throw upon the biblical evidence.

With extra-biblical *b'l* compounds it is often very difficult to establish whether such names are, in fact, Hebrew, a factor which needs to be constantly borne in mind. Of the 14 occurrences of the element *b'l* in extra-biblical names, as many as 11 are inscriptions from Samaria. These are:

'bb'l (SO 2,4 cf. *SSI*, 9,11). The name can either mean 'Baal is Father' or 'The Father is Lord (i.e. Y)'.

b'l' (SO 1,7; 31.3 cf. SSI, 10,12: SO 3,3; 27,3; 28,3 cf. *IH*, 292). Gibson (*SSI*, 11) suggests a likely sf. of *b'lyh* 'Y is Lord' for this name. Diringer (Dir, 43) and Lemaire (*IH*, 50) consider it to be an abbreviation of Baal (n. pr. div.) and an unknown second element.

b'l'zkr (SO 37,3; cf. Dir, 43 no. 17). Most consider the name to be a scribal error for *b'lzkr* 'Baal has remembered' cf. Dir, 43 no. 17, *IPN*, 239, 186-87, *IH*, 50. The name could also mean 'The Lord (i.e. Y) has remembered'. Vriezen and Hospers (VH, 27) consider it to be a place name. E. Lipiński, *BO* 35 3/4 (1978), 286, reviewing *IH*, claims that it is not correct to emend to *b'lzkr*, when there is a parallel *'Aštart-'azi* 'Astarté est ma force'. He writes, 'Le nom *'az* ou *'ōz* y est cependant déterminé par un autre substantif, et non par le suffixe pronominal. Ce substantif est *kar*, 'quai' ou 'entrepôt', vocable attesté en sémitique nord-occidental dés le début du XVe siècle a.n.è. (cf. RB 78, 1971, p. 87), sinon dès le IIIe millénaire (cf. OA 15, 1976, p. 13)'. Lipiński suggests this renders a meaning 'Baal est la force de l'entrepôt' and compares Akk. names of the type *Nabû-dūr-ālišu*, 'Nabû est le rampart de sa ville' (*APN*, 148b, Stamm, 227). Lipiński's suggested meaning, however, would be at variance semantically with other ideas expressed in the Heb. onomasticon, as well as formally, by producing a three part compound name. In Heb., the noun *kār* (root *kwr*) has a meaning 'basket-saddle' (cf. BDB, 468) and also attested are the nouns *kar* 'pasture' and *kōr* 'a measure' (both of dubious roots, cf. BDB, 499), as well as *kar* 'he-lamb', 'battering ram' (root *krr*, cf. BDB, 503).

b'lzmr (SO 12,2-3; Dir, 43 no. 16). The root *zmr* in BH exists only in the Piel 'to make music in praise of God', or 'to trim, prune' or perhaps 'sacred' cf. BDB, 274-75. In S. Arab. the same root means 'to protect'. Diringer considered the meaning of *zmr* to be 'to sing'. H. Michaud, *Sur la Pierre et l'Argile* (1958), 57, considers the element *zmr* to mean 'antelope' and, like Lemaire (*IH*, 31), has separated the two elements so that the second becomes a patronym.

mrb'l (SO 2,7 cf. *SSI*, 9,11). Gibson (*SSI*, 11) considers the name to be Meribaal 'Baal is (my) lord', which occurs in Samuel as Mephibosheth. Diringer (Dir, 46-47), comparing the name with the biblical *mryb b'l* 1 Chr. 9.40, considered the meaning of *mrb'l* as 'Adversary of Baal'. We should also bear in mind the element *mrr* in Ug. meaning 'to strengthen, bless, commend', cf. *UT Glossary*, 438 no. 1556 and Lemaire, *IH*, 53, who translates 'Baal a béni', although there is no reason why the idea 'to strengthen' should be excluded if the root *mrr* is to be preferred. Lipiński (*op. cit.*), in his review of Lemaire's work, claims that it is not possible to dissociate the name *mrb'l* from *mryb'l* (1 Chr. 9.40), *mryb b'l* (1 Chr. 8.34; 9.40) being a later interpretation. Lipiński supports Lemaire in a meaning 'Baal has blessed' suggested by the Ug. root *mrr*, and to strengthen his somewhat tenuous link between *mrb'l* and *mryb'l* states, 'Le suffixe *ī* nest pas marqué sur l'ostracon de Samarie, mais il y a toute raison de croire qu'il était prononcé'. W. Kornfeld (*WZKM* 71 [1979], 44) has an additional suggestion for the name *mrb'l* of a meaning 'Geliebt von Ba'al', the first element being derived from Eg. *mry*. His citation of Ug., Phoen. and Amor. names (*PTU*, 400f., *PNPPI*, 143 and *APNM*, 233 respectively) seems to suggest support for an Eg. origin, but these references make no mention of an Eg. etymology for the element *mr*, and it would seem unnecessary, here, to stray outside the Semitic field in search of a suitable meaning.

b'lm'ny (SO 27,3 cf. Dir, 43 no. 18). The name probably means 'Baal is a refuge', or 'The Lord is a refuge', root *'wn*, or 'Baal (or the Lord) is my answer' root *'nh* (see below, § 2.3). However, the name may also be gentilic, 'One from Ba'al Me'on' (cf. Dir, 43, *IH*, 50, W. Kornfeld, *WZKM* 71 [1979], 42).

b'r' (SO 43,2 = 45,2 = 46,2-3 = 47,1 cf. *IH*, 292). Like biblical *ba'ărā'* and the similar names *ba'ănā'*, *ba'ănāh* and *ba'šā'*, the element *b'l*, if it exists in this name, is not at all clear. Diringer (Dir, 44) considered the name to be a derivation from the root *b'r* with a possible meaning 'to shepherd', followed by an abbreviated divine element of Y or *b'l*, although accepting the root *b'r* for the first element makes the terminating *'ālep* no more representative of the divine element *b'l* than any other divine element. Noth (*IPN*, 40) considered the first element to be *b'l* with retention of only the first two letters. Other types of shortened forms, however, only attest the absence of a third letter when it is a guttural or *rēš* or from a Geminate root (see below, § 2.10).

All these names have the basic similarity of having been discovered on Samarian ostraca. Only three other names compounded with *bʿl* which occur extra-biblically, remain, two of which are very likely to be Phoenician rather than Hebrew names:

bʿlḥnn (Seal V, 36). A meaning 'Baal (or the Lord) has been gracious' is acceptable.

bʿlysp (Seal V, 219). 'Baal has added' or 'The Lord has added' are both possible as interpretations.

It should be noted that the forementioned extra-biblical inscriptions and seals are datable to a period following considerable Phoenician influence, by reason of the marriage of Ahab to Jezebel, daughter of the King of Sidonia (1 Kgs 16.31). It is very probable, therefore, that there were Phoenicians who resided in Samaria whose names may have survived upon ostraca and seals. The identification of these *bʿl* compound names with Hebrew persons, therefore, should not be too strongly pressed.

One other name occurs compounded with *bʿl*, this is:

ʿnybʿl (Inscr. MH 6,1 cf. *IH*, 268). Lemaire interprets this name as 'Baal a répondu' (p. 269) i.e. from a root *ʿnh* 'to answer', although the *yōd* seems to indicate a nominal form if the root is III *he*. The roots *ʿwn* 'to dwell', and *ʿnn* 'to appear' (?) may also be relevant, but no appropriate noun forms from these roots exist. Since the letters on the inscr. are not clear, no certain reading can be obtained.

Any analysis of these extra-biblical names compounded with *bʿl* cannot fail to take account of the high percentage of names from Samarian ostraca. The importance of this fact cannot be overestimated since, if we accept the element *bʿl* in these names to be the divine name, this evidence for the influence of Baal worship in Samaria accords well with the polemics delivered by the prophet Amos to the northern capital concerning the breach of covenant between Israel and Yahweh (Amos 2.6-8; 3.9-10; 4.1 etc.) and with those of Hosea, who blames the corrupt kingship and court for the religious decadence of the northern kingdom. Clearly, Baal worship was very evident at the northern capital of Samaria. Hosea writes:

> 'My people inquire of a thing of wood and their staff gives them oracles. For a spirit of harlotry has led them astray, and they have

> left their God to play the harlot. They sacrifice on the tops of the mountains, and make offerings upon the hills, under oak, poplar, and terebinth, because their shade is good'.
>
> Hos. 4.12-13

and, again, Hosea says of the Israelites that:

> 'they came to Ba'al-pe'or and consecrated themselves to Ba'al, and became detestable like the thing they loved'.
>
> Hos. 9.10b

The evidence for religious decadence attested by Amos and Hosea is therefore unquestionable, but what is questionable is the extent of it. Both prophets had a message for the northern kingdom and both prophets were concerned with the royal court and privileged classes which were at the core of the social and religious grievances of the time. They were, in fact, speaking to a specific class and, in the main, to a specific area—Samaria. It is with this outlook that the extra-biblical evidence correlates well, for we find many names compounded with *b'l* from Samaria, but only two or three are evident apart from these. Contemporary Judah for instance has yielded no such *b'l* compounds (cf. J. Bright, *A History of Israel*, SCM [1974], 257).

Combining the *b'l* compounds from biblical evidence and those from extra-biblical sources, then, it may be concluded that from the evidence of personal names, the absorption of Canaanite elements into Israelite religion is shown to be only localized and appertaining to two limited periods of time. Biblical names compounded with *b'l* do not in themselves imply syncretism beyond the royal family, while extra-biblical compounds with *b'l* suggest such syncretism only for the northern capital of Samaria, which the biblical accounts of Amos and Hosea attest during the last few years of the reign of Jeroboam II and perhaps in the decade of political instability after his death. If other periods of apostasy arose when the Canaanite god Baal was worshipped, personal names cannot be used as evidence for such. Indeed, they indicate only limited worship of the Canaanite deity and for the great numbers of ordinary individuals they cannot speak.

Other divine elements
(cf. Appendix, Tables 4.1, 4.14, 4.18, 4.19 and 4.20).
Throughout the Old Testament are attested 11 theophoric compound names borne by 20 Hebrew individuals, which have as their theophoric element a foreign deity. In some cases the non-theophoric

element could itself be Hebrew, as in *'azgād*, where the initial element *'az-* is akin to the Hebrew root *'zz*, but in most cases the entire name is foreign. Names compounded with foreign deities are:

ḥēnādāb Probably *ḥēn* + *hdd* 'Favour of Hadad', cf. BDB, 337, Geh, 378, KB, 319 and Noth, *IPN*, 243, who considered the name to be that of a tribe. Hadad was the name of an Aram. deity, and the name, which occurs only once in the OT, is attested for the post-Exilic period.

ḥarneper This Eg. name meaning 'Horus is good, merciful' (cf. Geh, 365, KB, 341) occurs only in 1 Chr. 7.36, referring to a person of the fifth generation in the tribe of Asher. He would, therefore, be assigned to the pre-Monarchical period although Noth (*IPN*, 64) saw the name as post-Exilic. BDB, 357 consider the name to be, in addition, a place name.

mordᵉkay This name, which was borne by two individuals of the Exilic and post-Exilic period, is possibly derived from the Bab. deity Marduk (*mᵉrōdak*) cf. BDB, 598, Geh, 634, KB, 598, *IPN*, 11, 63.

sismay The element *ssm* appears in Phoen. names as the name of a Phoenician god Sasam (cf. *PNPPI*, 368) from which *sismay* may be derived. This deity was also met at Ugarit (*PTU*, 187). The name is attested only by the Chronicler for the pre-Monarchical period or the time of the united Monarchy.

'ōbed 'ĕdôm This name is attested only by the Chronicler for one individual in the time of the united Monarchy and for one individual in the period of the divided Monarchy. The name probably means 'Servant of Edom', referring possibly to the Edom. deity, cf. BDB, 714. Geh, 677 translates 'Serving Edom', while Noth (*IPN*, 252 and 137) considered the name to be a reference to tribes, with the exception of the Gittite mentioned in 2 Sam. 6.10, 11, 12 (= 1 Chr. 13.13, 14; 15.25).

'azgād A meaning 'Gad is mighty or strong' is likely, referring to the Phoen. and Aram. deity (cf. BDB, 739, Geh, 81, *IPN*, 126). Another possibility, the Pers. *izgad* meaning 'messenger' is suggested by KB (1953), 694 (see also Zadok, *The Jews in Babylonia* [1979], 41). The name is attested for three post-Exilic individuals.

'ănātôt Most see this name as derived from the name of the goddess 'Anat (BDB, 779, Geh, 42) who is attested in Ug. (*PTU*, 111), Amor. (*APNM*, 200-201) and Phoen. (*PNPPI*, 382). Both *IPN*, 254 and KB (1953), 722 consider the name to refer to a tribe or place. The biblical references, however, refer to two individuals, one in the pre-Monarchical period and one post-Exilic individual.

pašḥûr This possibly Eg. name which Geh, 704 suggests means perhaps 'Portion of Horus', is the name given to 5 individuals in the OT, 2 in the period of the divided Monarchy, and 3 in the Exilic/post-Exilic period. S. Aḥituv ('Pashhur', *IEJ* 20 [1970], 95-96) translates the name as 'Son of Horus', the name being explained by Eg. *p^3 šri n ḥr* 'Son of Horus'. The *n*, he notes, is often dropped when signifying the genitive in Eg., which would account for its absence in the biblical name. The name also occurs extra-biblically.

šᵉmîdāʿ BDB, 1029 suggest questioningly 'The name knows' as the meaning of this name. However, Geh, 866 and *IPN*, 123 see the Phoen. deity *'šm* in the first element, in which the prosthetic *'ālep* can sometimes be absent. KB, (1953), 986 suggest a parallel in the name *šᵉmû'ēl* which they translate as 'The unnamed god is El'. Against this, see below §§ 2.6 and 2.7. *Šᵉmîdāʿ* is attested only once in the OT for the pre-Monarchical period.

šen'aṣṣar Geh, 866 and KB, (1953), 996 suggest 'Sin protect' as the meaning of this name. P.R. Berger ('Zu den Namen *ššbṣr* und *šn'ṣr*', *ZAW* 83 [1971], 98-100) suggests a possible derivation from Akk. *Šin-uṣur* 'Šin schütze' or, a sf. of *šarra-uṣur* 'Schütze den König', involving an interchange of *r* and *n*.

šēšbaṣṣar BDB, 1058 suggest Akk. *Šamaš-bal-uṣur* or *Sin-bal-uṣur* for this name, while Geh, 868 prefers Akk. *Sin-at-uṣur* 'O (moon god) Sin, protect the father', comparing the Gk. *Sabanasar*, *Sabanasaros*. However, concerning the element *šš*, Berger (*loc. cit.*) suggests: 'In den neubabylonischen Königsinschriften ist an einigen Stellen der Gottesname auch in der syllabischen Schreibung *Ša-aš-šu* belegt. Das würde die hebräische Wiedergabe gut erklären'. This would indicate *šaššu* (sun god) for the initial element and a meaning 'Šaššu, protect the Father' for the name. It is attested only once in the OT for an individual of the Exilic/post-Exilic period.

When the spread of these names throughout the OT is examined, most of them are found, as expected in view of the general spread of all names, in the post-Exilic period. However, in examining these names, their origin, that is to say the place of origin of the theophoric element, is of considerable importance. The spread of these names is as follows:

Pre-Monarchical period

Deity	*Origin*	
Horus	Egyptian	1 individual, Chr. only
Sasam	Phoenician	1 individual, Chr. only
'Anat	Ugaritic/Amorite/Phoenician	1 individual, Chr. only
Eshmum	Phoenician	1 individual

United Monarchy

Deity	*Origin*	
Edom	Edomite	1 individual, Chr. only

Divided Monarchy

Deity	*Origin*	
Edom	Edomite	1 individual, Chr. only
Horus	Egyptian	2 individuals

Exilic and post-Exilic period

Deity	*Origin*	
Hadad	Aramean	1 individual
Marduk	Akkadian	2 individuals
Sin	Akkadian	1 individual, Chr. only
Sassu	Akkadian	1 individual
Gad	Phoenician/Aramean	3 individuals
ʻAnat	Ugaritic/Amorite/Phoenician	1 individual
Horus	Egyptian	3 individuals

For the pre-Monarchical period, 3 names are seen to be of possible Phoenician origin. As a grandson of Benjamin, referred to by the Chronicler, *ʻănātôt* (1 Chr. 7.8) containing the divine name ʻAnat, is rather early to assume syncretistic ideas from Canaanite religious thought. The remaining two names, *sismay* and *šᵉmîdaʻ* are unlikely to suggest Phoenician religious influence to any extent since names compounded with the popular Phoenician element *bʻl* are virtually absent in biblical names from this early period. Similarly, one would hardly claim Egyptian influence in early Israelite thought from the presence of one Egyptian name (*ḥarneper*) in this pre-Monarchical period.

We should perhaps expect to find foreign deities evident in Hebrew personal names as a result of the foreign alliance marriages of Solomon, or as a result of the influence of the Phoenician wife of Ahab, Jezebel, but personal names do not suggest such, either for the period of the united Monarchy, or for the time of the divided Monarchy. For these periods only an occasional foreign name is mentioned, that of *ʻōbed ʼĕdôm* which occurs twice, one in each of these periods, and *pašḥûr* which is the name of two individuals in the time of the divided Monarchy. Also attested for the time of the divided Monarchy is *nᵉtan-melek* noted earlier in this section.

For the Exilic and post-Exilic period, the picture is a little different. With the Exile in Babylon, one would expect to see numerous examples of Babylonian influence; we find, in fact, only 4 individuals with Akkadian names (*mord^e^kay* 2 persons, *šen'aṣṣar* and *šēšbaṣṣar*). Indeed, the Phoenician/Aramean deity, Gad, is found almost as frequently with the 3 individuals who bear the name *'azgād*, to which may be added the Phoenician, as well as Ugaritic and Amorite deity, 'Anat, in the name *'ănātôt*. The possible Egyptian name *pašḥûr*, which was evident in the time of the divided Kingdom, is also seen to be the name of 3 individuals of this time.

Names compounded with foreign deities during the Exilic/post-Exilic period give the appearance of being merely sporadic. It is likely that the Jews in Babylon were not scattered within the local population, but were settled independently in southern Mesopotamia, and not actually in Babylon (cf. Ezek. 3.15; Ezra. 2.59; 8.17 and J. Bright, *op.cit.*, 346). Others may have fled to Egypt or to the other Israelite neighbouring countries so that one or two of these returning exiles may have brought with them foreign names. However uncertain the reason for the presence of these names amongst the returned members of the Jewish community, it is certain that they do not attest to any *specific* area of religious influence beyond Yahwism.

Amongst extra-biblical Hebrew names are also a number of other divine elements, though none is particularly prominent. The element *gd* is found in the names of 9 individuals and in at least two of these names it is certainly non-theophoric and occurs with the divine name *yhwh*. These two names are:

gdyhw (Seal P. Bordreuil, A. Lemaire, *Sem* 29 [1979], 71-72; inscr. *AI*, 71, 3). Like biblical *gaddî'ēl* (Num. 13.10), the name probably means 'Y is fortune'. The same meaning may be assigned the name:

gdyw (Insc. SO 2.2 prob. = 4.2 = 5.2 = 6.2 = 7.2 = 16a.2 = 16b.2 = 17a.2 = 17b.2 = 18.2; SO 33.2 = 34.2 = 35.2-3 cf. *IH*, 293; SO 30.2; SO 42.3 cf. *SSI*, 9, 10, 12). Gibson prefers a translation 'Gad is Y' (*SSI*, 11), and Lemaire (*IH*, 50) considers the name to be composed of the two theophoric elementes *yhwh* and *gd*.

The element *gd* is more doubtful in the following names on seals:

'bgd (V, 234). Translations 'Gad is Father' or 'The (divine) Father is fortune' are both possible, though the seal is probably not Heb. (cf. N. Avigad, *IEJ* [1968], 52f.).

'bgd hwzḥ (*IR*, 10). Since all the letters are in the order of the Heb. alphabet the whole name may not be authentic. However, the first part does constitute a known name, as the previous seal shows, and so should perhaps be noted here: see also below, §2.9.

gdmlk (V, 64). The interpretations 'Gad is King' or 'The King is fortune' are possible, see above, p. 52.

None of the extra-biblical names compounded with the element *gd*, therefore, contains with any certainty the name of the Phoenician/ Aramean deity, Gad. The theophoric element *ḥm* may be evident in the name:

ḥmy'dn (seal V, 324). The element *ḥm* may well be Heb. rather than foreign, meaning 'husband's father' 'paternal uncle' (cf. BDB, 327). The name could be entirely non-theophoric or the element *ḥm* could be used in the same way as *'b*, *'ḥ* and particularly *'m* (cf. N. Avigad *EI* 12, 66 no. 1 [Heb.]). The name would then mean 'The (divine) Uncle is delight'; cf. also the name *ḥmy'hl* (seal V, 412) 'The (divine) Uncle is a tent (i.e. protection)'.

pšḥr The name *pšḥr* which is attested biblically as noted above, has been found on two seals (V, 148, 152) and in one inscription (*AI*, 54). The meaning, like that of the biblical names, is possibly 'Portion of Horus', Horus being an Eg. deity (cf. Geh, 704), or 'Son of Horus' as suggested by S. Aḥituv (*IEJ* 20 [1970], 95-96).

The element *'ly*, which may be an abbreviated form of *'elyôn* 'Highest, Most High' (cf. BDB, 751), is probably an epithet for Yahweh in the name:

yḥw'ly (Inscr. SO 55.2). Gibson (*SSI*, 13) considers the first element to be a Piel jussive from the archaic root *hww* (later *ḥyy*) with the addition of the divine element *'ly*. The meaning would then be 'May the High One preserve alive' and would contain Yahweh as the subject. However, a Qal imf. of the root *ḥyh* for the initial element is to be preferred. This suggests a translation 'The High One lives' (see below §2.4 *ḥyh*).

A theophoric element has been seen by some in the name:

ṭbšlm This name is found on a seal (*IR*, 136) as well as on a number of ostraca from Lachish (L 1, 2 cf. *SSI*, 36, 37; L 7, 5-6; L 18, 1 cf. *IH*, 294, 94-95). Gibson (*SSI*, 37) considers the name to have meant originally 'Salem is good' and does not accept Torczyner's suggestion of 'Good he has repaid' (Torcz, 198). Lemaire (*IH*, 94-95) also prefers to retain *slm* as the theophoric element with *ṭwb* 'to be good' as predicate. The name is not conclusively Heb. but may well be Aram. It occurs also on an Aram. inscr. from Arad, for which J. Naveh suggests an abbreviated form of *ṭwb-šlm-'l* (J. Naveh 'The Aramaic Ostraca from Tel Arad', *AI*, 167 inscr. 39).

Extra-biblical names, therefore, reveal very few compound names containing a theophoric element which is conclusively non-Hebrew. Only the names *pšḥr* and possibly *ṭbšlm* can be identified more positively as possessing such pagan elements, and these are too few in number to suggest any pertinent areas of pagan infiltration of religious ideas into Israelite worship from the evidence of personal names.

The foregoing study of the various theophoric elements and divine appellations is an attempt to establish facts which remain valid irrespective of the problems of source analysis outlined in Section 2.1. Certain statements can, indeed, be made, and have been listed at the end of the discussion of each theophoric element. Nevertheless, the entire problem is far from solved and the nature of the names in Chronicles remains problematic.

In many ways, the evidence of those names recorded only in Chronicles, deviates drastically from that of the rest of the Old Testament. Nowhere is this more evident than in the large number of names compounded with *yhwh* which the Chronicler alone assigns to the pre-Monarchical period and, yet, abbreviated forms from the rest of the Old Testament would support the existence of such names in this early period (see above, p. 33). Indeed, this could indicate that the rest of the Old Testament is at variance in not assigning compounds with *yhwh* prior to the events at Sinai.

There are, however, many points on which the Old Testament and the Chronicler agree, and these should not be underestimated. Although there is no correlation between *yhwh* compounds attested only by the Chronicler for the pre-Monarchical period for example, there is a high correlation between the two for *'l* compounds in this time. Similarly, names compounded with *'b* and *'ḥ* and mentioned only by the Chronicler conform in general to the spread and use of these names throughout the rest of the Old Testament, that is, they are found predominantly early, in more prefixed cases than suffixed, and in mainly nominal, as opposed to verbal, forms. The Chronicler also reflects the popularity of the affix *yhw* in the period of the divided Monarchy.

The accusation that the Chronicler reflected his own period of the post-Exilic time to such an extent that he superimposed names of that age upon the earlier period has yet to be proved. The characteristics which are displayed by names attested by the Old Testament for the Exilic/post-Exilic period excluding the Chronicler's evidence, *are very different* from those names found only in Chronicles which are attested for the pre-Monarchical period and the time of the united Monarchy. The following table will elucidate this further. In this table, the ratios of names from the Old Testament alone are for the Exilic/post-Exilic period, and the ratios of names attested only in Chronicles (Chr.) are for the pre-Monarchical period (pre-M.) and the time of the united Monarchy (unit. M.). If the Chronicler truly reflects his own time, and this time is the post-Exilic period, we should expect the ratios to be very similar:

		approx.
OT	*yh* prefixed: *yh* suffixed	1:3
Chr. pre-M.	*yh* prefixed: *yh* suffixed	1:4
Chr. unit. M.	*yh* prefixed: *yh* suffixed	1:2
OT	*'l* prefixed: *'l* suffixed	1:2
Chr. pre-M.	*'l* prefixed: *'l* suffixed	1:2¾
Chr. unit. M.	*'l* prefixed: *'l* suffixed	1:1½
OT	*'b* prefixed: *'b* suffixed	2:1
Chr. pre-M.	*'b* prefixed: *'b* suffixed	4:1
Chr. unit. M.	*'b* prefixed: *'b* suffixed	1:2
OT	*'ḥ* prefixed: *'ḥ* suffixed	2:1
Chr. pre-M.	*'ḥ* prefixed: *'ḥ* suffixed	4:1
Chr. unit. M.	*'ḥ* prefixed: *'ḥ* suffixed	3:1
	Qal perfective	
OT	*yh* prefixed: *yh* suffixed	1:7
Chr. pre-M.	*yh* prefixed: *yh* suffixed	1:6
Chr. unit. M.	*yh* prefixed: *yh* suffixed	1:1¾
	Nominal	
OT	*yh* prefixed: *yh* suffixed	1:2½
Chr. pre-M.	*yh* prefixed: *yh* suffixed	1:2
Chr. unit. M.	*yh* prefixed: *yh* suffixed	1:1
	Compounds with *yh*	
OT	Nominal: Qal perfective	1:3¼
Chr. pre-M.	Nominal: Qal perfective	1:1¼
Chr. unit. M.	Nominal: Qal perfective	1:3
OT	*yh* construct forms: all others	1:5½
Chr. pre-M.	*yh* construct forms: all others	1:15
Chr. unit. M.	*yh* construct forms: all others	1:9

	Qal perfective	
OT	*'l* prefixed: *'l* suffixed	1:1½
Chr. pre-M.	*'l* prefixed: *'l* suffixed	3:1
Chr. unit. M.	*'l* prefixed: *'l* suffixed	1¾:1
	Nominal	
OT	*'l* prefixed: *'l* suffixed	2:1
Chr. pre-M.	*'l* prefixed: *'l* suffixed	1:1⅓
Chr. unit. M.	*'l* prefixed: *'l* suffixed	1:1
	Compounds with *'l*	
OT	Nominal: Qal perfective	1:1½
Chr. pre-M.	Nominal: Qal perfective	2:1
Chr. unit. M.	Nominal: Qal perfective	2:1
OT	*'l* construct forms: all others	1:11
Chr. pre-M.	*'l* construct forms: all others	1:6
Chr. unit. M.	*'l* construct forms: all others	1:12¾

Clearly, there is frequently a distinct difference between the character of post-Exilic names recorded by the rest of the Old Testament and the characteristics of names attested by the Chronicler for the pre-Monarchical and Davidic periods, particularly with *'l* compounds and construct forms. Thus, it simply cannot be claimed that the Chronicler's names reflect those of his own time for this early period.

The problem of the names in Chronicles must, however, remain unsolved for the present, since it is an aspect which demands a lengthy and separate study in itself. Nevertheless, it is to be hoped that the preceding chapters have at least shown that the Chronicler's evidence cannot be dismissed by an accusation of mere invention: this is a hypothesis which has in no way been proved.

2.3 *Nominal Sentence Names*

Nominal sentence names are names which consist of a subject and a nominal predicate, the subject in the following discussion being a theophoric element. The subject may occur in the first position e.g. *'ĕlîmelek* 'El is King', or in the second e.g. *malkî'ēl*.[18] Martin Noth's suggestion that 'die normale Stellung im semitischen Nominalsatz Subjekt-Prädikat ist' (*IPN*, 17) is one which needs qualification before proceeding, in view of the fact that this may not be the case in

Hebrew personal names and since the position of the subject varies with different types of theophoric elements.

In biblical Hebrew names the subjects *'l* and *yhwh* occur predominantly in the second position. Likewise, in nominal sentence names, the usual order for *'l* and *yhwh* compound names is predicate-subject. Although nominal sentence names are a marked feature of names in which the theophoric element is prefixed, the relative paucity of these makes the number of nominal compounds with suffixed *'l* and forms of *yhwh*, the greater.

The situation changes, however, when names prefixed and suffixed with *'b*, *'ḥ* and *'m* in biblical Hebrew are considered. These theophoric elements are found predominantly in the first position and more rarely in the second position, so for these nominal sentence names the word order is mainly subject-predicate. Since, too, nominal sentence names are a distinct feature of names compounded with *'b*, *'ḥ* and *'m*, their number is sufficient, when combined with those nominal compounds containing *'l* and forms of *yhwh*, to tilt the balance in favour of an order subject-predicate for nominal sentence names in biblical Hebrew. The fewer instances of names compounded with *'dn*, *mlk*, *b'l*, *ṣwr*, *šdy* and other theophoric elements, show a similar preference for the order subject-predicate.

The situation is again similar when the archaeological material is examined. Extra-biblical names affixed with *'l* and forms of *yhwh*, as in biblical Hebrew, occur mainly in the order predicate-subject and, likewise, names affixed with *'b*, *'ḥ* and *'m* are predominantly subject-predicate in order. Names affixed with other theophoric elements also show a slight preference for subject-predicate. However, unlike names in biblical Hebrew, the class of names compounded with *'b*, *'ḥ* and *'m*, when combined with elements affixed with *'l* and forms of *yhwh* and other divine elements like *b'l*, *mlk*, *'dn* etc., is not sufficient in number to alter the fact that the most prevalent order for Hebrew extra-biblical names is predicate-subject. Indeed, when these are added to those in biblical Hebrew, the total number of names still indicates an overall order of predicate-subject, and one must conclude, against Noth, that the usual order for the nominal sentence type of Hebrew personal names is predicate-subject. It is interesting to note that extra-biblical names are largely datable to the period of the divided Monarchy, for which time the order predicate-subject for nominal sentence names is a particular feature of biblical names. In all other periods, the converse order, subject-predicate, obtains.

The word order for Hebrew personal names with nominal predicates, then, does not reflect the more usual word order for nominal sentence names in other Semitic onomastica, which is subject-predicate for Ugaritic (*PTU*, 35), Phoenician (*PNPPI*, 217), Palmyrene (Stark, *passim*) and Aramaic. In Amorite names, however, the order is predominantly predicate-subject (*APNM*, 95) and in Akkadian names the order is subject-predicate for two-word compounds in the older names, predicate-subject in later names, and mainly predicate-subject for three-word theophoric compounds (Stamm, 108-109).

Neither is the order subject-predicate/predicate-subject in Hebrew personal names a haphazard occurrence, since a careful study of this order reveals some quite definite features peculiar to each. An examination of nominal predicates which occur only in the order predicate-subject in Hebrew theophoric names as a whole, reveals the following ideas:

dlt 'door'. This element occurs in the name *dltyhw* (seal, V, 331), 'Y is a door (i.e. refuge)'.

hr 'mountain' (*sanctuary*). *Hryhw* (seal, V, 273), 'Y is a mountain'.

ḥzq 'strength'. *Ḥzq[yw]* (inscr. Dir, 302 no. 16); *ḥ[z]qyhw* (inscr. Ophel 1), cf. *SSI*, 25, 26, where Gibson reads with a preformative *yōd* and with a verbal translation, and *IH*, 239, where Lemaire reads without the *yōd* but considers the name to be verbal, 'Yhwh a rendu fort'). Biblical occurrences of *ḥizqîyāhû* are probably abbreviated forms of *y^{e}ḥizqîyāhû* (see below, § 2.10). As a nominal form, the name would mean 'Y is strength'.

ḥlq 'portion'. BH *ḥilqîyāhû*; seals, V, 52, 150, 321, 325, 416, 417, 418; Herr, 136 no. 128; BL, 53 no. 21. 'Y is my portion', cf. BDB, 324, KB, 311, Geh, 392, *IPN*, 163.

ḥn 'favour, grace'. Seal *ḥnyhw* (V, 359). The name means either 'Y is grace, favour', or 'Grace, favour of Y'. Cf. also the name *ḥn'[b]* (SO 30.3 cf. *SSI*, 9, 12 and below § 2.9). The first element of this latter name may also be a noun from the root *ḥnn*, which would suggest a meaning 'The Father is grace or favour'. The BH name *ḥēnādāb*, which is usually interpreted as a construct form 'Favour of Hadad', cf. BDB, 337, Geh, 378, may indicate the same form for *ḥn'b*, although not with any certainty. More recently, Lemaire (*IH*, 33) has read *Gēra Ḥanna* on this ostracon.

ytr 'pre-eminence, abundance'. BH *yitr^e'ām*: 'The (divine) Kinsman is pre-eminence or abundance' as a meaning for this name is both semantically and formally suitable, cf. KB, 432. Noth (*IPN*, 197) preferred an imf. of the root *trh* not attested in BH but with a meaning 'to protect', suggested by Akk. *tarū*. Since the root *ytr* presents no formal or semantic problems, and since it is evident verbally in the BH name *'ebyātār* (see below, *ytr*) as well as being adequately attested in BH (cf. BDB, 452), it is to be preferred.

mbṭḥ 'confidence, trust'. Root *bṭḥ*: inscr. *mbṭḥyhw* (L 1.4 cf. *SSI*, 36). A meaning 'Y is confidence, or trust' is likely. Torcz, 198, however, preferred the meaning 'Trust in Y'.

mgd 'excellence'. BH *magdî'ēl*. The form of the name is difficult (see below, § 2.9): a meaning 'El is excellence' is acceptable, although a verbal form is also possible.

mḥsh 'refuge'. BH *maḥsēyāh*; inscr. *mḥs[yhw]* (*AI*, 23.6), *mḥs[yw]* (SS 4.1 cf. *IH*, 248). The name means 'Y is a refuge', cf. BDB, 340, KB, 541, *IPN*, 158.

mnḥm 'comforter'. Inscr. *m[n]ḥmyhw* (*AI*, 11.5). The meaning is possibly 'Y is a comforter'. However, Lemaire (*IH*, 170, 171) restores the line to *m(l)ḥm* 'some bread', but does not indicate any alternative reading for *yhw*. Aharoni (*AI*, 25) suggested that the *mēm* could indicate 'from': the name would then be *nḥmyhw* 'Y has comforted' (see below, § 2.4, *nḥm*).

m'wz 'refuge, protection'. Root *'wz*: BH *ma'azyāh* 'Y is a refuge', cf. Geh, 575, KB, 578, *IPN*, 157 and below § 2.9.

mr 'lord' (Aram.). The element *mr* in Hebrew names presents some difficulty. In the BH name *m^{e}rāyāh* it is probably a verbal form from the root *mrr*, attested in Ug. with a meaning 'to strengthen, bless, commend' (*UT Glossary*, 438 no. 1556). This root is not so obvious for the inscriptional names *mrnyw* (SO 42.3 cf. *SSI*, 10, 12) and *mrb'l* (SO 2.7 cf. *SSI*, 9, 11). The meaning of *mrnyw* may be 'Y has blessed/strengthened me' or, the Aram. noun 'lord' may be evident in the initial element, suggesting 'Y is our lord' (see also below, § 2.8, 5). However, Lemaire (*IH*, 35) reads *Adonyaw* for the name. Similarly, for the name *mrb'l*, the roots *mrr* or *mr* are both possible, suggesting 'Baal or the Lord has blessed/strengthened', or 'Baal is lord' (see also above, p. 61).

s'r 'storm, tempest, rage'. Inscr. *s'ryhw* (*AI*, 31.4). The name possibly means 'Y is rage or storm', perhaps against enemies, although Lemaire (*IH*, 200) interprets the name verbally. 'Yhwh a agité violemment, a provoqué la tempête'. W. Kornfeld (*WZKM* 71 [1979], 44) reads the name as *s'dyhw* with *d* instead of *r*, suggesting a meaning 'Yhw hat geholfen/gestützt', since Lemaire's suggestion finds no support from the rest of the Heb. onomasticon. A nominal form, however, with a meaning 'storm', would be in the same semantic group as names with *ḥrp* 'autumn' and *šḥr* 'dawn'. Y. Aharoni, (*BASOR* 197 [1970], 35) suggested a reading *sbryhw* but more recently preferred *s'ryhw* (*AI*, p. 57).

'dh 'ornament'. BH *'ădî'ēl* 'El is an ornament', cf. BDB, 726, Geh, 16. The first elements in the names *mô'adyāh* and *ma'adyāh* are also possibly nominal, although their forms are difficult (see below, § 2.9). Other occurrences in the initial position are probably verbal, while in the extra-biblical name *'d'l* (seal V, 146) the form could be verbal or nominal.

Root *ṣdq* 'righteousness'. BH *ṣidqîyāh(û)* 'Y is righteousness', cf. BDB, 843, KB (1953), 795, Geh, 1019. The same name possibly occurs on two inscr. L 11.5 cf. *IH*, 128, and Ophel 4 cf. *IH*, 239, 241, although Lemaire reads *Ṣedeqya(hu)* and prefers a verbal translation for the names.

Throughout these names the idea of God's protection seems to be evident: he is a 'door', a 'mountain or sanctuary', he is a 'refuge', 'comforter' and 'help' whose 'trust' and 'strength' can be relied upon. The idea contained in the concept of protection, is one of preservation and patronage or guardianship by the divine subject of the name. The Aramaic title *mr* for 'lord' enhances this notion of guardianship, although the form is not without difficulties, as noted above.

The idea expressed in the noun *meged* is that of 'excellence', but not in a transcendent sense since the noun is always used of the gifts of nature (cf. BDB, 550). Although the noun *yeter* 'pre-eminence, abundance', seems to suggest a transcendent concept of the deity in the idea of 'pre-eminence', such transcendence is perhaps modified by its synonym 'abundance'. The basic sense of the root *ytr*, 'to remain over', and the other uses of the noun *yeter* as 'remainder, excess' (BDB, 451) might suggest that 'abundance' is a more pertinent meaning.

The ideas depicted here, therefore, tend to reveal, in the main, the idea of God's protection, at the same time, they are neither characteristically anthropomorphic nor transcendent in semantic content.

Since stative verbs may also be considered as nominal sentence names, it is necessary to list here those stative verbs which occur as predicates only in the first position:

'br 'to be firm, strong'. Seal *'bryhw* (V, 330) 'Y is firm, strong'.

'mṣ 'to be strong'. BH *'ămaṣyāh(û)* 'Y is strong'.

gbr 'to be strong'. Insc. *gb*[*ryhw*] (*AI*, 60.5-6). The name may mean 'Y is strong'; cf. also the BH name *gabrî'ēl* below, § 2.9. A non-stative interpretation, as suggested by Lemaire (*IH*, 217), seems less probable in view of normal BH usage.

gdl 'to be great'. BH *g^e^dalyāh(û)*, *yigdalyāhû*; seals V, 100, 149, 218, 240, 421; inscr. *AI*, 21.2; *AI*, 110.2 cf. A.F. Rainey, *Tel Aviv* 4 (1977), 97-102. The names probably mean 'Y is great', cf. BDB, 153, Geh, 319.

ḥzq 'to be strong'. BH *ḥizqîyāh(û)/y^e^ḥizqîyāh(û)*: perhaps 'Y is strong'. Elsewhere, the name *y^e^ḥizqîyāh(û)* is variously interpreted: BDB, 306 suggest 'Y has strengthened', KB 292, suggest a nominal or verbal form, Geh, 385 'Y is strength', and *IPN*, 16 indicates a nominal form. However, the presence of the initial *yōd* makes a nominal form very unlikely.

ḥsd 'to be kind, good'. BH *ḥăsadyāh*; seal V, 220; inscr. R 2 cf. *IH*, 257-58. 'Y is kind' or 'Y has been gracious', cf. BDB, 339, Geh, 366.

ṭwb 'to be pleasing, good'. BH *ṭôbîyāh(û)* 'Y is good', cf. BDB, 375, Geh, 954; also *ṭôb 'ădônîyāh* 'Good is my lord Y' cf. BDB, 375, Geh, 954 and above, § 2.2 *'dn*. In extra-biblical names, the element is met verbally in *ṭb'l* (seal V, 376), *ṭbyhw* (inscr. L 3.19; 5.10 cf. *SSI*, 38, 41, 44, 45) as well as in the name *ṭbšlm* (seal *IR*, 136; inscr. L 1.2 cf. *SSI*, 36, 37; L 7.5-6; 18.1 cf. *IH*, 294, 94-95), which may be Aram. (see above, p. 68).

yph 'to be fair, beautiful'. Seal *ypyhw* (M, 80 no. 23). The root *yph* in BH means 'to be fair, beautiful' (cf. BDB, 421) but is not normally used with reference to Y. Nevertheless, the name may mean 'Y is fair, beautiful'.

knn 'to be firm, substantial'. BH *k^e^nanyāh(û)*. The root *knn* is rarely attested in BH, and never in verbal form. The parallel root *kwn*, probably meaning 'to be firm', is only found in derived conjugations (cf. BDB, 465). *K^e^nanyāh(û)*, however, is distinctly Qal perf. in form and should, therefore, be translated according to the basic sense of the verb, 'Y is firm', as BDB, 487 suggest. Against such an interpretation, KB, 461 suggest 'Y strengthens' and Geh, 157 'Y has established'; Noth (*IPN*, 179) also found a stative translation unacceptable.

'lh 'to go up, ascend, climb'. Seal *'lyh* (V, 157). A stative interpretation of the root *'lh*, to give a meaning 'Y is high, exalted', is perhaps best. The seal may, however, be Ammon. (cf. A.R. Millard, *BA* 35 [1972], 103 n. 19) or Edom.

'th 'to be proud, exalted'. BH *'ătāyāh*. This name perhaps means 'Y is proud' or 'Y is exalted', suggested by Arab. *'atā* (cf. Geh, 76). An alternative meaning, 'Y has shown himself excellent', may be possible (cf. Geh, 76, *IPN*, 191).

pl' 'to be wonderful, separate, unusual'. BH *p^e^lāyāh* and perhaps *p^e^lāyāh* which may belong here, or with the root *plh*), 'Y is wonderful', cf. Geh, 725, *IPN*, 191.

pr' 'to excel or to be noble' cf. Arab. *fara'a*. Seal *ypr'yw* (V, 177). The name could mean 'Y is noble' or 'Y excels', although the root *pr'* in BH, attested only once in verbal form, has the meaning 'to act as leader' (BDB, 828). The name, then, is only questionably stative.

rbb 'to be or become many, great'. BH *yārob'ām*; seal V, 68; inscr. Hazor B cf. *SSI*, 19. The names may mean 'The (divine) Kinsman is great', cf. Geh, 462, but are formally difficult (see below, § 2.9). The name *rbyhw*, on a seal (V, 161), can be translated more certainly as 'Y is great'.

š'l 'deep'. Seal *š'lyhw* (N. Avigad, *IEJ* 4 [1954], 235). An interpretation 'Y is deep' may be suggested by NH *š'l*, cf. BDB, 1043.

It is possible to suggest, here, a predominance of ideas concerning the transcendent nature and greatness of the deity. Two Hebrew roots, *gdl* and *rbb*, are used to express the greatness of God. It should be noted also, that nominal sentence names expressing greatness are exclusive to stative verbs in predicate-subject order. The same may be said of the roots *'br*, *'mṣ*, *gbr* and *ḥzq*, expressing the idea that the deity is strong. The idea of the deity as 'proud', 'exalted', 'wonderful', 'high' and 'noble', further indicate his transcendent nature. The concept of kindness and goodness expressed in Hebrew *ḥsd*, is one of no small import in the religious history of Israel, since it is one of those basic ideas belonging to the covenant relationship between Israel and her God (cf. W. Eichrodt, *The Theology of the Old Testament*, I, trans. J.A. Baker, SCM [1961], 232ff.).

An examination of those nominal elements occuring only in the second position, in the order subject-predicate, reveals the following:

gyl 'joy, rejoicing'. BH *'ăbîgayil*; seal *'bgyl* V, 62. The name is interpreted by BDB, 4 as 'My father is joy', and by Geh, 4 as 'The father is rejoicing', although BDB and Gehman recognize the uncertainty of the name. *IPN*, 39 considers *ayil* to be a caritative feminine ending in this name, causing the second element, as an abbreviated form, to be beyond recognition.

ḥyl 'strength, wealth, efficiency'. BH *'ăbîḥayil*; seals *yhwḥyl* (V, 42, 199) and perhaps *yhwḥl* (V, 198, 396). The names mean 'The (divine) Father/Y is might, strength', cf. BDB, 4, Geh, 4, KB, 5. As in the name *'ăbîgayil*, however, Noth (*IPN*, 39) considered the final *ayil* to be a caritative ending for this feminine name, although there seems no reason why a derivation from the root *ḥwl*/*ḥyl* should not be preferred.

ḥrp autumn. BH *'ělîḥōrep*. Although Noth (*IPN*, 237) considered the element *ḥōrep* as having nothing to do with autumn, the noun *ḥōrep* meaning 'harvest-time, autumn' (cf. BDB, 358) seems formally and semantically acceptable. BDB, 45 suggest 'Autumn God', KB, 54 'God rewards', or 'God is the giver of harvest-fruit', while Geh, 260 suggests 'God is (the giver of) autumn (fruit)'. The possibility that the second element is Eg. is noted by K.A. Kitchen, *NBD*, 1171b.

ṭwb 'goodness'. BH *'ăbîṭûb*, *'ăḥîṭûb*, 'The (divine) Father/Brother is goodness', cf. BDB, 4, 26, Geh, 7, 24, KB, 5, 32. When specifically a noun, *ṭwb* occurs only in the second position, but can occur in verbal form in first and second positions.

Root *yš'* 'salvation'. BH *'ĕlîšûaʿ*, *'ĕlîšāʿ*, *yᵉhôšûaʿ*, *yᵉhôšuaʿ* later *yēšûaʿ*, *'ăbîšûaʿ*, *malkîšûaʿ*; EB *'lyšʿ* (seal V, 41 (Ammon?), 271 (Heb?); inscr. SO 1.4; 1.7; 41.1 cf. *SSI*, 8, 10, 11; *AI*, 24.15; 24.19-20); *yhwšʿ* (seal V, 27); *ywyšʿ* (inscr. SO Dir, p. 311; SO 36.3 cf. *IH*, 52); *'bšwʿ* (seal V, 1). The names express that the deity is 'salvation'.

kbd 'glory'. BH *yôkebed*: 'Y is glory' is suggested by BDB, 222 and Geh, 498 as the meaning of this feminine name.

mwt 'death'. BH *'ăḥîmôt*. A meaning 'The (divine) Brother is death' is probable. 'My brother is death' is suggested by BDB, 27, while Geh, 24 considers the second element to be the proper name of the pagan deity Mot. The suggestion of Noth (*IPN*, 39, 40) that the *ōt* ending is a 'hypocoristic'[19] termination, should not be taken seriously: his suggested changeover of consonants in the second element of some names as, e.g. *'ăbîgayil* and *'ăbîḥayil* above, and the addition of a caritative or 'hypocoristic' ending, has no basis in the patterns displayed by abbreviated names as a whole (see below, § 2.10 Abbreviated Forms).

mʿṣ 'wrath'. BH *'ăḥîmaʿaṣ*; seals *'*[]*mʿṣ* (F.J. Bliss, *PEFQS* 32 [1900], 18); *'bmʿṣ* (V, 274). 'The (divine) Brother is wrath' is perhaps the best suggestion for this name, cf. BDB, 27, Geh, 23.

smk 'sustenance, support'. EB seal *'lsmky* (V, 129), 'El is my sustenance or support'. Lipiński (61) considers the seal to be Aram., however, while Herr (177 no. 11) considers it Phoen. The root is not otherwise found nominally in BH (cf. BDB, 701-702).

ʿdn 'delight, luxury'. BH *yᵉhôʿaddān*, *yᵉhôʿaddāyin*. An interpretation 'Y is delight or luxury' from a root *ʿdn*, seems the best possibility, cf. Geh, 450, KB, 379, *IPN*, 166. Nevertheless, the form of the second element must remain problematic (see below, § 2.9 *yᵉhôʿaddah*). The element is also found on a seal *ḥmyʿdn* (V, 324).

Root *ʿwd* 'witness'. BH *yôʿēd* 'Y is a witness', cf. BDB, 222, KB, 385, Geh, 498.

Root *ʿwn* 'refuge'. EB inscr. *bʿlmʿny* (SO Dir, 43 no. 18). An interpretation 'Baal is a refuge' or 'The Lord is a refuge' is likely, the second element being derived from the root *ʿwn*. Another possibility is a derivation of the second element from the root *ʿnh* and a meaning 'Baal is my answer' or 'The Lord is my answer' suggested by the noun *maʿăneh* ('answer', 'response', cf. BDB, 775). It is also possible that the name is a gentilic 'Man from *Ba'al Me'on*', (cf. *IH*, 50, Dir, 43 and W. Kornfeld, *WZKM* 71 [1979], 42).

ʿzr ʻhelp'. BH *'ĕlîʿezer, yôʿezer, 'ăbîʿezer, 'ăḥîʿezer*. The form is perhaps also nominal for the names *yhwʿzr* (seals V, 26; N. Avigad, *Qedem* 4 [1976], 7) and *ywʿzr* (inscr. Mur. B 4 cf. *SSI*, 32), although verbal forms are not impossible. The names express that the deity is a 'help'. The element *ʿzr* also appears in verbal form in the second position.

plṭ 'deliverance'. BH *'ĕlîpeleṭ* 'El is deliverance', cf. BDB, 45, KB, 54, Geh, 263, 265, *IPN*, 16, 156.

šbʿ 'oath, or fullness, good fortune'. BH *'ĕlîšebaʿ*, *yᵉhôšebaʿ/yᵉhôšabʿat*. An interpretation 'El is an oath' is possible, cf. BDB, 45, Geh, 264 or, more probably, 'El is fullness or good fortune' cf. Geh, 264. Alternatively, *šbʿ* may be used in the sense of perfection, cf. *IPN*, 46-47.

šwr 'wall (protection)'. BH *'ăbîšûr* 'The (divine) Father is a wall (i.e. protection, shield)', cf. BDB, 4, Geh, 7, KB, 6, *IPN*, 157.

Immediately apparent in the above list is the pronounced anthropomorphic nature of these predicates, showing God's involvement with man in his day to day life. This is expressed particularly in the ideas of 'joy', 'goodness', 'death', 'wrath', 'sustenance/support', 'delight' and perhaps 'good fortune'. The concept of rescue from need or danger is also evident in those names which describe the deity as a 'witness', a 'refuge', a 'help', as 'deliverance' and 'salvation'. Names from the root *yšʿ*, depicting the deity as 'salvation' need, perhaps, a special note, since this concept of salvation features so widely in Hebrew personal names. In Israelite religion, salvation is the epitome of God's involvement with man, since it lies at the beginnings of Israelite national consciousness, in the form of her deliverance from the land of Egypt (cf. J. Bright, *op. cit.*, 144ff.). It is interesting to note, also, that where the root *yšʿ* appears as a predicate in the first position, it is always verbal, supplying the meaning 'The deity has saved', as opposed to the nominal 'The deity is salvation'. The latter idea expresses continuity of involvement by God, whereas the former expresses an action which is complete in the past. The root has been studied by J.F.A. Sawyer, *Semantics in Biblical Research*, SCM (1972), but the study is not pertinent to personal names.

To turn now to the stative verbs occurring only in the second position, the following, relatively few, occurrences are found:

ytr 'to remain over'. BH *'ebyātār*. This name probably means 'The (divine) Father is pre-eminent', cf. Geh, 4, or 'The (divine) Father is abundance', cf. KB, 6 who, with *IPN* 193 suggest 'The Father gives abundance', a less probable alternative, since BH usage tends to support a stative interpretation.

ṣdq 'to be just, righteous'. BH *y(ᵉh) ôṣādāq*, 'Y is just or righteous', cf. BDB, 221, KB, 379, 386, Geh, 521, *IPN*, 189.

rwm 'to be high, exalted'. BH *y(ᵉh)ôrām*, *'ăbîrām*, *'abrām*, *'ăḥîrām*, *'amrām*, *'ădôrām/ădōnîrām malkîrām*; seals *'lrm* (V, 220, 217. V, 217 is possibly Ammon., cf. P. Bordreuil, *Syria* 50 [1973], 82; P. Bordreuil, A. Lemaire, *Sem* 26 [1976], 58, and Herr, 74 no. 44), *yhwrm* (Y. Aharoni, *Lachish V*, 22), *'brm* (V, 66). These names all express the idea that the deity is 'exalted'. The only occurrence of the root *rwm* in the initial position, is in the BH name *ramyāh*, the meaning of which is unclear, in view of its possible derivation from the root *rmh* (see below, § 2.5 *rmh/rwm*). The name *'brhm* remains enigmatic: Gen. 17.5 seems to suggest a word play with *hm/hmwn* 'crowd, multitude, abundance' (also 'sound, murmur, roar', cf. BDB, 242) perhaps suggesting a meaning *'ăbir hām* 'chief of multitude' (*ibid.*, 4). In this case, the name would be non-theophoric.

sgb 'to be (inaccessibly) high'. EB seal *'lśgb* (V, 59). The meaning of the name is perhaps 'El is exalted'. A less probable, non-stative interpretation, is suggested by *IPN*, 237. P. Bordreuil and A. Lemaire, *Sem* 29 (1979) 82, read the name as *'lšgb*. The authors follow E. Puech, *RB* 83 (1976), 80, in considering this seal to be Ammon.: 'cette identification proposée par E. Puech est vraisembable d'après la paléographie (cf. spécialement le *b* et le *m*) et l'iconographie que l'on peut rapprocher de cette de *Galling* 30'.

tmm 'to be perfect'. BH *yôtām* 'Y is perfect', cf. BDB, 222, KB, 386, Geh, 520. Noth (*IPN*, 189) suggested a non-stative interpretation, 'Y has shown himself upright'. KB, 386 also give a non-stative alternative.

The ideas contained in these names, in which a stative verb is peculiar only to the second position, are all similar: they illustrate, almost exclusively, the transcendent nature of the deity. The Israelite God is depicted as 'pre-eminent', 'righteous', 'inaccessibly high', 'perfect', and 'exalted', while anthropomorphic ideas are totally lacking.

No outstanding features are portrayed by those nominal predicates which can occur in the first and second positions except, perhaps, the concept of God as light in the Hebrew roots *'wr* 'light' or 'flame', *nr* 'lamp' and *šḥr* 'dawn'. The idea of the kingship of God expressed in the roots *hwd*, *mlk* and perhaps also in the stative verbs *ḥnn*, *ykl* and *ndb*, may also be present. Nominal elements occuring in first and second positions as predicates are:

'hl 'tent'. BH *'āhŏlî'āb*. The name probably means 'The (divine) Father is a tent (i.e. protection)', cf. Geh, 680, KB, 19, *IPN*, 158. The name *ḥmy'hl* occurs extra-biblically on a seal (V, 412). Such a figurative depiction of

divine protection is not unusual in the Heb. onomasticon; cf. names with *dlt* 'door' and *hr* 'mountain' above, *ṣwr* 'rock' (above, § 2.2 *ṣwr*), and *šwr* 'wall' above, also the comparable Amor. name element *madar* meanng 'dwelling' (see below, § 4.3, 3).

'wr 'light'. BH *'ûrî'ēl*, *'ûrîyāh(û)*, *šᵉdê'ûr*; EB *'wryw* (seals V, 184; Y. Aharoni, *IEJ* 9 [1959], 55); *'wryhw* (inscr. *AI*, 31.2; 36.2, cf. *IH*, 204; Ophel 8, cf. *IH*, 239, 241). The element may also be present in the name *yw'r* (seal V, 249) and in the inscr. *'ly'r* (*AI*, 21.2, but see below, § 2.5 *'rh/'wr*).

gd 'fortune' (and n. pr. div. Gad). BH *gaddî'ēl*, *'azgād*; EB *gdyhw* (seal P. Bordreuil, A. Lemaire, *Sem* 29 [1979], 71-72; inscr. *AI*, 71.3); *gdyw* (inscr. SO 2.2 prob. = 4.2 = 5.2 = 6.2 = 7.2 = 16a.2 = 16b.2 = 17a.2 = 17b.2 = 18.2; 33.2 = 34.2 = 35.2-3, cf. *IH*, 293; SO 30.2; 42.3, cf. *SSI*, 9, 10, 12); *'bgd* (seals V, 234 Heb?, 275); *gdmlk* (seal V, 64). Names in which the element *gd* is compounded with forms of *yhwh* or *'l*, and possibly *'b*, probably mean 'Y/El/The (divine) Father is fortune', cf. BDB, 151, although many would see the n. pr. div. Gad in such names (cf. Geh, 310, *IPN*, 126). This may be the case with *'azgād* (cf. BDB, 739, Geh, 81, *IPN*, 126, and above, § 2.2 *Other divine elements*) and with *gdmlk* (cf. Dir, 220).

hwd 'splendour, majesty'. BH *hôdwāh*, *hôdîyāh*, *'ăbîhûd*, *'ammîhûd*, *'ăḥîhûd*; EB *hwdyhw* (seals BL, 49 no. 9; N. Avigad, *IEJ* 25 [1975], 101 no. 1; Milik, *RB* 66 [1959], 551); *hwdyh* (seal V, 155). The names depict the deity as 'splendour' or 'majesty'.

mlk 'king'. BH *'ĕlîmelek*, *malkî'ēl*, *malkîyāh(û)*, *'ăbîmelek*, *'ăḥîmelek*, *malkîšuaʿ*, *malkîrām*, *nᵉtan-melek*; EB *'lmlk* (inscr. Hazor B 2, cf. *SSI*, 18, 19); *yhwmlk* (seal V, 162); *mlkyhw* (seals V, 176, 326, 406; Herr, 131 no. 113; P. Bordreuil, A. Lemaire, *Sem* 29 [1979], 72 no, 2; inscr. *AI*, 24.14; 39.2; 40.3); *'ḥmlk* (seals V, 139, 154, 292, 324, 358, 424; inscr. SO 22.2-3 = 23.2 = 24.1 = 25.2 = 26.1(?) = 27.2 = 28.2 = 29.2—48.2 cf. *IH*, 292; *AI*, 72.2); *gdmlk* (seal V, 64). In these names the deity is either depicted as a 'king', or *mlk* is used as a divine appellation. The verbal interpretation suggested by Lemaire (*IH*, 190, 206) for the Arad ostraca, seems unlikely in view of BH use of the noun in names. For a full discussion of the use of *mlk*, see above, § 2.2 *mlk*.

nr 'lamp'. BH *nērîyāh(û)*, *'abnēr*/*'ăbînēr*; EB *nryhw* (seals V, 19, 50, 56, 255, 281, 422; N. Avigad, *IEJ* 28 [1978], 53; Herr, 144 no. 151; BL, 46 no. 2; inscr. L 1.5 cf. *SSI*, 103; *AI*, 31.4); possibly *'bnṙ* (seal V, 163 cf. N. Avigad, *PEQ* [1950], 43-49). The names depict the deity as a 'lamp'.

nʿm 'pleasantness, delight'. BH *'elnāʿam*, *'ăbînōʿam*, *'ăḥînōʿam*; EB *nʿm'l* (seal V, 95); *'[ḥ]nʿm* (inscr. SO 10.2; 11.2; 19.4, cf. *SSI*, 11. For these ostraca, as well as SO 8.2, 9.2, Lemaire reads *'dnʿm*, cf. *IH*, 30-32).

'zz 'strength'. BH *'el'uzzî/'el'ûzay, 'uzzî'ēl, 'uzzîyāh(û)*; EB *'zyw* (seals V, 65.67; inscr. Dir, 274; Dir, 302 no. 15); *'zyhw* (seals V, 37, 356, 422; inscr. A 20.2, cf. *IH*, 184).

šḥr 'dawn'. BH *š^eḥaryāh, 'ăḥîšaḥar* 'Y/The (divine) Brother is dawn', cf. Geh, 863, 24, *IPN*, 169.

šlm 'welfare, peace, recompense'. BH *š^elumî'ēl, 'abšālôm/'ăbîšālôm*; EB *'mslm* (inscr. *AI*, 59.4); *šlm'l* (seal V, 145).

Stative verbs occurring as predicates in first and second positions are as follows:

hnn 'to be gracious, show favour'. BH *'elḥānān, ḥănam'ēl, ḥănanyāh(û), y(^eh)ôḥānān*; EB *'lḥnn* (seals V, 5, 28); *ḥnnyh* (seal V, 23, Ammon? cf. P. Bordreuil, A. Lemaire, *Sem* 29 [1979], 83); *ḥnnyhw* (seals V, 24, 25, 50, 218, 419, 429; inscr. *AI*, 3.3; 16.1; 36.4; Gib. 22, 32, 51 [probably all the same person] cf. *SSI*, 56; V. Fritz, *ZDPV* 91 [1975], 131-34; KM 3 cf. *IH*, 275); *ḥnn'l* (seal V, 157 Ammon?); *b'lḥnn* (seal V, 36). P. Bordreuil and A. Lemaire, *Sem* 29 (1979), 83 consider *'lḥnn* (V, 5) to be Ammon. although no suggestion of such an origin seems to be entertained elsewhere. They argue an Ammon. origin on the grounds that there are paleographical similarities, particularly the *nûn*, which corresponds to that in Ammon. *'dnnr* (V, 164), as well as the bull motif known from two other Ammon. seals, and the presence of the name *'lḥnn* on another Ammon. seal (*'lḥnn bn 'r'l*). Certainly, however, the name is attested biblically as Heb. (2 Sam. 21.19; 1 Chr. 20.5) and on a Heb. seal (V, 28).

ykl 'to be able'. BH *y(^eh)ûkal, y^ekolyāh(û)*; EB *yhwkl* (seal V, 253; Herr, 111 no. 63; inscr. *AI*, 21.1). 'Y is able'.

ndb 'to be noble, generous'(*cf. Arab naduba*). BH *y^ehônādāb, n^edabyāh, 'ăbînādāb, 'ăḥînādāb, 'ammînādāb*; EB *ndb'l* (seal V, 159, possibly Ammon. cf. P. Bordreuil, A. Lemaire, *Sem* 29 [1979], 81-82; Herr, 65 no. 18, V, 400); *yhwndb* (seal V, 336); *ndbyhw* (inscr. *AI*, 39.2); *'lndb* (seal V, 357). The meaning of these names may be suggested by Arab. *naduba*, a derivative verb from an Arab. nominal form, cf. BDB, 621.

'zz 'to be strong'. This root is certainly attested verbally in the BH name *'ăzazyāhû* and perhaps in *'azgād*. Extra-biblical occurrences of the root, however, are less certain formally. For the names *'l'z* (seal V, 170, possibly Ammon., cf. P. Bordreuil, A. Lemaire, *Sem*, 26 [1976], 56, P. Bordreuil, *Syria* 50 [1973], 185 and Herr, 72 no. 38), *'z'l* (seal V, 200) and *yhw^cz* (seal V, 156; inscr. *AI*, 49.7; 31.3) the form could be either nominal or verbal, since Geminate roots can either retain or lose the third root consonant (see below, § 2.5).

Here, again, the transcendent features in the character of the deity are emphasized and all the ideas conveyed are distinctly non-anthropomorphic.

The conclusions which can be drawn from the foregoing are suggested mainly by those nominal elements which occur only as predicates in the second position and, as such, portray a more anthropomorphic concept of the deity. The semantic content of those nominal predicates occurring only in the first position may be tentatively suggested as being concerned with the idea of protection. Stative verbs contain the more transcendent notions of the deity: such notions are clearly evident in those predicative elements occurring only in the initial position and are the only concepts present in predicative elements occurring solely in the second position.

In nominal sentence names in which both the subject and the predicate is a theophoric element, it is with considerable difficulty that the subject and predicate can be determined, so much so, that for many cases the results must remain inconclusive. It is difficult to say, for example in the name *'ăbî'ēl*, whether the subject is *'l* or *'b* and whether the interpretation is 'God is Father' or 'The Father is God'. Some are perhaps more positive; *'ĕlî'ēl* '(my) God is El' or 'El is (my) God' would indicate that the element *'l*, at least in this case, can occur as a predicate.

The work of Francis I. Andersen, *The Hebrew Verbless Clause in the Pentateuch*, Abingdon Press (1970), may be relevant here. If, as he states, the predicate is always definite in personal names (p. 46) then the name is one of identification and the word order is subject-predicate (p. 32). Indeed, the example which Andersen gives of such a clause of identification, 'I am YHWH' (§1 p. 52) suits this type of name, in which two possible theophoric elements are used, reasonably well. However, since other theophoric compound names do not conform to Andersen's classifications (see p. 171 n. 18), a word order subject-predicate for these names should not be accepted without considerable caution.

In an examination of theophoric elements which form predicates in first position only, second position only, and in first and second positions, however, no particular characteristics are evident to suggest that further elucidation here would be of any value. Nouns like *'b* 'father'. *'ḥ* 'brother', *'l* 'god', *b'l* 'lord', *mlk* 'king' and *'m* 'kinsman', which can also be theophoric elements, occur both in first and second positions in names, while *'dn* 'lord', occurs only in the initial position. For names containing these elements see the name list below, Appendix 3.

2.4 *Verbal Sentence Names in Hebrew*

Verbal sentence names in Hebrew are those consisting of a nominal subject, which is usually a theophoric element, and a verbal predicate: when these are combined, they form a short sentence. The verbal predicate can occur in the first or second position, e.g. ***neṯan'ēl***, ***'elnāṯān***, 'El has given'.

Although the most prevalent order for verbal sentence names is predicate-subject, names compounded with *'b* and *'ḥ*, whether in biblical or extra-biblical Hebrew, are always predominantly subject-predicate in order. However, in an examination of those verbal elements which only occur in the order subject-predicate, or predicate-subject, or both, unlike nominal sentence names, few outstanding characteristics of semantic content or form are displayed. It is possible to suggest a predominance of anthropomorphic ideas in those verbal elements found exclusively in the order subject-predicate, if we confine the analysis only to names occurring in biblical Hebrew; as soon as extra-biblical verbal names are added, such a suggestion is no longer tenable. It is noticeable that these biblical names are, in the main, very early, whereas the extra-biblical names are mostly datable to the time of the divided Monarchy. Verbal elements occurring only in the order subject-predicate in biblical Hebrew are:

'th	'to come' (poetical)	*'ĕlî'āṯāh*
dwd	'to love'	*'ĕlîdād*, *'eldād*
d'h	'to call' (cf. Arab. *da'ā*)	*'eldā'āh*
'wd	demon. 'to bear witness'	*'el'ād*
p'l	'to make, do'	*'elpa'al*

Also to be added are two roots which occur only in the second position in verbal names in biblical Hebrew, although they occur extra-biblically as verbal forms in the first position. These are:

'wš	'to lend, aid, come to help'	BH *yô'āš*; seals *'l'š* (V, 340); *'šn'l* (V, 88); *'šnyhw* (V, 125).
qnh	'to get, acquire, create'	BH *'elqānāh*; seal *qnyw* (V, 13).

Verbal elements of the names occurring only in biblical Hebrew are all prefixed with *'l* and, where a verbal form can be established (which is in every case), the form is Qal perfective. The roots *'th*, *dwd*, *d'h*, *'wš* and *qnh*, it is suggested, are anthropomorphic in idea. Further to be considered are verbal elements prefixed by *'b* and *'ḥ*, also occurring in the Qal perfective:

'wm	'to rule' (cf. Arab. *'āma*)	*'ăḥî'ām* (or root *'mm* 'to be wide, roomy').
'sp	'to gather'	*'ăbî'āsāp*, *'ebyāsāp* (or root *ysp* 'to add').
rwḥ	'to breathe'	*'aḥrāḥ* (on this name, see below, § 2.9).
šwr	'to behold, regard'	*'ăḥîšār*.

Verbal elements occurring only in the order subject-predicate in names found extra-biblically are:

'mn	'to support'	Seal *yw'mn* (V, 172).
bw'	'to come'	Inscr. *'lb'* (SO 1.6 cf. *SSI*, 11).
brr	'to purify, select'	Seals *'lybr* (V, 133, 397, see also below, § 2.4).
dll	'to direct' (cf. Arab. *dall*)	Inscr. (*'*)*mdl* (L 19.3 cf. *SSI*, 49). Lemaire, however, now reads *Mikal* for this name (cf. *IH*, 132, 133).
sḥr	'to go around, about'; or cf. Akk. *saḥāru* 'to turn'.	Inscr. [*yh*]*wsh*[*r*] (*AI*, 90). The name is perhaps verbal, but its form is difficult, see below § 2.9.

The ideas contained in these extra-biblical names as a whole are not predominantly anthropomorphic and therefore not similar to biblical names of the same type.

Many theophoric names in the Hebrew onomasticon contain verbal elements which are not attested in biblical Hebrew and whose meanings are, in the main, suggested by cognate languages. Of these, Arabic seems to predominate, as the following list of such roots will show:

'wm	'to rule' suggested by Arab. *'āma*.
'wš	'to bestow' cf. P. Bordreuil, *Syria* 52 (1975), 115-17, suggested by Arab. *'āsa*.

d'h	'to call' suggested by Arab. *da'ā*.
ḥbṣ	'to be joyful' suggested by Akk. *ḫabāṣu*.
ydh	'to show beneficence' suggested by Arab. *yadā*.
'zh	'to nourish' suggested by Arab. *ghadhā*.
'rš	'to plant' suggested by Akk. *erēšu* and Arab. *gharasa*.
'th	'to be proud, exalted' suggested by Arab. *'atā*.
qwt	'to nourish' suggested by Arab. *qāta*.
rml	'to adorn with gems' suggested by Arab. *ramala*.
šêzêb	Aram. 'to deliver'.

That verbal names compounded with such roots bear the stamp of foreign influence is not a necessary conclusion to be drawn from the above list. Rather, it is probable that these roots occurring only in names indicate a survival of elements in Hebrew which are now either no longer attested, or no longer attested with such nuances of interpretation (cf. Barr *Cp. Ph.*, 181-84).

Another interesting phenomenon concerning verbal elements in Hebrew theophoric names is the use of a verbal form which has no equivalent verbal aspect in biblical Hebrew. Most frequently, this involves a use of the Qal in the name, when such a verbal aspect is absent elsewhere. This phenomenon is evident in names from the following roots, while a discussion of each name including its form is to be found below.

'zn 'to hear'. The root occurs in the Qal in names, whereas in BH it exists only as a denominative verb in the Hiphil. It is used mainly poetically, especially of God listening favourably to prayers etc., cf. BDB, 24.

ṭll 'to cover over (protect)'. If the name *'ăbîṭāl*, which is derived from this root, is verbal (cf. below, p. 171 n. 23), the form is Qal, whereas in BH the root is attested only once, in the Piel, cf. BDB, 378.

yš' 'to deliver'. Attested in names in the Qal and Hiphil, this root is found in BH only in the latter, with the meaning 'to deliver', cf. BDB, 446.

kwn 'to establish'. This root is attested in names in the Qal and the Hiphil, whereas in BH it occurs only in derived conjugations.

mlṭ 'to deliver'. The use of the Qal in names is not attested in BH in which only the Niphal, with the meaning 'to escape', and the Piel, with the meaning 'to deliver', are found, cf. BDB, 572.

nḥm 'to comfort'. Occurring exclusively in the Qal in names, the root *nḥm* is attested in BH only in the Niphal 'to have compassion', and in the Piel 'to comfort, console', cf. BDB, 637.

str 'to hide, conceal'. The root *str* in BH is found mainly in the Hiphil and Niphal, but not in the Qal, cf. BDB, 711. For the name *ywstr* (V, 346) a Qal form is possible, 'Y is hidden', although a noun, *sēter*, meaning 'covering, hiding place' (cf. BDB, 712) may also be relevant.

pl' 'to be wonderful'. The verbal element in the name *p^{e}lā'yāh* from the root *pl'*, is Qal, while elsewhere the denominative verb indicates only use of the Niphal and Hiphil, cf. BDB, 810.

pll 'to judge'. The Qal, which occurs in names, is not found elsewhere in BH, where usage is confined to the Piel 'to mediate, judge' and Hithp. 'to intercede, pray', cf. BDB, 813.

Why this use of the Qal should be employed when the same sense is conveyed by a derived conjugation or a homonymous root in the Qal,[20] is not clear. It is possible that names which contain the Qal reflect a survival of the use of this verbal aspect which is no longer to be found outside the Hebrew onomasticon.

Also differing from normal usage of the root are instances in which a verbal element in names is attested when no verbal forms exist elsewhere, as the following show:

'br 'to be strong, firm'. In the name *'bryhw* (seal V, 330), *'br* probably means 'to be strong', although it is not attested verbally with this meaning in BH. However, cf. the adjectives *'ābîr* 'strong' and *'abbîr* 'mighty, valiant' (cf. BDB, 7).

'šh 'to support'. Names possibly derived from this root present formal difficulty (see below, § 2.5 *'šh/'wš*) and may belong to a root *'wš*. However, it is worth noting in this context, the absence of verbal forms from the root *'šh* in BH.

dwd 'to love'. Occurring in the Qal in names, the root is not attested biblically in verbal forms.

zbd 'to give'. Again, the Qal is attested in names when verbal forms from this root are absent in BH.

zmr 'to protect' (cf. S. Arab. *dhimr*). The root *zmr* exists in BH verbally with the meanings I 'to make music (in praise of God)' and II 'to trim, prune', cf. BDB, 274. It is likely that in names a Qal form is used, with a meaning suggested by a S. Arab. cognate *dhimr* 'to protect' for which no verbal forms are attested in BH.

ḥkl 'to be confused, vague'. If the BH name *ḥăkalyāh* is derived from the root *ḥkl* and not the root *ḥkh* (see below, § 2.8.1) no verbal forms from this root occur elsewhere in BH.

yšh 'to assist, support' (cf. Arab. *'asa'*). The BH name *yôšawyāh* may be derived from this root, which is not found in BH in verbal forms. The form of the name, however, is very difficult (see below, § 2.9).

ytn 'to be perpetual, never failing' (cf. Arab. *watana*). If the first element of the name *yatnî'ēl* is a verbal form from the root *ytn*, this is a root not attested elsewhere in BH in verbal form. The name, however, is difficult (see below, § 2.9).

knn 'to be firm, substantial'. The root *knn*, a parallel form of *kwn* 'to set up, establish', is not attested verbally in BH, whereas in the biblical name *k*ᵉ*nanyāh(û)* it appears to be found in the Qal perf.

rwḥ 'to breathe'. The form of the BH name *'aḥraḥ* is not clear (see below, § 2.9). A verbal form is not impossible although such forms are not attested in BH.

rmh 'to loosen' (cf. Akk. *ramû*). Names like BH *yirm*ᵉ*yāh*, which may be derived from the root *rmh*, are problematic in that it is often difficult to differentiate between a Hollow or III *hē* root as the source of the verbal element (see below § 2.5 *rmh/rwm*). If a III *hē* root is applicable for this name, with a meaning suggested by an Akk. cognate *ramû* 'to slacken' (G), 'to loosen' (D), it is not found in verbal forms in BH.

śakh/skh cf. NH 'to look out'. Again, the BH name *śāk*ᵉ*yāh* (LXX *śobyāh*) is difficult (see below § 2.9). If a verbal translation of the name is possible, it is not paralleled by any verbal usage with this root in BH.

š'l NH 'deep'. The element *š'l* appears in the name *š'lyhw* (seal N. Avigad, *IEJ* 4 [1954], 236). If an interpretation from the NH 'deep', 'depth' is correct (cf. BDB, 1043) it may be possible to suggest a stative verbal form for the meaning of the element, although verbal forms are not attested elsewhere in BH.

šrb 'to parch, be scorched'. A Piel perf. of the root *šrb* is suggested for the first element of BH *šērēbyāh* meaning, perhaps, 'Y has sent burning heat', cf. BDB, 1055, Geh, 867. The root is not found verbally elsewhere in BH. See also below, § 2.9.

A large percentage of the foregoing names display formal difficulty, but at least for roots such as *dwd*, *zbd*, *zmr*, *knn*, probably *rwḥ* and *šrb*, and from the former list illustrating the use of the Qal in names when the Qal is not found elsewhere, there is considerable evidence that verbal elements in names need not conform to the usage prevalent elsewhere in biblical Hebrew. This may well be due to the fact that personal names have retained a particular use of the root which is not otherwise extant, but which may have been in use at one time.

Verbal sentence names are the commonest type of name in the Hebrew onomasticon. They express statements about what the deity has done e.g. *'ĕlîšāmā'* 'El has heard', or continues to do, e.g. *yaḥzᵉyāh* 'Y sees', or what it is hoped the deity will do, e.g. *yᵉberekyāhû* 'May Y bless'. However, no conclusive formal rule can be established which would facilitate the classification of these names. One cannot say, for example, that all names with imperfective predicates express a wish formula, 'May the deity—', as Martin Noth has done (*op. cit., passim*). This, indeed, would deny to the Hebrew imperfective verb one of its basic functions, that of expressing habitual or customary action (cf. T.O. Lambdin, *Introduction to Biblical Hebrew*, DLT [1973], § 91 p. 100).

Categorization of these verbal forms is, therefore, better approached from a semantic point of view, but such an approach should not impose too much rigidity upon the kind of situation in which a name was given. Thus a name like *yᵉša'yāh(û)*, 'Y has saved', could refer to the successful birth of the child, to the deliverance of the parents or family in time of need, or perhaps even to a wider sense of deliverance of the whole people and a time of national importance. The confinement of these names by Noth to the categories of *Bekenntnisnamen, Vertrauensnamen, Danknamen*, and *Wunschnamen* (*op. cit.*, 135-213) places far too restrictive an interpretation upon the verbal names.

Moreover, it is possible that a great many names do no more than make a general statement about the deity, certainly about what the parents considered to be characteristic of their God, but not necessarily applicable to events which were paramount at the time the child was born. The following classification of verbal names, therefore, must remain flexible, as will be frequently pointed out.

A semantic analysis of the names seems to suggest that they are fairly equally divided between two main groups, those which possibly refer to the child or parents, and those which make more general statements about the deity. Most of the names which seem to refer to the child express the fact that the deity has made the birth of the child possible. A number of names seem to suggest that a parental request for offspring has been answered by the deity. Such names are portrayed in verbal forms from the following roots:

'zn 'to hear'. BH *'ăzanyāhû*, Qal perf. 'Y has heard', cf. BDB, 24, Geh, 79, *IPN*, 21, 185. The same meaning is likely for the element *'zn* in the EB name *ywzn* (seal BL, 50 no. 13).

šm' 'to hear'. BH *'ĕlîšāmā'*, Qal perf. 'El has heard', cf. BDB, 46, KB, 55 Geh, 264, *IPN*, 20, 185.
BH *š^ema'yāh(û)*, Qal perf. 'Y has heard', cf. Geh, 865, *IPN*, 21, 185. EB *'lšm'* seals (V, 59 [possibly Ammon., cf. P. Bordreuil, A. Lemaire, *Sem* 29 (1979), 82], V, 72, 100, 244, 423); *šm'yhw* seal (V, 40), inscr. (*AI*, 27.2; 31.5; 39.2; 39.7-8; Mur. B 4; L 4.6; 19.4, cf. *SSI*, 32, 49). The 28 people in the OT called *š^ema'yāhû* and the 14 extra-biblical occurrences of the name convey the idea that the deity 'has heard'. For the 42 people who bore this name it is likely that very different circumstances promoted the giving of each name. Some, at least, may refer to the granting of a child by the deity, but the name exemplifies well the flexibility which is needed in the approach to Hebrew names.

Names formed from the root *š'l* 'to ask', probably imply that the deity has answered the parents' request for a child:

š'l 'to ask, inquire'. BH *š^e'altî'ēl*, Qal perf. and *šaltî'ēl*, 'I have asked El', cf. Geh, 859, and BDB, 982, 1027 ('I have asked of God').

The roots *'zn*, *šm'* and *š'l* in names, express that the deity has heard the request of the parents for a child and has granted that request. Similarly, some names express that the deity remembered such a request:

zkr 'to remember'. BH *yôzākār*, Qal perf. 'Y has remembered', cf. BDB, 222, KB, 381, Geh, 521, *IPN*, 187.
BH *z^ekaryāh(û)*, Qal perf. 'Y has remembered', cf. Geh, 1010, 1014, KB, 260, *IPN*, 187.
EB *'lzkr* seals(V, 42, 43); *zkryhw* seals (V, 104, 167), inscr. (weight 11 cf. *SSI*, 69); [z]*kryw* seal (V, 323, cf. Herr, 108 no. 57), all Qal perf.

'nh 'to answer'. BH *'ănāyāh*, Qal perf. 'Y has answered', cf. Geh, 41, *IPN*, 185.
EB *'nyhw* seal (V, 273), perhaps also inscr. *'nyb'l* (MH 6.1 cf. *IH*, 68 and above § 2.2 *b'l*).

Names denoting that the deity 'has blessed' may well refer to the blessing of the parents by the gift of a child, as in the following names:

brk 'to bless'. BH *berekyāh(û)*, Qal perf. 'Y has blessed', cf. Geh, 105, *IPN*, 21, 183.
BH *bārak'ēl*, Qal perf. 'El has blessed', cf. Geh, 93, KB, 154.
EB *brkyhw* seals (V, 230; N. Avigad, *IEJ* 28 [1978], 53) and inscr. (*AI*, 22.1). Cf. also the name *m^erāyāh* below, § 2.9.

A similar idea is found in the name which denotes that the deity has shown kindness by granting a child:

ydh 'to do good, be beneficent' (cf. Arab. *yadā*). BH *yᵉdāyāh*, Qal perf. 'Y has shown kindness, has been beneficent'. The meaning of the name is suggested by an Arab. cognate *yadā*, cf. Geh, 449, KB, 373, *IPN*, 182.

Three Hebrew roots used in the Qal perfective express that the deity 'has given' the child to the parents. These are:

'wš 'to bestow' (cf. Arab. *'āsa*). BH *y(ᵉh)ô'āš*. Since the element *'āš-* displays the characteristics of a second position predicate from a Hollow root (see below, pp. 112f.) it is probably a Qal perf. from a root *'wš*. The meaning of the name could then be 'Y has bestowed', suggested by an Arab. cognate *'āsa*, cf. KB, 376, Geh, 495 and P. Bordreuil, *Syria* 52 (1975), 115-17. The same meaning is probable for the following extra-biblical names, but see below, pp. 112f. for the possibility of a root *'šh*.
EB *'šyhw* seal (V, 231, 281 = inscr. *AI*, 1.40 = 2.35 = 17.3 = 105.2 = 106.2 = 107.2; BL, 50 no. 12); inscr. (Y. Aharoni, *Lachish V*, 22; *AI*, 51.1); *'šyh* seal (V, 232). For *'šyhw* W. Kornfeld, *WZKM* 71 (1979), 42, suggests a parallel with *'ešbā'al* and a meaning 'Mann Yhw's' (see also above, pp. 57-58 and Y. Aharoni, *AI*, pp. 32-33), or the root *'wš* and a meaning 'gegeben von Yhw', following Lemaire, *IH*, 136. H. Parunak, *BASOR* 230 (1978), 29 IV 1 b ii, makes no mention of a root *'wš*, but notes *'îš* 'man' and following F.M. Cross, seems to prefer a derivation of the first element from *yš*, with a somewhat tenuous comparison with Ug. *'iṯ* 'lives', 'exists'.

zbd 'to bestow'. BH *'elzābād*, Qal perf. 'El has given, bestowed', cf. BDB, 44, KB, 53, Geh, 266.
BH *y(ᵉh)ôzābād*, Qal perf. 'Y has given, bestowed', cf. BDB, 220, KB, 378, 381, Geh, 454, *IPN*, 21, 47.
BH *zᵉbadyāh(û)*, Qal perf. 'Y has given, bestowed', cf. BDB, 256, KB, 250, Geh, 1012, *IPN*, 21, 46-47.
BH *'ammîzābād*, Qal perf. 'The (divine) Kinsman has given or bestowed', cf. BDB, 770, Geh, 37, *IPN*, 15 n. 2, 47.

ntn 'to give'. BH *'elnātān*, Qal perf. 'El has given', cf. BDB, 46, KB, 57, Geh, 265, *IPN*, 21, 170.
BH *nᵉtan'ēl*, Qal perf. 'El has given', cf. Geh, 653, *IPN*, 21, 92, 170.
BH *y(ᵉh)ônātān*, Qal perf. 'Y has given', cf. BDB, 220, Geh, 510, *IPN*, 20, 170.
BH *nᵉtanyāh(û)*, Qal perf. 'Y has given', cf. Geh, 660, *IPN*, 21, 270.
BH *nᵉtan-melek*, Qal perf. 'Melek has given', cf. Geh, 653, *IPN*, 21, 118 and above, § 2.2 *mlk*.
EB *'lntn* seal (V, 138, 189, 190, 306(?), 315 (?), 430); inscr. (L 3.15 cf. *SSI*,

38.40; L 11.2 cf. *IH*, 128; A.F. Rainey, *Tel Aviv* 4 [1977], 97-102 pls. 5-6); *ntnyhw* seals (V, 31, 32), inscr. (AI, 23.9; 56.1-2; Khirbet el-Kôm, cf. W.G. Dever, *HUCA* 40-41 [1969-70], 151-56; *ibid*., 156-57); *ywntn* inscr. (SO 45.3 cf. *IH*, 35. Diringer separates the *yw* and the *ntn* cf. Dir, 47 no. 36); *yhwntn* seal (V, 349).

Many names seem to express that the deity has created or made the child, and numerous Hebrew roots are employed for this purpose. Although the form of these names is predominantly Qal perfective, it is not exclusively so. Names referring to the creation of the child are indicated in the following:

bnh 'to build'. BH *b^{e}nāyāh*, Qal perf. 'Y has built, or created', cf. BDB, 125, *KB*, 134, Geh, 101, *IPN*, 21, 172.
EB *bnyhw* seals (V, 18, 299, 407, 431; Herr, 119 no. 82; *BL*, 46-47 no. 3); inscr. (L 16.4 cf. Torcz, 198; *AI*, 39.9; A 5.9 cf. *IH*, 167; A 74.4 cf. *IH*, 220); *ywbnh* seals (V, 197, 290) all Qal perf.
From the same root *bnh* comes the BH name *yibn^{e}yāh* in the imf. and meaning 'Y builds up, creates', cf. BDB, 125, KB, 367, Geh, 415. The suggestion of Noth (*IPN*, 212) that the name is one expressing a wish for more descendants seems an unnecessary assumption. Although such a meaning is possible, it is forced upon Noth by his adherence to the notion that names involving imperfectives should be translated as a wish.

br' 'to create'. BH *b^{e}rā'yāh*, Qal perf. 'Y has created', cf. BDB, 135, KB, 147, Geh, 104, *IPN*, 171.

qnh 'to create, acquire'. BH *'elqānāh*, Qal perf. 'El has created', cf. BDB, 46, who further suggest the possibility 'God has taken possession', KB, 58, *Geh*, 264, *IPN*, 20, 172.
EB *qnyw* seal (V, 13).

'śh 'to make'. BH *'el'āśāh*, Qal perf. 'El has made', cf. BDB, 46, KB, 57, Geh, 256/257, *IPN*, 21, 172.
BH *'ăśî'ēl*, Qal perf. 'El has made', cf. BDB, 795, Geh, 71. The suggestion of Noth (*IPN*, 28, 206) that the name is a sf. of *yā'ăśî'ēl* is not generally supported. BH *'ăśāh'ēl*, Qal perf. 'El has made', cf. Geh, 66.
BH *'ăśāyāh*, Qal perf. 'Y has made', cf. Geh, 66, *IPN*, 21, 172.
EB *yw'śh* seal (V, 171); *'śyhw* seals (V, 27, 62, 109; BL, 48 no. 7); The name *'śyhw* on the seal *'šyhw bn ḥwyhw* recorded by Bordreuil and Lemaire seems to belong here. However, the transcription of the name by these authors as *'šyhw*, with a meaning 'YHWH a fait', seems to show some confusion concerning the root *'śh* 'to do, make', which is obviously *'śh* with *ś* not *š*. The mistake is especially noticeable since they cite biblical *'ăśāyāh* (2 Kgs 22.12), which leaves no doubt as to the correct letter. Vattioni has also copied the error (V, 365), although citing other names which are clearly *'śjhw*, and has

also recorded the patronym *ḥwyhw* incorrectly as *ḥwhjhw*: inscr. (Y. Aharoni, *Lachish V*, 22); *'śyw* seal (V, 38), all Qal perf. The root *'śh* also occurs in the BH name *ya'ăśî'ēl* in the imf. Noth (*IPN*, 206) considered the name to express a wish that the deity should act or be concerned with the life of the child, but this seems awkward. Better, is a translation 'El makes', cf. Geh, 436, KB, 404; a simple statement by the parents to refer to God's creation of a child.

p'l 'to make'. BH *'elpa'al*. The second element of the name is difficult (see below, § 2.9) but is possibly Qal perf. This would indicate a meaning 'El has made', cf. KB, 58, Geh, 265, *IPN*, 172. The possibility 'God of doing' suggested by BDB, 46 seems unlikely; no other Heb. names have a theophoric element in construct with the following non-theophoric element.

rwḥ 'to breathe'. BH *'aḥrāḥ*. This name is discussed in detail below, § 2.9. A root *rû^aḥ* 'to breathe' is suggested for the second element, which conforms to the pattern of Hollow verb second position perfectives (see below, p. 112). A meaning 'The (divine) Father has breathed' is therefore possible, suggesting that the deity has breathed life into the child, i.e. created.

In a similar way, some names express that the deity has created the child by stating that he has 'accomplished' its creation. Thus we find names in the Qal perfective from the following roots:

gmr 'to accomplish'. BH *g^emaryāh(û)*, Qal perf. 'Y has accomplished', cf. BDB, 170, KB, 190, Geh, 320, *IPN*, 175.
Also EB inscr. (L 1.1; *AI*, 31.8; 35.4; 38.3; 40.1).

gml 'to accomplish'. The BH name *gamlî'ēl* is difficult (see below, § 2.9). If the form is Qal perf. a meaning 'El has accomplished or rewarded' is possible, cf. KB, 190, Geh, 315, *IPN*, 36. The suggestion of BDB, 168, 'Reward of God', is also possible, however, in view of the difficulty with these *qaṭlî'ēl* forms. The EB name *gmlyhw* (seal V, 169) is probably more decisively Qal perf. and vocalized *g^emalyāhû*, since *qaṭlî'ēl* types are almost exclusively suffixed with *'l* (see below, p. 134).

The root *'mr* 'to say' may well be used in names to indicate that the deity has created a child by command, in the same way that the expression *wayyōmer 'ĕlōhîm* is used in the creations depicted in the Genesis narrative (Gen. 1.3, 6, 9, 11 etc.).

'mr 'to say'. BH *'ămaryāh(û)*, Qal perf. 'Y has said, cf. Geh, 35, *IPN*, 21, 173. The use of the root *'mr* in the sense of 'to promise', is too infrequently attested to accept the suggestion of BDB, 57, 'Y has promised', as the meaning of this name.
EB *'l'mr* (seal V, 136); Herr, 180 no. 19 suggests that this name is probably

Phoen., but the root *'mr* is not otherwise attested in Phoen. names: *'mryhw* (seal V, 21; inscr. Gib. 14 cf. *SSI*, 56). The name *'ḥ'mr* possibly occurs on a seal (M, 76 no. 13 = Herr, 86 no. 9) although Moscati notes the alternative reading *'ḥsmk*, which seems to have been accepted by Vattioni (V, 280) also P. Lapp (*BASOR* 158 [1960], 12).

Some verbal names may refer to the actual birth of the child:

pqḥ 'to open'. BH *pᵉqaḥyāh*, Qal perf. 'Y has opened (the eyes)', cf. BDB, 824, KB, (1953), 775, Geh, 725. The name could be used in the sense of the deity opening the eyes of the newly born child, i.e. bringing it to life or, with Noth (*IPN*, 186), to express that the deity has opened his own eyes to the particular need of an individual.

ptḥ 'to open'. BH *pᵉtaḥyāh*, Qal perf. 'Y has opened (the womb)', cf. Geh, 740, *KB*, (1953), 788, *IPN*, 179.

rmh 'to loosen'. BH *yirmᵉyāh*; EB seals M, 74 no. 2; V, 58, 248; BL, 47-48 no. 6; Y. Aharoni, *IEJ* 18 (1968), 166-67; inscr. L 1.4 cf. *SSI*, 36; *AI*, 24.15-16. For the inscriptional name from Lachish, Lemaire (*IH*, 96) translates 'Yhwh relevera' i.e. from a root *rwm*. However, the name is difficult and an imf. from the root *rmh* is perhaps preferable (see below, § 2.5 *rmh*/*rwm*). BDB, 941 indicate a meaning 'Y loosens (the womb)', suggested by an Akk. cognate *ramû* (D). The suggestion of KB, 420, 'J gründete', from a root *rmh*, seems less likely, since such a meaning is not attested for the root in Heb. (cf. BDB, 941) and no cognate is suggested by KB. The idea may possibly have been suggested by Akk. *ramû* II (Š) meaning 'Fundament' (cf. *AHw*, 953). Elsewhere, a root *rwm* 'to exalt' is accepted cf. *IPN*, 201 n. 2, and Geh, 457, who also suggests 'Y founds, establishes'.

ḥlṣ 'to draw out'. EB seal *ḥlṣyhw* (V, 176). The root *ḥlṣ* means 'to draw off or out, withdraw' (cf. BDB, 322). The name is probably a Qal perf. from this root meaning 'Y has drawn (the child from the womb)'. The Piel of the root *ḥlṣ* sometimes has the meaning 'to rescue, deliver' when used poetically (cf. BDB, 322), but whether we are justified in pointing the name *ḥlṣyhw*, to suggest the Piel, is not possible to decide. However, it is possible that the name is meant in the sense of 'rescue' in the same way as the root *dlh* in Heb. names (see below, p. 97), and may refer to events other than the birth of the child.

Some roots are used verbally to express the idea that the deity has increased the number of children in the family, as in the following:[21]

ysp 'to add'. BH *'elyāsāp*, Qal perf. 'El has added', cf. BDB, 45, KB, 54, Geh, 259, *IPN*, 173. The element *ysp* is also met prefixed with *b'l* on the seal *b'lysp* (V, 219), 'Baal has added', but this seal may be Phoen. rather than Heb. The Hiphil imf. of the root *ysp* is also found in the BH name *yôsipyāh*

'Y adds'. The root *ysp* is often used in the Hiphil in BH in the same sense as the Qal (cf. BDB, 415). There seems no reason why the name should be translated 'May Y add', as Noth (IPN, 212) and Geh, 520 suggest.

rḥb 'to be or grow wide, large'. BH *r^eḥabyāh*. An interpretation 'Y has made wide or made room' (cf. Geh, 796, *IPN*, 193) probably suits the name best. This would be interpreting the Qal of the root *rḥb* in the same sense as the Hiphil. The element *rḥb* also exists in the BH name *r^eḥab'ām* for which the same meaning, 'The (divine) Kinsman has made wide', is preferable.

In a similar sense, it is possible that some names may express that the deity has replaced, or compensated for, a previously deceased child. Such an idea may be represented by the following roots:

šlm 'to recompense'. BH *šelemyāh(û)*, Piel perf.; also seal (V, 30 = inscr. *AI*, 108.3).
EB *šlmyh(w)* seals (V, 144, 333; inscr. L 9.7 cf. *SSI*, 47;. A 27.5 cf. *IH*, 198). The meaning of the BH and EB names is probably 'Y has recompensed', cf. KB, 613, *IPN*, 174.

šwb 'to restore'. BH *'elyāšîb*; EB seals *'lyšb* (V, 375, 231 = 282 = inscr. *AI*, 1.1 = 2.1 = 3.1 = 4.1 = 5.1 = 6.1 = 7.1 = 8.1 = 9.1 = 10.1 = 11.1 = 12.1 = 14.1 = 15.1-2 = 16.2—17.2 = 18.1-2—24.2. *AI*, 38.5; 47.1; 64.2; Y. Aharoni, *Lachish V*, 22-23 line 8). The biblical name means 'El restores', cf. BDB, 46, KB, 55, and is a Hiphil imf. This may also be the form of the EB names, although a Qal perf. is also possible. It is likely that the names refer to the replacement of a previously lost child. Geh, 259-60, however, prefers the translation 'El will restore'. Noth saw the names as a plea for the return of the dispersed Israel, or promotion of the earlier state, with an implied translation 'May El restore' (*IPN*, 213).

Also attested in Hebrew names is the idea that the deity 'returns', probably in the sense of returning to show favour. Such a concept is evident in the roots:

šwb 'to return'. The root *šwb* occurs in the Qal in the inscriptional name *šb'l* (Gib. 21 cf. *SSI*, 56). Gibson links the name with biblical *š^ebû'ēl* and translates 'Return to God', but the connection between the two is tenuous, and the name *š^ebû'ēl* is preferably construct (see below § 2.7). *Šb'l* is likely to consist of a Qal perf. form, with a meaning 'El has returned'. With the use of the Qal, the sense here is of the deity returning to show favour and is not connected with the Hiphil idea of restoring a child. Cf. also the name *šb'l(?) bn 'lyš'* (seal A.R. Millard, *Iraq* 24 [1962], 49 n. 55) which may be Heb. or Ammon. At one time, R. Zadok (*The Jews in Babylonia During the Chaldean and Achaemenian Periods According to the Babylonian Sources*, University of

Haifa [1979], 45-46) considered it Heb. More recently, however, Zadok suggests the stamp seal is Ammon., Moab. or Edom. ('Notes on the Early History of the Israelites and Judeans', *Orientalia* 51 [1982], 391-93). The root *šwb* is also attested in the BH name *yāšob'ām*, Qal imf. 'May the (divine) Kinsman return', cf. Geh, 447, KB, 425.

pnh 'to turn'. Perhaps similar to the above name is *pn'l* (inscr. B 1.2 cf. *IH*, 271). Lemaire considers the meaning to be verbal, 'El (dieu) s'est tourné vers, a regardé'. He equates the name with BH *p^enû'ēl* to which he assigns the same meaning since he believes a construct type name 'Face of El' makes no sense. While a verbal interpretation is likely for the EB name, however, *p^enû'ēl* is more likely to be construct (see below, §§ 2.6 and 2.7).

Some names seem to express the pleasure and joy of the parents in obtaining a child. Interestingly, names which seem to portray such an idea, occur mostly in biblical Hebrew, and rarely in extra-biblical names:

'śr 'to rejoice' (cf. Arab. *'aśira*). BH *'ăśar'ēl* Qal perf. (Cf. also *'ăśar'ēlāh*, 1 Chr. 25.2 which possibly has the same form and meaning). A meaning 'El has filled with joy', suggested by an Arab. cognate *'aśira*, seems the most preferable interpretation of this name, cf. *IPN*, 183, Barr *Cp. Ph.*, 181. The name perhaps expresses the joy of the parents concerning the birth of the child. The possibility of a derivation from a root *'sr*, meaning 'to tie, bind, imprison' (cf. BDB, 63), rendering 'God has bound', is suggested by Geh, 67.

ḥbṣ 'to be joyful' (cf. Akk. *ḫabāṣu*). BH *ḥăbaṣṣinyāh*. The form of this name is difficult, but the meaning of the first element may be suggested by an Akk. cognate *ḫabāṣu*, meaning 'to be joyful'. The addition of the *nûn* presents no problem if accepted as a 1st pers. sing. verbal suffix (see below, § 2.8.5), but the meaning would then need to be causative, 'Y has made me joyful (by the birth of the child)'.

ḥdh 'to rejoice'. BH *yaḥdî'ēl*, *yeḥd^eyāhû*. A meaning 'El/Y gives joy' is probably the best translation for both these names. For the latter name, however, BDB, 292 and *IPN*, 210 prefer 'May Y give joy', and Geh, 450 'Y will be glad'. For *yaḥdî'ēl*, BDB, 292 suggest 'God gives joy', while Geh, 442 interprets the name as 'May El give joy'. Noth (*IPN*, 210) seems to imply 'May El rejoice'.

'th 'to be proud' (cf. Arab. *'atā*). BH *'otnî'ēl*. The meaning of the first element in this name may perhaps be suggested by an Arab. cognate *'atā* meaning 'to be proud, exalted'. The *nûn* would represent a 1st pers. sing. verbal suffix (see below, § 2.8.5), suggesting a meaning 'El has made me proud, or exalted me'. The root also seems to occur in the Aram. name *'tr'th* (*PS*, 232).

ydh 'to praise'. BH *hôdawyāh(û)*, Hiphil imv. 'Praise or Thank Y', cf. BDB, 392, Geh, 401, KB, 231, *IPN*, 194, and B. Porten, *IEJ* 21 (1971), 48. The name is found once extra-biblically, in an inscr. (L 3.17 cf. *SSI*, 38, 41).

There are a number of verbal sentence names which are much more semantically ambiguous as far as the context in which they were given is concerned. They could refer to the newly born child as the object of the sentence, or to some particular circumstance of the parents. On the other hand, they could refer to circumstances affecting the whole family of the child or even, in a wider sense, be concerned with national events as, for example, some of the names which state that the deity 'has delivered'. This idea is expressed by five Hebrew elements:

plṭ 'to deliver'. BH *p^elaṭyāh(û)*, Qal perf. EB seals V, 379; P. Bordreuil, A. Lemaire, *Sem* 29 (1979), 74 no. 5, 'Y has delivered', cf. Geh, 725, *IPN*, 180.

yš' 'to deliver, save'. BH *y^eša'yāh(û)*, Qal perf. 'Y has delivered, saved', cf. Geh, 477, *IPN*, 176. The suggestion by BDB, 447 of a construct form 'Salvation of Y' is more doubtful.
BH *hôša'ăyāh*, Hiphil perf. 'Y has saved', cf. BDB, 448, Geh, 410.
EB *hwš'yhw* (seals V, 144, 423, 424; inscr. L 3.1 cf. *SSI*, 30, 38; MH 1.7 cf. *IH*, 261); *yš'yhw* (seals V. 52, 211, 294, 420, 426; Herr, 140 no. 140). The element *yš'* is also found suffixed with *'l* on the seal *yš''l* (V, 86) 'El has delivered' (although P. Bordreuil, A. Lemaire, *Sem* 29 [1979], 83, and Herr, 70 no. 34 suggest an Ammon. origin for this seal) and with *'m* on the seal *hwš'm* (B. Mazar, *Jerusalem Revealed* [1975], 38-40) 'The (divine) Kinsman has delivered'.

mlṭ 'to deliver, rescue'. BH *m^elaṭyāh*, Qal perf. 'Y has delivered, set free', cf. BDB, 572, KB, 558, Geh, 605, *IPN*, 180. In BH the Qal is not elsewhere attested, but both the Piel and the Hiphil can have the meaning 'to deliver' (cf. BDB, 572). It is not unusual for a Qal form to occur in names when elsewhere only derived forms exist (see above, pp. 86-87).

nṣl 'to deliver'. EB seal *hṣlyhw* (V, 186) Hiphil perf., also inscr. (L 1.1 cf. *SSI*, 36, 37) 'Y has delivered'.

dlh 'to draw'. BH *d^elāyāh(û)*, Qal perf. EB seal *'ldlh* (M, 20); inscr. *dl[yhw* (Y. Aharoni, *Lachish V*, 22); *dlyw* (Y. Yadin, *Hazor. The Rediscovery of a Great Citadel of the Bible*, 182-83). A meaning 'Y has drawn' is acceptable, cf. BDB, 195, KB, 213, Geh, 220. The Piel is attested once in BH with the meaning 'to draw up' (cf. BDB, 194). The name is thus probably to be interpreted with the implication that the deity has saved, a usage which corresponds to that of the same root in other Semitic onomastica (e.g. *APN*, 279). The element is also found in the imf. on the seal *ydlyhw* (V, 237), 'Y draws'.

Some names seem to express the idea that the deity has taken account of a situation, and that he has 'seen' the particular need of the parent or family, perhaps the need for a child. Similarly, names which express the idea that the deity has 'taken account' contain some notion of the reward of a child as a result of the pious life of the parents. The following roots contain such concepts:

hzh 'to see'. BH *ḥăzāyāh*, Qal perf. 'Y has seen', cf. BDB, 303, Geh, 370, *IPN*, 186.

r'h 'to see'. BH *r^e'āyāh*, Qal perf. 'Y has seen', cf. BDB, 909, Geh, 793, *IPN*, 186.

šwr 'to regard, behold'. BH *'ăḥîšār*, Qal perf. 'The (divine) Brother has beheld', see also below, § 2.9.

ḥšb 'to take account'. BH *ḥăšabyāh(û)*, EB inscr. *ḥsbyhw* (Yavn. 7 cf. *SSI*, 28, 30. The name is uncertain since the third letter could be ' not *b* and the name read *hwš'yhw* cf. *SSI*, 30). Qal perf. 'Y has taken account', cf. BDB, 364, KB, 347 Geh, 367, *IPN*, 189. The BH name *ḥăšabn^eyāh* probably has the same meaning with the addition of a 1st pers. sing. verbal suffix, 'Y has taken account of me' (see below, § 2.8.5).

š'r 'to reckon'. BH *š^e'aryāh*, Qal perf. also seal (V, 359). The name possibly means 'Y has reckoned'.

In some cases the imperfective of a verb and, in one case, the perfective (*ĕlîp^elēhû*, see below, *plh*), is used in order to express a wish for the future well-being of the child. Such names represent a request to the deity that he will undertake to care for the child in certain respects. Thus we find names from the roots *kwn*, *qwm* and *śwm*, expressing requests that the deity will establish the child in future life:

kwn 'to establish'. BH *y(^eh)ôyākîn*, *y^ehôyākin*, Hiphil imf. 'May Y establish', cf. *IPN*, 202. Elsewhere, translations differ; 'Y establishes' is preferred by Geh, 451; BDB, 220 have 'Y appointeth', KB, 378/381 suggest 'J. stellte sicher hin'.
BH *y^ekonyāhû* (sf. *konyāhû*), Qal imf. 'May Y establish'; BDB, 467 prefer 'May Yah be enduring' and Geh, 449 'Y establishes'.

Imperfectives from the root *qwm* may be used in names in the sense of a request that the child should be 'raised up' by the deity, perhaps in the sense of being established in dignity and power (cf. Isa. 49.6):

qwm 'to raise up, establish' (Hiphil). BH *'elyāqîm*, Hiphil imf. 'May El establish'. The name is not elsewhere uniformly interpreted. BDB, 45 suggest 'God sets up'; KB, 55 suggest 'G. liess erstehen'; Geh, 259 has 'God will establish'.
BH *y(ᵉh)ôyāqîm* and perhaps *yôqîm* (1 Chr. 4.22). Hiphil imf. 'May Y establish or raise up'. Elsewhere, 'Y raises up' is generally accepted, cf. BDB, 20 and Geh, 451. *KB*, 379, 386 suggest 'Y sets up'. Noth (*IPN*, 200) saw the name as expressing a wish for deliverance from misfortune, i.e. a 'raising up' from need and distress.
BH *yᵉqamyāh* Hiphil imf? 'May Y raise up, establish'. For this name Geh, 456 suggests 'Y will raise up, establish'. Cf. also the EB names *yqmyh(w)* seals (V, 53, 122, 153, 344; BL, 48 no. 8); inscr. (*AI*, 39.1; 59.2; 74.3; 80.2); *yqymyhw* seal (V, 366).
BH *yᵉqamʿām* 'May the (divine) Kinsman establish', cf. BDB, 880. Noth (*IPN*, 200) suggested a Hiphil imf. although a Qal imf. for this name, as well as for *yᵉqamyāh*, is not impossible. This would give the meanings 'The (divine) Kinsman/Y arises', and would not refer to the child. Since the Hiphil is so distinctive in the name *yqymyhw* (seal V, 366) a Qal form for the other names may be preferable.

śwm 'to establish'. BH *yᵉśîmî'ēl*, Qal imf. 'May El establish', cf. *IPN*, 202. Elsewhere, a translation 'El establishes' is preferred, cf. BDB, 964, KB, 422, Geh, 477.

In a similar sense, the use of the root *plh* may be considered as a request for the future establishment of the child in life:

plh 'to be separated, distinct'. BH *'ĕlîpᵉlēhû*. The form of the name is difficult (see below, § 2.9). Most interpret it as 'May El distinguish him' cf. BDB, 45, KB, 54, Geh, 263. An imv. with the addition of a suffix is suggested for the second element by Noth (*IPN*, 32 n. 2).

A request to the deity for the future nourishment of the child is expressed with the following imperfectives:

qwt 'to nourish' (cf. Arab. *qāta*). BH *yᵉqûtî'ēl*. An interpretation 'to nourish' for the root of the first element of this name is suggested by an Arab. cognate *qāta*, cf. Barr *Cp.Ph*, 182. A translation 'May El nourish' is not, therefore, improbable. From this same Arab. cognate, KB, 411 suggest the meaning 'El nourishes', and Geh, 456, 'El will nourish'. The suggestion of BDB, 429 'Preservation of God' from the root *yqh* 'to preserve, be pious', seems less attractive.

'zh 'to nourish' (cf. Arab. *ghadhā*). BH *ya'ăzî'ēl*, *ya'ăzîyāhû*, Qal imf. 'May El/Y nourish'. A root *'zh* is not extant in BH, but a meaning 'to nourish' is suggested by an Arab. cognate *ghadhā*. For the name *ya'ăzî'ēl*, a translation 'May God nourish' is suggested by Geh, 437 and *IPN*, 203. KB, 401 prefer 'God nourishes/ed', while BDB, 739 consider the name probably to be erroneous for *'uzzî'ēl*, 'My strength is El', though this suggestion seems unlikely, in view of the existence of the parallel *ya'ăzîyāhû*. For this name an interpretation 'May Y nourish' is suggested by Geh, 437. Again, the interpretation of BDB, 739, 'My strength is Y' (i.e. *'uzzîyāh(û)*), seems doubtful.

Other requests to the deity are for the strengthening, support, blessing and purifying of the child throughout its life:

ḥzq 'to strengthen'. BH *y^eḥezqē'l*, Qal imf. A translation 'May El strengthen' with *IPN*, 202 seems best. Elsewhere, an interpretation 'El strengthens' is preferred, cf. BDB, 306, KB, 388, Geh, 285.

smk 'to support'. BH *yismakyāhû*, Qal imf. 'May Y support', cf. *IPN*, 196. BDB, 702 suggest 'Y sustains', and Geh, 431 'Y supports'.

brk 'to bless'. BH *y^eberekyāhû*, Qal imf. 'May Y bless', cf. *IPN*, 195.

nzh 'to sprinkle'. BH *yizzîyāh*. The form is perhaps Qal imf. with the meaning of the Hiphil 'to sprinkle'. An interpretation 'May Y sprinkle' in the sense of purify, therefore, seems the most favourable, cf. Geh, 436, *IPN*, 245-46, BDB, 633. The BH name *y^ezî'ēl* is more problematic since a dagheshed *zayin* would be expected if the first element were to be derived from a root *nzh*, cf. Geh, 492, KB, 387, *IPN*, 245, and below § 2.9.

Interesting to note in the foregoing names, which portray requests for the future well-being of the child, is the almost total absence of extra-biblical names which contain this semantic concept. The only exceptions, indeed, are the names *yqmyh*(*w*) and *yqymyhw* from the root *qwm* (see above).

A large number of names seem to refer to general characteristics of the deity, characteristics which have been revealed to the parents through experiences in their everyday life. As already stated, such experiences may be confined to the parents themselves, or may be concerned with the wider concept of the family or even the nation. What is important, however, is the recognition that the original events which gave rise to a name cannot be determined with accuracy and that it is only possible to categorize names under very general headings. What is also probable is that the same name borne by different individuals may have been given by parents for entirely different reasons. It is also possible that some names reflect nothing more than a general statement concerning the deity, divorced from any particular connection with the birth of the child, but expressing what the parents of the child conceived to be the nature of the deity. A name may even have been given because of the mere attractiveness of the sound. It is therefore hazardous to suggest that the name 'The deity hears', for example, implies a hearing of the prayer for a child, or the deliverance from need, or the request for justice etc. The most which can be sensibly gained from such a name is a recognition that the deity displays the kind of personality which listened to the requests, needs, joys and cries of his people and this, in itself, is sufficiently important for the purpose of the present study.

Of the characteristics of the deity expressed in verbal sentence names, many express the deity's awareness of man in his everyday life, as shown in the following:

'zn 'to hear'. BH *ya'ăzanyāhû* (also *y^e^zanyāh(û)*, Qal imf. 'Y hears', cf. BDB, 24, Geh, 492; EB seals (V, 21, 69, 241); inscr. (L 1, 2, 3 cf. *SSI*, 36, 63-64; *AI*, 39.9). Noth (*IPN*, 198) interpreted the name as a wish, implying 'May Y hear'.
EB *yzn'l* seal (V, 28), Qal imf. 'El hears'.

šm' 'to hear'. BH *yišmā'ē'l*, *yišma'yāh(û)*, Qal imf. 'El/Y hears', cf. BDB, 1035, 1036, KB, 426, 427, Geh 430, 431. Noth (*IPN*, 198) interpreted both names as 'wish' names, 'May El/Y hear', which seems semantically unlikely: he assumed the names to be a cry for help from the parents because of some need or distress at the time of the birth. Such an interpretation, however, seems far too restrictive, and arises out of Noth's viewpoint that all imperfectives in names are to be interpreted as wishes, 'May the deity—'. Cf. also EB *yšm''l* seals (V, 45, 53, 418; Herr, 105 no. 48; K.G.O'Connell, *IEJ* 27 [1977], 197-99); inscr. (A 57.1 cf. *IH*, 214; Ophel, J. Prignaud, *RB* 77 [1970], 67).

yd' 'to know'. The element *yd'* always occurs in verbal sentence names in the Qal perf. and expresses the notion that the deity 'knows'. It occurs in the following names:
BH *'elyādā'* 'El knows', cf. BDB, 45. '—has known' is preferred by KB, 53 and Geh, 259.
BH *y^e^da'yāh* 'Y knows', cf. Geh, 449. '—has known' is preferred by KB, 375.
BH *y(^e^h)ôyādā'* 'Y knows', cf. BDB, 220, Geh, 451. '—has known' is preferred by KB, 378/381. For all biblical names containing the verbal element *yd'*, Noth (*IPN*, 181) considered the verb to have the nuance of meaning 'to care about, take care of', an unlikely suggestion since it is not a

meaning which the rest of the OT ascribes to this frequently attested verb. The root has been examined extensively by J.A.E. Emerton, 'A Consideration of some Alleged Meanings of *yd'* in Hebrew', *JSS*, 15 (1970), 145-80.
BH *b^e'elyādā'* 'Baal knows', cf. BDB, 128. An interpretation 'Baal has known' is suggested by Geh, 98, KB, 139. The element *yd'* also occurs in the EB names *yd'yhw* (seal V, 49; Herr, 129 no. 109; inscr. *AI*, 31,7; 39,4; 39,5) and *yd'yw* (inscr. SO 1,8; 42,2 cf. *SSI*, 1, 10, 11, 12 = SO 48,1 cf. *IH*, 36).

ḥzh 'to see'. BH *yaḥăzî'ēl*, Qal imf. 'El sees', cf. BDB, 303, KB, 388, Geh, 442. BH *yaḥz^eyāh*, Qal imf. 'Y sees', cf. BDB, 303, Geh, 442. Again, Noth (*IPN*, 198) preferred 'May Y see' for the meaning of both names. Cf. also the inscr. *yḥzẏ(ḣẇ* (*AI*, 3, 6; N. Avigad, *IEJ* 22 [1972], 1-9).

r'h 'to see'. BH *y^erî'ēl*, Qal imf. 'El sees', cf. KB, 418, Geh, 462. BDB, 436 suggest a construct form 'Founded of El', presumably from a root *yrh*, and emend to *y^erû'ēl*. However, the root *r'h* seems the better possibility, with the loss of the *'ālep* before the *'ālep* of the theophoric element. Thus, this letter is retained in the BH name *yir'îyâh*, Qal imf. 'Y sees', cf. BDB, 909, Geh, 423.

A number of verbal forms suggest that the deity approaches man. Such names convey the idea that the Israelite God not only has an awareness of the everyday experiences of man, as the previously listed names suggest, but that he *actively* approaches man, perhaps in order to help, support etc. This concept is illustrated in names from the following roots:

'th 'to come'. BH *'ĕlî'ātāh*, Qal perf. 'El has come', cf. BDB, 45, Geh, 260, KB, 53.

bw' 'to come'. Inscr. *'lb'* (SO 1.6 cf. *SSI*, 11), Qal perf. 'El has come'. The suggestion of Noth (*IPN*, 40) that this is a type of sf. seems an unnecessary complication for an otherwise satisfactory element. This may also be said of the view of Lemaire (*IH*, 49) and W. Kornfeld (*WZKM* 71 [1979], 41) that the name is probably a sf. with a terminating *a* for *Eliba'al* 'Baal est (mon) dieu'. Although Kornfeld cites the name *'lb'l* in Phoen. (*PNPPI*, 61) and Ug. (*PTU*, 369), neither of these references support a form *'lb'* as a sf. of *'lb'l*.

zrḥ 'to rise'. BH *z^eraḥyāh*, Qal perf. 'Y has risen' (perhaps like a star), cf. BDB, 280, KB, 270. An interpretation 'Y has shone forth' is suggested by Geh, 1022. The Qal perf. is also likely in EB *yhwzṙ[ḥ]* (seal V, 321). The element also occurs in the Qal imf. *yizraḥyāh* (BH), 'Y arises', cf. KB, 387, Geh, 436.

qwm 'to arise'. BH *'ăḥîqām*, Qal perf. 'The (divine) Brother has arisen', cf. BDB, 27 Geh, 23, KB, 33, *IPN*, 176.
BH *'ădōnîqām*, Qal perf. 'The Lord has risen', cf. BDB, 12, Geh, 17, KB, 16, *IPN*, 176.

EB *'lyqm* (seals V, 93, 108, 242, 277, 436); *yhwqm* (seals V, 335, 336); *ywqm* (seal V, 38); *'ḥqm* (seals V, 210; P. Bordreuil, A. Lemaire, *Sem* 29 [1979], 74 no. 5); *'ḥyqm* (inscr. *AI*, 31.5).
The possibility of a Hiphil vocalization for *'lyqm* is not improbable. This would suggest *'elyāqîm* instead of *'ĕlîqām*. However, the *yōd* is certainly retained in unvocalized EB names, as an intermediate vowel between the theophoric element *'l* and a following non-theophoric element, as in the names *'ly'r* (*AI*, 21.2) root *'wr*, *'lyš'* (V, 41, 271; inscr. SO 1.4; 1.7; 41.1; *AI*, 24.15; 24.19-20) root *yš'*, *'ly'm*[22] (V, 6) *'m*. Since the element *qwm* does appear in the Qal perf. in names, it may be as well to retain it for the unvocalized *'lyqm*, since the Qal perf. is by far the most predominantly used onomastic form, while bearing in mind the possibility of a Hiphil imf. The Arad inscr. *'ḥyqm*, therefore, is also likely to be Qal perf., although Aharoni (*AI*, p. 58) considered the name to be a contraction of *'ḥ-yqm*.

škn 'to settle down, abide, dwell'. BH *š^ekanyāh(û)*; also EB seal V, 327, Qal perf. 'Y has taken up his abode', cf. BDB, 1016, Geh, 860, *IPN*, 194. Lipiński's suggestion that the name means 'Neighbour of Yahu' is unlikely in view of the semantic difficulty of such an interpretation (Lipiński, 73).

y'd 'to appoint, assign'. The Niphal of this root means 'to meet by appointment', cf. BDB, 417. This may well be the meaning in the BH name *nô'adyāh*, Niphal perf. 'Y has met by appointment', cf. Geh, 671. Noth (*IPN*, 184) restricted the meaning of the name, rather unnecessarily, to the deity making himself known by the birth of the child, while BDB, 418 suggest an interpretation 'Meeting with Y', although a noun from the root *y'd* corresponding to this first element does not exist.

'nn 'to appear'. BH *'ănanyāh*, also EB seal (V, 254), Qal perf. 'Y has appeared', cf. Geh, 41, *IPN*, 184.

In this context belong names from the following root which express that the deity is permanently alive to man's requests and needs. Such names depict the living, real nature of a deity actively involved with man:

ḥyh 'to live'. BH *y^eḥî'ēl*, imf. 'El lives', cf. Geh. 450. Elsewhere, the formula 'May El live' is preferred, cf. BDB, 313, KB, 388 *IPN*, 206: cf. also the name *y^eḥî'ēlî* in 1 Chr. 26.21, 22.
BH *y^eḥîyāh*, Qal imf. 'Y lives', cf. Geh, 450. Again, BDB, 313, and *IPN*, 206 prefer 'May Y live'.
For the name *yḥw'ly* found on ostraca from Samaria (SO 55.2 cf. *SSI*, 10, 13; prob. = SO 60.1 cf. *IH*, 37) Gibson (*SSI*, 10) suggests a Piel jussive for the initial element, and a substitute for the divine name Yahweh in the second element. While this latter proposal is more certain, a Piel jussive, suggesting a translation 'May the High One preserve alive', is open to question. The

form, indeed, is difficult, but since an alternative form of the BH name *y^eḥî'ēl* is given as *y^eḥû'ēl* in Chr. 29.14, it is possible to suggest a Qal imf. of the root *ḥyh* for the initial element of the name *yḥw'ly*. A meaning 'The High One lives' is therefore preferred. Cf. also the name *'byḥy* below, § 2.9 and *yhw*[*ḥy*] (seal V, 253).

Many names express ways in which the deity was thought to have assisted man in his daily life, by protecting, supporting him etc. Again, names expressing such concepts probably refer to the very varied experiences of the parents, of the family, or may even refer to times of national import. Names of this type have verbal elements from the following roots:

mrr 'to strengthen'. BH *m^erāyāh*. The first element of the name is possibly a Qal perf. from a root *mrr*, the meaning of which may be suggested by the Ug. root *mrr* meaning 'to strengthen, bless, commend', cf. *UT Glossary*, 438 no. 1556. This is preferable to the suggestions of KB, 600, Geh, 608 and *IPN*, 250 that the name means 'obstinate'. (See also below, § 2.9.)

šmr 'to preserve, keep, watch'. BH *š^emaryāhû*, Qal perf. 'Y has preserved, kept', cf. BDB, 1037, Geh, 865, *IPN*, 177.
EB *šmryhw* (seals BL, 47 nos. 4, 5; inscr. *AI*, 18.4); *šmryw* (seal V, 214; inscr. SO 1.1 cf. *SSI*, 8.11, prob. = SO 13.2 = 14.2 = 21.1-2 cf. *IH*, 294).

A number of roots are used in Hebrew verbal names to suggest that the deity has supported or supports man, as the following show:

'mn 'to support'. EB seal *yw'mn* (V, 172), 'Y has supported'.

'šh 'to support'. BH *yō'šîyāh*(*û*)/*yō'ôšîyāhû*. If the root *'šh* is the correct etymology for this name, a possible Hiphil imf. may suggest a meaning 'Y supports', cf. BDB, 78. The name, however, remains problematic and is discussed fully below, § 2.5 *'šh*/*'wš*.

kwl 'to support, nourish, sustain' (Pilpel). EB seal *klklyhw* (V, 329), Pilpel, 'Y has supported or nourished'.

yšh 'to support, assist' (cf. Arab. *'asa'*). BH *yôšawyāh*. The form of the name is difficult, and the root *yšh* obscure (cf. BDB, 444). The idea 'to support' is only tenuously suggested by an Arab. cognate *'asa'*, but with this meaning, could be related to the root *'šh* above. See also below, § 2.9.

smk 'to support'. BH *s^emakyāhû*, *'ăḥîsāmāk*, Qal perf. 'Y/The (divine) Brother has supported', cf. BDB, 27, 702, KB, 33, 399, Geh, 24, 845, *IPN*, 176.
EB *smkyhw* (seal V, 239, 438; inscr. L 4.6; 13.2 cf. *SSI*, 41, 48; L 22.5 cf. *IH*, 136); *smkyw* (inscr. SS 4.3 cf. *IH*, 248).

Some verbal forms express the idea that the deity hides or protects man:

zmr 'to protect' (cf. S. Arab. *dhimr*). EB seal *zmryhw* (V, 54); inscr. *b'lzmr* (SO 12, Dir, 43 no. 16. Lemaire [*IH*, 31], however, separates the two elements so that *zmr* becomes a patronym). The meaning of the element *zmr* is perhaps best suggested by a S. Arab. cognate *dhimr* meaning 'to protect', cf. BDB, 275, *IPN*, 176.

ḥb'/h 'to hide'. BH *'elyaḥbā'*, Hiphil imf. 'El hides (i.e. protects)', cf. BDB, 45, KB, 53, Geh, 259. Noth (*IPN*, 197) interpreted the name as a wish, e.g. 'May the deity—'. On such an interpretation, see above, p. 89.
BH *ḥăbāyāh*, Qal perf. 'Y has hidden (protected)', cf. Geh, 354, KB, 274, *IPN*, 178.

str 'to hide, conceal'. EB seal *ywstr* (V, 346). Perhaps 'Y has hidden' (Qal), although the existence of a noun *sēter* 'covering, hiding place' (cf. BDB, 712) may suggest a nominal sentence name.

ṣpn 'to hide, treasure up'. BH *ṣ^{e}panyāh(û)*, Qal perf. 'Y has hidden', cf. Geh, 1020, *IPN*, 178. BDB, 861 prefer 'Y has treasured' (but for the name *'ĕlîṣāpān* 'God has protected' cf. BDB, 45).
BH *'ĕlîṣāpān*, Qal perf. 'El has hidden (protected)' cf. BDB, 45, KB, 45, Geh, 264, *IPN*, 178.
EB *ṣpnyhw* (seals V, 39, 258; M, 81 nos. 29, 30; inscr. *AI*, 59.5; Milik, *RB* 66 [1959], 551; Ophel 3 cf. *IH*, 240).

ṭll 'to cover'. BH *'ăbîṭāl*. The name is only questionably verbal: the second element conforms to the pattern of verbal forms in names from Geminate and Hollow roots and might indicate a meaning, 'The (divine) Father has covered (i.e. concealed, protected)'. See further below, p. 171 n. 23 and pp. 111-12.

The root *rp'* is used in verbal sentence names to portray the idea that the deity heals:

rp' 'to heal'. BH *r^{e}pāyāh*, *r^{e}pā'ēl*, Qal perf. 'Y/El has healed', cf. Geh, 798. There seems no reason why an interpretation 'to restore', in the sense of restoring a deceased child through the birth of another, should be relevant here, as Noth (*IPN*, 179) suggested. The nuance of meaning 'restore' is not otherwise attested for the root in BH.

Another characteristic of the deity revealed by verbal sentence names is the concept of the Israelite God as a redeemer or deliverer of man:

šêzêb (Aram.). BH *m^{e}šêzab'ēl*, part. 'El delivers', cf. BDB, 604, KB, 609, Geh, 612. See also below, § 2.8.2.

ḥml 'to spare'. EB *yḥmlyhw* (seals V, 51; N. Avigad, *EI* 69 no. 14). Qal imf. 'Y spares'. Diringer (Dir, 208-209), however, considered the vocalization to be *Jaḥmoljahu* and the meaning 'Y forgives'.

pdh 'to ransom'. BH *pᵉdah'ēl*, *pᵉdāyāh(û)*, Qal perf. 'El/Y has ransomed', cf. BDB, 804, Geh, 724, *IPN*, 180.
BH *yipdᵉyāh*, Qal imf. 'Y redeems', cf. Geh, 423, KB, 404.
BH *pᵉdāhṣûr*, Qal perf. 'The Rock has ransomed', cf. BDB, 804, Geh, 724, *IPN*, 180.
EB *pdyhw* (seals V, 45, 235; BL, 53 no. 5; inscr. *AI*, 49.15).

g'l 'to redeem'. Inscr. *g'lyhw* (*AI*, 39.5; 16.5). Although the *yōd* in the divine name is lacking on the seal *g'lhw* (V, 110), it is probably to be included here. The names mean 'Y has redeemed'.

Two roots are used verbally to express the idea that the deity 'has helped':

'wš 'to help'. BH *yô'āš*, Qal perf. 'Y has helped', cf. BDB, 222, KB, 386, Geh, 496, *IPN*, 176.
EB seals *'l'š* (V, 340), *'šn'l* (V, 88), *'šnyhw* (V, 125). The names on the last two mentioned seals probably mean 'El/Y has helped me'. For the pronominal suffix on verbal forms in names, see below, p. 130-31.

'zr 'to help'. BH *'el'āzār*, *'ăzar'ēl*, *'ăzaryāh(û)*, Qal perf. 'El/Y has helped', cf. BDB, 46, 741, Geh, 257, 80, *IPN*, 175.
EB *'zr'l* (seal V, 170 Ammon?); *'zryh* (seal V, 175); *'zryhw* (seals V, 24, 40, 188, 207, 270, 289; R. Amiran, A. Eitan, *IEJ* 20 [1970], 13; BL, 47 no. 4; Herr, 136 no. 128; N. Avigad, *IEJ* 4 [1954], 236; M. Heltzer, *AION* 31 [1971], 190 no. 26; Dir, 122 no. 5b; inscr. *AI*, 16.6; Gib. 1 cf. *SSI*, 56; M, 114 no. 2; L 18.2 cf. *IH*, 132; A 26.1 cf. *IH*, 197); *'zryw* (seals V, 228; Dir, 123 no. 5c prob. = V, 270); *'l'zr* (seals V, 310 (?), 312 (?); P. Bordreuil, A. Lemaire, *Sem* 29 [1979], 75 no. 7).

In one extra-biblical name the idea that the deity 'enlightens' is expressed with the root:

ngh 'to shine,enlighten'. EB seals *ygyh* (V, 272); *yg'l*? (V, 309). The initial element of both names is probably an imf. from the root *ngh*, suggesting a meaning 'Y/El has enlightened'. *Yg'l*, however, may be comparable to BH *yig'āl* (see below, p. 168).

That the deity forgets man's faults and sins is expressed by the root:

nšh 'to forget'. BH *yiššîyāh(û)*, Qal imf. 'Y forgets (sins)', cf. KB, 426. Both *IPN*, 211 and Geh, 434 prefer 'May Y forget'. The dagheshed *šīn* would not support Avigad's suggestion of *yēš*, 'exists', for the initial element (cf. above, p. 57 and the name *'šb'l*).

The merciful and compassionate nature of the deity is expressed in the following name-elements:

rḥm 'to have compassion' (Piel). BH *y^eraḥm^e'ēl*, Piel imf. 'El has compassion', cf. KB, 418. An interpretation 'May El have compassion' is preferred by BDB, 934, Geh, 456, *IPN*, 119. The same person is referred to on a seal (N. Avigad, *IEJ* 28 [1978], 53).

nḥm 'to comfort'. BH *n^eḥemyāh*, Qal perf. 'Y has comforted' cf. Geh, 657, *IPN*, 175; EB seal (V, 30); inscr. (*AI*, 31.3; 36.2; 40.1-2; 59.3).

Similarly, the idea of the deity providing comfort and well-being is portrayed in the following biblical name from the root:

yšb 'to dwell'. BH *yôšibyāh*, Hiphil imf. 'Y causes to dwell (in peace and security)' cf. KB, 386, Geh, 517, 518, BDB, 444, *IPN*, 202.

There are many verbal sentence names which describe the deity in terms of a ruler or judge, who defends and contends for man:

'wm 'to rule' (cf. S. Arab. *'āma*). BH *'ăḥî'ām*, Qal perf. The second element would appear to be from a Geminate or Hollow root (see below, pp. 111 and 114). A root *'wm* is suggested by a S. Arab. cognate *'āma* 'to rule' indicating a meaning 'The (divine) Brother has ruled'. For further discussion of the name and the possibility of a root *'mm* see below, *ibid.*

dyn 'to judge'. BH *dāni'ēl/dānîyē'l*, Qal perf. 'El has judged', cf. Geh, 202, *IPN*, 187. A nominal form 'El is my judge' is suggested by BDB, 193.
BH *'ăbîdān*, Qal perf. 'The (divine) Father has judged', cf. *IPN*, 187, KB, 4. BDB, 4 and Geh, 4 suggest a nominal form, but this is unlikely; the second element conforms to the pattern of verbal forms from Geminate and Hollow roots in second position in names (see below, pp. 111 and 112). An imf. of the root *dyn* is probable in the inscr. *ydnyhw* (*AI*, 27.4) 'Y judges' although Lemaire translates the name as 'Que Yhw juge' (*IH*, 198). W. Kornfeld, *WZKM* 17 (1979), 43, incorrectly cites this inscr. as Lachish 27.4 instead of Arad 27.4 (cf. *IH*, 198). Kornfeld follows Lemaire's interpretation of the name as well as adding an alternative 'Yhw stärke/stärkte'. The imf. is also probable for the name *'lydn* (seal V, 357).

pll 'to judge'. BH *'ĕlîpāl*, Qal perf. 'El has judged' cf. BDB, 45, Geh, 262, *IPN*, 187, KB, 54. The name is doubtfully a sf. of *'ĕlîpeleṭ* which KB, 54 suggest as an alternative and seem to misrepresent Noth (*op. cit.*) who does not suggest this connection with the root *plṭ* as authentic.
BH *p^elalyāh*, Qal perf. 'Y has judged, intervened', cf. BDB, 813, Geh, 725, *IPN*, 187.

špṭ 'to judge'. BH *'ĕlîšāpāṭ*, *y(^eh)ôšāpāṭ*, *š^epaṭyāh(û)*, Qal perf. 'El/Y has judged', cf. BDB, 46, 221, 1049, KB, 380, 386, Geh, 264, 452, 517, 866, *IPN*, 187;

EB seals *šptyhw* (V, 109, 438; BL, 50-51 no. 14).

dll 'to direct' (cf. Arab. *dall*). EB inscr. (')*mdl* (L 19.3 cf. *SSI*, 49). The meaning of the second element in this name may perhaps be suggested by an Arab. cognate of the root *dll*, meaning 'to direct, guide', cf. BDB, 195. This would indicate a translation 'The (divine) Kinsman has directed, guided'. The first and third letters of the name are unclear, however, and Lemaire, more recently, reads *Mikal* for this name (cf. *IH*, 132, 133).

'wd 'to testify'. BH *'el'ād*, Qal perf. 'El has testified', cf. BDB, 46, KB, 57, Geh, 257, *IPN*, 237. The root *'wd* is found elsewhere in BH only in the Hiphil with the meaning 'to testify'. A meaning 'El has turned' suggested by an Arab. cognate *'āda* 'to return' seems less likely. It would indicate a probable III *hē* root for the second element of the name and, as such, the *hē* is likely to be retained as suggested below, p. 111.

'md 'to take one's stand'. EB seal *'mdyhw* (V, 61), 'Y has taken a stand'. Why Noth (*IPN*, 32, 33) and Diringer (Dir, 218) should have seen the first element as the preposition *'m* is unclear.

ryb 'to strive, contend'. BH *y(ᵉh)ôyārîb*, Qal imf. 'Y contends', cf. BDB, 220, KB, 379/381. Geh, 452 and *IPN*, 201 interpret the name as 'May Y plead or contend'. For the name *yᵉrubba'al* see above, § 2.2 *b'l*.

śrh 'to persevere, persist (or to rule)'. BH *śᵉrāyāh(û)*, Qal perf. 'Y has persevered or persisted', cf. BDB, 976. Geh, 850 suggests 'Y has striven or ruled' (see also *IPN*, 191, 208). Indeed, the root *śrh* also seems to be attested in BH, although rarely, with the meaning 'to rule' (cf. BDB, 976), so that the translation 'Y has ruled' is not impossible. Verbal forms with this meaning, however, are not attested. The name is found, in addition, on two seals (V, 334; N. Avigad, *IEJ* 28 [1978], 56; the latter is identified with the person mentioned in Jer. 51.59). The root *śrh* also seems to be the most appropriate for the BH name *yiśrā'ēl*, Qal imf. 'El persists, perseveres', cf. BDB, 975, or 'El rules'. Cf. also Geh, 431, 'God strives' or 'Let God rule', and *IPN*, 207ff.

The concept of selection of certain people by the deity is expressed in names derived from a variety of roots:

'ṣl 'to lay aside, reserve'. BH *'ăṣalyāhû*, Qal perf. 'Y has reserved, set apart', cf. BDB, 69. A meaning 'Y has shown himself distinguished, noble', suggested by an Arab. cognate *'aṣula* is preferred by KB, 79, Geh, 79 and *IPN*, 193. The former suggestion, however, appears both formally and semantically suitable.

ḥṣh 'to divide'. BH *yaḥṣî'ēl/yaḥṣᵉ'ēl*, Qal imf. 'El divides', cf. BDB, 345, Geh, 442, *IPN*, 204. Both *IPN*, and KB, 390 suggest an alternative meaning of the root, as 'to favour, show kindness' suggested by an Arab. cognate *ḥaẓiia*.

ṭbl 'to dip (purify)'. BH *ṭᵉbalyāhû*, Qal perf. 'Y has dipped (purified)', cf. BDB, 371, Geh, 927. KB, 353 prefer the less satisfactory translation 'bei J. beliebt' from the root *ṭwb* with the addition of the preposition *lᵉ*.

brr 'to purify, select'. EB seals *'lybr* (V, 133, 397). Both these seals may be Ammon. rather than Heb. (cf. P. Bordreuil, A. Lemaire, *Sem* 29 [1979], 82; Herr, 69 no. 29. Against an Ammon. origin, however, cf. J. Teixidor, *Syria* 54 [1977], 261 no. 54). A meaning 'El has purified' and a Qal perf. of the root *brr* is probable. That the *yōd* can be retained in unvocalized EB Heb. names, as a suffix of the divine name *'l*, has been mentioned already (above, p. 135). The suggestion of P. Bordreuil and A. Lemaire (*JA* [1977], 18-19), of an imf. from the root *brr*, although possible is not, therefore, entirely conclusive.

d'h 'to call' (cf. Arab. *da'ā*). BH *'eldā'āh*. Qal perf. 'El has called', cf. BDB, 44, KB, 49, Geh, 256, Barr *Cp. Ph.*, 23-25. The root *d'h* with a meaning 'to call', is suggested by an Arab. cognate *da'ā*.

'sp 'to gather'. BH *'ăbî'āsāp/'ebyāsāp*, Qal perf. 'The (divine) Father has gathered', cf. BDB, 4, Geh, 3, KB, 4. A derivation from the root *ysp* 'to add' is preferred by *IPN*, 173, 234, and is given as an alternative by KB, 4.

drš 'to seek'. EB seals *dršyhw* (V, 212, 338, 434), 'Y has sought'.

pqd? The EB name *p̈q̈dyw* (seal V, 163) which may be from the root *pqd* 'to appoint', is possibly similar, although the first two letters of the name are obscure. The root *pqd*, however, has a variety of meanings, 'to attend to, visit, muster, appoint' (cf. BDB, 823) and so is only tentatively placed here.

The idea of more special selection by the deity is probably reflected in the following concepts:

dwd 'to love'. BH *'eldād/'ĕlîdād*, Qal perf. 'El has loved', cf. BDB, 44, KB, 49 (also 'G ist Oheim/Freund'), *IPN*, 183. Geh, 256, suggests 'Dad is god' for *'eldād*, and 'God has loved' for *'ĕlîdād* (p. 260), although the second elements in both names are identical. See also below, § 2.9.

'dh 'to adorn' BH *'el'ādāh*, Qal perf. 'El has adorned', cf. BDB, 46, KB, 57, Geh, 257, *IPN*, 182.
BH *'ădāyāh(û)*, Qal perf. 'Y has adorned', cf. Geh, 15, *IPN*, 182. A meaning 'Y has decked himself' is suggested by *BDB*, 726. Although the root is mainly used reflexively in the Qal in BH, it is not exclusively so used (cf. BDB, 725). The non-reflexive use is probably more suited to both the biblical names, in the sense of the adorning of a person by the deity, perhaps in the sense of special selection.
EB *'d'l* seal (V, 146, or nominal cf. above, p. 89); *'dyhw* seals (V, 148, 154, 417; BL, 50-51 no. 14; inscr. *AI*, 58.1); *'y'dh* (seal V, 151); *'l'dh* (inscr. Mur, B, 3 cf. *SSI*, 32). The pointing of the BH name suggests a III *hē* root for these EB names, as opposed to a Hollow root. This would make the alternative suggestion of W. Kornfeld, *WZKM* 71 (1979), 47 'Yhw ist Zeuge/hat sich wieder zugewendet' from a root *'wd*, unlikely.

rml 'to adorn with gems' (cf. Arab. *ramala*). The meaning of the root *rml* in the name *rmlyhw* on two seals (V, 19 cf. Herr. no. 51, who reads *dmlyhw*, also B. Porten, *IEJ* 21 (1971), 48, V, 60) and the BH name *r^emalyāh(û)*, may be suggested by Arab. *ramala* 'to adorn with gems'. This would indicate a translation 'Y has adorned' for the names. However, the BH name *r^emalyāh(û)* could be from a root *rwm* with the addition of the vocative particle *l* (see below, § 2.9).

Similar may be the idea that the deity has 'established' in names from the root:

kwn 'to establish'. BH *kônanyāhû/kŏnanyāhû*, Polel, 'Y has established', cf. Geh, 182, *IPN*, 179. EB occurrences of the name are probably Qal in the names *ywkn* (seals V, 108, 277); and *knyhw* (inscr. L 3.15 cf. *SSI*, 38, 40; *AI*, 49.4, reading uncertain).

Some verbal sentence names describe the deity in terms of nature with the use of the following roots:

zrh 'to scatter, fan, winnow'. EB seal *zryhw* (V, 301), 'Y has scattered'. Herr, 148 suggests that this seal may be a forgery, or perhaps 9th. cent., and only possibly Heb.

zr' 'to sow'. BH *yizr^e'e'l*, Qal imf. 'El sows', cf. BDB, 283, Geh, 492. KB, 387 and *IPN*, 213 prefer the less likely interpretation of the root *zr'* 'to make fruitful'.

'rš 'to plant' (cf. Arab. *gharasa* and Akk. *erēšu*). BH *ya'ărešyāh*, Qal imf. 'Y plants', cf. KB, 404, Geh, 436, *IPN*, 203, Barr *Cp. Ph.*, 182. This meaning for the root *'rš* is suggested by Arab. *gharasa* and Akk. *erēšu*.

šrb 'to parch, be scorched'. BH *šērēbyāh*, Piel perf. 'Y has sent burning heat', cf. BDB, 1055-56, Geh, 867.

Finally, there remain a few names which express characteristics of the deity which are not possible to group together. These are as follows:

glh 'to carry into exile' (Hiphil). EB seal *hglnyh* (V, 161), 'Y has carried me into exile'. A Hiphil perf. with the addition of the 1st pers. sing. suffix is suggested by A. Reifenberg, *PEQ* (1942), 111.

'ḥz 'to seize, grasp'. BH *y(^eh)ô'āḥāz*, *'ăḥazyāh(û)*, Qal perf. 'Y has seized', cf. BDB, 28, 219, KB, 32, 376, Geh, 22, 450, *IPN*, 179. The name may be figurative for protection or selection by the deity.
EB seals *'ḥzyh(w)* (M, 81-82 no. 31; V, 342); *yh'ḥz* (V, 252), possibly the son of King Josiah, 7th cent., cf. H.G. Herr, 'Paleography and the Identification of Seal Owners', *BASOR* 239 (1980), 69.

'ms 'to carry a load, bear'. BH *'ămasyāh*, Qal perf. 'Y has borne, carried', cf. Geh, 35. The name may be figurative for protection as Noth (*IPN*, 178) suggested.

2.5 *Difficulties with Hollow Roots*

A number of personal names in which the non-theophoric element appears to be derived from a Hollow root, are problematic in view of the fact that there are also other roots from which they could be derived. This usually involves a choice between a III *hē* or Geminate and, in some cases, I *yōd* root.

One factor does seem helpful in the choice of a Hollow or III *hē* root for the non-theophoric element in second position. This is the retention of the final *hē* in the III *hē* verbal form. Thus we find:

'eldā'āh	El has called	root *d'h*
'el'ādāh	El has adorned	root *'dh*
'el'āśāh	El has made	root *'śh*
'elqānāh	El has created	root *qnh*
ywbnh	Y has built (created)	root *bnh*
'ldlh	El has drawn	root *dlh*
yw'śh	Y has made	root *'śh*

When III *hē* verbal elements occur in the first position in names, however, the *hē-* is usually absent, cf:

b^enāyāh	Y has built (created)	root *bnh*
d^elāyāh(û)	Y has drawn	root *dlh*
ḥăzāyāh	Y has seen	root *ḥzh*
p^edāyāh(û)	Y has ransomed	root *pdh*

However, the *hē* can sometimes be retained:

p^edah'ēl	El has ransomed	root *pdh*
p^edāhṣûr	The Rock has ransomed	root *pdh*

Geminate roots most frequently retain the three root consonants in names, for example:

'elḥānān	El is gracious	root *ḥnn*
ḥănanyāh(û)	Y is gracious	root *ḥnn*
'ănanyāh	Y has appeared	root *'nn*
k^enanyāh(û)	Y is firm	root *knn*
'ăzazyāhû	Y is strong	root *'zz*
p^elalyāh	Y has judged	root *pll*

However, the duplication of the second letter of the root sometimes does not occur:

m^{e}rāyāh	Y has strengthened or blessed	root *mrr*
rbyhw	Y is great	root *rbb*
'ĕlîpāl	El has judged	root *pll*
yôtām	Y is perfect	root *tmm*

Hollow root verbs occurring in the second position usually have the form *CāC*, which the following selection of names will exemplify:

'eldād	El has loved	root *dwd*
'ĕlîdād	El has loved	root *dwd*
'el'ād	El has testified	root *'wd*
yô'āš	Y has helped	root *'wš*
y^{e}hôrām	Y is exalted	root *rwm*
'ăbîdān	The (divine) Father has judged	root *dyn*
'ăḥîqām	The (divine) Brother has risen	root *qwm*

Hollow root verbs in the initial position are much less widely attested. None occurs amongst biblical names apart from the more easily recognized imperfectives, and the problematic names to be discussed below. Among extra-biblical occurrences are the following:

ṭbyhw	Y is good	root *ṭwb*
ṭb'l	El is good	root *ṭwb*
knyhw	Y has established	root *kwn*
šb'l	Y has returned	root *šwb*

It will be seen, therefore, that there may be occasions when a name could be derived from a number of roots; the second element of the name *yôtām* for example, is from a Geminate root *tmm*, whereas an identically patterned *yô'āš* is derived from a Hollow root *'wš*. Roots presenting this particular type of problem are as follows:

'šh/'wš. The root *'šh* means 'to support' (cf. BDB, 78) but is not attested verbally in BH. The root *'wš* is not attested at all in BH, but an Arab. cognate *'āsa* may suggest a meaning 'to give, bestow'. A root *'yš* may also imply the interpretation 'to be strong' (*ibid*., 35), while another Arab. cognate *'asā* indicates the possible meaning 'to heal, cure'. For the name *y(^{e}h)ô'āš*, a root *'wš* is very probable, for a III *hē* root would involve the retention of the final *hē*. As far as the other names are concerned, however,

no conclusion can be reached. Biblical names containing the problematic element are *yō'šîyāh(û)* and *yō'ôšîyāhû*, while the same problem is applicable also in the following extra-biblical names:
'šyhw (seals V. 231, 281 = inscr. *AI*, 1.40 = 2.35 = 17.3 = 105.2 = 106.2 = 107.2; BL, 50, no. 12; inscr. Y. Aharoni, *Lachish V*, 22; *AI*, 51.1). For this name W. Kornfeld, *WZKM* 71 (1979), 42, suggests a meaning 'Mann Yhw's', similar to *'ešbā'al*, or follows Lemaire, *IH*, 136, with an interpretation 'gegeben von Yhw'. Parunak, *BASOR* 230 (1978), 29 IV B 1 b ii, makes no mention of the root *'wš* for this name, but notes *'îš* 'man' and, following F.M. Cross, seems to prefer *yš* cf. Ug. *'iṯ* 'lives', 'exists'. *'šyh* (seal V. 232).

'rh/'wr. The root *'rh* means 'to pluck, gather' (cf. BDB, 71) and although found only rarely in BH, it is semantically equivalent to theophoric names with the idea of the deity 'gathering' certain people (cf. *'sp* 'to gather' above, p. 147). From this same root *'rh*, is derived the noun *'ărî* meaning 'lion', while a second meaning of the root *'rh*, 'to burn', is the source of a noun *'ări'êl* 'hearth' (cf. BDB, 72). The root *'wr* means 'to be or become light' (*ibid*., 21), from which the nouns *'ôr* 'light' and, more rarely, *'ûr* 'flame' are derived. Where the *wāw* is retained in names, the root is obviously *'wr*, cf. *'ûrî'ēl*, *'ûrîyāh(û)*, but there are occasions when only the element *'r* exists, in which case it is rarely possible to establish a meaning. A name like biblical *'ărî'ēl* is often interpreted as 'Lion (or hearth) of El' (cf. BDB, 72, KB, 84, Geh, 61, *SSI*, 76, 79-80). However, the presence of the element *'r* in the second position in extra-biblical names like *'ly'r* (seal P. Bordreuil, A. Lemaire, *Sem* 29 (1979), 73-74 no. 4; inscr. *AI*, 21.2) and *yw'r* (seal V, 249), rather speaks against the interpretation 'lion' (*'ărî*). At the same time, a III *hē* root for the second element is most unlikely in view of the lack of a final *hē*, which would exclude a verbal form of the root *'rh* 'to pluck, gather'. The latter is not impossible for the element *'r* in first position, however, which would suggest a meaning 'The deity has gathered'. A root *'rr* meaning 'to curse' (cf. BDB, 76) is semantically improbable, which seems to leave only the root *'wr*. One would, however, expect the *wāw* to be retained for a nominal form 'light' or 'flame'. Parunak, *BASOR* 230 (1978), 29 IV B 1 a ii, considers the final element of the name *'ly'r* to be jussive or preterite, since the defective writing of the second element is unusual, but he seems to be unaware of the seal *yw'r* (V, 249). However, verbal forms for *'ly'r* and *yw'r*, 'El/Y is light', may also be possible. BH names which present difficulty are *'ărî'ēl* and *'ar'ēlî* which probably mean 'lion', while EB names cannot be determined with accuracy. These are: *'ryhw* (seal V, 207, 429, 430; Herr, 105 no. 48; 118 no. 79; inscr. L 16 obv. 5 cf. Torcz, 198; *AI*, 26.1; Khirbet el-Kôm cf. W.G. Dever, *HUCA* 40-41 [1969-70], 158-62).
'ryw (inscr. SO 50.2 cf. *SSI*, 10, 11; SS 4.4 cf. *IH*, 248).

rmh/rwm. The meaning of the root *rmh* in personal names may be suggested by an Akk. cognate *ramû* meaning 'to slacken' (G), 'to loosen' (D).

The root *rwm* is widely attested in the Heb. onomasticon, and means 'to be high, exalted, to rise' (cf. BDB, 926). Once again, second position elements present no problem because of the lack of the *hē* in names like *y(ᵉh)ôrām*, *'ăḥîrām* etc., which indicate a Hollow root *rwm*. With other names the matter is a little more complicated. The biblical name *ramyāh* could be from either root, although the vocalization of a III *hē* root would be *rᵉmāyāh*, which would suggest a slight preference for the root *rwm*. Biblical *yirmᵉyāh* seems to conform more to a III *hē* Qal imf. verb (*yiqṭeh*), rather than a Hollow verb, while the same possibly may be said for the extra-biblical occurrences of the name *yrmyhw* (seals V, 58, 248, 258, 411; BL, 47-48 no. 6; inscr. L 1.4 cf. *SSI*, 36; *AI*, 24.15-16), although the lack of vocalization makes such a form less certain.

In one case, the choice between a Hollow or I *yōd* root is evident with the roots:

yš'/šw'. From a formal point of view, the second elements of the names *'ăbîšûᵃ'*, *'ĕlîšûᵃ'*, *malkîšûᵃ'* and *yᵉhôšûᵃ'* could be from the root *yš'* 'to deliver' (Hiphil, BDB, 446) or *šāwa'* 'to cry out for help' (BDB, 1002). Semantically, however, the former root is more acceptable and, indeed, is used widely of the deity, whereas *šāwa'* is found only rarely, in the Piel. However, the noun *šûᵃ'* from the root *yš'* is also rarely attested (Job 30.24 (?), 36.19) though Gray *op. cit.*, 147-47 and BDB, 447 interpret it as 'opulence'. Gray assigned this meaning to the second element in all the above names, while the interpretations of BDB vary with 'My father is rescue or is opulence' for *'ăbîšûᵃ'* (BDB, 4), 'God is salvation' for *'ĕlîšûᵃ'* (*ibid.*, 46), 'My king (= Y) is opulence' for *malkîšûᵃ'* (*ibid.*, 575) and 'Y is salvation or opulence' for *yᵉhôšûᵃ'* (*ibid.*, 221). The adj. *šôᵃ'* '(free), independent, noble' (*ibid.*, 447) is also rarely attested, and would be an unlikely etymology for the second element of these names since adjectives do not feature elsewhere in Heb. name-giving. Noth (*IPN*, 154) preferred to think of the element more in the sense of being synonymous to *'zr* 'help' in Heb. names, and akin to Arab. *wś'* 'generous' and biblical *šāwah* noted above. More probably, the prevalence of the element in names may suggest a stronger connection with the idea of deliverance in the root *yš'* and an interpretation 'salvation, rescue' may be more pertinent.

Where the *yōd* is retained in names, other nouns from the root *yš'* may also be relevant. These are *yēša'* m. 'deliverance, rescue, salvation', also 'safety, welfare', and *yᵉšû'āh* f. 'salvation'. In the inscriptional name *'lyš'* the *yōd* is taken as consonantal by Gibson (*SSI*, 11). This is unlikely in view of the possibly parallel biblical name *'ĕlîšā'*, and since a *yōd* is often evident following the element *'l* in unvocalized, extra-biblical names when it is not a consonant of the following root (see above, p. 103): a nominal form for the name is therefore preferable. The inscriptional name *ywyš'* (SO Dir, 311)

should perhaps be vocalized *yôyēša'*, since a verbal form of the root *yš'* is found in no other name in the second position. Biblical names from the root *yš'* are *hôša'ăyāh*, *y^eša'yāh(û)*, *'ĕlîšû^a'*, *'ĕlîšā'*, *y^ehôšû^a'/y^ehôšu^a'/yēšû^a'*, *'ăbîšû^a'*, *malkîšû^a'*, and extra-biblical *'lyš'* (seals V, 41 [possibly Ammon.], 271, 375; inscr. SO 1.4; 1.7; 41.1 cf. *SSI*, 8, 10, 11; *AI*, 24.15; 24.19-20); *yš''l* (seal V, 86 considered Ammon. by P. Bordreuil, A. Lemaire, *Sem* 29 [1979], 83 and Herr, 70 no. 34); *yhwš'* (seal V, 27); *ywyš'* (inscr. SO Dir, 311; SO 36.3 cf. *IH*, 52. For this inscr. Diringer read *ywyšb/r*, Dir, 46 no. 30, and Noth, *IPN*, 189, read *ywyšr*); *hwš'yhw* (seals V, 144, 423, 424; inscr. L 3.1 cf. *SSI*, 30, 38; MH 1.7 cf. *IH*, 261); *yš'yhw* (seals V, 52, 211, 294, 420, 426; Herr, 140 no. 140); *hwš'm* (seal B. Mazar, *Jerusalem Revealed* [1975], 38-40).
In all names the form is likely to be verbal in first position and nominal in second position.

2.6 *Construct Form Names*

A significant group of personal names in Hebrew express relationship to the deity by the use of the construct form of the noun. In such names there are two elements, both nouns, which are placed in juxtaposition in order to show a modifying relationship. The first noun, the *nomen regens*, is in the construct state, while the second noun, the *nomen rectum*, forms the theophoric element, e.g. *'ōbadyāhû* 'Servant of Yahweh'.

The noun which occurs in the first position refers to the name-bearer, and often not only illustrated how man saw his position and relationship with God, but also stood as a declaration that he intended his child to become bound to that God, and to no other. This is seen in the following group of construct form names:

m^etûšā'ēl BH: 'Man of El', BDB, 607, KB, 618, Geh, 613. Cf. Bab. *mutu-ša-ili* and below, § 2.7.

gabrî'ēl BH: perhaps 'Man of El' (name of an angel), BDB, 150, KB, 169. On names of this type, see below, § 2.9. Against this interpretation, Noth (*IPN*, 36, 190) suggested a perf. + noun with an infixed *ī* = 'God has shown himself strong', cf. Bab. *El-gab(a)r(i)*, *Ilu-gabri/a* and *^dAddu-gabri*. Cf. also Geh, 309 who suggests 'Man of God' but prefers 'God has shown himself mighty'.

bityāh BH: possibly 'Worshipper of Y' cf. BDB, 124 = *bat yāh*. KB, 160, also Geh, 119, suggest 'Queen' cf. Eg. *Bj tj t*. As a 'daughter of Pharaoh' (1 Chr. 4.17) the name may be wholly Eg. and therefore not relevant here.

gryhw EB seals V, 243, Herr, 120 no. 83. For this latter seal V, 142 = *gdyhw*, but more recently Vattioni reads *gryhw* (Vattioni, *AION* 38 [1978],

254). The name means 'Client of Y', cf. Phoen. *gir/ger* 'client' or dweller' (*PNPPI*, 298). The parallel names in Phoen. are also construct forms.

*n*ᵉ*'aryāh* BH: 'Youth of Y', cf. KB, (1953), 624. *N'r* can also be used in the sense of 'personal attendant, servant' or 'retainer' (cf. BDB, 655); thus Noth (*IPN*, 139) has 'Servant of Y' and Geh, 655 'Attendant, armour bearer of Y'.

'ābdî'ēl, *'abd*ᵉ*'ēl*, *'ōbadyāh(û)* BH: 'Servant of El/Y', cf. BDB, 715, KB, (1953), 673f., Geh, 2, 676, and the name *'ōbed 'ĕdôm* above, § 2.2 *Other divine elements*. The element *'bd* also occurs widely on seals and inscriptions suffixed with *yh(w)* (V, 26, 32, 34, 35, 70, 281, 425; *AI*, 10.4; 27.2; 49.8; SO 50.2 cf. *SSI*, 10; Z. Meshel, C. Meyers, *BA* 39 [1976], 6-10 [Heb. or Phoen.]), and means 'servant'. It always appears in construct in names. Noth (*IPN*, 137) suggested that in later time this designation tended to take on a cultic association as an expression depicting the name-bearer as a worshipper of his God; cf. the n.m. *'ōbed*, *'ôbēd* 'worshipper' (BDB, 714). This may well be the interpretation of *'ōbadyāh(û)*.

*p*ᵉ*tû'ēl* BH: 'Youth of El'. Geh, 740, KB, (1953), 786 = *p*ᵉ*tî* 'youth'. The Heb. root *pth* means 'to be spacious, wide, open', cf. Arab. *fatuwa*, *fatiya*, 'to be youthful', n. m. 'young man' and BDB, 834. See also below, § 2.7.

Any one of these names when given to a newly born child by its parents, would have been tantamount to parental dedication of the child to the deity and, a posteriori, would have denoted similar parental dedication. Moreover, in expressing allegiance to that deity, there would be inherent in the name a hope for the protection and care by God throughout the life of the child.

Another significant group of construct form names refers to God's involvement in the birth of the child, and shows that the parents regarded their offspring as a manifestation of the divine creativity and blessing. This is expressed in the names:

mattanyāh(û) BH: 'Gift of Y', BDB, 682, Geh, 596, KB, 619, root *ntn*. The BH name *mattityāh(û)* may also be included here. The name is also found on a number of seals (M, 81-82 no. 31; BL, 49 nos. 9, 11; V, 268; K.J. O'Connell, *IEJ* 27 [1977], 197-99) and inscr. (L 1.5 cf. *SSI*, 103).

ma'ăśēyāh(û) BH: 'Work of Y', BDB, 796, Geh, 575, KB 583: also found on seals (V, 51, 55, 242, 294, 427). The BH name *ba'ăśēyāh* is perhaps also to be included here, cf. Geh, 85, BDB, 129.

bēdyāh BH: 'In the hand of Y', cf. also the seals *bdyhw* (V, 393), *bd'l* (V, 400) and the inscr. *bdyw* (SO 58.1 cf. *IH*, 37). J. Teixidor, *Syria* 54 (1977), 266 no. 82, considers this last inscr. to be Phoen. and to read *Bodyaw*, not *Bedyaw* as Lemaire suggests. The name *byd'l* is well attested as Ammon. and has more recently been attested on two new seals, V, 449 and V, 450 whose origin is unknown to the author at present. The patronym *'lmg* of V, 450 would, indeed, be new to Heb. name-giving and etymologically difficult, since the only appropriate root would be *mwg* 'to melt' (cf. BDB, 556). The form *bd* is interesting: Noth suggested a meaning 'branch' or 'shoot', taken from the imagery of plant life and depicting God figuratively as a tree, of which the child is a branch. As a 'branch of Y' the child would enjoy care and protection from the deity. He further suggested that the idea stems from the concept of the holy tree in Canaanite religion (*IPN*, 149-50). A more tenable interpretation is suggested by the Ammon. seal *byd'l bn tmk'l* (V, 17) 'In the hand of El' or 'By the hand of El', the addition of the preposition denoting the instrument or means of the birth of the child. The thought in the Heb. names, then, appears reminiscent of the creation narrative and the making of man by God like the moulding of clay by the potter (cf. BDB, 427 and Isa. 49.5, 43.7 etc.). The interpretation of the element *bd* as 'in the hand of' may also refer to protection by the deity, and this translation is also supported by the Ug. element *bd*, which also occurs in personal names with a similar meaning (cf. *UT Glossary*, 370-71 and *bdil* 'From-the-hand(s)-of-god', as well as *PTU*, 118). Relevant here, also, is the Aram. name *ḱlbyd'l* (P. Bordreuil, *Sem* 23 [1973], 95, 97), since it is the first instance in which names of this type have *kl* 'all' prefixed to the expression 'in the hand of' the deity. Although not identical, it is a good indication of the kind of meaning which is suitable for these names.

Another group of construct names depicts a more special, closer relationship between the name-bearer and the deity:

dôdāwāhû BH: 'Beloved or friend of Y'. Cf. also the name *ddyhw* which occurs on a seal (V, 325). For the BH name, BDB, 187 suggest *dôdîyāhû* as the best reading and a meaning 'Beloved of Y'. KB, 205 suggest *dōdîyāhû* 'Y is a friend' or 'Friend of Y' while Noth (*IPN*, 149) suggested 'Beloved or friend of Y', i.e. *dôdîyāhû*.

y^{e}*dîdyāh* BH: 'Beloved of Y', root *ydd*, BDB, 392, Geh, 449, KB, 373.

r^{e}*'û'ēl* BH: 'Friend of El'. Geh, 800 suggests a nominal sentence, 'God is a friend'. KB, (1953), 900 suggest *rē'eh* + *'l*. A nominal sentence name is also indicated by Phoen. *R'MLK R'MLK* 'Milk is (my/his) Friend' (*PNPPI*, 221) and by Noth (*IPN*, 153) 'My friend is God'. On this point, however, see the comment on this name below, § 2.7.

b^{e}*sôdyāh* BH: 'In the secret (council) of Y', cf. BDB, 126, KB, 135, Geh, 105, *IPN*, 152.

y^{e}*'î'ēl/y*^{e}*'û'ēl/y*^{e}*'iw'ēl* This name also is possibly to be considered in this context. If it is a construct type name (see below, pp. 121 and 125) and since no appropriate meaning can be ascertained from the Heb., it may mean

'Remembered of El', cf. Arab. *wa'ā* 'to keep in mind, remember', although Geh, 491 suggests a verbal translation, 'El has remembered', from this same Arab. root. KB, 401, however, suggest 'to be strong' from Safaitic *w'j* or Arab. *wa'ij*, or 'to heal' from Arab. *w'j*.

A stronger relationship between the deity and the name-bearer, in which the latter is more passively subject to the power of the deity, is expressed in the following four names:

'û'ēl BH: 'Will of El'? cf. BDB, 15, root *'wh*. The form of this name is dubious; cf. Geh, 963 and *IPN*, 235, where a contraction from *'ăbû'ēl* is suggested, as well as the comment on this name below, § 2.7.

d^e'û'ēl BH: 'Invocation of El', root *d'h* cf. Arab. *da'ā* 'to call'. Geh, 222 suggests 'Knowledge of God' (root *yd'*) or 'Invocation of God' cf. Arab. *da'ā* 'to call aloud'. KB, 219 also suggest *d'h* or *yd'*. B. Porten (*IEJ* 21 [1971], 47f.) classifies the name as one of 'encouragement' and the form as an imv. from the root *yd'*, 'Acknowledge God'. See also the discussion of this name below, § 2.7.

miqnēyāhû BH: 'Possession of Y', root *qnh*, cf. BDB, 889, KB, 594, Geh, 619. See also the seals V, 162, 272; F.M. Cross, *HTR* 55 (1962), 251, and inscr. *AI*, 60.4; A 72.1, cf. *IH*, 219. Noth (*IPN*, 172) suggested that *qnh* is used here with the sense 'to create', so that the noun is to be translated as 'Geschöpf'. In this context, cf. the Phoen. parallel MQNMLK (*PNPPI*, 230), which could mean 'Possession of Milk/the King' from the Phoen. root *qny* 'to acquire' or, alternatively, Ug. *qny* 'to create' may be relevant (cf. the Ug. name *bn qnmlk PTU*, 39 'Mlk has created'). The Phoen. name is clearly a construct form.

š^ebû'ēl, *šûbā'ēl* BH: 'Captive of El'. KB, (1953), 939 suggest the root *šbh* + *'l*; see also below, § 2.7. Some, however, suggest the root *šwb*, cf. Geh, 860 'Return O God', who follows the Gk. and 1 Chr. 24.20 (*šûbā'ēl*), also Noth (*IPN*, 257).

A small group of construct names implies that the deity has close knowledge and understanding of the name-bearer:

y^edî'ă'ēl BH: 'Known of El', cf. Geh, 449. KB, 373 suggest 'der den Gott kennt'. Noth (*IPN*, 181) suggested a pass. part. with independent genitive from the root *yd'*, 'to take care of, care about', on which point, see above, p. 101.

buqqîyāhû BH: 'Proved of Y', root *bqh* 'to test, prove', cf. BDB, 131. The name is not without difficulties: KB, 143 suggest *baqbuq* + *jā* from the root *bwq*. Geh, 128 suggests 'bottle, jar'! Noth (*IPN*, 226/105) considered the *yh* as an emphatic afformative since the name makes no sense when a theophoric ending is affixed. His citing of the name as *bqyh* rather than *bqyhw*, however, makes the termination, as well as the final interpretation, no less difficult. The name is also attested on an inscr. *bqyhw* (Ophel 1 cf. *SSI*, 25, 26). However, Lemaire (*IH*, 239, 241) no longer sees a name here, but translates *cardeurs*.

Another small group of construct names is concerned with personal aspects of the deity, and seem to describe the name-bearer as part of the deity or, more probably, may refer to the deity himself:

pᵉnû'ēl BH: 'Face of El', cf. BDB, 819, Geh, 733. The name is probably a construct form (see below, § 2.7). KB, (1953), 768 have *pāneh* + *'l*. Noth (*IPN*, 225) contested the relationship with *pnym*, but found the first element impossible to clarify. Cf. also Phoen. PNSMLT, a genitive form (*PNPPI*, 392).

qôlāyāh BH: 'Voice of Y', cf. BDB, 877. (For construct *qwl* see Gen. 3.8.) The name *qlyhw* also occurs on a seal (V, 233), as well as in an inscr. *qlyw* (SS 4.2 cf. *IH*, 248) which Lemaire transcribes as *qolyaw* and suggests is verbal. (For these EB names, see below, § 2.9.) Geh, 544 interprets the BH name verbally, 'Y has spoken', while Noth (*IPN*, 32 n. 1) suggested a cohortative *ā* for the final element, although the first element he found unclear.

šᵉmû'ēl BH: 'Name of El'. Geh, 828 and BDB, 1028 suggest 'Name of El' or 'His name is El'. KB (1953), 985 have *šm* + *'l* 'The unnamed god is El'. Noth (*IPN*, 123) considered the element *sm* as possibly theophoric with prosthetic *ālep*, thus *'sm* + *'l*. However, cf. the parallel W. Semitic *šumu-'Ay(y)a* 'Name of 'Ay(y)a'. *šumu-Suen* 'Name of Suen' etc., J.J.M. Roberts, *The Earliest Semitic Pantheon*, Johns Hopkins (1972), 20, 50, also Ug. *šu-mu-a-bi*, *šu-mu-a-sa*, *šu-mu-ra-bi* (*PTU*, 355). See also below, § 2.7. Whether the initial element refers to the deity or to the name-bearer is difficult to determine. The similar name *šm'b* 'Name of the (divine) Father' occurs on a seal (V, 128).

Two names have an animal as the *nomen regens*. These are:

'ărî'ēl BH: 'Lion of El'. Cf. also BH *'ar'ēlî*, and for the possibility of other EB additions with the same meaning, see above, § 2.5 *'rh/'wr*. Names formed with the root *'rh* are difficult since the possibility of a root *'wr* 'to be or become light' cannot be excluded. BDB, 72, KB, 84 and Geh, 61 suggest possibilities of 'Lion of El' or 'altar-hearth' (BDB, 'Hearth of El') although Geh, 61 prefers an Akk. origin *Arallu* (*Arallū*) 'which has a double sense of "underworld" and "Mountain of the gods", the cosmic mountain in which, according to an Assyrian text, the gods were born and reared. Heb. *har'ēl* means "mountain of God" and is thus a popular ety. of the Akkad. loan word'.

Whatever meaning is given to these names, it needs to be taken into account that the element *'r* can occur in second position, with a theophoric element in first position, which may suggest other possibilities (see above, § 2.5 *'rh/ 'wr*). The form *'r'l* occurs in the Meša inscr. 12 (cf. *SSI*, 75) followed by the n. pr. David, and is translated by Gibson as 'Lion figure of David' (*ibid.*, 76).

ḥannî'ēl BH: 'Favour or grace of El', cf. BDB, 337. The name may refer to the grace of the deity himself, or it may refer to the child as being a manifestation of divine grace or favour. Noth (*IPN*, 35, 187) and Geh, 363 suggest a verbal form. Noth considered the form to be perf. because of the presence of the *yōd*; however, on this point, cf. below, p. 135.

'glyw EB: SO 41.1 'Calf of Y'. Gibson (*SSI*, 12) suggests 'Y is a young bull' or, better, 'Calf of Y'. For the construct *'ēgel* see 1 Sam. 28.24. It is often used in similis, cf. Ps. 29.6; Ezek. 1.7, BDB, 722. Noth (*IPN*, 150) suggested a construct form and compared the many similar Akk. names e.g. *A-ga-al-Marduk*, 'Kalb (*agalu*) Marduks'. The distinction between a nominal sentence name 'Y is a calf', and a construct form, 'Calf of Y', is important for this name, since the former designates Yahweh by a term which was, for Israel, contrary to her normal worship (cf. 1 Kgs 12.28f.). The latter, however, makes the name-bearer himself the *nomen regens*. Moreover, the diminutive form of the animal would seem to be important and less disparaging that the designation 'bull' (*IPN*, 151) so that any suggestion that this name indicates image worship in the form of a bull in Israel is speculative. Indeed, Lemaire (*IH*, 53) notes that *'gl* was 'une désignation familière pour un jeune homme'.

Two construct form names appear to stand independently in semantic content. These are:

g^e'û'ēl BH: 'Majesty of El', root *g'h*. Cf. BDB, 145, and below, § 2.7. Geh, 326 suggests 'Majesty of God', or a sf. from the root *g'l* 'Redeemed of God'. This latter meaning was also suggested by Noth (*IPN*, 240) who cited the Gk Γουδιηλ for Γουλιηλ.

ḥaggîyāh BH: 'Feast of Y', cf. BDB, 291. The name is doubtfully theophoric: KB, 279 suggest *ḥag* + carit. ending, but against this cf. A. Vincent, *La religion des Judéo-Araméens d'Elephantine*, Paris (1937), 400, who suggests 'Y is my feast'. Geh, 357 prefers 'festal', i.e. born on a feast day, with a 'hypocoristic' ending as, also, *IPN*, 222 'born on a feast day', cf. *šabb^{e}tay* 'born on a Sabbath'.

We have seen above that some construct forms are preceded by the preposition *b^e*, as in BH *b^{e}sôdyāh* and *bēdyāh*. Two further names with this same preposition need to be included here. These are:

b^{e}ṣal'ēl BH: 'In the shadow (protection) of El', cf. BDB, 130, KB, 141, Geh, 114, *IPN*, 152.

b'd'l EB: seal (V, 48), 'In the testimony, witness of El'. Since no appropriate root *b'd* exists in Heb. it seems likely that the name involves the preposition *b^{e}* and the root *'wd* or *'dh*. The root *'wd* would suggest a meaning 'testimony' or 'witness of El', and does no violence to the sense when preceded by the preposition, 'in the witness, testimony of El'. The root *'dh*, however, is usually used in Heb. personal names with the meaning 'to ornament, deck oneself': the noun, usually collective, denoting 'ornaments'. This, however, makes little sense when the preposition precedes it, and gives preference to the root *'wd*. Perhaps also relevant is the preposition *b'd* 'away from, behind, about, on behalf of' (BDB, 126) but is possibly less semantically acceptable.

Finally, two names occur whose meanings are indiscernible but which are probably construct forms. These are *y^{e}mû'ēl* and *n^{e}mû'ēl*.

y^{e}mû'ēl BH: the meaning of this name is quite uncertain: KB, 396 suggest *yām* or *yôm* for the first element. Since the form *n^{e}mû'ēl* is given as an alternative reading, it may be a corruption of *n^{e}mû'ēl*, although the latter itself is uncertain. On the basis of a comparison with names like *p^{e}nû'ēl* and *r^{e}'û'ēl* one is tempted to suggest a III *hē* root and a construct form, although the roots *ymh* and *nmh* do not exist in Heb.: see also below § 2.7.

n^{e}mû'ēl BH: this name is equally obscure; Barr cites a root *nmh* 'to bring tidings', from Arab. *namā* (Barr *Cp. Ph.*, 182) although pointing out that this root 'is probably an idiosyncrasy of Arab. and seems to have no cognates in other Semitic languages' (*ibid.*, 193, n. 1).

The basic characteristic of all these construct names, with only few exceptions, is that they reveal much more about the name-bearer and, therefore, about the name-giver, than other types of names. This is because the actual construction of the names is such that the *nomen regens*, the non-theophoric noun, is bound to the *nomen rectum*, the theophoric element, revealing a close connection between name-bearer and deity, and depicting a degree of *involvement* between man and God. With the exception of the name *g^{e}'û'ēl*, such involvement makes the general nature of these names distinctly non-transcendent. God is shown to be prominently concerned with man's whole existence, just as man's existence is revealed as being bound to that of his God.

2.7 *Names of the Pattern q*^{e}*ṭû'ēl*

In thirteen biblical Hebrew names the initial element occurs in a pattern mainly formed of two consonants, the first carrying a *shewa*, the second being followed by the long vowel *û*. All the names of this type are suffixed with *'l* and do not occur suffixed with forms of *yhwh* or any other theophoric element. Neither do they occur extra-biblically.

What is interesting concerning these names is their apparent regularity of form, which would seem to suggest that they should all belong to a particular class of names with a common grammatical structure. Nevertheless, a variety of suggestions has been put forward for each one, as indicated in the following list:

g^{e}*'û'ēl*. BDB, 145 interpret the name as 'Majesty of El'. The same interpretation is suggested by Geh, 326, as well as the alternative of a sf. from the root *g'l* meaning 'Redeemed of God'. Other sff., however, do not indicate that a third radical can be omitted to shorten a name unless it is a guttural, *rēš*, or of a Geminate or Hollow root, cf. below § 2.10. KB, 161 suggest the noun *ga'ăwāh* + *'l*. Noth (*IPN*, 240) also preferred the interpretation 'Redeemed of God' (i.e. *g*^{e}*'ûl-'ēl*). The root *g'h* in BH means (1) 'to rise up', (2) 'to grow up (of plants)', (3) 'to be lifted up, exalted', from which are derived the fem. nouns *ga'ăwāh* 'majesty, pride' and *gē'ût* 'majesty', and the masc. noun *gā'ôn* 'exaltation, majesty, excellence'.

d^{e}*'û'ēl*. LXX, the Sam. text, and Num. 2.14, have *r*^{e}*'û'ēl*. Geh, 222 translates the name as 'Knowledge of God' (root *yd'*) or 'Invocation of God', cf. Arab. *da'ā* 'to call aloud'. KB, 219 also suggest the root *d'h* or *yd'*. B. Porten, *IEJ* 21 (1971) 47, prefers an imv. from the root *yd'*, 'Acknowledge God!' The root *d'h* 'to call', does not occur in BH except in the name *'eldā'āh*. Relevant nouns from the root *yd'* are *dē*^{a}*'* 'knowledge' (m.), and *dē'āh* 'knowledge' (f.).

y^{e}*'û'ēl*. Also *y*^{e}*'î'ēl* and *y*^{e}*'iw'ēl*. Geh, 491 suggests 'El has remembered', comparing Arab. *wa'a* 'keep in mind, remember'. KB, 401 compare Safaitic *w'j* 'to be strong', Arab. *wa'ij* 'strong', and Arab. *w'j* 'to heal'. The root *y'h* 'to sweep together' (cf. Arab. *wa'ay* 'to collect, gather') is used only once in BH in the Qal but would be semantically suitable in that it is similar to the root *'sp* 'to gather' in the BH name *'ăbîyāsāp/'ebyāsāp*.

l^{e}*mû'ēl*. Also *l*^{e}*môēl*. *L*^{e}*mô* is a poetical form of the preposition *l*^{e} (cf. BDB, 541). Most agree with an interpretation 'Belonging to El', cf. Geh, 556, KB, 505, *IPN*, 249. Less attractive is the suggestion of A. Jirku, *ZAW* 25 (1954), 151, that the initial element represents the deity *Lim*, popular at Mari, where it is attested in the names *Zimri-Lim*, *Išar-Lim*, *Iarim-Lim* etc. Indeed, the *form l^emô/l^emû* for the initial element of the BH name is of more significance than Jirku admits.

m^etûšā'ēl. BDB, 607 suggest 'Man of God' for this similar form, citing Bab. *mutu-ša-ili*. This interpretation is supported by Geh, 613 and KB, 618.

n^emû'ēl. *N^emûēl* occurs in Num. 26.12 and 1 Chr. 4.24 and is the name of a son of Simeon who, in Gen. 46.10 and Exod. 6.15 is called *y^emû'ēl*. The name also exists independently as that given to a Reubenite in Num. 26.9. Noth (*IPN*, 251) seemed to consider the name to be erroneous for *y^emû'ēl* which he believed to be the name of a tribe. Barr *Cp. Ph.*, 182 cites a root *nmh* meaning 'to bring tidings', but against this root Barr observes: (1) it gives no sense paralleled in Israelite names, and (2) forms *ymw'l* and *lmw'l*, which look related, count against a derivation from the root *nmh*.

y^emû'ēl. This name is only found as an alternative to *n^emû'ēl* in Gen. 46.10 and Exod. 6.15, as the previous name has shown. Geh, 307 suggests that the name is a corruption of *n^emû'ēl* while KB, 396 suggest either *yām* or *yôm* as the etymology of the first element.

p^enû'ēl. BDB, 819 suggest 'Face of God', also Geh, 733. In contrast, Noth (*IPN*, 255) contested the connection with *pnym* 'face' but found the first element unclear. Cf. also the Phoen. name PNSMLT, a genitive type name, vocalized *pānēsimlot*, meaning 'Face of the Ikon' (*PNPPI*, 230). Not to be taken seriously is the suggestion of B. Margulis (*Ug. Forsch.* 2 [1970], 131-38) that names such as *p^enû'ēl* contain a n. pr. div. *pn*, especially since he depicts the supposed god as 'a deity hitherto unattested at Ugarit, and unknown elsewhere'!

p^etû'ēl. Geh, 740 suggests the possible meaning 'A youth belonging to God'. KB (1953), 786 also suggest 'youth' for the initial element of the name. BDB, 834 list the name under the root *pth* 'to be spacious, wide, open', citing an Arab. cognate *fatuwa*, *fatiya* for this root with the meaning 'to be youthful, in the prime of life', from which is derived the noun 'young man'.

q^emû'ēl. KB (1953), 842 and Geh, 534 consider the first element to be derived from the root *qwm*, Gehman suggesting a meaning 'God has raised himself, stood up'. Probably, more correctly, BDB, 887 list the name under a hypothetical root *qmh*. R. Zadok (*WO* 9 [1977], 54) considers the name to mean 'Qam is God' but, again, the long vowel *û* seems to serve some specific purpose, making a divine name for the first element unlikely.

r^e'û'ēl. Most suggest 'El is a friend', cf. KB (1953), 900, Geh, 800, and Noth (*IPN*, 153-54) who suggested the addition of the 1st pers. sing. suffix. Cf. also the Phoen. names R'MLK, R'MLK, 'Milk is (my/his) friend' (*PNPPI*, 409-10). Also possible, however, is a construct form 'Friend of El'.

BDB, 944ff. also imply the root *r'h* for the etymology of the first element. This root has two basic meanings, (1) 'to pasture, graze', and (2) probably 'to associate with', from which are derived the masc. nouns *rē^a'* 'friend, companion', *rē'eh* 'friend', and *rē^a'* 'purpose, aim'.

š^ebû'ēl. This name, which was given to a son of Gershom in 1 Chr. 23.16 and 26.24, occurs as *šûbā'ēl* in 1 Chr. 24.20. Both Geh, 860 and Noth (*IPN*, 32, 257) consider the form *šûbā'ēl* to be the original, with a meaning 'Return O El'. KB, (1953), 939 and BDB, 986 cite the name under a root *šbh* which has the meaning 'to take captive' (cf. BDB, 986). Nouns from this root are *š^ebî* and *šibyāh* (f.) 'captivity, captives' (coll.), *š^ebît*, *š^ebût*(f.) with the same meaning, and *š^ebî* (f.) 'precious stone'.

š^emû'ēl. Most suggest 'Name of El' as the meaning of this name, cf. BDB, 1028, who also note the possibility of a caritative from *yišmā'ē'l* (a feature not exemplified elsewhere in Heb. names), and Geh, 828, who also gives the alternative 'His name is El'. KB (1953), 985 interpret the name as 'The unnamed God is El'. Cf also the Old Akk. names *šumu-Ay(y)a* (Name of Ay(y)a', Roberts, 14, 20), *šum-Malik* ('Name of Malik' *ibid.*, 43), *šumu-Suen* ('Name of Suen' *ibid.*, 50) and *šumu-ilum* (DINGIR), ('Name of the god' *ibid.*, 125). Also to be considered is the root *šmh* which does not exist in verbal form in BH, but an Arab. cognate *sama'* may suggest a meaning 'to be high, lofty' (cf. BDB, 1029). This indicates a possible 'Loftiness, exaltedness of El', an interpretation which is certainly semantically suitable. R. Zadok (*op. cit.*, 54) considers the name to mean 'Šem is god' because of its parallel with *q^emû'ēl*, whih he translates as 'Qam is god'. However, he fails to take into account the twelve other names of this type.

One further name may perhaps be considered in the above category. This is the name:

'û'ēl. A contraction of *'ăbû'ēl* is suggested by Geh, 963 and BDB, 15; this would give a meaning 'El is (divine) Father'. The alternative suggested by BDB, however, seems the better proposition. This involves a construct noun from the root *'wh* producing 'Will of El': This root has three possible meanings, (1) 'to betake oneself (to a place for dwelling)' suggested by an Arab. cognate *'away*, (2) 'to be tenderly inclined', also suggested by an Arab. cognate *'awaya*. From this latter source is derived the verb *'āwāh* 'to incline, desire', and the noun *'aw* 'desire' (construct *'ô*, rare), (3) 'to sign, mark, describe with a mark'.

In the foregoing names, it is possible that the *û* form may be a survival of an early case ending. GKC, 252 section 90k suggested that *û*, in certain compound proper names, is the old sign of the nominative case ending, as in the names *m^etûšā'ēl* (and probably *b^etû'ēl*) and *p^enû'ēl*. The evidence for this archaic nominative termination, however, has been deduced from only a few proper names and such evidence, when applied to the above list, continues to violate any formal classification on this basis. Indeed, one would expect theories advanced for any one of these names to be applicable to at least a few others of the same type. When this is not so, the theory itself may be questionable. For this reason, B. Porten's view that *d^e'û'ēl* is an imperative from the root *yd'* meaning 'Acknowledge God' (*op. cit.*, 47) is tenuous. Although the form *d^e'û* is attested as such (Num. 32.23 etc.) an imperative interpretation is by no means the norm for the other names in the above list and the imperatives of the relative roots of the remaining names never take this form.

Viewing the names as a class, there seems present a considerable preference for a III *hē* root for most of these names as, indeed, BDB have implied by placing them under such roots, even where these are not otherwise attested in biblical Hebrew. For the names *m^etûšā'ēl*, *'û'ēl*, *g^e'û'ēl*, *d^e'û'ēl*, *p^enû'ēl*, *r^e'û'ēl*, *p^etû'ēl* and *š^emû'ēl* a construct form plus theophoric element would seem to be the most attractive possibility and the most widely accepted. This suggests that some of the more doubtful forms may also be construct forms from a III *hē* root, for example, *y^e'û'ēl*, 'Remembered of El' (cf. Arab. *wa'a*), and *š^ebû'ēl* 'Captive of El'. Yet the names *n^emû'ēl*, *y^emû'ēl* and *q^emû'ēl* still remain obscure, while the form *lmw* in the name *l^emû'ēl*/*l^emô'ēl* seems, at present, better considered as a relative of *lā'ēl*, 'Belonging to El'. For the majority of names in this section, however, one can suggest a possible III *hē* root construct form for the non-theophoric element.

2.8 *Other Grammatical Forms*

1. *Imperatives*

The existence of imperatives in Hebrew name-giving is very rare, and since those examples which do exist are dubious, their occurrence in the Hebrew onomasticon should be considered with caution. Three possible names of this type arise:

ḥăkalyāh BH. This name is usually revocalized to render *ḥakkēlyāh* 'Wait for Y' (*ḥakkēh l^eyāh*), cf. BDB, 314, KB, 301, *IPN*, 32 n. 3, and B. Porten, 'Domla'el and Related Names', *IEJ* 21 (1971), 48. However, this radical alteration to the vocalization in order to obtain a viable interpretation is hardly justifiable. The root *ḥkl* has no attested verbal forms in BH, although from an Arab. cognate *hakala* a meaning 'to be confused, vague' may have suggested the translation 'Y is obscure' put forward by Geh, 355. The form of the name as it appears in Neh. 1.1, seems to be Qal perf. and there is a lot to be said for retaining this form and recognizing the root *ḥkl* as no longer containing any extant verbal meaning. The name *ḥklyhw* is also attested on an ostracon (L 20.2, cf. *IH*, 134).

dml'l EB seal (V, 233). The name *dmlyhw* is also attested on a non-Heb. seal (Herr, 144 no. 151). For *dml'l*, S.H. Horn ('An Inscribed Seal from Jordan', *BASOR* 189 [1968], 41-43) favours a reading *rml'l* (root *rwm*) and an interpretation 'May Y verily be exalted', as in *'Adôn-la-rām* (cf. *KAI*, 203). Horn also cites Diringer's connection of *dml* with the Arab. verb *damal* meaning 'to make peace, to heal, to cure' (see also *SSI*, 56). Horn also notes 'the name *Dml'l* may, like *Rmlyhw*, contain a precative *la* added to the verb *dwm* "to be silent" or better, the preposition, so that the name should be read *Dûmla'el* meaning "Wait on God"' (p. 43). The root *dwm* in Heb. has no attested verbal forms, although originally it may have had the meaning 'to whisper' (cf. BDB, 189). The similar root *dmm*, however, has the meaning 'to be or grow dumb, silent, still', and an imv. form *dôm* (cf. BDB, 198-99). This root suggests that the meaning of the name could be explained by Ps. 37.7: *dôm layhwh w^e^hitḥôlēl lô* 'Be still before the Lord, and wait patiently for him'. This interpretation has been suggested by B. Porten (*op. cit.*, 47).

yaḥl^e'ēl BH. It is possible that this name is derived from a root *yḥl* which occurs in BH in the Niphal 'to wait', and in the Piel 'to await'. No Niphal imv. is attested, although a Piel imv. (*yaḥēl*) occurs in Pss. 130.7 and 131.3 (cf. BDB, 403-404). An interpretation of the name as derived from this root would be 'Wait for God!' (cf. BDB, 404). More probable, however, is the derivation of the name from a root *ḥlh*, extant in BH with the meaning 'to mollify, appease, entreat the favour of' (cf. BDB, 318 II). This root occurs in NH, Aram. and Arab. with the meaning 'to be sweet, pleasant', and a derivation from this root would suggest 'May El show himself (or, El is) well-disposed, or friendly', cf. Geh, 442, *IPN*, 204.

2. *Participles*

A small group of names, which in most cases bears the trace of Aramaic and Akkadian influence, is characterized by a participial predicate. Names with such predicates tend to emphasize the active side of the divine nature, and the immediacy of this action may well indicate that the names are to be interpreted in the context of the birth of the child.

mahălal'ēl BH. The root *hll* in BH can mean 'to shine' (attested once in the Qal, but mainly in the Hiphil) or 'to praise' (Piel also rarely in the Qal with a meaning 'to be boastful'). The use of the Piel is found extensively in the OT with reference to Yahweh. However, for the Piel use 'to praise' in names, the theophoric element would need to be the object, not the subject of the name (cf. *IPN*, 205). However, see also below, p. 136, where the possibility of the deity as subject in the name *y^ehalel'ēl* is discussed further. BDB, 239, cite a noun *mahălāl* which is attested only once (Prov. 27.1) and interpret *mahălal'ēl* as a construct form, 'Praise of God'. This is semantically unlikely in view of the nature of construct type names which usually express the name-bearer as a subordinate of the deity, or depict some divine aspect (cf. above, § 2.6). The alternative is a Hiphil part. of the root *hll*, 'El shines forth', cf. Geh, 580, *IPN*, 31, 169 (205).

m^eḥûyā'ēl, *m^eḥîyâ'ēl* BH. Of the two etymologies possible for this name, the root *mḥh* with the meaning 'to strike', makes little sense. A Piel or Hiphil part. of the verb *ḥyh* 'to live', as suggested by KB, 538, however, renders a meaning 'El gives life', although the form remains obscure.

m^ehêṭab'ēl BH. The Aram. root *yṭb*, 'to be good, well, glad, pleasing', occurs in the part. element *mêṭîb* with the addition of Heb. *'l*, suggesting a meaning 'El benefits', cf. BDB, 406, Geh, 605. Retention of the *h* is a common feature of Aram., cf. A.R. Millard, *ZAW* 86 (1974), 15.

m^ešêzab'ēl BH. This name, which can be interpreted as 'El delivers', contains Aram. *šêzêb*, itself a loan-word from Akk. cf. *^dAdad-mu-še-zi-ib* and *^dŠamaš-mu-še-zi-ib* (Stamm, 221). Cf. also BDB, 604, KB, 609, Geh, 612, *IPN*, 31, 156.

m^ešelemyāh(û) BH. 'Y recompenses', cf. Geh, 612, KB, 613, *IPN*, 145. The idea of recompense may well be that of the substitution of a newly born child for a previously deceased one.

3. *Prepositions*

A small group of names contains prepositional elements. Such names frequently tend to express relationship between the name-bearer and the deity. In those names which have the prepostion *b^e* as the initial element, the second element is always placed in construct with the following theophoric noun, e.g. BH *b^eṣal'ēl* 'In the shadow (protection) of El'. (For names of this type, see above, § 2.6.) Other prepositional elements do not belong in the category of construct forms. The preposition 'with' is expressed in two names:

'itî'ēl BH. This name means 'God is with me', cf. BDB, 87, Geh, 434, and the Phoen. name (')TB'L, *PNPPI*, 223. Similar Akk. names are usually three-part, cf. *Itti-^dNabû-nuḫḫu*, translated by Stamm (Stamm, 230-31) as 'Bei Nabû ist das Beruhigen (des Zornes)' etc. Also relevant may be the name *'t'b* (seal V, 444), for which see below, § 2.9.

'immānû'ēl BH. This name, which means 'God is with us', cf. BDB, 769, Geh, 419, *IPN*, 33, is used only symbolically in Isa. 7.14; 8.8, 10 etc.

Two names have the preposition *l*[e] 'to' or 'belonging to' as their initial element. These are:

lā'ēl BH. A meaning 'Belonging to El' is widely accepted, cf. BDB, 522, KB, 488, Geh, 547, *IPN*, 153. Parallels also occur in Palm. LŠMŠ, LMLK' 'Belonging to Šamaš/Malka' (cf. Stark, 93), and Amor. *La-na-*^{d}*Da-gan* etc. (*APNM*, 223).

l[e]*mû'ēl*, *l*[e]*mô'ēl* BH. It is possible that *lmw* is a poetical form of *l*[e], cf. Prov. 31.1 and BDB, 541. This would suggest a meaning 'Belonging to El', cf. Geh, 556, KB, 505, *IPN*, 249 (= *lā'ēl*?). Note also the possibility of a construct form, above, § 2.7.

The placing of a preposition before the theophoric element has made the following two names unique in the Hebrew onomasticon. The middle element *yhwh*, nevertheless, occurs in both its usual forms of *yhw* and *yw*:

'ely[e]*hô'ênay*, *'elyô'ênay* BH. These names, which can be interpreted as 'Towards Y are my eyes', cf. BDB, 41, Geh, 260, KB, 53, are reflected in Akk. *Itti-*^{d}*Nusku-īnāya* translated by Stamm as 'Auf Nusku (ruhen; sind gerichtet) meine Augen' (Stamm, 230).

The preposition *k*[e] 'like', does not occur independently in Hebrew names; rather, it is found as a second element after the interrogative *my*, as the following illustrate.

4. *Interrogatives*

With one exception, the only interrogative attested in Hebrew theophoric compounds is *my*, 'Who?', which forms the first element of names of the pattern *my* + *k* + *'l* or *yh*(*w*), and various abbreviated forms arising from this pattern. Names of this type are: BH *mîkāyāh*(*û*), *mîkāy*[e]*hû*, and *mîkā'ēl* 'Who is like Y/El?', cf. BDB, 567-68, KB, 545-46, Geh, 614, 617. The name *mykyhw* also occurs extra-biblically on seals (V, 30; BL, 49 no. 10) and in two inscr. (L 11.3 cf. *IH*, 128; N. Avigad, *RB* 80 [1973], 579). The name *mîšā'ēl* (BH) 'who is as El?', cf. BDB, 567, KB, 547, Geh, 624, containing the element *ša* instead of *k*[e], reflects Akk. influence. Numerous parallels exist for these names elsewhere, particularly in Akk. (cf. Stamm, 341) and Palm. (cf. Stark, 94-95). Cf. also the ^{I}*man-nu-ki-i-la-ḫi-i* (probably *man-ki-'ilāhi*, 'Who is like my god?'), an Aram. name from the

Murašû Documents (cf. Coogan, 76). The seal *rpṭy yhw/k'l* (F.J. Bliss, *PEFQS* 31 [1899], 198) doubtfully contains the preposition *k*[e] in the second name. Bliss favoured a reading *yhw'l*.

5. *Pronominal Elements*

Another group of Hebrew names is characterized by a compound consisting of a pronominal element and a theophoric element. In such names the pronoun is likely to be the subject of the sentence, placing the divine element in the category of a predicate. Only one such pronominal element is attested, the third person masculine singular *hû'*. Instances of the use of *hû'* occur only in biblical Hebrew, in the names:

'ĕlîhû', *'ĕlîhû* 'He is God', cf. BDB, 45, Geh, 261. The reverse order, 'God is he', is preferred by KB, 53 and *IPN*, 18. Cf. also Ug. *hwil*, 'He is (my) god', *PTU*, 134.

yēhû' A probable contraction from *y(*[e]*h)ôhû'* 'He is Y', cf. KB, 376. A reverse order, 'Y is he', is suggested by BDB, 219, Geh, 454, *IPN*, 143.

'ăbîhû' 'He is (divine) Father', cf. BDB, 4, KB, 4. The order 'A Father is he', is preferred by Geh, 5 and, questioningly, by Noth (*IPN*, 18).

These three names are of considerable interest from the point of view of word order. Not only does the word order given by BDB, Geh and KB differ for each name, but these works are inconsistent in themselves. This indicates the impossibility of dictating a specific subject-predicate or predicate-subject word order for these names and for similar compounds like *'ăbî'ēl* and *'ĕlî'āb* etc. Compare, for example, the translation by BDB of *'ĕlîhû'* as 'He is (my) God', *yēhû'* as 'Y is he', and *'ăbîhû'* 'He is father'. Only Noth retained the first element in the initial position in translation, although there is no convincing evidence to suggest that the first element was necessarily the subject; cf. further, p. 171 n. 18 and p. 83.

Noth (*IPN*, 143) suggested that names of the above type imply an earlier idea of the existence of more than one deity. In this case, these names would have represented a statement by the name-bearer, and therefore the name-giver, in favour of the worship of El or Yahweh as opposed to any other deity. Noth further suggested that such names later came to represent a declaration of Yahweh as the only eixistent and true God. While this second suggestion of Noth's is certainly tenable, the former assumption rests entirely on an early date for these names which is not substantiated. Indeed, the only early name is *'ăbîhû'* which describes the deity (as being like a divine Father) in a totally different way.

Other occurrences of pronominal elements are as suffixes of a predicate. As such, they occur after a preposition as in *'îtî'ēl*, 'El is with me' and *'immānû'ēl*, 'God is with us' noted above and also after a verb in the name:

'ĕlîpᵉlēhû BH. The name is usually interpreted as 'May El distinguish him', cf. BDB, 45, Geh, 263, although the form is difficult. KB, 54 suggest a Qal form instead of a Hiphil of *plh*, 'El has distinguished him'. An imv. with a suffix suggested in *IPN*, 32 n. 2 seems unlikely. See also above, § 2.4 and below, § 2.9.

The first person plural suffix on a noun may be evident in the name:

mrnyw EB. (Inscr. SO 42.3 cf. *SSI*, 10, 12) 'Y is our Lord' or 'Our Lord is Y'. Cf. also Dir, 47 no. 31, *IPN*, 143 n. 2. Also possible, however, is a derivation of the first element from a root *mrr*, attested in Ug. with the meaning 'to strengthen, bless, commend' (*UT Glossary*, 438, 1556). The name would then mean 'Y has strengthened, blessed, commended me'. Cf. also Lemaire (*IH*, 35) who reads *Adonyaw* for this name.

It is also possible that in a few cases, a first person singular verbal suffix is attested. This was suggested some time ago by A. Reifenberg (*PEQ* [1942], 111) in remarks concerning the name:

hglnyh EB. (Seal V, 161). A meaning 'Y exiled me' (a Hiphil of the root *glh*) seems likely in this name. What is interesting about such an interpretation is the possibility of the same suffix on other verbally compounded names:

ḥăšabnᵉyāh BH. Most suggest a possible meaning 'Y has taken account of me', from the Heb. root *ḥšb* 'to think, account', with the addition of the 1st pers. sing. suffix *n*. Although Noth contested the existence of such a suffix on verbal name forms (cf. *IPN*, 189), there seems to be no apparent reason for rejecting it here.

ḥăšabnāh BH. The name is probably a sf. of the foregoing, cf. KB, 347, Geh, 367. An acceptance of the verbal suffix makes it unlikely that this name is simply erroneous for BH *ḥăšabyāh(û)* as *BDB*, 364 suggest.

šᵉbanyāh(û) BH. This name occurs also on numerous seals and inscriptions (see below, Appendix 3) and was obviously a widely used name. A root *šbn*, however, is not attested in BH or in any cognate language. A number of possibilities can be suggested:
1. The addition of a 1st pers. sing. verbal suffix suggested by A. Reifenberg

(*loc. cit.*).This would involve a root *šbh* 'to take captive', or a root *šwb* 'to return'. The meaning would then be 'Y has taken me captive', or 'Y has returned to me'.
2. An imv. of the root *šwb* 'Return O Y', cf. Geh, 860, and Amor. *šu-ub*^d^IM/-*na*-AN/-*na-lu-ú* where the *-na* is probably 'a precative particle serving to make the command more polite' (*APNM*, 86).
3. The first consonant may represent an archaic causative with the root *bnh* suggesting 'Whom Y has made to grow up'. This meaning, but with no mention of the causative, was suggested by Gesenius: cited by F.J. Bliss in *PEFQS* 32 (1900), 338f. However, some suggest that Heb. has no certain trace of the causative with *š* (Th. Noldeke, *CSL*, 4 and G.R. Driver, *CSL*, 16), although C. Rabin has suggested that since personal names may retain obsolete grammatical features, there is a possibility that the causative is retained, particularly with weak roots (*CSL*, 93).
4. The vocalization of the name appears to be a straightforward Qal perf. and the frequency with which this is retained in the names may suggest a root *šbn*, the meaning of which is no longer extant (cf. *IPN*, 258).

'otnî'ēl BH. The meaning of the first element in this name is entirely unknown. The nearest possible cognate is Arab. *'atā*, 'to be proud, exalted'. The addition of a Heb. 1st pers. sing. verbal suffix would suggest an interpretation 'El has exalted me' or 'El has made me proud' (by bestowing a child?), although a transitive interpretation for the Heb. is problematic.

ḥăbaṣṣinyāh BH. The meaning of the first element is perhaps suggested by Akk. *ḫabāṣu* 'to cause to increase, to be happy', cf. KB, 275. The addition of the verbal suffix suggests 'Y has made me happy' as the meaning of the name, although the form remains difficult, in view of the intransitive nature of the Akk. verb, cf. above, § 2.4.

Less problematic is perhaps the name:

'šnyhw EB. (Seal V, 125), also *'šn'l* (V, 88). These names are probably from the root *'wš* 'to lend aid, come to help', with the addition of the 1st pers. sing. verbal suffix, suggesting a meaning 'Y/El has helped me'.

2.9 *Difficult Forms*

Many of the theophoric names which occur in biblical Hebrew present difficulty with regard to their form or semantic content. Those which are mainly excluded elsewhere in this work as manifesting such difficulties are presented here, and an attempt has been made to elucidate some of these more difficult forms, by grouping them together according to type.

An outstanding group of such names, with the pattern *q^{e}ṭûēl* has been dealt with elsewhere (see above, § 2.7). Another type of form, also mainly suffixed with *'l*, is found in *qaṭlî'ēl* types: such names are fairly numerous and, thus, the form of some can be determined. This is the case with the name *'abdî'ēl* which, since a nominal or verbal interpretation is nonsensical when applied to the deity, can be nothing other than a construct form of the root *'bd* 'to serve', with the addition of the theophoric element *'l*, resulting in a meaning 'Servant of El'. Equally certain, however, is a nominal interpretation of a *qaṭli'ēl* form in a name like *malkî'ēl* which can only mean 'El is (my) King'. The element *malkî-* is the only one occurring in the pattern *qaṭlî* which occurs with a theophoric element other than *'l*, i.e. *malkîyāh*(*û*), as well as occurring as a theophoric element itself cf. *malkîšû^{a}'* and *malkîrām*. The question of the pronominal suffix in such names will be discussed below. At this point, it may be well to look at the names involved in the present discussion to discover whether a nominal, genitive or verbal predominance exists in these *qaṭlî'ēl* forms.

'aśrî'ēl. The root *'śr* is not found in BH, but an Arab. cognate *'ašr* 'to fill with joy' may be relevant. Noth (*IPN*, 167) suggested from this same Arab. root, a noun *'ašrun*, meaning 'rejoicing joy'. The interpretation of the name would then be 'El is rejoicing joy', a nominal sentence name. However, a construct form 'Rejoicing joy of El' is also semantically possible.

gabrî'ēl. The root *gbr* in BH means 'to be strong, mighty', from which the noun *geber* 'man' is derived. BDB, 150 and KB, 169 favour a construct form with an interpretation 'Man of God', while Geh, 309 and *IPN*, 36, 190, prefer a verbal translation 'God has shown himself mighty'. Noth's argument that the form is verbal as opposed to construct, was based on the unconvincing parallel cuneiform forms *Na-tan-ni-El*(UM) and *Na-tan-El* (BE IX). That the vowel *ī* occurs as a terminating sound for the first element of a verbally prefixed name is not disputed, but there is no evidence to suggest that in *qaṭlîēl* forms, with which we are dealing, the *ī* vowel has the same significance. It is impossible for this *ī* vowel to indicate conclusively a perfective form as Noth suggested (*IPN*, 36) since a verbal interpretation is not permissible for names such as *'abdî'ēl.*

gamlî'ēl. BDB, 168 suggest a construct form 'Reward of God', while KB, 190 and *IPN*, 182 prefer a verbal form, 'God has shown himself good'. Geh, 315 also prefers a verbal interpretation 'God has accomplished, rewarded'.

zabdî'ēl. In this case, Noth (*IPN*, 33) favoured a construct form 'Gift of God', suggesting that the *ī* vowel is a survival of an old case ending. BDB,

256, however, suggest a nominal form, 'My gift is God', the *ī* vowel being a pronominal suffix. Geh, 1010 proposes a verbal form 'El/God has given'.

magdî'ēl. The meaning of the root *mgd* can be determined from Arab. *majada* 'to be glorious, excel in glory'. The root is not used in BH in verbal form, but a noun *meged* exists meaning 'excellence', which is always used of the gifts of nature. Nevertheless, the interpretation by KB, 516 as 'Gift of God' seems unlikely since we have no evidence of the use of the noun specifically to mean 'gift'. A nominal form, 'El is excellence' suggested by Geh, 579, seems more probable, although a verbal interpretation, 'El is excellent', is also possible.

malkî'ēl. A nominal sentence name 'El is King' is accepted by BDB, 575, KB, 561, Geh, 582 and *IPN*, 36, although BDB seem to imply a use of the middle vowel *ī* as a pronominal suffix in their interpretation 'My king is El'.

malkîyāh(*û*). A meaning 'My king is Y', is suggested by BDB, 575, and 'Y is king', by KB, 561, Geh, 582 and *IPN*, 16, 141. Cf. also Phoen. MLKṢD 'Sid is (my?) king', *PNPPI*, 222.

'abdî'ēl. An interpretation 'Servant of El' is widely accepted, cf. BDB, 715, KB, (1953), 673, Geh, 2, *IPN*, 137. In this name Noth considered the long vowel *ī* to be a survival of the old genitive case ending.

'adrî'ēl. The root *'dr* is Aram., but the name may be Heb. (see below, § 4.4 *'dr*. Most accept a nominal interpretation 'El is help', cf. Geh, 18, KB, (1953), 685. Again, BDB, 727 seem to accept the *ī* as a pronominal suffix since they interpret the name as 'My help is God'. There is no semantic reason why the name could not be given a verbal interpretation.

'azrî'ēl. KB (1953), 697 and Geh, 82 interpret the name as nominal, 'El is help'. Again, BDB, 741 see the intermediate *ī* as a pronominal suffix, and suggest a meaning 'My help is El'. Noth (*IPN*, 18, 154) recorded the name as verbal, 'God has helped'. It is noticeable that all second position occurrences of *'zr* are nominal (see above, p. 79) which may favour a verbal or construct form for this first position predicate.

pag'î'ēl. The Heb. root *pg'* means 'to meet, encounter' in the Qal and 'to cause to entreat, make entreaty' in the Hiphil. Geh, 691 suggests an interpretation 'God has entreated', or 'God has met'. Noth (*IPN*, 16, 254) suggested a nominal or perf. form.

palṭî'ēl. A nominal form from the root *plṭ* 'to escape' (Piel 'to deliver') is suggested by *IPN*, 38 n. 1, 156, i.e. 'El is salvation'. Geh, 698 suggests a verbal form, 'El has delivered'.

qadmî'ēl. The root *qdm* means 'to be before, in front' and the same root is also present in the S. Arab. names *Ḳadam'il* and *'Ilḳadam*, 'El is preponderant’ (cf. Geh, 532). A verbal translation is suggested by Geh, 532, ‘God goes before, leads’, and a nominal interpretation by BDB, 870 ‘El is the Ancient One’. Noth remained undecided between a verbal perf. and a nominal form (*IPN*, 256).

šaltî’ēl. The root *š’l*, which means ‘to ask, inquire’, would suggest a construct form as probable for this name, ‘Asked of El’. The similar name *š^{e}’altî’ēl* is usually interpreted ‘I have asked of God’, cf. BDB, 982, Geh, 859.

yatnî’ēl. In view of the above names, it is possible that this name is from the root *ytn*, the meaning of which can be determined by an Arab. cognate *watana* meaning ‘to be perpetual, never-failing’ (cf. BDB, 450). Geh, 448, therefore, suggests an interpretation ‘God is constant’. In BH the root does not occur in verbal form and only the adj. *’êtān*, *’ētān* is extant. Whether the form in the name is verbal or nominal is not determinable. Another possibility is an imf. of the root *tnh* ‘to hire’, as BDB, 1072 suggest, with a verbal interpretation ‘El hires’. KB, 430 suggest the Phoen. root *ytn* corresponding to Heb. *ntn* (cf. *PNPPI*, 192, 328ff.).

With the name *yatnî’ēl*, the problem of a *qaṭlî’ēl* or *yaqṭî’ēl* form is not able to be solved. With other *yaqṭî’ēl* forms, the choice is less problematic, and with one group of names of this type we are able to designate the forms as Qal imperfectives of III *hē* verbs. Such names are:

yaḥdî’ēl	root *ḥdh* ‘to rejoice’	‘El gives joy’.
ya‘ăzî’ēl/ *ya‘ăzîyāhû*	root *‘zh* cf. Arab. *ghadhā* ‘to nourish’	‘May El/Y nourish’ (or ‘El/Y nourishes’).
yaḥṣî’ēl	root *ḥṣh* ‘to divide’	‘El divides, apportions’.
yaḥăzî’ēl	root *ḥzh* ‘to see’	‘El sees’.
ya‘ăśî’ēl	root *‘śh* ‘to make, do’	‘El makes’.

What is noticeable about the above list is the predominance of *’l* suffixes, which suggests that the intermediate *yōd* may have been an early phenomenon in this type of name. More important here, however, is the point that in these verbal *yaqṭî’ēl* forms, the intermediate *yōd* cannot be consistently indicative of a construct form, a pronominal suffix, or the survival of an old case ending. With some justification, therefore, we may contend that the *yōd* in similar *qaṭlî’ēl* names is not representative of any particular form whether nominal, verbal, construct, or pronominal, but may have been merely a terminal sound added to the first element in a theophoric compound name. This would then partly explain the difficulty of assigning *qaṭlî’ēl* names to any one category of nominal, verbal or construct type forms. The addition of this long vowel to the first syllable has perhaps caused changes in the vocalization of the first element so that its original nominal or verbal form is not clearly discernible, and only by semantic content can we occasionally assess the possible meaning of a name. The lack of a specific function for the intermediate *yōd* is exemplified further in the parallel forms in which it is absent. Thus we find, for example, *yaḥṣî'ēl* (1 Chr. 7.13) and *yaḥṣ*^{e}*'ēl*, (Gen. 46.24; Num. 26.48) two forms of the name given to the son of Naphtali, and the names *'abdî'ēl* (1 Chr. 5.15) and *'abd*^{e}*'ēl* (Jer. 36.26), although referring to different persons, are probably identical in form.

In all probability, this intermediate *yōd* is also to be found in nominal sentence names, particularly where the theophoric element is in the initial position. Numerous such examples are found, cf. *'ĕlî'āb*, *'ûrî'ēl*, *'ăbîhûd* etc. Similarly in verbal forms the same phenomenon exists, cf. *'ĕlî'ātāh*, *'ăbî'āsāp*, etc. While it is possible that in *some* cases a pronominal element may be involved, there are no criteria which would ascertain such cases, and we are not at liberty to assign pronominal suffixes at will.

To conclude, most of the names of the type *qaṭlî'ēl* must remain enigmatic, although we may with some certainty assign *malkî'ēl* and *malkîyāh(û)* to a nominal category and designate *'abdî'ēl* as a construct form.

Other names presenting difficulty either in form or in semantic content have been divided into two main groups, those in which the problematic non-theophoric element is prefixed, and those in which it is suffixed. Of the first group of prefixed elements, we find a small group of names which appear to be Qal perfective in form, but which are semantically perplexing. These are:

'ăśar'ēlāh. As in *'ăśar'ēl* (see above, § 2.4), the first element of this name is probably a Qal perf. possibly of the root *'sr* 'to bind', or could be related to Arab. *'aširа* 'to fill with joy'. No satisfactory reason for the terminating *-āh* seems evident. The name appears in a more dubious form, *y*^{e}*śar'ēlāh*, in 1 Chr. 25.14, with reference to the same son of Asaph.

r^{e}*malyāhû*. The root *rml* is not attested in BH, although BDB, 942 cite the name under a root *rml* meanng 'to adorn with gems', suggested by an Arab. cognate *ramala*. KB (1953), 894 also retain the root *rml*. The possibility of a root *rwm* with the addition of the vocative particle *l*, has been suggested by W.L. Moran. ('The Hebrew Language in its Northwest Semitic Background', *The Bible and the Ancient Near East*, ed.G.E. Wright, Doubleday (1961), 60-

61). This would inidcate a meaning 'Be exalted O Y'. The vocalization of the name may be very old, and the rendering of LXX as Πομελιου (2 Kgs 15.25, 27, 30, 32, 37; 16.1, 5; Isa. 7.1, 4, 5, 9; 8.6), and Πομελια (2 Chr. 28.6), may support the root *rwm*. However, note that LXX is not always indicative of form, cf. Barr *Cp. Ph.*, 267-69, 208-209, 261-62. The name is also found on two seals (V, 19, 60; for V, 19 Herr, 144 no. 51 reads *dmlyhw*, as, also, B. Porten, *IEJ* 21 [1971], 48).

m^e^rāyāh. The form of the initial element appears to be a Qal perf. of a root *mrh* or *mrr*. In BH the root *mrh* means 'to be contentious, refractory, rebellious', which is semantically difficult with reference to the deity. Most consider the name to mean 'obstinate', cf. KB, 600, Geh, 608, *IPN*, 250. However, the root *mrr* in Ug. means 'to strengthen, bless, commend' (*UT Glossary*, 438). The root can also mean 'strong' as well as 'bitter' (*ibid.*, and *PTU*, 160). This may suggest a meaning 'Y has strengthened or blessed (or commended)', or 'Y is strong, mighty, powerful'. See also above, § 2.4.

'ătalyāh(û). This name is very dubious: most connect the initial element with Akk. *etlu* 'great, lofty', suggesting a meaning 'Y is exalted', cf. BDB, 800, Geh, 77, *IPN*, 191. The connection, however, is tenuous, since the Akk. cognate is *eṭelu* and would imply a root *'ṭl*.

A number of prolematic names occur with imperfective forms as the first element of the name:

y^e^halel'ēl. Like the participial form in *mahălal'ēl* (see above, § 2.8.2) this name presents difficulties in that it is doubtful whether the theophoric element can be anything other than the subject in the name. The root *hll* can be used with a meaning 'to praise' or 'to shine', the former interpretation presenting semantic difficulties unless the theophoric element is made the object of the verb. Thus, BDB, 239 interpret the name as 'He shall praise God'. Noth (*IPN*, 205) preferred a Hiphil of the root *hll*, 'May El light up' or 'May El cause to shine'. The use of the Hiphil, however, seems precarious, since the form seems so obviously Piel. Indeed, the interpretations of KB, 380 as 'El leuchtet auf' and Geh, 450 with 'God will flash forth light', do not contain any causative nuance of meaning. If the Piel form is retained, extant Heb. forms indicate that it is more likely to be used with the meaning 'to praise', while the Hiphil is confined only to the meaning 'to shine'. It may well be, since this name is an early one, that the deity could have been the subject of the verb 'to praise', at an earlier time. If this is the case the meaning of the name would be 'May El praise (i.e. the child)'.

y^e^šôḥāyāh. No suitable form or meaning can be established for this name. A root *šḥḥ* means 'to bow, be bowed down, crouch', while *šḥh* also has the meaning 'to bow down'. The root *šû^a^ḥ* means 'to sink down', but all three roots are semantically difficult when the subject of the name is the deity.

yārob'ām. Both elements in this name present problems: a root *ryb* for the first element, 'The kinsman (or the people) contends', is formally difficult, while a root *rbb* meaning 'to be or become many, much', would indicate a meaning 'May the people become many'. Only if a causative theme could be justified with the root *rbb*, could the second element possibly be theophoric, 'May the (divine) Kinsman (cause to) increase'. With this same root, Geh, 462 suggests as a possible meaning 'May the people become numerous', but prefers a meaning 'The (divine) Kinsman is great'. Perhaps this interpretation follows *IPN*, 206, where Noth cites the use of the root *rbb* in Aram. and Arab. with the meaning 'to be great'. If this is the case, then the second element is justifiably theophoric and the first element a possible Qal imf. of this root. The name *yrb'm* is also attested extra-biblically (seal V, 68; inscr. Hazor B cf. *SSI*, 19.

yorq^e'ām. This name, which KB, 421 and *IPN*, 247 consider as a place name, may be from a root *rq'* meaning 'to beat, stamp, beat out, spread out', or from the root *yrq* meaning 'to grow green, pale'. Neither supplies an interpretation which is satisfactory semantically. Perhaps we should not exclude the possibility of a root *ryq* which is attested in BH only in the Hiphil, with a meaning 'to make empty, empty out'. The form and meaning, however, remain obscure.

y^{e}zî'ēl, *y^{e}zaw'ēl*. A root *yzh* is not attested in BH: a dagheshed *zayin* might suggest a root *nzh* 'to spurt, spatter', Hiphil 'to sprinkle', in which case the name would be interpreted 'El has sprinkled' (in the sense of purified), and would be comparable to the name *yizzîyāh* (Ezra 10.25). Otherwise, it must remain inconclusive.

A small group of names with the form *qaṭalyāh*, and in one case *'elqaṭal*, presents some difficulty with regard to form. These names are:

ma'azyāh. A root *m'z* is not attested in BH, but a noun *mā'ôz*, 'a place or means of safety, protection', from the root *'wz* 'to take or seek refuge' (cf. BDB, 731), may indicate a meaning 'Y is a refuge as Geh, 575, KB, 578, and *IPN*, 157 suggest.

ma'adyāh. This name, given to a priest of Zerubbabel's time in Neh. 12.5, is found in the form *mô'adyāh* in v. 17. On the basis of the above form *ma'azyāh*, we might suggest a noun from the denom. root *'wd* meaning 'to bear witness', although a noun corresponding to the first element does not exist. The root *'dh* meaning 'to ornament, deck oneself', has suggested to KB, 576 a meaning 'Ornament of Y'. Geh, 574 cites an Arab. cognate *wa'ada*, 'to promise' and interprets the name as 'Y promises'. The alternative form *mô'adyāh* may also suggest a root *y'd*, 'to appoint', from which is derived the n. m. *mô'ēd* 'appointed time, place, meeting'. On the other hand, BDB, 588 cite the name under a root *m'd* 'to slip, slide, totter, shake' which makes little sense semantically when applied to the deity. The variety of possibilities put forward by scholars reflects the difficulty and uncertainty in ascribing any exact meaning and form to the name.

ra'amyāh. The root *r'm* means 'to move violently' and the denom. verb *rā'am*, 'to thunder'. A noun *ra'am* also exists with the meaning 'thunder', and when attributed to Yahweh can be used figuratively of his display of might (cf. BDB, 947 and Job 26.14 [construct]). A meaning 'Thunder of Y' is suggested by BDB, 947 and a verbal interpretation, 'Y has thundered', by Geh, 788.

Perhaps to be included here is an *'elqaṭal* form in the name:

'elpa'al. The verb *p'l* means 'to do, make', and is usually employed as a poetical alternative to the verb *'śh*. The noun *pō'al* means 'doing, deed, work', although the suffixed position of the name-element makes a construct form impossible and a nominal form is semantically improbable as a divine attribute. KB, 58, Geh, 265 and *IPN*, 172 all suggest a verbal interpretation 'God has made or wrought'. Noth, in particular, emended to a Qal perf., *'elpā'āl*.

Other prefixed non-theophoric forms presenting difficulty indicate little regularity in form, and frequently must remain inconclusive. These are:

kil'āb. The name is very dubious: KB, 453 suggest *kol-'āb* 'All the Father', a semantically improbable name with no similar type in the Heb. onomasticon. A verbal form of the root *kll* 'to be complete, perfect' would be more suitable semantically, but the form remains obscure.

ḥăzī'ēl. In view of the intermediate *ī*, Noth (*IPN*, 27 n. 1) considered this form to be a sf. of *yaḥzī'ēl* since, he claimed, an archaic *ī* is often found at the end of III *hē* imfs. when followed by a noun. While this latter fact is certainly true, this intermediate *yōd* is also a feature of nominal, construct and perfective forms as indicated above (pp. 134f.), so that it is quite erroneous to claim that the presence of the vowel *ī* is evidence of a III *hē* imf. A construct form, 'Vision of El', is suggested by BDB, 303 but the form remains unclear.

ḥammû'ēl. For this obscure name, Geh, 360 compares the S. Arab. name *Ḥamay'il*, 'God protects'. This root *ḥmh* is not found in verbal form in BH and nouns derived from the root, *ḥām* 'husband's father' and *ḥômāh* 'wall', do not clarify the form. The root *ḥmm* which means 'to be or become warm' provides little help. Geh, 360 also suggests the n. pr. div. *Hammu* and the meaning 'Hammu is god'.

baqbuqyāh. The noun *baqbuq* from a root *bqq* 'to empty', means 'flask', which makes little sense with the addition of the theophoric element. Most consider the name to mean simply 'flask', cf. Geh, 90, *IPN*, 105, 226. An alternative meaning of the root *bqq* 'to be luxuriant', although semantically viable, is only attested once in BH (cf. BDB, 132).

ḥarḥăyāh. A root *ḥrḥ* does not exist in BH although a root *ḥrh* is evident, meaning 'to burn, be kindled (of anger)', cf. BDB, 354. Neither root suffices to elucidate this form.

pûṭî'ēl. The initial element in this name is generally considered to be Eg. Most suggest a meaning 'He whom God has given', cf. BDB, 806, Geh, 783, KB (1953), 754. The name *pṭyhw* occurs on an inscr. from En-gedi (*EAEHL*, II, 374).

qûšāyāhû. Akk. *qāšu* 'to present, give a gift', may suggest a meaning for the first element of this name, as Geh, 545 and KB, (1953), 834 note. More precarious, is the suggestion of J.R. Bartlett ('The Moabites and Edomites', *People of Old Testament Times*, OUP [1973], 245) that the first element is the Edom. deity Qaus.

rᵉ'ēlāyāh. No certain meaning can be established for this name. The root *r'l* means 'to quiver, shake, reel', which has suggested to Geh, 795 the possible meaning 'Y has shaken'. A parallel form *ra'amyāh* (see above) in Neh. 7.7, referring to the same person, is perplexing, although semantically similar.

śākᵉyāh (LXX *śobyāh*). This name seems totally obscure: LXX reading with a *b*, suggests to Geh, 816 a meaning 'Y is fullness' or 'Y has hedged about', although no suggestion as to the etymology is given. The root *śkh* can be explained, tentatively, by NH *skh* 'to look out'. Neither Gehman's nor Noth's suggestion ('umzäunt, umhegt hat Jahwe' *IPN*, 178) seems tenable. A further proposal, 'foreseer' or 'watchkeeper', has been put forward by Lipiński, 74.

šērēbyāh. A meaning 'Y has sent burning heat' has been suggested by BDB, 1055-56, and one can compare Akk. *Išribijāma* (*BEUP*, 10, 53). As Noth (*IPN*, 259) suggested, the form may be a Piel perf.

yôšawyāh. This name is quite problematic. The root *yšh*, which BDB, 444 interpret from a dubious Arab. cognate *'asa'* with a meaning 'to assist, to support', seems possible. KB, 386 suggest a corruption of *yôšabyāh*.

Problematic names whose non-theophoric elements occur in the second position fall into three main groups, those which have a non-theophoric element as *CaC*, those which have *CāC*, and a small group which has irregular forms. The difficulty presented by the first two groups is often a choice between a Hollow or Geminate derivation. Of the type *CaC*, three names occur:

'ĕlîpaz. The root *pzz* in BH, meaning 'to be refined' and extant only in the Hophal, may suggest a meaning 'El is fine gold' (BDB, 45). However, an Arab. cognate *fauz* meaning 'victory' is cited by KB, 54 and Geh, 262, to suggest a meaning 'El is victorious'.

'ăbîšag. The root *šgg* 'to go astray, commit sin, error', seems semantically improbable for the second element of this name unless the first element is non-theophoric. However, BDB, 4 translate 'My father is a wanderer' from the same root. The suggestion of Geh, 6, that the second element may be Sumer. *šag*, 'heart' producing a meaning 'The Father is love, is merciful', seems untenable, since very few Sumer. words passed into Heb.

'ăḥîman. A derivation of the second element from the root *mnh* seems unlikely, since a verbal translation of this root with a meaning 'to count, number, reckon, assign', would normally involve a retention of the final *hē* when the verbal element is in second position (see above, § 2.5). Neither can a suitable noun be found from the same root. Lidzbarski's suggestion (*Eph*, 18) of a sf. of *'ăḥîma'aṣ*, or similar, seems precarious. BDB, 27 propose, questioningly, 'My brother is a gift', suggested by an Arab. cognate *man*. However, the alternative form *'ăḥimān* in Josh. 15.14, referring to the same son of Anak, termed *'ăḥîman* in Num. 13.22 and Judg. 1.10, may endorse a Qal perf. of a Hollow or Geminate root (cf. below, and above, § 2.5). A Hollow root *mwn* does not exist in BH, but a root *mnn* could possibly have been the original root of the name although extant uses are rare, and it is problematic to discover an original meaning: BDB, 585 suggest 'to be bounteous' or 'to be separate'.

Those names whose second position, non-theophoric element is of the type *CāC* are numerous in biblical Hebrew. By grouping names of this type together, it is possible to see immediately the advantage of comparing difficult names with others of the same formal pattern *in the same onomasticon*. While comparisons with cognate languages play an important part in helping to determine the meaning of a problematic Hebrew name, such methods should fall secondary to any clarification which may be gained from the Hebrew onomasticon itself. Taken individually, the following names of the type *CāC* defy clarification. Taken as a group, however, many can be seen to display a regularity of form which has hitherto remained unnoticed. It is possible to find many names of such types which are non-problematic and which indicate certain forms; thus we find from Hollow roots:

'ăḥîqām	a Qal perf. of the root *qwm*
'ăḥîrām	a Qal perf. of the root *rwm*
'ăbîrām	a Qal perf. of the root *rwm*
*y*ᵉ*hôrām*	a Qal perf. of the root *rwm*
'amrām	a Qal perf. of the root *rwm*
yô'āš	a Qal perf. of the root *'wš*
'el'ād	a Qal perf. of the root *'wd*

Some are from Geminate roots:

yôtām	a Qal perf. of the root *tmm*
'ĕlîpāl	a Qal perf. of the root *pll*
'ăbîṭāl	a Qal perf. of the root *ṭll*[23]

From extra-biblical sources we may add, for example:

'lybr	root *brr* 'to purify, select'	seals V, 133, 397.[24]
yhw'z	root *'zz* 'to be strong'	seal V, 156; inscr. *AI*, 31.3; 49.7.
'l'z	root *'zz* 'to be strong'	seal V, 170 (possibly Ammon.).
'lyqm	root *qwm* 'to arise'	seals V, 93, 108, 242, 277, 436.
yhwqm	root *qwm* 'to arise'	seal V, 335, 336.
ywqm	root *qwm* 'to arise'	seal V, 38.
'ḥqm	root *qwm* 'to arise'	seals V, 210; P. Bordreuil, A. Lemaire, *Sem* 29 (1979), 74 no. 5.
'ḥyqm	root *qwm* 'to arise'	inscr. *AI*, 31.5.

With the evidence of these names in mind, an examination of those names of the same type which present formal or semantic difficulty, can now be undertaken.

'ăḥî'ām. The suggestions of Geh, 23 that the name may mean 'mother's brother', and that of KB, 32 that it is composed of *'ām* + *yām* seem unlikely. A root *'wm* or *'mm* is more than probable. The root *'wm* may be suggested by S. Arab. *'āma*, meaning 'to rule'; in this case, the form would be a Qal perf. and the name would mean 'The (divine) Brother has ruled'. On the other hand, a Qal perf. from the root *'mm*, the meaning of which may be suggested by Akk. *amāmu* 'to be wide, roomy', produces an interpretation 'The (divine) Brother has made wide' with which may be compared the semantically similar BH *r*ᵉ*ḥabyāh*, 'Y has made wide, or made room'. The name *'ḥy'm* also occurs on an inscr. A 35.3 cf. *IH*, 204. W. Kornfeld, *WZKM* 71 (1979), 46, prefers to see a n. pr. div. *y'm*/*ym* in the second element, but in view of the pointing of BH *'ăḥî'ām*, this seems to disregard, totally, the name pattern *'ăḥî*- so common in the Heb. onomasticon.

'ăḥîšār. KB, 33, following *IPN*, 189, have suggested the root *yšr* 'to be smooth, straight, right', for this name. BDB, 27 prefer the root *šyr* 'to sing' and suggest an interpretation 'My brother has sung', although the form of the second element is not that expected of a middle *yōd* verb, *šyr* in the Qal perf. However, a Qal perf. of the root *šwr* 'to behold, regard' would suggest a meaning 'The (divine) Brother has beheld or regarded', which seems both formally and semantically justifiable. Equally possible is a derivation of the name from a root *šrr*, cf. O. Aram. and Aram. 'to be firm, sound consistent'.

'ăbîdān. A choice between a nominal form and a verbal, classifies this name as a difficult form. BDB, 4 and Geh, 4 consider the name to be nominal, '(My) Father is a judge', while KB, 4 and *IPN*, 20 prefer a verbal form, '(My) Father has judged'. Since a noun *dān* 'judge' of the root *dyn* does not exist in BH (cf. BDB, 193), while the form of the name conforms to other types from Hollow roots, a Qal perf. seems quite in order.

'ĕlîdād, 'eldād. These names are probably derived from the root *dwd* meaning 'to swing, rock, dandle, fondle, love', although the root is not attested in verbal form (cf. BDB, 187). Semantic comparisons in personal names are met frequently in Akk. (*APN*, 67, 278; Stamm, 242), Amor, (*APNM*, 181-82) and Ug. (*PTU*, 122) mostly, however, in nominal or construct forms and nearly always in the first position. Although verbal forms of the root *dwd* are not attested in BH, elsewhere, names of this type from Hollow roots are always Qal perf. in form. There seems no reason for suggesting otherwise for these names: a meaning 'El has loved' is, therefore, acceptable; cf. BDB, 44, Geh, 260, *IPN*, 183.

'ĕlîqā'. For the second element in this name, most suggest a contraction of *'ĕlîqām* 'El has arisen', cf. Geh, 262, KB, 54, and Lidzbarski, *Eph*, 7. R. Zadok, *ZAW* 89 (1977), 226 suggests 'If one disregards the vocalisation of the *y* of *'lyq'*, then the name can be interpreted as *'El-yaqa* "El has guarded", cf. NA [*A-bi*]-*ia-qa*'.

'ăḥîrā'. A Geminate root for this name would indicate a meaning 'My brother is evil' from the root *r''*, as BDB, 27 suggest. Geh, 24 and KB, 33 consider the second element as a noun 'friend', from the root *r'h*, although recognizing the uncertainty of such an etymology. Indeed, we have no other evidence to suggest that this III *hē* root can produce a form of this kind. Noth (*IPN*, 16) also suggested a nominal form but indicated no root or meaning. A Hollow root *rû*^{a}*'*, which is only found in derived conjugations in BH, with a meaning 'to raise a shout', or 'to give a blast', is less satisfactory semantically.

Similar names, but lacking the intermediate *yōd* between the first and second elements are:

'aḥbān. The name has been interpreted in a variety of ways. BDB, 26 suggest 'Brother of an intelligent one', from a root *byn* 'to discern'. Geh, 23, KB, 29 and *IPN*, 225 suggest an Arab. cognate *ḫābin* 'strong' in which case the name would probably be non-theophoric. KB, 29 also suggest the possibility of the root *bnh* 'to build' or 'to create', with which can be compared the Akk. name *Aḫi-bāni*, 'My Brother is creator' (*APN*, 14b). None of these suggestions offers convincing evidence for a particular derivation: The root *byn* does not produce a verbal form *bān*, and a noun of the same root is also formally unconvincing. III *hē* roots used as second position elements in names, occur regularly with the final *hē* retained (see above, § 2.5) while no noun from the root *bnh* suggests itself for the second element. We may be left, therefore, with the alternative of a non-theophoric name from Arab. *ḫābin* meaning 'strong', or 'The Brother is strong', but any conclusion remains tenuous.

'ăbîdā'. Since a Geminate or Hollow root derivation for the second part of this name cannot be found, the form presents difficulties. Most favour the root *yd'* 'to know', BDB, 4 suggesting a meaning 'My Father took knowledge', Geh, 4 'The Father knows', and KB, 4 'The Father has known'. This really involves a revocalization to *'ābyādā'* or *'ăbîyādā'*. The root *d'h* (cf. Arab. *da'ā* 'to call') would also be difficult since, as indicated for the previous name, all III *hē* verbs used in the second position retain the final *hē*. No convincing form or meaning can, therefore, be ascertained.

'aḥrāḥ. This name is generally accepted as a corruption of *'ăḥîrām*, cf. BDB, 31, Geh, 21, KB, 35, and *IPN*, 236, although why the second element should be derived from the root *rwm* none of these sources makes clear. On the analogy of many of the above names we should expect a Qal perf. of the root *rḥḥ* or *rwḥ*. While the former does not exist in BH, the latter does, although always in nominal form. The basic idea of the root *rûaḥ* is 'to breathe, blow'. In its nominal form it is frequently used of God giving the breath of life (cf. Zech. 12.1; Job 27.3; Gen. 6.3 etc.). A verbal form for this name may suggest a meaning such as 'The (divine) Brother has breathed' (the breath of life into the child?). For existence of verbal elements in names where these are not attested elsewhere in BH, see above, pp. 86-87.

yôḥā'. The root and meaning of the second element in this name are very dubious. The possibility of *yô'āḥ* is suggested by BDB, 398, while KB, 381 and Lidzbarski, *Eph*, 7, suggest a sf. of *yôḥānān*.

Other difficult forms present individual idiosyncrasies of form which do not enable then to undergo comparison with other types of names in the Hebrew onomasticon. Such names are:

'ĕlîpᵉlēhû. The second element is usually accepted as being derived from the root *plh*, extant in BH only in the Niphal and Hiphil with the meaning 'to

be separated, distinct'. BDB, 45 and Geh, 263 suggest a meaning 'May God distinguish him'. KB, 54 prefer 'God has distinguished' with the use of the Qal instead of the Hiphil, while Noth (*IPN*, 32 n. 2) suggested an imv. with a suffix. See also above, §§ 2.4 and 2.8.5.

y^ehô'addāh. Because of the dagheshed *dālet* in this name, two etymologies are possible: the root *'dh* 'to ornament, deck oneself', and the root *'dd* 'to count, reckon'. To which root the name belongs, as well as its form and meaning, remains unclear.

y^ehô'addān, *y^ehô'addāyin*. Geh, 450, KB, 379 and *IPN*, 166 suggest a derivation from the root *'dn* for the two forms of this feminine name. This suggests a nominal sentence name with a meaning 'Y is delight', although both names retain their formal uncertainty.

'ăbîšay, *'abšay*. BDB, 5 suggest a meaning 'My father is Jesse', although KB, 6 indicates a derivation of the second element from the noun *yēš* which means 'substance, being, existence'. The name is unlikely to be a sf. of a name like *'ăbîšālôm* or *'ăbîšûr* as suggested by Lidzbarski (*Eph*, 13) since this type of abbreviation is not exemplified elsewhere in the Heb. onomasticon (cf. below, § 2.10).

'ăbî-'albôn. This very obscure name has been variously interpreted. Geh, 3 suggests that *albon* may be a scribal confusion from Shaalbonite, (2 Sam. 23.31). LXX has the reading *'ăbî'ēl* instead of *'ăbî-'albôn* in 2 Sam. 23.31, which is the name given the same individual in 1 Chr. 11.32. On the other hand, *KB*, 6 cite an Arab. cognate *'alaba* meaning 'to be hard', or 'to cut in, carve', and also suggest a corruption from *'ăbîba'al ben*.

'ăḥô^aḥ. The name may be a sf. (see below, § 2.10). It is given to a Benjaminite in 1 Chr. 8.4, but since the name *'ăḥîyāh* appears in v. 7, most suggest this as the proper form; cf. BDB, 29, Geh, 25, KB, 30, *IPN*, 235.

'adb^e'ēl. The meaning of the root *'db* may possibly be determined by an Arab. cognate *'adaba* meaning 'to invite, discipline', cf. BDB, 9. This may suggest an interpretation 'El has invited, or disciplined', cf. KB, 11, Geh, 16, although the form of the name remains difficult.

Extra-biblical names which present difficulty in form or semantic content have been separated from biblical names, because of their lack of vocalization. Frequently, it is the vocalization of biblical names which is problematic, while in extra-biblical names it is the lack of vocalization which makes a form more difficult to determine with any precision. In most cases, however, the biblical name can indicate the form and meaning of the unvocalized non-biblical name: the frequent occurrence of the construct form name *mattanyāh(û)* in BH, for example, suggests an identical identification as a construct form for extra-biblical *mtnyhw*. Some non-biblical names present difficulty because no basic etymology can be derived from their extant forms, or because the apparent root is semantically difficult when applied to the deity. This is the case with the following names:

'ḥ'mh. The name occurs on a seal (BL, 48 no. 8). The second element of the name seems to be derived from a root *'mh* which is not found in verbal form in BH, but in a nominal form *'āmāh* meaning 'handmaid' (BDB, 51). The only other possibility seems to be a noun from the root *'mm* which has the basic idea 'to be wide, roomy'. Nouns from this root, however, are not semantically applicable to the deity, cf. *'ammāh* n. f. = (1) 'mother city'; (2) 'ell, cubit'; (3) 'foundation' (dubious, cf. BDB, 52), and *'ēmmāh* n. f. 'tribe, people'. J. Teixidor, *Syria* 54 (1977), 262 no. 55 considers the name to be Aram. and to mean 'Brother's mother', which has no parallels in any other Semitic onomasticon, and is semantically very dubious.

[yh]wsḥ[r]. The uncertainty of the letters in this inscr. (*AI*, 90) may well account for the resulting difficulty in meaning presented by a root *sḥr* when applied to the deity. This root in BH means 'to go around, about, travel about in', which is semantically awkward when used with a theophoric element as subject. Akk. *saḫāru*, however, is attested in Akk. names (cf. *APN*, 299) with the meaning 'to turn' and is, perhaps, more likely to be the sense implied by this name. The root is also met in Ug. with the meaning 'to turn around' (*PTU*, 184).

mḥlyh. This name, which occurs in an inscr. (Y. Aharoni, *Lachish V*, 5ff.) would appear to be derived from a root *mḥl*. Aharoni cited the BH name *mḥly* in 1 Chr. 23.23, 24.30, but disputed Noth's connection of this name with Arab. *miḥālun* meaning 'craftiness' or 'prudence' (*IPN*, 249). He suggested that the name is a sf. of *Maḥalyahu*, 'Y has renounced'. However, the root *mḥl* does not exist in BH and it is difficult to see from where Aharoni derived such a meaning, itself semantically problematic with reference to the deity.

sryh. This name, which occurs on a seal (V, 33), seems to be derived from a root *swr* meaning 'to turn aside', or *srr* 'to be stubborn, rebellious', neither of which seems semantically satisfactory when the subject is a divine name. The former root, however, may imply the idea of the deity turning aside in order to help or notice the name-bearer or name-giver.

Other names present various difficulties:

'bgd hwzḥ. This seal (V, 275) is the work of an unskilled hand, and was probably a trial piece. The first part of the seal, *'bgd*, is attested elsewhere as a personal name (seal V, 234) but, since the letters represent the first part of

the Heb. alphabet, we may suppose that *hwzḥ* has no real value as an authentic name. Cf. also the similar *'bdgh//wzḥṭy* (Aram. BL, 54 no. 26) and *'bdghw//zḥṭykl* (Ammon. *ibid*., no. 37).

'byḥy. The name *'byḥy* occurs on one inscr. (*AI*, 39.11). Cf. also the seal *yhw*[*ḥy*] (V, 253). The second element is probably derived from the root *ḥyh* 'to live', and the form *ḥay* may be verbal (cf. Gen. 5.5), or adjectival (cf. Josh. 3.10). Since adjectives compounded with theophoric elements are non-existent elsewhere in the Heb. onomasticon, we may perhaps favour a verbal translation, 'The (divine) Father is living or lives'. Cf. also Lemaire (*IH*, 206, 207) 'Mon père est vivant'. W. Kornfeld (*WZKM* 71 [1979], 40) suggests as an alternative to Lemaire's interpretation, 'mein Vater ist mein Bruder', which is semantically nonsensical and unattested elsewhere. It would also involve a type of abbreviation (from *'by'ḥy*) with no parallels in the Heb. onomasticon.

'ḥy'yl. Inscr. (*AI*, 35.3). The root *'yl/'wl* in BH means 'to be in front of, precede, lead', cf. BDB, 17. A verbal translation, not attested in BH, might suggest, 'The (divine) Father has led', or perhaps better, 'is predominant' (cf. Ug., *PTU*, 103). A nominal interpretation, on the other hand, would indicate 'The (divine) Father is a leader or chief'. Lemaire (*IH*, 204), however, reads *Aḥyam*, and translates 'mon Frère a dominé'. H. Van Dyke Parunak (*BASOR* 230 [1978], 28 IV B 1 a i) considers a vocalization *'aḥî'ayl* unlikely, since other Arad names do not indicate 'internalised case endings and personal pronouns'. He prefers *aḥ*(*ī*)*ya'īl* i.e. Hiphil. On this point, however, cf. above, pp. 134f. Aharoni (*AI*, p. 65) transcribed the name as *Aḥi'eyal* (*'ăḥî'ĕyāl*), *'yl* representing 'strength', but there seems no evidence for such an interpretation, cf. BDB, 17ff., 33.

'ḥymh. Seal (V, 366). Bordreuil and Lemaire (BL, 48) suggest a comparison with *'ḥy'm* meaning 'Mother's brother' (cf. Geh, 23 and Aram. *'ḥmh*, *KAI*, 209. For a different interpretation of *'ḥy'm* see above, p. 141). The suggestion, however, seems unlikely, even if no appropriate etymology for the second element seems evident. Some connection with the equally difficult name *y*ᵉ*mû'ēl* (see above, § 2.7) may be possible, since a root *ymh*, although unknown, would suit both.

'nyhw. This name occurs on an inscr. discovered at Khirbet el-Kôm (W.G. Dever, *HUCA* 40-41 [1969-70], 158-59) and on a Heb. seal (N. Avigad, *BASOR* 246 [1982], 59-62. A root *'wn* in BH has no verbal forms, only the nouns (1) *'āwen* 'trouble, sorrow, wickedness' (BDB, 19) and (2) *'ôn* 'vigour, wealth' (BDB, 20). A verbal form of this latter noun would produce a semantically suitable meaning and has suggested an interpretation 'Yhwh est (ma) force, (ma) puissance', to Lemaire (*RB* 84 [1977], 602, cf. KB, 21 III and N. Avigad, *op. cit.*). The root *'ānāh* has the verbal meanings (1) 'to mourn' and (2) 'to be opportune, meet, encounter opportunely' found only in

derived conjugations (BDB, 58). A Qal interpretation from this latter meaning of the root might suggest 'Y has met', cf. the semantically similar BH name *nô'adyāh* 'Y has met by appointment' (see above, p. 103). A root *'nn*, extant only in the Hithpo., has a less suitable meaning 'to complain, murmur' (BDB, 59).

'ṣyh. This name, which occurs on the seal *'ṣyh brk ḥtm z* (V, 97), presents a number of problems. Not only is the seal questionably Heb., but the word division of the letters is debatable. A.F. Rainey (*IEJ* 16 [1966], 187f.) divides the letters so that the first name is non-theophoric, *l'sy hbrk h ḥtm z* and suggests that the seal is an ellipsis of a longer phrase, '(Belonging) to *'Aṣay* the blessed, this seal'. Diringer (*IEJ* 15 [1965], 224-25) also supports such a reading. A name *'ṣy* or *'ṣyh* has no parallel in BH but could possibly be derived from the root *'wṣ* meaning 'to make haste, press, be pressed'.

't'b. Seal (V, 444). The meaning of the name is uncertain. The initial element could be from a root *'th* 'to come' (cf. BDB, 87 and the BH name *'ĕlî'ātāh*) or could indicate the preposition 'with', suggesting a meaning 'With the father' (cf. Phoen. *'tb'l*, *PNPPI*, 281).

ḥwyhw. Seal (BL, 48 no. 7. Vattioni [V, 365], citing Bordreuil and Lemaire, has recorded the name erroneously as *ḥwhjhw*). Bordreuil and Lemaire translate this name as 'YHWH a fait vivre', but the translation is perhaps oversimplifying the form, although a derivation from the root *ḥyh* is possible. The initial element seems to suit a root *ḥwh* which, if not connected with *ḥyh* 'to live', could perhaps be determined from Arab. *ḥaway* 'to collect, gather' (cf. BDB, 295). *Ḥwh* also means 'to tell, declare', although in BH the verb is found only in the Piel, where it seems to have been confined to a late period and to poetic usage (*ibid*., 296). Also possible may be a sf. of *yḥwyhw*, similar to the name *yḥw'ly*.

ḥn'[b]. Inscr. SO 30.3 cf. *SSI*. 9, 12. Noth (*IPN*, 187) suggested that the name is possibly derived from the root *ḥnn* 'to show favour, be gracious'. In BH, names with this root usually retain the form *ḥnn* when verbal, cf. *ḥănanyāh(û)*, *y(ᵉh)ôḥānān*, *'elḥānān*, but a construct form *ḥannî'ēl*, also exists. A nominal form *ḥēn* meaning 'favour, grace' for the inscr. is probably preferable, giving a meaning 'The (divine) Father is grace or favour'. Recently, however, Lemaire (*IH*, 33) reads *Gera Ḥanna* on this ostracon, finding no trace of *ḥn'b*.

yr'wyhw. This name, which occurs on a seal (N. Avigad, *EI*, 12, 67 no. 5) is perhaps from the root *r'h* 'to see' or from the root *yr'* 'to fear' which, in the Niphal, is frequently used of Yahweh in the sense of reverential fear and awe. The form, however, remains uncertain. (Vattioni [V, 328] records the name incorrectly as *yr'yhw*, without the *wāw*).

yrmlk. Seal (V, 444). The initial element of this name is possibly derived from the root *yrh* 'to throw, shoot, cast', Hiph. 'to point out, show, direct, teach' (BDB, 434-35). Cf. also the possible sf. *yôray* below, § 2.10. The form of the EB name, however, is uncertain.

sb̆k̆yhw. Inscr. (L 11.4). Lemaire (*IH*, 129) finds in this name the root *sbk* 'to interweave'. However, to interpret the name, Lemaire cites the root *skk* 'to weave together' and places his interpretation 'pour désigner l'action de la divinité formant l'embryon dans le sein maternel', upon this root. He finally suggests therefore, a meaning 'Yhwh a entrelacé', i.e. 'Yhwh a formé l'embryon. While such an interpretation is certainly permissible for the root *skk*, perhaps more caution should be exercised in giving this same shade of meaning to the root *sbk*, at the same time, noting the problematic reading of the second and third letters of the name.

'byw. Seal (V, 174). The etymology of the name *'byw*, of Eg. provenance, is dubious. A root *'bh* in Heb. has the meanng 'to be thick, fat, gross', and may suggest a non-theophoric name 'fat, heavy built', while a n. m. *'āb* from a root *'wb* has the meaning 'dark cloud, cloud mass, thicket' (cf. BDB, 728, also *PTU*, 141 and the element *ǵl* 'thicket' in the names *abǵl* and *iḫǵl*). In Phoen. *'b* is sometimes a variant of *'b* or *'bd* (cf. *PNPPI*, 369), but the same phenomenon is not evident in Heb. names. Vattioni records the name incorrectly as *'byw*, but perhaps the original reading is dubious (cf. Reifenberg, *IEJ* 4 [1954], 139). The name remains very uncertain.

qlyhw. Seal (V, 233). The first element in the name is difficult to interpret. S.H. Horn (*BASOR* 189 [1968], 41-43) gives the various possibilities as:
1. variant of *qwl*, Qal perf. 'Y has spoken'.
2. root *qlh* 'to despise': since the second name of the man called Qelyah in Ezra 10.23 was *Kelita*, which may mean 'dwarf', the name *qlyhw* could be interpreted 'Y has despised him'.
3. W.F. Albright suggested the Ug. cognate *ql* 'to fall down', or 'to prostrate oneself (before someone)' and Akk. *qâlu* (*qwl*) 'to be silent (before god)' or 'to heed (a command of god)'. This would suggest a meaning 'Pay homage to Y'.

The name *qlyw* is found on an inscr. (SS 4.2 cf. *IH*, 248). Lemaire transcribes the name as *Qolyaw* and suggests 'Yhwh a parlé' (*IH*, 249). W. Kornfeld (*WZKM* 71 [1979], 46) also suggests a meaning 'der Schnelle (Bote) Yw's/ schnell ist Yw', presumably from a root *qll* 'to be slight, swift, trifling' (cf. BDB, 886). See also the BH name *qôlāyāh* above, § 2.6.

rbyhw. A number of etymologies are possible for this name which occurs on a seal (V, 161). It may be derived from the root *rbh* or the root *rbb*, both having a meaning 'to be or become much, many, i.e. great', or may be a Qal perf. of the root *ryb* 'to strive, contend'.

šnyw. Seal (V, 132). A choice between *śîn* and *šîn* for the first letter makes this name difficult. The only appropriate root seems to be *šnh* 'to shine, be beautiful', suggested by an Arab. cognate *sana'* (cf. BDB, 1040). This would indicate a meaning 'Y has shone or is beautiful', comparable to the name *ypyhw* (M, 80 no. 23) 'Y is beautiful, fair', root *yph*.

2.10 *Abbreviated Forms*

Throughout the Hebrew onomasticon there exist numerous abbreviated names, names which have been shortened in a variety of ways, from a previously existing full form. The term usually employed for such shortened forms, *hypococristica*, has been interpreted so widely that it has become a designation which is difficult to employ with any exact meaning (cf., for example, *APNM*, 130 and H. Ranke, *Early Babylonian Personal Names*, Philadelphia [1905], 7 n. 2). If the word is returned to its correct use, *hypocristica* must refer to 'pet names' or 'diminutives' (*OED*, 597 and H.W. Fowler, *Modern English Usage*, 2nd edition, Oxford: Clarendon [1965], reprinted [1974], 258). Since in the Hebrew onomasticon it is not possible to prove that each abbreviated name was a pet name, the term *hypocoristic* will not be used, and any name which appears to have been shortened by omitting a part of that name, or by omitting a part of the name and adding a different, terminating element, will be designated 'abbreviated' or 'shortened'. From the full forms *'ăḥazyāh(û)* and *y(ᵉh)ô'āḥāz*, for example, occur the abbreviated names *'āḥāz* and *'aḥzay*.

Many of the abbreviated names have a terminating *y*, *w*, *h* or *'* which, although in many cases indicate the presence of a shortened form (sf.), are not necessarily indicative of a shortened theophoric element. This can be seen clearly in names such as *rîbay* (BH) which is likely to be abbreviated from *yᵉhôyārîb*, *'lsmky* (seal V, 129: Lipiński, however, considers this seal to be Aram. [Lipiński, 61] while Herr [Herr, 177 no. 11] considers it Phoen.) which already has a prefixed theophoric element as has a name like *'ḥm'* (SO 32.3 = 37.2 = 38.2 = 39.2). Similarly, the shortened form *'uzzî* (BH) is usually accepted as an abbreviation of *'uzîyāh*, although a full name, *'el'uzzî* (BH), exists. Indeed, as will be seen in the following names, some of these terminations may have been primarily due to a question of form and sound, and any implication of a deity may have been of secondary consideration.

Attempts to suggest an original full form from the many extant short forms are, on the whole, purely speculative. Even where a number of abbreviated names can be grouped together under a specific type, we cannot conclude that every occurrence of this type is a shortened form. For example, the *qaṭlay* type of short form is frequent, cf. *'aḥzay*, *na'ăray* etc. Yet is is quite possible that other names of this type are not shortened forms at all, cf. for example, *ḥadlay*, 'fat, fleshy' (perhaps from Arab. *ḫadlun*, cf. Geh, 356, *IPN*, 226). In the same way, unless otherwise indicated by the text, care has to be taken that a shortened name is not allocated a specific theophoric element on the basis of very little, if any, evidence. This can be seen with a name like *mā'ay*, which lacks evidence to suggest that it is an abbreviated name. Nor is there evidence to suggest that it is an abbreviation from *ma'ăday* or *ma'adyāh*, as some have indicated (cf. *IPN*, 250 and *Eph*, 16). Similarly, with a name like *nātān*, which can occur prefixed or suffixed with both *'l* and forms of *yhwh*, it is simply not possible to suggest any legitimate full form.

Some abbreviated forms may be assigned to full forms with more reliability however. It seems likely that where the biblical text has two names attested for the same person, a shortened form and a full form, it is possible to suggest with more certainty the derivation of the abbreviated name. The paucity of such cases would seem to speak against Lidzbarski's view that such instances probably occurred as a result of textual emendation: 'Es könnte der Verfasser der einen Schrift, bzw. der Autor seiner Quelle, den ihm überlieferten Vollnamen in einer zu seiner Zeit beliebte Form abgeändert, oder auch umgekehrt eine vorgefundene Kurzform in eine volle umgewandelt haben' (*Eph*, 6). Indeed, there seems no substantial evidence to suggest that one person could not be known by two names, one abbreviated and one full. A full name was able to be shortened in a variety of ways (see below p. 169) and it would have been as difficult for a writer to know which shortened form a particular person used, as to know to which corresponding full form a specific abbreviated form should be allocated.

Such instances of abbreviated and full forms referring to the same person are not frequent in the biblical text but, although few, they serve to exemplify the manner in which names were shortened. These names are:

yēšû^{a}' (BH). Sf. of *y^{e}hôšû^{a}'* 'Y is salvation', cf. BDB, 221 and Geh, 518. *IPN*, 154 and KB, 379 prefer 'Y is help'. This name, given to the successor of Moses, is usually found in the form *y^{e}hôšu^{a}'* (Exod. 17.9-14 etc.), also as *y^{e}hôšû^{a}'* (Deut. 3.21; Judg. 2.7) and in Neh. 8.17 as *yēšû^{a}'*. Similarly, the high priest after the restoration is called both *y^{e}hôšu^{a}'* (Hag. 1.1, 12, 14 etc) and *yēšû^{a}'* (Ezra 2.2; 3.2, 8 etc.).

'ăbîyām (BH). The suffix *ām* here appears to replace part of the theophoric ending *yāhû* since the name is a sf. of *'ăbîyāh(û)*, the King of Judah, son and successor of Rehoboam. The alternative form *'ăbîyām* occurs in 1 Kgs 14.13; 15.1, 7, 8, and thus means 'Y is (divine) Father', cf. BDB, 4, Geh, 5, KB, 4. Noth (*IPN*, 234) contested the identification of *-ām* with *yhwh*. Other instances of this suffix as an abbreviated ending seem unlikely: the name *'ăḥuzzām*, for example, considered by *IPN*, 38, 179 as a sf. of *'ḥz* + theophoric element, seems better translated 'possessor', with BDB, 28 and Geh, 25.

'î'ezer (BH). A sf. of *'ăbî'ezer*, 'The (divine) Father is help', cf. BDB, 4, Geh, 4, KB, 5, *IPN*, 236. The full form of the name is given for its Manassite bearer in Josh. 17.2, Judg. 6.34; 8.2 and 1 Chr. 7.18, and the sf. in Num. 26.30.

'ăḥôaḥ (BH). Sf. of *'ăḥîyāh* 'Y is (divine) Brother', cf. Geh, 23, KB, 32, *IPN*, 235. The son of Ehud is referred to by the sf. in 1 Chr. 8.4, and the longer form in 1 Chr. 8.7.

yntn (EB seal V, 348). This name appears to have been a sf. of *yhwntn*, cf. N. Avigad, *IEJ* 25 (1975), 8-12.

'ûtay (BH). Sf. of *'ătāyāh* 'Y is proud, exalted', perhaps suggested by Arab. *'atā* 'to be proud, go beyond bounds'. Cf. also KB (1953), 692, Geh, 968, *IPN*, 191. *'ûtay* is attested in 1 Chr. 9.4, while the same person is referred to in Neh. 11.4 as *'ătāyāh*.

'ăbî m. and f. (BH, also inscr. Mur. B 2 cf. *SSI*, 32). Sf. of *'ăbîyāh(û)* 'Y is (divine) Father', cf. BDB, 4, KB, 4, Geh, 5. The mother of Hezekiah, to whom this name is ascribed in 2 Kgs 18.2, has the corresponding full form in 2 Chr. 29.1.

'āḥaz (BH, also seals V, 44, 141; inscr. SO 2.5 cf. *SSI*, 9. 11; SS 7.1 cf. *IH*, 250). The BH name is a sf. of *yehô'āḥāz* 'Y has seized', cf. BDB, 28 and KB, 31. The name of the Judean king *'āḥāz* is given its full form *Ja-u-ḫa-zi* in the list of tributaries of Tiglath-Pileser III, cf. *IPN*, 62. Geh, 22 also has 'Y has seized', but since he always gives translations of the Heb., one cannot be certain whether Gehman implies a suffixed or prefixed theophoric element.

zābād (BH). Sf. of *yôzābād* 'Y has given'. The name, given to one of the murderers of Joash of Judah, appears in 2 Chr. 24.26 as *zābād* and as *yôzābād* in 2 Kgs 12.22. KB, 250 and *IPN*, 46-47 also suggest a sf. of the root *zbd* and an unspecified theophoric element. Geh, 1010 suggests that the deity is semantically implied and BDB, 256 prefer 'He has given', or 'A gift'.

zeker (BH, also seals V, 46, 47, 171, 329; inscr. SO 31.3 cf. *SSI*, 10; *AI*, 67.5; 38.7; 48.3; KM 1 cf. *IH*, 275). The BH name is a sf. of *zekaryāh* 'Y has remembered', cf. Geh, 1019, KB, 260, and is found in 1 Chr. 8.31. The full form *z^e^karyāh*, referring to the same person, is found in 1 Chr. 9.37.

palṭî (BH). Sf. of *palṭî'ēl* 'El has delivered', cf. Geh, 698, KB (1953), 762, BDB, 812. The second husband of Michal, called *palṭî* in 1 Sam. 25.44, is called *palṭî'ēl* in 2 Sam. 3.15.

mîkā', *mîkāh* (BH). Sff. of *mîkāyāh* 'Who is like Y?', cf. BDB, 567, Geh, 614. The name *mîkā'* occurs in Neh. 11.17 and the full form *mîkāyāh* in 12.35 for the same person. Similarly, the Ephraimite *mîkāh* in Judg. 17.5-13, 18.2ff. etc., is called *mîkāy^e^hû* in 17.14, while the prophet Micah is given the sf. *mîkāh* (Mic. 1.1) as well as the full form *mîkāyāh* (Jer. 26.18). Cf. also the name *mîkāh* in 2 Chr. 34.20 = *mîkāyāh* in 2 Kgs 22.12, both referring to the same person. The name *mykh* is also as attested on a seal (V, 313).

'abdā' (BH, also seal V, 217 [Ammon.?]; inscr. SO 57.1 cf. *IH*, 292). The Levite who bears the name in Neh. 11.17, is referred to by the full form *'ōbadyāh*, 'Servant of Y', in 1 Chr. 9.16: cf. BDB, 715, KB, (1953), 673.

rāpāh (BH). Sf. of *r^e^pāyāh*, 'Y has healed'. The descendant of Saul who bears this name is referred to by the sf. in 1 Chr. 8.37, and the full form in 1 Chr. 9.43.

bārûk N. Avigad (*IEJ* 28 [1978], 53) has identified *brkyhw*, attested on a seal impression, with Baruch of Jer. 36 etc. This name, then, would be a sf. meaning 'Y has blessed'. The name *brwk* is also attested on a seal (V, 308).

šammû^a^' (BH). Sf. of *š^e^ma'yāh*, 'Y has heard', cf. KB, 985. The Levite who is called *šammû^a^'* in Neh. 11.17 is called *š^e^ma'yāh* in 1 Chr. 9.16.

šallûm (BH). The name is probably a sf. of (*m^e^*)*šelemyāh*(*û*) 'Y recompenses'. The Levite who bears the sf. in 1 Chr. 9.17, 17; Ezra 2.42 etc. is referred to by the full form *šelemyāhû* in Jer. 36.26. The same person is called (*m^e^*)*šelemyāh*(*û*) in 1 Chr. 9.21; 26.1, 29 cf. *IPN*, 174. Apart from the names *šallûm* and *šammû^a^'*, other forms of the *qaṭṭûl* type seem very dubious and contain no suggestion that they are necessarily theophoric in form or semantic content, or even simple abbreviations: cf. *ḥaššûb* 'considerate', *'azzûz* 'helpful', *pallû'* 'wonderful'. An exception may be *mallûk* which needs to be considered as a possible sf. of *mlk* + theophoric element (see above, § 2.2 *mlk*) and perhaps *yaddû^a^'* in which the deity may be semantically implied (see below).

qîšî (BH). A sf. of *qûšāyāhû*, 'Y has presented or bestowed', cf. Akk. *qāšu*. The Levite who bears the full form is referred to in 1 Chr. 15.17, while the sf. occurs in 1 Chr. 6.29, cf. Geh, 245, KB (1953), 834.

'uzzî'ēl (BH). This name, which occurs in 1 Chr. 25.4, is found in the form *'ăzar'ēl* in 1 Chr. 25.18 with reference to the same Levite. However, BDB,

739, *IPN*, 160 and Geh, 970 suggest a root *'zz* and a meaning 'My strength is El', while KB, (1953), 695 cite also an Arab. cognate *ghadhā* 'to nourish', i.e. a root *'zh*, not found in BH. We should not entirely exclude the possibility of the first element being a rare sf. of the root *'zr*. Indeed, the root *'zr* seems to have become attracted to the root *'zz* in some cases, cf. A.F. Rainey, 'Ilānu rēsūtni lillikū!', *Orient and Occident* (1973), 139-42 and references.

In some abbreviated forms the preformative *yōd* of the imperfective has been dropped, as shown in the following names:

ḥizqîyāh (BH). Sf. of *y^eḥizqîyāh*. The full form is the name given to the head of a family of returned exiles in Ezra 2.16, who is referred to by the sf. in Neh. 7.21. Similarly, King Hezekiah (2 Kgs 1.16 etc.) is known as *y^eḥizqîyāh* in Hos. 1.1 and Mic. 1.1. For the meaning of *ḥizqîyāh*, BDB, 306 suggest 'Y has strengthened or strengthens', KB, 292 'Y is my strength' or 'Y has strengthened me'. Geh, 385 has 'Y is strength'. Noth (*IPN*, 16) also preferred a nominal interpretation. If the name is a sf. of *y^eḥizqiyāh*, and the alternative forms *yḥ*/-*ḥ*- for the same person would seem to endorse this in at least two cases, then a verbal translation is necessary since the *yōd* indicates an imf. It may also be possible, however, that the name *ḥizqîyāh* exists in addition as an unabbreviated nominal form. Cf. also the seal *ḥzqyh̊w* (V, 321 = King Hezekiah). The inscr. *ḥzq*[*yw*] (Dir, 302 no. 16) is possibly nominal (see above, p. 73) as well as the inscr. name *h*[*z*]*qyhw* (Ophel 1 cf. *SSI*, 25, 26). Gibson reads this last name with a preformative *yōd*, Lemaire (*IH*, 239), however, without.

konyāhû (BH). The last but one king of Judah is given this sf. in Jer. 22.24, 28; 37.1. The full form *y^ekonyāh*(*û*), retaining the preformative *yōd*, occurs in Jer. 27.26; 24.1; 28.4; 29.2; 1 Chr. 3.16, 17; Esth. 2.6, with a meaning 'May Y establish'. BDB, 467 suggest a meaning 'May Y be enduring', Geh, 449 'Y establishes'. Cf. also Phoen. YKNŠLM 'May ŠLM establish or endure' (*PNPPI*, 128). See also above, § 2.4 *kwn*.

Apart from these cases of parallel short and full forms referring to the same persons, we have no firm basis on which to make any assertions as to which full form a particular abbreviated name belongs. Failure to recognize this fact has led to much over-simplification of this complex area of the Hebrew onomasticon. The uncertainty of assigning a shortened form to a full form with a *specific* theophoric element has been reflected in Noth's listing of the names by root, involving full forms compounded with that root, and then abbreviated forms (cf., for example, names under the root *ḥnn*, *IPN*, 187). It is important to note, however, that he rarely ascribed one of these abbreviated forms to any one particular full form. This has not frequently been noticed by the newer lexicon of Koehler and

Baumgartner, which displays a tendency to misrepresent Noth by listing, for example under the shortened form *ḥănānî*, the information 'Kf. v. *ḥănanyāhû* (Noth 38, 187)'. Other abbreviated forms meet the same fate (For example, *bunî*, *zeker*, *zikrî*, *yišmā'*, *yišmᵉray* [for which Noth indicates no full forms, *IPN*, 196], *yiš'î* etc.), which is beyond the scope of this study to pursue. What should be emphasized here, however, is the pronounced uncertainty of assigning any abbreviated name to a specific full form, unless we have textual or other evidence on which we can base such an assumption.

Similarly, BDB have a tendency to group together full and abbreviated forms under one heading, giving the impression that the short form is an abbreviation of the listed full forms. While this may be quite legitimate in certain cases when both forms refer to the same person, in other cases such listing is quite erroneous. Compare, for example, the placing together of: *yᵉhôyāqîm*, *yôyāqîm*, *yôqîm* (p. 220), when there is nothing to suggest that *yôqîm* is an abbreviation of the other two names; *yᵉhôrām*, *yôrām*, *yōrām* (p. 221), where *yōrām* does not conclusively contain a shortened theophoric element as opposed to an imperfective; *'ăḥazyāhû*, *'ăḥazyāh 'aḥzay* (p. 28), where *'aḥzay* does not conclusively contain the theophoric suffix *yh*(*w*). This is also seen to be the case with the names *'ăḥî* (p. 26), *ma'ăśay* (p. 796) and *'atlāy* (p. 800).

Neither can we allocate a short form to a corresponding full form simply because only one full form exists. The possibly abbreviated name *ḥubbāh* for example, has a seemingly corresponding full form *ḥăbāyāh*: no other names survive from this root, but this is not to say that there were no others. Indeed, the names known to us from the biblical text, and from extra-biblical seals and inscriptions may only represent a small portion of the whole Hebrew onomasticon.

Very often, however, the form of the name, its semantic content, and the prevalence of other similar theophoric compound names, tend to suggest that some abbreviated names once had an original theophoric element. Thus it is possible to *suggest* a large number of shortened names which were derived from theophoric compounds, although we are rarely at liberty to state what that theophoric element should be. These names will be examined according to their form which, as will be seen, may have played an important part in dictating the type of names which tended to be abbreviated.

Abbreviated names in which the first part, a theophoric element, may have been shortened in some way, seem to occur infrequently and, probably exclusively, with the theophoric elements *yhw*, *'ḥ* and *'b*:

ḥî'ēl (BH). For this name, BDB, 313 suggest 'El lives', or perhaps a sf. of *yḥy'l*, both involving the root *ḥyh* 'to live'. This, indeed, would seem to be the best etymology for the initial element of the name. However, cf. also BDB, 27 where a sf. of *'ăḥî'ēl* (not otherwise attested in Heb.), with a meaning 'Brother of El', is suggested for the same name! KB, 296 also prefer a sf. of *'ăḥî'ēl*, while Geh, 387 gives both possibilities, 'God lives' and 'God is a brother', noting LXX reading *Achiēl*. A construct form 'brother of' for the first element is unlikely: cf. above pp. 134f. for a discussion concerning the intermediate *yōd*.

ḥmlk (EB seal V, 124). Perhaps a sf. of *'ḥmlk* 'The (divine) Father is King'.

ḥîrām (BH). A sf. of *'ăḥîrām* has been suggested by some: BDB, 27 interpret *'ḥ* as non-theophoric and in construct, 'Brother of (the) lofty'. Geh, 393 suggests 'The brother is exalted', while KB, 300 also consider the original to have been *'ăḥîrām*, 'm. Br. ist erhaben'. The best interpretation is probably that of Gehman since, if the name is a sf. of *'ăḥîrām*, the intermediate *yōd* in this name is unlikely to have any grammatical significance (see above, pp. 134f.).

ḥmn (EB seals V, 30, 202). This name may be a sf. of a name like *'ăḥîmān*/*'ăḥîman* (see above §2.9).

'ēhûd (BH). The name is usually suggested as a contraction of *'ăḥîhûd* 'The (divine) Brother is majesty', cf. KB, 18 or, of *'ăbîhûd* (unattested) 'The (divine) Father is majesty', cf. Geh, 254, *IPN*, 235.

'y'dh (EB seal V, 151). A form *'ḥy'dh* would mean 'The (divine) Brother has adorned', though such a form is by no means certain. Cf. also *'î'ezer* above.

The theophoric elements *yhw* and *yw* may be shortened further when occurring in the first position, as in the names:

yēhû' (BH). Most suggest a contraction of *yᵉhôhû'* (unattested) or *yôhû'* (unattested) 'He is Y', cf. BDB, 219, KB, 376, Geh, 454. Cf. also the name *yēšûaʿ* above.

hôšāmāʿ (BH). A meaning 'Y has heard' is generally accepted, cf. BDB 221, Geh, 410, KB, 232, *IPN*, 107 n.3, 185. In this case the preformative *yōd* would have been dropped.

yōrām (BH, also seal V, 54); cf. BDB, 221, KB, 379/386, Geh, 452/512. The name is possibly a sf. of *yᵉhôrām* or *yôrām*, 'Y is exalted'. Cf. also

Gibson, *SSI*, 63, who suggests a sf. of *yhwyrym* (unattested), 'Y shall exalt'.

ytm (EB seals V. 131, 158). Perhaps a sf. of *ywtm*, 'Y is perfect'. However, cf. *SSI*, 61, where Gibson vocalizes as *yatōm*, i.e. 'the orphan', a name occurring in the Elephantine papyri.

y'wš (EB inscr. L 2.1 = 3.2 = 6.1 cf. *SSI*, 37, 38, 45). Gibson (*SSI*, 37) suggests a sf. of an imf. form prefixed with *'l* or *yhw* i.e. *yhw'wš* or *'ly'wš* (both unattested), 'Y/El shall grant'. Cf. also P. Bordreuil, *Syria* 52 (1975), 115-17, on the root *'wš*. Torcz, 198 suggested 'He is strong'. Also to be considered here is the inscr. *y*[*'*]*š* (Y. Aharoni, *Lachish V*, 5ff.).

y'š (EB inscr. SO 48.3 cf. Dir, 46 no. 32). Although a sf. of the root *'wš* 'to lend aid, come to help' + a theophoric element is suggested by some (cf. *IPN*, 196 and Dir, 46), the name may be an ordinary imf. as opposed to a sf. Lemaire (*IH*, 53) considers the name to be derived from *'śh* 'to do, make', although, presumably incorrectly, he records the root as '*'šh*, "faire"'.

The non-theophoric element can be shortened in a number of ways, but will be classified here mostly in two main groups, those which are biconsonantal in form, and those which are triconsonantal. Of the biconsonantal shortened forms, we find two names which have the third consonant omitted, the vowel of the first syllable lengthened to *û* and a vocalic ending added:

'ûzay (BH). Sf. of the root *'zn* + theophoric element. KB, 20, *IPN*, 185, and Geh, 969 suggest a sf. of *'ăzanyāhû*, 'Y has heard'. Cf. also the name *'ûtay* above.

bûnāh (BH). The form may be a sf. of the root *bnh* + theophoric element (*IPN*, 172). KB, 111 suggest a sf. of *b*^{e}*nāyāh*(*û*) 'Y has built', and BDB, 107, 'intelligent'. Cf. also the seal *bwnh*/*y* (V, 160) the final letter of which is uncertain.

Two nouns of this type are from Hollow roots:

'ûrî (BH). Sf. of *'wr* + theophoric element, cf. *IPN*, 38, 168, KB, 251. Geh, 967 suggests a sf. of *'ûrîyāh*, 'Y is my light'. BDB, 22 prefer 'fiery'.

sôdî (BH). Possibly the preposition *b*^{e} is also omitted, cf. *b*^{e}*sôdyāh*. A sf. of (*b*^{e})*sôdyāh* is accepted by BDB, 691 (without the preposition), and by KB, (1953), 651, and *IPN*, 152. Cf. also Geh, 890. BH *bēsay* and EB *bsy* (seal V, 247) may also be sff. of a name like *b*^{e}*sôdyāh*, 'In the secret (council) of Y'.

Other shortened forms consisting of two consonants may have a short, or long, first vowel and a vocalic ending *ī* or *ay*:

bunî (BH). Sf. of *bnh* + theophoric element (cf. *IPN*, 172). KB, 134 suggest a sf. of *b^e^nāyāhû*; Geh, 128 suggests perhaps 'built, erected (by Y)'.

bēṣay (BH, also seal V, 142). *IPN*, 152, KB, 141, *Eph*, 14 suggest a sf. of *b^e^ṣal'ēl*, 'In the shadow of El'.

'ēḥî (BH). BDB, 29 and Geh, 254 suggest a possible sf. of *'ăḥîrām*, 'The (divine) Brother is exalted'. Note also the inscr. *AI*, 93.6 which could be *'ēḥî* or *'ăḥî*.

bānî (BH). Sf. of the root *bnh* + theophoric element (cf. *IPN*, 172). KB, 134 suggest a sf. of *b^e^nāyāh*, 'Y has built'. Geh, 90 also suggests 'Y has built'.

mā'ay (BH). The name may be a sf. although of what full form it is not possible to say. *IPN*, 250, probably following *Eph*, 16, indicates *ma'ăday* or *ma'adyāh* as the original form, but equally possible would be *ma'azyāh* or *ma'ăśēyāh*.

šāray (BH). A possible sf.; *IPN*, 260 and *Eph*, 16 suggest a sf. of *šērēbyāh* or similar.

Frequently met are abbreviated names of the pattern *q^e^ṭî*. These forms occur mainly with biconsonantal nouns or III *hē* (and Geminate?) roots:

'ăḥî (BH, also inscr. *AI*, 93.6). Sf. of *'ḥ* 'brother' + theophoric element. KB, 32 and Geh, 23 suggest a sf. of *'ăḥîyāh*, 'Y is (my) brother'. BDB, 26 suggest 'Brother of Y', but the *yōd* following the element *'ḥ* in the full form, is unlikely to be indicative of either a pronominal suffix, or a construct form (see above, pp. 134f.). Cf. also the name *'ăbî* above, which is a sf. of the same type.

gry (EB seals V, 299, 407; also inscr. *AI*, 64.1). Perhaps a sf. of a name like *gryhw*, 'Client of Y'. For this full form, cf. the seals V, 243 also Herr, 120 no. 83 (for which V, 142 reads *gdyhw*).

nry (EB seal V, 127). Sf. of element *nēr* 'lamp' + theophoric element, cf. *nērîyāh(û)*, 'Y is a lamp'.

'śy (EB seal V, 243). Sf. of *'śh* + theophoric element, cf. *'ăśāyāh* and *'ăśî'ēl*, 'Y/El has made'.

Some similar forms have the final root letter omitted and the second radical doubled. The ending is usually *î*, *ay* or *ô*:

gaddî (BH). Sf. of *gd* 'fortune' + theophoric element. Geh, 310 suggests a sf. of Gaddiel. BDB, 151 prefer 'My fortune'. *IPN*, 126 suggests Gad (n. pr. div.) + theophoric element.

hidday (BH). The name may be a sf. of the noun *hwd* 'splendour', with a theophoric element; cf. Geh, 387, KB, 229, *IPN*, 39, 146. Lidzbarski (*Eph*, 14) suggested a sf. of *hădāyāh* (unattested). The parallel form *ḥûray* (1 Chr. 11.32) gives no further elucidation.

zakkay (BH). Sf. from the root *zkr* 'to remember' + theophoric element; cf. *z*ᵉ*karyāh* 'Y has remembered'. Geh, 1010 suggests a probable contraction of Zechariah. Cf. also Schottroff 105 (W. Schottroff, *Gedenken im Alten Orient und im Alten Testament*, Neukirchener Verlag [1964]), *IPN*, 39, 187, *Eph*, 16.

ḥaggay/ḥaggî (BH, also seals V, 2, 20, 203, 213, 355; B. Mazar, *Jerusalem Revealed* [1975], 38, 40; Herr, 119 no. 82). Perhaps a sf. of a name like *ḥagîyāh*, 'Feast of Y', cf. BDB, 291, although such a full form is not widely interpreted as theophoric, cf. KB, 279, Geh, 357, *IPN*, 222.

yiddô, *yadday* (BH). Sff. from the root *yd'* probably with a theophoric element (cf. *IPN*, 181). Geh, 415 favours 'Y has known'.

'attay (BH). Possibly a sf. of a name like *'ătāyāh*. The first element may mean 'to be proud, exalted', suggested by Arab. *'atā* 'to be proud', cf. *IPN*, 191, and Geh, 76 who proposes 'Y has manifested himself as lofty'.

radday (BH). Possibly a sf. of the root *rdh* 'to have dominion, rule, dominate' + theophoric element. A full form with this root is not attested. Geh, 790 suggests 'Y rules'; KB (1953), 875 also suggests *raddiyāh*.

šammay (BH). Possibly a sf. of *šm'* + theophoric element, cf. *IPN*, 185. Geh, 857 suggests perhaps 'Y has heard'.

Possibly also belonging here is the shortened form:

bûnnî (BH). Sf. of the root *bnh* 'to build' + theophoric element. KB, 111 consider the name to be a sf. of *b*ᵉ*nāyāh*, 'Y has built'. Geh, 128 suggests perhaps 'Built, erected, by Y'. Cf. also the EB name *bwnh/y* (seal V, 160) in which, since the final letter is uncertain, the form may be either *bûnāh* or *bûnnî*, cf. Moscati, M, 65. In BH, the form of the name *bûnnî* alternates with *bunnî* cf. Ezra 8.33; Neh. 10.10 = 9.4 (and possibly with *bānî* Neh. 8.7).

What is noticeable with this last group of abbreviated forms is the prevalence of III *hē*, III *'ayin*, III *rēš* or Geminate roots, which would seem to suggest that this kind of abbreviation had more to do with sound and form, than with any other factors. This may have been the case also with the following group of abbreviated forms, which again have an omission of the third consonant and a doubling of the second, but have a reduced first vowel and the ending *ā'*, *āh* and *î*. They belong to III *hē* or Geminate roots:

buqqî (BH). Root *bqh*, sf. of a name like *buqqîyāhû*, 'Proved of Y', cf. BDB, 31, KB, 143. Geh, 128 and *IPN*, 226, however, interpret the name as 'bottle, jar'.

ḥubbāh (BH). Possibly a sf. of the root *ḥbh* + theophoric element, cf. the name *ḥăbāyāh*, 'Y has hidden', and *IPN*, 178 n. 2.

ḥuppāh (BH). Sf. of an unattested full form from the root *ḥph* + theophoric element, 'x has hidden or covered' (in the sense of protected); cf. Geh, 412, who suggests a noun 'covering', and the meaning '(Y is) a covering'.

'uzzāh, *'uzzā'* (BH, cf. also *'z'*, seals V, 36, 205, 436; inscr. SO 1.5 cf. Dir, 48 no. 40; 308; *AI*, 72.4). The BH names are probably sff. of the root *'zz* + theophoric element, probably nominal, 'x is strength'. BDB, 739, Geh, 969, KB, (1953), 693/694 suggest sff. of *'uzzîyāh*.

'uzzî (BH, also seal V, 278). Sf. of the root *'zz* + theophoric element, 'x is strength', cf. *IPN*, 160. Geh, 969 suggests a meaning 'Y is strength'.

'unnî (*'unnô*) (BH). Sf. of the root *'nh* 'to answer' or *'nn* 'to appear' + theophoric element, cf. *IPN*, 185. Geh, 966 suggests a sf. of 'Y has answered' and Lidzbarski (*Eph*, 12) a sf. of *'ănāyāh* or *'ănanyāh* 'Y has answered', or 'Y has appeared', respectively.

A similar abbreviated form, though not strictly of the same pattern, occurs in the name:

'uzzîyā' (BH). Most suggest a sf. of *'uzzîyāh(û)*, 'Y is my strength', cf. BDB, 739. KB, (1953), 695 suggest that the name is late for *'uzzîyāh*. Geh, 969 interprets the name as 'Y is strength'.

Biconsonantal nouns, or nouns formed from Hollow roots, frequently have a suffixed *'ālep* in their abbreviated forms. Although this includes the theophoric elements *'b* and *'ḥ*, non-theophoric elements are also abbreviated in this way:

'b' (EB seal V, 160, 204). Sf. of a name like *'byhw*?

'ḥ' (EB seals V, 121, 295, 296; inscr. *AI*, 49.16; 67.4; 74.2; V. Fritz, *ZDPV* 91 [1975], 131-34; SO 51.3 cf. *SSI*, 10; KM 4 cf. *IH*, 275). Sf. of *'ḥ* + a theophoric element, cf. *'ăḥîyāhû*, *'ăḥîmelek* etc. and *SSI*, 13. Moscati (M, 83) suggests a probable *'ḥyh* as the full form.

'āsā' (BH). Possibly a sf. from the root *'sh*, cf. Arab. *'asā* 'to heal', Aram. *'āsā*, *'assā* 'physician', also Akk. *asû* 'to heal', suggesting 'x has healed'. *IPN*, 181f. prefers a root *'sp*.

'r' (EB seal V, 328). Possibly a sf. of the root *'rh* or root *'wr* + theophoric element, though the meaning is difficult, see above, § 2.5 *'rh*/*'wr*.

'š' (EB seal V, 316; inscr. SO 22.2 = 23.2 = 24.1 = 25.2 (?) = 26.1 = 27.1 = 28.1 = 29.1; 37.3 = 39.3; 102.1 cf. *IH*, 292). Gibson (*SSI*, 12) suggests that the first element may be a sf. with *'yš* 'man', cf. *'ešbā'al*, but considers the more likely possibility to be that *'š* = *yš*, 'The deity exists', cf. also Dir, 42. However, cf. the BH root *'šh* 'to support' or Arab. *'asā* 'to heal', as well as the most likely possibility of a root *'wš*, suggested by another Arab. cognate, *'āsa* 'to give'. This root is discussed by P. Bordreuil, *Syria* 52 (1975), 115-17.

nr' (EB seal V, 196). The name is probably a sf. or *nēr* 'lamp' + theophoric element, cf. BH *nērîyāhû* etc. and *SSI*, 56.

The imperfective of shortened forms of III *hē* or III *'ayin* roots have the third consonant omitted and the ending *ay*, *āw*, *āy* or *ô* added. The first consonant is also a guttural, *hē* or *ḥēt*:

yaḥmay (BH). Sf. of the root *ḥmh* + theophoric element. BDB, 327 suggest a possible sf. of *yaḥmᵉyāh*, 'May Y protect', or *yaḥmᵉ('ēl)* (both unattested), cf. KB, 389, Geh, 442. The meaning of the root *ḥmh* is suggested by an Arab. cognate *ḥamā* 'to protect', cf. S. Arab. *yaḥmi'il*, *ḥamayil*.

ya'ăśay, *ya'ăśāw* (BH). Sf. of the root *'śh* 'to do, make' + theophoric element. KB, 404 and *IPN* 206 indicate a sf. of *ya'ăśî'ēl*. Geh, 436 prefers 'Y makes'.

ya'nay (BH). Sf. of the root *'nh* 'to answer' + theophoric element, cf. KB, 402, *IPN*, 198. Geh, 446 proposes 'Y answers'.

yahdāy (BH). Sf. of the root *hdh* + theophoric element e.g. *yhdyh* (unattested) 'Y leads', cf. KB, 376. Geh, 442 supports 'Y leads'. The root *hdh* means 'to stretch out the hand', cf. BDB, 213.

yaḥday, *yaḥdô* (BH). Sff. of the root *ḥdh* + theophoric element (*IPN*, 210); cf. *yaḥdî'ēl* and *yeḥdᵉyāhû* 'El/Y gives joy', and above, § 2.4.

Perhaps also belonging here is the similar form which could be I *yōd* or imperfective:

yôray (BH). Possibly a sf. of the root *yrh* 'to throw, shoot', Hiphil 'to teach' + theophoric element. BDB, 436 consider the name to be equivalent to *yôrîyāh* (unattested), a Hiphil imf. of the root *yrh*. *IPN*, 40f. and KB, 386 prefer *yôyārîb* as the original name.

The remaining abbreviation of an imperfective full form in which the third consonant is absent, contains a suffixed *ā'*:

yišmā' (BH). Sf. of the root *šm'* + theophoric element. KB, 426, *IPN*, 19 specify a sf. of *yišmā''ēl*, 'El hears'.

Other abbreviated forms retain the three root consonants. The most simple shortened form of this type consists of the Qal perfective (cf. also *zābād* and *'āḥāz* above):

yādā' (BH, also inscr. L 3.20 cf. Torcz, 198). Sf. of the root *yd'* + theophoric element, cf. *yᵉhôyādā'*, *yᵉda'yāh*, *'elyādā'*, 'Y/El knows'.

yš' (EB seal M, 26). Sf. of the root *yš'* 'to deliver' with the addition of a theophoric element probably in second position, see above, §§ 2.3 and 2.5 *yš'/šw'*.

nādāb (BH). Sf. of the root *ndb* + theophoric element, cf. *IPN*, 163. KB, (1953), 596 propose a sf. of *nᵉdabyāh* 'Y is noble, generous'. BDB, 621 prefer 'generous, noble'.

nātān (BH). Sf. of the root *ntn* 'to give' + theophoric element, cf. *IPN*, 170. KB (1953), 644 suggest a sf. of *'elnātān* or *yᵉhônātān*.

smk (EB seals V, 139, 240, 292, 401, 432; M, 75 no. 7; Herr, 90 no. 17; 119 no. 80). Perhaps a sf. of a name like *smk'l* (unattested) or *sᵉmakyāhû*, 'El/Y supports'.

pālāl (BH). Sf. of the root *pll* + theophoric element, cf. *IPN*, 187f. *KB*, (1953), 763 propose a sf. of *pᵉlalyāh* 'Y has judged'.

ṣpn (EB seals V, 188, 274, 289, 410, 435; BL, 46 no. 2; Herr, 110 no. 59). Sf. of the root *ṣpn* + theophoric element, 'x has hidden, treasured', cf. Diringer, *PEQ* 73 (1941), 40 no. 1, 2, and Dir, 121.

rāpā' (BH, also seals V, 377, 378 and inscr. SO 24.2 cf. Dir, 49 no. 46). Sf. of the root *rp'* 'to heal' + theophoric element, cf. *IPN*, 179. *KB* (1953), 903 consider *rāpā'* as a sf. of *rᵉpā'ēl*.

šāmā' (BH, also seals V, 16, 68, 71, 72, 167, 245, 346, 416; N. Avigad, *EI* 9, 8 no. 19). Sf. of the root *šm'* 'to hear' + theophoric element, cf. Dir, 176 no. 16 and 231 no. 71. KB (1953), 992 consider the name to be a sf. of *yišma'yāhû*.

šāpāṭ (BH). Sf. of the root *špṭ* 'to judge' + theophoric element. KB (1953), 1003 consider *šāpāṭ* to be a sf. of *šᵉpaṭyāhû*, 'Y has judged'.

Another group of abbreviated names is formed on the patterns *qeṭel*, *qōṭel*, which are usually verbal (*'ebed* is a construct form; cf. also *zeker* above [verbal]).

ḥesed Most accept a sf. of *ḥăsadyāh*, 'Y is kind' or 'Y has been gracious', cf. *IPN*, 183. KB, 323 consider the meaning of the name to be 'Güte Js'.

'ebed (BH). Sf. of *'bd* 'servant' + theophoric element, cf. *IPN*, 137. BDB, 714 suggest a sf. of *'abdᵉ'ēl*, 'Servant of El'. Geh, 236 prefers 'servant'.

peleṭ (BH). A possible sf. of the root *plṭ* + theophoric element, 'The deity has delivered or is deliverance', cf. *IPN*, 156, Geh, 725.

šemer (BH). Possibly a sf. of the root *šmr* 'to guard, keep' + theophoric element, cf. Geh, 866, *IPN*, 177. KB, (1953), 994 propose a meaning 'rich yield'.

'ōhel (BH). A possible sf. of a name like *'āhŏlî'āb*, 'The (divine) Father is a tent i.e. protection', cf. *IPN*, 158. BDB, 14 suggest only 'tent'.

gōmer m. and f. (BH, also inscr. SO 50.1 cf. *SSI*, 12). Usually suggested is a sf. of *g^emaryāhû*, 'Y has accomplished', cf. KB, 190, *IPN*, 175, Torcz, 198.

rō'eh (BH). Possibly a sf. of a name like *r^e'āyāh*, 'Y has seen', cf. BDB, 909. Against this, Geh, 365 and KB (1953), 864 suggest 'seer'.

Other nouns in which the entire theophoric element is absent, and which have no vocalic ending are:

'ûr (BH). A possible sf. of *'wr* 'light' + theophoric element, cf. *IPN*, 37. Geh, 967 interprets the name as '(God is) light', and BDB, 22 as 'flame'.

hôd (BH). The meaning of the word as 'splendour', or 'majesty' may suggest that the name is a sf. with an original theophoric element, cf. *hôdîyāh* and Geh, 401, KB, 231.

mattān (BH). Sf. of the element *mtn* 'gift' (root *ntn*) + theophoric element, cf. *IPN*, 170.

ṣdq (EB seals V, 322; M, 75 no. 6; inscr. *AI*, 93). The names are possibly sff. of the element *ṣdq* + theophoric element, cf. *ṣidqîyāhû*, 'Y is righteousness', and N. Avigad, *IEJ* 25 (1975), 101.

The type of abbreviated form most frequently met is that which retains the three root consonants, has a shortened vowel in the first syllable, and the ending *āy*, *ay* or *î*. Such abbreviated forms represent verbal, nominal or construct full forms:

ḥelqāy (BH). Most suggest a sf. of *ḥilqîyāh(û)*, 'Y is my portion', cf. BDB, 324, KB, 311, Geh, 377.

'adlāy (BH). The name may be a sf. of an unattested full form such as *'ădalyāhû* from the root *'dl*, cf. Arab. *'adala* 'to act equitably'. Geh, 17 suggests 'Y is justice'. However, Noth (*IPN*, 231) preferred a meaning 'garden cress'.

'atlāy (BH). BDB, 801 and Geh, 78 suggest a sf. of *'ătalyāhû* the meaning of which is dubious. A connection with Akk. *etlu* 'great, lofty' (so BDB, 800, Geh, 77, Barr *Cp. Ph.*, 182), where the Akk. has *ṭ*, is very dubious. The name is better considered a sf. of the unknown root *'tl* + theophoric element.

na'ăray (BH). The form *pa'ăray* is found in 2 Sam. 23.35. Sf. of a name like *n*ᵉ*'aryāh*, perhaps 'Attendant, or youth of x'. KB (1953), 623 specify a sf. of *n*ᵉ*'aryāh* and Geh, 645 also translates as 'Attendant of Y'.

ma'ăśay (BH, also inscr. *AI*, 22.4). Sf. of *'śh* 'to do, make' + theophoric element, cf. *IPN*, 172. BDB, 796, KB, 583 and Geh, 575 prefer a sf. of *ma'ăśēyāh(û)*, 'Work of Y'. Gehman further suggests a possible accidental transposition of the letters in the name Amasai.

'aḥzay m. and f. (BH, also seal N. Avigad, *Qedem* 4 [1976], 6, 7, and inscr. SO 25.3 cf. *IH*, 48 and Dir, 41; SO Dir, 310). Sf. of the root *'ḥz* 'to seize, grasp' + theophoric element, cf. *IPN*, 179. BDB, 28, KB, 32 and Geh, 22 specify a sf. of *'ăḥazyāh(û)*, 'Y has seized'.

'amṣî (BH). Sf. of *'mṣ* 'to be strong' + theophoric element. KB, 63 and Geh, 41 translate as a sf. of *'ămaṣyāh(û)*, 'Y is strong'.

zabdî (BH). Sf. of the root *zbd* 'to bestow upon' + theophoric element, cf. *zabdî'ēl*, *z*ᵉ*badyāh* etc.

'abdî (BH, also seals V, 172, 291; M, 77 no. 14, 15). Sf. of *'bd* 'servant' + theophoric element, cf. *IPN*, 137. KB, (1953), 673 specify a sf. of *'abdî'ēl*, BDB, 715, and Geh, 2 a sf. of *'ōbadyāh*, 'Servant of El/Y' respectively.

pilṭay (BH). Sf. of *plṭ* 'to deliver' or noun 'deliverance' + theophoric element, cf. *IPN*, 156. Cf. also *palṭî* above.

'imrî (BH). Sf. of *'mr* 'to speak' + theophoric element. KB, 66 (and *IPN*, 173?) indicate a sf. of *'ămaryāhû*, 'Y has spoken'. BDB, 57 prefer 'tall? or eloquent'.

zikrî (BH, also seal V, 309 and inscr. Dir, 274 Weights and Measures). Sf. of the root *zkr* 'to remember' + theophoric element, cf. *IPN*, 187. KB, 260 specify a sf. of *z*ᵉ*karyāh(û)*, 'Y has remembered', and Geh, 1023 also has 'Y has remembered'. Cf. also Schottroff *op. cit.*, 105 n. 2.

zimrî (BH). Sf. of *zmr* + theophoric element, cf. *IPN*, 38, 176. Geh, 1024 suggests 'Y is active', or 'has helped' from Arab. *dhimr* 'active, always giving help'. KB, 263 also indicate a sf. of *zmryhw* Y has helped'.

ḥizqî (BH). Sf. of *ḥzq* + theophoric element, KB, 292 and *IPN*, 160 specify a sf. of *ḥizqîyāhû* 'Y is my strength', or verbal, 'Y has strengthened'.

yiš'î (BH). Sf. of the root *yš'* 'to deliver' + theophoric element, cf. *IPN*, 176. KB, 428 interpret the name as a sf. of *y*ᵉ*ša'yāh(û)*, 'Y has saved'. Geh, 430 also has 'Y has saved'.

sitrî (BH). The name may be a sf. from a verb *str* 'to hide, conceal' or a noun meaning 'hiding place' or 'refuge', with a loss of the original theophoric element. Geh, 887 suggests 'Y is a hiding place, or refuge', though there is no reason to suggest that the theophoric element should be *yhwh*.

šilḥî (BH). Possibly a sf. of an unattested full form *šlḥ* + theophoric element, 'The deity has sent (i.e. the child)', cf. Geh, 869, *IPN*, 173.

šimʿî (BH, also seal V, 308). Sf. of the root *šmʿ* 'to hear' + theophoric element, cf. *IPN*, 185. KB (1953), 992 specify a sf. of *šᵉmaʿyāh(û)* 'Y has heard'.

šimrî (BH). Sf. of *šmr* 'to keep, watch, preserve' + theophoric element, cf. *IPN*, 177, and *šᵉmaryāh(û)*, 'Y has kept, preserved'.

smky (EB seal M, 81 no. 29). Perhaps a sf. of the root *smk* 'to support' + theophoric element, cf. *sᵉmakyāhû* 'Y has supported', and Moscati *ibid*.

ʿezrî (BH). Sf. of the root *ʿzr* 'to help' + theophoric element, cf. *IPN*, 154. KB (1953), 697 specify a sf. of *ʿăzaryāhû* 'Y has helped'.

ʾoznî (BH). Possibly a sf. of a name like *ʾăzanyāhû*, 'Y has heard', cf. Geh, 691, KB, 27. Gen. 46.16 has *ʾeṣbôn*, though this seems no reason to exclude *ʾoznî* as a name, as did Noth (*IPN*, 235).

yoglî (BH). Most interpret this name as a Qal instead of Hophal from the root *glh* with a meaning 'to be manifest', 'to reveal' with a loss of the original theophoric complement, cf. Geh, 500, KB, 369, *IPN*, 244.

ʿotnî (BH). The name may be a sf. of *ʿotnîʾēl* or similar, but the meaning of this latter name is dubious: cf. Geh, 690, KB (1953), 748, *IPN*, 254 and above, § 2.8.

pqḥy (EB seal V, 44). Perhaps a sf. of *pqḥ* + theophoric element 'x has opened (the eyes)'.

Not strictly of the same form, but perhaps to be included here is the name:

mattᵉnay (BH). Most accept a sf. of *mattanyāh(û)* 'Gift of Y' cf. BDB, 682, KB, 619, Geh, 597, *IPN*, 170.

Abbreviations of verbal sentence names of mainly Geminate roots have a reduced first syllable vowel, a long second syllable vowel, and the ending *î*:

ḥănānî (BH). Sf. of the root *ḥnn* 'to be gracious' + theophoric element, cf. *IPN*, 187. BDB, 337 specify a sf. of *ḥănanyāhû*, 'Y has been gracious', also KB, 322.

kᵉnānî (BH). A sf. of *kᵉnanyāh(û)*, 'Y is firm', cf. above, § 2.3 *knn*, *IPN*, 179, KB, 461 and Geh, 157.

ʿănānî (BH). Sf. of the root *ʿnn* + theophoric element, cf. *IPN*, 184. KB, (1953), 772 and Geh, 41 specify a sf. of *ʿănanyāh*, 'Y has appeared'.

A similar type of abbreviated form occurs in the names:

'ămāśā'. variants: *'ămaśśay*, *'ămāśay* (BH, also seal *'mś'* V, 145). The names are possibly sff. of the root *'ms* + theophoric element (*IPN*, 178). Cf. *'ămasyāh*, 'Y has borne', and Geh, 35, KB (1953), 717.

Similar also, is the name:

'ămittay (BH). The name may be a sf. of the noun *'ĕmet* + theophoric element, 'The deity is truth, or faithfulness', cf. KB, 67, *IPN*, 162. Geh, 36 translates the name as 'Y is faithfulness, or truth'.

Certain abbreviated forms have a final *ā'* or *āh*, sometimes used interchangeably. For abbreviated forms *ba'ănā'*, *ba'ănāh*, *ba'ărā'* and *ba'šā'* see above, § 2.2 *b'l*. Cf. also *mîkā'* and *mîkāh* above, and *'dny* above.

šim'ā', *šim'āh* (BH). Sff. of *šm'* 'to hear' + theophoric element, cf. *IPN*, 185. KB, (1953), 992 specify sff. of *šᵉma'yāhû* 'Y has heard'.

šammā', *šammāh* (BH). The names may be sff. of the root *šm'* + theophoric element, cf. Geh, 857, *IPN*, 39 or perhaps *šmr* + theophoric element.

šebnā', *šebnāh* (BH, also seals V, 57, 168, 196, 223, 288; M, 78 no. 17, all with final *'ālep*. Sff. of *šbn* + theophoric element. Most suggest a sf. of *šᵉbanyāhû* (meaning dubious), cf. KB (1953), 942, *IPN*, 258, Geh, 860.

'šn' (EB seals V, 141, 413). The name may be a sf. containing the root *'wš* 'to give' (cf. P. Bordreuil and A. Lemaire, *Syria* 52 [1975], 115-17) + a theophoric element and the addition of the 1st. pers. sing. verbal suffix (see above, pp. 130-31).

mattattāh (BH). A sf. of *mattityāhû*, 'Gift of Y', is suggested by KB, 620 and *IPN*, 170.

dml' (EB seal V, 341; inscr. Gib. 21.28 cf. *SSI*, 56). Sf. of *dmm* + *l*, or root *dml* (cf. Arab. *damal* 'to make peace, heal, cure') + theophoric element. B. Porten (*IEJ* 21 [1971], 48) suggests a sf. of *dml'l* 'Be silent before God' or a sf. of *dmlyh* (unattested). Gibson (*SSI*, 56) also proposes a sf. of *dmlyhw* but with a meaning suggested by Arab. *damal*.

yᵉhûdāh (BH). Possibly a sf. of *yᵉhûdyāh* (unattested) or *yᵉhûd'ēl* (also unattested, Hophal of the root *ydh*), 'May Y/El be praised', cf. A.R. Millard, 'The Meaning of the Name Judah', *ZAW* 86 (1974), 216-18. Cf. also the seal *yhwd* (V, 184) which may be a similar sf.

yᵉdîdāh (BH). The name is usually accepted as meaning 'beloved' (so, BDB, 392, Geh, 449, KB, 373, *IPN*, 223). However, Noth admitted the possibility of a sf. of *yᵉdîdyāh* (*IPN*, 223 n. 1) which seems likely.

ḥsd' (EB seal M, 74 no. 2). Possibly a sf. of *ḥsd* + theophoric element, cf. *ḥăsadyāh*, 'Y is kind or has been gracious'.

yš' (EB seals V, 85, 425). A possible sf. of *yš'* + theophoric element, cf. *yᵉša'yāhû*, 'Y has saved'.

Abbreviated forms which retain the three root consonants and occur in the imperfective are rare:

yišmᵉray (BH). Possibly a sf. of an imf. of the root *šmr* + theophoric element. KB, 427 specify a sf. of *yišmaryāh(û)* (unattested), 'May Y keep, preserve'; cf. also Geh, 431, 'May Y keep'.

y'zn (EB inscr. *AI*, 59.5; A 58.4 cf. *IH*, 215). Possibly a sf. of a name like *ya'ăzanyāhû*, 'Y hears'.

Abridged forms of names compounded with the interrogative *my*, involving the vocalic ending *ā'*, have already been noted above. Other shortened forms involving this interrogative are:

mîkal f. (BH). The name is usually accepted as a sf. of *mîkā'ēl*, 'Who is like El', cf. BDB, 568, Geh, 617, KB, 546.

mk' (EB seal V, 322). A sf. of *mîkā'ēl*, 'Who is like El?' has been suggested by N. Avigad, *IEJ* 25 (1975), 102.

The remaining abbreviated forms do not display characteristics which enable them to be placed in any particular group:

bṣl (EB inscr. *AI*, 49.1). The name could be a sf. of the root *ṣll* + *bᵉ* with the addition of a theophoric element, cf. BH *bᵉṣal'ēl*.

hôšēᵃ' (BH, also seals V, 46, 181, 411, 423, 424, 428; inscr. Mur B 1 cf. *SSI*, 32). Most accept a sf. of *hôša'ăyāh*, 'Y has saved', cf. Geh, 406, KB, 233, *IPN*, 32. BDB, 448 prefer 'salvation'.

yôsēp (BH). The name is a possible sf. of the root *ysp* 'to add' + a theophoric element, cf. *yôsipyāh*, 'Y adds', and *yᵉhôsēp*, Ps. 81.6.

ywzn (EB seal BL, 50 no. 13). Bordreuil and Lemaire suggest a sf. of *yw'zn* (unattested), 'Y has given ear'.

yᵉrîbay (BH). Noth suggested a sf. of *y(ᵉh)ôyārîb* (*IPN*, 201) while Geh, 460 suggests a meaning 'Y contends, pleads'.

rîbay (BH). Sf. of the root *ryb* 'to strive, contend' + theophoric element. KB, 889 suggest a sf. of *yᵉrîbay*; *IPN*, 201 specified the name as a sf. of *y(ᵉh)ôyārîb* and Geh, 804 interprets the name as 'Y strives'.

pnbn yḥny (EB seal M, 79 no. 22; cf. also the seal V, 392). In this name Diringer saw a sf. of the name *pᵉnû'ēl*, or similar, in the form *pn/bn* (*PEQ* 73

[1941], 51). The name *yḥny* may also be a sf. from the root *ḥnn* 'to show favour, be gracious' and a theophoric element.

'aḥlay (BH). The name doubtfully belongs here: it may be an interjectional name, 'O that!' cf. Akk. *Aḫlapia* 'O! that I at last' and BDB, 29. However, Geh, 24 compares Akk. *Aḫ-iliya*, 'My god is a brother', and KB, 33 *Aḫlija 'ḥ* + *'l*?, Akk. *Aḫu-ilia* 'The brother is my god'. Noth (*IPN*, 236) interpreted the name as a sf. from *'aḥlāmāh*, 'precious stone?'

tîryā' (BH). Possibly a sf. meaning '(Y?) is watchful'. Cf. Geh, 951 who compares Akk. *Tīri-Yāma* which occurs in documents of the time of Artaxerxes I and Darius II, where *Yāma* corresponds to *Yhwh*. Noth (*IPN*, 260) also considered a probable connection of the first element with NH *tyr* 'watchful'.

'ḥm' (EB inscr. Dir, 41 no. 6 = SO 32.3 prob. = 37.2 = 38.2 = 39.2 cf. *IH*, 48). The initial element is probably theophoric, but it is not possible to determine the original second element. Kornfeld, *WZKM* 71 (1979), 41 suggests a sf. of names such as *'ḥymwt*, *'ḥymlk*, *'ḥm'ṣ*, and Lemaire (*op. cit.*,) considers the name to be a sf. of *'ḥymlk*.

šmyh (EB inscr. *AI*, 110.1, see also A. F. Rainey, *Tel Aviv* 4 [1977] 97-104). This hitherto unattested name may be a sf. of *šm'yh* or *šmryh*.

The above names have been grouped together because they appear to be abbreviated from a corresponding full form which is compounded with a theophoric element. There are many other names which have been considered in other studies as abbreviated forms of theophoric compound names, a full discussion of which is beyond the scope of this study. Names, for example, with the ending *āt* have not been considered as abbreviated, cf. *šimrāt* 'guarded' (by the parents?). Also *qaṭôl* forms like *'āmôṣ* 'strong' (cf. BDB, 55, Geh, 40) and *ṣādôq* 'righteous', have been rejected, although the latter may contain a semantic implication of a deity. The diminutive form *ôn* suggested by Lidzbarski (*Eph*, 18) and Noth (*IPN*, 38), has not been accepted as an abbreviation, since names like *šalmôn*, *heṣrôn*, *šim'ôn*, *šimrôn* and *šimšôn* do not contain reference to a deity, even if the formula diminutive form = abbreviated form, could be verified. Frequently, a number of ordinary imperfective forms have been considered as abbreviated names which originally contained a theophoric compound. Careful examination of such types, however, gives no indication that they should be accepted as such. Many may possibly contain a semantic idea of a deity, such as *yibḥar* (BH) 'He (the deity) chooses', or 'May he (the deity) choose', while others may pertain, not to a deity, but to the child itself, for example, *yimlā'/h* 'May he fulfil' (the wishes of his parents, or the like), *y*^{e}*'ûš* 'May he help', *yiṣḥar* 'May he shine' etc. The following additional names are included, not because they are shortened names with regard to *form*, but because the deity is possibly semantically implied in the nature of the name. Biblical names of this type are listed here, though they frequently occur elsewhere as shortened forms.

zābûd	'Given' (by the deity), cf. Geh, 1010.
z^{e}*bûdāh*	'Given' (by the deity), cf. Geh, 1013.
z^{e}*bîdāh*	'Given' (by the deity), cf. Geh, 1013.
zabbay	'He (the deity) has given', cf. Geh, 1010.
zakkûr	'He (the deity) has remembered.[25]
zimmāh	'He (the deity) has considered, purposed', cf. Geh, 1024, *IPN*, 39, 176.
ḥārim	'Consecrated' (to the deity)', cf. Geh, 364, *IPN*, 136.
yā'îr	'He (the deity) enlightens', cf. Geh, 442, KB, 365 or, 'May he (the deity) shine forth', *IPN*, 204.
yibḥār	'He (the deity) chooses', cf. BDB, 104, Geh, 415, KB, 366.
yaddu^{a}*'*	'Known' (of the deity), cf. Geh, 441.
yig'āl	'May he (the deity) redeem', cf. Geh, 418, KB, 368, *IPN*, 200.
yôb/yāšûb	'May he (the deity) return', cf. Geh, 447, KB, 381/425, *IPN*, 199. The meaning may also be 'He returns'.
yākîn	'He (the deity) establishes' or 'will establish', cf. Geh, 438, KB, 392.
yamlēk	'He (the deity) gives' or, 'May he (the deity) give dominion, power', cf. Geh, 418, KB, 397.
yimnāh	'May he (the deity) defend', cf. Geh, 420, KB, 397.
ya'ăqōb /ya'ăqōbāh	Possibly 'May he (the deity) protect', cf. Geh, 439, *IPN*, 177, also S. Arab. and Ethiopic *'akaba* 'to guard, protect'.
yapî^{a}*'*	'May he (the deity) cause to shine forth', cf. KB, 405, Geh, 446.
yaplēṭ	'May he (the deity) deliver', cf. Geh, 446, KB, 405, *IPN*, 199.
y^{e}*punneh*	'May he (the deity) be turned (favourable)', cf. 457, KB, 405.
yiptāḥ	'He (the deity) opens', cf. BDB, 836.
yāqîm	'May he (the deity) establish', cf. Geh, 443.
yārîb	'May he (the deity) contend', cf. Geh, 447, KB, 419. Noth (*IPN*, 201) specifies a sf. of *y*^{e}*hôyārîb*.
s^{e}*tûr*	'Hidden' (by the deity), cf. Geh, 853, *IPN*, 158.

'abdôn	'Servant' (of the deity), cf. Geh, 2, *IPN*, 137.
'ôbēd	'Worshipper' (of the deity), cf. KB, (1953), 685, *IPN*, 137.
'aqqûb	'(The deity is) protecting', cf. Geh, 26.
p[e]'ull[e]tay	'Work, recompense' (of the deity), cf. Geh, 740.
ṣill[e]tay	'(The deity is a) shadow' i.e. protection, cf. Geh, 1024.
r[e]ḥûb	'(The deity has shown) compassion', cf. Geh, 797, *IPN*, 187. BDB, 933 suggest 'compassionate, softness, gentleness'.
raḥam	'(The deity has shown) compassion', cf. Geh, 790, *IPN*, 187. BDB, 933 suggest 'girl (like)?'
šā'ûl	'Asked' (of the deity), cf. Geh, 836, BDB, 982.
šû[a]'	'(The deity is) salvation or help', cf. Geh, 877.
šû'ā'	'(The deity is) salvation or help', cf. Geh, 877, *IPN*, 38, 154.

Before concluding this section concerning abbreviated names, a number of points require comment. To begin with, several abbreviated forms are compounded with roots which are not attested in a full form with a theophoric element. Such, for example, are the names *'ămittay*, *yoglî*, *ḥuppāh*, *'adlay*, *radday*, *šilḥî*, *tîryā'* and *'aḥlay*. It is to be noted, too, that some names could probably be shortened in a variety of ways. The full forms *yišma'yāh(û)*, *š[e]ma'yāh(û)*, *'ĕlîšāmā'* and *yišma''ēl* occur alongside a variety of shortened forms, *šammay*, *šāmā'*, *šim'î*, *šim'ā'*, *šim'āh*, *šammû[a]'*, *šammā'*, *šammāh*, *yišmā'* and *hôšāmā'*, which seems to indicate that one full form could be shortened in several different ways. Nevertheless, we can rarely assign any of these shortened forms to a particular full form.

Finally, it should be observed that, although many shortened names cannot be attributed to a full form, the likelihood of their containing a theophoric element originally makes their inclusion in a study of the Hebrew concept of deity through proper names a relevant inquiry.

Notes to Chapter 2

1. I.e. without the names attested only in Chronicles.

2. I.e. with the names attested only in Chronicles.

3. Such a conclusion, however, depends upon the addition or subtraction of the 89 occurrences of names in 1 Chr. 23–27 which occur in the context of the Davidic administration, but which many suggest belong to a period of about the 4th century BC (cf. A.S. Herbert, 'I and II Chronicles', *Peake's Commentary*, 362, *et al.*). In the case in hand the addition of these names to the period of the united Monarchy would occasion sufficient occurrences of names at this time to outnumber those in the pre-Monarchical period.

4. A fact which Gray *op. cit*. 162, Tables 3 and 4. failed to note.

5. *'oznî 'ûrî buqqî gaddî gōmer hôšē*[a]*' y*[e]*hûdāh yoglî yôsēp mā'ay mîkāh nādāb sitrî sôdî šammāh šammû*[a]*' šim'î zabdî zikrî zimrî 'uzzî*. See also the table of short forms in the Appendix 4.2.

6. For example *y*[e]*hûdāh*, *yôsēp*, *hôšē*[a]*'*, while *mîkāh* and *šammû*[a]*'* are certainly abbreviations, at least in some cases, of a Yahwistic compound name; see p. 152.

7. The addition of the 41 occurrences of names suffixed with forms of *yhwh* in 1 Chr. 23–27 to the period of the united Monarchy would, however, occasion more such compounds in this period than in the pre-Monarchical period.

8. Actual numbers are not given here, in view of the constant addition of new names. Table 4.15 of the appendix gives the appropriate number of forms at the time of writing.

9. The addition of the 21 names in 1 Chr. 23–27, however, would occasion more Qal perfectives in the period of the united Monarchy than in the pre-Monarchical period.

10. The addition of the 10 names in 1 Chr. 23–27 to the period of the united Monarchy, however, would occasion sufficient occurrences of prefixed *yhwh* so that they, also, would exceed their number in Exilic and post-Exilic times, i.e. another divergence from the usual distribution of names.

11. Unless names in 1 Chr. 23–27 are placed in the Davidic period in which case more compound names with *'l* would be evident in the time of the united Monarchy than the Exilic/post-Exilic period.

12. Unless names from 1 Chr. 23–27 are included here, in which case, names suffixed with *'l* attested for the period of the united Monarchy would be only second in number to those of the pre-Monarchical time.

13. Or 1:5 if names in 1 Chr. 23–27 are included.

14. Or 1:6 if names in 1 Chr. 23–27 are included.

15. Unless names from 1 Chr. 23–27 are included in this period, in which case occurrences of names prefixed with *'l* are sufficient in this period to be second only to those of the united Monarchy in frequency.

16. Or 1:5 if names from 1 Chr. 23–27 are included.

17. The names and Heb. roots here, have been transcribed by the present writer.

18. In nominal sentence names where the theophoric element occurs in the 2nd position e.g. *'ădî'ēl*, there seems no need to place the theophoric element in the predicative position in translation, 'An ornament is El' (cf. BDB, 726). The parallel verbal forms *'el'ādāh* and *'ădāyāh* both mean 'El/Y has adorned', although the theophoric element as subject can be placed in first or second position. There is no reason why this cannot also be the case with nominal sentence names. We should note on the subject of such word order, the work of F.I. Andersen, *The Hebrew Verbless Clause in the Pentateuch*, Abingdon Press (1970), although the work is not easily applicable to personal names. If, as Andersen states, the predicate in personal names is always definite (p. 46), then the name clause is always one of identification and the order subject-predicate obtains (p. 32). One could hardly conclude, however, that the word order for *all* theophoric personal names is subject-predicate. As will be seen below, the word order in such names has more to do with the idea which is expressed about the deity than with any rule appertaining to the semantics of the Hebrew language as a whole.

19. For the mis-use of the term, see below, p. 149.

20. For *'zn*, cf. *šm'*; for *ṭll* cf. *ḥph*, *ḥpp*, *y'ṭ*, *ksh*, *l'ṭ*, *skk*, *skn*, *šwp*; for *kwn*, cf. *ysd*; for *pll*, cf. *dyn*, *špṭ*. The roots *nḥm*, *yš'* and *pl'* have no homonymous parallel in the Qal.

21. The final letter on the seal *'ldg*[ ] (Y. Aharoni, *Tel Aviv* 1 [1974], 157) is uncertain. The second element has been restored by Vattioni (V, 300) to *dgn*, but this is uncertain. Semantically, the roots *dgh* 'to multiply, increase' (cf. BDB, 185) as well as *dgl* 'to look, behold' (cf. BDB, 186) are both possible, but this is equally uncertain. Herr, 148 no. 160 also restores the final letter as *n*. He notes, also, that the seal is crude and could be a modern forgery, or of Philistine origin.

22. P. Bordreuil and A. Lemaire, *Sem* 29 (1979), 83, consider the seals V, 41 and V, 6 to be Ammon. For the latter seal they prefer a reading *'lh'm*. The intermediate *yōd* is also evident with other theophoric elements in the first position, cf. *'byḥy AI*, 39.11; *'ḥy'yl AI*, 35.3 (*'ḥy'm* A 35.3 in *IH*, 204); *'lyṣwr* B 2.1 cf. *IH*, 273.

23. The possibility of a Qal perf. from the root *ṭll* 'to cover, roof', would suggest a translation 'The (divine) Father has covered i.e. protected'. Elsewhere, the name is interpreted nominally, 'The (divine) Father is dew', cf. BDB, 4, Geh, 7, KB, 5. See also above, § 2.5 for the Qal perf. of Geminate roots.

24. P. Bordreuil and A. Lemaire, Sem 29 (1979), 82, consider these seals to be Ammon. However, against this, cf. J. Teixidor, *Syria* 54 (1977), 261 no. 54.

25. *Qaṭṭûl* forms are frequently attested in the Elephantine papyri, as Silverman has pointed out (Michael H. Silverman, *Jewish Personal Names in the Elephantine Documents: a study in onomastic development*, Ph.D. Dissertation, Brandeis University (1967), University Microfilms, p. 95). He considers these as shortened forms from strong verb perfectives (including I *'ālep* and III *yōd* roots). Certainly, BH attests a *qaṭṭûl* form *šammûaʿ* which is abbreviated from *šᵉmaʿyāh(û)*. Whether all *qaṭṭûl* forms are such abbreviations is not possible to say, but we should consider the possibility that some, at least, may be considered so. (Cf. also the *qaṭṭûl* forms *yaddûaʿ* and *ʿaqqûb* listed below.)

Chapter 3

THE CONCEPT OF DEITY AS REVEALED IN HEBREW PERSONAL NAMES

The foregoing sections of the present study have been devoted to an analysis of Hebrew theophoric personal names, primarily with regard to their formal characteristics. Each name, in addition, has revealed some aspect of the divine character, has expressed in some cases divine involvement with man, or has conveyed a particular kind of relationship between name-bearer and deity. Names are found, for example, which depict the deity as 'trust' (*mbṭḥ*) or 'light' (*'wr*), names which show that the deity 'supports' (with the roots *smk*, *'mn*, *'šh*), and names which portray the name-bearer as a 'servant of' the deity (*'bd*).

1. *Anthropomorphic concepts*

Many Hebrew names describe the deity anthropomorphically, attributing to the Hebrew God the characteristics of man. This is evident with the use of the elements *'b* 'father', *'ḥ* 'brother' and *'m* 'kinsman, uncle'. The deity is also depicted as a 'portion' (*ḥlq*), as 'ancient' or, perhaps, 'pre-eminent' with the root *qdm* (see above, §2.9 *qadmî'ēl*) as well as 'excellent' or 'excellence' with the use of the root *mgd*, a root which is not used in a transcendent sense, but is used in biblical Hebrew of the gifts of nature. Also anthropomorphic in character, are names which portray the deity as 'good fortune' (*šb'*, *gd*), 'confidence', 'trust' (*mbṭḥ*), 'death' (*mwt*), and as a 'witness' (root *'wd*). Less certain are the ideas of the Hebrew God as 'existence' (*yš* see above, §2.9 *'ăbišay*), as 'truth' in the possibly abbreviated name *'amittay* (*ibid.*, §2.10) and 'fine gold' (*pz ibid.*, §2.9 *'ělîpaz*). Relevant here, too, is the concept that the deity is kindled with anger (*ḥrh ibid.*, *ḥarḥăyāh*).

Also in the context of anthropomorphic concepts, or perhaps involved with the idea of the deity as a source of joy (see below), are names which depict the Hebrew God as a source of light, with the nouns *'wr* 'light' and *nr* 'lamp'. The deity is also portrayed as 'fair' and 'beautiful' in names containing the root *yph* 'to be fair, beautiful' and *šnh* 'to shine, be beautiful'. Similarly, some names portray the deity as 'pleasantness' and 'delight' with the use of the roots *n'm* and possibly *'dn* (see above §2.9 *y^ehô'addān*). The idea of the deity as 'luxuriant' may also be present in the name *baqbuqyāh*, although this is uncertain (*ibid.*, §2.9). Other anthropomorphic elements also occur, and will be noted in the following categories.

2. *Concepts involving nature*

Still anthropomorphically, some names seem to represent the deity in terms of nature: these involve the roots *zrh* 'to scatter, fan, winnow', *zr'* 'to sow', *'rš* 'to plant' (cf. Arab. *gharasa*, Akk. *erēšu*) and, perhaps, *šrb* 'to send burning heat' (Piel). Also to be considered are the concepts 'autumn' (*ḥrp*), 'dawn' (*šḥr*), and 'storm, rage, tempest' (*s'r*), as well as the idea that the deity 'has thundered' or is 'thunder' (*r'm* see above §2.9 *ra'amyāh*) and perhaps similarly, the use of the root *r'l* 'to quiver, shake' (*ibid.*, *r^e'ēlāyāh*). The root *š'l* 'deep' may also be relevant here (cf. NH 'deep, depth' [of the sea], BDB, 1043).

3. *Genitive elements*

Three nouns of anthropomorphic type occur in construct type names which, as such, may refer to characteristics of the deity, or may refer to the name-bearer. These are the nouns *pn* 'face', *šm* 'name' and *ḥg* 'feast'. The name-bearer is also depicted in relationship to the deity with construct type nouns portraying him as a 'man of' (*'yš*, *mt*, *gbr*), 'client of' (*gr* cf. Phoen.), 'youth, attendant of' (*n'r* and *pth* cf. Arab. *fatiya*) and 'servant of' (*'bd*) the deity. Other names of this type express closeness between God and man by describing the name-bearer as the 'friend of' (*r'*), 'possession of' (*mqnh*) and 'known of' (root *yd'*) the deity. Some names of this type are prefixed with the preposition *b^e* 'in', and express the name-bearer as 'in the testimony of' (*b* + *'wd*), 'in the hand of' (*b* + *yd*) and 'in the secret council of' (*b* + *swd*) the deity. Two names of animals, *'ry* 'lion' and *'gl* 'calf', are used to depict the name-bearer as a 'lion of' and 'calf of' the deity.

4. *Prepositional elements*

Similar, too, are names with the prepositions *'t* and *'m*, both meaning 'with'. which express that the deity is with man. The preposition *l^emô/l^e* 'belonging to' also depicts the name-bearer in close relationship with the deity. The names *'ely(^eh)ô'ênay* 'Towards Yahweh are my eyes' also involve the prefixing of the preposition *'l* 'to' and are the only examples in Hebrew names in which the theophoric element is not in the initial or final position.

5. *Deity approaches man*

Many names convey the idea that the Hebrew God approached man, as in names from the roots *'th* and *bw'* 'to come', *zrḥ* 'to rise', *qwm* 'to arise', *škn* 'to take up abode', *y'd* 'to meet by appointment' (Niphal), *pg'* 'to meet', and *'nn* 'to appear'. A root *glh* 'to manifest, reveal' is also evident in the Hebrew name *yoglî* but this may not be an abbreviation of a theophoric compound (see above §2.10).

6. *Perceptiveness of the deity*

A large percentage of Hebrew names indicate the perceptiveness of the Hebrew God. This concept that the deity observes or takes account of man, is evident in names from the roots *ḥzh* and *r'h* 'to see', *ḥšb* 'to take account' and *š'r* 'to reckon'. Less certain are the roots *šwr* 'to regard, behold' (see above §2.9 *'ăḥîšār*) and *śkh* 'to look out' (cf. NH and *ibid.*, *śāk^eyāh*). The root *tyr* 'to be watchful' (cf. NH) occurs in the name *tîryā'*, which may be an abbreviation of a theophoric compound (see above §2.10) but, again, this is uncertain.

Also revealing the idea of the perceptiveness of the deity are names incorporating the elements *yd'* 'to know', *'zn* and *šm'* 'to hear', as well as the root *š'l* 'to ask' which, since it is used with the deity as the object in the names *š^e'altî'ēl* and *šaltî'ēl* (*ibid.*, §2.9) belongs here in this context, also implying that the deity listens to, and is aware of, man. Also indicating a conception of the deity's perceptiveness are names involving the elements *zkr* and *y'd* (cf. Arab. *wa'ā* with the meaning 'to remember'.

Similar, are names containing the roots *'nh* 'to answer' and, perhaps, *brk* 'to bless' which show that the divine character was one which considered man's requests. The deity may be semantically the subject of the name *zimmāh* 'He has considered, purposed', although this is uncertain (*ibid.*, §2.10)

7. *Involvement of the deity in birth events*

Many Hebrew names seem to express some involvement of the deity in the birth of the child. The Hebrew God is frequently depicted as having created the child, an idea exemplified in anthropomorphic names with *bnh* 'to build, create', *br'* and *qnh* 'to create', *'śh* and *p'l* 'to make' and *rwḥ* 'to breathe (i.e. create)'. The thought that the deity gives life is possibly attested also in the name *m*ᵉ*ḥîyâ'ēl/m*ᵉ*ḥûyā'ēl* (see above, §2.8. 2).

The roots *šlm* 'to recompense' and *šwb* 'to restore' (Hiphil) in names, probably refer to the idea of compensation by the deity for a previously deceased child. Evidence for the belief that the deity 'gives' a child is found frequently in the name elements *'wš* (cf. Arab. *'āsa*), *zbd*, *ntn*, *qwš* (cf. Akk. *qāšu* and above, §2.9 *qûšāyāhû*) and *pwṭ* (Eg. in *pûṭî'ēl* and *pṭyhw*).

The roots *gml* and *gmr* meaning 'to accomplish' may also be connected with birth events, denoting that the deity has 'accomplished' the birth of the child. It is possible that the roots *'mr* 'to say' and, perhaps, *qwl* 'to speak' (see above, §2.9 *qlyhw*) express that the child has been created by command, in the same way as some of the creations of the Genesis narratives (Gen. 1.3, 6, 9, 11 etc.). Perhaps also in this context should be included the root *pqd* 'to appoint' which, however, is attested only in the difficult name *p̊q̊dyw* (see above, §2.4 *pqd*).

Also involved with the birth events are names with the roots *ptḥ* 'to open (the womb)' and perhaps *pqḥ* 'to open (the eyes)'. In the same context is the use of the element *rmh* 'to loosen (the womb)', although this root is problematic in Hebrew names (*ibid.*, §2.5 *rmh*/*rwm*). The root *rḥb* meaning 'to be or grow wide, large', may be used in names in the same way as *rmh*, suggestive of the enlarging of the womb although the element may involve the idea of enlargement of the family in the same way as the root *ysp* 'to add' in Hebrew names.

8. *Protection*

The Hebrew onomasticon contains many elements which characterize the deity as protection. This is an idea mainly represented anthropomorphically by the nouns *'hl* 'tent', *dlt* 'door', *hr* 'mountain', *ṣwr* 'rock' and *šwr* 'wall', while the concept of the deity as a 'refuge' is attested in the nouns *mḥsh* and *m'wz*, perhaps also, with the root *'wn* (see above §2.2 *b'l/b'lm'ny*). Also anthropomorphic is the thought of the name-bearer as 'in the shadow (protection) of' the deity in the name *beṣal'ēl*. Occurring, too, are names which symbolize protection by stating that the deity 'has hidden'. This is the case with the roots *ḥb'/h*, *str* and *ṣpn* and perhaps, similarly, with the root *ṭll* which states that the deity 'has covered' (*ibid.*, §2.4 *ṭll*). The specific idea that the deity 'protects' is to be found in names with the roots *zmr* (cf. S. Arab. *dhimr*) and, possibly, *ḥmh* (cf. S. Arab. *ḥamay*).

9. *Preservation and support*

The idea of preservation of, and support for, man was also incorporated in the Hebrew concept of deity. The notion of 'support' is attested in the roots *smk*, *'mn*, *'šh* and perhaps *yšh* (cf. Arab. *'asa'* and above, §2.9 *yôšawyāh*). Similar are the ideas that the deity 'nourishes' contained in names with the roots *kwl* (Pilpel), *qwt* (cf. Arab. *qāta*) and *'zh* (cf. Arab. *ghadhā*). and that the deity 'preserves' in the root *šmr*. An analogous thought is perhaps also evident in the use of the root *yšb* 'to cause to dwell (in peace and security)' (Hiphil).

10. *Strength*

Frequently attested are names which describe the deity as 'strong' with the elements *gbr*, *ḥzq*, *'zz*, *'br*, as well as *knn* 'to be firm'. The thought is conveyed nominally in the roots *ḥzq*, *'zz* and *ḥwl/ḥyl* 'strength'. Also found, are names which state that the deity 'strengthens', with the root *ḥzq* and perhaps *mrr* (cf. Ug. 'to strengthen, bless, commend').

11. *Salvation and help*

Occurring frequently also are names which characterize the deity as 'delivering' or 'rescuing' with the elements *yš'*, *plṭ*, *mlṭ*, *nṣl* (Hiphil) and Aram. *šêzêb*, as well as *ḥml* 'to spare', *dlh* 'to draw (i.e. rescue)' and, possibly, *ḥlṣ* 'to draw off, withdraw', although this last root may imply some connection with birth events (see above §2.4). Similar is the notion that the deity has 'ransomed' in names with the root *pdh* and that the deity has 'redeemed', with the root *g'h*.

A few names portray the deity as 'help', an idea attested in the elements *'zr*, *'wš* and *'dr*. The root *'ḥz* 'to seize' may also contain the similar thought that the deity 'seizes', perhaps in order to help. Relevant here, too, is possibly the root *'ms* 'to carry, bear', and the unusual thought 'to carry into exile' with the Hiphil of the root *glh*.

12. *Goodness, kindness, grace and compassion*

The divine characteristics of goodness, kindness and grace are reflected in another group of personal names with the roots *ḥnn* 'to be gracious, show favour', *ḥn* 'grace, favour', *ḥsd* 'to be kind, good, gracious', *ḥlh* 'to be pleasing, show oneself well-disposed, friendly', *ṭwb* 'to be pleasing, good', *yṭb* 'to benefit' (cf. Aram.), *ydh* 'to be beneficent, do good' (cf. Arab. *yadā*) and, perhaps also pertinent here, *ṣdq* 'to be just, righteous'.

The Hebrew God is also characterized as merciful and compassionate, an idea represented in names with the roots *rḥm* 'to have compassion' (Piel), *nḥm* 'to comfort' and *mnḥm* 'comforter'. Comparable may be the thought that the deity turns towards man, although this is not an idea attested with certainty in the name-elements *swr* 'to turn aside' (see above §2.9 *sryh*), *pnh* 'to turn' (*ibid.*, §2.4) and *sḥr* 'to turn' (*ibid.*, §2.9 [*yh*]*wsḥ*[*r*]). Possibly similar, is the idea that the deity has 'returned' with names involving the Qal of the root *šwb*.

Also analogous to the thought of the mercy of the deity are names from the root *nšh* 'to forget', in which the object is probably 'sins', as well as names from the root *rp'* stating that the deity 'heals'.

13. *The deity as a source of joy*

A small group of names is also evident in which the deity is portrayed as a source of joy. In Hebrew names this thought is probably depicted only causatively, rather than stating that the deity himself is joyful or rejoices. The root *'šr* is used to express the idea that the deity 'fills with joy' (cf. Arab. *'ašira*), and the noun *gyl* describes the deity as 'rejoicing joy'. Also attested is the root *ḥdh* 'to rejoice', and *ḥbṣ* 'to be joyful' in the name *ḥăbaṣṣinyāh* (see above §2.8). Relevant in this context may be the thought that the deity 'enlightens' with the use of the root *ngh*.

14. *The concept of selection*

There is also evident among Hebrew names some indication that the deity was thought to select certain people. Such a concept is attested in names with the elements *'ṣl* 'to reserve, lay aside', *ḥṣh* 'to divide', *d'h* 'to call', *'sp* 'to gather' and *drš* 'to seek'. Selection in a more ritualistic sense is perhaps exemplified in the use of the roots *brr* 'to purify, select', *ṭbl* 'to dip (purify)' and *nzh* 'to sprinkle'. The idea of special closeness between deity and man is found in names from the roots *dwd* and *ydd* depicting the name-bearer as 'beloved of' Yahweh, while the root *dwd* is also used verbally to denote that the deity 'has loved'.

Perhaps also connected with the idea of selection is the notion that the deity 'adorns' in names with the roots *'dh* and, possibly, the root *rml* 'to adorn with gems' (cf. Arab. *ramala* and above, §2.9 *r^emalyāhû*). The idea of the name-bearer as 'captive of' the deity may also depict the concept of selection in Hebrew names, although the root *šbh*, from which such a thought is derived, is not found with certainty (see above, §2.7 *š^ebû'ēl*). Applicable here, would also be the names *ḥārim* 'consecrated' and *yibḥar* 'He chooses' in which the deity may be semantically implied. However, this is not certain, and neither root is attested elsewhere with a theophoric element.

15. *Establishment by the deity*
The concept that the deity 'establishes' is found in Hebrew names with the roots *kwn* and *śwm*, while the Hiphil of the root *qwm* 'to raise up' expresses a similar idea, as well as the root *plh* 'to distinguish' in the name *'ĕlîp^elēhû* (see above, §2.9).

16. *Divine titles*
The title 'lord' is found in names as an appellation for Yahweh with the elements *b'l*, *'dn* and, perhaps, Aram. *mr'*, although this is uncertain (see above § 2.3 *mr*). Frequently attested, too, is the title 'king' with the noun *mlk*.

17. *Transcendent characteristics*
A large number of Hebrew names illustrate the transcendent nature of the deity, who is depicted as 'high, exalted' (*rwm*, and possibly *'lh*, see above, §2.3), 'inaccessibly high' (*śgb*), as 'proud or exalted' (*'th* cf. Arab. *'atā*), 'noble or excellent' (*pr'* cf. Arab. *fara'a*), 'pre-eminent or abundant' (*ytr*, verbal and nominal) and, perhaps, as 'preceding or predominant' (*'yl* see above §2.9 *'ḥy'yl*). The roots *gdl* and *rbb* portray the deity as 'great', while names with the elements *pl'* 'wonderful', *kbd* 'glory, honour' and *g'h* 'majesty' are also attested. The perfection of the deity is depicted in names with the root *tmm* 'to be perfect' and, possibly, *kll* 'to be complete' (see above §2.9 *kil'āb*). The Hebrew God is also described as 'perpetual, never-failing' with the root *ytn* (cf. Arab. *watana*), and as 'noble, generous' with the element *ndb*.

Also conveying the idea of the transcendent nature of the deity is the use of the pronoun *hw'* 'he' in names of the type *'ělîhû(')* 'He is God', as well as the use of the interrogative *mî* 'Who?' in the name-type *mîkāyāh(û)* 'Who is like Yahweh?'.

18. *Rulership and judgment*

Another group of names seems to express the idea of rulership, judgment and contention in the divine character. The concept that the deity 'rules' may be evident in the use of the root *'wm* (cf. S. Arab. *'āma*), although this root is uncertain in the name *'ăḥî'ām* (see above, §2.9). A possibly abbreviated name, *radday*, containing the root *rdh* 'to have dominion, rule, dominate' is also found, but the root does not exist elsewhere with a theophoric element and so may not be relevant.

The roots *dyn*, *pll* and *špṭ* express that the deity 'has judged', while the idea that the deity 'directs' is to be found, although not with certainty, in the roots *dll* (see above, §2.4) and the Hiphil of *yrh* (*ibid.*, §2.9 *yrmlk*). Similar in thought is the use of the roots *'wd* 'to testify', *'md* 'to take one's stand', *ryb* 'to strive, contend' and *śrh* 'to persevere, persist' (or 'rule'), while the name *'û'ēl* 'Will of God' (root *'wh* cf. Arab. *'awaya*) may also belong in this context, as well as the name *'adbe'ēl* which perhaps contains the root *'db* 'to invite, discipline' (cf. Arab. *'adaba* and above, §2.9).

19. *Imperatives*

A few name-elements are attested in the imperative. This is the case with the root *ydh* 'to praise' which occurs with the deity as the object, while the roots *dmm* 'to be still' (see above, §2.8. 1) and *ḥkh* 'to wait' (*ibid.*), which may contain imperative forms, are less certain.

Chapter 4

THE CONCEPT OF DEITY AS REVEALED IN OTHER ANCIENT SEMITIC ONOMASTICA

The second major division of the present study is devoted to an examination of the personal names found in Ugaritic, Phoenician, Amorite, Aramaic, Old Akkadian, Akkadian and Palmyrene, and a comparison between these various onomastica and Hebrew name-giving.

In each case, only theophoric names have been chosen, in other words, those names which reveal some concept concerning a deity. Usually, these names have been divided into those which have elements common to Hebrew and express similar ideas, those which have semantic similarities in Hebrew, and those containing concepts not reflected in Hebrew theophoric names. However, the format of each of the seven comparative sections is not identical since differences between the onomastica necessitate a fresh approach for each.

The extent to which abbreviated names can be used in the different onomastica also varies. In Akkadian, for example, where names often involve more than two parts and, therefore, contain fuller semantic content, it is easier to decide whether a name is an abbreviation of a theophoric compound. In a language such as Palmyrene, however, this same question is more difficult to determine in view of the presence of only two parts in compound names. Generally speaking, where a possible abbreviation of an originally theophoric compound is in question, the name is perhaps more acceptable as a shortened form if its non-theophoric element is attested elsewhere with a divine name. Otherwise, any decision in favour of an abbreviation of a theophoric compound should be considered speculative. Section 2.10 above, in the context of Hebrew names, has shown the precarious nature of many abbreviated forms.

It is rarely completely certain that any alleged short form originally contained a divine name. Evidence that the contrary was the case in other Semitic onomastica is unconvincing. In many instances, therefore, names considered as shortened forms in the non-Hebrew onomastica have been excluded, except in some cases where they affect conclusions reached concerning the concept of deity.

4.1 *A Comparison between the Concepts of Deity Revealed in the Ugaritic and Hebrew Onomastica*

A study of the Ugaritic onomasticon has been undertaken by Frauke Gröndahl in her work, *Die Personennamen der Texte aus Ugarit*,[1] and has greatly facilitated the present comparison between the concept of deity revealed in Hebrew and Ugaritic names.

1. The Hebrew and Ugaritic onomastica display many ideas and roots which are common to both, and which reveal similar thoughts concerning the large number of Ugaritic deities on the one hand, and the Israelite God on the other, as the following list illustrates:

Ug.	*PTU*	*Heb.*	
'b	86	*'b*	father
'dn	89-90	*'dn*	lord
'ḫ	91	*'ḥ*	brother
'wl	103	*'wl*	to be predominant[2]
'š	102	*'yš*	man[3]
bd	118	*bd*	in the hand of
bny/bnw	119	*bnh*	to build, create
b'l	114-17	*b'l*	lord
gmr	128	*gmr*	to accomplish
dyn	123	*dyn*	to judge
hw	134	*hw'*	pron. he
ḥwy/ḥyy	137	*ḥyh*	to live
ḥnn	135-36	*ḥnn*	to be gracious
ydd	143	*ydd*	to love[4]
yd'	142	*yd'*	to know
kbd	148	*kbd*	honour, glory
kwn	153	*kwn*	to be firm, stable[5]
mlk	157-58	*mlk*	king
mt	161	*mt*	man
ndb	164	*ndb*	to be generous, noble
ngh	164	*ngh*	to shine, enlighten
nyr/nwr	165	*nwr*	Ug. light, Heb. lamp

n'm	163	*n'm*	to be pleasant, delightful, lovely
n'r	163-64	*n'r*	youth, young warrior
'bd	104-106	*'bd*	servant[6]
'dr	113	*'dr*	to help
'zz/'zy	112	*'zz*	to be strong
'ly	108	*'lh*	to rise, ascend, be high[7]
'mm	109	*'m*	uncle, kinsman
pn	173	*pn*	face
ṣdq	187	*ṣdq*	to be just, righteous
qwm	178	*qwm*	to arise
qny	176	*qnh*	to create
rbb/rby	179	*rbb*	to be great, much
rwm/rym	182	*rwm*	to be high, exalted
rp'	180	*rp'*	to heal
šḥr	192	*šḥr*	dawn
šm	193	*šm*	name
šm'	194	*šm'*	to hear
tmm	201	*tmm*	to be complete, perfect

2. There are, however, a number of roots which are identical in both onomastica, but which either have totally different meanings or contain particular nuances of thought which portray slightly different concepts concerning the deity. Other roots common to both may have the same basic meaning, but may occur in different forms in the respective name-giving, as the following illustrate:

'mr 'to see' (*PTU*, 99). The root *'mr* in BH and in Heb. theophoric names means 'to say', as also the same root in Phoen. and Aram. The Ug. root, however, as in Akk. usage, means 'to see', comparable to the use of *ḥzh* and *r'h* in Heb. name-giving.

gr (*PTU*, 129). The element *gr* in Ug. means 'foreigner, charge, protégé', whereas the same element in Heb. names is probably more akin to Phoen. *gr* meaning 'client' (cf. *PNPPI*, 298). Both elements are found in construct with a following theophoric element. A meaning 'descendant, offspring' is, perhaps, also possible for the Ug. element (cf. J. Aistleitner, *Wörterbuch der ugaritischen Sprache*, Berichte über die Verhandlungen der Sächsischen Akademie der Wissenschaften zu Leipzig, Philologisch-historische Klasse, 106/3; Berlin (1963), 690 = 'Abkömmling').

gmr (*PTU*, 128). This element in Ug. names probably means 'to complete, execute', similar to the idea 'to accomplish' in Heb. names with the same root. Both Heb. and Ug. use the element verbally in names (see above, 1), while the Ug. root is also attested in nominal sentence names.

mlk (*PTU*, 157-58). Both Heb. and Ug. theophoric names contain the noun *mlk* 'king', but in Ug. names, the root is also used verbally, meaning 'to rule, advise'. The same concept 'to rule' may be evident in a root *'wm* in the BH name *'ăḥî'ām*. However, the second element of this name could also be derived from a root *'mm* (see above, §2.9).

mrr$_3$ (*PTU*, 159-60). For the meaning of this root, Gröndahl suggests 'stark, bitter sein', but lists no theophoric compound names under it. In the context of the element *mr*$_3$ (p. 159), however, with the same meaning 'stark, bitter', Gröndahl lists a number of theophoric names. There is no mention in the glossary of a meaning 'to strengthen, bless, commend' for the root *mrr*, which is noted by Gordon (*UT Glossary*, 437 no. 1540, and 438 no. 1556) and which is cited by Gröndahl elsewhere (p. 44). It is this latter root and meaning which probably serve to elucidate Heb. names like *m*^{e}*rāyāh*. Whether the use of *mrr* in Heb. theophoric names has any comparable counterparts in Ug., therefore, remains uncertain. Heb. theophoric names contain no parallel concept of 'bitter', although the idea of the deity as 'strong' or 'strength' is expressed in names with the roots *'zz*, *knn*, *'mṣ*, *gbr*, *ḥzq*, *ḥyl/ḥwl* and *'br*. The specific idea 'to strengthen' is found only in the root *ḥzq*, and *mrr* as mentioned. The idea 'to bless' in Heb. names is found only in the root *brk*, while 'to commend' is not attested.

nyr/nwr (*PTU*, 165). The Heb. root *nwr*, like the Ug. element, probably means 'to light, shine'. From this root, Heb. names attest a noun 'lamp', and Ug. names, a noun 'light' to describe the deity. However, Ug. names also use this element as the *nomen regens* in a construct type name, 'light of' the deity.

šlm (*PTU*, 193). The Ug. root *šlm*, meaning 'to be whole, intact' has, as a counterpart in Heb., the root *šlm* with the meaning 'to be complete, sound'. In Heb. theophoric names, however, the root is used in the sense 'to recompense' and is found in verbal and nominal forms. There is no evidence that the Ug. names can contain this same nuance of thought.

3. Many of the elements used in Ugaritic theophoric names are not found in the Hebrew onomasticon but, nevertheless, have semantic parallels. This is the case with the following elements:

'd 'father' (*PTU*, 89). This element is not attested in Heb. names which use the noun *'b* to describe the deity as a father; *'b* is also attested in Ug. (see above, 1).

ḥbb 'to love, grow fond of' (*PTU*, 134). A root *ḥbb* 'to love' occurs in BH, but is not found in theophoric compound names—in which the comparable concept is expressed with the roots *dwd* and *ydd*. The Heb. idea, however, does not contain the notion 'to grow fond of' which seems to be present in the Ug. root.

mdd 'beloved' (*PTU*, 156). Gröndahl lists the root *mdd* as meaning 'to apportion, help, stretch out'. The comparable root *mdd* in BH means 'to measure', but is not attested in personal names. Elsewhere, however, Gröndahl suggests for the Ug. element *mdd*, the more probable pass. part. of *ydd* 'to love' (*PTU*, 32, 76; cf. also *UT Glossary*, 409 no. 1074). In this case the element means 'beloved' and is comparable to the use of the root *ydd* in Heb. names. See also Gibson, *Canaanite Myths and Legends*, T. & T. Clark 2nd edn (1978), 150, who supports the derivation of *mdd* from a root *ydd* and the meaning 'beloved'.

tp 'friend, companion' (*PTU*, 201). The Akk. noun *tappu* 'friend, companion', suggests an interpretation 'God is a friend' for the name *il tappa*. The same idea is attested in Heb. theophoric names with the element *r'* 'friend', but in Heb. names the noun is always used in construct form to describe the name-bearer as a 'friend of' the deity. Both the Ug. name and the Heb. names, however, portray the idea of friendship between God and man.

gt 'luck' (*PTU*, 131). For the name *ilgt*, Gröndahl suggests that the second element may be an orthographic variant of *gd* 'luck', although the shift *d—t* is not elsewhere apparent in Ug. *Gd* 'fortune' is evident in Heb. theophoric names, but the form *gt* is not found. Gröndahl also cites a noun *gint* 'winepress' as a possible etymology for the second element of the name (cf. Heb. *gat*, BDB, 178). This noun is very frequent in Ug. place names, cf. *UT Glossary*, 382 no. 627.

ytn 'to give' (*PTU*, 147). The Ug. root *ytn* is a cognate of Heb. *ntn*. Both have the meaning 'to give' and both are used in theophoric compound names. The same concept is also expressed in Heb. names with the roots *'wš* 'to bestow' (cf. Arab. *'āsa*), as well as *zbd*, *qwš* (cf. Akk. *qāšu*) and the initial element in the name *pûṭî'ēl*, of Eg. origin (cf. also *pṭyhw*, above, §2.9), with the meaning 'to give'.

r'b 'to compensate' (*PTU*, 178). The idea that the deity 'compensates', probably refers to compensation for a previously deceased child. This would be comparable to Heb. names with the Hiphil of the root *šwb* 'to restore', and *šlm* 'to recompense'.

twr and *ṯwb* 'to return' (*PTU*, 200, 202). The notion that the deity has 'returned' is expressed in Heb. names with the Qal of the root *šwb*, a cognate root of the Ug. name-element *twb* with the same meaning. Similar ideas may be contained in the Heb. name *pn'l* from the root *pnh* 'to turn' (see above, §2.4), as well as the root *sḥr* 'to turn' (*ibid.*, §2.9 [*yh*]*wsḥ*[*r*]).

ḥdy 'to see' (*PTU*, 134). This Ug. root is cognate with the Heb. name-element *ḥzh* with the same meaning. The root *r'h* in Heb. names also expresses the same idea, while the roots *šwr* ('to regard, behold', see above, §2.9 *'ăḥîšār*) and *śkh* ('to look out', see above §2.9 *śākᵉyāh*) are attested less certainly among Heb. names.

yṯ' 'to help' (*PTU*, 147). The root *yt'* does not exist in BH, but there may be some connection with the Heb. root *yš'*, since the shift *š—ṯ* is attested elsewhere in Ug. (cf. *PTU*, 93). However, the root *yš'* in Heb. names means 'to deliver', while the idea that the deity 'helps' is portrayed by the roots *'zr*, *'wš* and, possibly, *'dr*. J.C. de Moor (*BO* 26 [1969], 106), notes that the existence of the root *yṯ'* 'to help' has not been proved in Ug., and that for a name such as *yṯ'd*, which would be the only tenable name to contain the root, the element *yṯ* may mean 'He exists', although *'d* is attested in other Ug. names (cf. *PTU*, 106f.).

'sy 'to heal' (*PTU*, 102). The root *'sh* is not attested with a meaning 'to heal' in BH, with the possible exception of the personal name *'āsā'*. Gröndahl suggests that the Ug. element *'sy* is derived from Akk. *asû* 'to heal'. This concept is portrayed in Heb. theophoric names only with the root *rp'*, a root also found in Ug. names (see above, 1).

ḏmr 'to protect' (*PTU*, 197): *'qb* 'to guard, protect' (*PTU*, 111). The Ug. root *ḏmr* is probably cognate with the element *zmr* in Heb. theophoric names, which also has the meaning 'to protect'. This interpretation of the Heb. root, however, is suggested by a S. Arab. cognate *dhimr*, since extant uses in BH suggest mainly, (1) 'to make music in praise of God', and (2) 'to trim, prune' (cf. BDB, 274-75). The idea 'to protect' is also found in Heb. theophoric names with the root *ḥmh*, although this meaning is suggested by an Arab. cognate *ḥamay*, and is not attested with certainty, cf. above, §2.9 *ḥammû'ēl*. Although the root *'qb* exists in BH, it has a meaning 'to follow at the heel' (BDB, 784), so that the Ug. name-element *'qb* 'to protect, guard', is paralleled in Heb. names only by the roots *ḥmh* and *zmr*.

mny 'to count, allot, define' (*PTU*, 159). The root *mnh* is extant in BH with the meaning 'to count, number, reckon', but is not attested in theophoric compound names. Similar may be the idea that the deity 'reckons', evident in the Heb. name-element *š'r*.

'dr 'to be mighty' powerful' (*PTU*, 90). Although the root *'dr* exists in BH with the meaning 'to be wide, great, high, noble, it is not attested in theophoric names. Heb. names express the similar idea, that the deity is 'strong' or 'strength', with the roots *ḥzq*, *ḥyl*/*ḥwl*, *'zz*, *'mṣ* and *'br*.

ṣhr/*ẓhr* 'to be above, high' (*PTU*, 183). For this Ug. root, semantic parallels in Heb. names are found in the roots *rwm* 'to be high, exalted', *'th* (cf. Arab. *'atā* 'to be proud, exalted'), *śgb* 'to be (inaccessibly) high', and perhaps *'lh*, although the name *'lyh* containing this root may not be Heb. (see above, §2.3).

yšr 'to be just, righteous' (*PTU*, 146). The Heb. root *yšr* means 'to be smooth, straight, right', but is not attested in theophoric personal names. The idea of the deity as 'justice' or 'righteousness' is conveyed in Heb. names by the root *ṣdq*.

škl 'to be judicious' (*PTU*, 192): *ṯpṭ* 'to judge' (*PTU*, 199). The root *škl* exists in BH, but with the meaning 'to be bereaved' (BDB, 1013). The idea 'to be judicious' is conveyed in Heb. names with the root *ṣdq* 'to be just, righteous', while the idea that the deity 'judges' is found in the roots *dyn*, *pll* and *špṭ*. This last root is cognate with the Ug. name-element *ṯpṭ* 'to judge'.

ina Akk. 'in, on, from, to' (*CAD*, I 141; *PTU*, 99). The Akk. preposition *ina* is found in the name *ina-pān-addi*, 'In the face of Addu' or 'Before Addu'. The preposition *b*[e] 'in', is evident in Heb. names of the type *b*[e]*ṣal'ēl* 'In the shadow of El' (cf. further above, pp. 120f.). The thought expressed in the Ug. name, however, is one not apparent in the Heb. onomasticon.

4. There also exist in Ugaritic a number of theophoric names in which the roots are formally or semantically difficult. These are as follows:

'd (*PTU*, 106). For the element *'d* in the Ug. names *'dmlk*, *'dršp* and *gl'd*, a number of roots are possible (cf. *PTU*, 106). Of relevance here, is the possibility of a root *'wd* 'to repeat, return', also attested in BH and in Heb. theophoric names with the Hiphil 'to testify', or the denominative 'to bear witness'. A noun from the Ug. root *'wd* would suggest a meaning 'witness', this same noun being evident in Heb. theophoric names. Gordon (*UT Glossary*, 453 no. 1817) also suggests a meaning 'witness' (although pointing out that this is usually *ypḥ* in Ug.) or 'eternal' as in the names *'dmlk* and *'dršp*. Another possibility is the root *'dh* 'to ornament, deck oneself', which is attested in Heb. names. Relevant, too, may be the root *'dd* cf. BH, 'to count, reckon', comparable to Heb. names with the root *š'r* 'to reckon' and perhaps *ḥšb* 'to take account'. The large number of other possibilities for the Ug. element *'d*, as outlined by Gröndahl, makes comparisons between Ug. and Heb. concerning these names very tenuous.

brd (*PTU*, 120). The initial element *brd* in the name *brdd* could mean 'hail', which is attested in BH but not in personal names. Gröndahl also suggests a meaning 'to offer, present', paralleled in Heb. names by the roots *'wš* 'to bestow' (cf. Arab. *'āsa*), *zbd*, *ntn*, *qwš* (cf. Akk. *qāšu*) 'to give', as well as the initial element in the names *pûṭî'ēl* and *pṭyhw* (see above, §2.9) which is derived from Eg. The same element *brd* is given the meaning 'to carve' by Gibson (*op. cit.*, 143) and 'to extend, offer' by Gordon (*UT Glossary*, 376 no. 508), but these meanings have no comparable ideas among Heb. names.

ḏr (*PTU*, 197). For this element, Gröndahl suggests the possibility of a comparison with Akk. *šarru* 'king'. This would be semantically comparable to Heb. *mlk*, 'king', which is found widely in theophoric names.

ytr 'to be unique, excellent' (*PTU*, 147). *Ytr* is extant in BH with the meaning 'to remain over', while relevant nouns from this root have the meaning 'remainder, excess, pre-eminence' and 'abundance' (cf. BDB, 451-52). The root is also found in the BH name *'ebyātār*, which suggests a verbal form, perhaps meaning 'The (divine) Father is abundant or pre-eminent'. This latter characteristic may well reflect the idea of uniqueness or excellence expressed in the Ug. element.

mrṯ (*PTU*, 160). The element is either from the root *yrṯ* 'to inherit, receive', which is not attested in Heb. names, or is derived from *mrṯ* meaning a 'wine product', which is unattested in BH. Neither possibility has any direct semantic parallel in Heb. names, although the root *qnh* 'to create, acquire', is perhaps similar to the idea suggested by the root *yrṯ*.

mšl/mṯl (*PTU*, 161). For the second element in the name *addu* (dU)-*mi-iš-lu*, Gröndahl suggests either the root *mṯl*, cf. Akk. 'to make similar', or the root *mšl* 'to rule'. The former root is cognate with BH *mšl* 'to represent, be like', cf. BDB, 605, the latter, with BH *mšl* 'to rule, have dominion, reign'. Neither root is used in theophoric names in Heb. For the root *mṯl*, Heb. names reveal no comparable semantic parallel. The idea that the deity 'rules', however, may be represented in the Heb. name *'aḥî'ām* which either contains the root *'wm* 'to rule' (cf. S. Arab. *'āma*) or a root *'mm* 'to be wide, roomy' (see above, §2.9).

'p (*PTU*, 111). This element is attested only in the name *'pṣpn*. It could be derived from a root *'wp* 'to fly' or *'pp*, which Gröndahl suggests is similar in meaning to the root *ǵẓy* 'to entreat (with gifts)' cf. Gordon *UT Glossary*, 463 no. 1958. The first possibility is not reflected in Heb. theophoric names, but the idea of a request to the deity, if this is the thought contained in the root *'pp*, may be paralleled in Heb. names with the root *š'l* 'to ask', which is used with the deity as the object. However, the Ug. name is too uncertain to draw any definite parallel.

ql (*PTU*, 176). The Ug. name *qldn* may be either *ql* + *dn*, with the second element meaning 'judge' (root *dyn*), or *ql* + *adn*, the latter meaning 'lord'. Otherwise, the name may be divided differently and may contain a root *qld* 'to put on a necklace': this would then be a non-theophoric name. If the name retains its theophoric nature, the element *ql* remains problematic. It could be derived from a root *qll* meaning 'to be small, light', 'to be swift', which has no equivalent in Heb. theophoric names, or from a root *qwl* 'to speak', which does occur as a noun 'voice' in Heb. theophoric compounds and, perhaps, verbally (see above, §2.9 *qlyhw*).

š (*PTU*, 191). For the element *š* in the names *šuba'al* and *šb'l*, Gröndahl suggests either Akk. *šu*, the 3rd pers. masc. sing. personal pronoun, or 'sheep'. The former suggestion would indicate a meaning 'He of Baal', a meaning not paralleled in Heb. names, which do not specifically use a pronoun as the *nomen regens* in a construct type name. The idea 'sheep' also has no parallel in the Heb. onomasticon.

šr (*PTU*, 196). For the element *šr* in the name *abšr*, Gröndahl suggests either Akk. *šarru* 'king', to which may be compared the Heb. name-element *mlk*, or the root *šyr* 'to sing', not found in Heb. theophoric compounds. (See above, p. 142 for the use of this root *šwr* in theophoric names with the possible meaning 'to behold'.) Cf. also the root *šrr* 'to let loose', and Gibson *op. cit.*, 159.

5. Ugaritic theophoric names contain many ideas which do not occur in the Hebrew onomasticon and which, therefore, portray characteristics of the Ugaritic deities which are not found to be characteristic of the Hebrew deity as far as the evidence of personal names is concerned. One of the most outstanding differences is the use in Ugaritic names of a feminine non-theophoric element to refer to the deity or the name-bearer, as the following show:

'dt 'lady' (*PTU*, 90). The noun is the feminine counterpart to *adn* 'lord'. The idea of a queen or goddess as a consort of the Heb. deity, is entirely absent.

'ḫt 'sister' (*PTU*, 92). Since it is uncertain whether the element *mlk* in the name *aḫat(u)-milki* is theophoric or not (cf. *PTU*, 157) the name may be a non-theophoric compound name, 'Sister of the king'. If *mlk* is a divine epithet, the name has no equivalent in Heb. name-giving.

'mm 'mother' (*PTU*, 99). Since there is a total absence of any female deities in Heb. religion Heb. names cannot portray the deity as a 'mother'. The Ug. element is the feminine counterpart to the idea of the deity as a 'father' found in the elements *'b* and *'d*. Also in Ug. names seems to be evidence that a masculine deity can be given a feminine predicate, as in the name *'ttr-um*, 'Aštar is mother' (*PTU*, 46).

bt 'daughter' (*PTU*, 119). Like the idea 'Son of' the deity in Ug. names, the concept 'Daughter of' the deity is not reflected in Heb. name-giving.

hy 'she' (*PTU*, 133). The 3rd pers. fem. sing. pronoun *hy* 'she', forms the initial element of the name *hyabn*, translated by Gröndahl as 'She is our father', for which Heb. names have no parallel. In spite of names like *'ttr-um* cited above, this particular interpretation of the Ug. name seems very tenuous.

There are numerous nominal elements apparent in Ug. names which have no semantic counterparts in the Heb. onomasticon. Absent in Heb. are names which depict the deity in such terms of natural phenomena as 'lightning' (*brq PTU*, 120), 'thicket'[8] (*ǵl PTU*, 14) and, similarly, 'garden'[9] (*gnn PTU*, 129) and 'field, plain' (*šd PTU*, 191-92). The Heb. deity is never depicted as an animal or bird unlike Ug. names containing the nouns 'lion'[10] (*lb' PTU*, 154) and 'falcon' (*nṣ PTU*, 169 [or genitive]). Also lacking in Heb. names are those anthropomorphic ideas of the Ug. deities in the name-elements 'soldier' or 'servant' (*mhr PTU*, 156), possibly 'ancestor, forefather' (*slp PTU*, 186, cf. Arab. *salafa* 'to be past'), 'hero' (*qrḏ* cf. J.C. de Moor, *BO* 26 [1969], 107), 'rider' (*rkb PTU*, 179) and 'image' (*ṣlm PTU*, 188). The Ug. noun *ṣn* (*PTU*, 189) with a meaning 'large shield' (cf. Heb. *ṣinnah*) or 'to cherish' (cf. Arab. *ṣanā*) is also not paralleled among Heb. names.

Genitive elements which are attested in Ug. names but have no semantic equivalents in Heb., amount to 'house' (*byt PTU*, 118), 'beard' (*dkn PTU*, 183), 'wing' (*knp PTU*, 150), 'wish, vow' (*ndr PTU*, 164), 'mouth, saying, command' (*p PTU*, 170), 'heaven' (*šmy PTU*, 194), 'son' (*bn PTU*, 118-19) and possibly 'root, shoot' (*šrš PTU*, 196).

Of verbal elements expressing ideas concerning the Ug. deities which have no parallel in Heb., one group is concerned with birth events. Such roots involve the concepts 'to be fruitful' (*pr*[11] *PTU*, 173-74 and *ṯmr*[12] *PTU*, 199), 'to announce, give a sign' (*mll PTU*, 39, 158), 'to call, name'[13] (*nb' PTU*, 164), 'to promise, name' (*qby PTU*, 175), 'to bore or break through' (*nqb PTU*, 168) and 'to make a path, level, smooth' (*pls PTU*, 172). Also attested only in Ug. are the verbal ideas 'to care for, manage'[14] (*skn PTU*, 185), 'to be pure' (*zky/zkw PTU*, 183), 'to shine, shine forth'[15] (*yp' PTU*, 144-45), 'to suffer want, become poor' or 'be orphaned'[16] (*yky/ykw PTU*, 143), 'to slay' *nky/nkw* (*PTU*, 166) and 'to avenge, revenge' (*nqm PTU*, 168). Some Ug. verbal ideas seem to suggest that the deity withdraws from man, as in names from the roots *s'p* 'to vanish' (*PTU*, 40, 184) and perhaps *syr/swr* 'to retreat, give way, journey'[17] (*PTU*, 184). Similar in thought is the use of the element *'y* 'where?' (*PTU*, 93) in names which ask the question 'Where is the deity?' for which there is no counterpart among Heb. names.

4.2 *A Comparison between the Concepts of Deity Revealed in the Phoenician and Hebrew Onomastica*

1. An initial glance at the Phoenician onomasticon as given in the work of F.L. Benz, *Personal Names in the Phoenician and Punic Inscriptions*,[18] reveals many roots and semantic ideas which are akin to Hebrew names. Phoenician and Hebrew names have a number of elements which are common to both and which are used to refer to the respective deities. These are:

Ph./Pun.	*PNPPI*	*Heb.*	
'b	257	*'b*	father
'br	259	*'br*	to be strong
'dn	260	*'dn*	lord
'hl	262	*'hl*	tent
'ḥ	263-64	*'ḥ*	brother[19]
'r	274	*'wr*	light, flame
't	281	*'t*	prep. with
bd	283-86	*bd*	from/by the hand of
bny/w	288	*bnh*	to build, create
b'l	288	*b'l*	lord
brk	291	*brk*	to bless
gd	294	*gd*	fortune (Phoen. also n. pr. div.)
gr	298	*gr*	client
hr	303	*hr*	mountain (i.e. sanctuary)
zkr	305-306	*zkr*	to remember
ḥzy	322	*ḥzh*	to look, see
ḥwy	308	*ḥyh*	to live
ḥlṣ	311	*ḥlṣ*	to deliver, save, rescue
ḥlq	311	*ḥlq*	portion
ḥnn	313-14	*ḥnn*	to show favour, be gracious
yd'	321	*yd'*	to know
ysp	323-24	*ysp*	to add
kbd	330	*kbd*	honour, glory
kwn	332	*kwn*	to establish[20]
mlk	344-45	*mlk*	king
mr	353-54	*mr*	lord[21]
mrr	354	*mrr*	to be strong, or, to strengthen, bless, commend, cf. Ug.
ndb	359	*ndb*	to be noble
n'm	362	*n'm*	pleasantness, delight
nr	363	*nr*	lamp
smk	366-67	*smk*	to support, sustain
'bd	369-72	*'bd*	servant
'd	373-74	*'d*	witness[22]
'z	374	*'zz*	to be strong, strength[23]
'zr	375-76	*'zr*	to help
'm	379	*'m*	paternal uncle, kinsman
'ms	379-80	*'ms*	to bear
pdy/w	389	*pdh*	to ransom
pṯ (Eg.)	389-90	*pṯ* (Eg.)	to give
plṭ	390-91	*plṭ*	deliverance; Heb. also verbal

pn	392	*pnh*	face, presence
p'l	393	*p'l*	to make, do
ṣdq	398-99	*ṣdq*	to be just, righteous
qm	404	*qwm*	to rise; causative, to establish
qny	404-405	*qnh*	to create, acquire; Phoen. also to possess
rm	408-409	*rwm*	to be high, exalted
šlm	417-18	*šlm*	to recompense.
šm	419	*šm*	name
šm'	421	*šm'*	to hear
šmr	421-22	*šmr*	to keep, preserve
špṭ	423-24	*špṭ*	to govern, judge
tmm	429	*tmm*	to be complete, perfect

Names represented by these roots present no markworthy formal differences between Hebrew and Phoenician usage. Generally speaking, where a nominal, verbal, or construct form is used in Hebrew, it is paralleled in Phoenician by the same form, with the exception of those noted.

2. Thus there exist in the Hebrew and Phoenician onomastica many ideas which are common to both, being used in Hebrew names to refer to Yaweh and in Phoenician to refer to the large number of Phoenician deities. To the above list may be added a number of more questionable similarities, uncertain because of difficulty of root or form, as the following show:

'š (*PNPPI*, 277-78). In some of the names occurring with this element, a meaning 'Man of' may be possible, comparable to the elements *'yš*, *mt*, and possibly *gbr* in Heb. theophoric names. Also possible for the element is a derivation from the root *'wš* 'to give' which is attested in the Heb. onomasticon. In the Punic name 'ŠB'L, however, a stative pass. part. is likely, 'Given by Baal', similar to Heb. *mattanyāh*(*û*) 'Gift of Y', root *ntn*.

ḥll (*PNPPI*, 310). For the Phoen. name 'BḤLL, Benz suggests a root *ḥyl* and cites Arab. *halal* 'turn', noting the link between Geminate and Hollow verbs as suggested by GKC, 67, 1. Heb. names have no certain comparison to this concept 'to turn' but may contain the roots *swr* 'to turn aside' (see above, §2.9 *sryh*) and the root *pnh* 'to turn' (*ibid.*, §2.4). Also relevant, but equally difficult, is the root *sḥr* with a meaning 'to turn' suggested by an Akk. cognate *saḫāru* (*ibid.*, §2.9 [*yh*]*wsḥ*[*r*]).

ḥm (*PNPPI*, 311). Phoen. theophoric names containing the element *ḥm* are quite uncertain. Benz considers the etymology probably to equate with that of the BH name *ḥammû'ēl*, which is itself difficult (see above, §2.9), the meaning of the initial element being suggested by Arab. *ḥamay* 'to protect'.

The possibility that the Phoen. element may represent a sf. is also noted by Benz.

yḥr (*PNPPI*, 322). Since the reading of the name YḤRB'L is uncertain, derivations from the root *yḥd* 'to give joy', *yhr* 'to be haughty', *yḥr* 'to rage', or *ḥrr* 'to be free', are all possible. With the root *yḥd*, 'to give joy', may be compared the related Heb. root *ḥdh* 'to rejoice', usually interpreted in the Heb. theophoric names *yaḥdî'ēl* and *yeḥdᵉyāhû* as 'El/Y gives joy'. Heb. theophoric names have no semantic parallel to Phoen./Punic *yhr* 'to be haughty', but with the root *yḥr* 'to rage', may be compared the Heb. root *ḥrh* 'to burn, be kindled (of anger)' which is a seemingly related root. The idea expressed in the root *ḥrr* 'to be free', has no formal or semantic parallel in Heb. in this stative sense.

yšb (*PNPPI*, 327). The Punic names YŠB'L and YŠBŠT have a number of possible etymologies, most of which are present in the Heb. nomenclature. A derivation from the root *yšb* 'to sit', is paralleled in the first element of the BH name *yôšibyāh* which is a Hiphil form of the root *yšb* 'to cause to dwell'. Another possibility for the Punic names, however, is a root *šwb* 'to return', which is also present in the Heb. onomasticon. The other alternative is *yēš* 'there is', which is not found in Heb. theophoric names (cf. above, §2.2 *b'l*/ *'ešbā'al*).

'n (*PNPPI*, 381). For the Punic name 'NB'L (f.) Benz suggests three alternatives one of which, a derivation from the root *'ny* 'to answer', is paralleled in Heb. names from the root *'nh*. Other suggestions for the Phoen. root are a possible replacement of the *'ayin* with *ḥēt* or, a defective spelling of 'YNB'L. This elision of the *yōd* in Phoen. *'yn* is met elsewhere, cf. C.F. Jean, J. Hoftijzer, *Dictionnaire des inscriptions sémitiques de l'ouest*, Leiden: E.J. Brill (1965), 207.

'p (*PNPPI*, 382-83). The element *'p* in the Punic names 'PŠḤR and 'PŠN is not easy to clarify. A Heb. root *'wp* 'to be dark' makes little sense with a theophoric element, which is the case, also, with the root *'wp* to fly'. A root *ḥpš* 'to free' is semantically suitable and similar to the idea 'to deliver' in Heb. names with the roots *yš'*, *mlṭ*, *nṣl* (Hiphil), *plṭ*, *ḥml* and Aram. *šêzêb* as well as, possibly, *dlh* 'to draw', i.e. 'rescue'. The element *'p* also exists in Ug. names, in which it is equally problematic (cf. above, §4.1.4).

'š (*PNPPI*, 385). The Punic names 'Š'ŠM[N] and 'ŠMLK have a number of possible etymologies. Benz prefers an interpretation of the first element *'š* as 'man', involving a change of *'ayin* to *'ālep* (a phenomenon attested elsewhere in Phoen./Punic names, cf. *PNPPI*, 203) which would then be paralleled in the Heb. name-elements *'yš*, *mt*, and perhaps *gbr*. Also suggested, however, is the root *'šy* 'to make', cognate with Heb. names from the root *'šh*. A change of *z* for *š* in the first element of the Punic names might suggest the idea *'az* 'strength' (cf. *PNPPI*, 374) which is also found in Heb.

names. Further possibilities are derivations from the root *'wš* 'to give', also occurring in the Heb. nomenclature, and a root *'wt* (cf. Aram. 'to restore') similar to Heb. names from the root *šwb* (Hiphil) 'to restore', and *šlm* 'to recompense'.

pl (*PNPPI*, 390). The Punic name PL'SR can be interpreted in a variety of ways. It may be derived from a root *p'l* 'to make, do', attested also in Heb. theophoric names. (The elision of the *'ayin* is found in other Phoen./Punic names; cf. *PNPPI*, 203.) Also possible is a root *pl'* 'to be miraculous', reflected in Heb. names with the same root. Alternatively, a root *pll* 'to judge' may be relevant, which is also found in Heb. theophoric names. The name may, however, be Ass., cf. *pl'sr* in Tiglath Pileser and *apil-ešarra* 'Son of the Temple of Ešarra' (see A.R. Millard, 'Assyrian Royal Names in Biblical Hebrew', *JSS* 21 [1976], 6-7).

ṣb (*PNPPI*, 397). For the Phoen. name 'ŠTRTṢB, Benz suggests a number of possible etymologies. A derivation of the second element from a root *nṣb*, and a Yiphil imf. form, would produce a meaning 'May Aštart establish'. This would correspond to the use of the Hiphil of the same root *nṣb* in Heb. (cf. BDB, 662) although the latter root is not found in Heb. theophoric names, which use the roots *kwn*, *qwm* (Hiphil), and *śwm* to express the same idea. However, the Phoen. name may also be derived from a root *ṣib*, cf. Amor. *ṣbw* 'desire' (*APNM*, 256). This has no counterpart in Heb. theophoric names, although a noun *ṣ*^{e}*bî* meaning 'beauty, honour, decoration' (and not 'ornament' as Benz [*PNPPI*, 397] following *APNM*, 256 suggests: cf. BDB, 840), and also 'gazelle', is found outside Heb. names. Another possibility for the Phoen. name is a derivation from a root *ṣb'* of unknown meaning.

r' (*PNPPI*, 409-10). Heb. theophoric names containing the root *r'h* 'to associate with, pasture, tend, graze', are formally problematic (see above, §2.7 *r*^{e}*'û'ēl*). No less difficult are names containing the element *r'* in Punic R'MLK, 'BDR', R'MLK and R'MT. In 'BDR and R'MLK, Benz suggests a likely representation of the Eg. deity *Re'a*, while in other names the element could mean 'friend', companion', or 'shepherd'. In Heb. names, the element is probably a construct noun meaning 'friend'.

š' (*PNPPI*, 423). The element *š'* in the two Phoen. names Š'B'L and 'DNŠ' is considered by Benz to equate to Heb. *šw'*, which Noth (*IPN*, 154 n. 2) considered a by-form of the root *yš'*. This latter root is frequently found in Heb. theophoric compound names. A better suggestion for the Phoen. names seems the alternative proposal by Benz of a root *š'y*, and a comparison with the BH root *š'h* 'to gaze', regard with favour', although this root is not used in Heb. theophoric names. The idea contained in the root, however, may be similar to Heb. names with the roots *ḥzh* and *r'h* 'to see' (cf. also the roots *šwr*, above, §2.9 *'ăḥîšār* and *śkh*, above, §2.9 *śāk*^{e}*yāh*).

3. Between the Phoenician and Hebrew onomastica, there exist a number of semantic parallels, as well as parallels which are semantically synonymous and very similar, though not identical, in form; compare for example, names from the Phoenician root *ytn* 'to give' and names from the Hebrew root *ntn*, also meaning 'to give'. Phoenician-Punic elements used in theophoric compound names, which have semantic counterparts in Hebrew theophoric names are as follows:

'd 'father' (*PNPPI*, 259). The Heb. equivalent to this element, is *'b* (also attested in Phoen., see above, 1) with identical meaning. The element *'d* in Phoen./Punic names is probably synonymous with the Ug. theophoric element, although Benz also considers the possibility that it is a sf. of *'dn* or *'dr*.

'dr 'mighty', glorious' (*PNPPI*, 261-62). The same root exists in BH but is not used in Heb. theophoric names, in which the concept of might and glory is attested in the element *kbd* 'glory'. This same root, as noted above (1) is also to be found in Phoen. names.

'rḥ 'to wander' (*PNPPI*, 320). The Punic name Y'RḤM is only questionably derived from this root meaning 'to wander, journey'. If this is the correct etymology, there may be some semantic similarity with the root *sḥr* 'to go around, about, travel about in', although Akk. *saḫāru* may suggest a meaning 'to turn' for the element in Heb. names (cf. above, §2.9 [*yh*]*wsḥ*[*r*]). Similar also in Heb. names, is the root *šgg*, found in the name *'ăbîšag*, for which BDB, 4 suggest the meaning 'My father is a wanderer'. This name, however, is also not without difficulties (see above, §2.9). Benz further suggests for the Punic name a meaning 'Hammon enlightens' to which may be compared the Heb. name-element *ngh* 'to shine, enlighten'.

gnn 'to protect' (*PNPPI*, 297). The same root, *gnn*, also exists in BH with a meaning 'to protect' (cf. BDB, 170) but it is not present in theophoric names. In Heb. names, the equivalent concept is expressed by the root *zmr* (cf. S. Arab. *dhimr*) and possibly by the root *ḥmh* (cf. S. Arab. *ḥamay*). In Phoen., the element is attested only once in a theophoric compound, in the Punic name 'SRGN.

ḥpṣ 'pleasure delight' (*PNPPI*, 316). This root is found only in the Phoen. name ḤPṢB'L. In Heb. the concept of 'pleasure' or 'delight' is found in theophoric names with the nominal elements *'dn* 'luxury, delight' and *n'm* 'delight, pleasantness'. Although the root *ḥpṣ* is attested in BH with a meaning 'to delight in' (cf. BDB, 342-43) it is not found in theophoric names.

Two Phoenician-Punic roots express the idea 'to give' in personal names, but have no formal counterpart in Hebrew. These are:

ytn 'to give' (*PNPPI*, 328): *mgn* 'to give, bestow, hand over', also appellation 'Benefactor, Suzerain' (*PNPPI*, 339). The element *ytn* is abundantly attested in Phoen./Punic names, as also its Heb. counterpart *ntn* in the Heb. nomenclature. From both these roots is attested a nominal name-element *mtn* 'gift'. The root *mgn* is not attested in BH. In Heb. names, the roots *'wš*, *zbd*, *ntn*, *qwš* (cf. Akk. *qāšu*), and the initial Eg. element of the names *pûṭî'ēl* and *pṭyhw*, are used to express the idea 'to give' or 'gift'. *Pṭ* is also found in Phoen. names, see above, 1.

mšl 'to rule' (*PNPPI*, 355). Although this root exists in BH, it is not found in Heb. theophoric names. Instead, the S. Arab. *'āma* 'to rule' may represent this idea in the name *'ăḥî'ām* although the second element could also be derived from a root *'mm* (cf. above, §2.9).

nn (*PNPPI*, 361). The Phoen. name 'BNN is problematic: Benz suggests a derivation from a root similar to Heb. *nwm* 'to propagate, increase' (BDB, 630) from which is derived a noun *nîn* meaning 'offspring'. The verbal idea 'to increase' is expressed in Heb. theophoric compound names by the root *ysp* 'to add' and perhaps by the root *rḥb* 'to make wide, enlarge', while the nominal idea 'offspring' is absent in Heb. names. Benz also suggests for the Phoen. name a sf. of 'BNTN, or a derivation from an original 'MNN.

'ṣ (*PNPPI*, 383-84). In the Punic names 'Ṣ'L, 'ṢB'L and 'ṢB'L, a change of the *'ayin* to *'ālep*, as suggested by Benz, would create a possible derivation from a root *'wṣ* which is paralleled in the Heb. theophoric name *'ṣyh* (seal V, 97). This name, however, is also not without difficulties (see above, §2.9). In BH, the root means 'to make haste, press, be pressed' (cf. BDB, 21).

pls 'to watch, level' (*PNPPI*, 391). In Phoen./Punic theophoric names, the element *pls* means 'to watch'. The root in BH probably has the basic meaning 'to be even, to balance' (cf. BDB, 813) and is not attested in personal names with a theophoric subject. Heb. names may express the idea 'to watch' as a characteristic of the deity with the root *šmr* (although this root tends to be used more in the sense 'to preserve'), and possibly with the obscure root *skh*/*śkh* (see above, §2.9 *śāk^{e}yāh*).

šyt 'to place, establish' (*PNPPI*, 426). This root, although met widely in BH, is not attested in theophoric names in Heb. in which *kwn*, *qwm* (Hiphil), and *śwm* are used to express the equivalent idea.

šlḥ 'to stretch, send', Piel 'to set free' (*PNPPI*, 416). This element is not attested in Heb. theophoric names although Noth (*IPN*, 173) accepted, with reservation, the name *šlḥy* as a sf. of an originally theophoric compound. If the Phoen. theophoric names from this root are in the Qal, with the meaning 'to stretch, send' they have no parallel in Heb. names. However, the Piel meaning 'to set free' is reflected frequently in the Heb. onomasticon (not necessarily in derived verbal forms) with the roots *ḥml* 'to spare', *yš'* 'to save', *mlṭ*, *nṣl* (Hiphil), *plṭ* and the Aram. element *šêzêb* to deliver', and the root *dlh* 'to draw', which is possibly figurative for the idea of rescue.

šlk 'to nourish, provide, (*PNPPI*, 416). The Heb. root *šlk* means 'to throw, fling, cast' (BDB, 1020) and is not an element found in Heb. theophoric names. The idea 'to nourish, provide', however, is expressed in Heb. names from the roots *'zh* and *qwt*, cf. Arab. *ghadhā* and *qāta* respectively.

tmk 'to support, hold fast' (*PNPPI*, 429). The root *tmk* is attested in BH with the meaning 'to grasp, support, attain', but is not used in theophoric names. To express the idea of support in Heb. names, the roots *'mn* and *'šh* are used, also the root *yšh* (cf. Arab. *'asa'*) although not with any certainty (see above, §2.9 *yôšawyāh*). The root *smk* in Heb. names, also meaning 'to support', is probably cognate with Phoen. *tmk*.

4. There remains a considerable number of Phoenician-Punic concepts contained in personal names which are not paralleled in the Hebrew onomasticon. These are of interest because they illustrate ideas which were held by the Phoenicians concerning their gods which, from the evidence of theophoric personal names, were not concepts applicable to the Hebrew God, Yahweh. Such ideas are attested in the Phoenician elements which follow.

Noticeably different from Heb. is the Phoen. use of feminine nouns depicting the goddesses as 'sister' (*'ḥt PNPPI*, 265, Punic), 'mother' (*'m PNPPI*, 269, Phoen./Punic) and 'queen, goddess' (*mlkt*, or 'kingship' *PNPPI*, 345-46, Phoen./Punic). However, also absent in Heb. are feminine construct nouns which act as the *nomen regens* in a construct type clause. This is evident in Phoen. *'mt* 'female servant' (*PNPPI*, 270, Phoen./Punic), *'ḥt* 'sister' (*PNPPI*, 265, Punic. To the list of names with this element should be added the Phoen. seal *'ḥtmlk* [V,63]) and *bt* 'daughter' (*PNPPI*, 293, Phoen./Punic).

Other nominal elements not attested in Heb. theophoric names are *'rš* 'request, desire' (*PNPPI*, 276, Punic), the divine appellation *zbl* 'prince' (*PNPPI*, 304, Phoen./Punic) and *nks* 'riches, treasures' (*PNPPI*, 359, Punic).[24] Certain nouns used in construct are also without any equivalent in Heb. These amount to *bn* 'son' (*PNPPI*, 287-88, Phoen./Punic), *'ḥ* 'brother' (*PNPPI*, 263-64, Phoen./Punic), *ml'k* 'messenger' (*PNPPI*, 344, Punic),[25] *'yn* 'eye' (*PNPPI*, 377, Phoen.) and *š* possibly 'sheep' (*PNPPI*, 412, Punic).[26]

Verbal elements expressing ideas without semantic equivalents in Heb. names are *ḥrm* 'to be holy' (also 'to devote' *PNPPI*, 318, Punic), *rkk* 'to be tender' (*PNPPI*, 326, Phoen.),[27] *ṣlḥ* 'to prosper' (*PNPPI*, 400, Phoen./Punic) and *š'n* 'to rest securely' (*PNPPI*, 412, Punic).

Other verbal elements may suggest that the Phoen. deities were conceived to be objects of fear and sources of adversity. Not attested in Heb. are semantic equivalents of Phoen. *ygr* 'to fear' (*PNPPI*, 321, Phoen./Punic),[28] *šmm* 'to be troubled' (*PNPPI*, 421, Punic)[29] and possibly *mgr* 'to overthrow' or 'tear down, destroy' (*PNPPI*, 339-40, Punic). Similar is the use of *'y* 'where?' (*PNPPI*, 265, Phoen./Punic) asking 'Where is?' the deity, and implying divine neglect of the name-bearer.

4.3 *A Comparison between the Concepts of Deity Revealed in the Amorite and Hebrew Onomastica*

For the present comparison between theophoric names in Hebrew and Amorite, the study of Amorite names by Herbert B. Huffmon, *Amorite Personal Names in the Mari Texts*,[30] has provided a thorough basis. However, such a comparison is not an easy task, since exact semantic values for Amorite onomastic elements are not possible and, in the majority of cases, the precise meaning of the name cannot be given. This problem, together with the early nature of the Amorite material, has resulted in many comparisons between the two onomastica being confined to the area of suggestion as opposed to the certainty of fact.

1. In Hebrew and Amorite name-giving, there exist many non-theophoric elements used in theophoric compound names which are common to both onomastica. These elements portray identical characteristics of the Amorite deities and of the Israelite God Yahweh, and are as follows:

Amor.	*APNM*	*Heb.*	
'b	154	*'b*	father
'ḫ	160	*'ḥ*	brother
'l/'l'	162, 165	*'l*	God
bl/(Akk.)	175	*b'l*	lord
gmr	180	*gmr*	to accomplish
dn	182	*dyn*	to judge
zmr	187-88	*zmr*	to protect[31]
ṭb	207	*ṭwb*	good
ytr	217	*ytr*	to be pre-eminent, abundant, surpassing: nominal, abundance
k_3	219	*k*	like
kn_1	221	*knn*	to be firm[32]

l	222-23	*l*	(belonging) to
mlk	230	*mlk*	king
nr₂	243	*nr*	lamp[33]
ntn	244	*ntn*	to give
ṣdq	256	*ṣdq*	to be just, right; righteousness
ṣr	258	*ṣwr*	rock[34]
qm	259	*qwm*	to rise; causative to establish
rm	261-62	*rwm*	to be exalted
rp'	263-64	*rp'*	to heal[35]
šb	266	*šwb*	to turn, return[36]
šd	267	*šdy*	Amor. 'mountain', Heb. n. pr. div.
špṭ	268	*špṭ*	to judge

A significant number of Hebrew name-elements containing *'ayin* are cognate with Amorite elements in which the *'ayin* is represented by cuneiform *ḫ*:

Amor.	*APNM*	*Heb.*	
ba(ḫ)l	174	*b'l*	lord
ḫbd[37]	189	*'bd*	servant, Amor. also slave
ḫzr	193	*'zr*	to help
ḫmm	196-98	*'m*	paternal uncle
ḫms	198	*'ms*	to bear
ydḫ	209	*yd'*	to know
zrḫ	188	*zr'*	to sow

Another change of consonants is evident in some of the Hebrew names which contain *š* as opposed to Amorite names containing *s*, as in the elements:

Amor.	*APNM*	*Heb.*	
skn	245	*škn*	to dwell
sm	247	*šm*	name
smḫ	249-50	*šm'*	to hear
smr	251	*šmr*	to guard, watch, preserve

Where the Hebrew name-element has a III *hē* root, in one case the Amorite counterpart has III *'ālep*:

Amor.	*APNM*	*Heb.*	
bn'	177	*bnh*	to build, create

2. Also evident in both onomastica are identical elements which either have entirely different meanings or have different formal

usage. Some examples of such have been noted in the foregoing lists, but this is also the case with the following:

zkr 'to remember, mention, name' (*APNM*, 187). The verbal forms *zakir*(*a*) and *zakur*(*a*) in Amor. names are uncertain (cf. *APNM*, 91f.) so that a comparison with Heb. names using the root *zkr*, 'to remember', is difficult. More certain, however, is a genitive use of the noun *zikr* in Amor. theophoric names meaning perhaps 'my remembrance', which has no parallel in Heb. names.

ḫw' 'to live' (*APNM*, 191). This Amorite element has as a counterpart in Heb. the root *ḥyh* with the same meaning. Heb. names with this root probably express that the deity 'lives' (see above, §2.4 *ḥyh*) whereas Amor. usage is possibly confined to a precative and causative interpretation. However, a causative nuance may also be present in Heb. part. forms with this root (cf. above, §2.8.2. *m*ᵉ*ḥûyā'ēl*).

mlk 'to rule' (*APNM*, 230). Both Amor. and Heb. theophoric names contain the element *mlk*, used nominally to describe the deity as a 'king'. In Amor. names, however, the root is also used verbally, with the meaning 'to rule, possess, counsel'. The same idea is possibly conveyed in Heb. names by the root *'wm* (cf. Arab. *'āma*, and above, §2.9 *'ăḥî'ām*).

nḥm 'favour' (*APNM*, 237). The root *nḥm* is attested widely in Amor. names, but only with the meaning 'favour' in theophoric names. Heb. names from the same root have the meaning 'pleasantness, delight', while the idea 'favour of' the deity, or that the deity 'is favour', is attested in names with the noun *ḥn*.

str 'protection' (*APNM*, 253-54). In Heb. theophoric names, the root *str* means 'to hide, conceal' and is a particularly figurative way of depicting divine protection. This difference from the notion 'protection' in the Amor. element is worth noting, since the Heb. element is distinctly more anthropomorphic, in spite of the cognate nature of both roots.

ql 'to speak' (*APNM*, 258). The element *ql* in Amor. names is attested as a verbal element. In Heb. theophoric names, however, the root *qwl* is formally problematic. It probably occurs in a construct type name, but is not attested with certainty in verbal sentence names (see above, §2.6 *qôlāyāh* and §2.9 *qlyhw*). More certainly, Heb. names depict that the deity 'has said', with the root *'mr*.

3. Many other elements in Amorite theophoric names have semantic counterparts in Hebrew which express the same, or similar, concepts about the deity:

'bl 'to bring, carry' (*APNM*, 154-55). Amor. *'bl* 'to bring, carry' is comparable to BH *ybl* (cf. BDB, 384-85). This latter root, however, is not

attested in Heb. personal names which express a similar idea with the root *'ms* 'to bear'.

'd 'father' (*APNM*, 156). This element is not found in Heb. names, in which the element *'b* depicts the deity as 'Father'. This latter noun is also attested in Amor. names (see above, 1).

bḫr 'to choose' (*APNM*, 175): *pḫr* 'to assemble'. The root *bḫr* is attested in BH as *bḥr* with *ḥēt* (cf. BDB, 103) but is not found in theophoric names. The idea portrayed in the Amor. element may be akin to the idea of selection by the deity, expressed in Heb. names from the roots *'ṣl* 'to reserve, set apart', *plh* 'to be separated, distinct', *ḥṣh* 'to divide' and, perhaps, *'sp* 'to gather', to which the Amor. name-element *pḫr* 'to assemble' (*APNM*, 254), is also semantically comparable.

dr_1 'to turn around, dwell, endure' (*APNM*, 183): *sqṭ* 'to rest' (*APNM*, 253). The root *dwr* in Amor. names means 'to turn around, dwell, endure'. The same root in BH means 'to dwell' but, in addition, 'to heap up, pile' (cf. BDB, 189) and is a root not attested in Heb. personal names. The idea 'to turn' is questionably evident in the Heb. onomasticon in the roots *swr* 'to turn aside' (see above, §2.9 *sryh*), *pnh* 'to turn' (*ibid.*, §2.4) and *sḥr* 'to turn' (*ibid.*, §2.9 [*yh*]*wsḥ*[*r*]). The idea that the deity 'dwells' is reflected in Heb. names with *škn* 'to take up an abode'. The root *yšb* 'to dwell' is only used in a causative sense in Heb. names, but in this sense is comparable to the causative use of the root *sqṭ* 'to rest' in Amor. theophoric names (cf. *APNM*, 253). The concept that the deity 'endures' is possibly reflected in the use of the root *ykl* 'to be able, have power, prevail, endure' in Heb. names. Also extant in Amor. names is a noun *madar* from the root *dwr* meaning 'dwelling'(?) in the sense of 'refuge', and is comparable to the idea of the deity as a 'tent' (*'hl*) in Heb. names.

ḫzb 'to rescue' (*APNM*, 192). The idea that the deity rescues is conveyed in Heb. names with the roots meaning 'to deliver' (*yš'*, *mlṭ*, *nṣl* [Hiphil], *plṭ* and Aram. *šêzêb*), 'to spare' (*ḥml*), 'to redeem' (*g'l*, *pdh*), and 'to draw' (*dlh*).

ḫqb 'to watch, protect' (*APNM*, 203): *mt'* 'to protect, guard' (*APNM*, 235). The root *'qb* in BH does not have the meaning 'to watch, protect', and does not occur with a theophoric element, while a root *mt'* is not attested in BH. However, the idea that the deity protects is reflected in Heb. names from the roots *zmr* (cf. S. Arab. *dhimr*) and, possibly, *ḥmh* (cf. S. Arab. *ḥamay*).

ysm 'to be pretty, ornamental' (*APNM*, 211): *šm* (*APNM*, 267): *spr* 'to be fair, shining' (*APNM*, 252). The element *yasim* is used frequently in Amor. theophoric names to describe the deity as 'beautiful'. Such a concept is reflected in Heb. names from the roots *yph* 'to be fair, beautiful', and possibly the root *šnh* 'to shine, be beautiful'. However, a derivation from a Hollow root *sym*, noted by Huffmon and suggested by Gelb (*Lingua*, 3.3.8.2.1), would suggest an interpretation 'to put', establish', paralleled in Heb. names by the same root *śwm*, as well as the semantically comparable roots *kwn* and *qwm* (Hiphil). From the root *ysm* may be derived the element *šm* in the names [*Y*]*a-ši-im-é-a*, *Ya-ši-im-ir-ra* and *Ya-*[*š*]*i-im-*^{d}*Da-gan* according to Dietrich and Loretz (*op. cit.*, 239), although the element is unexplained by Huffmon (*APNM*, 267). Also relevant here, is the Amor. name-element *spr* 'to be fair, shining' (*APNM*, 252).

ysr 'to be upright' (*APNM*, 212): *yšr* 'to be fair, just' (*APNM*, 216). Although the root *yšr* 'to be smooth, straight, right' is attested in BH (cf. BDB, 448), it is not found in theophoric personal names. The comparable idea is perhaps expressed in Heb. names by the root *ṣdq* 'to be just, righteous'.

yṣr 'to form, design' (*APNM*, 214). The notion that the deity 'forms' or 'designs' is similar in idea to Heb. names which suggest that the deity 'builds' (root *bnh*), or 'makes' (roots *'śh*, *p'l*) the child.

yšḫ 'help' (*APNM*, 215). Since Heb. ' is often represented in Amor. by *ḫ*, this root may be found in BH in the form *yš'*, which is attested in Heb. names with the slightly different meaning 'to deliver', 'deliverance'. The idea of the deity as 'help' is conveyed in Heb. names by the roots *'zr*, *'wš* and *'dr* (Aram.).

l'' 'to be able, strong; to prevail' (*APNM*, 224). Heb. names portray the concept of the deity as 'strong' with the roots *gbr*, *ḥzq*, *'zz*, *'br* and *'mṣ*. The root *ykl* is also attested in Heb. theophoric names with the meaning 'to be able'. A causative interpretation of the Amor. names with this element, with the idea that the deity 'has strengthened', would be paralleled in Heb. names from the roots *ḥzq* and, possibly, *mrr* 'to strengthen, bless, commend', cf. Ug.

mnn 'who?' (*APNM*, 231-32). The Amor. interrog. *manna* 'Who?' is used with the element *baltī* 'without', to ask the rhetorical question 'Who can be without' the deity? The interrog. *mî* 'Who?' is found in Heb. theophoric names, but is always used with the preposition *k*^{e}. This produces a rather different question, 'Who is like' the deity?

mrṣ 'to be sick, angry' (*APNM*, 233). A root *mrṣ* exists in BH meaning 'to be sick' (Niphal) and 'to be sickened' (Hiphil), perhaps in the sense of disturbing, vexing (cf. BDB, 599), but is not found in theophoric personal names. A possible comparison to this Amor. root is the root *ḥrh* 'to burn, be kindled (of anger)' in Heb. names (see above, §2.9 *ḥarḥăyāh*). M.C. Astour, *JNES* 26 (1967), 228 cites Akk. *marṣu* meaning 'taboo' which may shed some light on the Amor. names, although it has no counterpart in Heb. theophoric names, and is very uncertain.

nṭ' 'to plant' (*APNM*, 239). The root *nṭ'* occurs in BH (cf. BDB, 642) but is not attested in personal names, which use instead the root *'rš* 'to plant' (cf. Arab. *gharasa* and *Akk. erēšu*). Also comparable perhaps is the root *zr'* 'to sow, scatter seed'.

ns' 'to raise, lift up (oneself)' (*APNM*, 239-40). BH also attests a root *nś'* 'to lift, carry, take', but not in personal names, in which the idea that the deity raises or lifts up, is expressed with the Qal of the root *qwm*. The Heb. root *zrḥ* 'to rise, come forth', which is attested in personal names, is perhaps also applicable here, if the Amor. root is used in a reflexive sense.

nps 'breath, life' (*APNM*, 240). Cognate with this Amor. element is BH *npš* 'soul, life, living being, breath' etc. (cf. BDB, 659). The element is not, however, found in personal names. Nevertheless, the idea of the deity giving breath or life, may be evident in the Heb. root *rwḥ* 'to breathe' in the BH name *'aḥrāḥ* (see above, §2.9) and perhaps in the Piel or Hiphil of the root *ḥyh* (*ibid.*, §2.8 *mᵉḥûyā'ēl*).

nṣb 'to place, set up' (*APNM*, 241): st_1 'to put, place' (*APNM*, 253). The BH root *nṣb* means 'to take one's stand' and the Hiphil, 'to station, set', corresponds to the causative meaning of Amor. names from the root *nṣb*. Although the root is not attested in Heb. theophoric names, the comparable idea in such is expressed by the Heb. roots *kwn*, *qwm* (Hiphil) and *śwm*, containing the idea 'to establish'. This same concept is also evident in Amor. st_1 'to put, place' (cf. *APNM*, 253).

rb' 'to be or become large' (*APNM*, 260). This Amor. root may well be cognate with Heb. *rbb*, which is used in theophoric names to depict the deity as 'great'. However, Huffmon's suggestion of a G or causative imf. for the name *Ya-ar-bi*-AN, may indicate otherwise, since a causative interpretation is not paralleled in Heb. theophoric names. A meaning 'to be great' is possible for the Amor. element *rab* in the name *A-na-ra-a-bu*, although the initial element is not conclusively theophoric (cf. *APNM*, 168). Another possibility is that the root is semantically akin to the Heb. name-element *rḥb* 'to be or grow wide, large, make wide, make room', which probably refers to the events of the birth (see above, §2.4).

tr 'to return' cf. Akk. (*APNM*, 270). The Akk. verbal form *itur* occurs with an Amor. theophoric element in the name *I-túr-ás-du*. The idea that the deity has 'returned' is reflected in Heb. names with the root *śwb*.

4. Amorite names contain many elements in which the meanings or forms are difficult to determine. For many such elements often more than one etymology may be possible so that a comparison with Hebrew theophoric names is more problematic and tenuous as far as these names are concerned. A large number of such types is found in Amorite, as the following list shows:

'bn (*APNM*, 155). This element remained inexplicable to Huffmon. However, Astour (*op. cit.*, 227) suggests that it indicates a divinized stone, and he compares Ug. *Bn-Abn* 'Son of Stone', etc. The initial elements of the names containing the root *'bn*, *I-ba-el-a-ab-nu* and *Tu-tar-ab-nu*, are equally obscure, although Astour suggests a meaning for the former name as possibly 'He married the Stone' (!), and for the latter, 'The Stone has increased' (f.). Since such interpretations gain little support from other Semitic onomastica, and since an alternative meaning for *abn* as 'our father' (i.e. *'b* + 1st pers. plur. pronom. suffix *n*) is given by Gröndahl (*PTU*, 87), Astour's suggestions should not be taken too seriously.

'btl (*APNM*, 155). For this element in the name *I-la-ab-ta-lu-ú*, Huffmon notes two possibilities, a Gt form of *b'l* ('to rule'?), and Arab. *ibtahala* 'to humbly entreat'. The concept that the deity 'rules' is possibly evident in the Heb. name *'ăḥî'ām* (root *'wm* 'to rule', see above, §2.9), while the idea 'to humbly entreat' is not attested in Heb. theophoric names. Astour (*op. cit.*, 227) suggests for the Amor. name, however, an *'aqtal* form of a root *btl* 'to separate, devote oneself exclusively to one person or god'. This would be paralleled in Heb. names with the roots *'ṣl* 'to reserve, set apart', *ḥṣh* 'to divide', *plh* 'to be separated, distinct', and perhaps *'sp* 'to gather', but the Amor. name would need to be causative in order to supply the same meaning which these Heb. roots convey. Gelb (*Lingua*, 3.3.8.11) divides the name to suggest *Jilap-ṭalluhu*? which, presumably, would be non-theophoric.

'dn (*APNM*, 159). This Amor. element could represent the noun *'ad* 'father' with the addition of the suffix *-na*, paralleled in Heb. names by the noun *'b*. On the other hand, it could represent *'dn* 'lord', also attested in Heb. names, and semantically comparable to the Heb. name-elements *b'l* and, possibly, *mr* (Aram.) (see above, §2.3). Another possibility for the Amor. element is a variant of *ḫadun* which is itself uncertain (see *APNM*, 159).

'md (*APNM*, 167). This Amor. element occurs in the names *A-mu-ud-pi-*AN and *A-mu-ud-pi-i-la*. The BH noun *'emet* may suggest a meaning 'True is the word of god', while Arab. *'amad* 'eternity, period of time' suggests 'Enduring is the command of El'. Astour (*op. cit.*, 227) has suggested a meaning 'prophecy, oracular decision' in the name *A-mu-ut-pi-*AN. None of these suggestions has any parallel among Heb. names.

'mr (*APNM*, 168). It is uncertain whether this Amor. root follows the Heb., Phoen. and Aram. meaning 'to say' or the Ug. and Akk. meaning 'to see'. The former meaning 'to say' is reflected in Heb. theophoric names with the roots *'mr* and possibly *qwl* (see above, §2.9 *qlyhw*). The idea that the deity 'sees' is depicted by the roots *r'h*, *ḥzh* 'to see', perhaps *ś/skh* 'to look out' (dubious, see above, §2.9 *śāk^e yah*) and *šwr* 'to behold, regard' (see above, §2.9 *'ăḥîšār*).

's' (*APNM*, 169). This element appears in names such as *Ya-sú-*[d]IM and *Ya-sú-*[d]*Da-gan* and is unexplained by Huffmon. A root *'śy* is suggested by Dietrich and Loretz (*op. cit.*, 242) while Gröndahl (*Orientalia* 35 [1966], 455) compares *yasu-addu* (cf. Clay, *PNCP*, 196) or a root *'sy/w* 'to heal', a denominative verb from Akk. *asû* 'healer'. She also suggests, as Dietrich and Loretz, an imf. of the root *'śy/w* 'to make'.

'rs (*APNM*, 171). The element *'rs* may be compared with Arab. *'rz* 'to be firm (on a base)', a denominative verb from the noun *'arz* 'cedar'. The verbal idea has no semantic parallel in Heb. names with this particular nuance of meaning. Huffmon also cites Ug. *'rẓ* 'terrible, mighty', which may be compared with Heb. *gbr* containing the meaning 'mighty' but not 'terrible'. Also suggested by Huffmon is a derivation either from Arab. *ḥrs* 'to protect' which would be reflected in Heb. names by the roots *zmr* (cf. S. Arab. *dhimr*) and, possibly, *ḥmh* (cf. S. Arab. *ḥamay*), or from Amor. *ḥrz* 'to be strong' which, in Heb. names, is portrayed by the roots *'br*, *'zz*, *ḥzq*, *'mṣ*, *gbr* and *ḥyl/ḥwl*.

'š (*APNM*, 171). This Amor. element is also uncertain: Huffmon compares the root *ǵwṯ* 'to assist, repair', comparable to the root *'wš* 'to help' in Heb. names and semantically comparable to Heb. names containing the roots *'zr* and Aram. *'dr*. Huffmon favours this interpretation as opposed to a derivation from a root *'wš* 'to give' (cf. Arab. *'āsa*) which is attested in Heb. names. Heb. names also express that the deity 'has given' by use of the roots *zbd*, *ntn*, *qwš* (cf. Akk. *qāšu*) and the Eg. element *pṭ* in the BH name *pûṭî'ēl* (cf. also *pṭyhw* above, §2.9). Gelb (*Lingua*, 3.3.8.2.1.) prefers to associate the element with this root *'wš* as in the name *Ja'ūs-Haddu*, for which he suggests a qatal imf.

'škr (*APNM*, 172). Huffmon considers this element in the names *Aš-kur-*[d]IM and *mu-ut-aš-kur* to be a divine name. This may well be the case with the latter name, but an alternative of a root *zkr* with a meaning 'nennen, preisen', suggested by Akk. *zakāru*, is noted by Dietrich and Loretz, *op. cit.*, 241. No parallel seems evident among Heb. theophoric names.

bs' (*APNM*, 177). For the initial element of the name *Ya-ba-si-*[d]*Da-gan*, which is unexplained by Huffmon, Gröndahl (*Orientalia* 35 [1966], 455) suggests a comparison with O./M. Bab. *ibaš(š)i-ilum*. This would indicate a meaning such as 'There is a god!' which has no parallel among Heb. names.

ḫz' (*APNM*, 192). With this element Huffmon compares Arab. *ǵḏw* 'to nourish', the same cognate which suggests the meaning of the root *'zh* in Heb. theophoric names. It is also semantically comparable to the root *qwt* (cf. Arab. *qāta*) in Heb. names. However, Dietrich and Loretz (*op. cit.*, 242) suggest a root *'śy*, which seems less satisfactory in view of the supposed *z* for *ś*.

ḫl (*APNM*, 193-94). The Amor. name *Ya-ḫi-il-li-im* is uncertain. Huffmon suggests the possibility of two forms, *wa'(i)l* 'ibex', which has no parallel in Heb. theophoric names, or *y'l* 'to serve, help', reflected in Heb. names from the roots *'zr*, *'dr* (Aram.) and *'wš*. Also suggested by Huffmon is a root *ḫyl* 'to be in labour', which has no semantic parallel in Heb. theophoric names.

ḫms (*APNM*, 198). For the Amor. name *Ya-aḫ-mi-iṣ-*^{d}XX[X]? Huffmon compares the root *'mṣ* 'to press close' attested in Phoen./Punic names (cf. *PNPPI*, 380). No parallel to this root is evident in Heb. theophoric names, unless the uncertain root *'wṣ* 'to make haste, press, be pressed' is relevant here (see above §2.9 *'ṣyh*).

ḫnb (*APNM*, 199). The element *maḫnub* in the name *Ma-aḫ-nu-ub*-AN is difficult. A comparison with Akk. *ḫanābu* 'to grow abundantly', suggested by Huffmon would produce a meaning which is without parallel in Heb. M.C. Astour (*op. cit.*, 228) also cites Arab. *ḥaniba* 'to feel pity, compassion', paralleled in Heb. names by *rḥm* (Piel) 'to show compassion'.

ḫs (*APNM*, 201). The root *ḥws* 'to be compassionate' or *'śy/w* 'to make, do' may be present in the Amor. name *Ḫa-a-sú*-AN. The form of the name is suggested, questioningly, by Huffmon as a G part. The idea of the deity as compassionate in Heb. names is conveyed by the root *rḥm*, while the concept of the deity as a 'Maker', i.e. 'Creator', is expressed verbally with the roots *'śh* and *p'l* 'to make, do', *bnh* 'to build, create', and *br'* and *qnh* 'to create'. Dietrich and Loretz (*op. cit.*, 242) favour *'śy*.

ḫs' (*APNM*, 201): *ḫṣ'* (*APNM*, 202). The initial element of the name *Yi-iḫ-si*-AN is problematic and no meaning is suggested by Huffmon. Dietrich and Loretz (*op. cit.*, 242), however, suggest a root *ḥzy* 'to see', comparable to Heb. names from the roots *ḥzh* and *r'h* 'to see', possibly *šwr* 'to regard, behold' (see above, §2.9 *'ăḥîšār*) and, perhaps, *śkh* 'to look out' (*ibid.*, *śāk*^{e}*yāh*). For Amor. *ḫṣ'* Huffmon compares this same root *ḥzy* 'to see' (*APNM*, 202).

ḫṣn (*APNM*, 202). For this element in Amor. names such as *Ya-aḫ-ṣí-in-*^{d}*Da-gan* and *Ta-aḫ-ṣí-in-ad-mu* (f.), Huffmon compares Akk. *haṣānu* 'to shelter, protect', also *ḥḍn* 'to embrace, nourish'. The former concept is evident in Heb. names from the roots *zmr* (cf. S. Arab. *dhimr*) and, possibly, *ḥmh* (cf. S. Arab. *ḥamay*), the latter concept 'to nourish' attested in the roots *'zh* (cf. Arab. *ghadhā*) and *qwt* (cf. Arab. *qāta*), although the specific idea 'to embrace' is not evident in Heb. theophoric names.

ḫt' (*APNM*, 205). This element is unexplained by Huffmon in the name *Ya-ḫa-at-ti*-AN although he suggests a D imf. Gröndahl (*Orientalia* 35 [1966], 455), also suggests a D imf. but of the root *ḫṭ'* 'to compensate'. This would be similar to the roots *šlm* 'to recompense' and *šwb* (Hiphil) 'to restore' in Heb. names, the reference probably being to a previously deceased child.

ḫtr (*APNM*, 206-207). For this element Huffmon notes the possibility of Phoen. *'dr* 'mighty, chief' (cf. *PNPPI*, 261-62) which is reflected in Heb. names from the root *gbr*. Phoen. names with the element *'dr* also contain the idea of the deity as 'glorious', reflected in Heb. names from the roots *kbd* and *mgd*. A comparison with the root *'dr* 'to help' Huffmon considers to be more tenuous. Astour (*op. cit.*, 228) suggests that *ḫatr* also appears as *aṭr* with *ṭ*, to which can be compared Heb. *'aṭārā*, Phoen. *'ṭr* and Akk. *eṭru*, meaning 'crown, diadem' but this has no semantic complement in Heb. names.

y'n (*APNM*, 208). The element *ya'an* in the name *Ya-an*-AN could be nominal or verbal. Huffmon compares Arab. *wa'n* 'large', which has no direct counterpart in Heb. names, unless it can have the nuance of meaning 'great', which would be reflected in Heb. names from the roots *gdl* and *rbb*. Dietrich and Loretz (*op. cit.*, 243), however, consider the initial part of the name to be a verbal form from a root *'ny* 'to answer'.

yrḫ (*APNM*, 214). The element is uncertain: Huffmon notes Astour's connection of the root with OT *Y*^e^*rīḫō*, which Astour more recently (*op. cit.*, 228) retracts, preferring a comparison with Akk. *rēḫu* 'to fecundate, impregnate' in names such as *Ia-ri-ḫa-bu-um*. No semantic parallel seems evident among Heb. names.

kb (*APNM*, 219). The initial element in Amor. names such as *Ka-bi-*^d^IM and *Ka-bi-*^d^*Da-gan* may represent *Ka-'abī*, expressing the deity as 'like a father' or, Akk. *kāp* 'rock' may suggest a suitable interpretation. In Heb. theophoric names the preposition *k*^e^ 'like' occurs only with the interrogative *mî* 'Who?', e.g. *mîkā'ēl* and *mîkāyāhû* 'Who is like El/Y?' This usage is rather different from the Amor. names under discussion. If, on the other hand, the Amor. element is to be determined from Akk. *kāp* 'rock', then Heb. names containing the noun *ṣwr* 'rock', provide a semantic parallel.

kbs (*APNM*, 220). For the initial element in names like *Ki-ib-si-*^d^IM and *Ki-ib-si?-*^d^*Šamaš*, Huffmon cites a number of possible etymologies. A comparison with the root *qbḍ*, 'to assemble', may be semantically reflected in Heb. names which contain the root *'sp* 'to gather'. A derivation of the element from Akk. *kibs*, meaning 'step, path' suggested by Gelb (*Lingua*, 3.2.4.2.1) or Heb. *kebeš* 'footstool' would have no parallel in Heb. theophoric names.

l' (*APNM*, 224). The element *lu'u* is uncertain, but Huffmon suggests it is perhaps related to Akk. *le'û* 'strong' (cf. also Amor. *l'*' above, p. 202). This is a concept of deity expressed frequently in Heb. names with the roots *'br*, *'zz*, *ḥzq*, *'mṣ*, *gbr* and *ḥyl*/*ḥwl*. Huffmon also compares Arab. *lawā* 'to wait, turn, conceal'; the wide range of meaning of this root, however, makes a comparison with Heb. names tenuous. Another explanation cited by Huffmon is that of *la-hū* 'to, for him' which, in names such as ^d^*A-mu-um-lu-ú*, would have no semantic equivalent in Heb.

l'k. According to Dietrich and Loretz (*op. cit.*, 244), the name-element *malak*, which is attested in *Ma-la-ku-il* and *Ma-la-ak-ì-li*, is not derived from a root *mlk* as Huffmon suggests (p. 230) but a root *l'k* 'to send', cf. Ug. and Heb. *ml'k*. Such an idea has no counterpart among Heb. theophoric names: although a name *šilḥî* exists in BH and is possibly a sf. with the root *šlḥ* 'to send' (see above, §2.10 *šilḥî*), a full form with this root, i.e. containing a theophoric element, does not exist.

ms' (*APNM*, 232). This element is also uncertain: Huffmon notes Akk. *misû* 'to wash, purify', comparable to Heb. theophoric names from the roots *brr* 'to purify', *ṭbl* 'to dip' (purify) and *nzh* 'to sprinkle' (purify). Dietrich and Loretz (*op. cit.*, 244) suggest *mṣ'*, which would mean 'to find, attain to (something)' (cf. *APNM*, 232) and has no parallel among Heb. theophoric names. Gröndahl (*Orientalia* 35 [1966], 455-56) compares Akk. *mašû* 'to forget', which would be comparable to Heb. theophoric names containing the root *nšh*.

mr (*APNM*, 233). In the Amor. name *Ya-mu-ur-ad-du*, the initial element may be derived from *'mr* which, for Amor. names, could mean either 'to speak' or 'to see'. Both these concepts are reflected in Heb. names as discussed above (see *'mr* p. 204). Huffmon also suggests the Ug. root *mrr* 'to strengthen, bless, commend' (Huffmon cites only 'to bless'), which is also found in Heb. theophoric names. The root *ḥzq* is also used in Heb. names to denote the idea that the deity strengthens, while the idea 'to bless' is attested in the root *brk*. 'To commend' has no semantic equivalent in Heb. theophoric names.

sgb (*APNM*, 244-45). The element *sgb* in the Amor. name *Sa-ag-bi-*^{d}IM may reflect either West Semitic *śgb* 'to protect, make strong' or a noun 'élite, soldier', which Huffmon notes is attested in the Mari texts (Finet, *ARMT*, XV 252). This latter suggestion is not reflected in the Heb. onomasticon, while the former, 'to protect', is evident in the roots *zmr* (cf. S. Arab. *dhimr*) and, possibly, *ḥmh* (cf. S. Arab. *ḥamay*). 'To strengthen' occurs in Heb. names from the root *ḥzq* and, perhaps, *mrr* (cf. Ug.). Cf. also the root *śgb* 'to be (inaccessibly) high' in the Heb. name *'lśgb* (seal V, 59).

sṭ' (*APNM*, 245). The initial element in the name *Ya-sa-aṭ-ṭi*-AN is uncertain: Huffmon cites Akk. *ṣuddū* 'to nourish', reflected in Heb. names from the roots *'zh* (cf. Arab. *ghadhā*) and *qwt* (cf. Arab. *qāta*).

sl' (*APNM*, 246). Huffmon suggests a G or causative imf. for the initial element of the name *Ya-as-li*-AN but gives no indication as to the meaning of the root. Dietrich and Loretz (*op. cit.*, 244) propose the root *slḫ* which is given the meaning 'pardon' in Amor. names (cf. *APNM*, 246) perhaps similar to Heb. names with the root *nšh* 'to forget (sins)'. Gröndahl (*Orientalia* 35 [1966], 456) suggests a possible III Y form of *sll* 'Weg aufschütten, Bahn machen', which has no parallel among Heb. theophoric names.

smḫ (*APNM*, 250). Both Amor. and Heb. theophoric names express that the deity 'hears' by means of the root *smḫ* and *šm'* respectively. However, the element *samḫ* in the name *Sa-am-ḫi-li*-AN could also be derived from a root *śmḫ* 'to rejoice' (Heb. Ug.), 'to be high, haughty' (Arab.), 'to grow high, well' (Akk.). Huffmon also cites Akk. *šamḫ* 'abundant'. The idea that the deity *causes* man to rejoice is found in Heb. names from the roots *'śr* (cf. Arab. *'ašira* 'to fill with joy'), *ḥbṣ* (cf. Akk. *ḫabāṣu* 'to be joyful'), *ḥdh* ('to give joy, rejoice'), and the noun *gyl* ('rejoicing joy'). In Heb. names the idea is probably always causative, expressing the deity as a source of joy/rejoicing even in the nominal form *gyl*. The idea of the deity as 'high' in Heb. names is reflected in the roots *'lh* (but possibly Ammon. or Moab.) and *śgb* ('to be [inaccessibly] high'), as well as in names which express the deity as 'exalted' with the roots *'th* (cf. Arab. *'atā* 'to be proud, exalted') and *rwm* ('to be high, exalted'). The idea of the deity as 'haughty', however, does not appear to be contained in these Heb. roots, unless such a concept can be considered as synonymous with the idea of the deity as 'proud' which is, as noted, contained in the root *'th*. The Akk. suggestion, 'to grow high, well', is not reflected in Heb. theophoric names unless this concept contains the idea 'to be great', but the Akk. sense contained in *šamḫ* 'abundant' is possibly reflected in Heb. names with the noun *yeter* 'pre-eminence, abundance' (cf. above, §2.3 *ytr*). Huffmon also lists the Amor. name *Si-im-ḫi-*^{d}*Dagan*, and compares the element *simḫ* with Heb. *śimḥāh* 'joy' which, as noted, is a concept frequently attested in Heb. theophoric names. The numerous possibilities suggested for the Amor. element makes any comparison with Heb. names precarious.

sr' (*APMN*, 253). The element *sari'e* in Amor. names is uncertain. Noted by Huffmon is a comparison with Arab. *šariya* 'to shine, gleam', possibly paralleled in Heb. theophoric names by *šnh* 'to shine, be beautiful' (see above, §2.9 *šnyw*), although the Amor. element does not contain the nuance of meaning 'beautiful'. Another root cited by Huffmon is *šry* 'to loosen, release', which may be reflected in Heb. names from the difficult root *rmh* meaning 'to loosen' (*ibid.*, 2.5 *rmh*/*rwm*).

plḫ (*APNM*, 255). No suitable suggestion for this element in the name *Ya-ap-la-aḫ*-AN seems possible. A root *plh* exists in BH, and is found also in the theophoric name *'ĕlîp^{e}lēhû* meaning, probably, 'May El distinguish him', but any connection with the Amor. name is uncertain.

pls (*APNM*, 255). The element *puls* in Amor. theophoric names could be from *pls* 'to level' (cf. Heb. and Phoen.), which has no counterpart in Heb. names or, 'to view, consider' (cf. Akk.), which may be semantically similar to Heb. names from the roots *š'r* 'to reckon' and *ḥšb* 'to take account'.

ṣb (*APNM*, 256). The best suggestion for the meaning of this element in names is *ṣbw* 'to desire' (cf. Aram., Ug., Arab., Akk. Heb. *ṣ^{e}bî* means 'beauty, honour, decoration' and not 'ornament' as Huffmon suggests [cf. BDB, 840]). This concept has no counterpart in Heb. theophoric names. Other suggestions cited by Huffmon, *ḍb'* 'war' and *ḍibḥ* 'sacrifice' also have no parallel in Heb. names.

ṣpr$_1$ (*APNM*, 257). The initial element in the name *Ṣa-pur-sà-lim* may be determined by the Arab. cognate *ṣabūr* 'patient, steadfast'. This may be semantically similar to the Heb. name *yatnî'ēl* meaning perhaps 'El is constant', root *ytn* (cf. Arab. *watana*), although the form of the Heb. name is difficult (see above, §2.9).

ṣpr$_2$ (*APNM*, 258). The initial element of the theophoric name *Ṣú-up-ri-e-ra-aḫ* is problematic: Huffmon cites Akk. *ṣupr* 'claw', as well as *spr* (*špr*) 'to be fair'. Gröndahl (*Orientalia* 35 [1966], 456) compares the Ug. name *ṣupranu*, also meaning 'claw' (cf. *PTU*, 190). Only the idea 'to be fair' is met in Heb. names, with the use of the roots *yph* 'to be fair, beautiful' and, similarly, *šnh* 'to shine, be beautiful'.

r'p (*APNM*, 260). For this element in Amor. theophoric names, Huffmon suggests possibly *r'p* 'to be compassionate' (Arab.) comparable to Heb. names from the root *rḥm* 'to show compassion'. Another possibility is the root *r'b* 'to compensate' (Arab. 'repair': cf. also Dietrich and Loretz, *op. cit.*, 241), similar to the idea that the deity 'restores' (root *šwb*) or 'recompenses' (root *šlm*) in Heb. names, both roots probably referring to the restoration of a previously deceased child.

rsb (*APNM*, 263). This element in the name *Ya-ar-sa-ab-la*-AN is unexplained: Huffmon suggests, however, a root *ršp* 'to burn, kindle' which has a semantic complement in Heb. *ḥrh* 'to burn, be kindled (of anger)', a root which may be present in the problematic BH name *ḥarḥăyāh* (see above, §2.9).

5. Many Amorite theophoric names contain elements which have no semantic parallel amongst Hebrew name-elements. Such Amorite names express ideas about the deities, or about the relationship of the name-bearer to the deity, which have no counterpart in Hebrew and which, therefore, cannot be said to be characteristics of the Israelite God. Such concepts are as follows.

Absent in Heb. name-giving is any reference to the deity in terms of cosmic phenomena, found in the Amor. nominal elements *brq* 'lightning' (*APNM*, 178),[38] *sms* 'sun' (*APNM*, 250-51) and *kbkb* 'star' (*APNM*, 220). Neither is the Heb. deity depicted as an animal, as in Amor. *lb'* 'lion' (*APNM*, 225),[39] *ri-im* 'wild bull' (or construct; M.C. Astour, *op. cit.*, 226) and possibly *'sd*, which may mean 'lion' or 'warrior' (*APNM*, 169).[40] Absent, too, is the figurative idea of the deity as strength in Amor. *qrn* 'horn, strength' (*APNM*, 259). The Heb. onomasticon contains no evidence of a 'maternal uncle' in names, attested in Amor. *ḫl*$_3$ (*APNM*, 194): Heb. names depict the deity only as a 'Paternal Uncle' or 'Divine Kinsman'.

Construct nouns which are evident in Amor. but which have no semantic counterpart among Heb. names, portray the name-bearer as a 'son' (*bn APNM*, 175-76) and 'son-in-law' (*ḫtn*$_1$ *APNM*, 205), as a 'pledged person' (*lw' APNM*, 225) and perhaps as a 'girl' or 'servant' of the deity (*ḫlm APNM*, 195).[41] The Amor. element *p* 'mouth, command' (*APNM*, 254) is also not encountered in Heb. names.

Two prepositional expressions found in Amor. have no equivalent in Heb. names: these depict the name-bearer as 'behind, in favour of' the deity (*bḫd APNM*, 173) and 'under' (the authority of) the deity (*tḫt APNM*, 269). The interrogative *'y* 'where' (*APNM*, 161) asks 'Where is?' the deity and seems to suggest divine neglect of the name-bearer.

Amor. names contain many verbal elements which are not attested in the Heb. onomasticon. Connected with the birth events are the Amor. elements *nb'* 'to call, name, announce' (*APNM*, 236),[42] *gḫ* 'to break forth (of water)' or 'procreate' (Huffmon, *APNM*, 180 compares the causative, Syriac, use of the root), *spk* 'to pour out' (*APNM*, 252)[43] and *wṣ'* 'to go out' (G form or causative imf., *APNM*, 184). Other Amor. verbal elements used to describe the deities but with no equivalent in Heb. are *'w'* 'to be, become' (*APNM*, 159), *ḫln*$_2$ 'to be or become known' (*APNM*. 196),[44] *ypḫ* 'to be brilliant' (*APNM*, 212), *yqr* 'to be esteemed' (*APNM*, 214), *yḫd* 'one, unique' (*APNM*, 210), *rṣ* 'to be pleased, content' (*APNM*, 265),[45] *nḫ* 'to rest, be satisfied' (*APNM*, 237) and possibly *yrq* (= *wrq*?) 'to be green, yellow' (*APNM*, 215).[46] Two Amor. roots are used causatively to depict divine activity; these are *gd* 'to be, become good' (causative imf., *APNM*, 179) and *slm* 'to be well' (causative, *APNM*, 246). An imv. of the verb *ḫbb* 'to love' may be evident in Amor. *ḫbn*[47] but has no semantic counterpart in Heb. names. Other Amor. verbal elements not reflected in Heb. are *mṣ'* 'to find, attain to (something)' (*APNM*, 232),[48] *rḫ'* 'to pasture, guard, be a friend' (*APNM*, 260),[49] *rš'* 'to lament, feel pity' (*APNM*, 265),[50] *nqm* 'to vindicate, avenge' (*APNM*, 241),[51] and *rkb* 'to ride' (*APNM*, 261).

4.4 *A Comparison between the Concepts of Deity Revealed in the Aramaic and Hebrew Onomastica*

It has been the aim of the present study to compare the concept of the Hebrew God with that of other Semitic deities through an examination of the various onomastica. Nowhere is this more difficult to achieve than in the case of Aramean names, in view of the constant difficulty of assigning an Aramaic name to an Aramean person. The widespread use of Aramaic as a *lingua franca* meant that many Semitic and non-Semitic names were transcribed into Aramaic, so that a survey of such names cannot, in any way, yield a true reflection of the Aramean beliefs concerning their deities.

Although it is necessary, as far as possible, to establish Aramean ownership for an attested name, there are no criteria which enable this to be done with certainty. The Arameans constantly appropriated names and religious ideas from various sources, as the numerous examples of Aramaic names compounded with forms of *yhwh*, alone, illustrate (e.g. *'wryh br mḥsyah 'rmy zy swn*, Krael, 226 8.2). Attempts to establish such ownership by linguistic criteria or otherwise, therefore, are very precarious. For this reason, many of the names attested on the papyri from Elephantine are excluded from this immediate discussion but included, for reference, elsewhere (see Appendix, 2).

As far as possible, every attempt has been made to use Aramaic names which are thought to have belonged to Arameans, although it is feared that this may not always be the case. The lack of an up-to-date collection of all early Aramaic onomastic material has necessitated recourse to the works of many scholars. The collections and studies by Vinnikov,[52] Tallqvist[53] Donner and Röllig,[54] Gibson,[55] Cowley,[56] Driver,[57] and Kraeling[58] have been used extensively. Also utilized are the works of Grelot,[59] Silverman,[60] Lipiński[61] and the review of this last work by R. Zadok.[62] Zadok's work *On West Semites in Babylonia During the Chaldean and Achaemenian Periods: an Onomastic Study*[63] is also of some relevance here, though it does not solve the difficulty of assigning Aramaic names to Aramean owners. The same may be said of the work of W. Kornfeld, *Onomastica Aramaica aus Ägypten*.[64] Three articles by F.M. Fales[65] were also very useful, as well as an article by Driver on Aramaic names in Akkadian texts.[66] K. Deller[67] has suggested the presence of an Aramean settlement at Sultantepe in the New Assyrian period and has recorded theophoric names from this area. Also used are

Vattioni's lists of seals[68] while some Aramaic names are attested in the Old Testament.

1. There exist in Hebrew and Aramaic theophoric names many elements which are common to both and which, therefore, display similar concepts concerning the respective Israelite and Aramean deities. In the list of such elements which follows, Aramaic name-types are given in each case, in an attempt to draw up a complete list of names belonging to Arameans. Cuneiform names have been left in transliteration, others are transliterated from their W. Semitic characters.

Aram./Heb. *'b* 'father'. Cf. the Aram. names *A-da-bu-i*, which possibly means 'Ada(d) is my father', (*Fales*, 181, 8th/7th cent.), *Abā-il* (*APN*, 2, 7th cent.) and *'bgd*? (P. Bordreuil, A. Lemaire, *Sem* 26 [1976], 54 no. 25, but note *'bgdh//wzḥṭy ibid.*, no. 26).

Aram./Heb. *'wr* 'light'. Aram. *'wryh* (Krael. 226 8.2, Eleph. 5th cent.). Note the description of the owner of the name as *'rmy zy swn*.

Aram./Heb. *'ḥ* 'brother'. Aram. *'ḥš*[*y*], *Ḫa-Si-i* (Fales *OA 13*, 209).

Aram. *'lh*/ Heb. *'l* 'god'. Aram. *nbw'lh* (*PS*, 206) and *A-a-ila-a* (*APN*, 2); also *Na-šuḫ-ilu* (Deller, 474).

Aram./Heb. *'mr* 'to speak'. Aram. *Ilu-a-ma-*[*ra*? (Fales *OA 13*, 207, 228), and an unpublished seal *'l'mr*.

Aram./Heb. b^e 'in, with, by means of'. Aram. *byd'l* (*PS*, 205, V*Aug*, 9); *bydyh* (*PS*, 205).

Aram./Heb. *bnh* 'to build, create'. Aram. *'dbnh* (Fales *OA 13*, 205). The name *Ba-na-at-e-ma-šá-ma-šá* is translated questioningly by Fales (*OA 13*, 226) as 'la madre Šamaš(a)? crèo', which seems semantically difficult.

Aram./Heb. *b'l* 'lord'. Aram. *Amma-ba'li* (*APN*, 21, 268, 9th cent.); cf. also *Am-mi-pa-a'-li* (*APN*. 22).

Aram./Heb. *br'* 'to create'. Aram. *Bar-'a-ilu* [' '] (Fales, 182, 8th/7th cent.).

Aram./Heb. *brk* 'to bless'. Aram. *'lbr*[*k*] (V*Aug*, 8); *brkb'l* (V*Aug*, 17, Aleppo 7th or 6th cent.); *nbwbrk* (*PS*, 206, 5th cent.); *Bi-il-ba-rak-ki* (Deller, 475); *Ilu-bara-ku*[*ḫu*] (Fales *OA 13*, 207); *Še-er-ba-rak-ki*, [*ᴵŠe-er-b*]*a-rak-k*[*i*] (Deller, 475, Sultantepe 7th cent.); *Si-i'-pa-rak-ka* (Deller, 475).

Aram./Heb. *gd* 'fortune'. Aram. *gd'l* (*PS*, 224; V*Aug*, 9); *gdnbw* (*PS*, 225).

Aram./Heb. *dlh* 'to draw (rescue)'. Aram. *byt'ldlny* (*SSI II*, 22 rev. 2 4, Sefire 6th cent.); *nbwdlh* (*PS*, 206, Tell Ḥalaf 1, 7th cent.); *ndwdlny* (Grelot,

480, Eg. 5th cent.); *šmšdlh* (*KAI*, 236, Rs 7; *PS*, 253, Assur 7th. cent.); *šndlh* (Fales *OA 13*, 206); *Bêl-Harrān-di-li-i-ni* (Deller, 474); *Hadad-melek-di-li-i-ni* (*ibid.*); *Ilu-da-la-a* (*APN*, 96); *Na-suḫ-di-li-nu* (*ibid.*, 168); *Se-e-dàl-li-ni* (Fales *OA 13*, 207); *Se-e-dil-li-ni* (Deller, 474, Sultantepe 7th cent.); *Si-'-da-la-a* (*APN*, 194, 7th cent.); *Si-'-di-li-i-ni* (*APN*, 194).

Aram./Heb. *zbd* 'to bestow'. Aram. *'šmzbd* (Grelot, 464; *PS*, 214, Eg. 5th cent.); *byt'lzbd* (Grelot, 469, Eg. 5th cent.); *Mil-ki-il-za-ba-du* (R. Zadok, *BASOR* 230 [1978], 61); *Si-'-za-ba-di* (*APN*, 195, 7th cent.).

Aram./Heb. *ḥzh* 'to see'. Aram. *ḥz'l* (*SSI II*, Damascus 2.1, 5 A 4; *PS*, 217; *APN*, 87; Lipiński, 18; Deller, 475: cun. *Ḫa-za-ilu*, cf. also 2 Kgs 8.8, 13, 15, 29; 2 Chr. 22.6; 1 Kgs 19.15, 17 etc. 9th cent.); *La-aḫ-ze-ilu* (Fales *OA 13*, 207); *Si-e-ḫa-za-a* (*APN*, 194, 7th cent.).

Aram./Heb. *ḥlq* 'portion'. Aram. *ḥlqyw* (V*Aug*, 161). Heb. names with this element are nominal whereas the Aram. name could be nominal or verbal.

Aram?/Heb. *ḥml* 'to spare'. Aram. (?) *yḥmwlyh* (*PS*, 223, 5th cent.).

Aram./Heb. *ḥnn* 'to be gracious'. Aram. *Ḫa-nu-nu-ilu* (Fales *OA 13*, 206); *Ilu-ḫa-na-na* (*ibid.*); *Si-e-ḫa-an* (*APN*, 194, 7th cent.).

Aram?/Heb. *ḥsh* 'refuge'. Aram. *mḥsyh* (Krael, 226 8.2, Eleph. 5th cent.). Note the designation of the name-bearer as *'rmy zy swn*.

Aram./Heb. *ṭwb* 'to be good'. Aram. *'b(y)ṭb* (Grelot, 462; *KAI*, 268,2, Memphis 4th cent.); *'ḥ(w)ṭb* (*PS*, 194, 5th cent.); *ṭabrimmôn* (1 Kgs 15.18, cf. BDB, 372, 9th cent., also Zadok, *On West Semites*, 49); *ṭbšlm* (V*Aug*, 162); *Ṭa-ab-Si-i* (Fales *OA 13*, 206).

Aram./Heb. *yd'* 'to know'. Aram. *byt'lyd'* (*SSI II*, 22 obv. 2, Sefire 6th. cent.); *yd'l* (Lipiński, 105-106, Assur 5, 7th cent.); *Ia-da-a'-ilu* (Fales *OA 13*, 207).

Aram./Heb. *yš'* 'to deliver'. Aram. *mr'yš'* (V*Aug*, 24). The element *mr'* 'lord', however, need not be theophoric.

Aram./Heb. *k*^{e} 'like' and *mî* + *k*^{e} 'Who is like?' Aram sf.(?) *knbw* (V*Aug*, 43); *mkbnt* (Grelot, 477, Eg. 5th cent.).

Aram./Heb. *mlk* 'king' (Aram. perhaps also verbal). Aram. *'ḥmlk* (V*Aug*, 134); *'trmlky* (Grelot, 466 Eg. 5th cent.); *'l-mlk* (Deller, 475); perhaps *Al-Na-šuḫ-mil-ki* (*ibid.*, 474); cf. also S.A. Kaufman's suggestion of a possibly Aram. name *'dmlkly'*, *Ad-milki-ilayya*, 'Ad is King of the gods' (*JNES* 37 [1978], 109).

Aram. *mr'* Heb. *mr* (Aram. lw?) 'lord'. Aram. *mr'hdd* (V*Aug*, 15); *mr'yš'* (*ibid.*, 24); *Ma-ri-id-di* (*APN*, 134); *Mar-la-rim-me/Mar-la-ar-me* (Fales, *OA* 49; *APN*, 135, 7th cent.); *Mār-sūri* (*APN*, 135). Aram. names in which the corresponding element is non-theophoric may refer to a temporal lord rather than a deity. Heb. names do not conclusively contain Aram. *mr'* (cf. above, §2.3).

Aram. *nwr*, Heb. *nr* 'lamp'. Aram. *'ḥnwry* and *'ḥnry* (*PS*, 195) (or Akk.); *'lnwry* (V.*Aug*, 2); *'lnwry/'lnr* (Deller, 475); *byt'lnwry* (Grelot, 469, Eleph. 5th cent.); *nrš'*, *nrb'*[*l*] (Fales *OA 13*, 205, 210); ?*I*[d]*A-tar-nūri* (Deller, 473); *Mil-ki-nūrī* (R. Zadok, *BASOR* 230 [1978], 59, 7th cent.); *Se-e-nūri* (Deller, 475); [d]*Še-ri-nūri* (*ibid.*).

Aram./Heb. *ntn* 'to give'. Aram. *'dntn* (Fales *OA 13*, 205); *byt'lntn* (Grelot, 469, Eleph. 5th cent); *b'lntn* (*PS*, 214; V, 81-2; V.*Aug*, 21; Herr, 158 no. 8 considers this seal probably to be Moab.); *ḥrmntn* (Grelot, 474, Eleph. 5th cent.); *nbwntn* (Grelot, 480, Eleph. 5th cent.); *Bēl-na-tan* (*APN*, 61).

Aram./Heb. *smk* 'to support'. Aram. *'lsmk* (V.*Aug*, 179 no. 38; *SSI II*, 12 ii 1, Luristan, 8th cent.); *mrsmk* (Fales *OA 13*, 206, 220); *'trsmk* (*KAI*, 222 A 1.3. 14, Sefire 8th cent.), also *A-tar-šúm-ki* (Lipiński, 58ff.); *Ba'al-šá-ma-ka* (Fales *OA 13*, 207); *Si-'-ši-im-ki* (*APN*, 195). Heb. names with this root are only verbal; Aram. names are verbal and nominal.

Aram./Heb. *str* 'to conceal, hide'. Aram. *'lstr* (*SSI II*, 11 i 1, Luristan 8th cent.); *stryh* (*PS*, 221, Eleph. 5th cent.).

Aram./Heb. *'bd* 'servant'. Aram. *'bdb'lt* (*SSI II*, 6 ii 1, Hamath 9th/8th cent.); *'bdhdd* (V.*Aug*, 22); *'bdyrḥ* (V.*Aug*, 86); *'bdnbw* (*PS*, 223).

Aram./Heb. *'dh* 'to adorn'. Aram. *'dyh* (Grelot, 465; *PS*, 224, Eg. 5th cent.). The element is probably verbal in the Aram. name. Heb. names with this root are both nominal and verbal.

Aram./Heb. *'wd* 'witness'. Aram. *'d'd* (Fales *OA 13*, 208), 'The (divine?) Father is a witness'.

Aram./Heb. *'zz* 'to be strong'. Aram. *gd'zyz* (*PS*, 225, Eleph. 5th cent.). Heb. names containing this root are both verbal and nominal. Cf. also the possibly Aram. name *Šum-ma-uz-zi* (Fales *OA*, 50), and *'dm'zy* (Fales *OA 13*, 205), depicting the deity as a 'refuge/protection'.

Aram./Heb. *'zr* 'to help'. Aram. *'y'zr* (P. Bordreuil, A. Lemaire, *Sem* 29 [1979], 76); *b'l'zr* (*PS*, 214, Eleph. 5th cent.); *hdd'zr* (*PS*, 193; 2 Sam. 8; 1 Chr. 18,19; 1 Kgs 11.23, cf. BDB, 212, 9th cent.); *'tr'zr* (*PS*, 232; V.*Aug*, 25; A.R. Millard, *Iraq* 27 [1965], 14 no.7). Cf. also the Aram. cognate *'dr* below, 3.

Aram./Heb.(?) *'lh* 'to be high'. Aram. *dd'lh* (V.*Aug*, 46). The Heb. element, however, may be Ammon. or Edom., see above, §2.3.

Aram./Heb. *'m* 'with'. Aram. *Sam-si-im-me* (Fales, 186, 8th/7th cent.). Cf. Fales, 186 for the replacement of ' with *a* or *i*. However, more recently, Fales has preferred to interpret the second element of this name as 'mother', cf. below, p. 225.

Aram./Heb. *ʿm* 'kinsman'. Aram. *ʿmšzb* (*PS*, 229, Eleph. 5th cent.); *šdʿm* (*PS*, 245), perhaps 'The (divine) Kinsman is a mountain'; *A-me-A-tar* (Deller, 473); *A-tar-ḫa-mu/A-tar-ḫa-am* (Deller, 473; *APN*, 47, 7th cent.).

Aram./Heb. *ʿnh* 'to answer'. Aram. *ʿnʾl* (*PS*, 229).

Aram./Heb. *ʿnn* 'to appear'. Aram. *ʿnnyh* (Krael, 204 7.1, Eleph. 5th cent.). Note the designation of the name-bearer as *ʾrmy zy yb*.

Aram./Heb. *pṭ* (Eg.) 'to give'. Aram. *pṭsry* (*SSI II*, 30 A 9, 11, 27 B 1. Eg. Osiris + *pṭ* 'Osiris has given', Tema 5th cent.). The bearer of the name was probably an Aramean (cf. *SSI II*, p. 151).

Aram./Heb. *ṣdq* 'to be righteous', noun 'righteousness'. Aram. *ṣdqrmn* (*PS*, 228; V*Aug*, 3: for the Aramean deity Rammān/Rimmōn see J.C. Greenfield, *IEJ* 26 [1976], 195-98; *Ba-ṣi-id-qi-i/Bi-ṣi-id-qi-i* (Fales, 182, 8th/7th cent.). This last name possibly means 'The Father is justice, righteousness', although the initial elements *Ba/Bi* could represent the prep. b^e 'in', cf. Fales *OA 13*, 206, 225; *Ṣi-id-qi-ilu* (Fales *OA 13*, 206) nominal.

Aram./Heb. *qwm* 'to raise up, establish' (Hiph.). Aram. *bytʾltqm* (Grelot, 469; *PS*, 208, Eleph. 5th cent.); *A-tar-qa-mu* (*APN*, 47). This latter name, meaning 'Athar has risen', is reflected in Heb. in the Qal of the root *qwm* 'to arise'.

Aram./Heb. *qnh* 'to create'. Aram. *Qa-na-Si-i* (Fales *OA 13*, 207, 229).

Aram./Heb. *rbb* 'to be great'. Aram. *nbrb* (V*Aug*, 10); *Ra-ba-ilu* (Fales, 185, 8th/7th cent.); *Ra-man-ra-ba* (*APN*, 185, 7th cent.).

Aram./Heb. *rwm* 'to be exalted'. Aram. names with this root are *ʾšmrm* (*PS*, 214); *gdrm* (V*Aug*, 5); *šmrm* (*PS*, 253) which probably means ''*Ašim* is exalted'; *Ilu-a-a-ra-me* (Fales, 184, 8th/7th. cent.); *Mil-ki-i-ram*^{am} (R. Zadok, *BASOR* 230 [1978], 61); *Mil-ki-la-rim* (*ibid.*, 59); *Si-iʾ-ra-mu* (Fales, 186, 8th/7th cent.).

Aram./Heb. *rʿ* 'friend, companion'. Aram. *bytʾlrʿy* (Grelot, 469, Eg. 5th cent.); *nbwrʿy* (Grelot, 481, Eleph. 5th cent.); *rʿdd* (Fales *OA 13*, 205, 211); *A-bi-ri-i*, *Ḫa-an-da-ri-i* (*ibid.*, 211). Aram. nominal and construct, Heb. only construct.

Aram./Heb. *šʾl* 'to ask'. Aram. *Sa-al-ti-ilu* (Fales *OA 13*, 207, 226); *Su-u-li-i* (Fales, 186, 8th/7th cent.).

Aram./Heb. *šwr* 'wall'. Aram. *ʾdšry* (Fales *OA 13*, 205); *nbwšry* (V*Aug*, 13); *ʿtršwry* (Grelot, 466, Eleph. 5th cent.); *Aḫi-sūru* (*APN*, 17); *A-i-su-ú-ri* (*ibid.*, 19, 7th cent.); *A-tar-su-ri/ru* (*APN*, 47; Deller, 473, 7th cent.); *A-ta-su-ri* (*APN*, 47); *Mār-sūri* (*APN*, 135); *Na-ḫu-šu-su-ri* (= *Na-šu-ḫu-su-ri*) (Deller, 474); *Na-šuḫ-su-ri* (*ibid.*); *Si-iʾ-su* (= *Si-iʾ-su-*[*ri*]) (*ibid.*, 475).

Aram. *šzb* Heb. *šêzêb* (Aram. lw.), 'to deliver'. Aram. *'šmšzb* (Grelot, 464; *PS*, 214, Eg. 5th cent.); *byt'lšzb* (Grelot, 469, Eg. 5th cent.); *ḥrmšzb* (Kornfeld *OAA*, 51); *nbwšzb* (Grelot, 481, Eg. 5th. cent.); *nrglšzb* (Grelot, 483, Eg. 5th cent.); *'mšzb* (*PS*, 229, 5th cent.); *ṣlmšzb* (*SSI II*, 30 A 9, 11, 27; *PS*, 229, Tema 5th cent.); perhaps also *Mu-še-zib-ra-man* (*APN*, 141).

Aram./Heb. *šm'* 'to hear'. Aram. *yhwyšm'* (Grelot, 497, Eleph. 5th cent.); *šm''l* (*PS*, 252); *Ia-si-me-e'-ilu* (Fales *OA 13*, 207); *Na-aš-hu-sa-ma-'-a-ni* (*APN*, 168). The seal *yhwyšm' (bt šwššr'ṣr)* (V, 226, 6th cent.) may be relevant here. N. Avigad, 'Seals of Exiles', *IEJ* 15 (1965), 230-32, considers the owner of this seal to have been a Jewish woman. However, concluding the article, Avigad accepts his evidence for ownership as 'exceeding strictly scholarly analysis'.

2. Some Aramaic names are more problematic as far as meaning or form are concerned, or may involve some difficulty when compared with Hebrew theophoric names. This is the case with the following name-elements:

bb' ? In the possibly Aram. name *Adab-ba-ba-u* (*APN*, 7) the second element was considered by Tallqvist to mean *bābu* 'child' (*APN*, 274), although its position following the theophoric element makes its interpretation difficult. Heb. names contain no parallel to this idea. More suitable semantically would be the Aram. noun *bb'* meaning 'door, gate', symbolic for protection, and comparable to Heb. names with the element *dlt*, also meaning 'door'.

dyn 'to judge'. For the Aram. name *byt'ltdn* (Eleph. 5th cent.), Grelot (p. 469) suggests the root *'dn*, a cognate of Heb. *'zn* 'to hear' with a meaning 'Bêt'el can you hear?', although such a root is not attested elsewhere in Aram. This root *'zn* is found in Heb. theophoric names, as well as the root *šm'*, both meaning 'to hear'. A better suggestion, however, in view of its being well attested in Aram., is the root *dyn* 'to judge'. This is noted by Silverman *JAOS* 697, who interprets the element as a 2nd pers. sing. jussive. Heb. theophoric names also contain the idea 'to judge', expressed with the same root *dyn*, as well as with the roots *pll* and *špṭ*. The Aram. name *Da-na-ti*/*Da-na-ia-ti-ilu* (Fales *OA 13*, 207) also contains a perf. of the root *dyn*.

kdr 'eldest son'? For the name *'šmkdry* (5th. cent.), which could be Aram. or Akk., Grelot (p. 464) suggests a sf. of *'Ašim-kudurrî-uṣur* ''Ašim protect the eldest son', although other verbal elements would also be possible. The second element, however, remains quite uncertain.

kr' 'to decide'? The Aram. root *kr'* has three possible meanings, 'to bow down', 'to decide' and 'to weigh out' (cf. G.H. Dalman, *Aramäisch-NeuHebräisches Handwörterbuch*, J. Kaufmann, Frankfurt am Main [1922], 209). For the Aram. name *kr'dd* (V *Aug*, 97), the meaning 'to decide' i.e.

'Adad has decided' may be semantically preferable, but has no comparable thought among Heb. theophoric names.

m'd This root seems to be found in the Aram. names ^{d}*Ar-ú-ì?-ma-a-di* (Deller, 474, Sultantepe 7th cent.); ^{I}*X-ma-a'-di* (Deller, 474); ^{I}A.*X-ma-a-di* (*ibid.* Tallqvist [*APN*, 195] compared the Aram. element with the Heb. name *ma'adyāh*, which may be derived from a root *'dh* meaning 'to adorn', although this is uncertain [cf. above, §2.9]); ^{I}*Na-šu-ḫu-ma-a-di*, *Na-šu*[*ḫu-ma*]*-a-di* (Deller, 474, Sultantepe 7th cent.); [^{I}*Se*]*-e-ma-a-di* (*ibid.*); *Si-'-ma'di/mādi* (*APN*, 195, 7th cent.).

sl' For the meaning of the second element in the Aram. name *'bsly* (Grelot, 462; *KAI*, 267, 2, Saqqara 5th cent.) Grelot cites Noth's suggestion (*IPN*, 74) of an interpretation 'to restore, pay back', from Arab. *sala'a*. This may be similar in idea to Heb. names which suggest that the deity 'has recompensed' with the use of the root *šlm*, probably indicating the substitution of a previously deceased child. Similar in Heb. names is the Hiphil of the root *šwb* 'to restore'. The Aram. name is, however, very dubious.

sr The Aram. name *srgd* (V*Aug*, 61) can be variously interpreted. If the second element is theophoric and not a noun 'fortune' (cf. above), *sr* could mean 'prince', suggesting an interpretation 'Gad is prince'. Driver (*RSO*, 53), however, saw this initial element as *šâru* meaning 'breath', and translated the name as 'Breath of Gad'. Neither meaning has any parallel among Heb. theophoric names. However, also possible is an interpretation 'Assur is fortune', involving an elision of the initial *'ālep*.

'wt 'to help' or *'śh* 'to make'. For the Aram. name *byt'l'śny* (*SSI II*, 22 obv. 1, Sefire 6th cent.) a meaning 'Bêt'el has helped me', root *'wt*, or 'Bêt'el has made me', root *'śh*, is suggested by Gibson (p. 117). The former root would be cognate with the Heb. root *'wš*, which is attested in theophoric names with the same meaning. Also found with this meaning in Heb. names is the root *'zr*, as well as Aram. *'dr* in the Heb. name *'adrî'ēl* (see below, 3). The root *'śh* 'to make' is also attested in Heb. names, and semantically comparable would be the root *p'l* 'to make', as well as *bnh* 'to build, create' and *br'* and *qnh* 'to create'.

rgm This element, which occurs in the name *b'lrgm* (V*Aug*, 62), is not clear. Vattioni cites BH *regem*, which is a proper name also of uncertain meaning, although a noun 'friend' suggested by Arab. *rajmu* is cited by BDB, 920. Also to be considered, however, is a possible relation to Ug. *rgm* 'to say', from which a noun *rgm* 'word' is derived (cf. *UT Glossary*, 482 no. 2307), and the related Akk. *ragāmu* 'to call'.

Aram. *rp'* 'to make loose' or BH *rp'* 'to heal'. The root *rp'* means 'to loosen' in Aram. and, as such, would be semantically comparable to Heb.

names from the problematic root *rmh* (see above, §2.5 *rmh/rwm*). However, the existence of this root with this meaning in Aram. names is problematic in view of the presence of the Heb. root *rp'* 'to heal', which is attested in theophoric compound names and is also found in Amor., Ug. and Palm. Relevant names in Aram. are *yrp'l* (*PS*, 235; V*Aug*, 64) and *yrpyh* (*PS*, 235), which could mean 'God/Y heals (or loosens)' or 'May God/Y heal (or loosen)'; and *nbwrp'* (*PS*, 207), 'Nabû has healed (or loosened)'. Tallqvist seemed confident of a meaning 'to heal' in the name *Si-'-ra-pa-'* 'Si' has healed' (*APN*, 195) as, also, F.M. Fales in the name *Ra-pa-la* 'The god heals' (Fales, 185, 8th/7th cent.). Also relevant are the names *Adad-ra-pa-a'* (Deller, 474-75); perhaps *ᶠMārti-ra-pi-e* (*APN*, 135); *Mārtu-ra-pe-e* (Deller, 474); [ᴵGN]*-ra-pa-a* (or *-ra-pa-a'*) (*ibid.*); *Se-e-ra-pe-e* (*ibid.*, Sultantepe 7th cent.).

twr For the Aram. name *nbwtr* (V*Aug*, 171), Vattioni suggests the meaning 'Nabû is merciful'. However, the second element seems to be derived from a root *twr* 'to awaken', or perhaps NH *tyr* 'to be watchful', attested possibly in the Heb. name *tîryā'* (see above, §2.10), can suggest another alternative. The idea 'to awaken' has no comparable thought among Heb. theohporic names. Perhaps also relevant is Akk. *târu* 'to turn' (cf. Stamm, 147-49, 168, 190 etc.). This might suggest an interpretation 'Nabû has turned', cf. the Heb. name-elements *pnh* 'to turn' above, §2.4 and *sḥr* 'to turn' above, §2.9 [*yh*]*wsḥ*[*r*].

3. Many Aramaic names contain elements which have semantic counterparts in Hebrew, revealing similar ideas concerning the respective deities. Such name-elements are as follows:

'd 'father'. For the Aram. name *'dšy* (Assur 7th cent.), Lipiński suggests *'Addi-šī* 'My father is the Moon-god' (p. 102). Lipiński also cites the Old Aram. names *A-di-Èl*, *Ad-ra-me* (9th and 7th cent.), *Ad-di-id-ri* (7th cent.), *Ad-da-ia*, *Ad-da-a*, *'dg'y*, *'dm'zy*, *'dśmy*, *'dqr*, *'dbnh*, *'dntn*, *'dšry* (p. 101 n. 6): cf. also *'d'd* (Fales *OA 13*, 205) 'The father is a witness'. It may also be possible that the element *'d* is equivalent to Hadad in some of these names. Heb. names only depict the deity as a father with *'b*, which is also attested in Aram. names as noted above, 1.

bḥr 'to choose'. The root *bḥr* is attested in Heb. but not in theophoric names, although a deity may be implied in the name *yibḥār* (see above, §2.10). The idea contained in the Aram. name *ybḥr'l* (*PS*, 228) is similar to Heb. names from the roots *'ṣl* 'to reserve, lay aside' and *ḥṣh* 'to divide'.

bᵉtû'ēl This biblical name was borne by the Aramean son of Nahor, nephew of Abraham (Gen. 22.22, 23; 24.15, 24, 47, 50; 25.20; 28.25). Most emend the name to *mᵉtû'ēl*, cf. BH *mᵉtûšā'ēl*, 'Man of El', Akk. *Muti-ilu* (cf. below, p. 275 n. 101) and BDB, 143, KB, 159. Cf. also Geh. 113, who interprets the name as a nominal sentence 'El is a husband', from Akk. *Mutu-el*. Also to be compared is the element *mut* 'man' in Amor. names, and Ug. *mut-ba'al* (*PTU*, 31 and 161-62). Heb. names also use the element *'yš* 'man' and perhaps *gbr* (cf. also below, 4) to express the same idea.

g'h 'to be high, exalted'. This root is probably attested in the BH name *gᵉ'û'ēl* 'Majesty of El', but in the Aram. name *'dg'y* (Fales *OA 13*, 205, 218), the root has the meaning 'to be high, exalted' (*ibid.*, 218). Heb. names express this latter idea with the roots *'lh* (but possibly Ammon. or Edom.), *'th* (cf. Arab. *'atā*), *rwm* and *śgb*. Cf. also the Aram. name *brg'yh* 'Son of Majesty' (*KAI*, 222 A 1.2.7.13, mid 8th cent.) in which *g'yh* represents a divine name.

dkr 'to remember'. The root *dkr* in the Aram. name *Si-'-da-ki-ir* (*APN*, 194) is cognate with Heb. *zkr* 'to remember', which is attested in Heb. theophoric names.

dmr 'strength'. Grelot interprets the name *'trdmry* (Hermopolis 5th cent.) as 'Athar is my strength' (p. 466). Gibson, *SSI II*, 27 vii l reads *'trrmry*. The same element *dmr* is met in the name *Na-šuḫ-di-im-ri* (*APN*, 168). The Heb. use of the root *zmr* in names, which is suggested by S. Arab. *dhimr* 'to protect', is probably cognate, although not used in the sense 'to be strong'. The idea of the deity as 'strength' in Heb. names is expressed with the roots *ḥzq*, *'zz* and *ḥwl*/*ḥyl* (nominally), and *'br*, *'zz*, *ḥzq*, *'mṣ*, *gbr* (verbally, 'to be strong').

ḥwr 'to see'. The second element of the name *Si-i'-ḫa-ri* (Deller, 475; *APN*, 194, 7th cent.) is derived from Aram. *ḥwr* 'to see', comparable to Heb. theophoric names from the roots *ḥzh* (also attested in Aram. names, cf. above, 1) and *r'h* 'to see'. (Cf. also the possibility of a root *šwr* 'to regard, behold' in Heb. names, above, §2.9 *'ăḥîšār*). The BH name *'ammîḥûr* is also Aram. There seems no reason why the form *ḥwr*, as opposed to *hwd*, should not be retained if this is an Aramean name, especially in view of the name cited by Deller above. (For the preference *hwd* cf. Gray *op. cit.*, 43.) Note also the Aram. name *Adad-ḫa-ri* suggested by Kaufman (*JNES* [1978], 104-106), which he considers to be *'d'r*, in which cuneiform *ḫ* represents W. Semitic '.

ḥll 'to loosen, redeem' or 'to hollow out, bore out'. The root *ḥll*, which occurs in the name *ḥllyh* (V*Aug*, 121), could have three possible meanings according to Aram. usage (cf. Dalman *op. cit.*, 149). A meaning 'to hollow out, bore out' has no semantic counterpart in Heb. theophoric names, but is one semantically reflected in Ug. *nqb* (see above, §4.1. 5) with reference, perhaps, to divine participation in the birth of the child. A meaning 'to loosen' in the sense of 'redeem' is also possible for the root *ḥll*, and would be paralleled in Heb. names with *g'l* 'to redeem' and *pdh* 'to ransom, redeem'. The third meaning 'to change', seems less satisfactory semantically.

ṭwr 'mountain'. This Aram. element is used to depict the deity as a 'mountain' in the names *A-a-ṭu-ri* (*APN*, 2, 7th cent.); *A-du-ni-ṭu*[*-ri*] (*APN*, 13, 7th cent.); *Aḫ-ṭu-ri* (Fales, 182, 8th/7th cent.); and *Si-'-ṭu-ri* (*APN*, 195, 8th cent.). A comparable thought is expressed in Heb. names by use of *hr*. The Heb. noun *ṣwr*, 'rock', which is cognate with Aram. *ṭwr*, is attested in the Heb. names *'ĕlîṣûr*, *ṣûrî'ēl* and *ṣûrîšaddāy*.

yhb 'to give'. This element is found in the Aram. names *'lyhb* (*PS*, 201; V*Aug*, 70), *Ilu-ia-a-ab* (Fales *OA 13*, 229) and, possibly, *Ba-al-te-ia-a-ba-te* = *b'lt* + *yhbt* (*ibid.*, 207, 226), although the latter name may not be theophoric. The idea 'to give' is depicted in Heb. theophoric names with *'wš* (cf. Arab. *'āsa*), *zbd*, *ntn*, Eg. *pṭ*, and perhaps *qwš* (cf. Akk. *qāšu* and above §2.9 *qûšāyāhû*). The roots *zbd*, *ntn* and the Eg. element *pṭ* are also attested in Aram. names (see above, 1).

yqr 'to be precious, honoured'. The root *yqr* exists also in BH with this meaning, but is not attested in theophoric names. The Aram. name *Aḫ-ia-qa*[*r*] (Fales *OA 13*, 207, 229), which contains this root, is similar in thought to the Heb. name *yôkebed* 'Y is glory, honour'. Cf. also the name *šmhyqr* (*KAI*, 233. 10, 7th cent.) 'His name is precious', which may refer to a deity.

kwn 'to be right'. This element is attested in the name *Il-tam-meš-ki-i-ni* (Zadok *BO*, 228), which Zadok suggests is to be interpreted 'The sun-god is right'. Heb. names also use the root *kwn* but with the meaning 'to establish, appoint'. The idea that the deity is 'right' is perhaps reflected in Heb. names with the root *ṣdq* 'to be just, righteous'.

lkd 'to seize'. This element seems to be evident in the Aram. names *'ḥlkd* (*PS*, 195; V*Aug*, 51), *Adad²-lu-ki-di* (*APN*, 8) and *Si-'/e-lu-ki-di* (*APN*, 194; Fales *OA 13*, 219), which states that the deity 'has seized'. Heb. names express the same idea with the root *'ḥz*.

man(*nu*) 'who?'. Akk. *man*(*nu*) 'who?' is to be found in the Aram. names *Man-nu-ka-Si-i'* (Fales *OA 13*, 206) and *Man-ka!-Si-i* (*ibid.*). The identical idea is expressed in Heb. names of the type *mîkā'ēl* 'Who is like El' etc.

mnh 'to count'. *Mnh* occurs in the names *Na-šuḫ-ma-na-ni* (*APN*, 168), *Se-ir-ma-na-ni* (*ibid.*, 220), *Si-'-ma-na-ni* (*ibid.*, 195), *'ddmny* (Fales *OA 13*, 205, 227) and *'lmnny* (Lipiński, 118, Tell Ḥalaf 7th cent.). This last name Lipiński translates as 'El has counted me', in the sense of one of the living or as a protégé, and considers 'The expression might allude to the tally-keeper who counted the sheep as they came into the fold at night, to make sure that none was missing (cf. Jer. 33.13). In a religious context, it practically meant that the god "has predestined" the person', and here, Lipiński refers to Heb. *mny* 'fortune', 'and this acceptation seems to be attested also in Akkadian'. While this observation is interesting, we should note the total absence of the idea of 'predestination' anywhere in the Heb. theophoric onomasticon. The only comparable idea is that of 'fortune', contained in the element *gd*, and used to depict the Israelite God, who could hardly be termed predestined! Moreover, the idea of predestination or fortune is not to be found in Akk. *manû* (cf. *CAD*, M 1 221) and Lipiński's connection of this root with Akk. *menû* is tenuous. Lipiński writes, citing *AHw*, 645a and *menû(m)*, *manû(m)* 'The equivalences given in the lexical series are approximate and point to the acceptations "to predestinate" > "to love" and "fortune", "star". The root is the same as for the verb *manû*, "to count". Only the semantic field is different' (p. 118 n. 4). It is this last statement stressing the difference in the semantic field which is important, since while there *is* a difference here between the Akk. roots there is no justification for linking the two. The idea contained in the root *mnh* may be more akin to the use of the roots *ḥšb* 'to take account', and *š'r* 'to reckon' in Heb. names, which perhaps tend to indicate that the deity has taken account of a situation concerning the parents or name-bearer.

mt' 'to protect'. The root *mt'* does not occur in Aram. but may be determined by a S. Arab. cognate *mt'* meaning 'to save, protect' (cf. J.A. Fitzmyer, *The Aramaic Inscriptions of Sefire*, Rome PBI [1967], 25). The element occurs in the Aram. names *mt''l*, *mt'hdd*, *mt'š'* (Fales *OA 13*, 206, 221); *Ma-te-e-'-Si-i'*(Deller, 475); *Mati-ilāa* (*APN*, 136, 7th. cent.); *Ma-ti-'-il(u)* (Fitzmyer, *op. cit.*, Sefire 8th. cent.); *Ma-ti-i'-Si-i'* (Deller, 475, Sultantepe 7th cent.). Tallqvist (*APN*, 295) interpreted this same initial element in these names as *mty*/*mati* 'when' although the transcription of W. Semitic ' with ' may speak against this, and since it is written in Aram. *mt''l*, Tallqvist was clearly wrong. The idea 'to protect' is to be found in Heb. theophoric names with the roots *zmr* (cf. S. Arab. *dhimr*) and possibly *ḥmh* (cf. S. Arab. *ḥamay*). Cf. also *Mati'-'el* (A.R. Millard, *Iraq* 45 [1983], 103; Nimrud 8th cent.).

ngh 'splendour'. The root *ngh* is only attested verbally in Heb. names, with the meaning 'to shine, enlighten' whereas in the Aram. name *nsḥnghy* (Fales *OA 13*, 209), the deity is depicted as 'my splendour'. Perhaps similar among Heb. names are the ideas of the deity as 'wonderful' (*pl'*), 'glory' (*kbd*) and 'majesty' (*g'h*), although the specific idea of 'splendour' is not found. The root *ngh* is found verbally in the Aram. name *Na-ga-ḫa-(H)adad-milk* (Fales *OA 13*, 207), probably with the same meaning as the root in Heb. names.

nqy 'to purify'. The imv. of this root is evident in the name *Ú-qi-li-i*, translated by Fales as 'Purifica mio dio!' (Fales *OA 13*, 207, 227). In Heb. names the root *brr* 'to purify', as well as *ṭbl* 'to dip (purify)' and *nzh* 'to sprinkle (purify)', provide semantic parallels, but these are never found in the imv.

nśy 'to raise'. Fales considers a deity to be semantically understood in the name *Ia-ša-a* (Fales *OA 13*, 207, 228), containing the root *nśy* 'to raise'.

Comparable in Heb. names is the root *qwm* (Hiphil) 'to raise up' perhaps also *kwn* and *śwm* 'to establish'.

sgb. This Aram. root is evident in the second element of the name *Se-e-sa-gab* (Deller, 475). A root *śgb* is attested in Heb. theophoric names, with a meaning 'to be (inaccessibly) high', but in Aram. seems to be attested only with a meaning 'to make strong' (Pa. cf. Dalman *op. cit.*, 410). The idea 'to strengthen' is depicted in Heb. theophoric names with the roots *ḥzq* and, possibly, *mrr* (cf. Ug. 'to strengthen, bless, commend'). Lipiński discusses a noun *śagīb* meaning 'chief, ruler' and a verb *śagab* meaning 'to prevail' (Lipiński, 106-107). The idea of the deity as a 'chief' or 'ruler' is not attested among Heb. names, the nearest semantic thought being that of *mlk* 'king', while the root *ykl*, although meaning 'to be able, have power, prevail, endure', probably has only the first of these interpretations in Heb. names.

'dr 'to help'. This Aram. root is cognate with Heb. *'zr* which is also found in Aram. names (see above, 1) and is attested in Heb. theophoric names with the same meaning. The element *'dr* is met widely in Aram. names. cf. *'t'dry* (Grelot, 464, Eleph. 5th cent.); *b'l'dr* (*PS*, 214); *hdd'zr* (*PS*, 193, 9th cent.); *hr'dr* (Fales *OA 13*, 221); *zb'dry* (Grelot, 499-500, Eg. 5th cent.); *y'dr'l* (V, 84; V.*Aug*, 19); *nbw'dry* (*PS*, 207); *šmš'dry* (*PS*, 253; V.*Aug*, 38; Lipiński, 17, Tell Halaf 8th cent.); *Adad-idri* (*APN*, 8, 9th cent.); *Ad-di-id-ri* (*APN*, 12, 7th cent.); *A-ta(-a)-id-ri*, *A-tar-id-ri* (*APN*, 47); *A-u-id-ri* (*ibid.*, 48); *Bêl-Ḫarrān-id-ri* (Deller, 474, Sultantepe 7th cent.); *Mil-ki-i-di-ri* (R. Zadok, *BASOR* 230 [1978], 61, Tyre 6th cent.); *Na-aš-ḫu-id-ri* (*APN*, 168); *Ra-ma-nu-id-ri* (Fales *OA 13*, 210); *Sēr-idri* (*APN*, 220, 8th cent.); *Si-'-id-ri* (*APN*, 194); *Tam-meš-id-ri* (*APN*, 229, 7th cent.). See also Lipiński, 17 for the O. Aram. names *'dry'l* (10th cent.), *Id-ri-li-i* (7th cent.), and *^{d}Šá-maš-id-ri* (8th. cent.). The root *'dr* is also attested in the Heb. name *'adrî'ēl*, which is the name of a Meholathite (1 Sam. 18.19; 2 Sam. 21.8), probably a native of the village Meholah, perhaps Abel-meholah. Since this area was under heavy Aramean influence it is difficult to say whether the name is Heb. or Aram. Heb. theophoric names also express the idea 'to help' with the root *'wš*.

'wd 'to return' or 'to testify', cf. Heb. This root is not attested in Aram., but for the name *'wdnhr* (Eleph. 5th cent.), Grelot (p. 483) suggests a meaning 'Nahar has turned round', comparing the Heb. root *'wd*. This root has the meaning 'to return, go about, repeat, do again' (cf. BDB, 728), as well as a denominative meaning 'to bear witness' (*ibid.*, 729), which is attested in theophoric names. In this case, the Aram. name could mean 'Nahar has returned' comparable to Heb. names with the Qal of the root *šwb* 'to return'. Alternatively, it could mean 'Nahar has testified' in the same way as the root *'wd* in the BH name *'el'ād*. Both Heb. and Aram. names contain a nominal form 'witness' from this same root (see above, 1).

ʿqb ‘to protect’. The element *ʿqb* occurs in the Aram. names *byt'lʿqb* (Grelot, 468, Eleph. 5th cent.), *nbwʿqb* (*ibid.*, 480, Eleph. 5th cent.), and *Si'-aqab* (*APN*, 194), which express that the deity ‘has protected’ (cf. Amor. *ḫqb APNM*, 203). The root *ʿqb* in Heb. and in Aram. means ‘to follow at the heel’ (cf. BDB, 784). Theophoric names with this root are not attested in Heb., however, although the idea ‘to protect’ is found in names with the root *zmr* (cf. S. Arab. *dhimr*) and possibly *ḥmh* (cf. S. Arab. *ḥamay*), although this latter root is uncertain (see above, §2.9 *ḥammûʾēl*).

prs ‘to portion, share’. The name *Se-e-pa-ra?-si* (Deller, 475) may well be from a root *prs* ‘to portion, share’, indicating a meaning ‘Sē is my portion’. The same idea is depicted in Heb. with the name *ḥilqîyāh*(*û*) ‘Y is my portion’.

qtr ‘rock’. The deity is depicted as a ‘rock’ in the Aram. names *Ilu-qa-tar* (Deller, 475); *Na-aš-ḫu-qa-tar* (*ibid.*, variant *Na-aš-ḫu-qa-ta-ri*); *Se-e-qa-tar* (*ibid.*); *Si-'-qa-tar* (*APN*, 195); *X-qa-tar* (Deller, 475). The name *Aq-tu-ur-la-na-aš-ḫu* (*APN*, 25) possibly contains the preposition *la* ‘for’ and may mean ‘Rock for (i.e. of) Našḫu’, although the first element seems formally verbal. If the name-bearer is the subject of this name, it has no counterpart among Heb. names. If ‘rock’ refers to the deity, however, it would be comparable to the use of *ṣwr* ‘rock’ in Heb. theophoric names. (For the Aram. name *brṣwr*, see below, 4.)

rḥm ‘to love’. The root *rḥm* is attested in Heb. names with the meaning ‘to show compassion’, whereas the Aram. root *rḥm* means ‘to love, have affection for’ (cf. Krael, 4.4, 12 p. 168, 169; 7.1 p. 206, 207 etc.). With this meaning the root is attested in the Aram. names *'srḥm* (*PS*, 208); *Ab-ri-ḫi-me* (Deller, 474); *Ra-ḫi-me-ilu* (Deller, 474 Sultanepe 7th cent.); *Ri-ḫi-me-Hadad-Mlek* (*ibid.*). The idea ‘to love’ in Heb. theophoric names is depicted with the root *dwd*.

rmz ‘to speak’. The Aram. name *'lrmz* (V *Aug*, 113) means ‘God has spoken’. The same idea is portrayed in Heb. names with the root *'mr* ‘to say’, and possibly *qwl* ‘to speak’ (see above, §2.9 *qlyhw*).

śky ‘to pay attention’. Attested in the Aram. name *Adaḏ-sa-ka-a*, the root *śky* is semantically similar to *ḥšb* ‘to take account’ in Heb. theophoric names.

tkl ‘to trust’, noun ‘trust’. This element is present in the Aram. names *Adad-tak-kal* (*APN*, 11) = *hdtkl* (V *Aug*, 67); and *Ilu-a-a-ta-ka-*[*r*]*a?* or *Ilu-a-a-ta-ka-*[*ala*] (Fales, 185, 8th/7th cent.). Heb. names express the idea nominally with the noun *mbṭḥ* ‘to trust’.

4. Some Aramaic names contain ideas which are not reflected in Hebrew theophoric names and which, therefore, express ideas about

the various Aramean deities which are different from the Hebrew concepts of God. These Aramaic name-elements are as follows:

'm 'mother'. This element, unattested in Heb. theophoric names, is evident in the Aram. name *Ba-na-at-e-ma-šá-ma-šá*, translated by Fales as 'La madré Šamaš(a) crèo' (Fales *OA 13*, 207, 226). Cf. also the name *Sam-si-im-me* (above, 1), which Fales originally held to mean 'Šamaš is with me', but more recently interprets the second element as 'mother' (*OA 13*, 224).

'ḥt 'sister'. This element occurs in the name *'ḥtsn* (Grelot, 463, Eg. 5th cent.), 'Sister of Sin'. It has no counterpart in Heb. names, which never depict a female child in relationship with the deity.

b'lt 'lady'. Heb. names also have no semantic equivalent to the Aram. name *Ba-al-te-ia-a-ba-te* = *b'lt* + *yhbt* (Fales *OA 13*, 226, see also above, 3 *yhb*), in which *bd'lt* probably represents a divine name.

b'd 'for'. This element appears in the names *A-tar-bi-'-[di]* (*APN*, 47; Deller, 473); *A-tar-pi-i'-di* (Deller, 473); *Mar-bi-'-di* (*APN*, 127, although this name may not contain a theophoric element in *mr'* 'lord'), and *hrb'd* (Fales *OA 13*, 212), which Driver (*RSO*, 46) reads as *hdb'd* and compares with Ass. *Ilu-bi'dī*, *ilYa'u-bi'di* 'El or Yau is over me' (cf. *APN*, 96). These name-types probably have no parallel in the Heb. onomasticon. (However, cf. the name *b'd'l* above, pp. 121f.).

br 'son'. The idea of the child as a 'son of' the deity is not to be found among Heb. names but is frequently met in the Aram. onomasticon. Thus we find, *Bir-ḫ'a-a-nu* (*APN*, 64), *Bi-ir-a-tar* (*ibid.*), *Bir-Dadda* (Fales *OA*, 50; *APN*, 64, 7th cent.), *Bir-dSagale* (A.R. Millard, 'fŠa ekalli-šgl-dSagale', *Ugarit-Forschungen* 4 [1972], 161-62), *brhdd* cf. BH *ben-hădad* (1) son of Hadad 1 Kgs 15.18, 20 (9th cent.); (2) 1 Kgs 20.34, son of (1) (9th cent.); (3) son of Hazael 2 Kgs 13.3, 24, 25 (8th cent.). (Cf. also *SSI II*, Damascus 1 i 5 A, 4 5; Lipiński, 16). The name *brg'yh* (*KAI*, 221 A 1.2.7.13, Zenjirli 8th cent.) probably means 'Son of Majesty', in which the second element replaces a divine name. Similar are the names *brrkb* (*SSI II*, 14;1,15,19,20; 15 i 1; 16 ii 1; 17 iii 1, Panammu and Zenjirli 8th cent.), *brṣ(w)r* (*PS*, 219; *SSI II*, 14 1, Panammu 8th cent.) 'Son of the Rock'. Cf. also the name -type *Būr-Ramān* (*APN*, 66, 9th and 7th cent.).

gbr 'man, hero'. This element is probably nominal in the Aram. names *Ilu-gab-bi-ri* and *Ilu-gab-[bi-ri]* (Deller, 475, Sultantepe 7th cent.); *Si-'-gab-ba-ri* (*APN*, 194); *š'gbr* (Fales *OA 13*, 209). A meaning 'hero' is likely, but has no semantic equivalent among Heb. names. Although the root *gbr* occurs in the Heb. nomenclature, it is in the initial position as a construct noun 'man of' the deity, as well as being attested verbally with the meaning 'to be strong'.

zr' 'seed'. The Aram. name *zr'l* (Fales *OA 13*, 205, 211) can be compared with Akk. *Zēr-ili* which depicts the child as the 'seed of' the deity. Although the root *zr'* is attested among Heb. names, it is probably verbal, meaning 'to sow', while the idea 'seed of' the deity has no semantic counterpart elsewhere in the Heb. theophoric onomasticon.

Root *ḥmm* noun *ḫemtu* 'ardour'. The name *Hēmti-ilu* 'My ardour is the god' (*APN*, 88; Fales *OA*, 51) has no parallel among Heb. names.

kl 'all'. No parallel is evident among Heb. names for the Aram. name *klbyd'l* (Fales *OA 13*, 205, 212) meaning 'All is by/in the hand of god'. The Heb. name *kil'āb*, which looks similar, is problematic (cf. above, §2.9), and Heb. *byd'l* 'In the hand of El' seems to suggest a more pertinent reference to the name-bearer.

lwy 'to accompany'. This root is suggested by Fales (*OA 13*, 227) for the name *Se-e-la-u-a-*[*ni*] with the addition of the pronominal suffix *ni*. The same element is also to be found in Aram. *Na-šuḫ-la-ú-a-ni* (Deller, 474). No comparable thought seems to be expressed among Heb. names.

mṣr 'fortress'. The name *'trmṣrwn* (*SSI II*, 11 i 2, Luristan 8th cent.), meaning 'Athar is our fortress', has no parallel in Heb. theophoric names in which such figurative divine protection is depicted by concepts such as 'mountain', 'rock', 'refuge', 'wall', 'tent' and 'door'.

mārta 'lady'. There is no counterpart among Heb. names for the initial element attested in the name *ᶠMārti-ra-pi-e* 'My lady is a healer' (*APN*, 135) containing the fem. of the Aram. noun *mr'* 'lord'. The name may, however, be non-theophoric if, for example, the name of a slave or servant, although the idea of 'healing' is usually one attributed to a deity. For the root *rp'* in Aram., see above, 2.

1st pers. plur. suff. This is attested in the name *Se-e'-la-nu* which Fales (*OA 13*, 225) suggests is *šy-'l(h)n* 'Sē è il nostro dio'. The name has no parallel in the Heb. theophoric onomasticon.

'yn 'eye, source'. The Aram. name *A-i-in-ilu* is interpreted by Fales as 'la mia sorgente (*'yny*) è Dio' or, 'gli occhi di Dio (hanno visto ecc.)', (Fales *OA 13*, 206, 225). Neither interpretation, however, has any parallel among Heb. theophoric names.

Aram? *qry* 'to call, name'. Fales (*OA 13*, 227) finds the element *qry* 'chiamare' in the name *Na-šuḫ-qur-ri-ni* (cf. Deller, 474, Sultantepe 7th cent.) and also in the name *Qa-re-ilu* (Fales *OA 13*, 207, 229). Although Heb. theophoric names contain the idea 'to call' with the root *d'h* (cf. Arab. *da'ā*), this is not in the sense 'to name', which is the thought contained in *qry*. Indeed, Heb. names have no semantic counterpart for this idea.

r‘y ‘shepherd’. This element is met in the names *Adad*^{2}*-ra-ḫa-a-nu* (*APN*, 10), for which Tallqvist suggested a meaning ‘Adad is his shepherd’, and *Si-’-ra-ḫ’i-i* ‘Si’ is my shepherd’ (*ibid.*, 195). The idea of the deity as a ‘shepherd’ is not found in Heb. theophoric names, although it is expressed frequently in OT literature.

rqy‘ ‘far-famed’. For the name *hdrqy‘*, Driver (*RSO*, 47) suggests a noun *r*^{e}*qî*^{a}*‘* meaning ‘widespread, far-famed’, with the divine name Adad or Hadad. An interpretation ‘Hadad is far famed’ has no parallel in the Heb. onomasticon.

šdr ‘to send’. For the name *nbšdr* (Silverman *JAOS*, 699) ‘Nabû has sent’, there is no counterpart in Heb. name-giving. Although Heb. names depict that the deity has ‘created’, ‘made’ or ‘given’ a child, the particular idea ‘to send’ is only attested in the personal name *šilḥî* (see above, §2.10), but there is no evidence to suggest that this name is a sf. of an originally theophoric compound name.

škn ‘neighbour’? The initial element of the name *Šikin-’Ēl* (5th cent.) is interpreted by Lipiński as ‘neighbour’ (Lipiński, 73), which suggests a meaning ‘Neighbour of El’ for this name. Although Lipiński compares the name with Heb. *š*^{e}*kanyāh(û)*, to which he also gives the interpretation ‘Neighbour of Yahu’, the vocalization of the Heb. name does not do justice to Lipiński’s suggestion of a construct noun, and the meaning ‘Y has taken up his abode’ remains preferable.

4.5 *A Comparison between the Concepts of Deity Revealed in the Hebrew and Old Akkadian Onomastica*

A study of early Semitic deities attested in personal names and worshipped in Mesopotamia, has been undertaken by J.J.M. Roberts (*The Earliest Semitic Pantheon*, Johns Hopkins University Press [1972], referred to throughout as Roberts). This work has provided a considerable list of Old Akkadian theophoric personal names, which has facilitated the present comparison between the concepts of the Hebrew God and the various Old Akkadian deities. However, not all the interpretations suggested by Roberts for these Old Akkadian names have been followed, since the meanings of many must, in numerous cases, remain conjectural (cf. A.R. Millard, *JSS* 19 [1974], 88), a factor which Roberts has not always borne in mind. Considerable note has been taken, therefore, of the collection of personal names in the work of Gelb (I.J. Gelb, *Glossary of Old Akkadian: Materials for the Assyrian Dictionary*, University of Chicago Press [1957], hereafter Gelb).

1. The Hebrew and Old Akkadian onomastica have many elements in common, expressing identical, or very similar, concepts concerning the respective deities. These are as follows:

O. Akk.	*Heb.*	
abum	*'b*	father
urrum	*'wr*	light
aḫum	*'ḥ*	brother
ilum/elum	*'l*	god
banājum	*bnh*	to build (Akk. also nominal, 'Creator')
bēlum	*b'l*	lord
dâdum	*dwd*	beloved (Heb. also verbal)
diānum	*dyn*	to judge
ṭâbum	*ṭwb*	good
wadā'um	*yd'*	to know
watrum	*ytr*	excellent, surpassing (O. Akk.); pre-eminent (Heb.)
kunnum	*kwn*	to establish
nadānum	*ntn*	to give
nûrum	*nr*	light (O. Akk.); lamp (Heb.)
ammum	*'m*	paternal uncle
patā'um	*ptḥ*	to open
ṣillum	*ṣll*	shadow, protection
rabûm	*rbb*	to be great
rapā'um	*rp'*	to heal.[69]
šiāmum	*śwm*	to fix, appoint (O. Akk.); to establish (Heb.)
šamā'um	*šm'*	to hear

2. The forms in a few Old Akkadian names are difficult to determine, or present more than one possibility for interpretation. This is the case with the following:

barājum 'to look upon, watch over, inspect, observe' (Roberts, 16). This element is found in the O. Akk. name *Ibri-Amurru*, which is translated by Roberts as 'Amurru inspected'. However, the name-element more probably means 'to look upon, watch over' (cf. *CAD* B 115), synonymous with Heb. names from the roots *r'h* and *ḥzh* 'to see', *šwr* 'to behold, regard' and perhaps *skh/śkh* 'to look out'.

ḫadāwum 'joy' (cf. Gelb, 126). This O. Akk. element occurs in the name *Ḫadi-ilīšu*, which Roberts translates as 'Welcomed of his god' (p. 132), while the same name is listed by Gelb under *ḫadāwum* 'to rejoice' (p. 126). Heb. names do not contain the idea that the deity rejoices. Rather, the roots *'śr* 'to fill with joy' (cf. Arab. *'ašira)*, *ḥbṣ* 'to be joyful' (cf. Akk. *ḫabāṣu*), *ḥdh* 'to give joy, rejoice', with which the O. Akk. element is related, and the noun *gyl* 'rejoicing joy', all tend to be used causatively in Heb. names to suggest the deity more as a *source* of joy. If the O. Akk. element *ḫadi* is genitive, as Roberts suggests, with a meaning 'joy of' the deity, this has no comparison among Heb. names. A nominal interpretation, however (cf. *APN*, 83), would possibly imply the same sense as the Heb. name-element *gyl*, 'rejoicing joy'.

kînum (*cf. kuānum* 'to be firm'). The element *kīn* in names such as *Ab(b)a-kīn* is interpreted by Roberts as 'Ab(b)a is faithful' (p. 12), while the name *Ikūn-'Ay(y)a* is translated ''Ay(y)a proved true' (p. 20) and *Ilum*[DINGIR]-*kīn* as 'The god is reliable' (p. 126). However, it is likely that names of the type *Ikūn*-x are verbal forms of *kuānum* 'to be firm' (cf. Gelb, 138). Gelb interprets *kînum*, moreover, as 'established, regular, firm, well', meanings which have not quite the same nuance of thought as Robert's suggested 'faithful', 'reliable' or 'true'. Of all these suggestions, only the idea of the deity as 'firm' is depicted in Heb. names with the related root *knn*. Also without parallel in Heb. names is the name *Ninlil-iš-kīn* for which Roberts suggests an interpretation 'With Ninlil it is sure' (p. 47), but Gelb lists the name under *kînum* with the meanings noted.

inūnum 'punishment' (Gelb, 53). Roberts interpreted the name *Inu(n)-šadu* as 'The mountain granted a favour' (p. 50), semantically similar to Heb. names with the root *'nn* 'to answer'. However, Gelb interprets the initial element of the name as 'punishment' (Gelb, 53), which would have no equivalent among Heb. names.

mutum 'man' (Roberts, 17, 30, 37). This element is used in the genitive to depict the name-bearer as a 'man of' the deity, comparable to Heb. names containing the same element *mt*. However, in the name *Eštar-mutī*, the second position of the element, following the divine name, excludes the possibility of its being a genitive form. Roberts translates the name, questioningly, as 'Eštar is my man' (p. 37), but also possible is an interpretation 'warrior' (cf. *CAD*, M 313), which is noted by Roberts elsewhere (p. 158). However, the interpretation given by Gelb for this element as 'mate, husband' (Gelb, 186 cf. *CAD*, *loc. cit.*) may be preferable, since the idea of the deity as a 'spouse' may be reflected in later Akk. names, (see below, p. 256) and probably refers to the child of a widow.

šalālum 'to draw out'? Names such as *Išlul-Il* are translated by Roberts as 'Il drew out' (p. 31), which may be a reference to the child being drawn from the womb or, more probably, may be similar to the Heb. name-element *dlh* 'to draw' in the sense of rescue. Indeed, the characteristic of the deity Il as one involved with child-giving may be far less evident than Roberts was inclined to believe (cf. A.R. Millard, *JSS* 19 [1974], 89). The name could then be likened also to Heb. theophoric names with the ideas 'to deliver' (roots *yš'*, *mlṭ*, *nṣl* [Hiphil] and *plṭ*), 'to spare' (*ḥml*), and 'to rescue' (*ḥlṣ*). On the other hand, Gelb suggests a meaning 'to carry away' for the O. Akk. element, similar to the Heb. name-element *'ms* 'to bear', while von Soden (*AHw*, III, 1142) suggests 'fortführen'. This has no parallel in Heb. names.

3. The same ideas concerning the deities may be depicted in both onomastica by different elements. These semantically comparable elements are as follows:

addī 'father' (Roberts, 123). This element occurs in the name *Addī-ilum*[DINGIR] which Roberts translates as 'The god is my father', and would be comparable to *'b* 'Father' in Heb. theophoric names (see above, 1). However, note the Akk. name *Ad-di-li-ib-lu-uṭ* (O. Bab.), translated by Stamm as 'Mein Liebling(?) möge gesund sein' (Stamm, 154). The element *'d* 'father' occurs in Ug. (*PTU*, 88-89), Phoen. (*PNPPI*, 259-60), Amor. (*APNM*, 156) and Aram. (Lipiński, 101-102).

šarrum 'king' (Roberts, 13, 20, 48 etc.). Met frequently in O. Akk. names, the element *šarrum*, 'king', is comparable to the Heb. name-element *mlk* with the same meaning.

balāṭum 'life' (Roberts, 126). The O. Akk. name *Ilum-balāṭ* [DINGIR] 'The god is life', may depict the deity as a source or giver of life. This idea would be similar to Heb. *m*ᵉ*ḥûyā'ēl/m*ᵉ*ḥîyâ'ēl* 'El gives life', although the form of this Heb. name is difficult (see above, §2.8. 2).

išarum 'righteous' (Roberts, 49, 127, 129). Heb. names with the root *ṣdq* are semantically comparable to the O. Akk. name-element *išarum* 'righteous'.

damqum 'good' (Roberts, 38, 49, 122 etc.). Roberts interprets the element *damqum* as 'gracious, favourable', in O. Akk. names. The more usual interpretation of the element, however, is 'good', comparable to Heb. *ṭwb* and *ḥsd* in theophoric names, as well as, perhaps, 'beautiful' (cf. Gelb, 110f.) reflected in the Heb. name-elements *yph* and *šnh*. *Ṭwb* is also attested in O. Akk. names, (see *ṭâbum* above, 1).

ṣīnum, *rîṣum* 'help, helper'. O. Akk. *ṣīnum* appears in the name *Malik-ṣinšu*, 'Malik is his helper' (Roberts, 42). More widely attested is *rîṣum*, with the meaning 'help, helper' (*ibid.*, 20, 34, 38, 123, 125). The comparable idea in Heb. names is expressed with the roots *'zr*, Aram. *'dr*, and *'wš*.

enna 'mercy, grace'; *gamil* 'merciful'; *ipqum* 'grace'. The idea of divine mercy is depicted in O. Akk. names of the type *Enna-il* 'Mercy O Il' (Roberts, 31: cf. also the discussion of this element by Gelb, 51-52). Also attested is O. Akk. *gamil* 'merciful' from *gamālum* 'to save (spare)'. The root *gml* in Heb. names probably means 'to accomplish', but the comparable idea may be found in the Heb. name-elements *rḥm* 'to show compassion' and, perhaps, *nḥm* 'to comfort'. Also attested in O. Akk. names is *ipqum* 'grace' (Roberts, 31, 47), an idea depicted in Heb. names with the root *ḥnn*.

asûm 'physician' (Roberts, 37, 43, 122 etc.). This idea of the deity as a 'physician' is not directly paralleled in Heb. although, like O. Akk. names also, the root *rp'* 'to heal' is used in theophoric names to depict a similar idea (see above, 1).

karābum 'to bless' (Roberts, 20, 24). O. Akk. theophoric names with *karābum*, expressing the idea 'to bless', are paralleled by Heb. names with the root *brk* and perhaps *mrr* 'to strengthen, bless, commend' (cf. Ug.). The O. Akk. element, however, is also used nominally. (See also below, pp. 234f. for other uses of the element.)

alājum? 'to come up'. This verb meaning 'to come up' (cf. Gelb, 37) may be contained in the O. Akk. name *Ulli-ilum* [DINGIR]. Roberts's translation of this name as 'The god elevated' (p. 125) may be similar to Heb. theophoric names containing the idea 'to raise up' or 'to establish' with the roots *kwn*, *qwm* (Hiphil) and *śwm*. In Heb. names, the cognate root *'lh* (see above, §2.3) depicts the deity as 'exalted'.

šaṭāpum 'to preserve life' (Roberts, 31, 35, 40, 49 etc.). This O. Akk. element is comparable to *šmr* 'to preserve' in Heb. theophoric names. Roberts's connection of the element with birth events seems unlikely, cf. A. R. Millard, *JSS* 19 (1974), 89.

apārum 'to provide (with food)' (Roberts, 122). Similar to the above idea is the notion that the deity provides with food, exemplified in Heb. names with the roots *'zh* (cf. Arab. *ghadhā*) and *qwt* (cf. Arab. *qāta*), both meaning 'to nourish'.

imittum 'support' (Roberts, 38, 129). The concept of the deity as a support is expressed only verbally in Heb. names, with the roots *smk*, *'mn*, *'šh* and, possibly, *yšh* (cf. Arab. *'asa'*), although this root is problematic (see above, §2.9 *yôšawyāh*).

andullum 'protection'; *izammer* 'to protect'; *puzrum* 'shelter, security' *naṣārum* 'to watch, guard'. The idea of divine protection is depicted only verbally in Heb. names with the uncertain root *ḥmh* (cf. S. Arab. *ḥamay* and above, §2.9 *ḥammû'ēl*) and *zmr* (cf. S. Arab. *dhimr*). O. Akk. names depict the deity nominally as 'protection' with *andullum* (Roberts, 21, 34, 126) and, verbally, with the element *izammer*, which occurs only in the name *Izammer-Tišpak* (*ibid.*, 53). Gelb lists this name under the root *zamārum* 'to sing' (p. 308), while Roberts suggests that the root is Amor. *ḏmr* 'to protect', since the idea 'to sing' is semantically difficult (p. 165-66). Since the element seems to be cognate with the root *zmr* in Heb. names, the idea 'to protect' may be preferable. *Puzrum* is used very frequently to portray the deity as 'shelter' or 'protection' in O. Akk. names, but is always used in the genitive i.e. 'protection of' the deity. Although the Heb. roots *ḥmh* and *zmr* are not used in this way, they express the same concept of divine protection.

Naṣārum is attested nominally, describing the deity as a 'Protector', (Roberts, 127), as well as the name-bearer as 'guarded of' the deity (*ibid.* 129).

dūrum 'wall' (Roberts, 31, 35, 38, 49). Both O. Akk. *dūrum* and Heb. *šwr* in theophoric names depict the deity as a 'wall', which is figurative for protection.

ḫuršānum, *šadwum* 'mountain'. O. Akk. *ḫuršānum* (Roberts, 43) and, more frequently, *šadwum* (*ibid.*, 13, 20, 36, 38 etc.) are used to depict the deity as a 'mountain', comparable to Heb. theophoric names with the noun *hr*. Although *šdy* is attested in Heb. names it is found only as a divine name (see above, §2.2 *šdy*).

qiāpum, *tukkulum*, *takālum* 'to trust'. The O. Akk. name-elements *qiāpum* (Roberts, 125) and *takālum* (*ibid.*, 13, 16, 34, 36, 38 etc.) are usually found in imv. verbal forms with the deity as the object e.g. *Anda-iš-takal* 'Trust in Anda' (*ibid.*, 13). *Takālum* is also attested in nominal form (*ibid.*, 38, 131). A noun *mbṭḥ* depicting the deity as 'trust' is attested in Heb. names, but no verbal forms exist which are admonitions to 'trust' the deity. O. Akk. *tukkulum* is more difficult: for names of the type *Tukkil-Enlil*, Roberts translates 'Strengthen O Enlil' (p. 21), while Gelb, 295 lists this name under the root *tukkulum* 'to trust' which may suggest a meaning 'Trust in Enlil'.

wabālum 'to give pardon' (Roberts, 39, 123, 130). The O. Akk. idea that the deity has pardoned is similar to the Heb. element *nšh* 'to forget' (sins?) in theophoric names.

qabājum, *awājum* 'to speak'. The idea 'to speak' in Heb. theophoric names is contained in the root *'mr* (and perhaps *qwl*, see above, §2.9 *qlyhw*). In O. Akk. names, *qabājum* (Roberts, 50) is found only in the imv., whereas *awājum* (*ibid.*, 124) is used in the same way as the Qal of *'mr* in Heb. names.

ḫasāsum 'to remember' (Roberts, 123). *Ḫasāsum* 'to remember' is found in O. Akk. names in the genitive, depicting the name-bearer as 'Remembered of' the deity. Heb. names perhaps have a parallel in the use of *y'h* (cf. Arab. *wa'ā*) in the name *y^{e}'û'ēl* 'Remembered of El', but this is uncertain (cf. above, §§2.6 and 2.7). Although the root *zkr* 'to remember' is used only verbally with the deity as subject in Heb. names, like the Akk. element it shows that the deity was thought to remember man.

erāšum 'to wish, request' (Roberts, 126). This element is attested in the name *Ilam-ēriš* [DINGIR], translated by Roberts as 'He asked the god'. It is similar to the use of *š'l* 'to ask' in Heb. theophoric names.

riābum 'to compensate', *šanājum* 'to do something twice'. Both the O. Akk. elements *riābum* (Roberts, 49) and *šanājum* (*ibid.*, 121) probably refer to the birth of the child, *riābum* with the idea of the child being given as compensation for a previously deceased child, and *šanājum* for the giving of a second child (cf. Gelb, 278). Roberts's translation of the name *Išni-ilum* [I_3-lum] as 'The god repeated', however, seems to have missed this last point. The idea of recompense for a previously deceased child is evident in Heb. names with the roots *šlm* 'to recompense' and the Hiphil of *šwb* 'to restore', while the root *ysp* depicts the idea 'to add' (another child to the family).

šakānum 'to place' (*Roberts*, 18, 21, 124). This O. Akk. element seems formally cognate with Heb. *škn*, which is attested in the name *š^e^kanyāh(û)*. However, the meaning of this name, 'Y has taken up his abode', is semantically different, and the root in BH normally has the meaning 'to settle down, abide, dwell', cf. BDB, 1014. The O. Akk. idea 'to place' is perhaps similar to Heb. names with *qwm* (Hiphil), *kwn* and *śwm* 'to establish'.

dannum, *qarrādum/qurādum* 'strong'. The O. Akk. element *dannum* (Roberts, 15, 19, 38, 47 etc.) depicts the deity as 'strong, powerful' and has, as a semantic counterpart in Heb. names, the roots *'br*, *'zz*, *knn*, *'mṣ*, and *gbr*, as well as *ḥyl/ḥwl* (nominal, 'strength'). O. Akk. *qarrādum/qurādum* is translated by Roberts in all names as 'warrior', cf. *Ilum-qurud* (p. 121), *Erra-qarrād* 'Erra is a warrior' (p. 21) etc. This idea of the deity as a 'warrior' has no equivalent in the Heb. nomenclature. However, Gelb retains the meaning 'strong' in such names (pp. 226, 277), while it is also possible that the element means 'hero', cf. *AHw* (1972), 904.

ra'āmum 'to love'; *mani*, *narâmum* 'beloved'. The idea that the deity 'has loved' in Heb. names is expressed with the root *dwd*, while construct forms of this root and the root *ydd* express the name-bearer as 'beloved of' the deity. The latter concept is depicted in O. Akk. by the element *mani* in the name *Mani-(i)lī* 'Beloved of my god' (Roberts, 129), and by *narâmum* (*ibid.*, 49, 129). Cf. also *dâdum* above (1), while O. Akk. *ra'āmum* can be used in this way too (Roberts, 21), as well as verbally to express that the deity 'has loved' (*ibid.*, 18, 42). The first element of the O. Akk. name *Rīm-Ḫaniš* (*ibid.*, 29) may also be derived from *ra'āmum* and is listed by Gelb under *rîmum* 'love' (p. 231). Roberts, however, prefers to translate the name as 'Mercy of Ḫaniš' (p. 29), while also possible is a meaning 'gift' cf. *AHw*, II, 952.

tappā'um 'comrade, companion'; *banû* 'friendly'. Semantically equivalent to the element *r'* in the Heb. name *r^e^'û'ēl*, 'Friend of El', is the nominal use of the O. Akk. element *tappā'um* 'comrade, companion' (cf. Roberts, 127, 131). Similar is O. Akk. *banû* (*ibid.*, 126) which describes the deity as 'friendly', although a meaning 'fine, beautiful, splendid' is also possible (cf. *CAD*, B 81), comparable to Heb. names with the roots *šnh* 'to shine, be beautiful' (cf. Arab. *sana*) and *yph* 'to be fair, beautiful'.

karābum 'to worship, praise'; *dalālum*, *na'ādum* 'to praise'. The deity is the object of the verbal sentence in O. Akk. names with *karābum*, e.g. *Ilak-kur*[*ub*] 'Worship your god' (Roberts, 131), *dalālum* (*ibid.*, 124, 134) and *na'ādum*/*nu'udum* (*ibid.*, 13, 38, 127), the last element being used in the imv. in the same way as *karābum*. These ideas may be similar to Heb. names from the root *ydh* (Hiphil) 'to praise', in which the deity is also the object. A meaning 'to praise' for the imv. of *karābum* in names is likely (cf. *CAD*, K 192), as opposed to the idea 'to pray' to the deity (so Roberts, 17, 49, 51) or 'to bless' the deity (*ibid.*, 134).

buā'um 'to come' (Roberts, 126). This element is present in the O. Akk. name *Ilam-ba'ā* [DINGIR] translated by Roberts as 'Meet the god', comparable to Heb. *nô'adyāh* (root *y'd*). This name probably means 'Y has met or manifested himself' and is similar to the use of the O. Akk. element, although the action comes essentially from the deity in the Heb. name. The cognate root *bw'*, although attested in Heb. names, expresses the different idea that the deity 'has come'.

kašādum 'to arrive'; *tabā'um* 'to come up'; *napāqum* 'to come forth'. O. Akk. *kašādum* 'to arrive', has the child as the subject as well as the deity (cf. Roberts, 134). Heb. names do not specifically state that the deity 'has arrived', but the similar idea that the deity 'has come' is expressed with the roots *'th* and *bw'*. O. Akk. *napāqum* is perhaps present in the name *Enpiq-Ḫanīš* which is translated by Roberts as 'Ḫanīš came forth' (p. 29). Elsewhere (p. 165), Roberts considers the element to be Amor., although this is doubtful (cf. Westenholz, *op. cit.*, 290). Also relevant here may be O. Akk. *tabā'um* 'to come up, arise' in the name *Itbe-Laba* 'The Lion arose' (Roberts, 42). This further sense 'to arise' is reflected in Heb. *zrḥ* as well as the Qal of the root *qwm*.

tuārum 'to return' (Roberts, 18, 49). The idea 'to return', or pleas that the deity will 'return', are found in O. Akk. names with *tuārum*. This is paralleled in Heb. names with the Qal of the root *šwb*, and possibly by the roots *pnh* 'to turn' (see above, §2.4), *sḥr* (*ibid.*, §2.9 [*yh*]*wsḥ*[*r*]) and *swr* (*ibid.*, *sryh* 'to turn').

wardum 'slave, servant' (Roberts, 20, 53, 132). O. Akk. names which depict the name-bearer as a 'slave' or 'servant' of the deity are reflected in Heb. names with *'bd*, 'servant'.

ayarum 'young man'. *Ayarum* can be used in O. Akk. names to depict the name-bearer as a 'man of' the deity (Roberts, 20, 123: cf. also below, 4 for this element in a nominal sentence name). Heb. names express the same idea with *'yš* and *mt* 'man' (the latter also being attested in O. Akk., see above, 1), *pth* 'young man' (cf. Arab. *fatiya*), *n'r* 'youth, servant, attendant', and perhaps *gbr* 'man'.

liptum 'creation, craft' (Roberts, 129). This element is found in O. Akk. names which depict the child as a 'creation' or 'craft' of the deity. Although Heb. names do not use the genitive form in this way, the idea of divine creation is depicted verbally by the roots *bnh* 'to build, create', *br'* and *qnh* 'to create' and *'šh* and *p'l* 'to make'. *Bnh* is also found in O. Akk. (see *banājum*, above, 1).

bûrum 'calf' (Roberts, 43). The idea of the child as a 'calf' or 'young animal' of the deity, depicted in O. Akk. *bûrum*, is paralleled in Heb. by the name *'glyw* (SO 41,1 cf. *SSI*, 12) 'Calf of Y'.

4. There are many Old Akkadian name-elements which have no parallel semantic thought in Hebrew theophoric names. Names containing these elements express ideas concerning the deity which do not seem to be characteristics of the Israelite God, as far as the evidence of personal names is concerned, and are as follows.

Most conspicuous is the presence of feminine nouns to depict the O. Akk. female deities. Since a female divine consort for the Israelite deity, or a pantheon of gods, is not to be found in Israelite religion, Heb. names do not contain the feminine nouns *malkatum* 'princess' (Roberts, 38), *ummum* 'mother' (*ibid.*, 29, 37, 38, 39, 43 etc.), *šu'atum* 'lady' (*ibid.*, 43), *ši* 'she', as in *Ši-Mumma* (*ibid.*, 45), and *šarratum* 'queen' (*ibid.*, 43).

Absent in Heb. also, are names depicting a female child in relationship with the deity by a construct noun, as in the O. Akk. genitive elements *amtum* 'handmaid, female slave' (Roberts, 49) and *šat* 'she' in names of the type *Šat-Tišpak* 'She of Tišpak' (*ibid.*, 53). Also not attested among Heb. names are those which depict a male child as the son or heir of the deity, as in the O. Akk. genitive forms *šu* 'he' (*ibid.*, 13, 14, 16, 17, 18 etc., very frequent) and *aplum* 'heir, son' (*ibid.*, 132).

Genitive elements depicting the newly born child which are not attested among Heb. names are *naṣib* 'suckled' (*ibid.*, 129),[70] *šumum* 'name' (*ibid.*, 14, 20, 43, 50, 125)[71] and *nabā'um* 'to name', which occurs as a genitive element (*ibid.*, 49, 55) and verbally (*ibid.*, 13, 16, 21, 51, 56, 121, 123). In this context should be noted the verbal element *walādum* 'to beget' (*ibid.*, 52, 122), which is also without parallel in Heb. names.

Other genitive elements referring to the name-bearer which have no semantic equivalent in Heb. theophoric names are O. Akk. *migrum* 'favourite' (*ibid.*, 131), *tamkar* 'merchant' (*ibid.*, 130), *enbum* 'fruit' (*ibid.*, 23, 37), *kalbum* 'dog' (*ibid.*, 20), *meḫri* 'answer' (*ibid.*,

13), *ṣabi'um* 'soldier' (*ibid.*, 125; Gelb, 241 also 'worker') and *ubarum* 'guest, stranger' (Roberts, 18). Three other O. Akk. elements used in the genitive probably refer to the deity, not the name-bearer, and have no equivalent among Heb. names. These are *šepum* 'foot' (*ibid.*, 125), *šīrat* 'crescent' in *Šīrat-Su'en* 'Crescent of Su'en' (*ibid.*, 50) and *pum* 'mouth, word' (*ibid.*, 13, 18, 37, 43, 45 etc.).

Among nominal elements having no equivalent in Heb. are those which portray the deity as a 'city' (*ālum* Roberts, 15, 34, 37, 47, 48 etc.), 'clan' (*illatum* Roberts, 38, 51, 126, 126-27, 130: Gelb, 39 = 'power' or 'family'), 'house, household' (*bîtum* Roberts, 38, 49, 54, 126) and 'family' (*kimtum* Roberts, 126). The deity is never depicted as an animal in Heb. names, whereas this is evident in O. Akk. names with *labûm* 'lion' (Roberts, 36, 38, 46, 54 etc.). *lala'um* 'kid' (*ibid.*, 127), *šûrum* 'bull' (*ibid.*, 131) and *turāh* 'mountain goat' (*ibid.*, 45).

Other nominal forms used in O. Akk. names to describe the deity, but with no counterpart among Heb. names are *balangum* 'harp' (*ibid.*, 37), *ayyar* 'young man'[72] (*ibid.*, 48), *malkum* 'prince' (*ibid.*, 121, 131; or 'counsellor' cf. Gelb, 176), *sukkallum* 'vizier' (Roberts, 127, 131), *nuḫšum* 'wealth' (*ibid.*, 38, 131), *idum* 'arm' (*ibid.*, 124) and *qātum* 'hand'.[73]

Verbal elements with no semantic complement in Heb. names describe the deity as 'awe-inspiring' (*palḫum* Roberts, 125, 38; or 'feared' cf. Gelb, 214), 'eternal' (*dârijum* Roberts, 38), 'patient' (*arākum* Roberts, 129, or perhaps 'eternal' cf. Gelb, 64 'to be long') and 'wise' (*mūda* Roberts, 19, 38, 49, 51). Also without parallel in Heb. are *waṣā'um* 'to go out, go forth' (*Gelb*, 69-70),[74] *ra'āšum* 'to rejoice' (Roberts, 21),[75] *alālum* 'to acclaim' (*ibid.*, 124), *amārum* 'to see' (*ibid.*, 38, 42, 49, 51, 123),[76] *balālum* 'to mix' (*ibid.*, 31, 123),[77] *la'ājum* 'to prevail' (*ibid.*, 49; Gelb, 158 also 'to be strong'), *maḫārum* 'to receive' (Roberts, 52), *išu* 'to have' (Gelb, 72-3),[78] *magārum* 'to agree' (Roberts, 49), *ra'ājum* 'to shepherd' or 'provide with food' (*ibid.*, 12, 18, 43, 49, 51, 124, 127),[79] *pašāḫum* 'to become tranquil' (*ibid.*, 125), *ša'ārum* 'to battle, vanquish' (Gelb, 261), or nominal 'fighter' (Roberts, 121) and *uššurum* 'to release' (from sins?) (*ibid.*, 18).

O. Akk. *ali* 'where?' (*ibid.*, 16, 128, 129) asking the question 'Where is?' the deity, seems to suggest divine neglect of the name-bearer and is not reflected in Heb. names. Also without parallel in Heb. are the O. Akk. name-elements *kīma* 'like, as' in *Amurru-kīma-il* 'Amurru is like Il' (*ibid.*, 15), *man*, *manum* 'who' in *Man-balum-*

Dagan 'Who can be without Dagan?' (*ibid.*, 18), *kalum* 'all' (*ibid.*, 49, 126, 129) in names of the type *Kalî-ilī* 'My god is my all' (p. 126) and *maḫri* 'before, in front' in *Ili-maḫri* 'My god is before me' (*ibid.*, 131). O. Akk. *maṣiam* 'enough!' occurs in the name *Maṣiam-Eštar* 'Enough for me O Eštar' (*ibid.*, 39), which may suggest a time of parental stress or simply that no more children are wanted.

4.6 *A Comparison between the Concepts of Deity Revealed in the Akkadian and Hebrew Onomastica*

In the present comparison of the concepts of deity found in Akkadian and Hebrew theophoric names, three major works have been utilized. Akkadian names were studied by J.J. Stamm in 1939 (*Die Akkadische Namengebung*, Leipzig [1939], reprinted Darmstadt [1968], referred to throughout as Stamm) and by Knut Tallqvist in 1914 (*Assyrian Personal Names*, Hildesheim: Georg Olms [1914], reprinted [1966], referred to throughout as *APN*). A more recent work by C. Saporetti (*Onomastica Medio-Assira*, I, II Rome: Biblical Institute Press [1970], hereafter *OMA*) has also provided a substantial number of Middle Assyrian names.

Akkadian names are instantly seen to contrast sharply with Hebrew theophoric names, since the latter are mainly compounds involving two elements, with the exception of abbreviated names of one element, and only a few names prefixed with the preposition *'l*, which have three elements. Akkadian names, on the other hand, often contain three elements and are far more structurally complex. Although a name like Hebrew *b^{e}nāyāh* 'Yahweh has built (created)', for example, is reflected in Akkadian names like ^{f}*Tabni-Ištar* 'Ištar has created' (cf. Stamm, 28; *APN*, 275a-b; *OMA*, II 107-108), in which the common root *bnh* is used, other Akkadian names using this root are more involved, as in the name ^{d}*Marduk-tab-ta-ni-bul-liṭ* (N./L. Bab.) 'Marduk you have (just) created, keep (or make the child) healthy' (cf. Stamm, 154).

Akkadian names also give the impression of frequently relating the name-bearer or parent of the child, or some situation concerning these, more directly to the deity. In Hebrew names we are often left with a simple statement concerning the Israelite God, for example, *ḥăzāyāh* 'Yahweh has seen', *y^{e}ša'yāh*(*û*) 'Yahweh has saved' etc., in which any thought in the mind of the giver of the name cannot be ascertained with accuracy. Akkadian names, however, often tend to express more explicitly the psychological situation surrounding the name-giving, such as *^{d}Enlil-a-bi-en-ši* (M. Bab.) 'Enlil is father of the weak' (cf. Stamm, 240) and *^{d}Nabû-tultabši-līšir* (N. Bab.) 'Nabû you have caused him to be, may he prosper' (cf. Stamm, 155), which are types of names not paralleled in Hebrew. Another major contrast with Hebrew is the frequent Akkadian use of the vocative, imperative, or precative to express pleas or requests to the deities, as in *Ašur-māt-taqqin* 'O Aššur, order the country' (*APN*, 41b; *OMA*, II 164).

In Akkadian names, too, the name-bearer or parent is more frequently the subject of the sentence than is the case in Hebrew names, for example, *Ga-ma-al-^{d}Sin-lu-mur* (M. Bab.) 'May I see/experience the grace/kindness of Sin' (cf. Stamm, 168; *CAD*, G 21a). This creates considerable differences between Akkadian and Hebrew names. Compare, for example, the Hebrew name *mbṭḥyhw* (L 1,4) 'Yahweh is trust', with Akkadian *takālu* 'to trust', in the names *A-na-^{d}Šamaš-tak-la-ku* (O. Bab.) 'I trust in Šamaš (cf. Stamm, 196) and *A-na-a-mat-^{d}Bēl-at-kal* (N./L. Bab.) 'I trust in Bēl's word' (cf. Stamm, 199).

Some Akkadian three-part compound names do not contain a theophoric element, but the fuller sense of these names often suggests that a deity is implied. This may be seen, for example, in the name *^{f}Ina-Ekur-ba'-lat* (M. Bab.) 'In Ekur is she (the goddess) powerful' (cf. Stamm, 229).

1. The foregoing contrasts mean that some elements cannot be totally equated in both onomastica since, even where there are ideas common to both, there are often instances in which the Akkadian element has a further usage beyond that of Hebrew. This will be seen in the following list of common elements: where the Akkadian element is used in additional ways not reflected in Hebrew, this will be recorded in a footnote.

Akk.		*Heb.*
abu	Stamm, 54, 56, 208, 209, 222; *APN*, 263b; *OMA*, II 98-99.	*'b* father[80]
aḫu	Stamm, 22, 56; *APN*, 265b; *OMA*, II 100-101.	*'ḥ* brother[81]
āšu	*APN*, 265a.	*'wš* to help
(w)atru	*APN*, 281b.	*ytr* pre-eminent[82]

banû	Stamm, 28, 78, 98n.4, 139, 140, 154, 156, 217, 317; *APN*, 275a-b; *OMA*, II 107-108.	*bnh* to build, create[83]
bēlu	*APN*, 273b; *OMA*, II 110.	*b'l* lord[84]
dânu	Stamm, 172, 192, 221, 229, 370; *APN*, 279a.	*dyn* to judge[85]
enēnu	Stamm, 182; *APN*, 269b.	*ḥnn* to be gracious[86]
šūzubu	Stamm, 170, 191, 221; *APN*, 265a; *OMA*, II 119-20.	*šêzēb* Aram. lw. 'to save, deliver'
gadā	*APN*, 277a.	*gd* fortune
ḫāziru	Stamm, 213, 215.	*'zr* to help[87]
ḫammu	*APN*, 268b.	*'m* uncle
ḫinnu/annu	*APN*, 284b/269b.	*ḥn* grace
idû	Stamm, 198; *APN* 287a; *OMA*, II 124.	*yd'* to know[88]
ilu	*APN*, 267a.	*'l* god
itti	*OMA*, II 127.	*'t* with[89]
ka''ulu D	*APN*, 288b; *OMA*, II 129	*kwl* (Pilpel) to support
kunnu	*APN*, 288b.	*kwn* to establish
man(nu)	Stamm, 237-38; *APN*, 294a; *OMA*, II 135.	*my* who?[90]
nadānu	Stamm, 28, 38, 54, 56, 84, 85, 108, 136-37, 139, 217, 257; *APN*, 296 a-b; *OMA*, II 139.	*ntn* to give[91]
nūru/nīru	Stamm, 212; *APN*; *OMA*, II 144, 145.	*nr* light, lamp[92]
pānu	cf. A.R. Millard, *JSS* 21 (1976), 8.[93]	*pn* face
ṣillu	Stamm, 84, 85, 235, 276; *APN*,303b; [94] *OMA*, II 155.	*ṣl* shadow
qâšu	Stamm, 85, 139, 154, 160, 127; *APN*, 304a; *OMA*, II 149.	*qwš* to give[95]
rabû	Stamm, 84, 91, 224, 313; *APN* 305b; *OMA*, II 150.	*rbb* to be great[96]
šemû	Stamm, 78, 189; *APN*, 308b; *OMA*, II 158.	*šm'* to hear[97]
ṭâbu	Stamm, 291 n. 4 (verbal), 85, 224 (adj.); *APN*, 286a; *OMA* II 166.	*ṭwb* to be good[98]

2. A few Akkadian names present some difficulty with form or semantic content, making their comparison with Hebrew more problematic. This is the case with the following Akkadian elements:

'zl (*APN*, 265a). Tallqvist listed the name *A-zi-lu-/ilu* under this root, but no appropriate meaning seems evident. A plant (*azallu* cf. *CAD*, A 524; *AHw*, I, 92) is perhaps semantically unlikely, so the name remains obscure.

ālu 'city'. The name *^{d}Nabû-ana-āliya* (N./L. Bab.) seems semantically incomplete. Stamm suggests the name is a request that the deity should show the city how piety will be rewarded (p. 83). The name *Ili-ālum* is also uncertain and may contain *alum* 'Where?' (cf. Stamm, 90), but neither name has any parallel in Heb.

erēšu (*APN*, 271-72). Although Tallqvist recorded names such as *Ēreš-Ištar* (*APN*, 76a) and *Adad-ēreš* (*APN*, 7b) under the root *erēšu* 'to plant', which is cognate with the Heb. name-element *'rš* with the same meaning, it is possible that some of the names with this element belong in the context of *erēšu* 'to ask for, desire' (see below, p. 256).

erišu? (*APN*, 271b). This element may occur in the name *I-ri-su-īli^{pl}*, which Tallqvist suggested is possibly *ēriš* + šu. *Erēšu* normally means 'to ask for, request, desire', or 'to plant' (cf. Stamm, 125, 144, 192, 258 and *CAD*, E 281). Stamm, indeed, translates the MA name *^{d}Marduk-īris-su* as 'Marduk hat ihn gefordert' (p. 144). *Erēšu* 'to desire, ask for' is attested frequently in theophoric names in MA (cf. *OMA*, II 117-18), where it is usually found with a direct object.

ašāru (*APN*, 272b). Tallqvist considered this element to mean 'to be gracious' in the name *Li-šur-ṣa-la-Ašur*. However, *ašāru* seems to have had the meanings 'to muster', 'to provide with food', 'to be humble', or 'to release' (cf. *CAD*, A 2 420ff.). Stamm discusses *ašāru* at some length, concluding that the element should probably be interpreted 'mit Nahrung versorgen' (cf. Stamm, 181 and below, p. 252). The idea 'to provide with food' is similar to the concept in Heb. names that the deity 'nourishes', from the roots *qwt* (cf. Arab. *qāta*) and *'zh* (cf. Arab. *ghadhā*). The idea 'to release' would be paralleled in Heb. names from the difficult root *rmh* (cf. above, §2.5 *rmh*/*rwm*), or may be akin to the notion of salvation. The idea 'to muster' may be similar to Heb. *'sp* 'to gather', while 'to be humble' is not reflected in Heb. names.

ešāru (*OMA*, II 118). Saporetti interpreted this element as 'just' in the MA name *E-šar-dēn-Nusku*, presumably 'Just is the decision or judgment of Nusku', a name without parallel in Heb. The usual meaning of this root in names, however, is 'to thrive, prosper' (cf. below, p. 260), although a root *ešāru* 'to be right' would be semantically more suitable for such a name.

esēru 'to fetter, imprison' (Stamm, 251-52). The Akk. name *Asīr-^{d}Adad* (O. Bab.) is uncertain. If *asīru* is the correct derivation of the first element (cf. *CAD*, A 2 332b), a meaning 'Prisoner of Adad' may be similar to the Heb. name *š^{e}bû'ēl*, which is possibly derived from a root *šbh* 'to take captive' (see above, §2.7). The BH name *'ăśar'ēl* may have some connection with Heb. *'sr* 'to tie, bind, imprison', which is related to the Akk. root, but this is, again, uncertain (see above, §2.4 *'śr*).

manû (*APN*, 294b). The name *I-ma-ni-ilu* is listed by Tallqvist under the element *manû* 'to count', presumably as an improved etymology for 'Our *'m* is the god', which is given for the same name elsewhere (p. 100a). Tallqvist also compared the name *Im-ma-ni-Ašur*. Comparisons with Heb. *'ḥymn*, itself a difficult form (see above, §2.9) and names listed by Tallqvist under *mānu* (p. 294b) are too uncertain. Cf. also Ug. *mny*, above §4.1.2, and Aram. *mnh*, *ibid.* §4.4.3 'to count'.

mušētiq (*APN*, 273b). This part. form of *etēqu* Š is, according to Tallqvist, only attested in abbreviated names such as *Ašur-mušētiq* (*APN*, 42a), in which, since the divine name is retained, presumably the object of the verb has been dropped or is perhaps understood to be the child. *Etēqu* normally means 'to pass by or through', 'to exceed, surpass' (cf. *CAD*, E 384ff.), but a meaning 'Ašur averts (evil)' is also possible for the name (*ibid.*, 395). Stamm translates the element as 'vorübergehen (passieren)' and since the object 'light' (*urru*) is often supplied, Stamm suggests a translation 'Der Gott lässt das Licht vorübergehen (passieren)' (p. 319). This is an idea not attested among Heb. names.

nimru The element *nimru* is translated by Saporetti as 'splendore' (*OMA*, II 144), an idea which is not specifically attested in Heb. names, but the root *pl'* 'to be wonderful' possibly provides the nearest parallel. Nevertheless, other possibilities are also open for the interpretation of this element since the meanings 'leopard, panther', as well as 'light' are also attested for *nimru* (cf. *AHw*, II 790), while *CAD*, N 2 234, 235 lists names with *nimru* under 'light'. The former of these meanings has no parallel among Heb. names, but the latter is reflected in Heb. *'wr* 'light' and *nr* 'lamp' (cf. also *nūru/nīru* above, 1). These Heb. elements are, however, nominal, while the Akk. element may be genitive (cf. *OMA*, II 144).

ridū (*APN*, 305). *Ridū* occurs in the theophoric name *Tar-di-it-Ašur*, which is listed by Tallqvist under *ridū*, meaning 'child'. Semantically, the only suitable interpretation would be 'Child of Ašur', which has no equivalent in the Heb. onomasticon. However, cf. *rīdu*, meaning 'guidance' *AHw*, II 981.

rīmu (*APN*, 305a). Although the names *Nabû-rīm(AM)-ilāni* and *Ašir-ri-im-nišēšu* are listed by Tallqvist under the element *rīmu* 'bull' (ideogr. AM), we find the meanings differ in Tallqvist's alphabetical list. *Nabû-rīm-ilāni* is given the meaning 'Nabû is the wild ox of the gods' (p. 157b), which is the interpretation given to the name by Saporetti (*OMA*, II 153), and *Ašir-ri-im-nišēšu* is translated by Tallqvist as 'Ashir is favour for his people' (p. 32b). This name is discussed at length by Stamm, however, who favours 'Assur ist der Stier seines Volkes' (p. 228-29), a meaning also supported by von Soden (*AHw*, II 986). Heb. names have no parallel to the concept of the deity as a 'wild ox' or 'bull'.

sīqu (*OMA*, II 154). This element is found in the MA names *Si-qi-Adad/ ilāni*, and is translated by Saporetti as 'ginocchio grembo' ('knee', 'lap', 'bosom'), and by von Soden as 'Oberschenkel' ('thigh', *AHw*, II 1049). None of these meanings is reflected in the Heb. onomasticon.

šēpu 'feet' (Stamm, 277). The Akk. names *Še-ip-É-a* (O. Bab.) and *Ši-ip-*[(d)] *Sin* (O. Bab.), 'Feet of Ea/Sin'? are semantically problematic. Stamm suggests the possibility that the names are abbreviations. The idea is not reflected in Heb. names.

taḫḫum 'child' (Stamm, 38). The meaning of the name [d]*Nabû-taḫ-ḫi-še-me* is very uncertain. Stamm suggests a meaning 'child' for the second element, although an interpretation 'Ersatz(mann)' is suggested by von Soden (*Ahw*, II 1032). The final element, of uncertain reading (cf. Stamm, 38 n. 5), seems to be an imv. of *šemû* 'to hear'.

3. Many Akkadian names contain elements which have semantic equivalents among Hebrew theophoric names, expressing similar ideas concerning the many Babylonian and Assyrian deities. As previously noted, however, the Akkadian component frequently has a wider use than its Hebrew semantic counterpart, as many of the following will indicate:

ba'lu 'powerful, important'; *dannu* 'strong, powerful'; *emūqu*, *idu*, *qurdu*, *lītu* 'power, strength'; *gašru* 'strong, mighty'; *le'û* 'strong, able', *li'ū* 'mighty'; *li'ūtu* 'strength, might'. The idea of the deity as 'strong', 'powerful' and 'mighty' is a prevalent one in Akk. names. *Ba'lu* 'powerful' is found only in the name [f]*Ina-Ekur-ba'lat* (M. Bab., Stamm, 229), in which the deity may be implied semantically. *Dannu* usually refers to the deities as 'strong' or 'powerful' (Stamm, 224; *APN*, 280a; *OMA*, II 113), but in the name *Dan-ri-gim-šu* (N./L. Bab.) 'Powerful is his (Adad's) voice' (cf. Stamm, 235) it is the voice of the deity which is so described, which has no parallel in Heb. names. Also attested in Akk. names are *emūqu* 'strength' (Stamm, 212; *APN*, 268b; *OMA*, II 117), *gašru* 'strong, mighty' (*OMA*, II 121), *le'û* 'strong, able' (*OMA*, II 134; Stamm, 224) and *idu* 'power, strength' (cf. Stamm, 137, 212). Unlike Heb., this last element is also used in the sense of 'arm' in the name *A-ri-ik-i-di-*[d]*Enlil* (O. Bab.) 'Enlil's arm is long' (*ibid.*, 237), but is similar to Heb. usage in names of the type *A-šùr-i-di* (OA) 'Aššur is my strength' (*ibid.*,

212). Similar are *li'ū* 'mighty', and *li'ūtu* 'strength, might' (*APN*, 292a; *OMA*, II 133), the latter occurring in *Nabû-li-'ūti* 'Nabû is my strength' (cf. *APN*, 154a = 'power'). The name *Nabû-li-ūti-mārišu* 'Nabû is the power of his son' (*ibid.*), however, has no parallel in Heb. Relative, also, is the genitive use of *qurdu* 'strength' in Akk. names (Stamm, 322), as well as Akk. *lītu* 'strength' power' in the name *^{d}Šamaš-li-is-su* (M. Bab. 'Šamaš is his power' (cf. Stamm, 212), but the NA name *Li-it-Aššur-a-mur*, translated by Stamm as 'Den Sieg Assurs sah ich' (p. 184), has no equivalent in Heb. The verbal idea 'to be strong' is expressed in Heb. names with the roots *'br*, *'zz* and *'mṣ*, also 'to be strong, mighty' with *gbr*, and 'to be able, have power, prevail, endure' with *ykl*. Also to be considered is perhaps the root *knn* 'to be firm'. The nominal idea 'strength, might', is attested in Heb. *'zz* and *ḥwl*/*ḥyl*. For the idea 'to strengthen' in Akk. and Heb. names, see below, *danānu*, *patānu* etc.

muštarriḫu, *šarraḫu* 'proud'. These two Akk. elements are used to describe the divine personality as 'proud' (Stamm, 225), comparable to the Heb. name-element *'th* 'to be proud, exalted' (cf. Arab. *'atā*). *Šarraḫu* can also mean 'magnificent, glorious' (cf. *AHw*, III 1182), similar to Heb. names with the root *kbd* 'glory, honour' and possibly *pl'* 'to be wonderful'.

šaqû, *tizqar*, *ṣēru* 'to be exalted'; *nā'idu* 'lofty, high'. The deity is depicted as 'exalted' in Akk. names with *šaqû* (Stamm, 225, 226, although in the sense 'exalted of the gods' it has no complement in Heb. names) and *tizqar* (*ibid.*, 225). The element *ṣēru* is interpreted likewise by Stamm (p. 225) but normally means 'back' or 'over' (cf. *CAD*, Ṣ 138). The former of these meanings may imply protection (cf. *būdu* and *kutallu* below, p. 259), the latter perhaps suggesting 'exalted', comparable to Heb. names with *rwm* and *'lh* (Heb. ?) 'to be exalted, high', *'th* 'to be proud, exalted' (cf. Arab. *'atā*) and *śgb* 'to be (inaccessibly) high'. Similar, is Akk. *nā'idu* meaning 'lofty, high'.

kabtu 'honoured, important'; *ṣiru*. Akk. *kabtu* has been variously interpreted: Stamm preferred a meaning 'angesehen' (pp. 225, 226), while Tallqvist suggested 'lofty, mighty' (*APN*, 288a). Preferable is perhaps 'honoured, important' or, possibly, 'abundant' (cf. *CAD*, K. 24; *OMA*, II 127), semantically comparable to the Heb. name-element *kbd* 'glory, honour', and perhaps *ytr* 'pre-eminent', 'abundance'. Akk. *ṣiru*, attested in MA names, may also mean 'pre-eminent, excellent' (cf. *OMA*, II 156) or 'exalted' (cf. foregoing).

nirbi'u 'greatness'. Parallel with Heb. names which express the deity as 'great' with the roots *gdl* and *rbb* is the element *nirbi'u* 'greatness' in the MA name *Ištu-nir-bi-ja?-Aššur* (*OMA*, II 144).

(w)asāmu 'perfectly beautiful'? Akk. *(w)asāmu* normally means 'to be fitting, proper, suitable' and in the D theme 'to make fitting and suitable', ideas which have no equivalent among Heb. names. Stamm, however,

discusses the element at some length (p. 81), suggesting that for Akk. names a meaning 'vollendet schön' may be applicable. Similar in Heb. theophoric names are possibly *tmm* 'to be perfect', *kll* 'to be complete', as well as *yph* 'to be fair, beautiful', and *šnh* 'to shine, be beautiful', but exact semantic equivalents are not evident.

enû 'to change'. This Akk. name-element expresses that the deity does not change his word or promise (cf. Stamm, 206, 232). Possibly comparable in Heb. names is the root *ytn* 'to be constant' (cf. Arab. *watana*), although names from this root are formally difficult (see above, §2.9 *yatnî'ēl*).

etellu 'lord, prince' (cf. *APN*, 273a; *OMA*, II 119). The Heb. God is depicted in names as a 'lord' with the nouns *b'l*, *'dn* and possibly Aram. *mr* (see above, §2.3). The comparable idea is expressed in Akk. names with the element *bēlu* 'lord' (cf. above, 1), as well as with *etellu* 'lord, prince'. In many cases, however, the Akk. use of *bēlu* and *etellu* differs from Heb. usage (cf. below, p. 257).

šarru 'king' is used in the same way as Heb. *mlk*, as a title for the deity, only in MA names (cf. *OMA*, II 160), since the Akk. element usually occurs in name-types which have no equivalent in Heb. (cf. below, p. 257).

šū 'he'; *bašû* 'to be, exist'. Comparable to Heb. names of the type *'ĕlîhû'* 'He is God' is perhaps the MA name *Ilî-šu-ma* (*OMA*, II 162). Similar, is Akk. *bašû*, which is used with the deity as subject to express the belief that a god exists (Stamm, 135: see also below, p. 264, where similar usage has no parallel in Heb.). It is also found in a causative sense expressing that the deity has allowed a child to come into existence, perhaps akin to the thought in the Heb. name *'abšay/'ăbîšay* containing the element *yš* 'existence' and meaning 'The (divine) Father is existence' (i.e. the source of existence). *Nabšu*, a derivative of *bašû* occurs in names such as *Ibbaššâ-ša-ili* (M. Bab.), 'What the deity (has ordained) will materialize' (*CAD*, B 159b; cf. Stamm, 197), which has no parallel in Heb.

šanānu 'to be equal'. *Šanānu* is used in Akk. names together with the interrog. *mannu* 'Who?' to express that nothing is comparable to the deity, as in the name *Ma-an-nu-um-ša-ni-in-*^{d}*Ninurta* (O. Bab.) 'Who is comparable to Ninurta?' (cf. Stamm, 238). It can also be found without the interrogative in names such as *Sin-la-ša-na-an* (O. Bab.) 'Sin has no equal' (*ibid.*, 239). Heb. names such as *mîkāyāh* 'Who is like Y?' express the same idea.

namāru, *nebû* 'to shine'; *ṣarāru* 'to light up'; *ḫanābu* 'to be radiant'. Heb. *ngh* 'to shine, enlighten' is probably used in the latter sense in theophoric names, comparable to the use of *namāru* in Akk. names (cf. *APN*, 156a; *OMA*, II 141). Unlike Heb. usage, however, Akk. *namāru* 'to shine' is also used with the 'light of god' as the subject (Stamm, 184). It is also frequently used in the precative *liwwir* (*limmir*) (cf. Stamm, 85, 173, 231) with the child as the object e.g. *Li-wi-ra-am* (O. Bab.), which Stamm translates as 'Er (der Gott) möge mir leuchten' (p. 173). Also evident is the type *Itti-ᵈBēl-lummir, -limmir* (N./L. Bab.), 'May I shine with Bēl' (cf. Stamm, 231), as well as a causative form *nummuru* (*ibid.*, 192). It is doubtful whether Heb. names contain the specific idea 'to shine' since the root *ngh*, as noted, probably means 'to enlighten' in names, while the root *šnh* 'to shine, be beautiful' (cf. Arab. *sana*) may be used more in the sense of the root *yph* 'to be fair, beautiful'. The use of Akk. *nebû* 'to shine' in the name *ᵈNabû-ni-ib-a-na-ilē, -ana-ilē* (N./L/ Bab.), translated by Stamm as 'Nabû leuchtet den Göttern' (p. 185), therefore, would have no semantic complement in Heb. names. The same may be said of Akk. *ṣarāru* 'to flash' in the name *Šamaš-ṣa-ru-ri* (*APN*, 212a), since this element seems mainly to have been used of shooting stars (*CAD*, Ṣ 106) and may, therefore, refer to the deity in some cosmic sense. Similarly, *ḫanābu* 'to be radiant' in Akk. *ᶠI-na-Ì-si-in-ḫa-an-bat* (M. Bab.) 'She (the goddess) is radiant in Isin' (cf. *CAD*, Ḫ 76) is also a doubtful parallel to Heb. *ngh* and *šnh*.

šamḫu 'luxurious' (Stamm, 226). Akk. *šamḫu*, 'luxurious', can be compared with the Heb. use of the root *bqq* 'to be luxuriant', in the name *baqbuqyāh*, although the form and interpretation of this Heb. name are problematic (see above, §2.9).

tarāṣu 'to direct'. *Tarāṣu* is attested in names such as *Nabû-tāriṣ* 'Nabû directs' (*APN*, 162a). Comparable in Heb. names is the root *dll*, also stating that the deity has 'directed', but it is not attested with certainty (see above, §2.4). *Tarāṣu* may also be interpreted 'to set right' (see below, p. 259).

qabû 'to speak, announce, command'; *rigmu/rigimtu* 'voice'. Heb. names express that the deity 'has spoken' with the roots *'mr* (Akk. 'to see', see below, *amāru*) and perhaps *qwl* (see above, §2.9 *qlyhw*). Comparable is Akk. *qabû* 'to say' which occurs, in addition, with the object 'his life' in which the sense, unlike Heb., is nearer 'to announce, command' (cf. below, p. 258). *Qabû* also occurs in names such as *Ilu-gabbi-iqbi* 'The god has announced all' (*APN*, 97a) which, likewise, has no parallel in Heb.; nor does the imv. found in MA names *Qí-bi-Adad/Aššur/ilī/Šamaš* (*OMA*, II 147). *Rigmu/rigimtu* 'voice' in Akk. *Ri-gi-im-*, *Ri-gim-ᵈAdad* (M. Bab. Stamm, 277) 'Voice of Adad' is comparable perhaps to the use of the noun *qwl* in Heb. names. However, there is no equivalent in Heb. to Akk. names such as *Ṭà-ab-ri-gim-šu* (M. Bab.) depicting the voice of the deity as 'good', as well as those names describing the divine voice as 'mighty' and 'terrible'.

šâmu, kunnu, mukīnu, šakānu, elā'u Š 'to establish, appoint, place'; *pattanu* 'to set up, erect'. The idea 'to establish' or 'to appoint' is attested in Heb. names with the roots *kwn* 'to establish, appoint', *qwm* (Hiphil) 'to establish, raise up' and *śwm* 'to establish'. A similar concept concerning the deity is expressed with Akk. *šâmu* 'to fix, appoint' (Stamm, 145, 258), which is probably cognate with Heb. *śwm*. *Kunnu* is also used with the meaning 'to establish', and is cognate with Heb. *kwn* with the same meaning (see above, 1). A part. form of *kānu*, *mukīnu*, also conveys the idea that the deity 'establishes' (*APN*, 288b). Relevant here, also, with the meaning 'to place, establish' are *šakānu* (Stamm, 231) and *šakīnu* (*ibid.*, 219). *Šakānu*, however, also occurs with the objects 'a son', 'the king', 'mercy', 'name' or welfare' (*APN*, 307b). The Š part. form of the root *elā'u* with a meaning 'to establish' is attested in the MA names *Adad/Aššur/Šamaš-mu-še-ili* (*OMA*, II 116). Also relevant is perhaps Akk. *pattanu* 'to set up, erect'. This element is suggested by Stamm as a *qattalu* form of the verb *patānu* in *ᵈEa-pattanu* 'Ea richtet auf' (p. 221). *Patānu* normally means 'to strengthen' or 'to become strong' (cf. *AHw*, II 847 and below, p. 253), which may suggest some semantic similarity to the roots *ḥzq* 'to strengthen' and perhaps *mrr* 'to strengthen, bless, commend' (cf. Ug.) in Heb. theophoric names.

qerēbu 'to approach'. The idea that the deity approaches man, depicted in Akk. names containing *qerēbu* (Stamm, 193), is semantically similar to Heb. names with the idea 'to come' (roots *'th*, *bw'*), and 'to appear' (root *'nn*). For the name *Ilum-qé-ru-ub* (O. Bab.), however, Stamm suggests 'the god has divined' (cf. Stamm, 314), which has no equivalent in Heb., nor does the name *ᶠA-na-ša-si-e-qer-bet* 'She (the goddess) is near the caller' (cf. Stamm, 318-19, 241).

napāḫu 'to rise'. The Akk. name *ᶠIp-pu-ḫa-ni-bat*, *-ni-ba-a-at* (M. Bab.) 'She (*Ištar*) rose (and now) is bright' (*CAD*, N 1 266b, cf. Stamm, 185) is possibly comparable to the Heb. name-element *zrḥ* 'to rise, come forth'. However, the cosmic nature of the Akk. name need not necessarily be present in the Heb. name, even though the root *zrḥ* is sometimes used in Heb. with the sun as subject (cf. Judg. 9.33, 2 Sam. 23.4 etc.). A noun *nipḫu* is attested in Akk. *ᶠI-na-nipḫi* (KUR) *-ša-el-li-it* (M. Bab.) 'She is louder in her rising' (cf. Stamm, 185), but has no parallel among Heb. names.

ramû 'to dwell'. This element occurs in *ᶠIna-Esagil-ramât* (Stamm, 116) and *ᶠI-na-Ì-si-in-ra-mat* (M. Bab.) 'In Isin she lives' (cf. Stamm, 229). A comparable root *yšb* 'to dwell' is to be found in Heb. names but is always used causatively. The Heb. root *škn* 'to take up an abode', which is attested in theophoric names, provides a more pertinent parallel.

karābu 'to bless'; *kiribtu* 'blessing'. The idea 'to bless' in Heb. names is found in the roots *brk* and perhaps *mrr* 'to strengthen, bless, commend' (cf. Ug.). The idea is always expressed verbally. In Akk., *karābu* 'to bless' is also attested verbally (cf. Stamm, 192), while *kiribtu* 'blessing' expresses the similar idea of the child as a 'blessing of' the deity (*APN*, 290b; Stamm, 274). A verbal imv. is also attested in names such as OA *Ku-ru-ub-Ašùr/Ištar* and *Ilam*(AN)*-kur-ub* 'Bless the god!' (cf. Stamm, 204), which have no complement in Heb., although a meaning 'to praise' may be preferable for the imv. of this Akk. element (cf. *CAD*, K 192).

qâlu 'to pay attention to'; *qa''û* 'to wait for'; *paqû* D 'to pay attention to, watch for'; *dagālu pan* 'to wait for'. The Akk. name-element *qâlu* (Stamm, 195) can be found with the deity as subject and the name-bearer or parent as object, similar to Heb. names with *ḥšb* 'to take account'. It can also be found with the deity as the object, and in such name-types may be similar to the Heb. name *ḥăkalyāh*, which some have interpreted as 'Wait for Y' (see above, §2.8.1). Saporetti notes the imv. of *qu'ālu* in the MA name *Ana-Aššur-qa-al-la* (*OMA*, II 149-50), but considers the meaning to be 'to pay attention to, be silent'. This latter meaning is possibly reflected in the imv. of *dmm* in Heb. names, although the root is not attested with any certainty (see above, §2.8.1). Similar, may be Akk. *qu''û* 'to wait for' (Stamm, 195; *OMA*, II 149), which is found referring to the deity, the 'word' of the deity, and the 'sign' of the deity as objects, as well as *puqqu*, the D theme of *paqû*, 'to pay attention to, to watch for'. *Puqqu* is found in Akk. names of the type *ᵈBēl-ú-pa-qu* (N./L. Bab.), translated by Stamm as 'Ich schaue harrend auf Bēl' (p. 195), and *Ú-pa-qa-ana-Ištar* 'I pay attention to Istar' (*AHw*, II 879: Tallqvist = 'to wait for' *APN*, 242a). Relevant here, too, is Akk. *dagālu pan* meaning 'to wait for' (cf. *CAD*, D 21). This meaning is preferable to Tallqvist's suggestion 'to obey' in the name *Dugul-pān-ili* (NA), translated by Tallqvist as 'Obey the will of god' (*APN*, 71a).

mēšeru 'justice, redress'. Although Heb. names contain only the verbal idea 'to judge' with the roots *dyn*, *pll* and *špṭ*, the concept of the deity contained in this idea is similar to *mēšeru*, depicting the deity as 'justice' in the MA name *Ilī-mi-še-ru* (*OMA*, II 137).

takālu 'to trust'; *tukultu* 'trust'. The idea of the deity as 'trust' in Heb. names is expressed only with the noun *mbṭḥ*. In Akk. names, the concept is expressed verbally with *takālu* 'to trust' (cf. *APN*, 311a; *OMA*, II 164), which occurs with the name-bearer as subject and the deity as object, as well as in names of the type *Ta-kil-a-na-ili-šu* 'Trusting in his god' (*APN*, 228b) and *Nabû-natkil* 'Trust in Nabû!' (*ibid.*, 156b). A nominal form, *tukultu* 'trust', is also attested (*APN*, 311a; *OMA*, II 164). This translation of the noun is perhaps preferable to that of 'strength' suggested by Tallqvist (cf. *AHw*, III 1304). For other uses of *takālu* which are not attested in Heb., see below, p. 260).

damqu 'good'; *dummuqu* 'good, favourable, fine'. In Heb. names, the deity is depicted as 'good' in the sense of 'pleasing', by the root *ṭwb* and perhaps more in the sense of 'kind', by the root *ḥsd*. The comparable semantic elements in Akk. are *ṭâbu* (see above, 1) and *damqu* (Stamm, 236). *Damqu*, however, is also attested in names which have no equivalent in Heb., as in *Arkāt*(EGIR^{at})*-ili-damqā* (M. Bab. and N. Bab.) 'To be (or to go) behind god is good' (cf. Stamm, 236), *Šá-ᵈNabû-damqā* (N. Bab.) '(The works) of Nabû are good' (*ibid.*), and *Damqi-ilišu* (O. Bab.), translated by Stamm as 'Der von seinem Gott gut Behandelte' (*ibid.*, 258). The adj. *dummuqu*, meaning 'good, favourable, fine', is also attested in theophoric names (cf. Stamm, 212, 220, 234).

damāqu D 'to show favour, be gracious; *gamālu* 'graciousness, kindness'; *gimillu* 'favour, act of kindness'; *naplusu* 'to look graciously upon'; *ḫinnu*, *silmu*, *guzu* 'grace'; *damiq* 'favour, kindness'. The D theme of *damāqu* in Akk. names suggests that the deity 'shows favour' or 'is gracious' (cf. Stamm, 212, 220, 234; *APN*, 38b, 154b, 279b = 'merciful, friendly'; *OMA*, II 114; *CAD*, D 63b), semantically comparable to the roots *ḥnn* 'to be gracious' and *ydh* 'to do good, be beneficent' (cf. Arab. *yadā*) in Heb. theophoric names, although a name such as *Nabû-dumiq-ilāni* 'Nabû is the most gracious of the gods' (*APN*, 148a = 'friendly') has no parallel in Heb. Similar to *damāqu* D is Akk. *gamālu* 'graciousness, kindness', which is usually attested in the sense of a plea to the deity for graciousness (cf. Stamm, 57, 84, 85, 91, 168, 190, 220). Also found is *gimillu*, meaning 'favour, act of kindness' (cf. *OMA*, II 122: *APN*, 80b = 'present') which also occurs in the name *Ma-ad-gi-mil-Ištar* (O. Bab.) 'Great is the favour of Ištar' (cf. Stamm, 234), and *damiq* 'favour, kindness' (*CAD*, D 63). Akk. *naplusu* (Stamm, 167, 190) is used in the same way as *damāqu* and *gamālu*. Comparable to the noun *ḥn* 'grace, favour' in Heb. names are Akk. *silmu*, and *ḫinnu* (see above, 1), while the element *gūzu* in the name *Itti-^{d}Bēl-gūzu* (N. Bab., Stamm, 231) may also mean 'grace'. Note, however, the meaning 'Geborgenheit' given to this element by von Soden (*AHw*, I 300), while *CAD*, G 147 considers the meaning uncertain.

balāṭu, *napištu* 'life'. The Heb. name-element *ḥyh* probably suggests that the deity 'gives life', similar to the use of *balāṭu* 'life' (Stamm, 188, 239; *APN*, 108b) and *napištu* 'life' (Stamm, 219) in Akk. names, which describe the deity as a source of life.

epēšu 'to do, permit, build'; *liptu* 'creation, craft'. In Akk. theophoric names, *epēšu* is used mainly in the sense 'to create'. In some names, the object of this divine creation is a child (cf. Stamm, 193, 197; *APN*, 149a), who is depicted as a 'work of' the deity. Akk. *liptu*, 'creation, craft', is used in the same way. These elements are comparable to the Heb. name-elements *br'* and *qnh* 'to create', *bnh* 'to build, create' and, even more directly, *'śh* 'to make, do' (also nominal in *ma'ăśēyāhû* 'Work of Y') and *p'l* 'to make'. The Št part. form *muštepiš* is met in MA names of the type *Muš-te-piš-ilī* with similar meaning (cf. *OMA*, II 117). Some Akk. names with *epēšu*, however, have no similarity in Heb., e.g. when the object of creation is 'justice' (cf. Stamm, 172), and when the names describe the deity as 'creator of the gods', as in Akk. ^{d}*Ea-epiš-ilī* (N./L. Bab., Stamm, 65). *Epēšu* is also met in names of the type *Ila-mi-na-a-ēpuš* (O. and M. Bab.) 'What have I done, god?' (cf. Stamm, 164), *Ilu-ip-pa-aš* 'The god will execute or permit it' (*APN*, 97b) and *Sin-dīni-epuš* 'Sin has permitted my cause' (*ibid.*, 199a), which are also not reflected in Heb. theophoric names.

qīštu, *qīšu* 'present, gift'; *rīmūtu* 'gift'. Akk. *qīštu*, *qīšu* (cf. *APN*, 304a, *OMA*, II 149) and *rīmūtu* (Stamm, 259) depict the child as a 'gift of' the deity, comparable to the nominal use of the Heb. root *ntn*: (see also the discussion on the name *zabdî'ēl* above, §2.9). A cognate root *qwš* with a meaning 'to give' may also be evident in Heb. names (cf. above, §2.9 *qûšāyāhû*).

paṭāru, *pašāru* 'to loosen'. Both Akk. *paṭāru* (*OMA*, II 146) and *pašāru* 'to loosen' (*APN*, 303a) may refer to the birth of the child. However, *pašāru* is also used in the N theme meaning 'to be appeased' (see below, p. 263), which may suggest for the element the sense of 'loosening' from sin or present difficulties, a thought not expressed in the Heb. onomasticon. The root *rmh* 'to loosen' (the womb?) in Heb. names may provide a parallel but is not attested with any certainty (see the discussion on difficulties with Hollow/III *hē* roots above, §2.5 *rmh*/*rwm*).

radā'u D 'to increase'; *eṣēpu* 'to double, multiply'. Heb. names depict that the deity has 'added' or 'increased' (the number of children in the family) with the root *ysp*. The same idea is portrayed with Akk. *radā'u* D (cf. *OMA*, II 150) and with *eṣēpu*, in the name *Ṣí-pa-am-i-lí* (O. Bab.) 'Give me increase, my god' (cf. Stamm, 148).

râbu 'to compensate, recompense'; *kašāru* 'to compensate'; *tarībum*, *rībatu*, *kutallu* 'replacement, compensation'; *târu* 'to turn'; *šanû* 'to do twice'; *šalāšu* 'to do three times'. Akk. names containing *râbu* 'to compensate' or 'recompense' (Stamm, 28, 289; *OMA*, II 152; *APN*, 306a = 'reward') probably refer to compensation for a previously deceased member of the family. *Râbu* also occurs in names which are pleas to the deity for compensation (Stamm, 287) and in the genitive to refer to the child as 'compensation of (i.e. from) the deity' (*ibid.*, 258; *APN*, 306a). Tallqvist (*ibid.*), however, preferred a meaning 'reward' for the element. Akk. *kašāru* also means 'to give compensation' (cf. *CAD*, K 285), but can also mean 'to succeed', or 'achieve'. Tallqvist recorded the element as meaning 'to bring good luck' (*APN*, 291a), while Stamm preferred 'to give success' (Stamm, 221). The idea 'to compensate', however, seems more usual in personal names (cf. *CAD*, *loc. cit.*). The child is also depicted as 'replacement' or 'compensation' with the Akk. nominal elements *tarībum* (*APN*, 306a), *rībatu* (*ibid.*) and possibly with *kutallu* (*OMA*, II 133 'retro, rovescio', cf. *CAD*, K 603 'replacement': but cf. also below, p. 259). Similar ideas in Heb. are expressed with the root *šlm*, which is used in names with the meaning 'to recompense', and perhaps with the Hiphil of the root *šwb*, suggesting the deity 'has caused to return' or 'has restored'. Also relevant in Akk. names is *târu* 'to turn' which, in the context of some theophoric names, may refer to the idea that the deity gives back a previously deceased child, or gives another child (Stamm, 85, 147, 148, 287, 290). It is also met in the name *I-túr-pi-ilim* 'For the second time god's word (has come true)' cf. Stamm, 147).

Names such as *Li-tir-pi-*[d]*Šamaš* (O. Bab.) 'May the word of Šamaš (come true) abundantly' (cf. Stamm, 148), *Tu-ra-am-ì-li* 'Turn to me again, my god' (*ibid.*, 146, 168, 190) and [f]*A-na-*[d]*Šamaš-te-ir-ri* (O. Bab.), which Stamm suggests means 'Erstatte dem Šamaš (das dir erwiesene Gute) zurück!' (*ibid.*, 205), however, have no parallel in Heb. Although Heb. theophoric names express the thought that the deity has 'returned', with the Qal of the root *šwb*, it is doubtful whether the Heb. root implies that the deity has at some time turned away from the name-giver, which Akk. names such as *Tu-ra-am-i-li* seem to suggest: (cf. also the root *pnh* in Heb. names, above, §2.4, and the root *sḥr*, above, §2.9 [*yh*]*wsḥ*[*r*]). Interesting, is the use of *târu* in the name [d]*Ninurta-mu-tir-gimilli*(ŠU) (M. Bab.) 'Ninurta is avenger' (cf. Stamm, 290). This seems to suggest that the deity is depicted as an avenger because it gives back a previously deceased child and so avenges its death. No Heb. name portrays the deity as an avenger, however. Two other Akk. elements are also relevant, *šanû* 'to do twice' (*ibid.*, 146), and *šalāšu* 'to do three times' (*ibid.*, 161). These Akk. elements refer to the giving of a second or third child, similar to the use of the root *ysp* 'to add' in Heb. names, but could also involve the idea of compensation for previously deceased children.

kaspu 'ransom'. Akk. *kaspu* normally means 'silver, money, payment' (cf. *CAD*, K 245), although Stamm interprets the element in names as 'ransom', referring to the child as a 'ransom of' the deity (cf. Stamm, 301f.). This latter idea is comparable to the Heb. name-elements *pdh* 'to ransom, redeem' and *g'l* 'to redeem', although these Heb. roots are attested only verbally.

amāru 'to see'; *dagālu* 'to look upon'. The root *'mr* in Heb. means 'to say', which is also its meaning in Aram., Phoen. and Arab. *Amāru* in Akk. reflects Ug. usage, with the meaning 'to see'. This concept is expressed in Heb. names with the roots *r'h* and *ḥzh* 'to see', *šwr* 'to behold, regard' and perhaps *s/śkh* 'to look out'. In Akk. names, *amāru* is used in a variety of ways, most of which have no semantic equivalents in Heb. (see below, pp. 261f.). Indirectly comparable to the Heb. idea that the deity 'sees' are perhaps only those names which are a plea that the deity will look upon the name-giver or name-bearer (Stamm, 167; *APN*, 268b), and the MA name *Aššur-a-mi-ri* 'Aššur sees me' (*OMA*, II 103). A plea that the deity will 'look upon' the name bearer or name-giver is also found in Akk. names with *dagālu* (*APN*, 278b; *OMA*, II 114). The same element also appears in the name *La-da-gil-ilu* (NA), which Tallqvist translated as 'The god does not deal falsely' (*APN*, 120a), but a meaning 'The god does not look' is perhaps preferable, since 'to deal falsely' does not seem to be attested for the root elsewhere (cf. *CAD*, D 21). This name would have no equivalent in Heb. as, also, the use of *dagālu* in admonitions (see below, p. 264).

andullu, *ḫutnu*, *ṣulūlu*, *kidinnu*, *utlu* 'protection'; *emēdu* 'to take cover, refuge' Š 'to give refuge'; *ḫātinu*, *ḫaṣānu*, *paqādu*, *naṣāru* 'to protect'. The idea of divine protection, expressed verbally, occurs in Heb. names only with the roots *zmr* (cf. S. Arab. *dhimr*), and possibly *ḥmh* (cf. S. Arab. *ḥamay*), although the latter root is uncertain (cf. above, §2.9 *ḥammû'ēl*). Akk. *andullu* (Stamm, 211), *ḫutnu* (*APN*, 286a), *ṣulūlu* (*OMA*, II 156: cf. also above 1), *kidinnu* (Stamm, 85, 235; cf. *APN*, 288a; *OMA*, II 130), and *utlu* (genitive; Stamm, 276) occur only nominally, meaning specifically 'protection'. Names with *emēdu* express that the deity gives refuge or protection (cf. Stamm, 199), but *emēdu* is also used in names of the type *A-na-ṣilli*(GE$_6^{li}$)-^{d}*Sin-ēmid*(UŠ) (M. Bab.) 'I took refuge in the shadow of Sin' (cf. Stamm, 199), which has no equivalent in Heb., and ^{d}*Nabû-šu-un-mi-dan-ni* (N/L. Bab.) 'Nabû grant me support' (Š theme imv. of *emēdu CAD*, E 145a; cf. Stamm, 178). The Akk. element *ḫātinu* 'to protect' is found only in the name ^{d}*Šamaš-ḫa-tin-enši* (N. Bab., Stamm, 240). Also relevant are Akk. *ḫaṣānu* 'to shelter' (*APN*, 285a, cf. *CAD*, *Ḫ* 129) and *paqādu* 'to take care of, protect' (*APN*, 302b). This last root, however, may have the meaning 'to entrust, deliver up' (cf. *AHw*, II 824), and may refer to the delivering up or entrusting of the child to the parents. Much more frequently used in Akk. names is *naṣāru* 'to protect', which occurs with a large number of objects or persons which the deity is asked to protect (cf. Stamm, 84, 85, 91, 180, 216; *APN*, 297-98; *OMA*, II 143). Names in which the imv. *uṣur* is evident, however, with the objects of the sentence names as the 'word', 'command' or 'order' etc. of the deity (cf. Stamm, 204), have no equivalent in Heb. names. This may also be said of the name *Ma-an-nu-um-me* (*-e*)*-šu-li-ṣur*, translated by Stamm as 'Wer soll jetzt seine (Gottes) Ordnungen hüten (p. 286).

šadû 'mountain'; *bābu* 'gate, door'; *dūru* 'wall, stronghold'; *igāriš* 'like a wall'; *puzru* 'safety'. Heb. names often portray the deity more figuratively as protection, by the use of such nouns as *hr* 'mountain', *šwr* 'wall' and *dlt* 'door'. Similar concepts are present in Akk. names: *šadû* is used to describe the deity as a 'mountain' (Stamm, 85, 211, 226; *APN*, 307b; *OMA*, II 157), and *bābu* as a 'gate', 'door' (*APN*, 274a). In Heb., the element *šdy* is used as a theophoric element in names such as *šedê'ûr* ('Shadday is flame, light'), *'ammîšaddāy*, and *ṣûrîšadday*. See also, the discussion of the element by J. Hoftijzer, G. Van der Kooij (editors) *Aramaic Texts from Deir 'Alla*, Leiden: E.J. Brill (1976), 275f. and references. *Dūru*, meaning 'wall, stronghold', is attested frequently (cf. Stamm, 211; *APN*, 279a) and, in addition, is used to depict the deity as a 'stronghold for the weak' (*APN*, 184b), 'the frail' (*ibid.*), 'lamenting' (*ibid.*), and for 'the settlement' (*ibid.*) It also occurs in the name ^{d}*Šamaš-du-ur-a-li*[*šu*] (O. Bab.) 'Šamaš is the wall of his city' (cf. Stamm, 227). Cf. also *OMA*, II 116 for the element in MA names, as well as for the description of the deity as 'like a wall' with *igāriš* (*OMA*, II 124). Less figurative is the use of *puzru* 'safety' in the name *Puzur-Akšak* (O. Bab., Stamm, 84), in which the deity may be represented by the city Akšak.

imdu/*imittu* 'support'. Heb. names describe the deity as support with the roots *smk*, *'mn*, *'šh* 'to support', *kwl* (Pilpel) 'to support, nourish', and perhaps *yšh* (cf. Arab. *'asa'* and above, §2.9 *yôšawyāh*). In Akk. theophoric names a cognate of the root *kwl* is also used in the D theme, meaning 'to support' (see above, 1), as well as the nominal elements *imdu/imittu* 'support' from the root *emēdu* (*APN*, 268a; *OMA*, II 125; Stamm, 211).

epēru 'to provide for'; *ašāru* 'to provide for, take care of'; *zāninu* 'provider'; *kaṣāru* 'to preserve'; *šalāmu* 'to keep safe, preserve'; *ḫâṭu* 'to watch over, take care of'; *šaṭāpu* 'to preserve life'. In Heb. names, the concept that the deity preserves is attested in the root *šmr*, and a similar idea that the deity nourishes, in the roots *'zh* (cf. Arab. *ghadhā*) and *qwt* (cf. Arab. *qāta*). Akk. names express equivalent ideas with *epēru* 'to provide for' (Stamm, 54, 189, 213, 222; *APN*, 270b; *OMA*, II 117), *ašāru* 'to provide for, take care of' (Stamm, 181), *zāninu* 'provider' (*ibid.*, 213), and *kaṣāru* 'to preserve' (*APN*, 290b), which is also found with the objects 'a wall' and 'a name' (*ibid.*, 151b). *Kaṣāru* normally means 'to tie, bind together, collect, organise, gather', and D 'to assemble' (*CAD*, K 257). However, the accusative elements in the names suggest that Tallqvist's interpretation 'to preserve' is perhaps preferable since no other meaning seems appropriate: (see also below, p. 258). Also attested in Akk. are *šalāmu* D 'to keep safe, preserve' (*APN*, 308a; *OMA*, II 157-58), which also occurs with the objects a 'brother', 'son', 'king' or 'father', *šaṭāpu* 'to preserve life' (Stamm, 207) and *ḫâṭu* 'to watch over, take care of', which is found in the name *Ì-lí-ḫi-ṭa/ṭá-an-ni* (O. Bab.) 'Watch over me my god' (*CAD*, Ḫ 159b; Stamm, 167).

asû, *ašâtu* 'physician, healer'. Akk. *asû* and *ašâtu* are used to depict the deity nominally as a 'physician, healer' (Stamm, 216, 223; *APN*, 270a; *OMA*, II 106). Heb. names reflect the idea only verbally with *rp'*, stating that the deity 'has healed'.

eṭēru, *gamālu*, *ḥws* 'to save, spare'. The idea 'to save' is one expressed widely in Heb. theophoric names, with the roots *yš'*, *mlṭ*, *nṣl*, *plṭ* and Aram. *šêzêb* (cognate with Akk. *šūzubu*, see above, 1) 'to deliver', *ḥml* 'to spare', possibly *ḥlṣ* 'to draw off' (i.e. rescue?) and *dlh* 'to draw' (rescue). Both *yš'* and *plṭ* are used nominally in Heb. names to describe the deity as 'deliverance'. Similar in thought are Akk. *eṭēru* 'to save' (Stamm, 170, 191; *APN*, 266a; *OMA*, II 119) and *gamālu* 'to save, spare' (*APN*, 277-78). *Eṭēru* also occurs nominally in the name *^{d}NN-bēl-eṭēri* (N./L. Bab.), in which the deity is portrayed as the 'lord of rescue', but such a name has no direct parallel in Heb. Tallqvist also cited a root *ḥws* with the meaning 'to spare' (*APN*, 283b).

danānu, *patānu* 'to strengthen'; *taqānu* D 'to order, strengthen'; *kiṣru* 'strengthened'. The idea that the deity strengthens is evident in Heb. names with the roots *ḥzh* and possibly *mrr* 'to strengthen', bless, commend' (cf. Ug.). Akk. names express the equivalent idea with *danānu* 'to strengthen', in names such as *Ašur-mātka-danin* 'O Ašur, strengthen your country' (*APN*,

280a, 41b), although Heb. names have no direct object. Also attested in Akk. names are *patānu* 'to strengthen' (Stamm, 178; *AHw*, II 847 although Tallqvist preferred a meaning 'to protect' in the name *Ašur-pa-tin-um* [*APN*, 303a]), which mostly occurs with a direct object, and *taqānu* D 'to order, strengthen', found in the latter sense in the name *Adad-bēl-taqqin* 'O Adad, make the lord firm!' (*APN*, 7b). The pass. verbal adj. *kiṣru* 'strengthened' is evident in Akk. names such as *Ki-ṣir-*^{d}*Bēl*, -^{d}*Nabû* (NA and N. Bab., Stamm, 321) and *Ki-ṣir-Aššur* (Stamm, 321; *OMA*, II 132), while the element is verbal in the name ^{d}*Šamaš-ik-ṣur* (Stamm, 258).

nārāu, rēṣu, tillatu, usātu, kitru, ḫamātu 'help'. Heb. names depict that the deity 'has helped', with the roots *'wš*, *'zr* and probably *'dr*, and nominally as 'help', with the noun *'zr*. Comparable in Akk. names are the nominal elements *nārāru* (Stamm, 212, 212 n. 4, 367; *APN*, 298a; *OMA*, II 144), *rēṣu*/ *reṣūtu* 'help' (Stamm, 212; *APN*, 305b; *OMA*, II 151, also attested verbally), *tillatu* (Stamm, 212), *usātu* (Stamm, 212; *OMA*, II 168), *kitru* (Stamm, 212: or 'ally', cf. below, p. 257), and *ḫamātu* 'help', rescue' (*APN*, 284a). Although Tallqvist recorded this last root as meaning 'refuge', the idea 'help, rescue' is better attested (cf. *CAD*, Ḫ 61).

ṣabātu 'to seize'. *Ṣabātu* 'to seize' often occurs in Akk. names with the object 'hand' (*qāta*) (Stamm, 171, 221; Cf. *APN*, 303a and *CAD*, Ṣ 5), indicating figuratively that the deity has helped or saved, similar to Heb. names with the root *'ḥz* 'to seize'. The MA names *Aššur-šuma-aṣ-bat* and *Ina-Aššur-šuma-aṣbat* (*OMA*, II 154) and *Šepa-Ašur-aṣbat* 'I seize the feet of Aššur' (cf. *APN*, 220a), however, have no comparable thought in Heb.

mêšu 'to forgive' (cf. Stamm, 170). Akk. use of *mêšu* in theophoric names is with the direct object 'sins'. The Heb. name-element *nšh* denotes the similar idea that the deity 'forgets', probably implying the same object.

nasḫuru 'to turn, turn around'; *târu* 'to turn'; *tu'āru* 'to return'. Akk. *saḫāru* N normally means 'to turn, turn around', also 'to search for, dwell' (cf. *AHw*, II 1005). In names, the element probably means 'to turn to (in mercy)', as indicated by Tallqvist in his translation of the name *Na-as-ḫir-Bēl* (*APN*, 299a: cf., however, the meaning 'benevolent attention' *CAD*, N 2 25b). The root may be cognate with *sḥr* in the uncertain Heb. name [*yh*]*wsḥ*[*r*] (see above, §2.9). Also uncertain in Heb. names are the roots *pnh* 'to turn' (*ibid.*, §2.4) and *swr* 'to turn aside' (*ibid.*, §2.9 *sryh*). *Nasḫuru* also occurs in MA names in the imv. and vent. as a plea that the deity will turn towards the parent (cf. *OMA*, II 142), while *târu* is also found in the imv. and vent. in the MA names *Adad-tu-ra* and *Ištar-tu-*[*ra*]? (*OMA*, II 165), as well as *tu'āru* 'to return' (*ibid.*).

rēma rašu 'to show pity'; *rêmu* 'to pity'; *rēmēnû, tayāru* 'merciful'; *rīmu* 'mercy, grace'. The Babylonian and Assyrian deities were depicted as merciful in Akk. names such as *Ili*(AN.MU)-*rišâ* (TUK[a])-*ri-ma* (M. Bab.) 'My god, look on me with pity' (cf. Stamm, 167). Similar, are Akk. names with *rêmu* 'to have pity on' (*ibid.*, 149, 167, 190; *APN*, 305a-b; *OMA*, II 151), *rēmēnû* 'merciful' (Stamm, 220), *tayāru* 'merciful' (*APN*, 32b, 107b, cf. Stamm, 220 = 'versöhnlich'), and *rīmu* 'mercy, grace' in *Nabû-šakin-rēmu* 'Nabû provides mercy' (*APN*, 158a). The comparable thought is expressed in Heb. names with *rḥm* 'to show compassion' and perhaps with *nḥm* 'to comfort'.

râmu 'to love'; *narāmu*, *tarāmu* 'beloved, favourite'. Akk. *râmu* 'to love; is usually attested with a direct object viz. 'the living being', 'the people', 'the seed', 'the king', 'the faithful', 'the just', 'living descendants', and 'the city of Ur' (*APN*, 305a; *OMA*, II 150; Stamm, 218, 221, 227, 239). The genitive forms *narāmu* (Stamm, 263; *OMA*, II 142) and *tarāmu* (Stamm, 84-85) 'beloved, favourite of' the deity, are also attested. In Heb. names, the idea 'to love', expressed verbally, is found in the root *dwd*, while the idea 'beloved of' is attested in nouns from the roots *dwd* and *ydd*.

tappû 'companion'. *Tappû* is used in Akk. names to depict a relationship of friendship between deity and man (cf. *APN* 311b; *OMA* II 164; Stamm, 84), comparable to Heb. names which describe the name-bearer as a 'friend of' the deity, with the element *r'*.

amru. This element is attested in the MA names *Am-ru-Adad/Aššur/Šerū'a*, and is interpreted by Saporetti as 'seen, considered' (genitive, viz. 'guardato, visto' *OMA*, II 103) but probably means 'checked, accounted for' or more semantically suitable, 'selected' (cf. *CAD* A 2 78). This idea of a child being selected by the deity may be reflected in Heb. names from the roots *'ṣl* 'to reserve, lay aside' and *ḥṣh* 'to divide', although the specific statement that the deity has 'selected' is not evident among Heb. names.

marāṣu 'to suffer, be angry' (Stamm, 166). *Marāṣu* is found in Akk. names of the type *Lim-ra-aṣ-lib-bi-ili* (NA) 'May god become angry'. In this case, it would perhaps be similar to the root *ḥrh* 'to burn', be kindled (of anger)' which may occur in the Heb. name *ḥarḥăyāh*/*ḥarhăyāh* (see above, §2.9).

awīlu 'man' (Stamm, 263). This element is used in the genitive to describe the name-bearer as a 'Man of' the deity. Comparable names in Heb. contain the nouns *'yš*, *mt*, and perhaps *gbr*.

(*w*)*ardu* 'servant'. Both Akk. and Heb. theophoric names depict the name-bearer as a 'servant of' the respective deities. In Akk. this is done with the element (*w*)*ardu* (Stamm, 262; *APN*, 281a; *OMA*, II 167), in Heb. with the noun *'bd*.

būru/*bīru* 'calf' (*APN*, 274a). The idea of the child as a 'calf of' the deity is found in Akk. names with the element *būru*/*bīru*, comparable to the Heb. name *'glyw* (inscr. SO 41.1).

upnu 'palm'; *īnu* 'eye'; *uznu* 'attention'. Although Akk. *upnu* 'palm' (Stamm, 196) has no semantic equivalent in Heb. theophoric names, the name-type *A-na-^{d}Nabû-ú-p*[*i*]*-ni-ya* (N./L. Bab.) 'Towards Nabû is my palm (opened)' is similar to the Heb. names *'ely(^{e}h)ô'ênay* 'Unto Y are my eyes (directed)'. Similar also is the Akk. use of *īnu* 'eye' in the name-type *Itti-^{d}Nusku-īnā-ya* (N./L. Bab.) 'My eyes are on Nusku' (cf. Stamm, 230). *Īnu*, however, is also met in names of the type *^{d}NN-īnāya* 'God NN is my eye' (*ibid.*, 212), and names which refer to the deity as the 'eye of the land' and the 'eye of the state' (*ibid.*, 227): such names are not reflected in Heb. (see also below, p. 258). Also relevant is perhaps Akk. *uznu* 'attention' (Stamm, 196) in names such as *Ibašši*(GÁL^{ši})*-uz-ni-a-na-ili*(AN) 'My attention is directed on god'.

zittu 'face' (Stamm, 371). Akk. names containing this element, meaning 'face of' the deity, are paralleled in Heb. names by the noun *pnh* with the same meaning. Note, however, the interpretation of *zittu* given by *CAD*, Z 139, as 'share of an inheritance', which may be similar to the use of the noun *ḥlq* 'portion' in Heb. theophoric names.

bunna 'thank'; *dalālu*, *nâdu*, *šitammuru* 'to praise'; *mu'û* 'to praise, adore'. The thought expressed in the Akk. names *Bu-un-na-iliya*(AN.MU)*-ab-luṭ*, *-abluṭ*TI^{uṭ}) (M. Bab.) 'Thanks to my god, I recovered' (cf. Stamm, 188) is similar to the Heb. name *hôdawyāh*/*hôdaywāhû*, from the root *ydh* meaning 'Praise or thank Y', although unlike the Akk. name, the Heb. does not indicate the reason for the thanks. The meaning of the Akk. element, however, is uncertain (cf. *CAD*, B 317). Similar in Akk. are names with *dalālu* (Stamm, 202), *nâdu* (*ibid.*, 202, 204, 224), and *šitammuru* (*ibid.*, 202), meaning 'to praise', and *mu'û* 'to praise, adore' (*CAD*, M 2 321; *OMA*, II 138), the object of the praise being the deity as in the Heb. name *hôdawyāh*/*hôdaywāhû*.

4. A large number of Akkadian name-elements remain, containing ideas about the Akkadian deities which were not characteristic of the Hebrew God as far as the evidence from personal names is concerned. These ideas are as follows.

One of the most outstanding differences is the total lack in Heb. names of any connection between the Israelite God and a female consort, or even between the Israelite God and a female child. There is no Heb. equivalent, therefore, to the Akk. nominal elements *šarratu* 'queen' (Stamm, 223, 229; *APN*, 310a), *ummu* 'mother' (Stamm, 83, 209; *APN*, 268b; *OMA*, II 167), *bēltu* 'lady' (Stamm, 227; *OMA*, II 110), and *etellūtu* 'lady' (*APN*, 273a). Genitive elements depicting a female child in relationship to the deity, in Akk. *mārat* 'daughter' (Stamm, 260), *amtu* 'female servant, slave' (*ibid.*,

262; *APN*, 268a; *OMA*, II 103), and *šāt* 'she' (Stamm, 263) also have no equivalent in Heb.

Heb. bears no trace of a name which suggests that the owner was a priestess, a practice illustrated in the use of Akk. *erēšu*, which occurs in the genitive 'request of' the deity (*ibid.*, 125) and in names such as *ᶠDan-erēssa* (O. Bab.) 'Strong is her (the goddess's) claim' (cf. Stamm, 125).[99] Akk. *šeriktu*, *šerku* suggests that the female child was 'given to' or a 'gift' to the deity (Stamm, 259). Similar dedication of a male child may be implied in the Akk. phrase *īna našû* suggesting divine 'desire' or 'demand' (*ibid.*, 125), the G. part. of *rašā'u* 'to have, receive, acquire' (*OMA*, II 151), but more obviously in Akk. *šangû* 'priest' (*APN*, 309a).

Many attributes given to Akk. deities are found to be absent among Heb. names. This is the case with Akk. *apkallu* 'wise man' (Stamm, 226-27; cf. *APN*, 264a; *CAD*, A 2 171), *nēmuqu* 'wisdom' (*OMA*, II 144), *emqu* (*ibid.* 117), *ḫāsisu* (Stamm, 220), and *mūdû* 'wise' (*ibid.*, 225), *kēnu* 'true, truth' (*APN*, 288b; *OMA*, II 129), *etellu* 'princely' (used of the word of Marduk, Stamm, 232), *muštālu* 'well-considered' (*ibid.*, 225; or 'judicious, thoughtful, full of concern' cf. *CAD*, M 1 283), *(w)aqru* 'precious, beloved' (Stamm, 229; *APN*, 281a[100]), *ašaridu* 'first' (often in the sense of 'the most predominant of the gods', Stamm, 225, 226; *APN*, 272b; *OMA*, II 120), *(w)atru* 'pre-eminent, rich' (used of the word of Šamaš, Stamm, 232), and *dārū* 'everlasting' (*APN*, 278a). Akk. *gabbu* (*-ile'i*) describes the deities as 'totality, almighty' (*ibid.*, 277a; cf. *OMA*, II 120), and similar is *il naphāri* 'god of totality' (*APN*, 301b).

Absent among Heb. names is the idea of the deity as a building, unlike Akk. *bītu* 'temple' (used instead of a divine name, Stamm, 91) and *ekallu* 'palace' (*ibid.*, 211; *OMA*, II 116). Also not attested in Heb. are names which describe the deity as a 'family' or member of the family, perhaps indicating compensation for a deceased person, as in Akk. *ellatu* 'family, clan' (Stamm, 299), *kimtu* 'family' (*ibid.*, 277), and *qinnu* 'nest, family' (*ibid.*, 231). Perhaps in the same context may be added *mūtu* 'spouse'[101] (*ibid.*, 298), *talīmu* 'favourite brother' (*ibid.*, 102), and *ḫālu* 'maternal uncle' (*OMA*, II 122).

Absent in Heb. are names which describe the deity as an animal, unlike Akk. *rīmu*/*rīmtu* 'wild bull/cow' (Stamm, 83, 226), *būru*, 'calf' (*OMA*, II 112; also genitive, see above, 3), *yālu* 'mountain goat' (*APN*, 286b), *barḫu* 'he goat' (*ibid.*, 276a; cf. *CAD*, B 110, where the element is uncertain), and *lab'u* 'lion' (*OMA*, II 112). Other Akk.

elements not attested in Heb. are *kitru* 'ally' (*APN*, 291b), *lamassu* 'guardian angel' (Stamm, 210, 308; *APN*, 293a), *bāštu* 'angel'[102] (Stamm, 210, 226, 308), *qurādu*/*qarradu* 'hero' (Stamm, 225, 226; *OMA*, II 148; cf. *APN*, 304b[103]), *dipāru* 'torch' (Stamm, 212; *APN*, 286a = *ṭipāru*), *šamšu* 'sun' (Stamm, 212; *APN*, 308b; *OMA*, II 159), *uqnu* 'lapislazuli' (*APN*, 266b), *qarnu* 'horn' (i.e. 'strength, power', Stamm, 212; *OMA*, II 148), *libbu* 'heart' (*OMA*, II 134), and *gugallu* 'irrigation official' (*OMA*, II 122; *CAD*, G 121).

Akk. names often contain additional elements which modify the sense within the name to provide a further contrast with Heb. names. Thus Heb. has no equivalent to the Akk. name-elements *šarḫu* 'magnificent', in the sense of 'the most magnificent of the gods' (Stamm, 226), *kuzbu* 'luxuriance, abundance, attractiveness',[104] *elû* 'to be high, exalted', where the object is the 'claim', 'demand' or 'throne' of the deity (*ibid.*, 187, 234), *banû* 'good, excellent',[105] which is used to describe certain attributes of the deities rather than the deities themselves (*ibid.*, 65, 236), and *arāku* 'to be long, last long' in names such as *Arik-dēn-ilu* 'Long is the judgment of god' (*APN*, 29b; *OMA*, II 105; cf. Stamm, 237). Also with no equivalent in Heb. are the Akk. elements *edēšu*, which Stamm suggests means 'in neuem Glanze erstrahlen' (Stamm, 62), and *muttabbilu*, a Gtn form of *'bl*, probably meaning 'active' (*CAD*, M 2 302; *OMA*, II 138; cf. Stamm, 213-14, 223).

Although Heb. names suggest that the deity *causes* man to rejoice, there is no indication that the deity himself was thought to rejoice. This latter idea is evident in Akk. *rêšu* (Stamm, 186; *OMA*, II 152: also nominal *rēštu*/*rēšu* 'joy'),[106] and *ṣâḫu* 'to laugh' (Stamm, 80, 85). Akk. *ḫadû* 'to be pleased', occurs in *Ḫa-di-a-me-ir-^{d}Šamaš* (N./L. Bab.) 'He was happy to see the sun' (*CAD* Ḫ 21a; cf. Stamm, 185), a name again not reflected in Heb.

Attested in Heb, and Akk. are names which state that the deity is 'King' or Lord' (see above, 1 and 3). Akk. *šarru* 'king' is more frequently used in the genitive, however, and describes the deity as 'king of justice' (Stamm, 221), 'king of the gods' etc. (*ibid.*, 226 cf. 227; *APN*, 309-10; *OMA*, II 160-61). Akk. *bēlu* 'lord' is also better attested in genitive type names which depict the deity as the 'lord of descendants', of 'people', 'well-being', 'justice' etc. (cf. Stamm, 212, 217, 218, 221, 223, 228; *APN*, 273b; *OMA*, II 110). The Akk. use of an additional element in these names tends to confine the power of the deities to certain contexts. Relevant also is Akk. *etellu* 'lord, prince', used to portray the deity as 'lord of heaven and earth' (*APN*, 273a; *OMA*, II 119).

Also with no semantic equivalent in Heb. are Akk. names containing *qātu* 'hand' (Stamm, 183, 231), symbolic of the power of the deity, *pû* 'mouth, word' (*APN*, 301; *OMA*, II 147) in names such as *Kīn-pi-Šamaš* 'True is the word of Šamaš' (cf. *APN*, 115b), *īnu* 'eye' (*APN*, 266a) in *E-ni-ilu* 'Eye of the god' (*ibid.*, 74a), and *šēpu* 'feet' in the MA name GÌR-*Adad* (*OMA*, II 161; see also above, 2). Remaining are four genitive elements in which the *nomen regens* refers to the deity: these are *palû* 'reign' in names such as *Ṭāb*(DUG.GA)-*pa-la-*[d]*Šamaš* (N./L. Bab.) 'Good is the reign of Šamaš' (cf. Stamm, 236), *inbu* 'fruit' in [fd]*Taš-me-tum-i-ni-iḫ-i-la-ti*[*m*] (O. Bab.) 'Tašmētu is the fruit of the goddesses' (*ibid.*, 226; cf. also *APN*, 269a), *šulmānu* 'gift' in the MA name *Šùl-ma-nu-Adad* (*OMA*, II 162), and *muštašimu*, which may be derived from *tašīmtu* 'careful reflection' (Stamm, 322). None of these concepts has any semantic equivalent in Heb.

Akk. names contain many genitive types in which the *nomen regens* represents the name-bearer. Markworthy are numerous names, totally absent in Heb., which refer to the name-bearer as a child or offspring etc. of the deity. This idea is attested in the elements *aplu* 'inheritance, heir, son' (Stamm, 260; *APN*, 270b; *OMA*, II 104), *māru* 'son'[107] (Stamm, 38; *APN*, 134b; *OMA*, II 136), *pir'u* 'offspring' (Stamm, 221, 260), *lāḫu* 'offspring' (*APN*, 292b), *ṣeḫru* 'child' (Stamm, 260-61), *waldu* 'child' (*ibid.*, 261; see also *ridū* above, 2), *urkattu* 'late-child/fruit' (*OMA*, II 167; cf. Stamm, 49, 158), *zārūt* 'begotten' (*APN*, 282b), *zēru* 'seed' (*APN*, 282b; *OMA*, II 169 acc.), *inbu* 'fruit' (Stamm, 260), and *šū* 'he' in *Šù-A-šur* (*ibid.*, 263). Other Akk. genitive elements referring to the name-bearer which have no semantic equivalent in Heb. are *nēmelu* 'prize' (*ibid.*, 262), *tanattum*/*tanittum* 'prize' (*ibid.*, 277), *ubāru* 'guest, stranger' (*ibid.*, 264), *migru* 'favourite' in *Migrat-*[d]*Sin* (O. Bab., *ibid.*, 274-75),[108] and *rāmu* 'grace' (*APN*, 186a; *OMA*, II 167).

Many names in Heb. and Akk. were concerned with the events of the birth: the following ideas, however, are peculiar to Akk. names. *Adannu* '(appointed) time' (Stamm, 147) and *sanāqu* 'punctual' (*ibid.*, 233) probably suggest that the deity has fulfilled a promise of a child. In the same context are Akk. *qabû* 'to say, promise, order' (*ibid.*, 147, 206), *kaṣāru* perhaps 'to firmly ordain' (cf. Stamm, 188),[109] *magāru* 'to approve, grant' (*OMA*, II 135; *CAD*, M 1 34ff.), *nabû* 'to name, call' (Stamm, 142; also genitive Stamm, 258; *APN*, 160b), *zākiru/zakāru* 'to name' (Stamm, 84, 85, 142, 215, 218; also genitive Stamm, 257), *(w)abālu* 'to bring' (*ibid.*, 140, 182), *abāku* 'to send' (*OMA*, II 98),[110] *(w)alādu* 'to beget' (Stamm, 140; *OMA*, II 166), also nominal *mu'allidu* 'begetter' (*APN*, 68b), *šapāku* (*zēr*) 'to pour out (seed)' (Stamm, 218; *APN*, 309a), and *aṣû* 'to come out' (*APN*, 281a; also causative 'to bring forth', *APN*, 154b).[111] These Akk. name-elements occur with the child as the object, suggesting that the birth has been brought about by the deity. Similar in thought is the use of Akk. *ša'āmu* 'to purchase', suggesting that the parents have purchased a child from the deity (presumably through pious behaviour) (*OMA*, II 156-57).[112] Also peculiar to Akk. names are those which suggest an exclamation uttered at the time of birth, as in *ennam/ennum* 'lo! behold!' (Stamm, 133), perhaps, similarly, *išû* 'to have' (*ibid.*, 131; *APN*, 287b; *OMA*, II 126),[113] and *kašādu* 'to be there' (Stamm, 132; *OMA*, II 128).[114]

Many Heb. and Akk. names involve the idea of the deity as protection, either directly or figuratively (see above, 3 *andulla* etc.). In the latter context are Akk. *būdu* (Stamm, 231) and *kutallu* (*ibid.*, 231 n. 1) meaning 'back',[115] *itû* 'boundary' (*ibid.*, 212), *kibru* 'shore' (*ibid.*, 212, 322), *birtu* 'fortress' (*OMA*, II 111), and *šummannu* 'rope' (Stamm, 322), this last element perhaps suggesting figuratively that the deity guides or directs. Such figurative expressions are without equivalent in Heb. names.

Other Akk. names indicate that there are aspects of divine activity not expressed in Heb. names. This is the case with Akk. *paḫāru* 'to unite, assemble, gather' (*ibid.*, 287, 290; *OMA*, II 145; *APN*, 301b[116]), probably referring to the uniting of the family by the deity, *re'û* 'to pasture' (Stamm, 189), *rē'û* 'shepherd' (Stamm, 214, 223; *APN*, 305a; *OMA*, II 152), *utullu* 'shepherd'[117] (Stamm, 293), and *šabā'u* D 'to satisfy' (*OMA*, II 157). Although Heb. names state that the deity 'has loved', the Akk. element *menû* 'to love, become fond of' is used differently in the names *ᵈSin-im-na-an-ni* (O. Bab.) 'Sin has become fond of me' (*CAD*, M 2 19b; cf. Stamm, 192) and *ᵈNa-bi-um-pa-li-iḫ-šu-i-ma-an-ni* (O. Bab.) 'Nabû loves him who fears him' (cf. Stamm, 193).

Some Akk. elements contain the idea that the deity brings circumstances into order, 'sets right' or intercedes in some way for man. This is evident in Akk. *dabābu* 'to speak' (*ibid.*, 212) in the M. Bab. name *ᵈŠamaš-dābibi*, *tarāṣu* 'to set right' (*ibid.*, 178), *tuqqunu* 'to bring in order' (*ibid.*, 177; *APN*, 312a; *OMA*, II 164), and *mušteširu*, probably also 'to bring in order' (Stamm, 224-25). These ideas are without equivalent in Heb. names. This is also the case with Akk. names suggesting that the deity acts as an adviser, with *malāku* 'to advise' (*ibid.*, 145, 166), also *maliku* 'adviser, counsellor' (*ibid.*, 145, 166, 215-16, 223; *APN*, 294a; *OMA*, II 135), *milku* 'counsel, advice, order, decision' (Stamm, 230; *APN* 294a), and *tamlaku* 'adviser' (Stamm, 226). Similar are *ṭēmu* 'decision' (*ibid.*, 231), *apālu* 'to intercede for, answer' (*ibid.*, 171),[118] and *izuzzum* 'to stand, stand beside' (*ibid.*, 171, 178, 193).

Heb. names often involve the idea that the deity cares for and helps man in various ways. Absent in Heb., however, is any thought that the deity causes man to prosper, as in Akk. *ešēru* 'to prosper, thrive', (*ibid.*, 101, 179; *APN*, 287b; *OMA*, II 118, 119), *naḫašu* 'to prosper' (Stamm, 240), *kāširu* 'success' (*ibid.*, 221, 222), *ḫanābu* D (*OMA*, II 123) and *šamāḫu* D 'to cause to thrive, prosper', and *šarā'u* D 'to make rich' (*ibid.*, 160).

Some Akk. names suggest a time of need or anxiety on the part of the parent. Heb. theophoric names contain no suggestion of a cry to the deity, unlike Akk. names with *šašu* 'to call to' (Stamm, 77, 200, 318-19), *še'û* 'to search for' (*ibid.*, 200), *šutēmuqu* (*ibid.*, 203), and *panû* (*ibid.*, 201) 'to turn to'. In these names, the deity is the object of the sentence name. Similar, too, is the Akk. use of *takālu* 'to trust' (*ibid.*, 196, 199, 205, 258).[119]

Many Akk. names represent pleas to the deity by the parents, who ask for help in time of distress or whose requests are pertinent to the future life of a child. Akk. *balāṭu* 'to be healthy' can be used as a plea for the health of the name-bearer (*ibid.*, 154, 177; *APN*, 8lb, 209b), but is also used more generally to suggest that the deity is a source of health (Stamm, 187), as well as in the D theme *bulluṭu*, meaning 'to keep alive' (*APN*, 7a, 11b, 41b, 95b; *OMA* II 107). A nominal form, *bulṭu* 'health', occurs in names of the type *Ina-qāt-*^{d}*Nabû-bul-ṭu* 'Health is in the hand of Nabû' (cf. Stamm, 231). Pleas for health are also found in Akk. *bu'āru* 'to be healthy' (*OMA*, II 111-12), and for safety in Akk. *šalmu* (Stamm, 176), which is also used more generally to describe the deity as a source of safety (*ibid.*, 85, 120, 187, 219, 240). None of these names has any parallel in Heb. name-giving.

Similar, also, are pleas for the recovery of a child, in names with Akk. *napāšu* 'to breathe, be wide' (*ibid.*, 172).[120] From this root is attested the noun *nipšu* 'breath', in *Ṭāb-nipšu* (N./L. Bab.) 'Pleasant is the breath (of god)' (cf. Stamm, 370 and *CAD*, N 2 248b, 'Pleasant is the mention of him'). A request that the child will be perfect is evident in Akk. names with *šuklulu* (Stamm, 156), while the presence of *bâru* in names may imply a plea that the child will be 'bright', although a meaning 'to establish' is also possible (cf. *CAD*, B 125).

Akk. *kânu* 'to establish' (or 'to be firm') is used in pleas for the establishment of the child, progeny, or the 'word' of the deity (Stamm, 146, 150 n. 3; *APN*, 81b). A part. form in the name *Mukīn-šarrūte-ilu*, translated by Tallqvist as 'Establisher of the kingship is the god' (cf. *APN*, 139b), also has no parallel in Heb. names, as also the name *Gula-zāri-li-kun*, translated by Tallqvist as 'O Gula, may the begetter stand fast' (*ibid.*, 81b, or cf. *CAD*, K 161b 'O Gula, may my progeny last'. Representing pleas in the time of distress are Akk. names with *zaqāpu* 'to lift up' (Stamm, 177; *OMA*, II 168), *našû* 'to lift up' (*APN*, 298a; *OMA*, II 143-44), and *kullu* 'to hold' (Stamm, 171, 191). Pleas to the deity that the lord of the slave will live long are found in Akk. names with *dārû* 'to be everlasting, eternal' (*ibid.*, 311), and that the child will live long with *labāru* (*ibid.*, 158; *APN*, 292a-b).

Also without equivalent in Heb. are those Akk. names requesting that the deity will answer a prayer, evident in names with *maḫāru* 'to receive, accept'[121] (Stamm, 167), as well as a request for understanding, with *lamādu* 'to understand' (*ibid.*, 166), and for wealth, with Akk. *šušru* 'to be rich' (*ibid.*, 179). Heb. also has no equivalent to the Akk. names *ᵈBēl-*, *ᵈNabû-ana-mēreḫ(ē)tum* (N./L. Bab.), which may well be sff. perhaps meaning 'Show the insolent how the pious are rewarded' or similar (cf. Stamm, 83, 180).

Widely attested in Akk. names is *amāru* 'to see', which is mainly used with an accusative element, often in requests that the name-bearer or parent should 'see' (experience) divine grace, well-being, justice etc. (*ibid.*, 168, 172). It is also found in names which express that the name-bearer or parent 'sees' various aspects of the divine character, such as 'divinity', 'godliness', 'power', 'might' etc. (*ibid.*, 183-84; *APN*, 46a), the deity itself (Stamm, 183), or the 'faces' of the deities (*ibid.*, 203). *Amāru* is also attested in the name *Innammar-dīn-ili* (MA) 'The god's decision is made clear' (*CAD*, A 2 25b; cf. Stamm, 197). An imv. representing a plea to the deity to look upon the name-bearer or parent, is also evident (Stamm, 167; *OMA*, II 103: for semantic equivalents in Heb., see above, §2.8.2). Similar may be the use of *naṭālu* 'to look at, see', in names of the type *Ì-lí-li-*

ṭul (O. Bab.), suggested by Stamm to mean 'Mein Gott möge ein Einsehen haben (= möge dies nicht dulden)' (Stamm, 165: cf. the idea 'to witness' in *CAD*, N 2 122b). Akk. *kullumu* D 'to cause to see' suggests that the deity allows the light to be seen (*ibid.*, 221), and occurs in names which are pleas to this effect (*ibid.*, 174) as well as in names such as *Ašur-kal-lim-an-ni* 'O Aššur, let me see (a child)' (*APN*, 41a; or cf. *CAD*, K 525a 'make me free'). In this context perhaps, belong the Akk. names ^{d}*Bēl-mušētiq*-UD.DA and ^{d}*Nabû-mušētiq*-UD.DA, translated by Stamm as 'Der Gott lässt das Licht vorübergehen' (Stamm, 319: cf. *CAD*, E 395a 'It is Nabû who averts UD.DA').

Markworthy in Akk. names are those in which the parent questions the deities concerning some kind of distress or anxiety. Such concepts are evident in Akk. *adi mati* 'How long? (*ibid.*, 162; *APN*, 12b; *OMA*, II 99), *mati* 'When?' (Stamm, 162f.), *minsu* 'How?', 'For what reason?' in *Min-su-ili* (N. Bab.) 'How is it possible, O god?' (cf. Stamm, 162), *ammēni* 'Why?' (Stamm, 162; *APN*, 22a), *mīnu* 'How?', 'What?' asking 'How have I sinned?' or 'What have I done?' (cf. Stamm, 164; *APN*, 138a),[122] *ali alum* 'Where?' in *A-lí-ḫa-aṭ-ili* and *A-lí-ḫaṭ-ili* (O. Bab.) 'Where is the rule of god?' (*CAD*, Ḫ 155a; cf. Stamm, 165), and *maṣi* 'Enough!' (*ibid.*, 163). This last reference may be to some particular difficulties of the name-giver or simply to the production of too many children. Also evident are names which state more specifically that the context of the giving of the name was one of distress, evident in Akk. *anāhu* 'to be tired' (*ibid.*, 163; *OMA* II 104), or 'to have had enough' (cf. *CAD*, A 2 103), *aḫulap* 'enough' (Stamm, 162) and *(w)ēdu* 'solitary, alone' (*ibid.*, 163).

Some names state that the deity 'releases', or are requests for release from burdens or sins, illness or misfortune. These concepts are reflected in Akk. *nasāḫu* 'to take away' (*ibid.*, 170), *paṭāru/pāṭiru* 'to loosen' (*ibid.*, 169, 221, 368), and *ušāru* D 'to release' (*ibid.*, 170; *OMA*, II 168).[123] Relevant here, also are perhaps those names containing fears of being shamed or humiliated by the deities, reflected in Akk. *bâšu* 'to shame' (Stamm, 166, 174-75, 199) and *enēšu* 'to be shamed, humiliated' (*ibid.*, 175). *Bâšu* is also used in names such as *Nabû-kar-ṣi-ú-ba-aš* 'Nabû has put the slander to shame' (*ibid.*, 151b) and *Nabû-šarḫu-ubāša* 'Nabû has put the mighty to shame' (*ibid.*, 159a). Akk. *saḫāru* 'to turn' is also evident in names which suggest some distress owing to divine neglect of the name-bearer or parent (cf. Stamm, 168, 190). Names of this type, suggesting some kind of questioning of the deity concerning the vicissitudes of daily life, often involving the idea that the deities are responsible for such adversities, are not evident among Heb. names.

A number of Akk. names suggest that the deities had adverse characteristics. *Mašû* 'to forget' is attested in such names as *dŠamaš-Larsa-e-ta-am-ši* (O. Bab.) 'Šamaš do not forget Larsa' (*ibid.*, 83), which assumes, perhaps, that the deity is capable of forgetting the city. *Mašû* is also attested in names of the type *Ilu-ul-am-ši* (M. Bab.) for which the vocative 'O god, I have not forgotten', or the accusative 'The god, I have not forgotten' (Stamm, 292), are possible (cf. also *APN*, 295a; *OMA*, II 136). The implication that the various deities are to be feared is evident in the use of *adāru* 'to fear' (*APN*, 264b), in the names *La-a-di-ru-ilu* 'He who does not fear the gods' (cf. Stamm, 268), an appropriate name for a captain of brigands, and similarly, *Lā-e-du-ur-Aššur* (*OMA*, II 99) and *La-taddar-ila* 'Do not fear god!' (Stamm, 268).

Akk. names suggesting that the deities are actively harmful to man contain the elements *nêru* (Stamm, 180; *APN*, 296a) and *di'āšu* D (*OMA*, II 115) 'to destroy', *tuktû* 'to revenge', although this element was considered by Stamm to indicate avengement of the death of a person by the replacement of another child (p. 290; cf. *târu* above, 3), *šalālu* 'to rob, deprive' (*ibid.*, 291), *kašādu* 'to conquer' in the name *Šamaš-kāšid-ayāba*, interpreted by Tallqvist as 'Shamash defeats the enemy' (*APN*, 210b),[124] and *kanāšu* 'to conquer, subdue' (*OMA*, II 128).[125] Akk. deities are also portrayed as a 'binder' (i.e. 'troubler') with *kāmi* (Stamm, 63, 291), as 'vehement' with *tišmar/šitmar* (*ibid.*, 225; *OMA*, II 165), 'heroic, ferocious' with *dāpinu* (*CAD*, D 104; Stamm, 225, 250 suggests 'gleissend'),[126] and as 'lamentation'(?) with *kirū* (*APN*, 291a).[127] Perhaps connected with thunderstorms or other such phenomena is Akk. *šagāmu* 'to roar' (Stamm, 63; *APN*, 307a; also nominal, Stamm, 63, 225).

In a similar context are those Akk. names which suggest that the deities become quiet or peaceable, with *nâḫu* 'to be quiet, appeased' (*ibid.*, 169, 230, 291), *pašāḫu* 'to calm down' (*ibid.*, 168), *salāmu* 'to be peaceable' (*ibid.*, 169, 190; *OMA*, II 153),[128] *pašāru* N 'to reconcile, be reconciled with, appeased' (Stamm, 168, 190, 221; *APN*, 303a; *OMA*, II 142), and *tayyāru* 'to be reconciled, to turn around' (Stamm, 220). Such elements involve ideas which are not evident in Hebrew theophoric names.

Also not attested in Heb. names are admonitions to pray to or worship the deity, or statements that a particular deity is worshipped or prayed to. These concepts are evident in Akk. names with *dagālu* 'to look' perhaps in the sense of being obedient to the deity (Stamm, 250),[129] *palāḫu* 'to worship' (*ibid.*, 204, 234; *OMA*, II 145-46), *suppû* 'to pray' (Stamm, 167, 201), *ṣullû* D 'to pray, implore' (Stamm, 234; also nominal 'prayer' Stamm, 167; *APN*, 303b), and *dalālu* 'to pray, beg, ask, worship' (*OMA*, II 114). Similar is the use of Akk. *egû* in names of the type *Lā-tēgi(-ana)-Ištar*, translated by Tallqvist as 'Do not sin against Ishtar' (*APN*, 121a, cf. *OMA* II 116).

Remaining, are various Akk. elements which have no equivalent thought in Heb. and which do not fall into any particular semantic grouping. Unlike Heb. *my* 'Who?', attested in names which ask 'Who is like God?', Akk. *mannu* occurs with an additional thought, as in *Mannu-kī-ili-rabū* 'Who is like the god, great?' (*APN*, 126b), *Mannu-kī-Ištar-li* 'Who is like Ištar, mighty?' (cf. *APN*, 126a), *Ma-nu-gēr-Aššur* 'Who is adversary of Aššur?' (*OMA*, II 135), and *Mannu-gēri-*^{d}*Šamaš* 'Who can make war on Šamaš?' (cf. Stamm, 238). Heb. also has no parallel to the use of Akk. *šumma* 'if, indeed' in such names as *Sum-man-la-*^{d}*Marduk* (O. Bab.) 'Were it not Marduk? (who else)!' (cf. Stamm, 136), *Šu-ma-li-ba-Ašur*, *- Ašùr* and *Šu-ma-li-be-i-li-a*, for which Stamm suggested 'So mein Gott will (wird es gut gehen)' (*ibid.*, 197). Cf. also *Šum-ma-Adad*, *Sum-ma-ilānu* (*OMA*, II 162) and *Šum-ma-ibašši-ilāni* 'Indeed, there are gods' (cf. Stamm, 135). To this last name may be added Akk. *bašû* 'to be, exist, happen, be in existence', in names such as *Ibašši-ilāni* 'There exist gods' (*APN*, 93a). *Bašû* is also used in the precative, expressing a wish for a child (*OMA*, II 109) and in the causative, suggesting that the deity has caused the child to be (Stamm, 145, 148, 218). It is also found in the name *Ittabši-din-*^{d}*Aššur* 'The judgment of Ašur is established (cf. Stamm, 192).

Although Akk. *itti* 'with' has usages in names comparable to Heb. *'t* (see above, 1), it also occurs in other contexts, as in *Itti-*^{d}*Nabû-pa-ši-ru* 'With Nabû is my secret' (Stamm, 230; see also *APN*, 273; *OMA*, II 127). Names such as *Itti-Adad-anīnu* 'With (or from) Adad are we' (*APN*, 108b; cf. *OMA*, II 144) have the personal pronoun as the subject, unlike Heb. names with *'t*, which have the deity as subject. *Arki* 'behind' is found in such names as *Arkāt*(EGIR^{at})*-ili-damqā* (M., N. and L. Bab.), interpreted by Stamm as 'Hinter Gott zu sein (zu gehen) ist schön' (Stamm, 236) and by *CAD*, D 69b as 'It is pleasant to follow the god'. These meanings have no parallel in Heb., nor has *alāku* 'to go', in names of the type *I-na-ili-ya-al/a-lak* 'With my god I walk' (*APN*, 100b; *OMA*, II 102), *ᵈAššur-ālik-panī* 'Aššur is (my) leader' (*APN*, 35a; *OMA*, II 102), and *I-na-šar-ᵈNusku-allakᵃᵏ* (M. Bab.) 'In the breath of wind of Nusku I go' (cf. Stamm, 196). *Šāru* 'breath of wind' is also evident in names such as *Ša-ar-Ištar* (*ibid.*, 276; *OMA*, II 161) and *Ṭà-ab-ša-ri-ili*(AN) 'Pleasant is the breath of wind (scent) of god' (*ibid.*, 234-35, 235; *OMA*, II 161). *Šāru* is also found with the imv. and vent. of *zi'āqu* 'to blow' (*OMA*, II 169), a root which is possibly evident in the difficult name *Adad-za-qa-a* (*APN*, 282a).

Akk. *annu*, 'indeed, yes' perhaps expresses the idea of a promise or assent from the deity, in names such as *An-ni-ilum*(AN) (O. Bab.) 'Indeed/yes, O god' (cf. Stamm, 136) and *Anum*(AN)-*pî*(KA)-*ᵈMarduk* (O. Bab., Stamm, 233-34). *Šamû* 'heaven' also has no complement among Heb. names: it is used to describe the deities as the 'light of heaven and earth' and as 'lord of heaven' (Stamm, 81; *OMA*, II 159). *Šumu* 'name, son, line' (*AHw*, III 1274) is used in Akk. to refer to both the deity and the name-bearer. As the former, it is found in names such as *Ṭāb*(DÙG.GA)-*šum*(MU)-*ᵈAdad* 'Good is the name of Adad' (cf. Stamm, 236), and as the latter, it describes the name-bearer as a child of the deity (*ibid.*, 261). In the name *Šu-mi-ì-lí-ya* (O. Bab.) 'Name of my god' (*ibid.*, 303), the reference may be to the replacement of a deceased father. Although *šm* is attested in Heb. names of the type 'Name of El/the (divine) Father', the *nomen regens* here probably refers to the deity and doubtfully contains the nuance of meaning 'son', depicting the name-bearer as an offspring of the deity, since this is a feature totally absent elsewhere in Heb. names.

Heb. names have no parallel to the name-element *nâšu* 'to totter', in *ᶠAi-inūš-šadû* in which the deity is possibly semantically implied in the epithet 'mountain' (*šadû*). A meaning 'Der Berg möge nicht wanken' is suggested by Stamm (pp. 82, 198 n. 1) perhaps in the sense that the truth will not be shaken, while *CAD*, N 2 113b suggests 'Let not the mountain quake'.

4.7 *A Comparison between the Concepts of Deity Revealed in the Palmyrene and Hebrew Onomastica*

The study of the Palmyrene onomasticon undertaken by J.K. Stark,[130] has greatly facilitated the present comparison between theophoric names in Palmyrene and those found in the Hebrew onomasticon.

1. In these two languages, there exists a number of name-elements which are common to both, as the following list shows:

Palm.	*Stark*	*Heb.*	
'b	76	*'b*	father
'ḥ	66	*'h*	brother[131]
't	73	*'t*	with
brk	74	*brk*	to bless
gd	81, 98	*gd*	fortune
zbd	74, 98, 100, 107	*zbd*	to give
ḥzh	74, 76	*ḥzh*	to see
ḥnn	77, 89, 107	*ḥnn*	to be gracious
yd'	75, 76, 98	*yd'*	to know
l	93	*l/lmw*	belonging to
m	94	*my*	who?
mlk	95	*mlk*	king
mr	98	*mr*	lord[132]
nwr	99, 108	*nr*	light (Palm.); lamp (Heb.).
ntn	108	*ntn*	to give
'bd	102, 103	*'bd*	servant
'azīz (Arab.)	99	*'zz*	to be strong, powerful
'alīy (Arab.)	106	*'lh*(?)	to be high, exalted
rby	111	*rbb*	to be great (Heb. Geminate)
rm	115	*rwm*	to be exalted
rp'	75, 112, 115	*rp'*	to heal

In Palmyrene and Hebrew names in which non-theophoric elements are derived from the above roots, the forms of the names are identical except where noted. Also common to both onomastica may be the following three roots:

pny 'to turn' (Stark, 73). A verbal perf. of *pny* 'to turn' is attested in the Palm. name *'TPNY*. The same root is used in Heb. *p^{e}nû'ēl*, perhaps as a construct form, 'Face of El' (see above, §2.7), and possibly verbally in *pn'l* (see above, §2.4 *pnh*). However, A. Caquot (*RHR* 182 [1972], 201) has doubted the presence of the fem. divine name *'Ate* as the initial element of the Palm. name 'TPNY, which raises the question of its relevance here.

šlm 'safety' (Stark, 114). Palm. *šlm* is found in genitive form in the name ŠLMLT, 'Safety given by Allat'. Although this meaning of the root exists in BH (cf. BDB, 1022), it is attested in Heb. names with a meaning 'to recompense' in verbal and nominal (but not construct) forms.

zdq 'to be just' (Stark, 86). Since in Palm. *zdq*, *z* represents Heb. *ṣ*, the element is cognate with *ṣdq* in Heb. name-giving, with the same meaning 'just, righteous'.

2. Some non-theophoric elements in Palmyrene names have semantic rather than formal parallels in Hebrew. These are as follows:

yhb 'to give' (Stark, 76); *ndb* 'to grant' (Stark, 99); *wahb* 'gift', cf. Arab. (Stark, 85). Although the root *yhb* is attested in BH, it is not found in Heb. names in which the verbal idea 'to give' is represented with *'wš* (cf. Arab. *'āsa* 'to bestow'), *zbd*, *ntn*, possibly *qwš* (cf. Akk. *qāšu* and above, §2.9 *qûšāyāhu*) and the initial Eg. element of the names *pûṭî'ēl* and *pṭyhw* (see above, §2.9). Similar in thought is Palm. *ndb* 'to grant'. Although *ndb* is attested in Heb. names, it probably means 'to be noble, willing, generous' (cf. Arab. *naduba* and BDB, 621). The element *wahb* 'gift' (cf. Arab.) in Palm. names is used in the genitive, comparable to the use of *ntn* in Heb. names.[133]

'auḏ 'protection' cf. Arab. (Stark, 104); *'qb* 'to protect' (Stark, 73, 77, 108). The idea 'Protection of god' expressed in the Palm. name 'WD'L is similar to Heb. names containing the verbal idea 'to protect' in the roots *zmr* (cf. S. Arab. *dhimr*) and perhaps *ḥmh* (cf. S. Arab. *ḥamay* and above, §2.9 *ḥammû'ēl*). Semantically comparable to the verbal forms in Heb. names is Palm. *'qb* 'to protect', a root which is attested in BH but not in theophoric compound names.[134]

p^eṣā' 'to open (the womb)' cf. Aram. (Stark, 109). A root *pṣh* exists in BH with the meaning 'to part, open', cf. BDB, 822, but is not attested in theophoric names, which convey the same idea with the root *ptḥ*.

rg' 'luck' (Stark, 106-7); *š'd* 'luck' (Stark, 115). Although the idea 'luck' is not attested as such in Heb. theophoric names, the similar idea of the deity as 'fortune' is found in *gd* 'fortune' and *šb'* 'fulness, good fortune'. These Heb. name-elements are attested nominally, as Palm. *rg'* 'luck'. Palm. *š'd* 'luck' is, however, a genitive form.

šwr 'stronghold' (Stark, 77). The Heb. name-element *šwr* 'wall', is probably semantically and formally cognate with Palm. *šwr*. The Heb. element, however, does not have the meaning 'stronghold' (cf. BDB, 1004), although both are figurative for the idea of protection. This figurative idea of protection in Heb. names is further exemplified in the roots *ḥsh*, *'wz* and *'wn* 'refuge', *ṣwr* 'rock', which also seems to contain some etymological link with Palm. *šwr*, *hr* 'mountain' and *'hl* 'tent'.

tym 'servant' (Stark, 116, 117). The idea 'servant of' the deity is exemplified in Heb. names by the element *'bd*,[135] an element also attested in Palm., see above, 1.

3. There are many elements which exist in Palmyrene names which have no analogy in Hebrew names. These are as follows.

Markworthy, is the Palm. concept of the female deities as 'mother' (*'m* Stark, 107) as well as feminine genitive compound elements depicting the name-bearer as a 'daughter' (*bt* Stark, 80, 81) and 'maid' of the deity (*'mš* Stark 70). Similarly, the masculine genitive elements *'ḥ* 'brother' (*ibid.*, 66) and *br* 'son' of the deity (*ibid.*, 78-80) are also without parallel in Heb. theophoric names. This may be said also of the genitive elements *'wyd* 'refugee' (*ibid.*, 105) and *naṣr* 'help' (cf. *Arab.*, Stark, 100).[136]

Verbal elements not attested in Heb. are *'th* 'to bring' (Stark, 67),[137] *gᵉram* 'to decide' (cf. Syr. Stark, 115) and *rᵉwaḥ* 'to feel easy' (cf. Aram., Stark, 111).[138] Also with no semantic complement among Heb. names is Palm. *kā'* 'here' in 'TYK' 'Athe is here' (cf. Aram. Stark, 108).

4. Evident throughout the work of Stark are many abbreviated forms, the use of which, in the present context, is questionable. Conclusive proof that an abbreviated form is, indeed, an abbreviation of a theophoric compound name seems to be lacking. One would expect at least the non-theophoric element of a so-termed abbreviated name to be attested elsewhere with a theophoric element, and while this is the case with some elements, it is by no means the case with all. Some abbreviated forms in Palmyrene names would necessitate no alteration whatever to the foregoing comparison between Hebrew and Palmyrene theophoric names, simply because they would have corresponding full forms already discussed above. Yet there remains a group of names which Stark considers to be abbreviations of theophoric compound names, but which have no corresponding full forms in which the non-theophoric element occurs with a divine name.[139] These represent concepts not already covered in the foregoing analysis. While it is not suggested that the evidence for the inclusion of these names is by any means satisfactory, it is felt that such names should not remain entirely unnoticed in the present context, and they are therefore outlined below. The following are those with semantic parallels in Hebrew.

Palmyrene	*Hebrew semantic equivalents*
	Genitive elements
'mr 'man' (Stark, 69)	*mt*, *'yš*, *gbr*.

Palmyrene	*Hebrew semantic equivalents*
	Verbal elements
bnh 'to build' (Stark, 64)	*bnh* 'to build, create'
	qnh, *br'* 'to create'
	p'l, *'śh* 'to make'
dyn 'to judge' (Stark, 83)	*dyn*, *pll*, *špṭ*
dkr 'to remember' (Stark, 83)	*zkr*
hd' 'to guide' cf. Syr. (Stark, 84)	*dll* 'to direct'? and cf. *yahdāy*, which may be a sf. 'Y leads', root *hdh*
ḥbb 'to love' (Stark, 87)	*dwd*
nš' 'to raise, lift up (oneself)' (Stark, 110)	*qwm* (Hiphil)
ṣ'd 'to rise' (Stark, 109)	*zrḥ* 'to rise, come forth'
	qwm (Qal)
rḍy 'to be content' (Stark, 112)	*ḥdh* 'to give joy'
	'šr 'to fill with joy' cf. Arab. *'ašira*
	ḥbṣ 'to be joyful' cf. Akk. *ḫabāṣu*
	gyl 'rejoicing joy'
	n'm 'delight, pleasantness'
	'dn 'luxury, delight'
	possibly *ḥlh* 'to be sweet, pleasing' cf. Arab. *ḥalā*
šm' 'to hear' (Stark, 75, 115)	*šm'*, *'zn*

5. Three roots used in abbreviated names have no semantic parallels among Hebrew names. These are *mlk* 'to rule', which is causative in YMLKW 'N.N. shall cause to rule' (Stark, 91), *mšk* 'to take possession' (cf. Aram. Stark, 97)[140] and possibly *'qb* 'to reward' (Stark, 68).

Notes to Chapter 4

1. Studia Pohl Dissertationes Scientificae de Rebus Orientis Antiqui, I Rome (1967), referred to throughout as *PTU*.
2. For the root in Heb. names, see above, §2.9 *'ḥy'yl*.
3. J.C. de Moor suggests, however, that it is questionable whether *'iš* 'man' occurs in Ug. and also notes the possibility that *'išb'l* is a dialectical form of *'itb'l*, cf. *BO* 26 (1969), 106 and references.
4. Heb. construct, 'beloved'.
5. Heb. causative with the meaning 'to establish'.
6. Ug. may also contain the idea 'slave'.
7. However, the seal *'lyh* may not be Heb., see above, p. 76.
8. However, the noun *'āb* 'dark, cloud, cloud mass, thicket' may be evident in the Heb. name *'byw*, but this is doubtful, see above, p. 148.
9. The Heb. name *'ldg*[ ] is uncertain, see above, p. 171 n. 21.
10. Although the element *'ry* 'lion' is found in Heb. names, there is no evidence to suggest that it can be used in any other form than a construct noun and, as such, refers to the name-bearer rather than the deity.
11. It is uncertain whether the initial element of the Ug. name *prqdš* is from a root *pry* 'to be fruitful', noun *pr* 'fruit', or is a noun from the root *prr* meaning 'young bull'.
12. Names with this element are difficult: the root seems to depict the deity as a giver, or god, of fruitfulness.
13. Although the root *d'h* is found in Heb. personal names with a meaning 'to call', suggested by an Arab. cognate *da'ā*, the root has not the nuance of meaning 'to name'.
14. Heb. names tend to be more specific in describing the care of the deity; cf. the ideas 'to nourish', 'strengthen', 'support', 'deliver'.
15. The Heb. name-element *ngh* is used causatively 'to enlighten', while *šnh* 'to shine, be beautiful' (cf. Arab. *sana*) is more akin to BH *yph* 'to be fair, beautiful' (also attested in theophoric names) and, therefore, are unlike the Ug. idea.
16. In the name *ṣalmeki*: however, cf. Akk. *ṣalāmu* 'to become dark' *CAD*, *Ṣ* 70, suggesting a meaning 'I am dark', also W. Richter, *ZDMG* 119 (1970), 354.
17. For the possibility of a root *swr* (*śwr*) 'to turn aside' in Heb. names, see above, §2.9 *sryh*.
18. Studia Pohl Dissertationes Scientificae de Rebus Orientis Antiqui: Rome (1972), referred to throughout as *PNPPI*.
19. Phoen. nominal and construct, Heb. only nominal.
20. The Phoen. element, however, is stative.
21. The element is not clear in Heb. names, see above, §2.3 *mr*.
22. Benz seems to have confused the Heb. root *'wd*, from which the noun *'d* 'witness' is derived, and the root *'dh* 'to ornament', which are not related.

He has, accordingly, misrepresented Noth (*IPN*, 182, 204) where the references are only concerned with the root *'dh*.

23. Phoen. only nominal.

24. The element is difficult, cf. Heb. *nksym* BDB, 647. Benz also suggests a reading *nws*, of unknown meaning.

25. The BH name *mal'ākî* is uncertain, cf. BDB, 522. It could mean 'My messenger' or it could be a sf. of 'Messenger of Y', cf. Geh, 581, but there remains no clear example of the noun with a theophoric element.

26. The element is obscure: other possibilities are a root *'š* (cf. *PNPPI*, 277-78), or the relative particle 'of'. Cf. also the element *š* in the BH name *m^e tûšā'ēl* 'Man of El' (see above, §2.6).

27. in the name ṢDYRK: however, the element may be a cognate of the Heb. root *'rk* 'to be long' (of time, cf. BDB, 73) indicating a meaning 'May Ṣd lengthen (life?)', a concept also without parallel in Heb. theophoric names.

28. in the names Y'GRYST[R]T and YGR'ŠM[N]: a root *grh* 'to incite, provoke' may also be possible but, likewise, has no semantic parallel in the Heb. nomenclature.

29. in the name B'LSMM: Benz also suggests that the element may be erroneous for *šm'* or *šmr*.

30. *APNM*, Baltimore (1965).

31. Amor. also nominal, whereas Heb. is always verbal.

32. Amor. Hollow root, Heb. Geminate. The root *kwn* in Heb. names is used with the meaning 'to establish, appoint'.

33. Amor. 'light'

34. Amor. also 'mountain', cf. Heb. *hr* in theophoric names.

35. Amor. also nominal, meaning 'health, restoration, healing'.

36. Amor. also 'to answer', cf. Heb. *'nh* in theophoric names.

37. The initial element of the name *Ḫa-ba-du*-AN, listed by Huffmon under *ḫbd*$_2$ (*APNM*, 189-90) as unexplained, is considered a variant of *Ḫa-ba-du*-AN 'servant', slave', by M. Dietrich and O. Loretz, in their review of Huffmon, *OL* 61 (1966), 244.

38. The element can occur as a theophoric element, cf. R. Zadok, *On West Semites in Babylonia During the Chaldean and Achaemenian Periods: An Onomastic Study*, Jerusalem: H.J. and Z. Wanaarta and Tel-Aviv University (1977), 51.

39. On the use of *'ry* in Heb. names, see the comment above, p. 270 n. 10.

40. Dietrich and Loretz (*op. cit.*, 241) suggest a root *ysd* and compare Akk. *išdu* 'Fundament', but this, also, is not attested in Heb. theophoric names.

41. The element is uncertain in the name *Ḫa-li-ma*-AN: Huffmon compares Ug. *ǵlmt* 'girl, servant'.

42. The root *d'h* (cf. Arab. *da'ā*) in Heb. names does not have this nuance of meaning 'name' or 'announce', and is therefore different.

43. Huffmon suggests that the element *sibk* in the name *Si-ib-ku-na*-^{d}IM is

also from this same root *spk*. However, Gelb (*Lingua*, 2.3.5) transcribes the name as *Si-ip-qú-na-*^{d}IM suggesting perhaps the root *śpq* 'to be abundant', similar to the Heb. name-element *ytr* (see above, 1).

44. The root *yd'* in Heb. names is not used in this same, stative, sense.

45. However, Gröndahl (*Orientalia* 35 [1966], 456) suggests the root *rw/yṣ* '(zu Hilfe) eilen', found in Akk., Ug., Heb. and O. Ass., although it has no semantic equivalent in Heb. names.

46. The element is difficult in the name *Ya-ar-qa-*A[N]: also possible is an imf.

47. Gröndahl (*Orientalia* 35 [1966], 455) suggests an imv. of the verb *ḥbb* 'to love' with the 1st pers. sing. pron. *nī* (cf. Akk.) comparable to Ug. *ilḥbn* 'Gott/El hat mich lieb gewonnen'. Huffmon (*APNM*, 190) leaves the element unexplained.

48. In *Ya-am-si-*AN the element could be a G or causative imf. of a root *mṣ'* or a root *mẓy* 'to reach, arrive', which is also without parallel in Heb. names.

49. Uncertain in the name *I-la-ra-ḫi-ya* (*I-la-ra-ḫi-e*). The root *r'h* is attested in Heb. names but as a construct noun, 'friend of' the deity.

50. The element is uncertain: Huffmon suggests a G or causative form in names such as *Ya-ar-si-*AN. Only the idea 'to feel pity' would be reflected in Heb. names with the root *rḥm* 'to show compassion'. Dietrich and Loretz (*op. cit.*, 241) suggest 'haben, gewinnen', connecting *Ya-ar-si* with *rsi*, used in Akk. names; this also has no semantic equivalent in Heb. names.

51. It is possible that the name may involve the idea of recompense for a previously deceased member of the family, but this is uncertain.

52. I.N. Vinnikov, *Palestinski Svornik* 3 (1958), 171-216 ('); 4 (1959), 196-240 (*b-d*); 7 (1962), 192-237 (*h-y*); 9 (1962), 140-58 (*k-l*), 11 (19 3), 189-232 (*m-'*); 13 (1965), 217-62 (*p-t*), hereafter *PS*.

53. *APN*.

54. H. Donner, W. Röllig, *Kanaanäische und Aramäische Inschriften II u. III*, Wiesbaden: Otto Harassowitz (1964), hereafter *KAI*.

55. J.C.L. Gibson, *Textbook of Syrian Semitic Inscriptions II*, Oxford (1975), hereafter *SSI II*.

56. A. Cowley, *Aramaic Papyri of the Fifth Century BC*, Oxford (1923).

57. G.R. Driver, *Aramaic Documents of the Fifth Century BC*, Oxford (1957), revised edn (1965).

58. E.G. Kraeling, *The Brooklyn Museum Papyri*, Yale University Press, New Haven (1953), hereafter Krael.

59. P. Grelot, *Documents Araméens d'Egypte*, Les Éditions du Cerf (1972), hereafter Grelot.

60. M.H. Silverman, 'Aramaean Name-types in the Elephantine Documents', *JAOS* 89 4 (1969), 691-709, hereafter Silverman *JAOS*.

61. E. Lipiński, *Studies in Aramaic Inscriptions and Onomastics*, Leuven University Press (1975), hereafter Lipiński.

62. *BO* 33 no. 574 May-July (1976), 227-31.

63. Jerusalem: H.J. and Z. Wanaarta and Tel-Aviv University (1977), hereafter Zadok, *On West Semites*.

64. Vienna: Österreichische Akademie der Wissenschaften (1978), hereafter Kornfeld OAA.

65. F.M. Fales, 'On Aramaic Onomastics in the Neo-Assyrian Period', *OA* 16 (1977), Fac. 1, hereafter Fales OA, and F.M. Fales, 'West Semitic Names from the Governor's Palace', *Annali di ca' Foscari*, 13 3 (1974) (Serie Orientale 5), 179-88, hereafter Fales, also F.M. Fales, 'L'onomastica aramaica in età neo-Assira: raffronti tra il corpus alfebetico e il materiale cuneiforme', *OA* 13 (1978), 199-229, hereafter Fales *OA 13*.

66. G.R. Driver, 'Aramaic Names in Accadian Texts', *RSO* 32 (1957), 41-57, hereafter Driver *RSO*.

67. K. Deller, 'Neuassyrisches aus Sultantepe', *Orientalia* 34 (1965), 473-75, hereafter Deller.

68. F. Vattioni, 'I sigilli ebraici', *Biblica* 50 (1969), 357-88 abbreviated throughout as V, and F. Vattioni, 'I sigilli, le monete e gli avori aramaico', *Augustinianum* 11 (1971), 47-87, hereafter V.*Aug*.

69. Roberts considers this element, which is only attested in the name *Tarpa-iltum* [DINGIR], to be Amor. (p. 166). However, cf. A. Westenholz, *JNES* 34 (1975), 290, whose review of Robert's work considers the presence of Amor. elements in O. Akk. names to be less acceptable, and cf. the O. Bab. name *Ta-ar-pí-Annunītum*, *AHw*, II, 956.

70. Gelb interprets the element as 'an object of metal' (p. 207), but Roberts's translation is preferable, cf. *naṣābum* '(ein)saugen', *AHw*, II, 755.

71. Akk. names suggest that the element is used in the sense of 'creation/named' of the deity, referring to the name-bearer not the deity. In the BH name *šᵉmû'ēl*, 'name of El', the *nomen regens* is likely to refer to the deity, and so is different.

72. Nominal in the name *Su'en-ayyar* 'Su'en is a young man', but also found in genitive form where it corresponds to Heb. 'man of', see above, 3 *ayarum*.

73. In *Qāssu-ālum* 'the city is his hand'? (Roberts, 124). *Idum* and *qātum* are probably figurative for protection.

74. Roberts considers the initial element of *Iṣi-Anda* 'Anda went out' (Roberts, 13) to be Amor. (cf. *APNM*, 184-85). However, Gelb lists names with this element under *waṣā'um* 'to go out, go forth' (pp. 69-70). On the doubtful presence of Amor. elements in O. Akk. names, cf. Westenholz, *op. cit.*, 290.

75. See the discussion concerning O. Akk. *ḫadāwun* above, p. 228. The element also occurs as a genitive, 'joy of' the deity (Roberts, 13).

76. Always used with the deity as the object.

77. Probably used figuratively to describe divine creation of the child.

78. Roberts interprets the names *Išu-Il* (p. 31) and *Išu-ilum* [DINGIR] (p. 124) as 'Il/the god exists', disputing a meaning 'to have' for the initial element (p. 90 n. 210). Cf., however, the similar OA and Akk. names with this same element, and the possibility of a nominative or accusative meaning for the divine name (Stamm, 130, 132).

79. Also nominal 'shepherd' (Roberts, 18, 19). Note, however, Gelb's interpretation 'to pasture', 'to provide with food', perhaps similar to Heb. 'to nourish' in the name-elements *'zh* (cf. Arab. *ghadhā*) and *qwt* (cf. Arab. *qāta*). 'To pasture' is a more figurative expression for the care of the deity, however.

80. Akk. also designates the deity as 'father of the weak' (cf. Stamm, 240).

81. Akk. also 'brother of the lost' (*ibid.*, 241).

82. Cf. perhaps also the name *Atri-ilu* (*APN*, 281b).

83. Akk. names also contain the noun 'Creator'.

84. For Akk. usage not reflected in Heb., see above, p. 257.

85. Akk. also nominal 'judge', while Heb. is only verbal: cf. also *OMA*, II 113.

86. Akk. may be more in the sense 'to grant a favour', cf. *CAD*, E 164.

87. Heb. also nominal: the element *ḫāziru* may be an Amor. lw. (cf. Stamm, 215).

88. Also used differently in Akk. names such as *Ì-lí-ki-nam-i-di* 'My god knows the righteous' (*ibid.*, 239-40), *[d]Ea-ḫi-i-ti-ul-i-di* 'Ea, my offence I know not' (*ibid.*, 164), and *Šá-[d]Nabû-idûšu* (N. Bab.) 'Whom Nabû knows' (*ibid.*, 370). The element in this last name may have the sense 'to care for' cf. *CAD*, I 28a.

89. For Akk. usage not reflected in Heb., see above, p. 264.

90. Akk. use of the element with no equivalent in Heb. is found in names such as *Mannu-gēri-[d]Šamaš* (N./L. Bab.) 'Who can make war on Šamaš?' (cf. Stamm, 238), *Mi-nu-ú-a-na-[d]Bēl-da-a-ni* (N. Bab.) 'What is strong (enough) against Bēl?' (*ibid.*, 238; *AHw* II 656a), and *Ma-nu-um-ba-lum-ilum* (AN), -*[d]Šamaš* (O. Bab) 'Who can be without god/Šamaš?' (cf. Stamm, 238). See further, above, p. 264.

91. Verbal and genitive elements are attested in both Heb. and Akk., but the latter also has a nominal form, referring to the deity as 'Giver' (cf. Stamm, 217). Unlike Heb., Akk. names are also found with the objects 'brother', 'son', 'lord', 'king', 'name' and 'progeny'.

92. Akk. also found in the genitive (Stamm, 275; *OMA*, II 144). Also not attested in Heb. are Akk. names of the type *Sin-nūr-māti-šu* (M. Bab.) 'Sin is the light of his land' (cf. Stamm, 227) and *[d]Šamaš-nūra-kul-li-man-ni* (M. Bab.) 'Šamaš, let me see the light' (*ibid.*, 174).

93. In the name *Pān-ashur*: the element also occurs in the accusative in names such as *Pān-Ašur-lāmur* 'May I see the face of Ašur' (*APN*, 179b).

94. Tallqvist saw the numerous names of the type *Ṣil*-deity, as abbreviated

forms. However, genitive types, 'Shadow/Protection of Adad/Aššur/Bēl/Bēlit/Ištar' etc., may be possible since, in view of the frequency of such names, we might expect some evidence of an original full form, although this seems to be absent (cf. *APN*, 205-206). Genitive forms would seem to be supported by MA usage (cf. *OMA*, II 155).

95. The Akk. element is probably to be found in the Heb. name *qûšāyāhû*, the form of which is problematic (see above, §2.9). Akk. also attests a genitive form (Stamm, 257) and the element is also found with the objects 'progeny' and 'name' as well as in the names *dGu-la-ta-qi-še-lib-luṭ* 'O Gula, may the child that thou has presented live' (*APN*, 81b) and *dMarduk-qi-šá-an-ni* 'Marduk, reward me' (cf. Stamm, 178).

96. Also used differently in Akk. to describe the 'word' of the deity (Stamm, 232), the 'rescue' (*ibid.*, 234), 'shadow' (*ibid.*, 235), 'throne' (*ibid.*, 236) and 'works' of the deity (*ibid.*, 237). Cf. also the verbal precative in *Sippar-lirbi/Lirbi-Sippar* (O. Bab.) in which Sippar, as the name of a city, may represent a theophoric element (cf. Stamm, 84-85). A causative sense also seems to be evident in the names *Adad-rabā-iddin* (*APN*, 305b; *OMA*, II 150) and *Aššur-iddin-ra-ba* (*OMA*, II 150), expressing that the deity gives greatness. Such names also have no parallel among Heb. names.

97. Akk. also with the objects 'prayer' (Stamm, 167, 189) and 'the pious' (*ibid.*, 241). Cf. also the elements *šēm(m)i*, *šēm(m)eat* (*ibid.*, 85, 91, 219, 220).

98. Different from Heb. is the Akk. use of this name-element to describe the 'breath' (or 'scent') of the deity (Stamm, 235; *OMA*, II 166), the 'voice', 'shadow' (i.e. protection), 'divine security' of the deity (Stamm, 235), and the 'name' and 'reign' of the deity (*ibid.*, 36). Also not attested in Heb. is a name such as *Ṭāb-a-šab-Marduk*, translated by Stamm as 'Schön ist es, bei Marduk zu sitzen' (p. 236).

99. *Erēšu* 'to request' is also found in names suggesting that the deity has requested the birth of the child (cf. Stamm, 144), and 'justice' (*ibid.*).

100. Tallqvist preferred a meaning 'glory' in names of the type *Aqar-Bēl-lūmur*, which he translated as 'May I see the glory of Bēl' (*APN*, 25a). The element normally means 'precious, valuable, dear' (cf. *CAD*, A 2 207), although a nominal form would be expected .

101. *Mūtu* is perhaps found in names of children of widows, who would depict the deity as a husband, cf. *Mu-ti-ilum*(AN) (O. Bab.) 'My spouse is god' (cf. Stamm, 298). However, *CAD*, M 2 316 indicates a meaning 'man, warrior' which, if genitive, would be comparable to Heb. names with *'yš*, the cognate element *mt*, and perhaps *gbr*.

102. See, however, the comment on *'šb'l*, above, §2.2 *b'l*.

103. Tallqvist preferred a meaning 'to be strong', although 'warrior, hero' is well attested, cf. *AHw*, II 905.

104. In *dA-a-ku-zu-ub-ma-tim* (O. Bab.) 'Aja is the abundance or luxuriance of the land' (cf. Stamm, 227) and *Nabû-kuzub-ilāni* (*APN*, 153b).

105. Note, however, the meanings 'well-formed, well-made, splendid, fine, beautiful, friendly' given by *CAD*, B 81.

106. The element is also used to describe the 'splendour' and the 'rising' etc. of a deity (Stamm, 186).

107. *Māru* is also found in the name *Māram*(TUR)-*ib-ni* (O. Bab.) 'He (the deity) has created a son' (cf. Stamm, 38).

108. The element is also met in the name *fTukīn-ḫaṭṭi-migriša* 'She (the goddess) has established the rule of her favourite' (cf. *CAD*, M 2 49b; Stamm, 122).

109. The usual meanings of *kaṣāru*, however, are 'to tie, bind together' collect, organise, gather' or 'to assemble' cf. *CAD*, K 257, which may suggest similarity to the Heb. name-element *'sp* 'to gather' (see also above, 3).

110. The BH name *šilḥî* (see above, §2.10) is not attested with a theophoric element and is uncertain as an abbreviated form.

111. Also used in names of the type *Lūṣâ-ana-nūr-dMarduk* (Stamm, 151). It is found nominally in *Ri-eš-a-ṣu-šu* 'Joyful is its (the deity's) rising' (cf. Stamm, 186, but cf. also *CAD*, A 2 369b 'Happy is its (the star's) going forth'.

112. An imv. of *ša'āmu* in the name *Sîn-šá-am* (*OMA*, II 156-57) seems to make little sense.

113. in names of the type *dNinurta-ni-šu* (M. Bab.), which could mean 'Ninurta, we have (a child)', or 'We have Ninurta' (cf. Stamm, 131).

114. *Kašādu* also occurs in the name *Ḫa-da-an-šu-li-ik-šu-ud* (O. Bab.), translated by Stamm as 'Möge sein (des Gottes) Termin eintreffen' (p. 149). For a meaning 'to conquer', see above, p. 263.

115. *Kutallu* may mean 'replacement', however, cf. *CAD*, K 606 where the name *Ku-tal-la-a-dNabû* (N. Bab.) is cited, and above, p. 249. This would be comparable to *šlm* 'to recompense' and *šwb* (Hiphil) 'to restore' in Heb. names.

116. Tallqvist interpreted the D theme in names as 'to strengthen', but this is unlikely, cf. *AHw*, II 810.

117. Found only in the name *Ilum-ú-túl-la*(*m*)-*ni-šu* (O. Bab.) 'O god, we have a shepherd', but it is not clear whether 'shepherd' refers to the deity or the child.

118. Also attested in names such as *Ì-lí-a-pi-li* (O. Bab., Stamm, 213), in which it may mean 'the one who satisfies me' or 'rewards me' (cf. Stamm's interpretation of *Ilum-a-pil* as 'Der Gott belohnt [das Kind]', *ibid*., 223).

119. Cf. also Akk. *mutakkilu*, in names such as *Mu-tak-kil-dMarduk* (M. Bab.) 'Marduk inspires trust' (cf. Stamm, 222), and a part. D form in names such as *Aššur-mu-ta-kil* (*OMA*, II 164), perhaps suggesting the idea 'to encourage'. For the G theme 'to trust', see above, 3.

120. *Napāšu* is also found in the name *dNabû-muneppiš-ugārī* 'Nabû allows the fields to flourish' (cf. Stamm, 66 n. 2), but a meaning 'Nabû extends the field' is perhaps also possible.

121. Also found in names of the type *Ì-lí-am-ta-ḫ[ar]* (O. Bab.) 'I was beseeching my god continually' (*CAD*, M 1 67; cf. Stamm, 201).

122. Cf. *ḫaṭû* 'to sin' in *Aššur-la-ta-ḫa-t[i* (*OMA*, II 123) and *ᵈEa-ḫi-i-ṭi-ul-i-di* 'Ea, my offence I know not' (cf. Stamm, 164).

123. Tallqvist preferred to interpret *uššuru* in *Nabû-la-tú-šir-a-ni* as 'to cast down' (*APN*, 153b).

124. The element normally means 'to arrive, happen', see above, p. 259.

125. For the sense of this kind of name cf. the NA sf. *Mušekniš* 'Who makes submit!' (*CAD*, K 144).

126. *Dāpinu* may be a theophoric element referring to the planet Jupiter.

127. Cf., however, *kirû* 'garden, orchard', *CAD*, K 411.

128. Also attested in names of slaves which are pleas to the deity that the lord of the slave will be peaceable (cf. Stamm, 311).

129. The element has a quite difference sense in *Pan-ᵈBēl adaggal* (N. Bab.), which Stamm suggests means 'Ich harre Bels' (p. 195). See also above, 3.

130. *Personal Names in Palmyrene Inscriptions*, Oxford (1971), referred to throughout as Stark.

131. The noun *'ḫ* 'brother', occurs in nominal sentence names in both Heb. and Palm., but is found in genitive compounds only in Palm. names.

132. The element is problematic in Heb. names, and a root *mrr* may be preferable, see above, §2.3 *mr*.

133. Cf. also the possible sf. 'WŠY 'Gift of N.N.', root *'wš* 'to give'. On abbreviated forms in Palm. see below.

134. A sf. HM', which Stark suggests has a meaning N.N. protects' (cf. Arab. *hamā*, Stark, 89) may also be noted here, as well as the Palm. name *ḤPRY*, which Stark suggests is a sf. with Arab. *ḥafara* 'to protect'.

135. The Palm. name Š'', which Stark (p. 115) considers to be a sf. meaning 'Servant of God' (i.e. Š''L), should also be noted here.

136. The genitive form of the element in NṢRLT 'Help from Allat' is perhaps different from the verbal idea 'to help' expressed in Heb. *'wš*, *'zr* and *'dr*.

137. An Aphel perf. of *'th* in 'YTYBL 'Bēl has brought (the child)'. The same root in Heb. *'ělî'ātāh* is used in the Qal, 'El has come'.

138. *Pa''el* in RWḤBL 'Bel gives rest': contrast Heb. *yôšibyāh*, 'Y causes to dwell (in peace and security)', which contains a slightly different nuance of thought.

139. Stark also refers to a number of sff. which are pass. parts., as in the name ZBWD 'Given by N.N.' (Stark, 86). On such forms in the Heb. onomasticon, see above, p. 168). These, however, reveal no semantic concepts which are not already covered by full forms or other suggested sff. in Palm.

140. The Heb. root *'ḥz* 'to grasp, take hold, take possession' probably contains the first of these meanings in theophoric names, and expresses

figuratively that the deity has 'grasped' or 'seized' (by the hand) in order to help, cf. the Akk. use of *ṣabātu* 'to seize' (by the hand) above, §4.6.3.

Chapter 5

CONCLUSION:
A COMPARISON BETWEEN THE CONCEPTS OF DEITY IN HEBREW AND OTHER ANCIENT SEMITIC ONOMASTICA

It would not seem unreasonable to expect, amongst the ancient Semitic onomastica, certain similarities in semantic ideas. The vicissitudes of life would have made concepts such as protection and graciousness or kindness, for example, essential ingredients of a divine personality, which we would expect to occur in each of the Semitic onomastica. For many ideas, however, there is considerable variance; the idea of salvation, for example, is evident in all Semitic name-giving except Palmyrene and, while such a concept is rare in Ugaritic, Amorite, Phoenician and Old Akkadian, it is more frequent in Aramaic and Akkadian, and most widely met in Hebrew names.

The semantic content of Hebrew theophoric names has been examined above (§3) under a number of sub-headings, and we are now in a position to compare these ideas with those of the remaining Semitic onomastica, in the same categories. Excluded, for the time being, will be those concepts which are either used differently from, or have no semantic equivalent in, Hebrew names; these will be dealt with separately below. As the previous comparative sections will have shown, many elements present considerable difficulty, so that their comparison with Hebrew elements has been problematic. This is particularly noticeable with Amorite names, which often have a wide variety of possible etymologies. When this is the case, the root will be noted as a difficult form (Df.), followed by references to sections where other possibilities are suggested. Semantic equivalents will be denoted by the sign ^{s}/eq. In the following lists, name-elements are grouped, as far as possible, according to semantic criteria.

A. *Concepts attested in Hebrew names with cognates or semantic equivalents in other ancient Semitic onomastica*

1. *Anthropomorphic concepts*

Heb. *ḥlq* 'portion'.	Also Phoen.; Aram. (or verbal): ^{s}/eq. Aram. *prs*; perhaps Akk. *zittu* 'share of inheritance'.
Heb. *gd* 'fortune'.	Also Phoen.; Aram.; Palm.; Akk. *gadā*; Ug. *gt* (Df. cf. below, A 12): ^{s}/eq. Palm. *rg'* 'luck', *š'd* 'luck', (the last element is gen. while all the other elements are nominal).
Heb. *šb'* 'good fortune, fulness, perfection'.	For ^{s}/eq. cf. *gd*.
Heb. *yš* 'existence'.	in the dubious name *'ăbîšay/'abšay*: however, cf. Akk. *bašû* 'to be, exist' which can be used to depict the deity as a source of existence.
Heb. *mbṭḥ* 'trust'.	^{s}/eq. Aram. *tkl* (verbal); O. Akk./Akk. *takālu* (verbal and nominal). Verbal elements have the deity as object.
Heb. *'wd* 'witness'.	Also Phoen.; Aram.; Ug. *'d* (Df. cf. below, A 14, A 18).
Heb. *ḥrh* 'to burn, be kindled (of anger).	^{s}/eq. Phoen. *yḥr* 'to rage' (Df. cf. below, A 13, B 7, B 21); Amor. *mrṣ* 'to be sick, angry' (Df.), *rsb* (= *ršp*?) 'to burn, kindle' (Df.); Akk. *marāṣu* 'to be sick, angry'.
Heb. *'wr* 'light'.	Also Phoen.; Aram.; O. Akk. *urrum*.
Heb. *nr* 'lamp'.	Also Ug. (and gen.); Phoen.; Amor.; Aram.; O. Akk./Akk. *nūru*; Palm.
Heb. *'m* 'kinsman'.	Also Ug.; Phoen.; Amor. *ḫmm*; Aram.; O. Akk. *ammum*; Akk. *ḫammu*.
Heb. *ḥm* 'paternal uncle.	For ^{s}/eq. cf. *'m*.
Heb. *'b* 'father'.	Also Ug.; Phoen.; Amor.; Aram.; O. Akk./Akk. *abu*; Palm.: ^{s}/eq. Ug. *'d*, also Phoen. (Df.), Amor., Aram., O. Akk. *addi*; Amor. *'bn* (Df.), *'dn* (Df. cf. below, A 16).

Heb. *'ḥ* 'brother'.	Also Ug.; Phoen.; Amor.; Aram.; O. Akk./Akk. *aḫu*; Palm.
Heb. *yph* 'to be fair, beautiful'; *šnh* 'to shine, be beautiful'.	^{s}/eq. Amor. *ṣpr*$_2$ 'to be fair' (Df. cf. below, B 7), *ysm*, *šm* (Df.) 'beautiful', *spr* 'to be fair, shining', *sr'* cf. Arab. *sariya* 'to shine, gleam' (Df. cf. below, A 7); O. Akk. *banû* 'fine, beautiful, splendid' but perhaps 'friendly' in names (cf. below, A 3).
Heb. *'dh* 'ornament'.	^{s}/eq. Aram. *m'd* (Df.).
Heb. *n'm* 'pleasantness, delight'.	Also Ug.; Phoen.: ^{s}/eq. Phoen. *ḥpṣ* 'pleasure, delight'.
Heb. *'dn* 'delight, luxury'.	For ^{s}/eq. cf. *n'm*.
Heb. *bqq* 'to be luxuriant' (Df.).	^{s}/eq. Akk. *šamḫu*.
Heb. *ytr* 'abundance.	^{s}/eq. Amor. *spk* (= *śpk*? Df. cf. below, B 15).
Heb. *pn* 'face'.	Also Ug.; Phoen.; Akk. *pānu*.
Heb. *šm* 'name'.	Also Ug.; Phoen.; Amor. *sm*.

There remains a number of anthropomorphic ideas which are unique to Hebrew. The root *qdm* probably depicts the deity as 'ancient', while the root *mgd*, meaning 'excellent' or 'excellence', is used in biblical Hebrew of the gifts of nature, so that its use to describe the Hebrew deity is essentially anthropomorphic, rather than transcendent in meaning. Only Hebrew names portray the deity as 'death' (*mwt*), and as 'fine gold' (*pz*), while also peculiar to Hebrew is the name *ḥagîyāh* 'Feast of Y'.

2. *Concepts involving nature*

Heb. *zr'* 'to sow'.	Also Amor. *zrḫ*.
Heb. *'rš* 'to plant'.	Also Akk. *erēšu*: ^{s}/eq. Amor. *nṭ'*.
Heb. *šḥr* 'dawn'.	Also Ug.

Several ideas remain peculiar to Hebrew; these are contained in the roots *zrh*, 'to scatter, fan, winnow', *šrb* (Piel) 'to send burning heat', *ḥrp* 'Autumn' *s'r* 'storm, rage, tempest', *r'm* 'thunder', *r'l* 'to quiver, shake, reel' and *š'l* 'deep' (of the sea).

3. *Genitive elements*

Heb. *'yš* 'man'.	Also Ug. *'š*; Phoen. *'š* (Df. cf. below, A 7), *'š* (Df. cf. below, A7): ^{s}/eq. Akk. *awīlu*; Palm. *'mr* (sf. only): cf. also *mt*.
Heb. *mt* 'man'.	Also Ug.; perhaps Aram. in the name *b^{e}tû'ēl* (=*m^{e}tû'ēl*?); Akk. *mūtu* (or spouse): for ^{s}/eq. cf. *'yš*.
Heb. *gbr* 'man'.	For ^{s}/eq. cf. *'yš* and *mt*.
Heb. *n'r* 'youth, servant, attendant'.	Also Ug.: ^{s}/eq. O. Akk. *ayarum* 'young man'.
Heb. *pth* 'youth'.	For ^{s}/eq. cf. *n'r*.
Heb. *'bd* 'servant'.	Also Ug.; Phoen.; Amor. *ḫbd*; Aram.; Palm.: ^{s}/eq. O. Akk./Akk. *(w)ardu*; Palm. *tym*, *š'* (sf. only).
Heb. *gr* 'client'.	Also Phoen.
Heb. *b* + *yd* 'in the hand of'.	Also Ug.; Phoen.; Aram.
Heb. *'gl* 'calf'.	^{s}/eq. O. Akk./Akk. *būru*.
Heb. *r'* 'friend'.	Also Phoen. (nominal Df.); Aram. (nominal and construct): ^{s}/eq. Ug. *tp* (cf. Akk.); O. Akk./Akk. *tappû* 'companion' (nominal); O. Akk. *banû* 'friendly' (or 'fine, beautiful, splendid' cf. above, A 1).

Two construct nouns preceded by a preposition are found to be attested only in Heb. names: these are *b* + *'wd* 'in the testimony, witness of' and *b* + *swd* 'in the secret council of' the deity. Also occurring only in Hebrew are construct nouns from the roots *qnh* 'possession of' and *yd'* 'known of' the deity, while *'ry*, depicting the name-bearer as a 'lion of' the deity, is also not attested elsewhere.

4. *Prepositional elements*

Heb. *'t* 'with'.	Also Phoen.; Palm.; Akk. *itti*.
Heb. *'m* 'with'.	Also Aram. (Df.): for ^{s}/eq. cf. *'t*.
Heb. *l*/*lmw* 'belonging to'	Also Palm.; Amor.

Heb. *'l* 'towards'.	The Heb. name *'ely(^{e}h)ô'ênay* 'Towards Y are my eyes' is semantically similar to the Akk. names ^{d}*Nabû-ú-p[i]-ni-ya* 'Towards Nabû is my palm opened', *Itti-*^{d}*Nusku-īnā-ya* 'On Nusku (rest or are directed) my eyes' and *Ibašši* (GÁL*ši*)*-uz-ni-a-na-ili* (AN) 'My attention is directed on god'.

5. *Deity approaches man*

Heb. *'th*, *bw'* 'to come.	^{s}/eq. O. Akk. *kašādum* 'to arrive', *napāqum* 'to come forth'; Akk. *qerēbu* 'to approach'.
Heb. *zrḥ* 'to rise'.	^{s}/eq. Amor. *ns'* (if reflexive); O. Akk. *tabā'um* 'to come up, arise'; Akk. *napāḫu* 'to rise'; Palm. *ṣ'd* 'to rise' (sf. only).
Heb. *qwm* 'to arise'.	Also Ug.; Phoen.; Amor.: for ^{s}/eq. cf. *zrḥ*.
Heb. *škn* to take up abode'.	Also Amor. *skn*: ^{s}/eq. Amor. dr_1 'to turn around, dwell, endure'; Akk. *ramû* 'to dwell'.
Heb. *'nn* 'to appear'.	Also Aram.

Only Hebrew names contain the idea that the deity 'meets' man. This thought is evident in the Niphal of the root *y'd* 'to meet by appointment', *pg'* 'to meet', and possibly *'nh* 'to meet' (see above, §2.9 *'nyhw*). Also unattested in other ancient Semitic name-giving is the idea that the deity has 'sought', found in Hebrew names with the root *drš* 'to seek'.

6. *Perceptiveness of the deity*

Heb. *ḥzh* 'to see'.	Also Ug. *ḥdy*; Phoen. *ḥzy*; Amor. *ḫs'* (Df.); Amor. *ḫṣ'* (Df. cf. below, A 14); Aram.; Palm.: ^{s}/eq. Ug. *'mr*, perhaps also Amor.; Aram. *ḥwr*; Akk. *amāru* 'to see', *dagālu* 'to look upon'; Phoen. *š'* (= *š'y*?) 'to gaze, regard with favour' (Df. cf. below, A 11); Aram. *twr* 'to be watchful' (Df. cf. BH *tîryā'* and below, A 8, A 12).
Heb. *r'h* 'to see'; *šwr* 'to regard, behold' (?); *śkh* 'to look out' (?).	For ^{s}/eq. cf. *ḥzh*.

Heb. *ḥšb* 'to take account'; *š'r* 'to reckon'.	^{s}/eq. Ug. *mny*, Aram. *mnh*, Akk. *manû* (Df.) 'to count'; Amor. *pls* 'to view, consider' (Df. cf. below, B 15); Akk. *qâlu* 'to pay attention to'; Aram. *śky* 'to pay attention'.
Heb. *yd'* 'to know'.	Also Ug.; Phoen.; Amor. *ydḫ*; Aram.; O. Akk. *wadā'um*; Akk. *idû*; Palm.
Heb. *šm'* 'to hear'.	Also Ug.; Phoen.; Amor. *smḫ*; Aram.; O. Akk. *šamā'um*; Akk. *šemû*; Palm. (sf. only).
Heb. *'zn* 'to hear'.	For ^{s}/eq. cf. *šm'*.
Heb. *s'l* 'to ask, inquire'.	Also Aram.; ^{s}/eq. Ug. *'p* (=*'pp*?) 'to request a gift' (Df. cf. below, B 20); O. Akk. *erāšum* 'to wish, request'.
Heb. *zkr* 'to remember'.	Also Phoen.; Amor. (Df. cf. below, B 7) Aram. *dkr*; Palm. *dkr* (sf. only).
Heb. *y'h* 'to remember'.	Heb. construct: ^{s}/eq. O. Akk. *ḫasāsum* (gen.).
Heb. *'nh* 'to answer'.	Also Phoen. *'n* (Df.); Amor. *y'n* (Df. cf. below, B 7); Aram.; O. Akk. *inu*(*n*) 'to grant a favour' (Df. cf. below, B 24): ^{s}/eq. Amor. *šb*; Palm. *ndb* 'to grant'.
Heb. *brk* 'to bless'.	Also Phoen.; Aram.; Palm.: ^{s}/eq. O. Akk./Akk. *karābu* 'to bless', (O. Akk. also nominal); Akk. *kiribtu* (gen.).

7. *Involvement of the deity in birth events*

Heb. *bnh* 'to build, create'.	Also Ug.; Phoen.; Amor. *bn'*; Aram.; O. Akk./Akk. *banû*; Palm. (sf. only): Akk. also nominal 'Creator'.
Heb. *br'* 'to acquire, create'.	Also Aram.: ^{s}/eq. Ug. *mrṯ* (root *yrṯ*) 'to inherit, receive' (Df.).
Heb. *qnh* 'to create, acquire'.	Also Ug.; Phoen.; Aram.: ^{s}/eq. possibly Ug. *mrṯ* (*yrṯ*) 'to inherit, receive' (Df.).
Heb. *'śh* 'to make', also construct 'work'.	Also Phoen. *'š* (= *'šy*? Df. cf. above, A 3, and below) Amor. *'s'* (Df. cf. below, A 12), *ḫs* (Df. cf. below, A 12) and *ḫz'* (Df. cf. below, A 9); Aram. (Df.): ^{s}/eq. O. Akk./Akk. *liptu* 'creation, craft'; Akk.

	epēšu 'to do, permit'; Amor. *yṣr* 'to form, design'.
Heb. *p'l* 'to make'.	Also Phoen.; Phoen. *pl* (Df. cf. below, A 17, A 18, B 6): for ^{s}/eq. cf. *'śh*.
Heb. *rwḥ* 'to breathe (create)' (Df.).	^{s}/eq. Amor. *nps* 'breath, life'.
Heb. *ḥyh* 'to give life' (Df.).	^{s}/eq. Amor. *nps*, Akk. *napištu* 'breath, life', O. Akk./Akk. *balāṭu* 'life'.
Heb. *šlm* 'to recompense'.	Also Phoen.: for ^{s}/eq. cf. *šwb*.
Heb. *šwb* Hiphil 'to restore'.	^{s}/eq. Ug. *r'b* 'to compensate'; Amor. *r'p* (= *r'b*? Df. cf. below, A 12); O. Akk./Akk. *râbu* 'to compensate'; Phoen. *'š* (Df. cf. above A 3, and Heb. *'wš* below); Amor. *ḫt'* (= *ḫṭ'*?) 'to compensate' (Df.); Aram. *sl'* 'to restore, pay back' (Df.) Akk. *kutallu*, *rībatu*, *tarībum* 'compensation, replacement', *kašāru* 'to compensate'.
Heb. *gmr* 'to accomplish'.	Also Ug. (verbal and nominal); Amor.
Heb. *gml* 'to accomplish'.	For ^{s}/eq. cf. *gmr*.
Heb. *'mr* 'to say'.	Also Amor. (or 'to see'); Aram.: ^{s}/eq. Aram. *rgm* 'to say' (Df.), *rmz* 'to speak'; O. Akk. *awājum* 'to speak'; Akk. *qabû* 'to speak, announce, command'.
Heb. *qwl* 'voice'.	(Heb. perhaps also verbal 'to speak'). Also Ug. *ql* (Df.); Amor. *ql* (verbal): ^{s}/eq. Akk. *rigmu*/*rigimtu* 'voice'.
Heb. *'wš* 'to bestow'.	Also Palm.; Phoen. *'š* (Df. cf. above, A 3), *'š* (Df. cf. above, A 3, A 7); Amor. *'š* (Df. cf. below, A 11): ^{s}/eq. Ug. *brd* 'to offer, present' (Df.); Phoen. *mgn*; Aram. *yhb*: cf. also *ntn*, *zbd* and *qwš*.
Heb. *zbd* 'to bestow'.	Also Aram.; Palm.: for ^{s}/eq. cf. *'wš*, *ntn* and *qwš*.
Heb. *ntn* 'to give' construct 'gift'.	Also Amor.; Aram.; Palm.; O. Akk./Akk. *nadānu*; Ug. and Phoen. *ytn*: for ^{s}/eq. cf. *'wš* and *zbd*; also Akk. *rīmūtu*, *qīštu*, *qīšu* 'gift'; Palm. *wahb* 'gift', *yhb* 'to give'.

Heb. *qwš* 'to give a gift, present' (Df.).	Also Akk. *qâšu*: for ^{s}/eq. cf. *'wš*, *zbd* and *ntn*.
Heb. *pṭ* (Eg.) 'to give'.	Use of this Eg. element is also attested in Phoen. and Aram. names. For ^{s}/eq. cf. *'wš*, *zbd*, *ntn* and *qwš*.
Heb. *ptḥ* 'to open (the womb)'.	Also O. Akk. *patā'um*; Palm. *p^{e}ṣā'*.
Heb. *rmh* 'to loosen'.	^{s}/eq. Ug. *šr* (= *šrr*?) 'to let loose' (Df. cf. below, A 11, A 16, B 21); Amor. *sr'* (= *šry*?) 'to loosen' (Df. cf. above, A1); Aram. *rp'* 'to loosen' (or 'to heal' Df.); Akk. *ašāru* 'to release' (Df. cf. below, A 9).
Heb. *rḥb* 'to make wide, make room, be wide, large'.	^{s}/eq. perhaps Amor. *rb'* 'to be or become large' (or = *rbb* 'great').
Heb. *ysp* 'to add'.	Also Phoen.; Akk. *eṣēpu* 'to double, multiply': ^{s}/eq. Phoen. *nn* 'to propagate, increase' (Df.); O. Akk. *šanājum* 'to do something twice'; Akk. *radā'u* 'to increase'; *šanû* 'to do twice', *šalāšu* 'to do three times'.

Extant only in the Hebrew nomenclature, is the idea that the deity opens the eyes, with the use of the root *pqḥ*, a concept which may belong here in the context of bringing the child into the world, or may involve the sense of enlightening. The root *sbk*, perhaps 'to interweave', is also peculiar to Hebrew usage, but its relevance to birth events is questionable and the uncertainty of the name has been noted above (§ 2.9 *sḃk̇yhw*).

8. *Protection*

Heb. *'hl* 'tent'.	Also Phoen.: ^{s}/eq. Amor. *dwr* (noun *madar*) 'dwelling'.
Heb. *dlt* 'door'.	^{s}/eq. Aram. *bb'* 'door, gate' (Df.); Akk. *bābu* 'door, gate'.
Heb. *hr* 'mountain' (sanctuary).	Also Phoen.: ^{s}/eq. Amor. *šd* 'mountain', *ṣr* 'mountain, rock'; Aram. *ṭwr*, O. Akk. *huršānum*; O. Akk./Akk. *šadû*.
Heb. *mḥsh* 'refuge'.	Also Aram.

Heb. *'wn* 'refuge' (Df.).	For s/eq. cf. *mḥsh*.
Heb. *šwr* 'wall'.	Also Aram.; Palm. ('stronghold'); O. Akk./Akk. *dūru*: s/eq. Akk. *igāriš* 'like a wall'.
Heb. *b* + *ṣll* 'in the shadow of'.	Cf. O. Akk/Akk. *ṣillu*.
Heb. *ṣwr* 'rock'.	Also Amor. 'rock, mountain': s/eq. Amor. *kb* (Df.); Aram. *qtr*.
Heb. *zmr* 'to protect'.	Also Ug. *ḏmr*; Amor. (verbal and nominal); O. Akk. *zamārum* (*izammer*): s/eq. Ug., Aram. and Palm. *'qb* Amor. *ḫqb* 'to guard, protect'; Aram. *mt'* 'to guard, protect'; Amor. *mt'* 'to protect'; Phoen. *gnn*, Amor. *'rs* (= *ḥrs*? Df. cf. below, A 10, B 27), *sgb* (Df. cf. below, A 10), Akk. *ḫātinu*, *naṣāru*, *emēdu* (S), Palm. *hm*, *ḥpr* (Df.) 'to protect'; Amor. *str*, O. Akk./Akk. *andullu*, Akk. *utlu*, *kidinnu*, *ḫutnu*, *ṣulūlu*, Palm. *'auḏ* 'protection'; Amor. *ḫṣn* (Df. cf. Heb. *'zh*, below) and Akk. *ḫaṣānu* 'to shelter, protect'; Akk. *paqādu* 'to take care of, protect' (Df.), *ḫâṭu* 'to watch over, take care of'; Phoen. *pls* 'to watch, level'; Aram. *twr* 'to be watchful' (Df. cf. above, A 6, below, A 12); O. Akk. *barājum* 'to look upon, watch over, inspect, observe'; Akk. *amru* 'seen, guarded' (Df. cf. below, A 14); O. Akk./Akk. *puzru* 'security'; O. Akk. *naṣārum* nominal, 'Protector', 'guarded'.
Heb. *ḥmh* 'to protect' (Df.).	Also Phoen. *ḥm* (Df.): for s/eq. cf. *zmr*.
Heb. *str*, *ḥb'*, *ṣpn* 'to conceal, hide'.	Also Aram. *str*.

Remaining in Hebrew names alone, may be the anthropomorphic idea of protection expressed by the root *ṭll* 'to cover'.

9. *Preservation and support*

Heb. *šmr* 'to preserve, keep'.	Also Phoen.; Amor. *smr*: S/eq. O. Akk./ Akk. *šaṭāpu* 'to preserve life'; Akk. *kaṣāru* 'to preserve', *šalāmu* 'to keep safe, preserve'.
Heb. *'zh* 'to nourish'.	Also Amor. *ḫz'* (Df. cf. above, A 7): S/eq. Phoen. *šlk* 'to nourish, provide'; Amor. *sṭ'* 'to nourish', *ḫṣn* (= *ḥḍn*?) 'to embrace, nourish' (Df. cf. Heb. *zmr* above); O. Akk. *apārum*, Akk. *epēru* 'to provide for'; Akk. *ašāru* 'to provide with food', *zāninu* 'Provider'.
Heb. *qwt* 'to nourish'.	For S/eq. cf. *'zh*.
Heb. *smk* 'to support, sustenance, support'.	Also Phoen.; Aram.; Phoen. *tmk*: S/eq. O. Akk./Akk. nouns from *emēdu*, 'support'.
Heb. *'mn*, *'šh*, *yšh* (Df.) 'to support'.	For S/eq. cf. *smk*.
Heb. *kwl* Pilpel 'to support, sustain, nourish'.	Also Akk. *ka''ulu* (D): S/eq. cf. *smk* and *'zh*.
Heb. *yšb* 'to cause to dwell (in peace and security)'.	Also Phoen. (Df. cf. below, A 12, B 2): S/eq. Amor. *sqṭ* 'to rest'.

10. *Strength*

Heb. *mrr* 'to strengthen' (or 'bless, commend').	Also Ug.; Phoen. ('to be strong'); Amor. *mr* (Df.): S/eq. Amor. *l''*, *sgb* (Df. cf. above, A 8); Aram. *sgb* (Df. cf. below, B 7); Akk. *patānu. danānu*, *taqānu* (D).
Heb. *ḥzq* 'to strengthen'.	For S/eq. cf. *mrr*.
Heb. *'zz* 'to be strong, strength'	Also Ug.; Phoen.; Aram.; Palm.: S/eq. Phoen. *mrr*, Amor. *ḫtr* (Df. cf. below, A 11, B 7), *l'* (Df. cf. below, B 28), *'rs* (= *ḥrz*? Df. cf. above, A 8, below, B 27), Aram. *dmr* 'to be strong'; O. Akk. *qarrādum/ qurādum*, O.Akk./Akk. *dannu*, Akk. *emūqu*, *le'û*, *gašru* 'strong'; Akk. *qurdu*, *idu*, *li'ūtu*, *kiṣru* 'strength'; Akk. *lītu* 'power, strength, *ba'lu* 'powerful, important', *li'ū* 'mighty'; Ug. *'dr* 'to be mighty, powerful'.

Heb. *ḥwl/ḥyl* 'strength'.	For ^{s}/eq. cf. *'zz*.
Heb. *'wn* 'strength' (Df.).	For ^{s}/eq. cf. *'zz*.
Heb. *ḥzq*, *'mṣ* 'to be strong'.	For ^{s}/eq. cf. *'zz*.
Heb. *knn* 'to be firm'.	Also Ug. *kwn*; Amor. *kn*$_1$; O. Akk. *kînum*.
Heb. *'br* 'to be firm, strong'.	Also Phoen.: for ^{s}/eq. cf. *'zz* and *knn*.
Heb. *ykl* 'to be able, prevail'.	^{s}/eq. Amor. *l''* 'to be able, strong, prevail'.

11. *Salvation and help*

Heb. *yš'* 'to deliver, save'.	Also Aram.: ^{s}/eq. Ug. *šr* (= *šrr*?) 'to let loose' (Df. cf. above, A 8, below, A 16, B 21); Phoen. *š'* (Df. cf. above, A 6), *šlḥ* 'to set free'; Akk. *eṭēru* 'to save', *gamālu* 'to save, spare', *ḥws* 'to spare'; cf. also *plṭ*, *ḥml* and *šêzêb*.
Heb. *plṭ* 'to deliver'.	Also Phoen.: for ^{s}/eq. cf. *yš'*.
Heb. *nṣl* Hiphil 'to deliver.	For ^{s}/eq. cf. *yš'*, *plṭ* and *šêzêb*.
Heb. *ḥml* 'to spare'.	Also Aram.: for ^{s}/eq. cf. *yš'*.
Heb. *šêzêb* (Aram. lw. 'to deliver'.	Also Aram.; Amor. *ḫzb* 'to rescue'; Akk. *šūzubu*: for ^{s}/eq. cf. *yš'* and *plṭ*.
Heb. *dlh* 'to draw'.	Also Aram.: ^{s}/eq. O. Akk. *šalālum* 'to draw out' or 'carry away' or 'continue' (Df.).
Heb. *ḥlṣ* 'to draw off'.	Also Phoen. 'to deliver': for ^{s}/eq. cf. *dlh*.
Heb. *pdh* 'to ransom'.	Also Phoen.: ^{s}/eq. Akk. *kaspu* 'ransom'.
Heb. *g'l* 'to redeem'.	^{s}/eq. Aram. *ḥll* 'to loosen, redeem' (Df. cf. below, B 15).
Heb. *'zr* 'to help'.	Also Phoen.; Amor. *ḫzr*; Aram.: ^{s}/eq. Ug. *yṯ'* (Df.); Amor. *ḫtr* (= *'ḏr*? Df. cf. above, A 10, below, B 7), *yšḫ*, *ḫl* (Df. cf. below, B 10); O. Akk. *ṣīnum*, *rîṣum* 'help'; Akk. *ḫāziru* (Amor. lw.), 'to help', *kitru*, *narāru*, *rēṣu*, *tillatu*, *ḫamātu* 'help'; cf. also *'dr* and *'wš*.

Heb. *'dr* 'to help'.	Also Ug.; Aram.: for ^{s}/eq. cf. *'zr*.
Heb. *'wš* 'to help'.	Also Amor. *'š* (Df. cf. above, A 7); Aram. *'wt* (Df.); Akk. *āšu* 'to help', *usātu* 'help': for ^{s}/eq. cf. *'zr* and *'dr*.
Heb. *'ḥz* 'to seize'.	^{s}/eq. Aram. *lkd*; Akk. *ṣabātu* 'to seize' (by the hand).
Heb. *'ms* 'to carry a load, bear'.	Also Phoen.; Amor. *ḫms*: ^{s}/eq. Amor. *'bl* 'to bring, carry' (or refers to birth events).

In this semantic group, one idea remains which is attested only in Hebrew theophoric names: this is the thought that the deity has 'carried into exile' contained in the Hiphil of the root *glh*.

12. *Goodness, kindness, grace and compassion*

Heb. *ḥnn* 'to be gracious, show favour'.	Also Ug.; Phoen.; Aram.; Akk. *enēnu*; Palm.: ^{s}/eq. Akk. *naplusu* 'to look graciously upon'; *damāqu* (D) 'to show favour'.
Heb. *ḥn* 'grace, favour'.	Also O. Akk. *enna*, Akk. *ḫinnu/annu*: ^{s}/eq. Amor. *nḥm*; O. Akk. *ipqum*; Akk. *gimillu*, *damiq*, *gūzu* (Df.), *silmu*; *gamālu* 'graciousness, kindness'.
Heb. *ḥsd* 'to be kind, good, gracious'.	For ^{s}/eq. cf. *ḥnn* and *ṭwb*.
Heb. *ḥlh* 'to be sweet, pleasing, show oneself well-disposed, friendly'.	For ^{s}/eq. cf. *ḥnn*.
Heb. *ṭwb* 'to be good'.	Also Amor.; Aram.; O. Akk./Akk. *ṭâbu*: ^{s}/eq. O. Akk./Akk. *damqu* 'good'; Akk. *dummuqu* 'good, favourable, fine'.
Heb. *yṭb* 'to benefit', *ydh* 'to be beneficent, do good'.	For ^{s}/eq. cf. *ḥnn* and *ṭwb*.
Heb. *ṣdq* 'to be just, righteous'.	Also Ug.; Phoen.; Amor.; Aram.; Palm. *zdq*: ^{s}/eq. Ug. *yšr*; Amor. *ysr*, *yšr*, O. Akk. *išarum*; Ug. *škl* 'to be judicious'; Aram. *kwn* 'to be right'.
Heb. *rḥm* Piel 'to have compassion'; *nḥm* 'to comfort'.	^{s}/eq. Amor. *r'p* (Df. cf. above, A 7), *ḫnb* (Df.), *ḫs* 'to be compassionate' (Df. cf. above, A 7); O. Akk. *gamil* 'merciful';

	Akk. *rēma rašu* 'to show pity', *rêmu* 'to have pity on', *rēmēnû* 'merciful', *rīmu* 'mercy, grace', *tayāru* 'merciful'.
Heb. *šwb* 'to return'.	Also Ug. *ṯwb*; Phoen. *yšb* (= *šwb*? Df. cf. above, A 9, below, B 2); Amor. (also 'to answer'): ^{s}/eq. Ug. *twr*; Amor. *tr*; Aram. *'wd* (or 'to testify'); O. Akk./Akk. *tu'āru*.
Heb. *swr* 'to turn aside' (Df.).	^{s}/eq. Phoen. *ḥll* 'to turn'; Amor. dr_1 'to turn around, dwell, endure'; Aram. *twr* 'to turn' (Df. cf. above, A 6, A 8); Akk. *târu* 'to turn'.
Heb. *pnh* 'to turn' (Df.).	Also Palm.: for ^{s}/eq. cf. *swr*.
Heb. *sḥr* 'to turn' (Df.).	Also Akk. *saḫāru* (N): ^{s}/eq. cf. *swr* and *pnh*.
Heb. *nšh* 'to forget (sins)'.	^{s}/eq. Amor. *ms'* 'to forget' (Df. cf. below, A 14), *sl'* (= *slḫ*?) 'to pardon' (Df. cf. below, B 15); O. Akk. *wabālum* 'to pardon'; Akk. *mêšu* 'to forgive (sins)'.
Heb. *rp'* 'to heal'.	Also Ug.; Amor.; Aram. (Df.); Palm.; O. Akk. *rapā'um*: ^{s}/eq. Ug. *'sy*; O. Akk./Akk. *asû* 'physician, healer', Akk. also *ašâtu*; Amor. *'s'* (Df. cf. above, A 7). The root *'sh* is attested only in a sf. in Heb. names.

13. *The deity as a source of joy*

Heb. *ḥdh* 'to rejoice, give joy'.	Also Phoen. *yḥr* (= *yḥd*? Df. cf. above, A 13, below, B 7, B 21); O. Akk. *ḫadāwum* 'joy': ^{s}/eq. Amor. *simḫ* 'joy' (Df. cf. below A 17, B 21); Palm. *rḍy* 'to be content' in sf. only with the meaning 'to delight'.
Heb. *gyl* 'rejoicing joy'; *'śr* 'to fill with joy'; *ḥbṣ* 'to be joyful (causative?).	For ^{s}/eq. cf. *ḥdh*.

14. *The concept of selection*

Heb. *'sp* 'to gather'.	^{s}/eq. Amor. *pḫr*, *kbs* (Df. cf. below, B 7) 'to assemble'; Akk. *ašāru* (Df.) 'to muster', 'to provide with food', 'to be humble', 'to release', *kaṣāru*? 'to tie, bind together, collect, organize, gather' (Df.).

Heb. *ḥṣh* 'to divide'.	Also Amor. *ḫṣ'* (Df. cf. above, A 6): ^{s}/eq. Amor. *btl* 'to separate, devote oneself exclusively to one god' (Df.); perhaps Akk. *amru* 'checked, accounted for' (Df. cf. above, A 8).
Heb. *d'h* 'to call'.	^{s}/eq. Amor. *bḫr*, Aram. *bḥr* 'to choose' (*bḥr* = sf. only in Heb. names).
Heb. *'ṣl* 'to reserve, lay aside'.	For ^{s}/eq. cf. *ḥṣh*.
Heb. *brr* 'to purify, select'; *ṭbl* 'to dip (purify)'; *nzh* 'to sprinkle (purify)'.	^{s}/eq. Amor. *ms'* 'to wash, purify' (Df. cf. above A 12); Aram. *nqy* (imv.) 'to purify'.
Heb. *ydd* 'beloved'.	Also Ug. (verbal 'to love'), *mdd* (pass. part.): ^{s}/eq. O. Akk. *mani*; O. Akk./Akk. *narāmu*; Akk. *tarāmu* cf. also *dwd*.
Heb. *dwd* 'to love, beloved'.	Also O. Akk. *dadum* 'beloved': ^{s}/eq. Ug., Palm., *ḥbb* 'to love'; Aram. *rḥm* 'to love, have affection for'; O. Akk./Akk. *râmu* 'to love'; cf. also *ydd*.
Heb. *'dh* 'to adorn'.	Also Ug. *'d* (Df. cf. above, 1, below, 18); Aram.
Heb. *rml* 'to adorn with gems'.	For ^{s}/eq. cf. *'dh*.
Heb. *šbh* 'captive'.	^{s}/eq. Akk. *esēru* 'to fetter, imprison' (gen.).

15. *Establishment by the deity*

Heb. *kwn* 'to establish'.	Also O. Akk./Akk. *kunnu*, Akk. *mukīnu*: ^{s}/eq. Phoen. *šyt*, *ṣb* (= *nṣb*? Df.); Amor. *nṣb* 'to place, set up', *st_1* 'to put, place'; Aram. *nśy* 'to raise'; O. Akk. *alājum* 'to elevate'; Akk. *elā'u* (Š) 'to establish', *pattanu* 'to set up, erect'; O. Akk./Akk. *šakānu* 'to establish'; Palm. *nš'* (sf. only); cf. also *qwm* and *śwm*.
Heb. *śwm* 'to establish'.	Also Amor. (Df.); O. Akk./Akk. *šâmu* 'to appoint'; for ^{s}/eq. cf. *kwn* and *qwm*.

Heb. *qwm* Hiphil 'to raise up'.	Also Phoen.; Amor.; Aram.: for s/eq. cf. *kwm* and *śwm*.
Heb. *plh* 'to distinguish (be separated)'.	Also Amor. (Df.).
Heb. *ngh* 'to enlighten'.	Also Ug.; Aram.: s/eq. Phoen. *'rḥ* (Df.); Akk. *namāru* 'to shine' (precative, also plea).

16. *Divine titles*

Heb. *b'l* 'lord'.	Also Ug.; Phoen.; Amor. *bl* (Akk.), *ba(ḫ)l*; Aram.; O. Akk./Akk. *bēlu*: s/eq. Akk. *etellu* 'lord, prince'; cf. also *'dn* and *mr*.
Heb. *'dn* 'lord'.	Also Ug.; Phoen.; Amor. (Df. cf. above, A 1): for s/eq. cf. *b'l* and *mr*.
Heb. *mr* 'lord' (Df. Aram. lw.?).	Also Phoen.; Aram. *mr'*; Palm.: for s/eq. cf. *b'l* and *'dn*.
Heb. *mlk* 'king'.	Also Ug.; Phoen.; Amor.; Aram.; Palm.: s/eq. O. Akk./Akk. *šarru*; Ug. *ḏr*, *šr* (Df. cf. above, A 7, A 11, below, B 21).

17. *Transcendent characteristics*

Heb. *rwm* 'to be high, exalted'.	Also Ug.; Phoen.; Amor.; Aram.; Palm.: s/eq. Ug. *ṣhr*/*ẓhr* 'to be above, high'; Amor. *smḫ* (= śmḫ?) 'to be high, haughty' (Df. cf. above, A 13, below, B 21); Aram. *g'h* 'to be high, exalted'; Akk. *ṣēru*, *šaqû*, *tizqar* 'exalted', *nā'idu* 'exalted, lofty'; cf. also *'lh*.
Heb.? *'lh* 'to be high, exalted'.	Also Ug.; Aram.; Palm.: for s/eq. cf. *rwm*.
Heb. *śgb* 'to be (inaccessibly) high'.	For s/eq. cf. *rwm*, *'lh* and *'th*.
Heb. *'th* 'to be proud, exalted'; *pr'* 'to be noble, excel'.	s/eq. Akk. *muštarriḫu*, *šarraḫu* 'proud'; cf. also *rwm* and *'lh*.
Heb. *ytr* 'to be pre-eminent'.	Also Ug. ('to be unique, excellent', but as 'unique', cf. below, B 7); Amor.; O. Akk./Akk. (*w*)*atru*; Akk. *ṣiru* 'pre-eminent', 'exalted' or 'excellent'.

Heb. *'yl* 'to be predominant' (Df.).	Also Ug.
Heb. *rbb* 'to be great'.	Also Ug.; Amor. *rb'*; Aram.; O. Akk./Akk. *rabû*; Palm. *rby*: ^{s}/eq. Akk. *nirbi'u* 'greatness'.
Heb. *gdl* 'to be great'.	For ^{s}/eq. cf. *rbb*.
Heb. *ytn* 'to be perpetual, never-failing, constant'.	^{s}/eq. Amor. *ṣpr*$_1$ 'patient, steadfast' (Df.); Akk. *enû* 'to change' (+ negative).
Heb. *ḥyh* 'to live'.	Also Ug. *ḥwy/ḥyy*; Phoen. *ḥwy*.
Heb. *ndb* 'to be noble, generous'.	Also Ug.; Phoen.
Heb. *tmm* 'to be perfect'.	Also Ug.; Phoen.: ^{s}/eq. Akk. *(w)asāmu* 'perfectly beautiful'.
Heb. *kll* 'to be complete' (Df.).	For ^{s}/eq. cf. Heb. *tmm*.
Heb. *g'h* 'majesty'.	Also Aram.: ^{s}/eq. Aram. *ngh* 'splendour'; Akk. *nimru* 'splendour'.
Heb. *kbd* 'honour, glory'.	Also Ug.; Phoen.; Akk. *kabtu* 'honoured, important': ^{s}/eq. Phoen. *'dr* 'majestic, glorious'; Aram. *yqr* 'to be honoured, precious'; Akk. *šarraḫu* 'proud, glorious, magnificent'.
Heb. *pl'* 'to be wonderful'.	Also Phoen. *pl* (= *pl'*?) 'to be miraculous' (Df. cf. above, A 7, below, A 18, B 6).
Heb. *hw'* 'he'.	Also Ug.: ^{s}/eq. Akk. *šū* (in names of the type 'He is x').
Heb. *my* 'who?' + *k*^{e} 'like'.	Also Amor.; Aram.; Palm.; Akk. *man(nu)* (also Aram.): ^{s}/eq. Akk. *šanānu* 'to be equal' (+ interrog.).

18. *Rulership and judgment*

Heb. *'wm* 'to rule' (Df.).	^{s}/eq. Ug. *mlk*, also Amor.; Aram. Phoen. *mšl*; Ug. *mṯl* (= *mšl*?) (Df.); Amor. *'btl* (= *b'l*? Df. cf. below, B 18).
Heb. *dyn* 'to judge'.	Also Ug.; Amor.; Aram.; O. Akk./Akk. *dânu* (Akk. also nominal); Palm. (sf. only): ^{s}/eq. Akk. *mēšeru* 'justice'; cf. also *pll* and *špṭ*.

Heb. *pll* 'to judge'.	Also Phoen. *pl* (Df. cf. above, A 7, A 17, below B 6): for s/eq. cf. *dyn* and *špṭ*.
Heb. *špṭ* 'to judge'.	Also Ug. *ṯpṭ*; Phoen.; Amor.: for s/eq. cf. *dyn* and *pll*.
Heb. *dll* 'to direct' (Df.).	s/eq. Akk. *tarāṣu* 'to direct'; Palm. *hd'* 'to guide' (sf. only, cf. Heb. *ḥdh* 'to lead' sf. only).
Heb. *'wd* 'to testify'.	Also Ug. *'d* (Df. cf. above, A 1, A 14); Aram. (or 'to return').

Some roots in this semantic group are peculiar to Hebrew. This is the case with *ryb* 'to strive, contend', *'md* 'to take one's stand', *śrh* 'to persevere, persist' (or 'to rule'), while the 'will of' the deity is depicted with the root *'wh*. None of these ideas has any equivalent in the other Semitic onomastica.

19. *Imperatives and names in which the deity is accusative*

Heb. *ydh* 'to praise, thank'.	s/eq. O. Akk./Akk. *dalālu*, *nâdu* 'to praise', *karābu* 'to praise, worship'; Akk. *šitammuru* 'to praise', *bunna* 'thank!' (Df.), *mu'û* 'to praise, adore'.
Heb. *ḥkh* + *l* 'to wait for' (Df.).	s/eq. Akk. *qâlu* 'to pay attention to, be silent', *paqû* (D) 'to pay attention to', *naṭālu* 'to look at, see', *qa''û* 'to wait for, pay attention to', *dagālu pān* DN 'to wait for'.
Heb. *dmm* 'to be still' or 'to make peace'.	s/eq. Akk. *qâlu* 'to pay attention to, be silent'.

20. *Others*

Heb. *'wṣ* 'to make haste, press, be pressed'.	Also Phoen. *'ṣ* (Df.): s/eq. Amor. *ḫms* (= *'mṣ*?) 'to press close' (Df. cf. below, B 28).

The root *'db* 'to invite, discipline' (cf. Arab. *'adaba*) is not attested with certainty in Hebrew names (see above, § 2.9 *'adb^{e}'ēl*), but has no semantic parallel in the other ancient Semitic onomastica.

In summary, it may be concluded that there are some ideas which are attested only in the Hebrew onomasticon. These are mainly anthropomorphic notions, and ideas concerning Nature. They involve the concept of the deity as 'ancient' (*qdm*), 'death' (*mwt*), 'abundance' (*ytr*), 'fine gold' (*pz*) and 'excellence' (*mgd*, of the gifts of Nature). The Hebrew name *ḥagîyāh* 'Feast of Y' is also not attested elsewhere. Not occurring in other ancient Semitic names are semantic equivalents of the Hebrew roots *zrh* 'to scatter, fan, winnow', *šrb* (Piel) 'to send burning heat', *ḥrp* 'Autumn', *š'l* 'deep', *s'r* 'storm, rage or tempest', *r'm* 'thunder' and *r'l* 'to quiver, shake, reel'.

Of genitive elements, describing the relationship between name-bearer and deity, Hebrew names alone make use of the idea of the name-bearer as 'in the testimony, witness of' the deity (*b* + *'wd*), 'in the secret council of' the deity (*b* + *swd*), and as 'possession of' (*qnh*), 'known of' (*yd'*) and 'lion of' (*'ry*) the deity.

Peculiar to Hebrew names is the use of the root *drš* 'to seek', while the idea that the deity 'meets' man is also conveyed only by Hebrew names with the roots *y'd* (Niphal), *pg'* and perhaps *'nh*. Probably concerned with events of the birth of the child, the root *pqḥ* 'to open (the eyes)' is found only in Hebrew names.

While the concept of divine protection is widely attested throughout ancient Semitic name-giving, only Hebrew theophoric names portray the anthropomorphic idea 'to cover', with the root *ṭll*. The thought that the deity has 'carried into exile' (root *glh*) is also found only in Hebrew names.

Divine determination seems evident in Hebrew names with the roots *ryb* 'to strive, contend', *'md* 'to take one's stand', *śrh* 'to persevere, persist' (or 'to rule'), and *'wh* 'will' (construct), which are concepts not attested in other ancient Semitic onomastica. Two other roots, of some uncertainty, are also peculiar only to Hebrew: these are *'db* 'to invite, discipline', and *sbk* 'to interweave'.

It is at this point that many scholars are prepared to leave the study of onomastics, reaching a conclusion that, because so many name-elements and ideas have equivalents throughout the entire Semitic onomastica, there is little to differentiate the religious throught in one onomasticon from that of another. M.D. Coogan (*West Semitic Names in the Murašû Documents*, Scholars Press [1976], 122), for example, while concluding that there were few names which were unique to the West Semitic community at Nippur, quotes A. Caquot's remarks concerning Palmyrene names, 'The testimony of proper names is always subject to question in view of the conservative character of onomastics . . . But names, although traditional, remained intelligible, and nothing forces us to see in them the reflections of an extinguished piety. Still, this piety is no more specifically Palmyrene or Aramaic than that of the personal names of the Old Testament is specifically Israelite. The parallels which we have encountered in passing come from the most diverse horizons of the Semitic domain . . . Could we not then speak of a Semitic piety?' (Cf. A. Caquot, 'Sur l'onomastique religieuse de Palmyre', *Syria* 39 [1962], 256.)

The absurdity of this statement will be demonstrated below. What Coogan and Caquot failed to observe, and what occasional visitors to the field of onomastics also fail to realize, is that what identifies a language as unique, is not the parallels, but the *differences*. In the light of Caquot's statement, for example, we may note the absence of numerous anthropomorphic features in Palmyrene theophoric names, the total absence of the idea of salvation, mercy, compassion, the paucity of transcendent concepts, and the absence of ideas of divine preservation and support. Such absences surely place religious ideas of the Palmyrene onomasticon out of the category of a *general* 'Semitic piety'!

In the case of Hebrew names, the ideas contained in other ancient Semitic onomastica which are not apparent in Hebrew are remarkably numerous, and indicate crucial differences between Hebrew religion and that portrayed by the other Semitic nomenclatures. It is this important material which is now to be examined.

B. *Ideas attested in Semitic onomastica which do not occur in Hebrew*

1. *Polytheistic concepts*

Unlike the other Semitic religions, Hebrew religion was not polytheistic. Names which display polytheistic ideas, mainly Akkadian three-part compounds, are without parallel in Hebrew. Akkadian names depict the deities as 'Creator of the gods' (*epēšu*), 'Exalted of the gods' (*šaqû*), 'King of the gods' (*šarru*), 'Most friendly of the gods' (*damiq*), 'Almighty of the gods' (*gabbu-ile'i*), and 'Luxuriance or abundance of the gods' (*kuzbu*), while the Aramaic name *'dmlkly'* (*Ad-milki-ilayya*) perhaps also depicts the deity as 'King of the gods'. Possibly to be included here is the Old Akkadian name *Amurra-kīma-il* 'Amurra is like god'. None of these ideas, or anything comparable with them, is attested in Hebrew names.

2. *Names depicting the existence of gods*

Hebrew has no parallel to those names in other Semitic onomastica which state that gods exist, or which declare the name-bearer or parents as worshippers of a particular god. These ideas are evident in Akkadian names with *bašû* 'to be, exist' and perhaps Amorite *bs'* (Df.). *Šumma* 'if, even, indeed' is used with similar meaning in Akkadian names, perhaps also Amorite *'w'* 'to be, become' (Df.) and $\underline{h}ln_2$ 'to be or become known'. The element *yēš* 'there is' (= *yšb* Df. cf. above, A 9, A 12) in Phoenician names perhaps also depicts the same idea 'There is a god', while the Aramaic name *Se-e'-la-nu* (*šy-'l(h)n*) 'Se is our god' and Amorite *bḫd* 'in favour of', seem to express worship of one particular god. Also relevant here may be the Akkadian name *Itti-Adad-anīnu* 'Wih Adad are we'.

3. *References to female deities*

The lack of a polytheistic concept in Hebrew worship meant the absence from the Hebrew onomasticon of titles of female deities. Not attested in Hebrew names, then, are the elements:

queen	O. Akk./Akk. *šarratu*; Phoen. *mlkt*.
mother	O. Akk./Akk. *ummu*; Phoen., Aram., Palm. *'m*; Ug. *'mm*.
lady	Akk. *bēltu*, *etellūtu*; Aram. *b'lt*, *mārta*; O. Akk. *šu'atum*.
princess	O. Akk. *malkatum*.
sister	Phoen. *'ḥt*
she	O. Akk. *ši*; Ug. *hy* (Df.).

4. *Feminine genitive elements*

Conspicuously absent among Hebrew names is a feminine noun as the *nomen regens* of a construct type name. No comparisons can be found in Hebrew for the following genitive elements in the other Semitic nomenclatures:

female slave	O. Akk./Akk. *amtu*; Phoen. *'mt*; Palm. *'mš*.
girl, servant	Amor. *ḫlm* (Df.).
daughter	Ug., Phoen. Palm. *bt*; Akk. *mārat*.
she	O. Akk./Akk. *šat*.
sister	Ug. *'ḫt*, Phoen., Aram. *'ḥt*.
lady	Ug. *'dt* (Df.).

5. *Names referring to priests and priestesses*
Some Akkadian names belonged to priestesses: such names incorporated genitive elements from *erēšu* 'to summon, demand, request', *īna našû* suggesting divine desire or demand and *šeriktu*, *šerku* 'given to, gift of' the deity. Similar is the Akkadian genitive use of *šangû* 'priest', perhaps Amorite *lw'* 'pledged person' and Ug. *ndr* 'vow, wish'. Such genitive elements have no equivalent in Hebrew names.

6. *Masculine genitive elements*
Totally absent in Hebrew names is the concept of a male child as a 'son of' or offspring of the deity, although it is evident in all the other Semitic languages. Hebrew names, then, have no parallel to the following genitive elements:

son	Ug., Phoen., Amor. *bn*; Aram., Palm. *br*; O. Akk./Akk. *aplu*, Phoen. *pl* (Df. cf. above, A 7, A 17, A 18); Akk. *māru*.
child	Akk. *seḫru*, *waldu*, *ridū* (Df.).
name	O. Akk./Akk. *šumu*; O. Akk. *nabā'um*.
root	Ug. *šrš*.
seed, progeny	Aram. *zr'*, Akk. *zēru*.
late child/fruit	Akk. *urkattu*.
offspring	Akk. *pir'u*, *lāḫu*.
suckled	O. Akk. *naṣib*.
he	Ug. *š* (= *šu*? Df. cf. below, B 10); O. Akk. *šu*.
begotten	Akk. *zārūt*.

Other genitive elements depicting the name-bearer in relationship with the deity which are not attested in Hebrew are:

favoured or granted	O. Akk./Akk. *migru*.
grace	Akk. *rāmu*.
prize	Akk. *tanattum/tanittum*, *nēmelu*.
answer	O. Akk. *meḫri*.
fruit	O. Akk./Akk. *inbu*.
joy	O. Akk. *ra'āšum*.
guest, stranger	O. Akk./Akk. *ubāru*.
refugee	Palm. *'wyd*.
foreigner, charge, protégé	Ug. *gr* (or 'descendant', 'offspring').
merchant	O. Akk. *tamkar*.
soldier	O. Akk. *ṣabi'um*.
neighbour	Aram. *škn*.

brother	Phoen., Palm. *'ḥ*.
son-in-law	Amor. *ḫtn*$_1$
dog	O. Akk. *kalbum*.
help	Palm. *naṣr*.

7. *Divine titles and attributes*
Many of the titles which are given to the deities, mostly in Akkadian, do not occur in Hebrew names. Although Hebrew names refer to the deity as a 'King', there is no equivalent in Hebrew for the use of *šarru* in Akkadian when this element is used to describe the deity as 'king of justice', 'king of the people' etc. Similarly, *bēlu* and *etellu* 'lord' are used in Akkadian to portray a particular deity as 'lord of' a certain sphere, for example, of 'descendants', of 'justice', of 'progeny', of 'heaven and earth'.

Other titles for the deity having no parallel in Hebrew are the following:

prince, counsellor, adviser	O. Akk. *malkum*; Aram. *sr* (Df.); Phoen. *zbl*; Akk. *malāku* (nominal and verbal), *tamlaku*, also *milku* 'counsel, advice, order, decision'.
vizier	O. Akk. *sukkallum*.
chief, ruler	Aram. *sgb* (Df. cf. above, A 10).
messenger	Phoen. *ml'k*.
angel	Akk. *bāštu* (but cf. the Heb. name *'šb'l*, above, § 2.2 *b'l*).
guardian deity	Akk. *lamassu*.

Attributes of Semitic deities which are not attested in Hebrew theophoric names are as follows:

esteemed	Amor. *yqr*.
wisdom	Akk. *nēmuqu*.
wise	Akk. *emqu*, *apkallu*, *ḫāsisu*; O. Akk./Akk. *mūdû*.
careful reflection	Akk. *muštašimu* (Df.).
princely	Akk. *etellu* (used of the word of Marduk).
far-famed	Aram. *rqy'*.
well-considered, thoughtful	Akk. *muštālu*.
first	Akk. *ašaridu*.
rich	Akk. *watru* (of the word of Šamaš).
wealth	O. Akk. *nuḫšum*; Phoen. *nks* (Df.).
precious, beloved	Akk. *(w)aqru*.
true, truth	Akk. *kēnu*.
everlasting	O. Akk./Akk. *dārū*.

magnificent	Akk. *šarḫu* (in the sense of the most magnificent of the gods).
awe-inspiring	O. Akk. *palḫum*.
patient	O. Akk. *arākum* (or 'eternal'?).
holy	Phoen. *ḥrm*.
haughty	Phoen. *yḥr* (= *yhr*? cf. above, A 1, A 13, below, B 21).
tender	Phoen. *rkk* (Df.), or 'to be long'.
active	Akk. *muttabbilu* Gtn of *'bl* (Df.).
one, unique	Amor. *yḫd*.
large	Amor. *y'n* (Df. cf. above, A 6).
established	Phoen. *kwn*; Akk. *bâru*.
all	O. Akk. *kalum*; cf. also Aram. *klbyd'l*. 'All is by/in the hand of god', and Akk. *il napḫāri* 'god of totality'.
gift	Akk. *šulmānu*.

Other, nominal, name-elements which are used to depict the deity and which have no semantic equivalent in Hebrew are:

young man	O. Akk. *ayarum* (also gen.).
claw	Amor. *ṣpr*$_2$ (Df. cf. above A 1).
image	Ug. *ṣlm*.
ancestor, forefather	Ug. *slp*.
step, path or footstool	Amor. *kbs* (Df. cf. above, A 14).
remembrance	Amor. *zkr*.
request, desire	Phoen. *'rš*.
harp	O. Akk. *balangum*.
lapislazuli	Akk. *uqnu*.
crown, diadem	Amor. *ḫtr* (Df. cf. above, A 10, A 11).

8. *Edifices*

Hebrew names never depict the deity in terms of a building as the elements:

bītu	temple	O. Akk./Akk.
ekallu	palace	Akk.
ālu	city	O. Akk./Akk.
byt	house	Ug. (gen.).

9. *Names depicting the deity as a member of the family or as a family*

Although Hebrew names describe the deity as 'Brother', 'Father' or 'Kinsman', the following ideas have no counterpart in the Hebrew nomenclature:

family	O. Akk./Akk. *ellatu*, *kimtu*; Akk. *qinnu*.
maternal uncle	Akk. *ḫālu*; Amor. *ḫl*$_3$.
spouse	Akk. *mūtu* (or 'man, warrior').
favourite brother	Akk. *talīmu*.

Other, similar, nouns which are used to depict the deity and which are not found in Hebrew are:

soldier, servant	Ug. *mhr*.
ally	Akk. *kitru*.
inspector of canals	Akk. *gugallu*.

10. *Animals*

Hebrew names never refer to the deity as any kind of animal, whereas this is a phenomenon met in other onomastica:

ibex	Amor. *ḫl* (Df. cf. above, A 11).
sheep	Ug. *š* (Df. cf. above, B 6); Phoen. *š* (Df.). Cf. perhaps, in addition, Amor. *š APNM*, 265.
lion	Amor. *'sd* (or 'warrior'); Ug., Amor. *lb'*; O. Akk./Akk. *lābum/lab'u*. Cf. also Canaanite *'bdlb't*, J.T. Milik, F.M. Cross, 'Inscribed Javelin-Heads from the Period of the Judges: A Recent Discovery in Palestine', *BASOR* 134 (1954), 5-15.
mountain goat	O. Akk. *turāḫ*; Akk. *yālu*, *barḫu*.
calf	Akk. *būru*.
kid	O. Akk. *lala'um*.
wild bull/cow	Akk. *rīmu/rīmtu*; Amor. *ri-im*; O. Akk. *šûrum*.
leopard, panther	Akk. *nimru* (Df. cf. above, A 17).
falcon	Ug. *nṣ*.

11. *Anatomical names*

Although Hebrew names refer to the name-bearer as 'in the hand of' the deity, there is no semantic equivalent for names with the following descriptions of the deity:

heart	Akk. *libbu*.
eye	Akk. *īnu*; Aram. *'yn* (or 'source'); Phoen. *'yn* (gen.).
mouth	Ug., Amor., O. Akk./Akk. *pû* (gen.).
foot	O. Akk./Akk. *šēpu*.

hand	O. Akk./Akk. *qātu*: (Akk. used in the sense that health [*bulṭu*]/everything is in the hand of the deity).

12. *Names involving Nature*

Hebrew names do not describe the deity as the following:

field, plain	Ug. *šd*.
thicket	Ug. *ǵl* (Df.). However, cf. the comment on the name *'byw*, above, pp. 148, 270 n. 8
green, yellow	Amor. *yrq* (= *wrq*?) (Df.).
fruit	Akk. *inbu*.
shepherd	O. Akk. *ra'āyum*, Akk. *re'û*, 'to shepherd, pasture', also nominal; Aram. *r'y*; Amor. *rḫ'*; Akk. *utullu* (or 'child').
breath of wind	Akk. *šāru*.
plant	Akk. *azallu* (Df.).
garden, orchard	Akk. *kirū* (Df.); Ug. *gnn*.
winepress	Ug. *gt* (Df. cf. above, A 1).

13. *Fertiliy and land*

The following ideas are not attested in Hebrew theophoric names:

luxuriance, abundance, attractiveness	Akk. *kuzbu* (used to depict the deity as the luxuriance etc. of the land).
to breathe, be wide	Akk. *napāšu* (causative).
to blow, waft	Akk. *zâqu* (of breath of deity) (Df.).
to be fruitful	Ug. *pr* (= *pry*?) or *prr* 'young bull' (Df.); Ug. *ṯmr* (god of, or giver of fruitfulness).

14. *Cosmos*

Hebrew names do not refer to the deity in astronomical terms and have no equivalent to the following:

sun	Amor. *sms*; Akk. *šamšu*.
heaven	Ug. *šmy* (gen.); Akk. *šamû* (in names of the type 'DN of heaven' etc.).
to be brilliant	Ug. *yp'*, Amor. *ypḫ*.
crescent	O. Akk. *šīrat* (Df.).
star	Amor. *kbkb*.
light	Ug. *nyr*/*nwr* and Akk. *nūru* (gen. as opposed to nominal forms in Heb.).
lightning	Ug., Amor. *brq*.

to shine	Akk. *nebû*, *namāru*.
to shine in a new light	Akk. *edēšu*.
to be radiant	Akk. *ḫanābu*.
to light up	Akk. *ṣarāru*.

Although Hebrew names depict the deity as 'light', Ugaritic and Akkadian usage, which is genitive and in the sense that the deity is the light of the land etc., is different from Hebrew. In the context of the idea of the deity as 'light', should be noted Akkadian *diparu/ ṭipāru*, describing the deity as a 'torch', which is also without parallel in Hebrew. This is also the case with Akkadian *mušētiq* 'to allow past', which is used with the object 'light', and Ugaritic *zky/w* 'to be bright, clean, pure'.

15. *Birth events*

Ideas expressing divine participation in events of the birth of the child which are not attested in Hebrew are the following:

to approve, grant	O. Akk./Akk. *magāru*.
to send	Akk. *abāku*; Aram. *šdr*; Amor. *l'k* (Df.).
to bring	Amor. *'bl*; Akk. *(w)abālu*; Palm. *'th*.
to summon, demand, request	Akk. *erēšu*.
to announce	Ug. *mll*.
to order	Akk. *qabû*.
to reward	Palm. *'qb* (sf. only).
to say, promise	Ug. *qby*, Akk. *qabû*.
to beget	O. Akk./Akk. *(w)alādu*; Akk. also nominal *mu'allidu*.
to do, permit	Akk. *epēšu*.
to call into life	Akk. *bulluṭu*.
to name, call	Ug., Amor. *nb'*, O. Akk./Akk. *nabû*; Amor. *'škr* (Df.); Akk. *zākiru/zakāru*; Aram. *qry*.
punctual	Akk. *sanāqu* (of time of birth).
(appointed) time	Akk. *adannu*.
indeed, yes	Akk. *annu* (refers to birth of child).
lo! behold!	Akk. *ennam/ennum* (refers to birth of child).
to be there	O. Akk./Akk. *kašādu* (obj., child at birth).
to reach, arrive	Amor. *mṣ'* (= *mẓy*? Df.).
to have	O. Akk./Akk. *išû* (obj. 'brother' or deity).

to look, be expected	Akk. *dagālu* in the sense 'I am the expected of the deity', also with the child as obj.
to be, exist, happen	Akk. *bašû* (causative).
to break forth (of water)	Amor. *gḫ*.
to make a way, path	Amor. *sl'* (Df. cf. above, A 12); Ug. *pls*; Amor. *pls* (Df. cf. above, A 6).
to come, go out	Amor. *wṣ'* (causative imf. or G); Akk. *aṣû* (precative).
to hollow out	Aram. *ḥll* (Df. cf. above, A 11).
to bore, break through	Ug. *nqb*.
to seize	Akk. *ṣabātu* (obj. a name, son).
to pour out	Amor. *spk* (Df. cf. above, A 1); Akk. *šapāku* (*zēr*).
to mix	O. Akk. *balālum*.
to purchase	Akk. *ša'āmu*.
to fecundate, impregnate	Amor. *yrh* (Df.).

16. *Interrogatives*

The only interrogative which is found in Hebrew theophoric names is *my*, which is used rhetorically in names of the type *mîkāyāhû* 'Who is like Yahweh?', expressing the idea that no one is like the Hebrew deity. Evident in the other Semitic onomastica, however, are rhetorical questions which are not reflected in Hebrew. This is the case, also, with those names in other ancient Semitic name-giving, which question the deity because of some exigency or difficulty of the parent or name-bearer. Frequently, such names imply impatience on the part of the parent, or infer a plea questioning why the deity has not taken notice of the needs and difficulties of the parents. Such concepts are found in names with the following interrogatives:

how? what?	Akk. *mīnu* 'What have I done?', 'What is strong against?', 'How have I sinned?'; *minsu* 'How is it possible?'.
where?	O. Akk./Akk. *ali alum*; Ug., Phoen., Amor. *'y* 'Where is the deity?'.
who?	Amor. *mnn*, O. Akk./Akk. *mannu*; Amor. and Akk. 'Who can be without the deity?'; Akk. 'Who can make war on the deity?', 'Who is like the deity, great/ mighty?', 'Who is adversary of the deity?'.
how long?	Akk. *adi mati*.
when?	Akk. *mati*.
why?	Akk. *ammēni*.

Probably in this context, belongs the Akk. name ^{d}*Ea-ḫi-i-ṭi-ul-i-di* 'Ea, my offence I know not' and, similar, are the interjectional names, also without parallel in Hebrew, which state that the parents have 'had enough':

enough!	Akk. *aḫulap*; O. Akk./Akk. *maṣi*.

17. *Imperatives*

Only three roots are attested in Hebrew names which are possibly imperative: these are *ydh* 'to praise' and, more doubtfully, *ḥkh* 'to wait', and *dmm* 'to be still', all used with the deity as object. In other ancient Semitic name-giving, particularly Old Akkadian and Akkadian, such imperatives were frequent. The following, all with the deity as the object, are ideas not attested in Hebrew:

to fear	Phoen. *ygr*; Akk. *adāru*.
to come, meet	O. Akk. *buā'um*.
to look (be obedient to)	Akk. *dagālu*.
to worship	Akk. *palāhu*.
to protect	Akk. *naṣāru* (obj. e.g. the 'orders' of the deity).
to trust	O. Akk./Akk. *takālu*; O. Akk. *qiāpum*.
to be neglectful, careless	Akk. *egû* (+ negative).
to see	Akk. *amāru*.

In three cases, the imperative is directed to the deity, with the name-bearer or parent as the object:

to love	Amor. *ḥbb* (Df.).
to turn	Akk. *târu*.
to speak	O. Akk./Akk. *qabû*.

The deity is not addressed this way in Hebrew names, which never command God.

18. *Laments and pleas*

Although the imperfective is sometimes attested in Hebrew names to express a wish that the deity will promote the child in some way—May the deity establish, distinguish, nourish, strengthen, support, bless etc.—other onomastica contain ideas of this type which express different wishes. Laments such as the following three concepts, however, are entirely absent from Hebrew:

to be tired	Akk. *anāḫu*.
to suffer want, become poor, orphaned	Ug. *yky/ykw*.
solitary, alone	Akk. *(w)ēdu*.

Pleas to the deity are very frequent, particularly in Akkadian names. The following are without parallel in Hebrew:

to be healthy, keep alive	Akk. *balāṭu*, *bu'āru*; Amor. *ḫw'* 'to live'; (pleas for health and life).
to breathe	Akk. *napāšu* (plea for recovery of the child).
to establish	Akk. *kânu* (plea for progeny).
to turn	Akk. *târu* (plea that the word [promise] of the deity will be fulfilled).
to stand firm	Akk. *kānu* (plea that the begetter will stand firm).
to exist, happen	Akk. *bašû*.
to hold	Akk. *kullu* (plea to 'hold' name-bearer, i.e. help).
to totter	Akk. *nâšu* (plea that the mountain will not totter).
to understand	Akk. *lamādu*.
to receive, accept	Akk. *maḫāru* (obj. prayer).
to look at, see	Akk. *naṭālu*, *amāru* (name-bearer subj., grace, justice, face of god, objs.).
to forget	Akk. *mašû* (plea that deity should not forget name-bearer/parent).
to be, become old	Akk. *labāru* (plea for child).
to be everlasting, eternal	Akk. *dārû* (plea of slave for lord).
to be rich	Akk. *šušru* (plea for child).
to prosper	Akk. *ešēru* (plea for child and lord).
to be perfect	Akk. *šuklulu* (plea for child).
to become great	Akk. *rabû* (plea for city).
to take away	Akk. *nasāḫu* (obj. burden).
to loosen	Akk. *paṭāru/pāṭiru* (obj. sin, burden).
to release	Akk. *ušāru* (D) (plea for name-bearer).
to lift up	Akk. *zaqāpu*, *našû* (obj. head).
to humbly entreat	Amor. *'btl* (Df. cf. above, A 18).

19. *Verbal elements with an accusative*

The existence of three-part compounds inAkkadian has meant that many verbal sentence names have an additional accusative element supplied. This often results in interpretations of names which are dissimilar to Hebrew two-part verbal compounds, even if the verbal element is cognate or semantically equivalent. Hebrew *rbb* 'to be great', for example, and Akkadian *rabû* are cognate, and attested in both onomastica, but the Hebrew element describes the deity as 'great', while the Akkadian names add the accusative elements 'word' and 'throne' to depict these as great. These accusative elements, entirely absent in Hebrew, occur with the following verbal ideas in Akkadian and Amorite. (The accusative elements for each are added in parenthesis):

to establish	Akk. *kunnu* (kingship), *kânu* (word).
to do, permit	Akk. *epēšu* (justice).
to be, last long	Akk. *arāku* (justice; arm of the deity).
to be fair, just	Akk. *ešāru* (decision).
to be good, excellent	Akk. *banû* (divine acts); *ṭâbu* (name; voice; shadow; reign; breath of wind; breath; protection; to sit by the deity and to worship the deity); *damqu* (works; to go behind [*arki*] the deity).
to be high, exalted	Akk. *elû* (claim; throne).
rich, pre-eminent	Akk. (*w*)*atru* (word).
to be great	Akk. *rabû* (word; rescue; shadow; throne; works).
strong, powerful	Akk. *dannu* (voice).
to be, exist, happen	Akk. *bašû* (will; justice).
to be true, enduring	Amor. *'md* (mouth; word) (Df.); Akk. *kēnu*/*kittu* 'just, righteous, true' (word).

20. *Other verbal elements with the deity as subject*

The following concepts have no parallel in Hebrew:

to be whole, intact	Ug. *šlm*; Amor. *slm* 'to be well' (causative).
to become fond of	Akk. *menû* (obj. those who fear the deity); Ug. *ḥbb*.
to unite, gather, assemble	Akk. *paḫāru* (obj. family).
to develop trust	Akk. *takālu* (D).
to loosen	Akk. *paṭāru*, *pašāru* (obj. probably sin, evil, burden).
to release	O. Akk. *uššurum* (obj. sin, evil); Akk. D stative.
to care for, manage	Ug. *skn*.

to know	Akk. *idû* (obj. righteous).
to speak (announce)	Akk. *qabû* (obj. all).
to go out, go forth	O. Akk. *waṣā'um*.
to receive	O. Akk. *maḫārum*.
to be troubled	Phoen. *šmm* (Df.).
to accompany	Aram. *lwy*.
to ride	Ug., Amor. *rkb*.
to desire	Amor. *ṣb* (= *ṣbw*? Df.).
to prosper	Phoen. *ṣlḥ* (Qal perf!).
to fly	Ug., Phoen. *'p* (Df.).
to retreat, give way, journey	Ug. *syr*/*swr*.
to have, receive, acquire	Akk. *rašā'u*.
to acclaim	O. Akk. *alālum*.

21. *Elements expressing that the deity rejoices*
Whereas Hebrew names convey the idea that the deity is a source of joy, the concept that the deities themselves rejoice or are pleased is sometimes depicted in other ancient Semitic name-giving as the following ideas show:

to rejoice	O. Akk./Akk. *rêšu*; Amor. *smḫ* (= *śmḫ*? Df. cf. above, A 13, A 17).
to be pleased, content	Amor. *rṣ* (Df.).
to laugh	Akk. *ṣâhu*.
to rest, be satisfied	Amor. *nḫ*; Phoen. *s'n* 'to rest securely'.
to sing	Ug. *šr* (Df. cf. above, A 7, A 11, A 16).
to feel easy	Palm. *r^e^waḥ* (cf. Aram.).
to be free	Phoen. *yḥr* (= *ḥrr*? Df. cf. above, A 1, A 13, B 7).

22. *The deity as a source of prosperity, order and success*
Hebrew names never express the idea that the deity causes man to thrive, succeed and prosper. These shades of meaning seem to indicate developing prosperity rather than the more static type of consistent welfare implied in Hebrew names. The following elements have no semantic equivalents in Hebrew theophoric names:

to cause to thrive, prosper	Akk. *šamāḫ* (D), *ḫanābu* (D); Akk. *nahāšu* (subj. he who obeys).
to cause to succeed	Akk. *ešēru* (Š), *mušētiq*, *kāširu* 'success' (given by the deity).

to make great	Amor. *rb'*; Akk. *rabû*.
to make rich	Akk. *šarā'u*.
to satisfy	Akk. *šabā'u* (D).
to set right	Akk. *tarāṣu*.
to bring in order	Akk. *tuqqunu*, *muštēširu*.
to cause to see	Akk. *kullumu* (obj. light).
to cause to rule	Palm. *mlk* (sf. only).
to be, become good	Amor. *gd* (causative).

23. *Intercession and decision*

Hebrew names have no semantic equivalents for the following ideas of intercession and decision by the deity:

to summon, demand ask for	Akk. *erēšu* (obj. justice).
to decide	Aram. *kr'* (Df.); Palm. *gᵉram* (cf. Syr.); Akk. *ṭemu* 'decision' (in names of the type 'With DN lies the decision').
to intercede for, answer	Akk. *apālu*.
to stand, stand beside	Akk. *izuzzum*.
to fix, appoint	Akk. *šâmu* (objs. right and order).
to speak (dispute for).	Akk. *dabābu*.

24. *Adverse attributes of the deities*

Hebrew names contain no thought that the deity can be harmful to man, which is an idea attested in other onomastica, as the following show:

to shame	Akk. *bâšu*, *enēšu*.
to destroy	Akk. *nêru*, *di'āšu*.
to slay	Ug. *nkw/y*.
to conquer	Akk. *kanāšu*, *kašādu*.
to battle, vanquish	O. Akk. *ša'ārum* (or nominal 'fighter').
to revenge	Akk. *tuktû*; Ug., Amor. *nqm*.
to roar/roarer	Akk. *šagāmu*.
vehement	Akk. *tišmar*, *šitmar*.
heroic, ferocious	Akk. *dāpinu*.
to overthrow	Phoen. *mgr* (cf. Aram. or 'to tear down' cf. BH).
to take possession	Palm. *mšk* (sf. only).

to vanish, or come to an end, cease	Ug. *s'p*.
punishment	O. Akk. *inūnum* (Df. cf. above, A 6).
binder (troubler?)	Akk. *kāmi*.
to look (+ negative)	Akk. *dagālu* ('The god does not look').
to rob, deprive	Akk. *šalālu*.
warrior	O. Akk. *mutum* (Df. cf. above, A 3).

25. *Appeasement of the deity*

The concept that the deity needs to be appeased or calmed is one not found among Hebrew names, but is evident in the following Semitic name-elements:

to be quiet, appeased	Akk. *nâḫu* (also used with the deity as subj. and anger as obj.).
to calm down	O. Akk./Akk. *pašāḫu*.
to be peaceable	Akk. *salāmu*.
to turn	Akk. *saḫāru* (in name implying that the deity has neglected the name-bearer).
to reconcile, be reconciled	Akk. *pašāru*, *târu* (*tayyāru*).
to lament (or feel pity?)	Amor. *rš'* (Df.).

26. *Names with the deity as accusative*

In Hebrew names, the deity is rarely the object in a compound name (cf. above B 17). This phenomenon however, as noted, is a frequent occurrence in Akkadian imperative forms. In many names, also, the name-bearer is the subject of the sentence name, in which he declares some aspect of his relationship with the deity. This is evident in the following ideas which have the name-bearer (or parent) as subject, and the deity as object:

to worship	Akk. *palāḫu*.
to turn to, devote oneself to	Akk. *panû*.
to pray	Akk. *suppû*, *ṣullû*, *dalālu*.
to call to	Akk. *šasû*.
to search for	Akk. *še'û*.
to trust	Akk. *takālu*.
to seize	Akk. *ṣabātu* (obj. feet of the deity).
to forget	Akk. *mašû* (Df. cf. above, B 18).
to see	O. Akk./Akk. *amāru*, Akk. also with the objs. power, greatness, divinity, godliness and victory of the deity.
to fly, flee (to)	Akk. *šutēmuqu*.

27. *Strength*

Although Hebrew names portray the idea of the deity as 'strong' or 'strength', the following elements, which are figurative for these ideas, are not found in Hebrew theophoric names:

horn	Amor. *qrn*, Akk. *qarnu*.
hero	Ug. *qrd*; O. Akk. (Df. cf. above, A 10)/ Akk. *qurādu/qarradu*; Aram. *gbr*.
arm	O. Akk. *idum*.
beard	Ug. *dkn*.
ardour	Aram. *ḫemtu*.
to be firm (on a base)	Amor. *'rs* (Df. cf. above, A 8, A 10).
to prevail	O. Akk. *la'ājum*.

28. *Protection*

The concept of the deity as protection is met in all the Semitic onomastica. Many elements, however, are figurative expressions of protection, some of which are not found in Hebrew. These are:

back, shoulder	Akk. *būdu*.
boundary	Akk. *itû*.
shore, bank	Akk. *kibru*.
rope	Akk. *šummannu*.
knee, lap, bosom	Akk. *sīqu*.
fortress	Akk. *birtu*; Aram. *mṣryn*.
wing	Ug. *knp*.
large shield	Ug. *ṣn*.
leader	Akk. *alāku* + *panī*.

Similar to these concepts may be the following ideas:

to press close	Amor. *ḫms* (or cf. Heb. *'wṣ* above, A 20).
for, over	Aram. *b'd* depicting that the deity is 'for, over' the name-bearer.
to, for him	Amor. *l'* (=*la-ḫū* Df. cf. above, A 10).
under (the authority of)	Amor. *tḫt*.

29. *Other names*

More unusual names, which have no equivalent in Hebrew and which do not appertain to any particular semantic group, contain the following ideas:

here	Palm. *kā'* (deity subj.).
before, in front	O. Akk. *maḫri* (deity subj.).

in the face of	Ug. *ina-pān-addi* (cf. Akk.).
to go, walk	Akk. *alāku* (in the breath of wind of the deity and 'With my god I walk').
to be pleased	Akk. *ḫadû* (subj. he who sees the sun).
safe, sound	Akk. *šalmu* (of worshippper of the deity).
safety	Palm. *šlm* (gen.).
favourite	Akk. *migru* (in a name expressing that the deity has made her favourite's sceptre stable).
secret	Akk. *pašīru* ('With DN is my secret').
to protect	Akk. *naṣāru* (obj. the commands of the deity); also *emēdu* (subj. name-bearer, obj. shadow of deity cf. Stamm, 199).
to turn, restore	Akk. *târu* (imv. deity obj.).
if, even, indeed	Akk. *šumma*.
insolent	Akk. *merēḫtu* (in ^{d}*Nabû-ana-mēreḫ(ē)tum* possibly a sf. with a meaning 'Show the insolent how the pious are rewarded' or similar).

This substantial corpus of material which is not attested in Hebrew names is of considerable importance for the assessment of the concept of the deity revealed in the Hebrew nomenclature, and the relationship between Hebrew name-giving and other Semitic onomastica. From the many differences which obtained between Hebrew and other Semitic theophoric names, as outlined above, some are worthy of extra notice.

Hebrew religion was unique in that it was monotheistic, and no suggestion that it was otherwise can be gained from personal names. Hebrew names never convey any doubt as to the existence of Yahweh, while names of other onomastica often imply such an idea by the expression 'There is a god'. Moreover, Hebrew names never imply worship of Yahweh while accepting the existence of other gods by a name motif such as 'x is our god'.

Because Hebrew religion is monotheistic there is no divine consort for the Israelite God, so that titles of female deities are totally lacking in Hebrew. This seems to be taken a stage further in that, also conspicuously absent, is a female child expressed as the *nomen regens* of a construct type name. Thus there is no instance in the Hebrew onomasticon when close relationship between a female name-bearer and the deity is expressed. In this context, too, should be noticed the absence of names of priestesses and priests.

Markworthy is the complete absence of the thought of a child as an offspring of the deity. This is an idea which is very frequent in the other Semitic onomastica, particularly the depiction of the name-bearer as a 'son of' the deity. Although Hebrew names state that Yahweh has 'created' or 'made' the child, the idea is always one which is divorced from the notion of 'begetting' the child and is one, in contrast, more akin to the creations of the Genesis narrative in the sense of creation by fiat, or of moulding man as the potter moulds clay.

Totally absent is any connection of Yahweh with the concept of fertility: the Hebrew God lacks a divine consort, and does not beget a divine family or an earthly one. No Hebrew child can, therefore, be referred to as a son or daughter of the deity, and the idea of a close relationship between a female child and Yahweh, expressed in construct type names, must have been wholly alien to the Hebrew mind. Also noticeable, however, is the absence of the idea of a male child as a 'brother of' the deity. This, too, seems to be a type of close relationship which was not acceptable to Hebrew thought.

Theophoric names in Hebrew show no sign that the deity was ever conceived to take the form of an animal, and indicate a distinct difference between Hebrew and other Semitic religions. Animal worship was widespread in Israel's neighbouring kingdoms, where the deity was frequently considered to manifest itself in animal form.

Also absent from Hebrew are names which portray the deity as an edifice of some kind, a temple, house, palace or city. Indeed, while Yahweh's presence may have been connected so strongly with tabernacle and temple, these objects themselves were never deified in Israelite worship.

Unattested, too, in Hebrew names, is any identification of the Hebrew deity with astronomical phenomena. Since the idea of Yahweh was as the creator of the universe, of the sun, moon and stars, his identification or manifestation as one of these phenomena would not have been encompassed in Israelite religious thought: indeed, the writer of Genesis 1 is careful to make this clear.

Whatever the vicissitudes of human existence, Hebrew names contain no notion of questioning the deity concerning difficulties experienced at the time the child is born. This feature, however, seems particularly evident in Akkadian interrogative name-elements. Indeed, laments and pleas to the deity are also characteristic mainly of Akkadian names, but any kind of complaint on the part of the parent, is totally lacking in Hebrew theophoric names.

The idea that the deity can be vengeful against man, or harm man in some way, is not evident in the Hebrew onomasticon. Similarly absent is any suggestion that the Hebrew deity needs to be appeased after a period of vehemence, which seems to be characteristic of Old Akkadian, Akkadian and Amorite names.

Far from concluding a general Semitic piety for all Semitic names, no two onomastica are alike. It has been the purpose of this study to differentiate between the religious ideas incorporated in Hebrew names and those revealed in other ancient Semitic languages, and this examination has revealed sharp contrasts. However, contrast will also exist between the other Semitic onomastica, a matter which is beyond the terms of reference of this study. What can be noted here, however, are the main differences between the Hebrew theophoric onomasticon and the name-stores of the other languages, apart from the dissimilarities already indicated in part B above.

Ugaritic names contain far fewer anthropomorphic ideas than Hebrew names, while the concept of the deity as salvation—a well attested idea in Hebrew—is probably absent in Ugaritic. (Cf. the difficult element *šr*, which may be from a root *šrr* 'to let loose' or could be Akk. *šarru* 'king'. The idea 'to let loose' could also refer, not to salvation, but to birth events, or to the 'loosening' of sin or a burden.) There is also no reference to divine compassion and mercy as characteristics of Ugaritic deities who, in addition, do not seem to be sources of joy, preservation, support or nourishment.

Phoenician names lack the richness of transcendent ideas of the deity which are contained in Hebrew names and, also, the idea of compassion, mercy and love of the deity. To be noted, in addition, is the tenuous nature of semantic similarities between Phoenician and Hebrew, in view of the numerous etymologies possible for Phoenician name-elements with formal or semantic difficulties.

Many problems are in evidence in a comparison between Hebrew and Amorite names. The lack of material extraneous to the Amorite onomasticon has made the meaning of many names difficult to determine with accuracy, and these names often have a number of possible etymologies. However, absent from Amorite theophoric names are many transcendent qualities, which describe the deities as splendour, majesty, glorious, wonderful and noble.

Aramaic names, too, present difficulty in that, in many cases, it is not possible to ascertain Aramean ownership of a name. Since, too, the Arameans were constant borrowers from their Near Eastern neighbours, linguistic and morphological criteria are unequal to the task of establishing such ownership: this, indeed, was found to be the case with the Elephantine material. Absent from the Aramean onomasticon is the idea, contained in Hebrew names, that the deities are a source of joy, or that they are compassionate.

In Old Akkadian names there are few transcendent ideas and an abundance of anthropomorphism. Such anthropomorphism, however, is of a very different kind from that which obtains in the same class of names in Hebrew. There are for example, as noted, no Hebrew names which depict the deity as an animal, whereas this is a characteristic of Old Akkadian names. Such differences, again, give the impression that Hebrew religious thought was of a very different character.

Sharp contrasts are evident between the Akkadian and Hebrew onomastica. Many Akkadian names are three-part compounds, which has meant that the context of the name-giving can be ascertained more easily than is the case with Hebrew two-part compound names, and frequently gives a meaning to a name which is without semantic equivalent in Hebrew. Akkadian names, moreover, appear to be more man-orientated than Hebrew names: this, again, is the result of an addition of a third, accusative, element in verbal sentence names, as well as the result of a tendency to place the name-bearer or parent as the subject of verbal sentence names with the deity as object, a practice which is rare in Hebrew.

Outstanding in Palmyrene names is the absence of the concept of salvation, as well as ideas of preservation, support, selection and compassion as divine characteristics. Palmyrene names constitute the most recent material of all the ancient Semitic onomastica, for they take us beyond the Old Testament period. It is perhaps for this reason that they lack, as a characteristic, the same kind of anthropomorphism which is evident in Hebrew names. At the same time, however, Hebrew names reveal a more transcendent picture of the deity.

In the foregoing comparisons between Hebrew theophoric names and those in other Semitic languages, it is important to remember the accidental nature of all occurrences: the similarities and differences which characterize the various onomastica would appear to be a true reflection of the formal and semantic points of contact, as well as illustrating, fairly accurately, similar and distinctive concepts concerning the respective deities.

As far as the relationship between Hebrew and other ancient Semitic onomastica is concerned, it may be safely concluded that while there is certainly a framework of similitude, there is, equally certainly, a substantial amount of evidence to suggest that the Hebrew theophoric onomasticon incorporated no thoughts that were incongruous with the mainstream of Israelite religion. There are sharp distinctions between the religious thought discernible in Hebrew theophoric names and other ancient Semitic names, distinctions which claim for Hebrew an individuality among the Semitic nomenclatures. This factor may do much to offset the prevalent view of the semantic conformity of Semitic onomastics as a whole. Indeed, far from speaking of a general 'Semitic piety' discernible from the corpus of ancient Semitic theophoric names, it is possible to claim a degree of individuality for each onomasticon. It is to be hoped that this study has won for the Hebrew onomasticon the claim to such individuality.

As to the Hebrew names themselves, a few points in conclusion need to be raised. The research has revealed that, on a strictly formal basis, Hebrew names do not always conform to grammatical rules of extant biblical Hebrew. Many names occur verbally from roots which have no verbal use apart from its evidence in names, and many incorporate a verbal aspect where that aspect is not attested elsewhere for the root. Names often reflect older forms and usages of an element, as well as semantic ideas which no longer obtain in biblical Hebrew: we should, therefore, exercise extreme caution in forcing formally and semantically obscure names into the existing pattern of our knowledge of Hebrew. It is perhaps for this reason that many studies relevant to the Old Testament are not pertinent to the study of personal names. This was the case, for example, with F.I. Andersen's work *The Hebrew Verbless Clause in the Pentateuch* (1970), while casual references to personal names, within the compass of studies outside the field of onomastics, usually fall very short of fact.

A study of the concepts of deity revealed in theophoric names has the advantage that such concepts indicate what the *ordinary* man conceived to be characteristics of his God, and such characteristics are not bound by ritualistic or formal ideas. We should note, too, the semantic congruence between biblical and extra-biblical Hebrew names: this is a guarantee that the biblical evidence is a good reflection of ancient Hebrew onomastics.

Much has been said by others about the evidence for religious syncretism reflected in Hebrew personal names (see above, p. 55) but, as the examination of theophoric elements has revealed, this cannot be substantiated, and is an opinion which should be regarded as a scholarly misinterpretation that has gained currency through repetition, rather than through systematic research. Indeed, what Hebrew theophoric names do show, is a congruity in thought with what is revealed as the character of the Israelite God throughout the Old Testament.

APPENDIX

1. *The Jews in Babylonia*

A careful study of the Murašû material presented by M.D. Coogan (*West Semitic Personal Names in the Murašû Documents*, Scholars Press [1976]), as well as Jewish names in the Chaldean and Achaemenian periods examined by Ran Zadok (*The Jews in Babylonia During the Chaldean and Achaemenian Periods According to the Babylonian Sources*, Studies in the History of the Jewish People and the Land of Israel, Monograph Series III, University of Haifa [1979]: hereafter Zadok) has suggested that names from these sources are better excluded from the main body of the Hebrew onomasticon because of the difficulty of identifying them, beyond doubt, as Jewish. In the examination of the names presented by these two authors, the problem of differentiating between Arameans and Jews never appears to be adequately solved.

Since the Arameans displayed a 'tendency toward syncretistic assimilation of originally non-Aramaean deities into their pantheon' (Coogan, 48), this, no doubt, extended to an assimilation of Yahwistic elements in the Aramean onomasticon (see below). Likewise, Coogan already notes that many of the names compounded with *'el* are Aramaic and not Hebrew (*ibid.*, 46), so that any distinction between Aramaic and Hebrew names as regards this compound is rarely possible.

Both Coogan and Zadok accept as Jewish any name with a Yahwistic element although there is no reason why such names should always belong to Jews. The Arameans, for example, certainly bore compound names containing forms of *yhwh* (see above, §4.4 *passim*), so to claim with Zadok (Zadok, 4-5) and Coogan (Coogan, 119) that only Jewish names contain this element, is simply untrue. Thus, for example, Zadok considers the name *Ha-ta-a-ma* (Zadok, 8, 14, 20, 39, 40) to be Jewish, even though its predicative element is distinctly Aramaic: while *Ha-ta-a-ma*'s son's name is Akkadian,

Nabû-aha-uṣur his marriage is into a family bearing wholly Aramaic names (*ibid.*, 40). It is not impossible that *Ha-ta-a-ma* was also an Aramean, despite the Yahwistic ending of the name.

Moreover, of 34 Nippur names which Zadok classifies as Hebrew, 15 contain predicative elements which are common to Hebrew and Aramaic (Zadok, 14, 101 no. 48). Zadok justifies accepting these 15 names as Jewish because the predicates are found in pre-exilic Hebrew names, though he fails to indicate why earlier Arameans are denied use of these predicative elements, some of which are certainly attested in pre-exilic Aramaic names (*'b* [see above, p. 213], *zbd*, in two of the names [*ibid.*, 214], *ḥnn* [*ibid.*], *yd'* [*ibid.*], and *nr* [*ibid.*, 215]).

Other criteria for Jewishness of names are equally suspect: for example, *Nidinti*-[. . .] and *Bēl-ia-a-da-ah*, sons of *Mannu-kī-Nanā*, despite the Akkadian and Aramaic names of the sons are believed by Zadok to be Jewish because their *partner*(!) *Aq-bi-ia-a-ma* also has an Akkadian patronym, *Bau-ēṭir*! Because he believes there would have been no non-Jewish partners in a family inherited bow fief, and that *Aq-bi-ia-a-ma* is Jewish, Zadok argues that all the other persons are Jewish. On the basis of these names, however, there seems more evidence for the non-Jewishness of the whole family, and it is likely that *Aq-bi-ia-a-ma*, the only Jewish one of the 5 names here, may not have been borne by a Jew: indeed, the root *'qb* is not attested in the Hebrew onomasticon with a theophoric element, so the name, if accepted as Jewish, would be new.

Similarly, genealogical information, where this is available, does not produce sufficient evidence for concluding which individuals were Jewish, as opposed to Babylonian or Aramean. Like Coogan, Zadok places far too much emphasis upon evidence of Jewishness from patronyms. While father and son hold a Babylonian and Yahwistic name, it cannot be concluded that the family is either Jewish or Babylonian or Aramean. (For example, *Ni-ri-ia-a-ma* son of *Bēl-zēra-ibni* [Zadok, 44], *Ia-a-da-ah-ia-a-ma* son of *ᵈTam-miš-la-di-in* [*ibid.*, 73], *Ma-at-tan-nu-ia-a-ma* son of *Bēl-uballiṭ* and *Ba-rak-ku-ia-a-ma* son of *Bēlšunu* [*ibid.*, 68] see also Coogan, 121. *Ha-na-ni/nu-ia-a-ma* is classed as a Jew by Zadok [Zadok, 65] despite his Iranian patronym *Ú(-'-)da-ar-na-'*). If onomastic syncretism took place, we are not able to conclude whether that syncretism affected only one language. Indeed, in spite of earlier presumptions, Coogan states, 'it is therefore impossible for the most part to identify the Jews among the West Semites at Nippur' (Coogan, 121).

The question of mixed marriages also speaks strongly against assigning, with certainty, a Hebrew name to a Jewish owner. *U-se-'*, whom Zadok considers Jewish (Zadok, 36 no. 9), for example, probably had two foreign wives ^{f}*Ba-di-a* and ^{f}*Me-'-sa-a*. There certainly seems to be a mixture of names in many families: *Ia-še-'-ia-ama* (also considered Jewish by Zadok) and his wife ^{f}*Ha-la-'a* (*Zitta?*) have a daughter ^{f}*Tābat-*^{d}*Iš-šar* (*ibid.*, 44), while *Šu-zu-bu* names his sons *Il* (DINGIR^{MEŠ})*-ga-bar/ba-ri* and ^{d}*Nabû-na-a* etc. Nevertheless, Zadok claims, 'I am in no position to state whether there were mixed marriages between Jews and Gentiles' (*ibid.*, 83).

Against the Jewishness of some of these names it should be noted, too, that 'twelve documents which belong to the Murašû Archive were issued on Jewish holidays, although it would not be expected that Jews would work on a feast day' (*ibid.*, 49, cf. pp. 76, 82, 125 n. 155).

It is worth mentioning here, also, that Zadok considers the percentage of Jews with Yahwistic names found at Nippur to correlate with that of the Yahwistic names in Judea. The latter is determined by obtaining the percentage from each of six lists in Ezra and Nehemiah. However, the percentages of Yahwistic names in these separate lists range from as low as 25% to as much as 75%, indicating that Yahwistic names are not themselves correlative in the biblical lists! (Cf. Zadok, 79-80.)

The following list of name-types is therefore included for comparison and interest, its contents not being incorporated in the discussion of the preceding sections. The theophoric element *'el* occurs in the cuneiform of the Murašû documents as DINGIR.MEŠ. (For its relation to the Hebrew theophoric element *'l*, see Coogan, 43-47.) Hebrew *yahū* occurs in the form ^{d}*ya-a-hu-* or ^{d}*ya-a-hu-u* and *yaw* was written *-ya-a-ma* with variants ^{d}*ya-a-ma*, *-ya-ma* and *a-ma* (see Coogan, 49f., 52; Zadok, 7ff.). The transliteration of the names given by Coogan and Zadok has been followed although improvements of Coogan's readings have been suggested by Zadok in his review of Coogan's work, *BASOR* 231 (1978), 73-74.

NAME LIST

(Names cited by Zadok are indicated: the remainder are to be found in Coogan's alphabetical glossary.)

'b 'father'. *'abiyaw*.

'wr 'light'. *Ur-mil-ki* Zadok, 39.

'ḥ 'brother'. *'aḥiyaw*.

'l 'god'. *Ìl-ia-a-u* Zadok, 10, 37.

bd 'in (or from?) the hand of'. *Ba-da-yaw*: Coogan (p. 68) considers the element to be a common Northwest Semitic contraction, *bayad* > *bad* > *bȯd* (> Phoen. *bōd*), cf. Phoen. and Ug.

bny 'to build, create'. *'ēlbanā*; *banā'ēl*; *banāyaw*. *Bāniya* Zadok, 56. Common to Akk. and West Semitic; impossible to determine where names can be assigned, cf. Coogan, 68.

b'l 'lord, master'. *Ba-li-yaw*? Coogan notes, 'Since the theophorous element *-yaw* is Hebrew, it is not surprising that the word *b'l* appears in its West Semitic form (as opposed to *bēl*). This ending also makes it likely that the first element is the common noun used as an epithet of Yahweh ("Y. is lord") rather than the proper name ("Y is Baal"); cf. the biblical name *bᵉ'alyāh* (I Chr. 12.6)' (p. 69).

brk 'to bless'. *'elbarak*; *barīk'ēl*; *barakyaw*; *barīkyaw*: 'The single most common element in the West Semitic Murašû onomasticon' (Coogan, 69).

gbr 'to be strong, be a hero, warrior'. *'ēlgabar*.

gd 'fortune' or n. pr. div. Gad. *Ga-di-'-il* Zadok, 39.

gdl 'to be great'. *Gadalyaw* (see also Zadok, 77); *yigdalyaw*: *gdl* is attested only in Heb. names, cf. Coogan, 70.

gr 'client'. *Gir-re-e-ma* Zadok, 17, 34; *Gír-ia-u* Zadok, 17, 35.

gmr 'to accomplish'. *Ga-mar-ia-a-ma* Zadok, 44; *Ga-mir-i[a(?)-a-ma]*(?) Zadok, 47.

dyn 'to judge'. *'ēlyadīn*.

zbd 'to give'. *'ēlzabad*; *yahūzabad*; *zabadyaw*. Coogan writes concerning this element, which he considers Aram., 'This root occurs only rarely in biblical names from pre-Exilic sources'. BH *zᵉbadyāh(û)*, however, seems to have been attested for 7 pre-Exilic individuals, *'elzābād* for 2 individuals, *zabdî'ēl* for 1 individual, *yᵉhôzābād* for 8 individuals and *'ammîzābād* for 1 individual, the remaining 8 instances when the name-element occurs with a theophoric element being Exilic/post-Exilic occurrences. This may contradict

Coogan's statement, 'We are dealing with an originally Aramaic element which became popular in the Israelite onomasticon during the Exile; the large number of names at Nippur with ZBD reflect this tendency' (p. 71).

zkr 'to remember'. *Za-kar-ia-a-ma* Zadok. 49 no. 15.

ḥzh 'to see'. *Ḥazā'ēl.*

ḥyh 'to live'. *Ia-u-hi-e* Zadok, 37.

ḥlq 'to share, divide'. *Hi-il-qi-a/ia(-u)* Zadok, 36. The seal *nḥm br ḥlqyw* is also considered Heb. by Zadok (Zadok, 45) and Avigad (*IEJ* 15 [1965], 230-31): there seems to be no certain evidence for its inclusion as Heb., however.

ḥnn 'to be gracious, to favour'. *Ḥananyaw.*

ḥsh 'to seek refuge', n. 'refuge'. *Mah-si-ia-a-u* Zadok, 36.

ṭāb (Akk. and Aram.), *ṭōb* (Heb.) 'good'. *Ṭu-ub-ya-a-ma*. Coogan considers the name to equate with Heb. *ṭôbîyah(û)*, 'the orthography shows that the scribes were reproducing Hebrew *ṭōb* rather than its Akkadian or Aramaic cognate' (p. 74).

yd' 'to know'. *Yadī''ēl*; *yada'yaw*; *yadī'yaw.*

yhb (Aram.) 'to give'. *'ēlyahab*; *yahab'ēl*. Coogan considers such names to contain the earliest certain examples of the root in personal names (p. 76).

yš' 'to deliver'. *Ia-še-'-ia-a-ma* Zadok, 21, 44.

lakim uncertain. ^{d}*Ya-a-ḫu-ú-la-ki-im* and ^{d}*ya-a-ḫu-la-ki-im* = *yahūlakim.* Coogan explains the names as 'Y is for you' (cf. Ruth 2.4 etc.) (p. 60 n. 40), while A. Caquot (*Syria* 55 [1978], 396) reads *-la-qi-im*, suggesting a root *qwm*. Zadok proposes an Aram. *laqtil* form, parallel to Heb. *yaqtil*, i.e. an imf. of the root *qwm*, perhaps representing the name *yhwyqym* (Zadok, 18).

mī 'who?' (interrog. pron.). Akk. *mannu*, Ug. and Aram. *man*, Heb. *mī*; *mīkayaw.*

mlk 'king'. *Ma-la-ki-a-ma* Zadok, 47.

ndb 'to be noble, willing, liberal, generous' cf. Arab. *naduba*. *Na-ad-bi-ia-a-ú* Zadok, 35.

ndr 'to promise, vow, be generous'? *'ēl-lindar*; *'ēlnadar*. D.B. Weisberg in reviewing Coogan's work (*JAOS* 99 2 [1979], 389-92) has noted that *lindar* cannot be a 'precative imperfect' as Coogan states, since this is 'a confusion in terminology from several languages'. Weisberg also notes that an Akk. precative could not be described as 'imperfect' 'since it is built on either a stative or preterite, and the verb *nadāru* occurs with rare exceptions for other periods only in the N and Ntn forms (*AHw*, 703b). The form may be an Aramaic verb with *lamed* prefix or perhaps Canaanite or Phoenician.' (p. 390).

nūr (Aram.) 'light'. *Ni-ri-ia-a-ma* Zadok, 15, 44; *Ni/Né-ri-ia-u* Zadok, 37.

n'm 'to be pleasant, lovely, delightful'? *Nim-ia-u* Zadok, 37, 99.

ntn 'to give', n. 'gift'. *'ēlnatan*; *natan'ēl*; *yahūnatan*; *mantanyaw/mattanyaw*. *Na-ta-nu-ia-a-ma* Zadok, 46. M. Stolper, 'A Note on Yahwistic Personal Names in the Murašû Texts', *BASOR* 222 (1976), 25 adds the name *^{d}Ḫu-ú-na-tan^{an}-na*, considering *Hū-* to be a sf. of *Yahū-*. Stolper also includes *Man-nu-dan-ni-ia-a-ma* and *Man-nu-dan-na-ia-a-ma* as equivalents to *mantanyaw/mattanyaw*, suggesting a 'reshaping' of the name *Mattan-ia-a-ma* ('Gift of Y') to *Mannu-danni-ia-a-ma* ('Who is stronger than Y?'), giving a quasi-Babylonian form, a name sounding both Jewish and Babylonian.

smk 'to lean, lay, rest, support'. *Sa-ma-ku-ia-a-m*[*a*] Zadok, 39.

'dr (Aram., Heb. *'zr*) 'to help'. *'ēl'adar*; *'ēl'idrī*; *ya'darnī'ēl*; *'adar'ēl*; *'idrī'ēl*: see also *A-a-u-id*-[*r*]*i*Zadok, 21, 36.

'nh 'to answer'. *'anā'ēl*; *'anānī'ēl/'anānī* (sf.) which are either from this root with addition of a 1st pers. sing. suffix, or the root *'nn* 'to appear'.

'qb 'to guard, protect'. *'aqab'ēl*; *'aqqabyaw*; *'aqūbiya*, *'aqqūb* (sff.).

pdh 'to ransom, save'. *Padāyaw*. *Pa-da-'-ia-a-ma* Zadok, 77.

pl' 'to be wonderful, extraordinary. *Pillīyaw* (probably Piel perf. 'Y has worked wonders') or root *pll* 'to judge'. Zadok suggests a nominal form 'My wonder is Yhw' (Zadok, 16).

plṭ 'to escape'. *Pal-ṭi/ṭi-ia/iá-u* Zadok, 37.

pll 'to judge'. *Pi-il-lu-ia-a-ma* Zadok, 16, 20: Zadok suggests a genitive *qitl* form of *pll*.

ṣpy uncertain. *Ṣi-pa-'-ia-a-ma* Zadok, 17. Zadok suggests a meaning 'Expect, hope for Yhw', a Qal imv. 2nd pers. sing. masc. of a root *ṣpy*.

qny 'to get, acquire'. *Qa-na-a-ma/Qa-na-'-a*-[*ma*] Zadok, 38.

qtr 'rock'. *'ēlqatar*.

rikat unexplained. *Rikat-'ēl* (*ri-i-kat-'el*).

rp' 'to heal'. *Ra-pa-'-ia-u* Zadok, 37.

rḥb 'to be wide'. *Ra-'-bi-ēl* = *raḥab'ēl*; the orthography is difficult, since West Semitic *ḥ* is usually represented by Akk. *h*.

rḥm 'to be merciful, compassionate'. *Raḥīm'ēl*.

šbn unknown. *Šu-bu-nu-ia-a-ma* Zadok, 16, 47.

šwb 'to turn back, return', Hiphil 'to restore'. *Ia-a-šu-bu* Zadok, 77.

skn 'to dwell'. *Šikin'ēl* (may be West Semitic).

slm 'to be complete, sound'. *Šá-lam-ia-a-ma* Zadok, 39.

šn' 'to be or become high, exalted in rank'; 'to shine' cf. Arab. *saniya*. *Ša-ni-ia-a-ma* Zadok, 22, 39. An active part. of *šn'* is suggested by Zadok.

šrb 'to send burning heat' or cf. Syr. Pa. 'to propagate, produce' and BDB, 1056. *yišribyaw*.

tīr(*a*) (Pers.) 'power'. *Tīr*(*i*)*yaw*. Stolper *op. cit.*, 27 suggests that the name was originally wholly Pers.; see also the literature cited by Stolper, p. 27 n. 15. Zadok also considers the name to be Iranian, *Tīrī-ama-* 'Having Tīrī's force' (Zadok, 22).

2. *Jewish Names in the Elephantine Documents*

Names contained in the papyri from Elephantine, where a Jewish garrison existed, have often been included as part of the Hebrew onomasticon (so, e.g., *IPN*, *passim*). However, to accept these Elephantine names as Jewish, without reservation, would seem as unwise as to accept religious ideas expressed in the names as indicative of the religion of Israel. This view is expressed well by Kaufmann, 'The garrison was founded before the Persian conquest of Egypt in 525; the Jews of Elephantine had spent over a century isolated in an alien environment by the time of the papyri. No Israelite writing was found among them, although the pagan Ahikar romance was. They had become assimilated linguistically and intermarried with their neighbors. Whatever "idolatry" they brought with them from their native land cannot but have heightened in these circumstances. In contrast to the Babylonian colony of exiles they had no prophets among them, though they did have priests. Their religion can therefore be used only in a most qualified way to reconstruct the popular religion of Israel in Palestine' (Y. Kaufmann, *The Religion of Israel*, translated and abridged by Moshe Greenberg, London: Allen & Unwin [1961], 149).

Names from the Elephantine papyri have been studied by M.H. Silverman (*Jewish Personal Names in the Elephantine Documents*: *a study in onomastic development*, Ph.D. Dissertation, Brandeis University [1967], University Microfilms). However, although he has attempted to extract Jewish names from the Elephantine onomasticon, his results do not appear sufficiently conclusive to justify the inclusion of any Elephantine names in the Hebrew onomasticon with which this study is involved.

To begin with, Silverman's division of the total number of Elephantine names is questionable. He extracts Egyptian, Persian and Babylonian names and then classifies the remainder as West Semitic (*ibid.*, 46-47). His criterion for such divisions is a linguistic one, i.e. the etymology of the non-theophoric element should belong to one of the four classes. He also localizes, where possible, the theophoric element, and uses this to determine the class into which a name should be placed. Yet for the distinction between a Jewish and a non-Jewish name, Silverman admits that sure criteria cannot be found and, with the exception of Yahwistic names, nearly all could be ascribed to both Jews and pagan Arameans or Phoenicians. In spite of this he writes: 'Even if the justification seems conjectural, a methodology must be chosen that will assist in making this distinction: For our purposes, I have chosen the following: all West-Semitic names emanating from the colony ought to be considered Jewish unless proven otherwise' (*ibid.*, 162). The precariousness of this 'conjectural' methodology becomes even more apparent when we note that Silverman fails entirely to recognize that a linguistic criterion for assigning a name to the class 'Jewish' or 'non-Jewish', does not determine *whether a Jewish or non-Jewish person bore that name*.

This question of identifying the name-bearer is important since, as we have noted with reference to the names from the Murašû archives (see above, Appendix 1), the Arameans were constant borrowers from the religions of others. It is, therefore, inconceivable that Arameans did not borrow from the Jewish onomasticon at Elephantine. Moreover, they certainly borrowed names compounded with a Yahwistic element (see above, §4.4) so that the criterion of using the theophoric element to ascertain the origin of a name on any grounds other than linguistic, is entirely suspect. The impossibility of assigning each name to its racial bearer is pointed out by Silverman himself: 'Both non-Semitic, Babylonian and West-Semitic names exist in the same famililies (*sic*) to such a degree that no ethnic decisions based on patronymics alone may be admitted. Indications of nationality, such as *'rmy* ("an Aramean"), *bbly* ("the Babylonian"), *yhwdy* ("a Jew"), etc. and specification of places of garrison, like . . . *zy swn* ("of Syene") or . . . *zy yb* ("of Elephantine"), often contradict the evidence of the language in the name itself, or themselves change in unordered fashion. Note that *hddnwry* is called a Babylonian, even though his name is Aramaic, and that *mšlm br zkwr* is termed *'rmy zy swn* ("Aramean of Syene") in B2.2, but *yhwdy zy yb* ("Jew of Elephantine") in B5.2. In these circumstances, the only reliable criterion is linguistic' (*op. cit.*, 12). It should be noted here that if, as he states, indications of nationality 'often contradict the evidence of the language in the name itself', then the converse is also true, i.e. the language, *or linguistics*, of the name will contradict indications of nationality, so demonstrating that linguistic criteria, also, cannot be 'reliable'.

Furthermore, we must suspect Silverman of reading far too many West Semitic and Semitic meanings into names: when linguistic criteria fail to establish the origin of a name, Silverman relies upon 'other factors', i.e. 'in resolving the ambiguities, the Semitic explanation will always be preferred, and within the Semitic sphere, the West-Semitic one will be chosen. Although this may appear arbitrary, it seems best to assign as many names as possible to these categories because they are our primary concern. Furthermore, those appellatives of mixed origin will be thought West-Semitic for the same reason' (*ibid.*, 47). Need it be said that 'concern' can in no way replace concrete evidence for assessing the origin of a name on any grounds, linguistic or otherwise!

Silverman assigns most of the West Semitic names to the category of 'Jewish-Aramaic', names which are structurally suited to Jewish or Aramaic origins (*ibid.*, 15, 171). Purely Hebrew as opposed to Aramaic names, both of which he labels 'Jewish' (*ibid.*, 61), he extracts by phonological, morphological and lexicographical criteria. Again, however, we are not able to conclude that a specific Hebrew or Aramaic name was borne by a correspondingly Hebrew or Aramean individual. That phonological criteria fail to establish such a relationship between name and bearer is indicated, for example, by the use of the element *'zr* (Hebrew) and *'dr* (Aramaic): both these elements mean 'to help' and both are probably used in biblical Hebrew in compound names of Hebrew individuals, as well as in Aramaic names of Aramean individuals (see above, p. 215). It is quite possible that the Elephantine onomasticon could reflect the same phenomenon. Indeed, even where names morphologically reflect Hebrew usage or where a particular root exists only in Aramaic or in Hebrew and not in other cognate languages, we cannot be certain that in the Elephantine colony no interchange of names between ethnic groups took place.

In conclusion, one fails to find satisfactory criteria for establishing that Jewish names from the Elephantine documents were, in fact, borne by Jewish individuals. The Elephantine onomasticon must remain, therefore, extraneous to the basic material with which this work is concerned. Nevertheless, as was found with the Murašû material, these names are certainly of interest, and have been appended as such.

In the following name-list, the meanings of roots and comments are generally those suggested by Silverman. Many of the abbreviated forms included by Silverman should be accepted with caution (see below, for example, p. 331 n. 3). Any discussion, or relevant notes concerning the name-list, are appended.

*Theophoric Names from the Elephantine Documents**

'b 'father'. *'ḥ'b*[1]; *'byhw*,[2] *'byhy* (f); sff. *'b'*; *'bh*.

'wṣ 'to urge, hasten' (Heb. only). *y'ṣyh*.

'wr 'light'. sf. *'wry*;[3] *yhh'wr*; *yhw'wr*; *'wryh*; *'ryh*;[4] *hwry'*;[5] *'rymlk*.

'wš 'strong, manly'.[6] *y'wš*; *y'šyh*.

'zn 'to hear'. *'znyh*; *y'znyh*; *yznyh*.

'ḥ 'brother'. *'ḥyh*.

'sr 'to bind'. *'srmlk* 'Osiris is king' (Eg.), or 'Prisoner, servant of Mlk'.

'ṣl uncertain, cf. Arab. *aṣala* 'to be distinguished, noble, chief'. sf. *'ṣwl* 'God is/has proven noble'.

bṭḥ 'to trust'. *mbṭḥyh*.

bnh 'to build, create'. *bnyh*.

swd. sf. *bs'*: sf. of *bswdyh*?[7]

b'd 'behind, after, on behalf of, for'. *b'dyh*.[8]

brk 'to bless'. *brkyh*; *nbwbrk*.

bt 'house'. sf. *bty* 'House of Y' i.e. 'Worshipper of Y' or '(My) house is Y'.

gdl 'to be great' (Heb. and Ug. only). *gdlyh*; sff. *ygdl*; *gdwl* (*qattûl*); *gdl*.

gmr 'to accomplish, finish'. *gmryh*.

*Notes to this appendix follow on pp. 331ff.

hdr 'glory, honour'. *yhhdry*.

zbd 'to give, grant, bestow'. *zbdyh*; *'šmzbd*; *byt'lzbd*; sff. *zbdy*; *zbwd* (*qattûl*).

zkr 'to remember' (Aram. *dkr*). *zkryh*; sf. *zkwr* (*qattûl*).

ḥg 'holyday'. sf. *ḥgy* (with *ay* 'hypoc.' or gentilic suffix).

ḥlq 'portion'. *ḥlqyh*.

ḥnn 'to show favour, be gracious'. *yhwḥn* (f.); *ḥnnyh*; *ḥnmyh*; sff. *ḥwny* (*qûtay*); *ḥnn*; *ḥnny*.

ḥsy 'to seek refuge'. *mḥsyh*; sf. *mḥsh*.

ṭb 'good' (Aram.). *'ḥwṭb*; *'ḥṭḇ*.

ṭl 'shelter, protection', (cf. Heb. *ṣl*). *yhwṭl*.[9]

ydh 'to confess, laud, praise' (Hiphil). *hwdwyh*; sf. *hwdw*.

yš' 'to save, deliver'. *yš'yh*; *'wš'yh*; *hwš'yh*; sff. *'wš'*; *hwš'*.

kwl/kll 'to contain, supply, sustain' Pilpel 'to sustain, feed, support'. *klklyh*.

my + *k* 'who?' *mykyh*; *mkyh*; sff. *myk'*; *mykh*; *mky*.

mlk 'king'. *mlkyh*; *'trmlky*; sf. *kyh*.

nṣl Hiphil 'to save, deliver'. sf. *hṣwl* (*qattûl*).

n(*w*)*r* 'light' (Heb. lacks *wāw*). *nryh*; *byt'lnwry*; *hddnwry*; *šmšnry*; sf. *nry*.

ntn 'to give'. *yhntn*; *yhwntn*; *byt'lntn*; *ḥrmntn*; *nbwntn*; *byt'lnd*[*n*]; *byt'ltdn*; sff. *ntwn* (*qattûl*), *ntn*, *mtn*.

smk 'to lean, lay, rest, support'. sf. *smky*.

str 'to hide, conceal'. sf. *stry*.

'zz 'stronghold' or *'wz* 'place of refuge'. *m'zyh*; *m'wzyh*; *gd'zyz*.

'zr 'to help' (Aram. *'dr*). *'zryh*; *b'l'zr*; *'t'dry*; *zb'dry*; *nśk'dry*; sf. *'zwr* (*qattûl*), *'dry*.

'lh 'to rise, ascend', hence 'be exalted'. *yhw'ly* (f.).

'm + *n* 'with us'. *'mnyh*.[10]

'nh 'to answer'. sf. *'ny*.

'nn uncertain. *'nnyh*.[11]

'qb 'to guard, protect' (or 'to follow'). *byt'l'qb*; *nbw'qb*.

'šr 'to abound, enrich'. *'b'šr*.

pdh 'to redeem, save' (common Semitic except Aram.). *pdyh*; sf. *pd'*.

plṭ 'to rescue, deliver, save'. *plṭyh*; sff. *plṭw? plṭy*.

pll 'to judge'. *pllyh*; *plwlyh*; *plplyh*; sf. *plwl*.

pny 'to face, turn to'. *pnwlyh* imv. + *l* 'Turn to Y!'

ṣpl uncertain, perhaps *ṣpn*. *ṣply'*; *ṣplyh*.

ṣpn 'to hide', hence 'to treasure, protect, shelter'. *ṣpnyh*.

qw' 'to await, expect, hope' (Heb., Akk., Aram.). *qwylyh* (f.) Piel imv. + prep. *l* = 'Hope in Y'; *tqwty'* 'Hope of Y'.

qwl 'voice' (Heb. includes *wāw*). sf. *qwl'*.

qwm 'to rise'. *byt'ltqm*.

qnh 'to buy, acquire or create'. *qnyh*; *qwnyh*; sff. *qny'*, *qwn* (Heb. includes *wāw*).

rwm 'to be high, exalted'. *'šmrm*; *šwhrm*; sf. *rmy*.

r'y/r'w 'to lead, pasture, be friendly', noun 'friend'. *r'wyh*;[12] *byt'lr'y*; *nbwr'y*; sf. *r'y'*.

rp' 'to heal'. *yrpyh*; sff. *rp'*, *rpy*.

śkh 'to look out'. *śk'l*.[13]

śmḥ 'to rejoice, be happy'. sff. *śmwḥ* (*qattûl*); *śmwḥ*.

śrr noun 'prince, king', or 'rule'. *śry*[*h*] (f.).

šdr 'to send'. *nbwšdr*.

šwr 'wall'. *byt'lš*[*wry*]; *'tršwry*.

šzb 'to save, rescue'. *'šmšzb*.

šwb 'to return, answer'. *yšbyh*; sff. *yšwb*; *šbh*; *šwby* (*qûtay*); *šybh*.

šlm 'to be complete, to restore, pay', (common Semitic). *šlmyh*; sff. *šlwm* (*qattûl*); *šlm*; *šlmm* (noun).

šm' 'to hear'. *yhwyšm'* (f.); *yhwšm'* (f.); *šm'yh*; sf. *šmw'* (*qattûl*).

špṭ 'to judge'. [*šp*]*ṭyh*.

tmm 'to be complete, finished'. sff. *ytwm*; *ytwmh* (f.); *ytm'*.

Notes to Appendix §2

1. Silverman's interpretation 'The Father is a/the/my brother' (p. 113) or vice versa, is by no means certain. His criterion for accepting the elements as theophoric, is based solely on the unconvincing argument that because the elements have theophoric status in some names, they have the same status in all names (p. 175). The usual rendering 'Father's brother' (i.e. 'uncle' [not divine cf. BDB, 26, Geh, 20, KB, 29]) is reflected in Akk. *Aḫi-abiya*, 'My uncle' (Stamm, 302) and *Aḫi-abi* 'Uncle' (Stamm, 302, *APN*, 14a). Similarly, the Akk. onomasticon also includes the obviously non-theophoric 'aunt' in the names *Aḫāt-abi-ša* (*ibid.*) and *Aḫāt-abi-šu* (Stamm, 302). Such an interpretation of 'Father's brother' may be endorsed by the fact that the elements never occur in reverse order, and the name is therefore unlike *'ăbîyāh(û)/yô'āb*, *'ăbî'ēl/'ĕlî'āb* etc. A secular name is, then, preferable.

2. Two possible meanings are suggested by Silverman for the name *'byhw*, 'Yahū is (my) Father' or 'He is my Father' (p. 113). The former interpretation is amply attested in BH, where the forms appear *with a dagheshed yōd* signifying duplicated value for this letter, and endorsing a consonantal value for the second *yōd*. Thus, the suggestion that the second element could be the 3rd pers. masc. pronoun *hw'* is highly unlikely. Silverman further suggests for the name *'byhy*, the meanings 'Yāh is my Father', with the addition of a 'hypocoristic suffix *ay* or, if the form could be considered as a fem. of *'byhw*, a meaning 'She is my Father'. Though the form *'byhy* is unusual, to suggest the 3rd pers. fem. sing. pronoun *hy'* for the second element seems formally unlikely as well as producing a meaning ('She is my Father') which is semantically ridiculous.

3. Silverman considers that *hypocristica* 'are usually formed from two element sentence names by omitting the theophorous element, and adding a suffix to the remaining nominal or verbal component', while other abbreviated names consist of a verb alone (p. 106). While these factors are not untrue per se, Silverman's contention that where a root exists in a name with the addition of a theophoric element, other names formed from that root, without the theophoric element, must be abbreviated forms, seems very questionable. He writes, it 'seems natural to assume that a root having a sense suitable for sacred appellatives would usually not suddenly assume a different meaning, one apt for profane names' (p. 174). Such a notion is impossible to prove: where a root occurs with a theophoric element, it is, in practically every case, semantically logical when applied to the divine personality. Naturally, any names formed from the same roots without the theophoric element are also semantically applicable to the deity, but such suitability alone, does not justify the tenuous suggestion that these roots can never be profane in an onomastic context. Equally speculative is the assumption that the suffix *y* is at times 'a phonetic rendering of the remnant of the theophorous element *yh*' (p. 130, cf. p. 205): it has been shown

elsewhere, that such a theory is most precarious (see above, p. 149).

4. Silverman considers the name to have been written defectively (pp. 114-15). However, cf. Section 2.5 'Difficulties with Hollow Roots' and names from the roots *'wr* and *'rh*.

5. The Heb. onomasticon has no parallel for this apparent interchange of *h* and *'* in the non-theophoric element.

6. Silverman finds preferable a root *'wš* meaning 'strong', 'manly', for the two names *y'wš* and *y'šyh*. (For difficulties with the root *'wš* and *'šh*, see above, §2.5.) He chooses this interpretation 'because it would be intelligible to the Jews of Eleph.' (p. 115), presumably since they employed the word for 'man'. However, a root *'yš*/*'wš* for the noun *'yš* (man) is by no means a certainty and, since a meaning 'to be strong' is suggested mainly by an Akk. cognate, there seems no reason to exclude cognates in other languages. Silverman is in error in suggesting that BDB indicate that *many* BH words containing the idea strength or support may be connected with the root *'wš*/*'yš*, in fact, BDB (35b) conclude the contrary, discussing only feminine and plural forms of *'yš* (man) as from a root *'nš* or *'wš*/*'yš*. Silverman's objection to the Arab. and Ug. cognate *'wš* meaning 'to give' is, therefore, without firm foundation. This is the case, also with his criticism of a derivation from the root *'šh* for the name *y'šyh* which Noth (IPN, 212) connects with Arab. *'asā* 'to cure'. Noth certainly does not formulate the equation *'šh* = 'cure', as Silverman suggests, and equally certainly draws no comparison between the Heb. name and Akk./Aram. as Silverman also indicates. It is better to recognize the present unfathomable nature of these names rather than append to them interpretations which can only be based on speculation.

7. That *bs'* is a shortened form of *bswdyh* 'In the counsel/secret of Y' should be accepted with more reservation than Silverman suggests. He is quite erroneous in saying that Lidzbarski has *shown* that *bsy* is a drastic contraction of *b*^{e}*sôdyāh*—Lidzbarski merely lists *bsy* as a sf., adding, in parenthesis, the note to *compare b*^{e}*sôdyāh* (*Eph*, 14).

8. A better suggestion for this name is the meaning 'In the testimony, witness of El', involving the preposition *b*^{e}, followed by the noun from the root *'wd* and the theophoric element (cf. further the seal *b'd'l* V, 48, above, p. 121).

9. The BH name *'ăbîṭāl* is usually interpreted as 'The Father is dew', cf. BDB, 4, Geh, 7, KB, 5. In the attested Elephantine name *yhwṭl*, Silverman endorses a root *ṭll* which he derives from a 'Proto-Semitic' root *ẓll* meaning 'shelter', 'protection'. The root *ṭll* with the meaning 'to cover, cover over, roof' is attested in BH as a borrowed Aramaism (cf. BDB, 378 II *ṭll*). The vocalization of the BH name indicates that the element *-ṭl* conforms to second position Qal perf. types from Geminate roots (cf. above, pp. 105 and 171 n. 23). A verbal translation 'Y has covered, i.e. protected' is not, then, inconceivable, although Silverman prefers a nominal interpretation, 'Yahu is the protector/protection'. The Elephantine name also demonstrates the

difficulty in ascertaining whether an Aram. or Heb. individual bore this name; clearly, the root *ṭll* was used in the Heb. onomasticon and equally clearly it is Aram. in form.

10. The name is interesting in that it parallels BH *'immānû'ēl*, showing that the biblical name could have been included in an everyday onomasticon, in spite of its special significance in the prophetic ministry of Isaiah (Isa. 7.14; 8.8, 10).

11. Silverman prefers a root *'nh* 'to answer' with the addition of the 1st pers. sing. suffix, i.e. 'Yah has answered, or answered me'. The BH name *'ănanyāh* is usually accepted as derived from the root *'nn* which, in verbal form, has the probable meaning 'to appear', suggested by an Arab. cognate.

12. Silverman derives the name from the root *r'w/r'y* meaning 'to lead, pasture, be friendly', and interprets the name as 'Yah leads', or 'is the friend'. The Heb. root *r'w* contains in its verbal forms, only the meaning I 'to pasture, tend, graze', II 'to associate with' and III 'to take pleasure (in), desire' (cf. BDB, 944-46). There is no evidence to suggest that the Heb. names can be interpreted in the sense which Silverman has done here (cf. further, the note on *'ăḥîrā'* above, p. 142).

13. Cf. *sākᵉyāh* above, p. 139.

3. *List of Ancient Hebrew Personal Names*

The following is a list of ancient Hebrew theophoric personal names occurring in the Old Testament, as well as those from extra-biblical sources. The names are classified according to the root of the non-theophoric element. After each biblical name a number in brackets signifies the number of people to whom such a name was given. The grammatical form of the name is also given, for example, nominal (n.), Qal perfective (Q. perf.), shortened form (sf.), or difficult form (Df.) etc. Names in biblical Hebrew are listed under the subheading BH, and extra-biblical names under EB.

Name List

'b father nominal.
BH *'abî'ēl* (2) *'abîyāh(û)* (8) m. & f. *'ăbîmelek* (4)
'ăbîmā'ēl (1) *'ĕlî'āb* (6) *yô'āb* (3)
Sff. *'ăbî* (1) *'ăbîyām* (1)

EB	*'byh*	Inscr. Gezer marg. cf. *SSI*, 2, 4.
	'byhw	Seal N. Avigad, *EI*, 12 68; inscr. *AI*, 27, 6.
	'byw	Seals V, 65, 123.
	yw'b	Seal V, 9.
	yhw'b	Inscr. *AI*, 39.10; 49.9; 59.1.
	'bb'l	Inscr. SO 2.4 cf. *SSI*, 2, 11.
	'bgd	Seals V, 234, 275 (?).
Sff.	*'b'*	Seals V, 160, 204.
	'by	Inscr. Mur. B 2 cf. *SSI*, 32.

'br to be firm, strong.
EB *'bryhw* Seal V, 330 Stative Q. perf.

'db cf. Arab. *'adaba* to invite, discipline.
BH *'adb^{e}'ēl* (1) Df.

'dn lord nominal.
BH *'ădōnîyāhû/'ădōyyinăh* (3)

EB	*'dnyh*	Seal V, 75
	'dnyw	Inscr. SO 8.2
	'dn'm	Inscr. SO 8.2; 9.2; 10.2-3; 11.2?; 19.4.
Sf.	*'dny*	Seal V, 96.

'hl tent nominal.
BH *'āhŏlî'āb* (1)
Sf. *'ōhel* (1)
EB *ḥmy'hl* Seal V, 412.

'wh (1) to incline, desire; (2) to sign, mark; or cf. Arab. to betake oneself or to be tenderly inclined, root *'wj*.
BH *'û'ēl* (1) prob. constr.

'yl/'wl to be in front of, precede, lead.
EB *'ḥy'yl* Inscr. *AI*, 35.3. Lemaire, *IH*, 204 reads *Aḥyam*.

'wm to rule cf. Arab. *'āma*.
BH *'ăḥî'ām* (1)

EB *'ḥy'm* Inscr. A 35.3 cf. *IH*, 204.
Q, perfs., or root *'mm* 'to be wide, roomy'.

'wṣ to press, be pressed, make haste.
EB *'ṣyh* or *'ṣy* Seal V, 97 Df.

'wr to be, become light; n. light.
BH *'ûrî'ēl* (2) n. *'ûrîyāh(û)* (4) n. *šᵉdê'ûr* (1) n.
Sff. *'ûrî* (3) *'ûr* (1)
EB *'ly'r* Seal P. Bordreuil, A. Lemaire, *Sem* 29 (1979), 73-74 no. 4 Df.
yw'r Seal V, 249 n?
'wryw Seals V, 184; Y. Aharoni, *IEJ* 9 (1959), 55 n.
'wryhw Inscr. *AI*, 31.2; A 36.2 cf. *IH*, 204; Ophel 8 cf. *IH*, 239, 241 n.

'wš to bestow, give cf. Arab. *'āsa*.
BH *y(ᵉh)ô'āš* (6) Q. perf.
EB *'šyhw* Seal V, 231, 281 = inscr. *AI*, 40.1 = 35.2 = 17.3 = 105.2 = 106.2 = 107.2; BL, 50 no. 12; inscr. Y. Aharoni, *Lachish V*, 22; *AI*, 51.1.
'šyh Seal V, 232 Q. perf.
y'wš Inscr. L 2.1=3.2 = 6.1 cf. *SSI*, 37, 38, 45 Df.
y[']š Inscr. Y. Aharoni, *Lachish V*, 5ff. Df.
For EB names cf. the possibility of a root *'šh* 'to support', also Arab. *'asā* 'to nurse, cure'.
Sff. *'š'* Seal V, 316; inscr. SO 22.2 = 23.2 = 24.1 = 25.2 (?) = 26.1 = 27.1 = 28.1 = 29.1; 37.3 =39.3; 102.1 cf. *IH*, 292.
'šn' Seal V, 141, 413.

'zn denom. to give ear, listen, hear (Hiphil).
BH *'ăzanyāhû* (1) Q. perf. *ya'ăzanyāhû/yᵉzanyāh(û)* (5) Q. imf.
Sff. *'oznî* (1) *'ûzay* (1)
EB *yzn'l* Seal V, 28 Q. imf.
y'znyh Seals V, 21, 241 Q. imf.
y'znyhw Seal V, 69; inscr. L 1, 2, 3 cf. *SSI*, 36, 63-4; *AI*, 39.9 Q. imf.
ywzn Seal BL, 50 no. 13 Q. perf.
Sff. *y'zn* Inscr. *AI*, 59.5; A 58.4 cf. *IH*, 215.

'ḥ brother nominal.
BH *'ăḥîyāh(û)* (10) *'ăḥîmelek* (2) *yô'āḥ* (5)
yôḥā' (2) Df.

Sff.	*'ăḥôªḥ* (1) *'aḥlay* (2) m. & f. *ḥî'ēl* (1)? *'ăḥî* (1)	
EB	*'ḥyhw*	Seal V, 246; inscr. Ophel 2; L 3.17 cf. *SSI*, 25, 38; R 1 cf. *IH*, 257; Q 1.2-3 cf. *IH*, 252 and *SSI*, 17.
	'ḥyw	Seals V, 183, 339.
	'ḥmlk	Seals V, 139, 154, 292, 324, 358, 424; Herr, 90 no. 7; inscr. SO 22.2-3 = 23.2 = 24.1 = 25.2 = 26.1 (?) = 27.2 = 28.2 cf. *IH*, 292; SO 48.2 cf. *IH*, 292; *AI*, 72.2.
Sff.	*'ḥ'*	Seals V, 121, 295, 296; inscr. *AI*, 49.16; 67.4; 74.2; V. Fritz, *ZDPV* 91 (1975), 131-34; SO 51.3 cf. *SSI*, 10; KM 4 cf. *IH*, 275.
	'ḥy	Inscr. *AI*, 93.6.
	ḥmlk	Seal V, 124.

'ḥz to grasp, take hold, take possession.

BH	*'ăḥazyāh(û)* (2) Q perf. *y(ᵉh)ô'āḥāz* (4) Q. perf.	
Sff.	*'āḥāz* (2) *'aḥzay* (1)	
EB	*'ḥzyhw*	Seals V, 342; M, 81-82 no. 31 Q. perf.
	yh'ḥz	Seal V, 252 Q. perf..
Sff.	*'ḥz*	Seals V, 44, 141; inscr. SO 2.5 cf. *SSI*, 9, 11; SS 7.1 cf. *IH*, 250.
	'ḥzy	Seal N. Avigad, *Qedem* 4 (1976), 6, 7; inscr. SO 25.3 cf. *IH*, 48 and Dir, p. 41; Dir, SO 310.

'yš man.

BH *'ešbā'al/'îš-bōšet* (1) constr.

'l El/God nominal.

BH	*'ĕlî'ēl* (8) *'ĕlî'āb* (6) *'ēlîyāh(û)* (4) *'ĕlîmelek* (1) *'ĕlî'ām* (2) *'ĕlîṣûr* (1) *'ăbî'ēl* (2) *'ăbîmā'ēl* (1) *yô'ēl* (14) *'ammî'ēl* (4) *malkî'ēl* (1) *ṣûrî'ēl* (1)	
Sff.	*ḥî'ēl* (1) *'aḥlay* ? (2)	
EB	*'lyhw*	Seal C. Graesser, *BASOR* 220 (1975), 63-66; P. Bordreuil, A. Lemaire, *Sem* 29 (1979), 73 no. 3.
	'ly'm	Seal V, 6 (Ammon.?).
	'lyṣwr	Inscr. B 2.1 cf. *IH*, 273.
	'lmlk	Inscr. Hazor B 2 cf. *SSI*, 18.19.
	yhw'l	Seals V, 256; F. J. Bliss, *PEFQS* 31 (1899), 198 = *yhw'/kl* Df.

Names cited are confined to those in which both elements can be theophoric.

'mh unknown

EB *'ḥ'mh* Seal BL, 48 no. 8 DF.

'mn to confirm, support.
EB *yw'mn* Seal V, 172 Q. perf.

'mṣ to be stout, strong, bold, alert.
BH *'ămaṣyāh(û)* (4) Stative Q, perf.
Sf. *'amṣî* (2)

'mr to utter, say.
BH *'ămaryāhû* (8) Q. perf.
Sf. *'imrî* (2)
EB *'mryhw* Seal V, 211; inscr. Gib. 14 cf. *SSI*, 56 Q. perf.
'l'mr Seal V, 136 Q. perf.
'ḥ'mr Seal M, 76 no. 13 = V. 280 Q. perf.
(or *'ḥsmk*)

'mt truth, firmness, faithfulness.
BH Sf. *'ămittay*

'nn to be opportune, meet, encounter opportunely.
EB *'nyhw* Seal N. Avigad, *BASOR* 246 (1982), 59-62; inscr. Khirbet el Kôm, W.G. Dever, *HUCA* 40-41 (1969-70), 158-69 Df.

'sh to heal cf. Arab. *'asā*.
BH Sf. *'āsā'* (1)

'sp to gather, remove.
BH *'ăbî'āsāp/'ebyāsāp* (1) Q. perf.

'ṣl to join: denom. to lay aside, reserve, withdraw, withhold.
BH *'ăṣalyāhû* (1) Q. perf.

'rh to pluck, gather; to burn; n. lion.
BH *'ărî'ēl* (3) constr. *'ar'ēlî* (1) Df.
EB *'ryhw* Seals V, 207, 429, 430; Herr, 105 no. 48; 188 no. 79; inscr. L 16, obv. 5 cf. Torcz, 198; *AI*, 26.1; W.G. Dever, *HUCA* 40-41 (1969-70), 158-62 constr.?
'ryw Inscr. SO 50.2 cf. *SSI*, 10, 11; SS 4.4 cf. *IH*, 248. Lemaire prefers a meaning 'Y is my light' (*IH*, 36, 49), while Gibson considers the *r* a mistake for *b*. constr.?
Sf. *'r'* Seal V, 328 (or root *'wr*).

'śr to fill with joy cf. Arab. *'ašira*.
BH *'ăśar'ēl* (1) Q. perf. *'ăśar'ēlāh* (1) Q. perf.
'aśrî'ēl (1) Df. *y^eśar'ēlāh* (1) Df.

'šh to support (or *'wš* to give).
BH *yō'šīyāh(û)/yō'ôšīyāhû* (2) Df.

't prep. with.
BH *'ītī'ēl* (2) prep.
EB *'t'b* Seal V, 444 Df.

'th to come (poet.).
BH *'ělī'ātāh* (1) Q. perf.

bw' to come.
EB *'lb'* Inscr. SO 1.6 cf. *SSI*, 11 Q. perf.

bṭḥ to trust; n. trust.
EB *mbṭḥyhw* Inscr. L 1.4 cf. *SSI*, 36 n.

bnh to build
BH *b^e^nāyāh* (11) Q. perf. *yibn^e^yāh* (2) Q. imf.
Sff. *bûnāh* (1) *bûnnî* (4) *bānî* (9) *bunî* (3)
EB *bnyhw* Seals V, 18, 299, 407, 431; Herr, 119 no. 82; BL, 46-47 no. 3; inscr. L 16.4 cf. Torcz, 198; *AI*, 39.9; A 5.9 cf. *IH*, 167; A 74.4 cf. *IH*, 220 Q. perf.
ywbnh Seals V, 197, 290 Q. perf.
Sf. *bwnh/y* Seal V, 160.

b'l lord/n. pr. div. Baal nominal.
BH *ba'alyāh* (1) *b^e^'elyādā'* (1) *'ešbā'al/'īš-bōšet* (1) *y^e^rubba'al* (1) *m^e^rîb ba'al* (2)
EB *b'l'* Inscr. SO 1.7; 31.3 (cf. *SSI*, 10, 12); 3.3; 27.3; 28.3 (cf. *IH*, 292),
b'lzmr Inscr. SO 12.2-3, Dir, 43 no. 16. Lemaire, *IH*, 31, separates the two elements.
b'lḥnn Seal V, 36.
b'lysp Seal V, 219 possibly Phoen.
b'lm'ny Inscr. SO 27.3, Dir, 43 no. 18, *IH*, 33.
b'l'zkr Inscr. SO 37.3, Dir, 43 no. 17.
'bb'l Inscr. SO 2,4 cf. *SSI*, 9, 11.
mrb'l Inscr. SO 2,7 cf. *SSI*, 9, 11.
'nyb'l Inscr. MH 6,1 *IH*, 268, 269.

b'n?
BH *ba'ănā'* (3) Df. *ba'ănāh* (4) Df.

b'r?
BH *ba'ărā'* (1) Df.
EB *b'r'* Inscr. SO 43.2 = 45.2—46.2-3—47.1 cf. *IH*, 292.

b'š?
BH *ba'šā'* (1) Df.

bqh to test, prove.
BH *buqqîyāhû* (1) constr.
Sf. *buqqî* (2)
EB *bqyhw* Inscr. Ophel 1 cf. *SSI*, 25, 26 constr. (for a different reading cf. *IH*, 239, 241).

bqq (1) to empty. (2) to be luxuriant.
BH *baqbuqyāh* (1) Df.

br' to shape, create.
BH *b^{e}rā'yāh* (1) Q. perf.

brk to kneel, bless.
BH *bārak'ēl* (1) Q. perf. *berekyāhû* (6) Q. perf.
y^{e}berekyāhû (1) Q. imf.
Sf. *bārûk*
EB *brkyhw* Seals V, 230; Avigad, *IEJ* 28 (1978), 53; inscr. *AI*, 22.1 Q. perf.
Sf. *brwk* Seal V, 308.

brr to purify, select.
EB *'lybr* Seals V, 133, 397 (Ammon.?) Q. perf.

bt worshipper?
BH *bityāh* (1) f. constr.

g'h to rise up; n. majesty.
BH *g^e'ûēl* (1) constr.

g'l to redeem, act as kinsman.
EB *g'lyhw* Inscr. *AI*, 16.5; 39.5 Q. perf.
g'lhw Seal V, 110 Q. perf.

gbr to be strong, mighty; n. man.
BH *gabrî'ēl* (1) Df. prob. constr.
EB *gb[ryhw]* Inscr. *AI*, 60.5-6 Stative Q. perf.

gd fortune/n. pr. div. Gad. nominal.

BH *gaddî'ēl* (1) *'azgād* (3)
Sf. *gaddî* (1)
EB *gdyhw* Seal P. Bordreuil, A. Lemaire, *Sem* 29 (1979), 71-72; inscr. *AI*, 71.3 (inscr. reading uncertain).
gdyw Inscr. SO 2.2 prob. = 4.2 prob. = 5.2 prob. = 6.2 prob. = 7.2 prob. = 16a.2 = 16b.2 prob. = 17a.2 prob. = 17b.2 prob. = 18.2; 33.2 = 34.2 = 35.2-3 cf. *IH*, 293; 30.2; 42.3 and *SSI*, 9, 10, 12.
gdmlk Seal V, 64.
'bgd Seals V, 234, 275.

gdl to grow up, become great.

BH *g*^{e}*dalyāh(û)* (6) Stative Q. perf. *yigdalyāhû* (1) Stative Q. imf.
EB *gdlyhw* Seals V, 100, 149, 218, 240; inscr. *AI*, 21.2 Stative Q. perf.
gdlyh Inscr. Arad, A. F. Rainey, *Tel Aviv* 4 (1977), 97-102. Stative Q. perf.
ygdlyhw Seal V, 421 Stative Q. perf.

gyl to rejoice; n. rejoicing joy

BH *'ăbîgayil* (2) n.
EB *'bgyl* Seal *V*, 62 n.

glh to uncover, remove; Hiphil to carry away into exile. Qal to be manifest, reveal.

BH Sf. *yoglî*
EB *hglnyh* Seal V, 61 Hiphil + 1st pers. sing. suffix.

gml to deal fully, to deal adequately with, to deal out to.

BH *gamlî'ēl* (1) Df.
EB *gmlyhw* Seal V, 169 Q. perf.

gmr to end, come to an end, complete, accomplish.

BH *g*^{e}*maryāh(û)* (2) Q. perf.
Sf. *gōmer* (2) m. & f.
EB *gmryhw* Inscr. L 1.1; *AI*, 31.8; 35.4; 38.3; 40.1 Q. perf.
Sf. *gmr* Inscr. SO 50.1 cf. *SSI*, 12.

gr client cf. Phoen.

EB *gryhw* Seals V, 243; Herr, 120 no. 83 (V, 142 = *gdyhw*) constr.
Sff. *gry* Seals V, 299, 407; inscr. *AI*, 64.1.

dgh to multiply, increase, or *dgl* to look, behold. ?

EB *'ldg*[ ] Seal V, 300 Df.

dwd to swing, rock, dandle, fondle, love.
BH *'eldād* (1) Q. perf. *'ĕlîdād* (1) Q. perf. *dôdāwāhû* (1) constr.
EB *ddyhw* Seal V, 325 constr.

dyn to judge.
BH *dāni'ēl/dānîyē'l* (4) Q. perf. *'ăbîdān* (1) Q. perf.
EB *ydnyhw* Inscr. *AI*, 27.4 Q. imf.?
'lydn Seal V, 357 Q. imf.?

dlh to draw (rescue); n. *dlt* door.
BH *d*[e]*lāyah(û)* (5) Q. perf.
EB *dl[yhw* Inscr. Y. Aharoni, *Lachish V*, 22 Q. perf.
dlyw Inscr. Y. Yadin, *Hazor. The Rediscovery of a Great Citadel of the Bible*, 182-83.
ydlyhw Seal V, 237 Q. imf.
dltyhw Seal V, 331 n.
'ldlh Seal M, 20 Q. perf.

dll to direct cf. Arab. *dall.*
EB (*'*)*mâl* Inscr. L 19.3 cf. *SSI*, 49 Q. perf. Lemaire, *IH*, 132, 133, now reads *Mikal* for this name.

dmm to be silent, still, dumb; or cf. Arab. *damal* to make peace, heal, cure.
EB *dml'l* Seal V, 233 imv. + prep.?
Sff. *dml'* Seal V, 341; inscr. Gib. 21.28 cf. *SSI*, 56.

d'h to call cf. Arab. *da'ā*
BH *'eldā'āh* (1) Q. perf. *d*[e]*'û'ēl* (1) constr.

drš to resort to, seek.
EB *dršyhw* Seals V, 212, 338, 434 Q. perf.

hbn to be strong? cf. Arab. *ḫābin.*
BH *'aḥbān* (1) Df.

hdh to stretch out the hand cf. Arab. to lead, guide.
BH Sf. *yahdāy* (1)

hw' 3rd pers. sing. pron. he.
BH *'ĕlîhû(')* (5) *yēhû'* (5) *'ăbîhû'* (1)

hwd n. m. splendour, majesty nominal
BH *hôdwāh* (1) *hôdîyāh* (4) *'ăbîhûd* (1)

'ăḥîhûd (1) *'ammîhûd* (4)
Sff. *hidday* (1) *hôd* (1) *'ēhûd* (2)
EB *hwdyhw* Seals BL, 49 no. 9; N. Avigad, *IEJ* 25 (1975), 101 no. 1; Milik, *RB* 66 (1959), 551.
hwdyh Seal, V, 155.

hwh to become, perhaps root of divine name *yhwh*.
BH *yô'āb* (3) *yô'āḥ* (5) *yôḥā'* (2) Df.
yô'ēl (14) *'ăbîyāh(û)* 8 m. & f.
'ēlîyāh(û) (4) *'ăḥîyāhû* (10) *'ădōnîyāhû/'ădōyinâh* (3)
ba'alyāh (1) *malkîyāhû* (11)
EB *yhw'l* Seal Y. Aharoni, *IEJ* 18 (1968), 166-67.
yw'b Seal V, 9
yhw'b Inscr. *AI*, 39.10; 49.9; 59.1.
'lyhw Seals V, 344; P. Bordreuil, A. Lemaire, *Sem* 29 (1979), 73 no. 3.
'byhw Seal N. Avigad, *EI* 12 68; inscr. *AI*, 27.6.
'byw Seals V, 65, 123, 174; inscr. SO 50.2 read *'ryw* by Lemaire *IH*, 36.
'ḥyhw Seal V, 246; inscr. Ophel 2; L 3.17 cf. *SSI*, 25, 38; R 1 cf. *IH*, 257; Q 1.2-3 cf. *IH*, 252 and *SSI*, 17.
'ḥyw Seals V, 183; N. Avigad, *EI* 12 70 no. 16.
'dnyh Seal V, 75.
'dnyw Inscr. SO 8.2.
gdyhw Seal V, 142; inscr. *AI*, 71.3 (uncertain).
gdyw Inscr. SO 2.2 prob. = 4.2 = 5.2 = 6.2 = 7.2 = 16a.2 = 17a.2 = 17b.2 = 18.2; 33.2 = 34.2 = 35.2-3 cf. *IH*, 293; 30.2; 42.3 cf. *SSI*, 9, 10, 12.
mlkyhw Seals V, 176, 326, 406; N. Avigad, *EI* 12 62 no. 3; Herr, 131 no. 113; inscr. *AI*, 24.14; 39.2; 40.3.

Names cited are confined to those in which both elements can be theophoric.

hll (1) to shine (Qal, Hiphil). (2) to be boastful (Qal), to praise (Piel).
BH *y^ehalel'ēl* (2) Df. *mahălal'ēl* (2) part.

hr mountain
EB *hryhw* Seal V, 273 n.

zbd to bestow upon, endow with.
BH *zabdî'ēl* (2) Df. *z^ebadyāh(û)* (9) Q. perf.
'elzābād (2) Q. perf. *y(^eh)ôzābād* (13) Q. perf.
'ammîzābād (1) Q. perf.

Sff. *zabdî* (4) *zābād* (7)

zkr to remember.

BH *z^{e}karyāh(û)* (28) Q. perf. *yôzākār* (1) Q. perf.
Sff. *zakkay* (1) *zikrî* (12) *zeker* (1)
EB *zkryhw* Seals V, 104, 167; inscr. weight 11 cf. *SSI*, 69 Q. perf.
[z]kryw Seal V, 323 cf. Herr, 108 no. 57 Q. perf.
'lzkr Seals V, 42, 43 Q. perf.
b'l'zkr Inscr. SO 37 Dir, 43 no. 17 Df.
Sff. *zkr* Seals V, 46, 47, 171, 329; inscr. SO 31.3 cf. *SSI*, 10; *AI*, 38.7; 48.3; 67.5; KM 1 cf. *IH*, 275.
zkr[Inscr. Tell Masos, V. Fritz, *ZDPV* 91 (1975), 131-34.
zkry Seal V, 309; inscr. Dir, 274 Weights and Measures.

zmr to protect cf. S. Arab. *dhimr*.

BH Sf. *zimrî*
EB *zmryhw* Seal V, 54 Q. perf.
b'lzmr Inscr. SO 12 Dir, 43 no. 16 Q. perf. Lemaire, *IH*, 31, separates the name into two elements i.e. *b'l* + patronym *zmr*.

zrh to scatter, fan, winnow

EB *zryhw* Seal V, 301 Q. perf.

zrḥ to rise, come forth.

BH *z^{e}raḥyāh* (2) Q. perf. *yizraḥyāh* (2) Q. imf.
EB *yhwzṙ[ḥ]* Seal V, 321 Q. perf.

zr' to sow, scatter seed.

BH *yizr^{e}'e'l* (2) Q. imf.

hb'/h to withdraw, hide.

BH *'elyāḥbā'* (1) Hiphil imf. *ḥăbāyāh* (1) Q. perf.
Sf. *ḥubbāh* (1)

ḥbṣ to be joyful? cf. Akk. *ḫabāṣu*.

BH *ḥăbaṣṣinyāh* (1) Df.

ḥg feast.

BH *ḥagiyāh* (1) constr.
Sff. *ḥaggay* (1) *ḥaggî* (1)
EB Sf. *ḥgy* Seals B. Mazar, *Jerusalem Revealed*, (1975), 38, 40; V, 2, 20, 203, 213, 355; Herr, 119 no. 82

ḥdh to rejoice.
BH *yaḥdî'ēl* (1) Q. imf. *yeḥdᵉyāhû* (2) Q. imf.
Sff. *yaḥday/yaḥdô* (1)

ḥyl/ḥwl to be firm, strong.
BH *'ăbîḥayil* (5) n.
EB *yhwḥyl* Seals V, 42, 199 n.
yhwḥl? Seal V, 198, 396 n. (Vattioni records the seal 396 erroneously as *yhwhl* with *hē*.)

ḥzh to see, behold.
BH *ḥăzāyāh* (1) Q. perf. *ḥăzî'ēl* (1) Df.
yaḥzᵉyāh (1) Q. imf. *yaḥăzî'ēl* (5) Q. imf.
EB *yḥzẏhẇ* Inscr. *AI*, 6.3 Q. imf.
yḥzyhw Inscr. N. Avigad, *IEJ* 22 (1972), 1-9.

ḥzq to be or grow firm, strong.
BH *yᵉḥezqē'l* (2) Q. imf.
yᵉḥizqîyāh(û)/ḥizqîyāhû) (5) Stative Q. imf.
Sf. *ḥizqî* (1)
EB *ḥzqyhẇ* Seal V, 321. Since the person on this seal is the biblical King Hezekiah, the name would be stative Q. perf. with a loss of the preformative *yōd*.
ḥ̇[z]qyhw Inscr. Ophel 1 cf. *SSI*, 25.26. Lemaire (*IH*, 239) reads without an initial *yōd*, Gibson (p. 26) with the *yōd* n.?
ḥzq[*yw*] Inscr. Dir, 302 no. 16 n?

ḥyh to live.
BH *yᵉḥî'ēl* (8) Q. imf. *yᵉḥî'ēlî* (1) Q. imf.
yᵉḥîyāh (1) Q. imf. *mᵉḥûyā'ēl/mᵉḥîyâ'ēl* (1) Df.
EB *ḥwyhw* Seal BL, 48 no. 7 Df.
yḥw'ly Inscr. SO 55.2 (cf. *SSI*, 10, 13) prob. = SO 6.1 (cf. *IH*, 37) Q imf.?
yhw[*ḥy*] Seal V, 253 Df.
'byḥy Inscr. *AI*, 39.11 Df.

ḥkl to be confused, vague?
BH *ḥăkalyāh* (1) Q. perf. or root *ḥkh* + *l* Piel imv.
EB *ḥklyhw* Inscr. L 20.2 cf. *IH*, 134 Df.

ḥlh to be sweet, pleasing cf. Arab. *ḥalā*.
BH *yaḥlᵉ'ēl* (1) Df.

ḥlṣ to draw out (rescue).
EB *ḥlṣyhw* Seal V, 176 Q. perf. (or Piel?).

ḥlq to share, divide.
BH *ḥilqîyāh(û)* (7) n.
Sf. *ḥelqāy* (1)
EB *ḥlqyhw* Seals V, 52, 150, 321, 325, 416, 417, 418; Herr, 136 no. 21; BL, 53 no. 21 n.

ḥmh to protect, guard cf. S. Arab. *ḥamay*.
BH *ḥammû'ēl* (1) Df.
Sf. *yaḥmay* (1)

ḥml to spare.
EB *yḥmlyhw* Seals V, 51; N. Avigad, *EI* 69 no. 14 Q. imf.

ḥnn to show favour, be gracious.
BH *ḥănanyāh(û)* (14) Stative Q. perf.
ḥannî'ēl (2) constr.
ḥănam'ēl (1) Stative Q. perf.
y(ᵉh)ôḥānān (15) Stative Q. perf.
'elḥānān (2) Stative Q. perf.
Sf. *ḥănānî* (5)
EB *ḥnnyh* Seal V, 23 (Ammon.?) Stative Q. perf.
ḥnnyhw Seals V, 24, 25, 50, 218, 419, 429; inscr. *AI*, 3.3; 16.1; 36.4; Gib. 22, 32, 51, (prob. all the same person) cf. *SSI*, 56; V. Fritz, *ZDPV* 91 (1975), 131-34; KM 3 cf. *IH*, 275 Stative Q. perf.
ḥnyhw Seal V, 359 n.
ḥnn'l Seal V, 157 (Ammon.? or Edom.?) Stative Q. perf.
ḥn'[b] Inscr. SO 30.3 cf. *SSI*, 9, 12 n. (However, Lemaire, *IH*, 33, now reads *Gera Ḥanna*.)
'lḥnn Seals V, 5 (Ammon.?), 28 Stative Q. perf.
b'lḥnn Seal V, 36 Stative Q. perf.

ḥsd to be kind, good.
BH *ḥăsadyāh* (1) Stative Q. perf.
Sf. *ḥesed* (1)
EB *ḥsdyhw* Seal V, 220; inscr. R 2 cf. *IH*, 257-58 Stative Q. perf.
Sf. *ḥsd'* Seal M, 74 no. 2.

ḥsh to seek refuge; n. refuge.
BH *maḥsēyāh* (1) n.
EB *mḥs[yhw]* Inscr. *AI*, 23.6 n.
mḥs[yw] Inscr. SS 4.1 cf. *IH*, 248 n.

ḥph to hide, cover.
BH Sf. *ḥuppāh* (1)

ḥṣh to divide.
BH *yaḥṣᵉ'ēl/yaḥṣî'ēl* (1) Q. imf.

ḥrh to burn, be kindled (of anger) or root *ḥrḥ*.
BH *ḥarhăyāh/ḥarḥăyāh* (1) Df.

ḥrp to gather fruit, pluck; to reproach; to remain in harvest time n. harvest-time, autumn.
BH *'ĕlîḥōrep* (1) n.

ḥšb to think, account.
BH *ḥăšabyāh(û)* (8) Q. perf. *ḥăšabnᵉyāh* (2) Q. perf.
Sf. *ḥăšabnāh* (1)
EB *ḥšbyhw* Inscr. Yavn. 7 cf. *SSI*, 30, 128 Q. perf.

ṭbl to dip
BH *ṭᵉbalyāhû* (1) Q. perf.

ṭwb to be pleasing, good.
BH *ṭôb 'ădônîyāh* (1) Stative Q. perf.
ṭôbîyāh(û) (4) Stative Q. perf.
'abîṭûb (1) n. *'ăḥîṭûb* (2) n.
EB *ṭbyhw* Inscr. L 3.19; 5.10 cf. *SSI*, 38, 41, 44, 45 Stative Q. perf. (For L 3.19 Torcz, 198 and Aharoni, *Lachish V*, 19 read *ndbyhw*.)
ṭb'l Seal V, 376.
ṭbšlm Seal *IR*, 136; inscr. L 1.2 cf. *SSI*, 36, 37 (prob. Aram.); L 7.5-6; 18.1 cf. *IH* 94-95, 294 Stative Q. perf.

ṭll to cover, protect.
BH *'ăbîṭāl* (1) Q. perf.

yd hand + *bᵉ* in.
BH *bēdyāh* (1) prep. + noun.
EB *bdyhw* Seal V, 393.
bdyw Inscr. SO 58.1 cf. *IH*, 37.
bd'l Seal V, 400.
byd'l Seals V, 449, 450 (Ammon.?).

ydd to love.
BH *yᵉdîdyāh* (1) constr.
Sf. *yᵉdîdāh* (1) f.

ydh to do good cf. Arab. *yadā*.
BH *y^edāyāh* (2) Q. perf.

ydh to throw, cast; Hiphil to praise (in ritual worship).
BH *hôdawyāh/hôdaywāhû* (4) Hiphil imv.
Sf. *y^ehûdāh* (5)
EB *hwdwyhw* Inscr. L 3.17 cf. *SSI*, 38, 41 Hiphil imv.
Sf. *yhwd?* Seal V, 184.

yd' to know.
BH *y^eda'yāh* (5) Q. perf. *y^edî'ă'ēl* (3) constr.
'elyādā' (3) Q. perf. *y(^eh)ôyādā'* (4) Q. perf.
'ăbîdā' (1) Df. *b^e'elyādā'* (1) Q. perf.
Sff. *yadday/yiddô* (2) *yādā'* (1)
EB *yd'yhw* Seals V, 49; Herr, 129 no. 109; inscr. *AI*, 31.7; 39.4; 39.5 Q. perf.
yd'yw Inscr. SO 1,8; 42.2 (cf. *SSI* 1, 10, 11, 12) = SO 48.1 (cf. *IH*, 36) Q. perf.
Sf. *yd'* Inscr. L 3.20 cf. Torcz, 198.

yṭb to be good, well; to be glad, pleasing.
BH *m^ehêṭab'ēl* (2) m. & f. part.

ykl to be able, have power, prevail, endure.
BH *y^ekolyāh(û)* (1) f. Stative Q. perf.
y(^eh)ûkal (1) Stative Q. perf.
EB *yhwkl* Seals V, 253; Herr, 111 no. 63; inscr. *AI*, 21.1 Stative Q. perf.

ymh unknown.
BH *y^emû'ēl* (1) constr.?
EB *'ḥymh* Seal V, 366 Df.

ysp to add.
BH *yôsipyāh* (1) Hiphil imf. *'elyāsāp* (2) Q. perf.
Sf. *yôsēp* (5)
EB *b'lysp* Seal V, 219 (possibly Phoen.) Q. perf.

y'd to appoint.
BH *nô'adyāh* (2) m. & f. Niphal perf.

y'h to remember? cf. Arab. *wa'a*.
BH *y^e'û'ēl/y^e'îēl/y^e'iw'ēl* (10) constr.

yph to be fair, beautiful.
EB *ypyhw* Seal M, 80 no. 23 Stative Q. perf.

yrh to throw, shoot, Hiphil to teach.
BH Sf. *yôray* (1)
EB *yrmlk* Seal V, 444 Df.

yš existence, being, substance.
BH *'ăbîšay/'abšay* (1) Df.

yšb to sit, remain, dwell.
BH *yôšibyāh* (1) Hiphil imf.

yšh to assist, support? cf. Arab. *'asa'*.
BH *yôšawyāh* (1) Df.

yš' to deliver; n. salvation, opulence.
BH *yᵉša'yāh(û)* (7) Q. perf. *hôša'ăyāh* (2) Hiphil perf.
'ĕlîšûᵃ' (1) n. *'ĕlîšā'* (1) n.
yᵉhôšûᵃ'/yᵉhôšuᵃ'/yēšûᵃ' (9) n.
'ăbîšûᵃ' (2) n. *malkîšûᵃ'* (1) n.
Sff. *yiš'î* (4) *hôšēᵃ'* (5)
EB *yš''l* Seal V, 86 (Ammon.?) Q. perf.
yš'yhw Seals V, 52, 211, 294, 420, 426; Herr, 140 no. 140. Q. perf.
hwš'yhw Seals V, 144, 423, 424; inscr. L 3.1 cf. *SSI*, 30, 38; MH 1.7 cf. *IH*, 261 Hiphil perf.
hwš'm Seal B. Mazar, *Jerusalem Revealed* (1975), 38-40 Hiphil perf.
'lyš' Seals V, 41 (Ammon. ?), 271 (Heb.?); A.R. Millard, *Iraq* 24 (1962), 49 n. 55 (Ammon.?) inscr. SO 1.4; 1.7; 41.1 cf. *SSI*, 8, 10, 11; *AI*, 24,19-20, 24.15, n.
yhwš' Seal V, 27 n.
ywyš' Inscr. SO Dir, p. 311; SO 36.3 cf. *IH*, 52 n.
For SO 36.3, Diringer reads *ywyšb/r* (Dir, 46 no. 30), and Noth *ywyšr* (*IPN*, 245).
'bšw' Seal V, 1 n.
Sff. *hwš'* Seals V, 46, 181, 410, 423, 428; inscr. Mur. B 1 cf. *SSI*, 32.
yš' Seal M, 26.
yš'' Seal V, 85, 425.

ytn to be perpetual, never-failing cf. Arab. *watana*.
BH *yatnî'ēl* (1) Df.

ytr to remain over; n. abundance.
BH *yitrᵉ'ām* (1) n. *'ebyātār* (1) Stative Q. perf.

kbd to be heavy, honoured.
BH *yôkebed* (1) f. n.

kwl Pilpel to support, sustain, nourish.
EB *klklyhw* Seal V, 329 Pilpel.

kwn to set up, establish (Hiphil).
BH *y(ᵉh)ôyākîn/yᵉhôyākin* (1) Hiphil imf.
yᵉkônyāh(û)/konyāhû/yᵉkonyāh (1) Q. imf.
kônanyāhû/kŏnanyāhû (2) Polel.
EB *knyhw* Inscr. L 3.15 cf. *SSI*, 38, 40; *AI*, 49.4 (reading uncertain) Q. perf.
ywkn Seals V, 108, 277; Q. perf.: cf. also *Ia-ku-ú-ki-ni/Ia-'-(u)kin*, Zadok, *The Jews in Babylonia, 19.*

kll to be complete, perfect.
BH *kil'āb* (1) Df.

knn to be firm, substantial.
BH *kᵉnanyāh(û)* (2) Stative Q. perf.
Sf. *kᵉnānî* (1)

l to, for.
BH *lā'ēl* (1) prep. *lᵉmû'ēl/lᵉmô'ēl* (1) prep.

mgd to be glorious, excel in glory.
BH *magdî'ēl* (1) Df.

mwg to melt.
EB *'lmg?* Df. possibly Ammon.

mwt death.
BH *'ăḥîmôt* (1) n.

mḥl unknown.
EB *mḥlyh* Inscr. Y. Aharoni, *Lachish V*, 5ff. Df.

my interrog. Who?
BH *mîkā'ēl* (11) *mîšā'ēl* (3)
mîkāyāh(û) (6) m. & f. *mîkāyᵉhû* (3)
Sff. *mîkāh* (7) *mîkā'* (3) *mîkal* (1) f.

EB *mykyhw* Seals V, 30; BL, 49 no. 10; inscr. L 11.3 cf. *IH*, 128; N. Avigad, *RB* 80 (1973), 579.
Sff. *mk'* Seal V, 322.
mykh Seal V, 313.

mlṭ Niphal to slip away; Hiphil to be delivered, escape; to deliver.
BH *m*^{e}*laṭyāh* (1) Q. perf.

mlk king nominal.
BH *malkî'ēl* (1) *malkîyāh(û)* (11) *malkîšû*^{a}*'* (1)
malkîrām (1) *'ĕlîmelek* (1) *'ăbîmelek* (4)
'ăḥîmelek (2) *n*^{e}*tan-melek* (1)
Sff. *mallûk* (5) *m*^{e}*lûkî* (1)
EB *mlkyhw* Seals V, 176, 326, 406; P. Bordreuil, A. Lemaire, *Sem* 29 (1979), 72 no. 2; Herr, 131 no. 113; inscr. *AI* 24.4; 39.2; 40.3.
'lmlk Inscr. Hazor B 2 cf. *SSI*, 18, 19.
yhwmlk Seal V, 162.
'ḥmlk Seals V, 139, 154, 292, 324, 358, 424; P. Bordreuil, A. Lemaire, *Sem* 29 (1979), 73 no. 3; Herr, 90 no. 17; inscr. SO 22.2-3 = 23.2 = 24.1 = 25.2 = 26.1 (?) = 27.2 = 28.2 = 29.2; 48.2 cf. *IH*, 292; *AI*, 72.2.
ḥmlk Seal V, 124.
gdmlk Seal V, 64.

mnn to be bounteous?
BH *'ăḥîmān/'ăḥîman* (2) Df.
EB Sff. *ḥmn?* Seals V, 30, 202.

m'ṣ wrath.
BH *'ăḥîma'aṣ* (2) n.
EB *'bm'ṣ* Seal V, 274 n.
'[ ]m'ṣ Seal F. J. Bliss, *PEFQS* 32 (1900), 18.
Sf. *'ḥm'?* Inscr. Dir, 41 no. 6 = SO 32.3 prob. = 37.2 = 38.2 = 39.2 cf. *IH*, 34-35.

mrr to strengthen, bless, commend cf. Ug.
BH *m*^{e}*rāyāh* (1) Q. perf.
EB *mrnyw* Inscr. SO 42.3 cf. *SSI*, 10, 12. Df. (or Aram. *mr* 'lord'); cf. also Lemaire, *IH*, 35, who reads *Adonyaw*.
mrb'l Inscr. SO 2.7 cf. *SSI*, 9, 11 (or Aram. *mr*).

mt male, man.
BH *m*^{e}*tûšā'ēl* (1) constr.

ngh to shine.
EB *ygyh* Seals V, 272; F.M. Cross, *HTR* 55 (1962), 251 Q. imf.
yg'l Seal V, 309.

ndb to be noble, willing, liberal, generous cf. Arab. *naduba* and BDB, 621.
BH *n^{e}dabyāh* (1) Stative Q. perf.
y^{e}hônādāb (2) Stative Q. perf.
'ăbînādāb (3) Stative Q. perf.
'ăḥînādāb (1) Stative Q. perf.
'ammînādāb (3) Stative Q. perf.
Sf. *nādāb* (4)
EB *ndb'l* Seals V, 159 (Ammon.?), 400 Stative Q. perf.
ndbyhw Inscr. *AI*, 39.3 Stative Q. perf.
yhwndb Seal V, 336 Stative Q. perf.
'lndb Seal V, 357 Stative Q. perf.

nr lamp nominal.
BH *nērîyāh(û)* (1) *'abnēr/'ăbînēr* (1)
EB *nryhw* Seals V, 19, 50 56, 255, 281, 422; N. Avigad, *IEJ* 28 (1978), 56; Herr, 144 no. 151; BL, 46 no. 2; inscr. L 1.5 cf. *SSI*, 103; *AI*, 31.4.
'bnr *Seal V, 163.*
Sff. *nr'* Seal V, 196.
nry Seal V, 127.

nzh to spurt, spatter, Hiphil to sprinkle.
BH *y^{e}zî'ēl/y^{e}zaw'ēl* (1) Df. *yizzîyāh* (1) Df.

nḥm to be sorry, console oneself.
BH *n^{e}ḥemyāh* (3) Q. perf.
EB *nḥmyhw* Seal V, 30; inscr. *AI*, 31.3; 36.2; 40.1-2; 59.3 Q. perf.
m[n]ḥmyhw Inscr. *AI*, 11.5 n. (However, Lemaire, *IH*, 170, 171, restores the line to *m(l)ḥm* 'some bread'.)

nmh unknown.
BH *n^{e}mû'ēl* (2) constr.

n'm to be pleasant, lovely, delightful.
BH *'elnā'am* (1) n. *'ăbînō'am* (1) n.
'ăḥînō'am (2) f. n.
EB *n'm'l* Seal V, 95 n.?
'[ḥ]n'm Inscr. SO 10.2; 11.2; 19.4 cf. *SSI*, 11 n.
For these ostraca, as well as SO 8.2; 9.2, Lemaire reads *'dn'm* (*IH*, 30-32).

n'r youth.
BH *n^{e}'aryāh* (2) constr.
Sf. *na'ăray* (1)

nṣl to deliver (Hiphil).
EB *hṣlyhw* Seals V, 186, 419, 420; inscr. L 1.1 cf. *SSI*, 36, 37 Hiphil perf.

nšh to forget.
BH *yiššîyāh(û)* (5) Q. imf.

ntn to give n. gift.
BH *n^{e}tan'ēl* (9) Q. perf. *n^{e}tanyāh(û)* (4) Q. perf. *n^{e}tan-melek* (1) Q. perf. *mattanyāh(û)* (12) constr. *mattityāh(û)* (4) constr. *y(^{e}h)ônātān* (17) Q. perf. *'elnātān* (4) Q. perf.
Sff. *nātān* (9) *matt^{e}nay* (3) *mattān* (2) *mattattāh* (1)
EB *ntnyhw* Seals V, 31, 32; inscr. *AI*, 23.9; 56.1-2; Khirbet et-Kôm W. G. Dever, *HUCA* 40-41 (1969-70), 151-56; *ibid*., 156-57 Q. perf.
mtnyhw Seals V, 268; M 81-82 no. 31; BL, 49 nos. 9. 11; K. G. O'Connell, *IEJ* 27 (1979), 197-99; inscr. L 1.5 cf. *SSI*, 103 constr.
'lntn Seals V, 138, 189, 190, 306, 315, 430; inscr. L 3.15 cf. *SSI*, 38, 40; L 11.12 cf. *IH*, 128; Arad, A. F. Rainey, *Tel Aviv* 4 (1977), 97-102 pls. 5-6 Q. perf.
yhwntn Seal V, 349 Q. perf.
ywntn Inscr. SO 45.3 cf. *IH*, 35 (Dir, 47 no. 36 separates the *yw* and *ntn*) Q. perf.
yntn Seal V, 348 Q. perf.

sbk to interweave ?
EB *sbkyhw* L 11.4 cf. Lemaire, *IH*, 128 Df.

swd cf. Syr. friendly, confidential speech.
BH *b^{e}sôdyāh* prep. + constr.
Sff. *bēsay* (1) *sôdî* (1)
EB Sf. *bsy* Seal V, 247.

swr to turn aside.
EB *sryh* Seal V, 33 Df.

sḥr to go round, about, or cf. Ass. *saḫāru* to turn.
EB [*yh*]*wsḥ*[*r*] Inscr. *AI*, 90 Df.

smk to lean, lay, rest, support.

BH	*s^e^makyāhû* (1) Q. perf. *yismakyāhû* (1) Q. imf.	
	'ăḥîsāmāk (1) Q. perf.	
EB	*smkyhw*	Seals V, 239, 438; inscr. L 4.6; 13.2 cf. *SSI*, 41, 48; L 22.5 cf. *IH*, 136 Q. perf.
	smkyw	Inscr. SS 4.3 cf. *IH*, 248 Q. perf.
	'lsmky	Seal V, 129 n.
	'ḥsmk	(or *'ḥ'mr*) seal V, 280 Q. perf.
Sff.	*smk*	Seals V, 139, 240, 292, 401, 432; M, 75 no. 7; Herr, 90 no. 17.
	smky	Seal M, 81 no. 29.

sm' unknown.

EB	[ ]*'lsmk*	Seal V, 224 Df. perhaps = *'lšm*?

s'r storm, rage.

EB	*s'ryhw*	Inscr. *AI*, 31.4 n.

str to hide, conceal.

BH	Sf. *sitrî* (1)	
EB	*ywstr*	Seal V, 346 Q. perf.

'bd servant, always constr.

BH	*abd^e^'ēl* (1) *'abdî'ēl* (1) *'ōbadyāh(û)* (12)	
	'ōbed 'ĕdôm (2)	
Sff.	*'ebed* (2) *'abdā* (2) *'abdî* (2)	
EB	*'bdyhw*	Seals V, 26, 32, 34, 35, 70, 281, 425; inscr. *AI*, 10.4; 27.2; 49.8.
	'bdyw	Inscr. SO 50.2 cf. *SSI*, 10; Z. Meshel, C. Meyers, *BA* 39 (1976), 6-10 (Heb. or Phoen.)
Sff.	*'bd'*	Seal V, 217 (Ammon.?); inscr. SO 57.1 cf. *IH*, 292.
	'bdy	Seals V, 172, 291.

'bh to be thick, fat, gross. ?

	'byw	Seal V, 174.

'gl calf.

EB	*'glyw*	Inscr. SO 41.1 cf. *SSI*, 10, 12 constr.

'dh to ornament, deck oneself.

BH	*'ădî'ēl* (3) n. *'ădāyāh(û)* (8) Q. perf.
	mô'adyāh/ma'adyāh (1 or 2) Df.
	'el'ādāh (1) Q. perf. *y^e^hô'addāh* (1) Df.
Sff.	*ma'ăday* (1) *mā'ay* (1)

EB	*'dyhw*	Seals V, 154, 148, 417; BL, 50-51 no. 14; inscr. *AI*, 58.1 Q. perf.
	'd'l	Seal V, 146 Q. perf.
	'y'dh	Seal V, 151 Q. perf.
	'l'dh	Inscr. Mur. B 3 cf. *SSI*, 32 Q. perf.

'dl to act equitably? cf. Arab. *'adala*.
BH Sf. *'adlay* (1)

'dn luxury, dainty, delight.
BH *ye hô'addān/ye hô'addāyin* (1) Df.
EB *ḥmy'dn* Seal V, 324 n.

'dr to help Aram.
BH *'adrî'ēl* (1) Df.

'wd to return, repeat; denom. to bear witness, Hiphil to testify.
BH *'el'ād* (1) Q. perf. *yô'ēd* (1) n.
EB *b'd'l* Seal V, 48 n. + prep.

'wd to take or seek refuge.
BH *ma'azyāh* (2) n.

'wn to dwell; n. refuge.
EB *b'lm'ny* Inscr. SO Dir, 43 no. 18 n.

'wš to lend aid, come to help.
BH *yô'āš* (2) Q. perf.

EB	*'šn'l*	Seal V, 88 Q. perf. + 1st pers. sing. verbal suffix.
	'šnyhw	Seal V, 125 Q. perf. + 1st pers. sing. verbal suffix.
	'l'š	Seal V, 340 Q. perf.
Sf.	*y'š* ?	Inscr. SO 48.3, Dir, 46 no. 32.

'zz to be strong.
BH *'uzzî'ēl* (6) n. *'ăzāzyāhû* (3) Stative Q. perf.
'uzzîyāh(û) (5) n. *'azgād* (3) Stative Q. perf.
'el'ûzay/'el'uzzî (1) n.
Sff. *'uzzā'/'uzzāh* (4) *'uzzîyā'* (1) *'uzzî* (5)

EB	*'z'l*	Seal V, 200 Stative Q. perf.
	'zyw	Seals V, 65, 67; inscr. Dir, p. 274; Dir, 302 no. 15 n.
	'zyhw	Seals V, 37, 356, 422; inscr. A 20.2 cf. *IH*, 184 n.
	'l'z	Seal V, 170 (Ammon.?) Stative Q. perf.?
	yhw'z	Seal V, 156; inscr. *AI*, 31.3; 49.7 Stative Q. perf.
Sff.	*'z'*	Seals V, 36, 205, 436; inscr. SO 1.5 Dir, 48 no. 40; Dir,

308; *AI*, 72.4.
'zy seal V, 278.

'zh to nourish cf. Arab. *ghadhā*.
BH *ya'ăzî'ēl* (1) Q. imf. *ya'ăzîyāhû* (1) Q. imf.

'zr to help.
BH *'ăzar'ēl* (5) Q. perf. *'azrî'ēl* (3) Df.
'ăzaryāh(û) (21) Q. perf. *'el'āzār* (6) Q. perf.
'ĕlî'ezer (10) n. *yô'ezer* (1) n.
'ăbî'ezer (2) n. *'ăḥi'ezer* (2) n.
Sff. *'ezrî* (1) *'î'ezer* (1)
EB *'zr'l* Seal V, 170 (Ammon.?) Q. perf.
'zryhw Seals V, 24, 40, 188, 207, 289; M. Heltzer, *AION* 31 (1971), 190 no. 26, Dir, 122 no. 5b; A. Eitan, *IEJ* 20 (1970), 13; BL, 47 no. 4; Herr, 136 no. 128; N. Avigad, *IEJ* 4 (1954), 236; inscr. *AI*, 16.6; Gib. 1 cf. *SSI*, 56; M, 114 no. 2; L 18.2 cf. *IH*, 132; A 26.1 cf. *IH*, 197 Q. perf.
'zryw Seals V, 228; Dir, 123 no. 5c (prob. = V, 270) Q. perf.
'zryh Seal V, 175 Q. perf.
'l'zr Seals V, 310, 312; P. Bordreuil, A. Lemaire, *Sem* 29 (1979), 75 no. 7 Q. perf.? or n.?
yhw'zr Seals V, 26, 421; N. Avigad, *Qedem* 4 (1976), 7 n.
yw'zr Inscr. Mur. B 4 cf. *SSI*, 32 n.

'yn eye.
BH *'elyᵉhô'ênay* (2) *'elyô'ênay* (6) n. + prep.

'lh to go up. ascend, climb.
EB *'lyh* Seal V, 157 (possibly Ammon. or Edom.) Stative Q. perf.

'm kinsman nominal
BH *'ammî'ēl* (4) *'ammîšaddāy* (1) *'ĕlî'ām* (2)
EB *'ly'm* Seal V, 6 (Ammon.?)
'dn'm Inscr. SO 8.2; 9.2; 10.2f.; 11.2; 19.4.

'm prep. with.
BH *'immānû'ēl* (1)

'md to stand, take one's stand.
EB *'mdyhw* Seal V, 61 Q. perf.

'ms to load, carry away.
BH *'ămasyāh* (1) Q. perf.
Sff. *'ămāśā'* (2) *'ămāśay* (4) *'ămaššay* (1)
EB Sf *'ms'* Seal V, 145.

'nh to answer, respond.
BH *'ănāyāh* (1) Q. perf.
Sff. *'unnî/ô* (2) *ya'nay* (1)
EB *'nyhw* Seal V, 273 Q. perf.
'nyb'l Inscr. MH 6.1 cf. *IH*, 268.

'nn to appear, intervene.
BH *'ănanyāh* (1) Q. perf.
Sf. *'ănānî* (1)
EB *'nnyhw* Seal V, 254 Q. perf.

'rš to plant cf. Arab. *gharasa*.
BH *ya'ărešyāh* (1) Q. imf.

'śh to do, make.
BH *'ăśah'ēl* (4) Q. perf. *'ăśî'ēl* (1) Q. perf.
'ăśāyāh (3) Q. perf. *ya'ăśî'ēl* (2) Q. imf.
ma'ăśēyāh(û) (19) constr. *ba'ăśēyāh* (1) constr.
'el'āśāh (4) Q. perf.
Sff. *ya'ăśāy/ya'ăśaw* (1) *ma'ăśay* (1)
EB *'śyhw* Seals V, 27, 62, 109; BL, 48 no. 7; inscr. Y. Aharoni, *Lachish V*, 22 Q. perf.
'śyw Seal V, 38 Q. perf.
m'śyhw Seals V, 51, 55, 294 constr.
m'śyh Seals V, 242, 427 constr.
yw'śh Seal V, 171 Q. perf.
Sff. *'śy* Seal V, 243.
m'śy Inscr. *AI*, 22.4.

'th to be proud, exalted cf. Arab. *'atā*.
BH *'ătāyāh* (1) Stative Q. perf.
'otnî'ēl (1) Q. perf. + 1st pers. sing. verbal suffix.
Sff. *'ûtay* (2) *'attay* (3) *'otnî* (1)

'tl unknown.
BH *'ătalyāh(û)* (3) m. & f. Df.
Sf. *'atlāy* (1)

pg' to meet, encounter, reach.
BH *pag'î'ēl* (1) Df.

pdh to ransom.
BH *p^e^dāh'ēl* (1) Q. perf. *p^e^dāyāh(û)* (7) Q. perf.
p^e^dāhṣûr (1) Q. perf. *yipd^e^yāh* (1) Q. imf.
EB *pdyhw* Seals V, 45, 235; BL, 53 no. 5; inscr. *AI*, 49.15 Q. perf.

pṭ Eg. to give.
BH *pûṭî'ēl* (1)
EB *pṭyhw* Inscr. En-gedi, *EAEHL*, II 374.

pzz to be refined (Hophal).
BH *'ĕlîpāz* (2) Df.

pl' to be separate, unusual, wonderful?
BH *p^e^lā'yāh* (1) Stative Q. perf.
p^e^lāyāh (1) Stative Q. perf.

plh to be distinct, separated.
BH *'ĕlîp^e^lēhû* (1) Df.

plṭ to escape (Piel causative).
BH *palṭî'ēl* (1) Df. *p^e^laṭyāh(û)* (3) Q. perf.
'ĕlîpeleṭ (5) n.
Sff. *peleṭ* (2) *pilṭay* (1) *palṭî* (2)
EB *plṭyhw* Seals V, 379; Lemaire, *Sem* 29 (1979), 74 no. 5 Q. perf.

pll to intervene, interpose.
BH *p^e^lalyāh* (1) Q. perf. *'ĕlîpāl* (1) Q. perf.
Sf. *pālāl* (1)

pnh to turn n. face.
BH *p^e^nû'ēl* (2) constr.
EB *pn'l* Inscr. B 1.2 cf. *IH*, 271-72 Df.
Sf.? *pnbn* Seal M, 79 no. 22 cf. V, 392.

p'l to do, make.
BH *'elpa'al* (1) Q. perf.

pqd to attend to, visit, muster, appoint.
EB *p̊q̊dyw* Seal V, 163 Q. perf.

pqḥ to open (usually the eyes).
BH *p^e^qaḥyāh* (1) Q. perf.
EB Sf. *pqḥy* Seal V, 44.

pr' to excel, be noble cf. Arab. *fara'a.*
EB *ypr'yw* Seal V, 177 Stative Q. imf.

pšh Eg.?
EB *pšḥr* Seals V, 148, 152; inscr. *AI*, 54 Df.

pth to be youthful n. m. young man cf. Arab. *fatuwa, fatiya.*
BH *p^etû'ēl* constr.

ptḥ to open.
BH *p^etaḥyāh* (3) Q. perf.

ṣdq denom. to be just, righteous.
BH *ṣidqîyāhû* (6) n. *y(^eh)ôṣādāq* (1) Stative Q. perf.
EB *ṣdqyhw* Inscr. L 11.5 cf. *IH*, 128; Ophel 4 cf. *IH*, 239, 241 n.?
Sff. *ṣdq* Seals V, 322; M, 75 no. 6; inscr. *AI*, 93.

ṣwr rock, cliff nominal.
BH *ṣûrî'ēl* (1) *ṣûrîšaddāy* (1) *'ĕlîṣûr* (1)
EB *'lyṣwr* Inscr. B 2.1 cf. *IH*, 273.
'ḥṣr Seal N. Avigad, *BASOR* 189 (1968), 44-47.

ṣl shadow.
BH *b^eṣal'ēl* (2) prep. + constr.
Sf. *bēṣay* (1)
EB Sff. *bṣy* Seal V, 142.
bṣl Inscr. *AI*, 49.1.

ṣpn to hide, treasure up.
BH *ṣ^epanyāh(û)* (4) Q. perf. *'ĕlîṣāpān* (2) Q. perf.
EB *ṣpnyhw* Seals V, 258; M, 81 nos. 29, 30; V, 39; inscr. *AI*, 59.5; Milik *RB* 66 (1959), 551; Ophel 3 cf. *IH*, 240 Q. perf.
Sff. *ṣpn* Seals V, 188, 274, 289, 410, 435; BL, 46 no. 2; Herr, 110 no. 59.

qdm to be before, in front.
BH *qadmî'ēl* (1) Df.

qwl n. m. voice, sound.
BH *qôlāyāh* (3) constr.
EB *qlyhw* Seal V, 233 Df.
qlyw Inscr. SS 4.2 cf. *IH*, 248 Df.

qwm to arise, stand (up), Hiphil to raise, raise up.
BH *y^eqamyāh* (2) Hiphil imf. *y^eqam'am* (1) Q. imf.

'elyāqîm (3) Hiphil imf. *'ĕlîqā'* (1) Df.
y(^{e}h)ôyāqîm (2) Hiphil imf. *yôqîm* (1) Hiphil imf. or sf.?
'ăḥîqām (1) Q. perf. *'ădōnîqām* (1) Q. perf.

EB *yqmyhw* Seals V, 53, 122, 344; BL, 48 no. 8; inscr. *AI*, 39.1; 59.2; 74.3; 80.2 Q. or Hiphil imf..
yqymyhw Seal V, 366 Hiphil imf.
yqmyh Seal V, 153 Q. or Hiphil imf.
'lyqm Seals V, 93, 108, 242, 277, 436; Q. perf.?
yhwqm Seals V, 335, 336 Q. perf.
ywqm Seal V, 38 Q. perf.
'ḥqm Seals V, 210; P. Bordreuil, A. Lemaire, *Sem* 29 (1979), 74 no. 5 Q. perf.
'ḥyqm Inscr. *AI*, 31.5 Q. perf.

qwš to present, give cf. Akk. *qāšu*.
BH *qûšāyāhû* Sf. *qîšî* (1) Df.

qwt to nourish cf. Arab. *qāta*.
BH *y^{e}qûtî'ēl* (1) Q. imf.

qmh unknown.
BH *q^{e}mû'ēl* (3) constr.?

qnh to get, acquire.
BH *miqnēyāhû* (1) constr. *'elqānāh* (8) Q. perf.
EB *mqnyhw* Seals V, 162, 272; F. M. Cross, *HTR* 55 (1962), 251; inscr. *AI*, 60.4; A 72.1 (?) cf. *IH*, 219 constr.
qnyw Seal V, 13 Q. perf.

r'h to see.
BH *y^{e}rî'ēl* (1) Q. imf. *yir'îyâh* (1) Q. imf.
y^{e}rîyāh(û) (1) Q. imf. *re'āyāh* (3) Q. perf.
Sf. *rō'eh*
EB *yr'wyhw* Seal N. Avigad, *EI* 12 67 no. 5 Df.

rbb to be or become much, many.
BH *yārob'ām* (2) Stative Q. imf.
EB *rbyhw* Seal V, 161 Stative Q. perf.
yrb'm Seal V, 68; inscr. Hazor B cf. *SSI*, 19 Stative Q. imf.

rdh to rule, have dominion.
BH Sf. *radday* (1) ?

rwḥ to breathe?
BH *'aḥrāḥ* (1) Q. perf.

rwm to be high, exalted, to rise; names are all Stative Q. perf.
BH *ramyāh* (1) Df. *y(ᵉh)ôrām* (5) *'abîrām/'abrāhām* (1) *'ăḥîrām* (1) *'amrām* (2) *'ădōnîrām/'ădôrām* (1) *malkîrām* (1)
Sff. *yōrām* (1) *'ēḥî?* (1) *ḥîrām* (3)
EB *'lrm* Seals V, 217 (Ammon.?), 220.
yhwrm Seal Y. Aharoni, *Lachish V*, 22.
'brm Seal V, 66.
Sf. *yrm* Seal V, 54.

rḥb to be or grow wide, large.
BH *rᵉḥabyāh* (1) Q. perf. *rᵉḥab'ām* (1) Q. perf.

rḥm denom. Piel to have compassion.
BH *yᵉraḥmᵉ'ēl* (3) Piel imf.
EB *yrḥm'l* Seal N. Avigad, *IEJ* 28 (1978), 53 Piel imf.

ryb to strive, contend.
BH *yᵉrubba'al* (1) Df. *mᵉrîb ba'al* (2) Df.
y(ᵉh)ôyārîb (3) Q. imf.
Sff. *rîbay* (1) *yᵉrîbay* (1)

rmh to loosen.
BH *yirmᵉyāh* (8) Df.
EB *yrmyhw* Seals V, 58, 248, 258, 411; BL, 47-48 no. 6; inscr. L 1.4 cf. *SSI*, 36; *AI*, 24.15-16 Df.

rml to adorn with gems cf. Arab. *ramala*; or root *rwm*.
BH *rᵉmalyāhû* (1) Df.
EB *rmlyhw* Seals V, 19, 60.

r'h to associate with; pasture, tend, graze, n. m. friend.
BH *rᵉ'û'ēl* (4) constr. *'ăḥîrā'* (1)? Df.

r'l to quiver, shake, reel.
BH *rᵉ'ēlāyāh* (1) Df.

r'm to move violently; denom. to thunder.
BH *ra'amyāh* (1) Df.

rp' to heal.
BH *rᵉpā'ēl* (1) Q. perf. *rᵉpāyāh* (5) Q. perf.

Sff. *rāpā'* (1) *rāpāh* (1)
EB Sf. *rp'* Seals V, 377, 378; inscr. Dir, 49 no. 46 = SO 24.2.

rq' ?
BH *yorqᵉ'ām* (1) Df.

śgb to be (inaccessibly) high.
EB *'lśgb* Seal V, 59 (Ammon.?) Stative Q. perf.

śwm to put, place, set, establish.
BH *yᵉśîmi'ēl* (1) Q. perf.

śkh to look out, cf. NH *skh*.
BH *śākᵉyāh* (LXX *śobyāh*) (1) Df.

śrh to persist, exert oneself, persevere.
BH *yiśrā'ēl* (1) Q. imf. *śᵉrāyāh(û)* (11) Q. perf.
EB *śryhw* Seals V, 334; N. Avigad, *IEJ* 28 (1978), 56 (= Jer. 51.59) Q. perf.

š'l to ask, inquire.
BH *šᵉ'altî'ēl* (1) Q. perf. *šaltî'ēl* (1) Df.

šbh to take captive.
BH *šᵉbû'ēl*/*šᵉbu'ēl*/*šûbā'ēl* (1) constr.

šbn unknown.
BH *šᵉbanyāh(û)* (4) Q. perf.
Sff. *šebna'*/*šebnāh* (1)
EB *šbnyhw* Seals V, 15, 20, 61, 143, 257, 270, 332, 356; Y. Aharoni, *IEJ* 18 (1968), 166-67; Dir 122 no. 5b; M. Heltzer, *AION* 31 (1971), 190 no. 27; inscr. *AI*, 27.4; 60.3; Silwan 1 cf. *SSI*, 24 Q. perf.
šbnyh Seal Dir, 123 no. 5c (prob. = V, 270).
šbnyw Seal V, 67.
Sf. *šbn'* Seals V, 57, 168, 196, 223, 288; M, 78 no. 17.

šb' n. seven, oath or abundance, fulfilment, good fortune, cf. Akk.
BH *'ĕlîšeba'* (1) f. n. *yᵉhôšeba'*/*yᵉhôšab'at* (1) f. n.

šgg to go astray, commit sin or error.
BH *'ăbîšag* (1) f. Df.

šdy n. pr. div. Shadday nominal.
BH *'ammîšadday* (1) *ṣûrîšaddāy* (1)

šwb to turn back, return, Hiphil to restore.
BH *yāšob'ām* (1) Q. imf. *'elyāšîb* (6) Hiphil imf.
EB *šb'l* Seal A. R. Millard, *Iraq* 24 (1962), 49 n. 55; inscr. Gib. 21 cf. *SSI*, 56, readings uncertain Q. perf.
'lyšb Seals V, 231, 282, 375; inscr. *AI*, 1.1 = 2.1 = 3.1 = 4.1 = 5.1 = 6.1 = 7.1 = 8.1 = 9.1 = 10.1 = 11.1 = 12.1 = 14.1 = 15.1-2 = 16.2 = 17.2 = 18.1-2 = 24.2; *AI*, 64.2; 38.5; 47.1; Y. Aharoni, *Lachish V*, 22-23 line 8 Hiphil imf. (or Q. perf.).

šwr to behold, regard n. wall.
BH *'ăbîšûr* (1) n. *'ăḥîšār* (1) Q. perf.

šzb to deliver Aram.
BH *m^{e}šêzab'ēl* (3) part.

šḥḥ to crouch, bow, be bowed down, humbled.
BH *y^{e}šôḥāyāh* (1) Df.

šḥr dawn nominal.
BH *š^{e}ḥaryāh* (1) *'ăḥîšaḥar* (1)

škn to settle down, dwell, abide.
BH *š^{e}kanyāh(û)* (6) Q. perf.
EB *šknyhw* Seal V, 327 Q. perf.

šlḥ to send.
BH Sf. *šilḥî* (1)

šlm to be complete, sound, Piel to recompense.
BH *š^{e}lumî'ēl* (9) n. *šelemyāh(û)* (1) Piel perf.
m^{e}šelemyāh(û) (1) part. *'ăbîšālôm/'abšālôm* (2) n.
Sf. *šallûm* (15)
EB *šlm'l* Seal V, 145 n.
šlmyhw Seals V, 144, 333; inscr. L 9.7 cf. *SSI*, 47; A 27.5 cf. *IH*, 198 Piel perf.
šlmyh Seal V, 30 = *AI*, 108.3 Piel perf.?
'mšlm Inscr. *AI*, 59.4 n.?

šm name.
BH *š^{e}mû'ēl* (3) constr.
EB *šm'b* Seal V, 128 constr.

šm‘ to hear

BH *š^{e}ma‘yāh(û)* (28) Q. perf. *yišma‘yāh(û)* (2) Q. imf.
yišmā‘ē'l (6) Q. imf. *hôšāmā‘* (1) Q. perf.
'ĕlîšāmā‘ (6)

Sff. *šammû^a‘* (3) *šammā'* (1) *šammāh* (4)
šāmā‘ (1) *šammay* (3) *šim‘î* (18)
šim‘ā'/*šim‘āh* (4) *yišmā'* (1)

EB *šm‘yhw* Seal V, 40; inscr. *AI*, 27.2; 31.5; 39.2; 39.7-8; Mur. B 4; L 4.6; 19.4 cf. *SSI*, 32.49 Q. perf.
yšm‘'l Seals V, 45, 53, 418, 427; Herr, 105 no. 48; K.G. O'Connell, *IEJ* 27 (1977), 197-99; inscr. A 57.1 cf. *IH*, 214; Ophel, J. Prignaud, *RB* 77 (1970), 67 Q. imf.
'lšm‘ Seals V, 59 (Ammon.?), 72, 100, 244, 423 Q. perf.

Sff. *šm‘* Seals V, 16, 68, 71, 72, 167, 245, 346, 416; N. Avigad, *EI* 9 p. 8 no. 19.
šm‘y Seal V, 308.
šmyh Inscr. *AI*, 110.1, see A.F. Rainey, *Tel Aviv* 4 (1977), 97-104.

šmr to keep, watch, preserve.

BH *š^{e}maryāhû* (4) Q. perf.

Sff. *šimrî* (4) *šemer* (4) *yišm^{e}ray* (1)

EB *šmryhw* Seals BL, 47 nos. 4 and 5; inscr. *AI*, 18.4 Q. perf.
šmryw Seal V, 214; inscr. SO 1.1 cf. *SSI*, 8, 11; prob. = SO 13.2 = 14.2 prob. = 21.1.2 cf. *IH*, 294 Q. perf.

šnh to shine, be beautiful cf. Arab. *sana*.

EB *šnyw* Seal *V*, 132 Df.

š‘l deep cf. NH.

EB *š‘lyhw* Seal N. Avigad, *IEJ* 4 (1954), 236 Stative Q. perf.?

š‘r to reckon, calculate.

BH *š^e‘aryāh* (1) Q. perf.

EB *š‘ryhw* Seal V, 359 Q. perf.

špṭ to judge, govern.

BH *š^{e}paṭyāh(û)* (9) Q. perf. *'ĕlîšāpāṭ* (1) Q. perf.
y(^{e}h)ôšāpāṭ (6) Q. perf.

Sf. *šāpāṭ* (5)

EB *špṭyhw* Seals V, 109, 438; BL, 50-51 no. 14 Q. perf.

šrb to parch, be scorched.

BH *šērēbyāh* (1) Piel perf.

Sf. *šāray* ? (1)

tyr to be watchful cf. NH.
BH Sf. *tîryā'* (1)

tmm to be complete, finished.
BH *yôtām* (3) Stative Q. perf.
EB Sff. *ytm* Seals V, 131, 158.

Possible occurrences of foreign deities in BH names
cf. Section 2.2 above.

Name	*Meaning*	*Source*	*Form*
ḥēnādāb (1)	Favour of Hadad	Aram.	constr.
ḥarneper (1)	Horus is good, merciful	Eg.	
mord^ekay (2)	perh. from n. pr. div. Marduk	Akk.	
sismay (1)	prob. from Phoen. god Sasam	Phoen.	
'ōbed 'ĕdôm (2)	Servant of Edom.?	Edom.	constr.
'azgad (3)	Gad is mighty, strong.	Phoen./Aram.	Stat. Q. perf.
'ănātôt (2)	plur. of goddess Anath.	Phoen./Eg.? Syr.	
pašhûr (5)	perh. Portion of Horus, or Son of Horus	Eg.	constr.
š^emîdā' (1)	The name knows, or Eshmun has known	Phoen./Sidon	Q. perf.
šen'aṣṣar (1)	Sin protect! or Protect the king	Akk.	
šēsbaṣṣar (1)	Sin or Šaššu, protect the father	Akk.	

4. *Classification of Names according to Form and Date*

In the following tables, the Old Testament has been divided into four major periods of time. These are:

Period A—pre-Monarchical
B—the united Monarchy
D—the divided Monarchy
E—Exilic and post-Exilic period.

Period C represents 1 Chronicles 23–27 which, as stated above (p. 31) is possibly post-Exilic in content, while referred by the Chronicler to the Davidic period. Two sets of figures are given; first, *all* theophoric names in the Old Testament and, secondly, alongside each total, those theophoric names found only in Chronicles (C). For example, in table 4:1, showing the distribution of BH names according to date, in Period A, 16 names are found prefixed with *yhwh*, 13 of which are referred to only by the Chronicler. Also in the same period A, occur 46 names suffixed with forms of *yhwh*, of which 45 are mentioned only by the Chronicler. Altogether, this means that of the 62 persons bearing names compounded with forms of *yhwh* in Period A, 58 of these occur only in Chronicles. It should also be noted that all totals refer to numbers of individuals and not name-types.

TABLE 4:1

DISTRIBUTION OF BH NAMES ACCORDING TO DATE

	A				B				C				D				E				Total			
			Total				Total				Total				Total				Total				Total	
	All	C	All	C	All	C	All	C	All	C	All	C	All	C	All	C	All	C	All	C	All	C	All	C
pref. *yhwh*	16	13	62	58	29	15	71	45		10		51	42	16	194	86	35	1	261	28	132	55	639	268
suff. *yhwh*	46	45			42	30				41			152	70			226	27			507	213		
pref. *'l*	29	12	107	46	34	16	62	38		8		32	15	8	46	34	24	2	71	5	110	46	318	155
suff. *'l*	78	34			28	22				24			31	26			47	3			208	109		
pref. *'b*	21	8	26	10	17	1	22	3		1		1	6	1	6	1	2		3		47	11	58	15
suff. *'b*	5	2			5	2											1				11	4		
pref. *'ḥ*	15	8	17	10	17	3	18	4				1	2		5	2	2	1	2	1	36	12	43	18
suff. *'ḥ*	2	2			1	1				1			3	2							7	6		
pref. *'m*	8	1	9	2	3	2	8	3		2		3			2		2	1	2	1	15	6	24	9
suff. *'m*	1	1			5	1				1			2								9	3		
pref. *'dn*					2		2						1	1	2	2	2		2		5	1	6	2
suff. *'dn*													1	1							1	1		

pref. *b'l*	1	1			6	1							1				3				11	2		
			2	1			8	1							1				3				14	2
suff. *b'l*	1				2																3			
pref. *mlk*	2	1			1				1				1				9	1			14	3		
			4	1			5	1			1				2				10	1			22	4
suff. *mlk*	2				4	1							1				1				8	1		
pref. *ṣwr*	2																				2			
			5																				5	
suff. *ṣwr*	3																				3			
pref. *šdy*	1																				1			
			3																				3	
suff. *šdy*	2																				2			
pref. Other Deities	4	3															5	1			9	4		
			4	3			1	1							3	1			12	1			20	6
suff. Other Deities					1	1							3	1			7				11	2		

		All	C		All	C		All	C		All	C		All	C		All	C
Totals	pref.	99	47	pref.	109	38	pref.		22	pref.	68	26	pref.	84	7	pref.	382	140
	suff.	140	84	suff.	88	58	suff.		67	suff.	193	100	suff.	282	30	suff.	770	339
	All	239	131	All	197	96	All		89	All	261	126	All	366	37	All	1152	479

The addition of columns A, B, C etc. does not result in the exact total of theophoric names found in each period. This is because certain names are included more than once in the above enumeration; the fourteen individuals with the name *yô'ēl*, for example, will be listed in the sections 'pref. *yhwh*' as well as 'suff. *'l*'. When such names are subtracted, the total occurrences of names, without repetitions, is as follows:

A	B	C	D	E	Total
210	168	83	248	350	1057

To this total should also be added the 8 individuals who bore the names *'ly(h)w'yny*, that is with infixed *y(h)w*, resulting in a final total of 1066.

TABLE 4:2

DISTRIBUTION OF SHORT FORMS ACCORDING TO DATE

A		B		C		D		E		Total	
ALL	C	ALL	C	ALL	C	ALL	C	ALL	C	ALL	C
85	63	44	24	15	15	42	17	83	10	269	129

TABLE 4:3

DISTRIBUTION OF BH NAMES ACCORDING TO FORM AND DATE

Form	A		B		C		D		E		Total			
yhwh	All	C	All	C	All	C	All	C	All	C	All	C	All	C
Noun														
Prefix	8	6	6	3		4	7	4	10		35	17	104	38
Suffix	11	11	9	3		5	20	2	24		69	21		
Qal Perf.														
Prefix	4	3	15	7		4	17	6	14		54	20	296	128
Suffix	19	19	17	12		20	72	44	114	13	242	108		

Form	A		B		C		D		E		Total			
yhwh	All	C	All	C	All	C	All	C	All	C	All	C	All	C
Qal Imf.														
Prefix									3		3		39	21
Suffix	5	5	6	6		7	8	1	10	2	36	21		
Stat. Qal Perf.														
Prefix	1	1	6	3		2	10	4	7	1	26	11	65	27
Suffix	2	2	2	2		3	14	5	18	4	39	16		
Stat. Qal Imf.														
Prefix							1				1		8	2
Suffix						1	4	1	2		7	2		
Construct														
Prefix													59	28
Suffix	4	4	6	5		4	16	11	29	4	59	28		
Hiphil Perf.														
Prefix													2	
Suffix									2		2			
Hiphil Imf.														
Prefix	1	1					2		1		4	1	8	4
Suffix	1	1					1	1	2	1	4	3		
Hiphil Imv														
Prefix													4	3
Suffix	1	1							3	2	4	3		
Piel Perf.														
Prefix													10	1
Suffix						1	4		5		10	1		

Form	A		B		C		D		E		Total			
yhwh	All	C	All	C	All	C	All	C	All	C	All	C	All	C
Niphal Perf.														
Prefix													2	
Suffix									2		2			
Polel														
Prefix													2	2
Suffix							2	2			2	2		
Interrog.														
Prefix													9	2
Suffix	1						6	2	2		9	2		
Part.														
Prefix													1	1
Suffix									1	1	1	1		
Prep.														
Prefix													2	
Suffix									2		2			
Pronoun														
Prefix	1	1	1	1			3	1			5	3	5	3
Suffix														
Difficult Forms														
Prefix	1	1	1	1			2	1			4	3	23	8
Suffix	2	2	2	2			5	1	10		19	5		
Prep.														
Infixed	2	2				1			5	1	8	4	8	4
Totals	64	60	71	45	52	52	194	86	266	29			647	272

TABLE 4:4

OCCURRENCES OF YHWH AS AN AFFIX IN BH NAMES

	A		B		C		D		E		Total	
	All	C	All	C	All	C	All	C	All	C	All	C
Prefixed												
y^e^hô	1		7			4	16	7	6		34	11
yô	14	12	17	13		4	13	8	23	1	71	38
yô and *y^e^hô*			4	1			9		2		15	1
yē	1	1	1	1		1	3	1	4		10	4
yō						1					1	1
yû and *y^e^hû*							1				1	
Suffixed												
yāhû	5	4	12	11		24	65	32	17	3	123	74
yāh	40	40	21	16		12	64	37	203	23	340	128
yāh and *yāhû*	1	1	9	3		5	23	1	6	1	44	11

TABLE 4:5

DISTRIBUTION OF BH NAMES ACCORDING TO FORM AND DATE

Form *'l*	A		B		C		D		E		Total			
	All	C	All	C	All	C	All	C	All	C	All	C	All	C
Noun														
Prefix	12	6	16	9		2	5	3	8		43	20	88	50
Suffix	18	9	10	8		5	7	7	5	1	45	30		
Qal Perf.														
Prefix	16	6	11	5		3	8	5	8	1	46	20	76	35
Suffix	6	2	3	3		5	5	5	11		30	15		

Form *'l*	A		B		C		D		E		Total			
	All	C	All	C	All	C	All	C	All	C	All	C	All	C
Qal Imf.														
Prefix													33	24
Suffix	8	5	5	5		5	10	9	5		33	24		
Stat. Qal Perf.														
Prefix			2								2		3	
Suffix									1		1			
Construct														
Prefix													41	19
Suffix	21	8	5	3		3	4	3	8	2	41	19		
Hiphil Imf.														
Prefix			1			1	2		6	1	10	2	10	2
Suffix														
Piel Imf.														
Prefix													3	2
Suffix	1	1				1	1				3	2		
Interrog.														
Prefix													14	9
Suffix	7	6	1	1		1	1	1	4		14	9		
Part.														
Prefix													7	
Suffix	2								5		7			
Prep.														
Prefix													7	
Suffix	2						1		4		7			
Pronoun														
Prefix			2	1		2			1		5	3	5	3
Suffix														

Form *'l*	A		B		C		D		E		Total			
	All	C	All	C	All	C	All	C	All	C	All	C	All	C
Difficult Forms														
Prefix	1		2	1					1		4	1	31	11
Suffix	13	3	4	2		4	2	1	4		27	10		
Totals	107	46	62	38	32	32	46	34	71	5			318	155

TABLE 4:6

Form *'b*	A		B		C		D		E		Total			
	All	C	All	C	All	C	All	C	All	C	All	C	All	C
Noun														
Prefix	15	8	9	1		1	5	1	2		32	11	42	15
Suffix	5	2	4	2					1		10	4		
Qal Perf.														
Prefix	2		1								3		3	
Suffix														
Stat. Qal Perf.														
Prefix	2		4				1				7		7	
Suffix														
Pronoun														
Prefix	1										1		1	
Suffix														
Difficult Forms														
Prefix	1		3								4		5	
Suffix			1								1			
Totals	26	10	22	3	1	1	6	1	3				58	15

TABLE 4:7

Form *'ḥ*	A		B		C		D		E		Total			
	All	C	All	C	All	C	All	C	All	C	All	C	All	C
Noun														
Prefix	7	4	14	3			1		1		23	7	28	11
Suffix	1	1				1	3	2			5	4		
Qal Perf.														
Prefix	2	1	2				1				5	1	5	1
Suffix														
Stat. Qal Perf.														
Prefix	1		1								2		2	
Suffix														
Difficult Forms														
Prefix	5	3							1	1	6	4	8	6
Suffix	1	1	1	1							2	2		
Totals	17	10	18	4	1	1	5	2	2	1			43	18

TABLE 4:8

Form *'m*	A		B		C		D		E		Total			
	All	C	All	C	All	C	All	C	All	C	All	C	All	C
Noun														
Prefix	5		2	1		1			1	1	9	3	12	3
Suffix			3								3			
Qal Perf.														
Prefix						1					1	1	2	1
Suffix			1								1			

Form *‘m*	A		B		C		D		E		Total			
	All	C	All	C	All	C	All	C	All	C	All	C	All	C
Qal Imf.														
Prefix													1	1
Suffix			1	1							1	1		
Stat. Qal Perf														
Prefix	3	1	1	1					1		5	2	5	2
Suffix														
Stat. Qal Imf.														
Prefix													2	
Suffix							2				2			
Hiphil Imf.														
Prefix													1	1
Suffix						1					1	1		
Difficult Forms														
Prefix													1	1
Suffix	1	1									1	1		
Totals	9	2	8	3	3	3	2		2	1			24	9

TABLE 4:9

Form *’dn*	A		B		C		D		E		Total			
	All	C	All	C	All	C	All	C	All	C	All	C	All	C
Noun														
Prefix			1				1	1	1		3	1	3	1
Suffix														

Form *'dn*	A		B		C		D		E		Total			
	All	C	All	C	All	C	All	C	All	C	All	C	All	C
Qal Perf.														
Prefix									1		1		1	
Suffix														
Stat. Qal Perf.														
Prefix			1								1		2	1
Suffix							1	1			1	1		
Totals			2				2	2	2				6	2

TABLE 4:10

Form *b'l*	A		B		C		D		E		Total			
	All	C	All	C	All	C	All	C	All	C	All	C	All	C
Noun														
Prefix			1	1							1	1	1	1
Suffix														
Stat. Qal Perf.														
Prefix			1								1		1	
Suffix														
Construct														
Prefix													1	
Suffix			1								1			
Difficult Forms														
Prefix	1	1	4				1		3		9	1	11	1
Suffix	1		1								2			
Totals	2	1	8	1			1		3				14	2

TABLE 4:11

Form *mlk*	A		B		C		D		E		Total			
	All	C	All	C	All	C	All	C	All	C	All	C	All	C
Noun														
Prefix	2	1	1			1	1		8		13	2	20	3
Suffix	2		4	1					1		7	1		
Qal Perf.														
Prefix													1	
Suffix							1				1			
Stat. Qal Perf.														
Prefix									1	1	1	1	1	1
Suffix														
Totals	4	1	5	1	1	1	2		10	1			22	4

TABLE 4:12

Form *ṣwr*	A		B		C		D		E		Total			
	All	C	All	C	All	C	All	C	All	C	All	C	All	C
Noun														
Prefix	2										2		3	
Suffix	1										1			
Qal Perf.														
Prefix													2	
Suffix	2										2			
Totals	5												5	

TABLE 4:13

Form *šdy*	A		B		C		D		E		Total			
	All	C	All	C	All	C	All	C	All	C	All	C	All	C
Noun														
Prefix	1										1		3	
Suffix	2										2			
Totals	3												3	

TABLE 4:14

Form	A		B		C		D		E		Total			
Other Deities	All	C	All	C	All	C	All	C	All	C	All	C	All	C
Construct														
Prefix													8	2
Suffix			1	1			3	1	4		8	2		
Qal Perf.														
Prefix	1										1		1	
Suffix														
Stat. Qal Perf.														
Prefix													3	
Suffix									3		3			
Difficult Forms														
Prefix	3	3							5	1	8	4	8	4
Suffix														
Totals	4	3	1	1			3	1	12	1			20	6

TABLE 4:15

DISTRIBUTION OF EB NAMES ACCORDING TO FORM

Type	Pref. *'l*	Suff. *'l*	Pref. *yhwh*	Suff. *yhwh*	Total
Noun	14	3	18	80	115
Q.Perf.	29	6	15	170	220
Q.Imf.		11		20	31
Stat.Q.Perf.	6	5	6	28	45
Stat.Q.Imf.	1		2	3	6
Q.Imv.		1			1
Construct		1		42	43
Piel Perf.				5	5
Hiphil Perf.				12	12
Hiphil Imf.	7			2	9
Hiphil Imv.				1	1
Pilpel				1	1
Interrog.		1		4	5
Prep.		4		2	6
Difficult Forms	1		7	33	41
Total	58	32	48	403	541
Short Forms					109
					650

TABLE 4:16

EB OCCURRENCES OF YHWH AS AN AFFIX

	Seals	Inscr.	SO	Total
Pref. *yhw*	20	7		27
Pref. *yw*	12	1	3	16
Pref. *y*		4		4
Pref. *yh*	1			1
Total	33	12	3	48
Suff. *yhw*	211	121		332
Suff. *yh*	19	2		21
Suff. *yw*	20	4	18	42
Suff. ?	1			1
Total	251	127	18	396*

*The difference between this number and the total figure for suffixed forms of *yhwh* in Table 4:15 (403), results from a preference to include the 6 instances of the names *b'r'* and *b'l'* as difficult forms rather than abbreviated forms, and to consider the possibility of an original suffix *yhw*, on analogy with the BH name *b'lyh*.

DISTRIBUTION OF EB NAMES ACCORDING TO FORM

TABLE 4:17

Type	Pref. *'b*	Suff. *'b*	Pref. *'ḥ*	Suff. *ḥ*	Pref. *'m*	Suff. *'m*	Total
Noun	13	5	19		1	2	40
Q. Perf.			6		1		7
Stat. Q. Perf.	1						1
Stat. Q. Imf.						2	2
Construct		1					1
Hiphil Perf.						1	1
Difficult Forms	2	1	3				6
(Short Forms	3		12				15)
Total	19	7	40		2	5	73

Repeats (i.e. compounds with *yhwh/'l*) 19 + 12 sff.

TABLE 4:18

Type	Pref. *'dn*	Suff. *'dn*	Pref. *b'l*	Suff. *b'l*	Pref. *gd*	Suff. *gd*	Total
Noun	3		2	2	7	2	16
Q. Perf.			2				2
Stat. Q. Perf.			1				1
Difficult Forms			7				7
(Short Forms	1						1)
Total	4		12	2	7	2	27

Repeats (i.e. compounds with *yhwh/'l/'b/'ḥ* etc.) 14 + 1 sf.

TABLE 4:19

Type	Pref. *ḥr*	Suff. *ḥr*	Pref. *ṣwr*	Suff. *ṣwr*	Pref. *mlk*	Suff. *mlk*	Total
Noun				1	5	11	17
Difficult Forms		3				1	4
(Short Forms						1	1)
Total		3		1	5	13	22

Repeats (i.e. compounds with *yhwh/'l/'ḥ 'm/'dn* etc.) 17.

TABLE 4:20

Type	Pref. *'ly*	Suff. *'ly*	Pref. *šlm*	Suff. *šlm*	Pref. *ḥmy*	Suff. *ḥmy*	Total
Noun					1		1
Stat. Q. Perf.				4	1		5
Q. Imf.		1					1
Total		1		4	2		7

Total 121—60 repeats = 61.

The elements cited above are not, in all cases, theophoric elements: many, such as *'b*, *'ḥ* etc. occur as predicates with certain theophoric elements like *'l* and *yhwh*, as well as occurring as theophoric elements themselves. Others, such as *gd*, possibly never occur as a theophoric element among Hebrew names. These factors, and instances of names in tables 4:17, 18, 19 and 20, are discussed in Section 2:2, *Theophoric Elements*.

SELECT BIBLIOGRAPHY

Aharoni, Y., *Arad Inscriptions* (Judean Desert Studies), Jerusalem: The Israel Exploration Society (1981).

—*Beer-sheba I 1969–1971 Seasons*, Institute of Archaeology: Tel Aviv University (1973).

—*et al. Investigations at Lachish: The Sanctuary and the Residency* [*Lachish V*], Institute of Archaeology: Tel Aviv University (1975).

—'Three Hebrew Seals', *Tel Aviv* 1 (1974), 157-58.

—'Trial Excavation in the 'Solar Shrine' at Lachish', *IEJ* 18 (1968), 157-69.

Aistleitner, J., *Wörterbuch der ugaritischen Sprache* (Berichte über die Verhandlungen der sächsischen Akademie der Wissenschaften zu Leipzig, Philologisch-historische Klasse 106/3), Berlin (1963).

Albright, W.F., 'The Oracles of Balaam', *JBL* 63 (1944), 207-33.

Amiran, R., Eitan, A., 'Excavations in the Courtyard of the Citadel, Jerusalem, 1968–1969 (Preliminary Report)', *IEJ* 20 (1970), 9-17.

Andersen, F.I., *The Hebrew Verbless Clause in the Pentateuch*, Nashville, Tennessee: Abingdon Press (1970).

Aro, J., review of F. Gröndahl, *Die Personennamen der Texte aus Ugarit*, Rome (167), *ZA* 61 (1971), 172-74.

Astour, M.A., review of H.B. Huffmon, *Amorite Personal Names in the Mari Texts*, Baltimore: Johns Hopkins (1965), *JNES* 26 (1967), 225-29.

Avigad, N., 'A Bulla of Jonathan the High Priest', *IEJ* 25 (1975), 8-12.

—'A Group of Hebrew Seals', *EI*, 9 (1969), 1-9.

—'Ammonite and Moabite Seals', *NEATC*, New York: Doubleday (1970), 284-92.

—'Baruch the Scribe and Jerahmeel the King's Son', *IEJ* 28 (1978), 52-56.

—'New Names on Hebrew Seals', *EI* 12 (1975), 66-71.

—'Seals of Exiles', *IEJ* 15 (1965), 224-25.

—'The Priest of Dor', *IEJ* 25 (1975), 101-105.

—'The Seal of Jezebel', *IEJ* 14 (1964), 274-76.

—'Three Ornamented Hebrew Seals', *IEJ* 4 (1954), 236-38.

Bartlett, J.R., 'The Moabites and Edomites', D.J. Wiseman (ed.), *Peoples of Old Testament Times*, Oxford: OUP (1973), 229-58.

Barr, J., *Comparative Philology and the Text of the Old Testament*, Oxford: OUP (1968).

Benz, F.L., *Personal Names in the Phoenician and Punic Inscriptions* (Studia Pohl Dissertationes Scientificae de Rebus Orientis Antiqui 8), Rome (1972).

Berger, P.R., review of F. Gröndahl, *Die Personennamen der Texte aus Ugarit*, Rome (1967), *WO* 5/2 (1972), 271-82.

—'Zu den Namen *ššbṣr* und *šn'ṣr*', *ZAW* 83 (1971), 98-100.

Bliss, F.J., 'First Report on the Excavations at Tell-es-Sâfi', *PEQ* 31 (1899), 188-99.

Bordreuil, P., 'Inscriptions sigillaires ouest-sémitiques I', *Syria* 50 (1973), 181-95.

—'Inscriptions sigillaires ouest-sémitiques II', *Syria* 52 (1975), 115-17.

Bordreuil, P., Lemaire, A., 'Deux nouveaux sceaux nord-ouest sémitiques', *Journal Asiatique* (1977), 18-19.

—'Nouveaux Sceaux Hébreux, Araméens et Ammonites', *Semitica* 26 (1976), 45-63.

Bright, J., *A History of Israel*, 2nd edn, SCM (1972).
Brown, F., Driver, S.R., Briggs, C.A., *A Hebrew and English Lexicon of the Old Testament*, 1972 edn, Oxford: Clarendon Press (1974).
Caquot, A., review of J.K. Stark, *Personal Names in Palmyrene Inscriptions*, Oxford (1971), *RHR*, 182 (1972), 200-202.
Clay, A.T., *Personal Names from Cuneiform Inscriptions of the Cassite Period*, New Haven (1912).
Coogan, M.D., *West Semitic Personal Names in the Murašû Documents* (Harvard Semitic Monographs 7), F.M. Cross Jr (ed.), Missoula, Montana: Scholars Press (1976).
Cowley, A., *Aramaic Papyri of the Fifth Century BC*, Oxford (1923).
Cross, F.M., 'Leaves from an Epigraphist's Notebook', *CBQ* 36 (1974), 493-94.
—'Yahweh and the God of the Patriarchs', *HTR* 55 (1962), 225-59.
Dalman, G.H., *Aramäisch-Neuhebräisches Handwörterbuch*, Frankfurt am Main: J. Kaufmann (1922).
Deller, K., 'Neuassyrisches aus Sultantepe', *Orientalia* 34 (1965), 473-75.
Dietrich, M., Loretz, O., review of Huffmon, *Amorite Personal Names in the Mari Texts*, Baltimore: Johns Hopkins (1965), *OL* 61 (1966), 235-44.
Diringer, D., *Le Iscrizioni Antico-Ebraiche Palestinesi*, Firenze, Felice le Monnier (1934).
—'On Ancient Hebrew Inscriptions Discovered at Tell ed Duweir (Lachish)'—I, *PEQ* 73 (1941), 38-56, II, *ibid*., 89-109.
Donner, H., Röllig, W., *Kanaanäische und Aramäische Inschriften*, II & III, Wiesbaden: Otto Harrassowitz (1964).
Douglas, J.D., (ed.), *The New Bible Dictionary*, London: The Inter-Varsity Fellowship (1962).
Driver, G.R., *Aramaic Documents of the Fifth Century B.C.*, Oxford: Clarendon Press (1957), revised edn (1965).
—'Aramaic Names in Accadian Texts', *RSO* 32 (1957), 41-57.
—'Semitic Languages', *CSL*, 15-19.
Edzard, D.O., review of F. Gröndahl, *Die Personennamen der Texte aus Ugarit*, Rome (1967), *OL* 67 (1972), 551-55.
Emerton, J.A.E., 'A Consideration of some Alleged Meanings of *yd'* in Hebrew', *JSS* 15 (1970), 145-80.
The Englishman's Hebrew and Chaldee Concordance of the Old Testament, London: Bagster (reprinted 1971).
Fales, F.M., 'L'onomastica aramaica in età neo-Assira: raffronti tra il corpus alfabetico e il materiale cuneiforme', *OA* 13 (1976), 199-229.
—'On Aramaic Onomastics in the Neo Assyrian Period', *OA* 16 Fasc. 1 (1977), 49-55.
—'West Semitic Names from the Governor's Palace', *Annali di ca' Foscari*, XIII/3 (1974), (Serie Orientale 5), 179-88.
Fitzmyer, J.A., *The Aramaic Inscriptions of Sefîre*, Rome: PBI (1967).
Fowler, H.W., *Modern English Usage*, 2nd edn, revised by Sir Ernest Gowers, Oxford (1968).
Fritz, V., 'Ein Ostrakon aus Hirbet el-Mšāš', *ZDPV* 91 (1975), 131-34.
Gehman, H.S., (ed.), *The New Westminster Dictionary of the Bible*, Philadelphia: Westminster (1970).
Gelb, I.J., *Glossary of Old Akkadian* (Materials for the Assyrian Dictionary 3), Chicago, Illinois: University of Chicago Press (1957).
—'La lingua degli Amoriti', *Atti della Accademia Nazionale dei Lincei, Rendiconti*

della Classe de Scienze morali, storiche e filologiche, Serie 8, XIII (1958), 143-64.

Gelb, I.J., Landsberger, B., *et al.*, *The Assyrian Dictionary of the Oriental Institute of the University of Chicago*, (1956—).

Gibson, J.C.L., *Canaanaite Myths and Legends*, 2nd edn, Edinburgh: T. & T. Clark (1978).

—*Textbook of Syrian Semitic Inscriptions. I Hebrew and Moabite Inscriptions*, Oxford: Clarendon Press (1971).

—*Textbook of Syrian Semitic Inscriptions. II Aramaic Inscriptions*, Oxford: Clarendon Press (1975).

—*Textbook of Syrian Semitic Inscriptions. III Phoenician Inscriptions*, Oxford: Clarendon Press (1982).

Gordon, C.H., *Ugaritic Textbook Glossary*, Rome: PIB (1965).

Graesser, C., 'The Seal of Elijah', *BASOR* 220 (1975), 63-66.

Gray, G.B., *Studies in Hebrew Proper Names*, London: A. & C. Black (1896).

Greenfield, J.C., 'The Aramean God Rammān/Rimmōn', *IEJ* 26 (1976), 195-98.

Grelot, P., *Documents Araméens d'Égypte*, Paris: Les Éditions du Cerf (1972).

Gröndahl, F., *Die Personennamen der Texte aus Ugarit* (Studia Pohl Dissertationes Scientificae de Rebus Orientis Antiqui, I), Rome (1967).

—review of H.B. Huffmon, *Amorite Personal Names in the Mari Texts*, Baltimore: Johns Hopkins (1965), *Orientalia* 35 (1966), 449-56.

Heltzer, M., Ohana, M., *The Extra-Biblical Tradition of Hebrew Personal Names (From the First Temple Period to the End of the Talmudic Period)*, University of Haifa (1978) (Hebrew).

Herr, L.G., *The Scripts of Ancient Northwest Semitic Seals* (Harvard Semitic Monograph Series 18), F.M. Cross, Jr (ed.), Missoula, Montana: Scholars Press (1978).

—'Paleography and the Identification of Seal Owners', *BASOR* 239 (1980), 67-70.

Hestrin, R., Dayagi, M., *Inscribed Seals—First Temple Period*, Jerusalem (1979).

—'A Seal Impression of a Servant of King Hezekiah', *IEJ* 24 (1974), 27-29.

Hirsch, H., review of H.B. Huffmon, *Amorite Personal Names in the Mari Texts*, Baltimore: Johns Hopkins (1965), *WZKM* 61 (1967), 177-78.

Horn, S.H., 'An Inscribed Seal from Jordan', *BASOR* 189 (1968), 41-43.

Huffmon, H.B., *Amorite Personal Names in the Mari Texts. A Structural and Lexical Study*, Baltimore: Johns Hopkins (1965).

Jean, C.F., Hoftijzer, J., *Dictionnaire des inscriptions sémitiques de l'ouest*, Leiden: Brill (1965).

Kaufman, S.A., 'The Enigmatic Adad Milki', *JNES* 37 (1978), 81-201.

Kautzsch, E. (ed.), *Gesenius' Hebrew Grammar*, 2nd English edn (1910), trans. A.E. Cowley, Oxford: OUP (1976).

Koehler, L., Baumgartner, W., *Hebräisches und Aramäisches Lexikon zum Alten Testament*, 3rd edn (2 vols.), Leiden: Brill (1967, 1974).

—*Lexicon in Veteris Testamenti Libros*, Leiden: Brill (1953).

Kornfeld, W., *Onomastica Aramaica aus Ägypten*, Vienna: Österreichische Akademie der Wissenschaften (1978).

—'Zur althebräischen Anthroponomastik ausserhalb der Bibel', *WZKM* 71 (1979), 39-48.

Kraeling, E.G., *The Brooklyn Museum Papyri*, New Haven: Yale University Press (1953).

Lambdin, T.O., *Introduction to Biblical Hebrew* London: DLT (1973).

Lemaire, A., *Inscriptions Hébraïques. I. Les Ostraca*, Paris: Les Éditions du Cerf (1977).
Lidzbarski, M., *Ephemeris für semitische Epigraphik II*, Giessen: Töpelmann (1908).
Lipiński, E., *Studies in Aramaic Inscriptions and Onomastics I*, Leuven University Press (1975).
Margulis, B., 'A New Ugaritic Farce (RS 24.258)', *UF* 2 (1970), 131-38.
Mazar, B., Yadin, Y. (eds.), *Jerusalem Revealed: Archaeology in the Holy City 1968*–1974, Jerusalem: Israel Exploration Society (1975).
Michaud, H., *Sur la Pierre et l'Argile*, Neuchâtel: Delachaux et Niestlé (1958).
Milik, J.T., Notes d'épigraphie et de topographie palestiniennes', *RB* 66 (1959), 551-75.
Millard, A.R., 'Assyrians and Arameans', *Iraq* 45 (1983), 101-108.
—'Assyrian Royal Names in Biblical Hebrew', *JSS* 21 (1976), 1-14.
—review of E. Lipiński, *Studies in Aramaic Inscriptions and Onomastics I*, Leuven University Press (1975), *JSS* 21 (1976), 174-78.
—review of J.J.M. Roberts, *The Earliest Semitic Pantheon*, Baltimore: Johns Hopkins (1972), *JSS* 19 (1974), 87-90.
—review of C. Saporetti, *Onomastica Medio-assira*, (I & II), Rome: PIB (1970), *BO* 30 (1973), 58-60
—'The Assyrian Royal Seal Type Again', *Iraq* 27 (1965), 14 n. 7.
—'The Meaning of the Name Judah', *ZAW* 86 (1974), 15.
de Moor, J.C., review of F. Gröndahl, *Die Personennamen der Texte aus Ugarit* (Studia Pohl Dissertationes Scientificae de Rebus Orientis Antiqui, I), Rome (1967), *BO* 26 (1969), 105-108.
Moran, W.L., 'The Hebrew Language in its Northwest Semitic Background', G.E. Wright (ed.), *The Bible and the Ancient Near East*, New York: Doubleday (1961), 54-72.
Moscati, S., *L'epigrafia Ebraica Antica 1935*–1950, Rome: PIB (1951).
Naveh, J., review of F.L. Benz, *Personal Names in the Phoenician and Punic Inscriptions* (Studia Pohl Dissertationes Scientificae de Rebus Orientis Antiqui VIII), Rome (1972), *IEJ* 25 (1975), 183-84.
—review of L.G. Herr, *The Scripts of Ancient Northwest Semitic Seals* (Harvard Semitic Monographs 18; Missoula, Montana: Scholars Press, [1978]), *BASOR* 239 (1980), 75-76.
Nöldeke, Th., 'Semitic Languages', *CSL*, 1-14.
Noth, M., *Die israelitischen Personennamen im Rahmen der gemeinsemitischen Namengebung*, Hildesheim: G. Olms (1966), reprint of Stuttgart (1928) edn.
Peake's Commentary on the Bible, Nelson (reprinted 1967).
Porten, B., 'Domla'el and Related Names', *IEJ* 21 (1971), 47-49.
Postgate, J.N., *The Governor's Palace Archive* (Cuneiform Texts from Nimrud II), British School of Archaeology in Iraq (1973).
Pritchard, J.B. (ed.)., *Ancient Near Eastern Texts Relating to the Old Testament*, 3rd edn with Supplement, Princeton, New Jersey: Princeton U.P. (1969).
—*Gibeon. Where the Sun Stood Still*, Princeton, New Jersey: Princeton U.P. (1962).
—*Hebrew Inscriptions and Stamps from Gibeon*, Philadelphia (1959).
Rabin, C., 'The Origins of the Subdivisions of Semitic', *CSL*, 89-94.
Rainey, A.F., 'Ilānu rēsūtni lilliku', *Orient and Occident*, (1973), 139-42.
—'Private Seal Impressions: A Note on Semantics', *IEJ* 16 (1966), 187-90.
—'Three Additional Hebrew Ostraca from Tel Arad', *Tel Aviv*, 4 (1977), 97-104.
Reifenberg, A., 'Ancient Hebrew Seals III', *PEQ* 74 (1942), 109-12.
Richter, W., review of F. Gröndahl, *Die Personennamen der Texte aus Ugarit* (Studia

Pohl Dissertationes Scientificae de Rebus Orientis Antiqui, I), Rome (1967), *ZDMG* 119 (1970), 351-55.

Roberts, J.J.M., *The Earliest Semitic Pantheon*, Baltimore: Johns Hopkins (1972).

Rosenthal, F., *An Aramaic Handbook*. Part 1/2 Glossary, Wiesbaden: Otto Harrassowitz (1967).

Sanders, J.A., (ed.), *Near Eastern Archaeology in the Twentieth Century*, New York: Doubleday (1970).

Saporetti, C., *Onomastica Medio-assira*, I & II, Rome: PIB (1970).

Sawyer, J.F., *Semantics in Biblical Research* London SCM (1972).

Schottrof, W., *'Gedenken' im Alten Orient und im Alten Testament*, Neukirchen-Vluyn: Neukirchener Verlag (1964).

Segal, J.B., review of J.K. Stark, *Personal Names in Palmyrene Inscriptions*, Oxford (1971), *PEQ* 104 (1972), 71-73.

Silverman, M.H., 'Aramaean Name-types in the Elephantine Documents', *JAOS* 89 (1969), 691-709.

—'Hebrew Name-types in the Elephantine Documents', *Orientalia* 39 (1970), 465-91.

—*Jewish Personal Names in the Elephantine Documents: A Study in Onomastic Development*, Ph.D. Dissertation Brandeis Univ. (1967), University Microfilms.

von Soden, W., *Akkadisches Handwörterbuch* Unter Benutzung des lexikalischen Nachlasses von Bruno Meissner (1868–1947), Wiesbaden: O. Harrassowitz, 3 vols. (1965, 1972, 1981).

Stager, L.E., 'El-Bouqei'ah', *RB* 81 (1974), 94-96.

Stamm, J.J., *Die Akkadische Namengebung*, Darmstadt (1968). First published 1939.

Stark, J.K., *Personal Names in Palmyrene Inscriptions*, Oxford: Clarendon Press (1971).

Stieglitz, R.R., 'The Seal of Ma'aseyahu', *IEJ* 23 (1973), 236-37.

Stolper, M., 'A Note on Yahwistic Personal Names in the Murašû Texts', *BASOR* 222 (1976), 25-28.

Strelcyn, S., review of J.K. Stark, *Personal Names in Palmyrene Inscriptions*, Oxford (1971), *JSS* 18 (1973), 165-68.

Tallqvist, K.L., *Assyrian Personal Names*, Hildesheim: G. Olms (1966). First published 1914.

Torczyner, H., *et al.*, *Lachish I. The Lachish Letters*, Oxford OUP (1938).

Tsevat, M., 'Ishbosheth and Congeners', *HUCA* 46 (1975), 71-87.

Ussishkin, D., 'Tel Lachish 1976', *IEJ* 27 (1977), 48-51.

Van Dyke Parunak, H., 'The Orthography of the Arad Ostraca', *BASOR* 230 (1978), 25-31.

Vattioni, F., 'Epigrafia aramaica', *Augustinianum* 10 (1970), 493-532.

—'I sigilli ebraici', *Biblica* 50 (1969), 357-88.

—'I sigilli ebraici II', *Augustinianum* 11 (1971), 447-54.

—'I sigilli le monete e gli avori aramaici. 1. I sigilli aramaici', *Augustinianum* 11 (1971), 47-87.

—'Sigilli ebraici III', *Annali dell' Istituto Orientali di Napoli* 38 NS 28 (1978), 227-54.

de Vaux, R., *Ancient Israel. Its Life and Institutions* 2nd edn, trans. J. McHugh, London: DLT (1968).

Vincent, A., *La religion des Judéo-Araméens d'Elephantine*, Paris: Geuthner (1937).

Vinnikov, I.N., *Palestinskii Svornik*, 3 (1958), 171-216; 4 (1959), 196-240; 7 (1962), 192-37; 9 ((1962), 140-58; 11 (1963), 189-232; 13 (1965), 217-62.

Vriezen, Th. C., Hospers, J.H. (eds.), *Textus Minores XVII Palestine Inscriptions*, Leiden: Brill (1951).

Westenholz, A., review of J.J.M. Roberts, *The Earliest Semitic Pantheon*, Baltimore: Johns Hopkins (1972), *JNES* 34 (1975), 288-93.

Whitaker, R.E., *A Concordance of the Ugaritic Literature*, Cambridge, Massachussetts: Harvard University Press (1972).

Yadin, Y., *Hazor. The Rediscovery of a Great Citadel of the Bible*, Weidenfeld and Nicolson (1975).

Zadok, R., 'Historical and Onomastic Notes', *WO* 9 (1977), 35-56.

—'Notes on the Early History of the Israelites and Judeans', *Orientalia* 51 (1982), 391-93.

—*On West Semites in Babylonia During the Chaldean and Achaemenian Periods. An Onomastic Study*, Jerusalem: H.J. and Z. Wanaarta and Tel-Aviv University (1977).

—'Phoenicians, Philistines, and Moabites in Mesopotamia', *BASOR* 230 (1978), 57-65.

—review of M.D. Coogan, *West Semitic Personal Names in the Murašû Documents*, Scholars Press (1976), *BASOR* 231 (1978), 73-78.

—review of E. Lipiński, *Studies in Aramaic Inscriptions and Onomastics I*, Leuven University Press (1975), *BO* 33 574 (1976), 227-31.

—*The Jews in Babylonia During the Chaldean and Achaemenian Periods According to the Babylonian Sources* (Studies in the History of the Jewish People and the Land of Israel, Monograph Series, III), University of Haifa (1979).

Zevit, Z., 'A Chapter in the History of Israelite Personal Names', *BASOR* 250 (1983), 1-16.

INDEX

Index of Hebrew Names

(Names are listed alphabetically in the order of the Hebrew consonants only.)

Ugaritic Name-Elements

Amorite Name-Elements

Aramaic Name-Elements

Akkadian Name-Elements

tamlaku 260, 300
tanattum 258, 299
tappû 254, 282
taqānu D 252-53, 288
tarāmu 254, 292
tarāṣu 245, 259, 295, 310
tarībum 249, 285
târu 249, 253, 291, 306, 307, 311, 313
tayāru 253-54, 291
tayyāru 263, 311
tillatu 253, 289
tišmar/šitmar 263, 310
tizqar 243, 293
tu'āru 253, 291
tuktû 263, 310
tukultu 247, 280
tuqqunu 259, 310
ṭâbu 239, 290, 308
ṭēmu 260, 310
ubāru 258, 299
ummu 255, 298
upnu 255, 283
uqnu 257, 301
urkattu 258, 299
usātu 253, 290
ušāru D 262, 307, 308
utlu 250-51, 287
utullu 259, 303
uznu 255, 283
(w)abālu 259, 304
(w)alādu 259, 304
waldu 258, 299
(w)aqru 256, 300
(w)ardu 254, 282
(w)asāmu 243, 294
(w)atru 238, 256, 293, 300, 308
(w)ēdu 262, 307
yālu 256, 302
zākiru/zakāru 259, 304
zāninu 252, 288
zaqāpu 261, 307
zâqu (zi'āqu) 265, 303
zārūt 258, 299
zēru 258, 299
zittu 255, 280

Palmyrene Name-Elements

'b 266, 280
'wš sf. 277n133, 285
'ḥ 266, 268, 281, 300
'm 268, 298
'mr sf. 268, 282
'mš 268, 298
't 266, 282
'th 268, 304
bnh sf. 269, 284
br 268, 299
brk 266, 284
bt 268, 298
gd 266, 280
g^e^ram 268, 310
dyn sf. 269, 294
dkr 269, 284
hd' sf. 269, 295
hm (cf. Arab. *hamā*) sf. 277n134, 287
wahb 267, 285
zbd 266, 285
zdq 267, 290
ḥbb sf. 269, 292
ḥzh 266, 283
ḥnn 266, 290
ḥpr (cf. Arab. *ḥafara*) sf. 277n134, 287
yd' 266, 284
yhb 267, 285
kā' 268, 312
l 266, 282
m 266, 294
mlk, + sf. 266, 269, 293, 310
mr 266, 293
mšk 269, 310
ndb 267, 284
nwr 266, 280
naṣr 268, 300
nš' sf. 269, 292
ntn 266, 285
'bd 266, 282
'auḏ 267, 287
'wyd 268, 299
'azīz 266, 288
'alīy 266, 293
'qb (to protect) 267, 287
'qb (sf. to reward) 269, 304
pny 266, 291
p^e^ṣā' 267, 286
ṣ'd 269, 283
rby 266, 294
rg' 267, 280

Ammonite Theophoric Names

’byḥy bt ynḥm (V, 103)
’bndb š ndr l‘št bṣdn tbrkh (*Sem* 29 [1979], 80)
’dnnr ‘bd ‘mndb (V, 164)
’dnplṭ ‘bd ‘mndb (V, 98)
’w’ bn mr’l (V, 194)
’ḥndb (*Sem* 29 [1979], 80)
’l’ bn ḥtš (*Syria* 50 [1973], 184)
’l’mṣ bn ’lš‘ (V, 115)
’lyš‘ bn grgr (V, 317)
’lmšl (V, 389)
’lndb (V, 442)
’lndb bn ’lydn (*Sem* 26 [1976], 56)
’lntn bn ytyr (V, 388)
’l‘z bn mnḥm (V, 353)
’lrm bn tm’ (V, 94)
’lšm‘ bn b—’l (V, 448)
(a) ’lšm‘: (b) *’lšm‘ bn b‘r’* (V, 386)
’lšm‘ pll (V, 352)
’ltmk? (*Sem* 26 [1976], 56)
’ltmk bn ‘ms’l (V, 443)
’ltš (V, 117)
’mr’l bn ynḥm (V, 259)
’nmwt ’mt dblks (V, 116 or Moab.)
’nmwt ’št dblbs (NEATC, 285)
[ ]*b’l l’bn[db]* (*Syria* 50 [1973], 184)
bd’l bn ndb’l (V, 400)
byd’l bn tmk’l (V, 17)
byd’l ‘bd pd’l (V, 403)
btš n‘r brk’l (V, 221)
ḥn’l bn ’wr’ (*Sem* 29 [1979], 82)
ḥtm l/ng’dt brk lmlkm (V, 229)
ḥtm mng’nrt brk lmlkm (V, 225, but cf. J. Naveh, *BASOR* 239 [1980], 76 = Aram.)
ltnr(?) bn ’l’mn (*Sem* 26 [1976], 57)
mkm’l (V, 445)
mnḥm bn mgr’l (V, 387)
mnḥm bn smk ‘bd mlk (V, 401)
ndb’l bn ’ddm (V, 29)
ndb’l bn ’l‘zr (V, 263)
ndb’l bn ‘ms’l (V, 201)
ndb’l bn tmk’ (V, 383)
‘ms’l (*Syria* 50 [1973], 185)
pd’l (V, 135)
plṭ(?) (V, 385)
plṭy bn š‘l (V, 446)
šb’l (V, 165)
šm‘ (V, 440)
šm‘l bh plṭw (*Syria* 50 [1973], 189)
tmk(’) bn mqnmlk (V, 318)
tmk’l (V, 382)
tmk’l bn ḥgt (V, 347)
tmk’l bn yš‘ (*Sem* 29 [1979], 84)
tmk’l br mlkm? (Herr, 15 no. 10)
tmk’l bn plṭy (V, 384)
tmk’l ‘bdmlkm (*Sem* 26 [1976], 57)

Edomite Theophoric Names

b‘zr’l ‘bdyb‘l (V, 118)
qws’ (V, 395)
qwsg[br] mlk ’[dm] (V, 227)
qwsynqm (J. Naveh, *AI*, 161 inscr. 20)
qws‘nl ‘bd hmlk (V, 119)

Moabite Theophoric Names

’mṣ hspr (*Sem* 26 [1976], 54)
kmš (V, 451)
kmšyḥy (V, 111)
kmšm’š (V, 266)
kmšntn (V, 265)
kmš‘m kmš’l hspr (V, 113)
kmšpṭ (V, 267)
kmšṣdq (V, 112)
nṣr’l hṣrp ? (V, 102)

JOURNAL FOR THE STUDY OF THE OLD TESTAMENT
Supplement Series

20 THE PSALMS OF THE SONS OF KORAH
M.D. Goulder

21 COLOUR TERMS IN THE OLD TESTAMENT
A. Brenner

22 AT THE MOUNTAIN OF GOD:
STORY AND THEOLOGY IN EXODUS 32–34
R.W.L. Moberly

23 THE GLORY OF ISRAEL:
THE THEOLOGY AND PROVENIENCE OF THE ISAIAH TARGUM
B.D. Chilton

24 MIDIAN, MOAB AND EDOM:
THE HISTORY AND ARCHAEOLOGY OF LATE BRONZE AND IRON AGE JORDAN AND NORTH-WEST ARABIA
Edited by J.F.A. Sawyer & D.J.A Clines

25 THE DAMASCUS COVENANT:
AN INTERPRETATION OF THE 'DAMASCUS DOCUMENT'
P.R. Davies

26 CLASSICAL HEBREW POETRY:
A GUIDE TO ITS TECHNIQUES
W.G.E. Watson

27 PSALMODY AND PROPHECY
W.H. Bellinger

28 HOSEA: AN ISRAELITE PROPHET IN JUDEAN PERSPECTIVE
G.I. Emmerson

29 EXEGESIS AT QUMRAN:
4QFLORILEGIUM IN ITS JEWISH CONTEXT
G.J. Brooke

30 THE ESTHER SCROLL: THE STORY OF THE STORY
D.J.A. Clines

31 IN THE SHELTER OF ELYON:
ESSAYS IN HONOR OF G.W. AHLSTRÖM
Edited by W.B. Barrick & J.R. Spencer

32 THE PROPHETIC PERSONA:
JEREMIAH AND THE LANGUAGE OF THE SELF
T. Polk

33 LAW AND THEOLOGY IN DEUTERONOMY
J.G. McConville

34 THE TEMPLE SCROLL:
AN INTRODUCTION, TRANSLATION AND COMMENTARY
J. Maier

35 SAGA, LEGEND, TALE, NOVELLA, FABLE:
NARRATIVE FORMS IN OLD TESTAMENT LITERATURE
Edited by G.W. Coats

36 THE SONG OF FOURTEEN SONGS
M.D. Goulder

37 UNDERSTANDING THE WORD:
ESSAYS IN HONOR OF BERNHARD W. ANDERSON
Edited by J.T. Butler, E.W. Conrad & B.C. Ollenburger

38 SLEEP, DIVINE AND HUMAN, IN THE OLD TESTAMENT
T.H. McAlpine

39 THE SENSE OF BIBLICAL NARRATIVE II:
STRUCTURAL ANALYSES IN THE HEBREW BIBLE
D. Jobling

40 DIRECTIONS IN BIBLICAL HEBREW POETRY
Edited by E.R. Follis

41 ZION, THE CITY OF THE GREAT KING:
A THEOLOGICAL SYMBOL OF THE JERUSALEM CULT
B.C. Ollenburger

42 A WORD IN SEASON: ESSAYS IN HONOUR OF WILLIAM McKANE
Edited by J.D. Martin & P.R. Davies

43 THE CULT OF MOLEK:
A REASSESSMENT
G.C. Heider

44 THE IDENTITY OF THE INDIVIDUAL IN THE PSALMS
S.J.L. Croft

45 THE CONFESSIONS OF JEREMIAH IN CONTEXT:
SCENES OF PROPHETIC DRAMA
A.R. Diamond

46 THE BOOK OF THE JUDGES: AN INTEGRATED READING
B.G. Webb

47 THE GREEK TEXT OF JEREMIAH:
A REVISED HYPOTHESIS
S. Soderlund

48 TEXT AND CONTEXT:
OLD TESTAMENT AND SEMITIC STUDIES FOR F.C. FENSHAM
Edited by W. Claassen

49 THEOPHORIC PERSONAL NAMES IN ANCIENT HEBREW
J.D. Fowler

50 THE CHRONICLER'S HISTORY
M. Noth

51 DIVINE INITIATIVE AND HUMAN RESPONSE IN EZEKIEL
P. Joyce

52 THE CONFLICT OF FAITH AND EXPERIENCE IN THE PSALMS:
A FORM-CRITICAL AND THEOLOGICAL STUDY
C.C. Broyles

53 THE MAKING OF THE PENTATEUCH:
A METHODOLOGICAL STUDY
R.N. Whybray

54 FROM REPENTANCE TO REDEMPTION:
JEREMIAH'S THOUGHT IN TRANSITION
J. Unterman

55 THE ORIGIN TRADITION OF ANCIENT ISRAEL:
THE LITERARY FORMATION OF GENESIS AND EXODUS 1–23
T.L. Thompson

56 THE PURIFICATION OFFERING IN THE PRIESTLY LITERATURE:
ITS MEANING AND FUNCTION
N. Kiuchi

57 MOSES: HEROIC MAN, MAN OF GOD
G.W. Coats

58 THE LISTENING HEART: ESSAYS IN WISDOM AND THE PSALMS
IN HONOR OF ROLAND E. MURPHY, O. CARM.
Edited by K.G. Hoglund

59 CREATIVE BIBLICAL EXEGESIS:
CHRISTIAN AND JEWISH HERMENEUTICS THROUGH THE CENTURIES
B. Uffenheimer & H.G. Reventlow

60 HER PRICE IS BEYOND RUBIES:
THE JEWISH WOMAN IN GRAECO-ROMAN PALESTINE
L.J. Archer

61 FROM CHAOS TO RESTORATION:
AN INTEGRATIVE READING OF ISAIAH 24–27
D.G. Johnson

62 THE OLD TESTAMENT AND FOLKLORE STUDY
P.G. Kirkpatrick

63 SHILOH: A BIBLICAL CITY IN TRADITION AND HISTORY
D.G. Schley

64 TO SEE AND NOT PERCEIVE:
ISAIAH 6.9-10 IN EARLY JEWISH AND CHRISTIAN INTERPRETATION
C.A. Evans

65 THERE IS HOPE FOR A TREE:
THE TREE AS METAPHOR IN ISAIAH
K. Nielsen

66 THE SECRETS OF THE TIMES:
RECOVERING BIBLICAL CHRONOLOGIES
J. Hughes

* Out of print